Sandra Day O'Connor
College of Law
at Arizona State University

Sandra Day O'Connor College of Law
at Arizona State University

1965 to 2020

Gary L. Stuart
FOREWORD BY DEAN DOUGLAS SYLVESTER

Copyrighted Material

Sandra Day O'Connor College of Law at Arizona State University: 1965 to 2020

Copyright © 2021 by Gary L. Stuart. All Rights Reserved.

No part of this publication may be reproduced, stored in a retrieval system or transmitted, in any form or by any means—electronic, mechanical, photocopying, recording or otherwise—without prior written permission from the publisher, except for the inclusion of brief quotations in a review.

For information about this title or to order other books and/or electronic media, contact the publisher:

Gleason & Wall Publishing
7000 N. 16th St.
Suite 120
Phoenix, AZ 85020

ISBN: 978-1-7368946-4-4

Printed in the United States of America

Cover and Interior design: 1106 Design

TABLE OF CONTENTS

Foreword — xi

Author's Note — xv

Prologue — xvii

PART ONE: *The Pedrick Years—1965 to 1975* — 1

Chapter 1
Creating the Arizona State University College of Law — 3

Chapter 2
Studying and Teaching Law in the 1960s — 21

Chapter 3
Willard Hiram Pedrick—Founding Dean—1965 — 33

Chapter 4
What is Notable—What to Include—What to Exclude — 49

Chapter 5
Beginning the Study of Law — 55

Chapter 6
The ASU Law Society—1966 to 1997 — 59

Chapter 7
Armstrong Hall—1966 to 1968 — 63

Chapter 8
Inaugural Faculty—1967 to 1970 — *73*
- Willard H. Pedrick — *75*
- Richard C. Dahl — *76*
- William C. Canby, Jr. — *79*
- Edward W. Cleary — *81*
- Richard W. Effland — *83*
- Dale B. Furnish — *84*
- Harold C. Havighurst — *84*
- Alan A. Matheson — *86*
- John P. Morris — *88*
- Jonathan Rose — *95*
- Michael A. Berch — *97*
- Milton R. Schroeder — *99*

Chapter 9
Dean Willard Pedrick's Report—1967 to 1968 — *107*

Chapter 10
Inaugural Graduates—1970 through 1976 — *117*
- Michael Gallagher, '70 — *118*
- Hon. Michael Daly Hawkins, '70 — *119*
- Joe Sims, '70 — *122*
- Jimmie Dee Smith, '70 — *123*
- Robert Blakley, Jr., '71 — *124*
- Hon. Cecil B. Patterson, Jr., '71 — *126*
- Hon. Roslyn Silver, '71 — *129*
- Les Schiefelbein, '71 — *131*
- Fritz Aspey, '72 — *134*
- Hon. Redfield T. Baum, '72 — *135*
- Lou Diesel, '73 — *137*
- Harold L. Watkins, '73 — *138*
- Ambassador Hattie C. Babbitt, '72 — *138*
- Barry MacBan, '72 — *140*

Table of Contents

Tom Chauncey, II, '73 — *141*
William K. "Bill" Culbertson, '73 — *142*
Marty Harper, '73 — *145*
Terrance P. "Terry" Woods, '73 — *146*
H. Bartow Farr III, '74 — *147*
Hon. Ruth McGregor, '74 — *148*
Ed Pastor, '74 — *152*
Bill Sandweg, '74 — *154*
Hon. Barry G. Silverman, '76 — *154*
William F. Atkin, '75 — *159*
Michael G. Bailey, '75 — *160*
Hon. Charles G. Case, Jr., '75 — *161*
Hon. James Alan Soto, '75 — *161*
Terry Goddard, '76 — *163*
Michael Grant, '76 — *164*
Ambassador Barbara Barrett, '78 — *165*
Hon. Douglas L. Rayes, '78 — *171*

Chapter 11
The Starsky Saga—1968 to 1970 — *197*

Chapter 12
The First Two Years—1967 to 1969 — *209*

Chapter 13
The Indian Law Program—1967 — *219*

Chapter 14
Dean Pedrick's 1971–72 Report — *229*

Chapter 15
ASU Law's First Graduating Class—1970 — *235*

Chapter 16
Dean Pedrick's Last Report 1974 to 1975 — *243*

PART TWO: *The Growth Years—1976 to 2000*   255

Chapter 17
    Dean Ernest Gellhorn 1976 to 1978   *257*

Chapter 18
    John R. Bates & Van O'Steen—Legal Advertising—1976   *271*

Chapter 19
    Dean Alan Matheson 1978 to 1984   *283*

Chapter 20
    Coach Frank Kush—The Legend—The Saga—1978 to 2000   *291*

Chapter 21
    ASU Law Skills Training—1970s   *307*

Chapter 22
    ASU Law Journals 1970 to 2020   *315*

Chapter 23
    ASU Law Center for Law, Science, & Technology, 1984   *319*

Chapter 24
    Dean Paul Bender, 1984 to 1989   *333*

Chapter 25
    The James Hamm Saga 1993 to 2005   *355*

Chapter 26
    Dean Richard Morgan, 1989 to 1997   *367*

Chapter 27
    ASU Law School Celebrates Its 25th Anniversary, 1970 to 1992   *379*

PART THREE: *The Success Years—2000 to 2020*   389

Chapter 28
    Dean Patricia White, 1997 to 2007   *391*

Table of Contents

Chapter 29
    The Arizona Innocence Project & Larry Hammond, 1998   *403*

Chapter 30
    Associate Justice Sandra Day O'Connor Names the Law School. 2006   *411*

Chapter 31
    Dean Paul Schiff Berman. 2007 to 2010   *421*

Chapter 32
    Dean Douglas Sylvester, 2007 to present   *431*

Chapter 33
    The ASU Alumni Law Group, 2014   *449*

Chapter 34
    The Arizona Legal Center   *453*

Chapter 35
    The Sandra Day O'Connor College of Law at Washington, DC, 2015   *457*

Chapter 36
    Sandra Day O'Connor College of Law Legal Centers,
    Clinics & Programs   *461*

Chapter 37
    Sandra Day O'Connor College of Law Donations & Endowment   *479*

Chapter 38
    The Beus Center for Law & Society as of 2019   *489*

Epilogue   *509*

Acknowledgments   *515*

Index   *517*

FOREWORD

by Dean Douglas Sylvester

"Legacy" is a heavy word. It is something you inherit from the giants that have come before. You receive it, hope to live up to the values and achievements it represents, and then, if you are very lucky, you get the chance to add to it. Legacy is a gift, but it is also a burden. It is a privilege and an obligation.

Here in ASU Law's fiftieth (ish) year, it is clear all who currently enjoy the privilege of calling themselves alumni, students, staff, faculty or, least of all dean, are inheritors of a tremendous legacy. The youngest law school in the top 25. An alumni group that is the envy of schools a hundred years older. A law school staff dedicated to the success of all our graduates and its community. And a faculty that has produced scholarship that has made a real difference.

This awesome history was not happenstance. The legacy of fifty years that we now inherit was the conscious and deliberate action of a generation of law professors, staff, students, alumni, and administrators to make it so. The narrative of this law school's rise and impact is a compelling story—and it would have made sense to speak about it, as many others have, through an omnipotent narrator. That is not, however, how our author decided to approach this topic, and I personally believe he made entirely the right choice. The focus should not, today, be on the institution of the law school as an abstract entity—made of stone, wires, and fabric. Instead, Gary Stuart has rightly focused on the individuals who have forged its history.

I am very proud to call Gary a friend. The position he currently holds here at the Sandra Day O'Connor College of Law is one he held before I knew him—as Special Advisor to the Dean, appointed by Arizona State University President

Michael Crow. As you can imagine, when I first became interim dean in May of 2011 I was a little worried to meet Gary. I didn't know him (other than through reputation, which was also daunting) and, well, I feared his role was to spy on me for the president! Even worse, he was a graduate of that, um, other law school. Now, after a decade of close work and cooperation, if he is a spy, he is the best since Kim Philby—one would never suspect! Gary has proven a great friend to me and to this law school, and this latest project is one last gift he is giving all of us.

For those who don't know Gary, he is a dynamo of energy. Whether he is writing four novels a year, inspiring our students through his teaching, or starting organizations to improve our profession, he is always creating something. When he first approached me about his idea to create a work that would celebrate our fifty years, I didn't hesitate for a second. I knew that he would not only do the work that needed to be done, he would bring to bear his unique viewpoint on our history and the individuals who created it. This work is the result of that perspective and that passion, and I could not be more grateful for his work or more honored for being asked to write this foreword.

As the eighth dean of ASU Law, and only the third of the Sandra Day O'Connor College of Law (renamed in 2006), I know, intimately, the challenges of running a law school. In just the decade I have been dean, we have witnessed a crisis in legal education that called into question the very existence of dozens of law schools around the country. We have experienced massive change in how law graduates are trained and employed. And, in just the time since Gary began this work, we have experienced the worst public health crisis in a century and the greatest social movement to increase social justice in more than half a century. The Sandra Day O'Connor College of Law has emerged from all of these crises stronger than when it entered. We have become a true model for legal education and are poised to make even greater impacts in the next fifty years to come.

We have not done this alone. We have done this on the shoulders of those who forged the foundations for this school. Those foundations, and the contributions of all memorialized in this work (and so many more),[1] are the reason we persevered and thrived while others struggled. It is their zeal for a law school that would be different, that would be impactful at every level, and that would reflect our greatest mission to serve our students and community that allowed those who work here now to never lose sight of why we serve. That is our legacy, and that is why this law school will remain one of the greatest institutions for legal education in the world.

Foreword

I could easily thank hundreds of our faculty, alums, staff, and friends. I won't do so here, but I hope many of you know how much the history of this law school is linked to your passion. However, I have to single out three people. First, thank you, Gary Stuart, for taking on this momentous task. This history would not exist without you, and I hope all take a moment to let him know our gratitude. Second, thanks to our founding Dean, Willard Pedrick. He crafted a unique, mission-driven law school focused on our students and community, and we will never lose sight of that. Finally, thanks to our namesake, Justice Sandra Day O'Connor. Your historic career, your passion for public service, and your constant passion to force the United States legal system to recognize its global commitment to humanity inspire us to larger visions and ambitions every single day.

We are so lucky to have this volume. The legacy we've inherited is now ours to extend, preserve, improve, and create for the next generation to carry on. Let's embrace that challenge, and the next fifty years, with the same enthusiasm, passion, and brilliance of those who have gone before. We do so with thanks to our greatest inspirators and we urge our readers to consider, closely, the stories of these giants. It is with specific thanks and inspiration that I wish to end.

---

1 It would not be an essay from a law professor without at least one footnote! This one is to say that we have created a website to collect the stories and histories of those we have neglected to include in this published volume.

AUTHOR'S NOTE

Some might wonder why a graduate of Arizona's other law school is writing ASU Law's history. True enough—I was a third-year law student in 1967 at the other one. However, over the last fifty years I have interacted with thousands of ASU Law's students, faculty, benefactors, and graduates. My thirty-year stint at Jennings Strouss & Salmon gave me the opportunity to practice with and against hundreds of ASU grads as opposing counsel, judges, and colleagues in bar-related activities and CLE programs. I have been on ASU's adjunct faculty since 1994. I've given advice to three deans and countless students. Consequently, I was thrilled when asked write its history.

The book's scope encompasses all aspects of legal education and lawyer skills training at ASU over the last half century. No work of history can ever pretend to be comprehensive or universal. There are written records revealing the imagining, conjuring, and convening of the law school between 1965 and 1967. And there are archival and digital sources from then to now. However, barring the invention of time travel, no legal historian can experience the past firsthand, or recreate its conditions in a laboratory setting. We rely on fragmentary records that survive from the period under study, which necessarily reveals just part of the story.

Writing the history of this law school required extensive research, analysis, selection, and interpretation. I went through a comparable educational experience at Arizona's other law school, at substantially the same period of time, took the same basic curriculum, taught by legal scholars of comparable talent and focus. I hope my selections and interpretations fit and the book feels comfortable to those who actually attended ASU Law. I know I benefited greatly from attending the other law school and from teaching at this one. My research and long relationship with the school convinces me that thousands of ASU Law's graduates served Arizona and our country at the highest levels. That said, readers are like jurors—they get the last say.

While I had help from students, graduates, teachers, administrators, librarians, and many lawyers and judges, I alone am responsible for selection and interpretation. That's how history is made. This book is chock-full of subjective decisions I made about what to include, exclude, and how best to present the college's historical story. Disagreeing about history is its essence. Importantly, other scholars, teachers, and students will surely find mistakes and omissions in the text. I've written five other books about Arizonans and their legal cases, events, and histories; each bears the scars of subjective selection. I see legal history writing as an ongoing argument over the unavoidable process of selection and interpretation. I hope my book fully demonstrates the vision of President Homer Durham and Dean Willard Pedrick. And I hope it meets the exacting standards of two good friends, President Michael Crow and Dean Douglas Sylvester. Their collective dreams evolved into today's Sandra Day O'Conner College of Law at Arizona State University.

PROLOGUE

This is a story about launching a legacy. Fifty years in the making, one lawyer at a time. It was pure concept in 1965. No building, no faculty, no curriculum, no students, and no assurance. Legal education history is a complex calculus of committed people, big ideas, and access to the world of lawyers. It's bewildering at first, then with time, merely difficult. The prize, a *Juris Doctorate* degree and a license to practice law, is priceless to those who earn it, and invaluable to those they represent. Its costs pale against its rewards—advancing the rule of law, the rule of nations, and access to justice. In 1960s Arizona, the law was a multicolored umbrella covering every aspect of life in the Valley of the Sun. The challenge was daunting, but the founders were fit for the task.

All it took was a great dean, excellent teachers, bright and eager students, doggedness, self-confidence, and trust in one another. Each of the eight inaugural faculty members was chosen for their solid teaching credentials, but none had actually created a law school from scratch. The inaugural student body knew they were an experiment but had no fear. Together, they built a band of talented instrumentalists who would occasionally confront legal order while always advancing the rule of law. They would surpass all expectations as they took their place in law practice, commerce, government, community outreach, and scholarly output. They made their university proud, rendered high service to central Arizona, and achieved national prominence. Little did its designers know they would compose their own score, drive their own stakes in the desert, and mature as the *Sandra Day O'Connor College of Law at ASU.*

What they sketched out on legal pads in 1965 would become a safe haven for questing legal assumptions, dashing legal fantasies, and a sky-high talent pool of determined, forceful, and committed advocates. Those inaugural teachers, scholars, planners and students didn't age—fifty years decorated them. Today we see them as legends in law and accessories to justice in our civil and criminal systems. It took two years, 1965 and 1966, to find a facility, design a curriculum, recruit a student body, and make good on that first promise—we will teach the law in ways not yet seen in American legal education. That first class would literally become the second promise—practice-ready lawyers—eager to deliver on time and on point—they advanced the rule of law.

It was not a peaceful time. No one could have predicted just how raucous and explosive America would become in the sixties. The placid Tempe campus, graced by palm fronds and wide walking boulevards, became contested ground. Nestled among thousands of undergraduates, the new law students hunkered down. It would take grit and purpose; they had plenty of both. They settled into new classrooms learning old law. There was a common sense their educations would test old paradigms, accepted norms, and a restless nation seeking long-withheld justice for people of color, victims of economic distress, and the decay of intolerance and bigotry. It all happened during the height of the Vietnam War, and just before the oncoming train wreck that plagued the Nixon administration and tested America's vaunted rule of law. Graduates in those early years not only read the news about Vietnam, many served there and came home maimed but determined to succeed in law practice and in government service.

The sixties also showcased the growing gap between "haves" and "have-nots" in the United States. In too many states, the shredding of the economic safety net was scarring and searing. It was not entirely about the racial gap, but the 1960s played a huge role in expanding that gap. It was a time of political assassination and soaring eloquence. JFK, Bobby Kennedy, and Martin Luther King had lived at the intersection of poverty, race, and the importance of education. The first law school graduating class of 1970 knew they had to face down legal barriers to equality. It was a testing time. Watergate was not yet on the legal horizon, but its building blocks were. Education, health care, jobs, and an all-out attack on the justice system from within was steaming. Would America have the national will to implement solutions? ASU's first law graduates would take their place in restoring confidence in our justice systems.

The Warren Court handed down a series of decisions between 1961 and 1969 that expanded citizens' due process rights and limited police powers. Some police

Prologue

administrators complained that Fourth, Fifth, and Sixth Amendment limits on police powers to question, arrest, search, and seize made it too difficult for police to fight crime. Civil liberties advocates heralded the revolution in criminal procedure as a way to ensure that police treated those accused of crimes fairly. The first three classes at ASU Law, starting with the first graduating class in 1970, took up the challenges and tremors in Arizona courtrooms. The law college also delivered transactional lawyers to ever-expanding cities in Arizona.

A century and a half earlier, law professorships, proprietary law schools, and bar associations were formed in every state of what would become a divided nation, at war with itself. Unfortunately, in 1828, the country took a backward step into populism. Andrew Jackson was elected as the seventh President of the United States in 1828. He was a lawyer, but claimed to be a champion of the common man. State legislatures capitulated, disavowing what the common man saw as elitist and reasserting authority over lawyers and law practice, earlier delegated to bar associations. Men who could claim "good moral character" became lawyers notwithstanding their utter lack of legal knowledge. They practiced law by the seat of their pants. Bar examinations were perfunctory, and the law ailed. But post-Civil War measures brought new standards to legal education.

Justice Joseph Story served on the U.S. Supreme Court from 1812 to 1845. He simultaneously taught law at Harvard Law School from 1829 to 1845. That augured Harvard's emergence as the first modern law school. Exactly one hundred years before the ASU class of 1970 graduated, Christopher Columbus Langdell became Dean of Harvard Law School, essentially launching the modern era of legal education. The Class of 1970 was educated along the lines established a century before.

Dean Langdell believed law could be taught as a science. Rather than listening passively to lectures and reading treatises, his students dissected lawsuits and criminal charges. Using a technique known as Socratic dialogue, professors bombarded their students with questions, forcing them to analyze the facts, reasoning, and law in each case. In addition, Langdell grouped related cases together, devoting separate books to different topics. Dean Langdell's method of instruction through dialogue and case study was adopted by Dean Willard Pedrick for ASU's new law school.

Dean Pedrick adopted Dean Langdell's method while at the same time creating a new dialogue and case study that would last fifty years and is still emerging, changing and making history.

PART ONE

The Pedrick Years: 1965 to 1975

Matthew Hall circa 1965

CHAPTER 1

CREATING THE ARIZONA STATE UNIVERSITY COLLEGE OF LAW

Creating ASU's College of Law followed the usual circuitous route that historically defined the relationship between Arizona's two largest cities—Phoenix and Tucson. Both cities were proxies for the *University of Arizona* in Tucson and *Arizona State College* in Tempe. They fought intensely for everything—prestige, power, and money. Both wanted a medical school. Only one would be chosen by the governing entity—the *Arizona Board of Regents*. The fight began in 1958 with a charitable donation of $565,700.00 to establish a medical school in Arizona. The donation was made to Arizona State College in Tempe, then Phoenix's suburb to the east.[1] But as the proxy war was fought out in ABOR hearings, the Tucson Medical Center offered to convey its facilities to start a medical school on two conditions: that it would become the hospital, and the medical school would be established at the University of Arizona in Tucson. Bragging rights were at stake between ABOR's flagship university in Tucson and its younger sibling, Arizona State College, in Tempe.

ABOR commissioned a long study to be conducted by a neutral expert. It selected Dr. John F. Volker, Director of Research and Graduate Studies at the University of Alabama Medical Center, to conduct the study. He submitted his report to ABOR in 1961 recommending that the medical college be built at the University of Arizona in Tucson.[2] Naturally, ASU's President, Dr. G. Homer Durham, took umbrage, but saw the loss as an opportunity for ASU to get a law school, which the University of Arizona might oppose, given its College of Law in Tucson had been supplying the state's lawyers and judges since 1915. Did the state need two law schools? In October 1964, without dissent, the Regents approved colleges of law and fine arts on ASU's Tempe campus.[3] Dr. Durham promptly hired Willard H. Pedrick, a law professor since 1946 at Northwestern University in Evanston, Illinois, to be the first dean at ASU's College of Law.

THE PHOENIX METROPOLITAN AREA

The Phoenix metropolitan area in the mid-1960s was on the cusp of national standing. That included its favorite suburb, Tempe. Both grew, one by leaps and bounds, the other by streets and blocks, after World War II, but collectively they exploded in what is now known as its "modern era." Nineteen seventy, the year ASU Law graduated its first class, was particularly growth oriented. The dry Salt River meandered along the northern edge of the ASU campus in Tempe, down through Phoenix's southern edge. There was little to differentiate the boundary lines between Phoenix and Tempe. The Valley that both called home gently sloped up and down the riverbed, punctuated by mountain ranges on both sides.

Substantial growth in both cities between the late forties and the mid-sixties came from "the desire of ex-servicemen stationed in the area during the war to return; improvements in air conditioning; charter government in Phoenix, which allowed a small pro-growth business group to gain power; and aerospace and electronics firms siting facilities, in part because of the federal government's designation of Fort Huachuca as the principal proving ground for electronic defense equipment. The modern period began around 1970, when a maturing metro area coincided with the baby-boom generation reaching adulthood. The result was even more rapid growth that has continued to the current time. Rapid growth of the Phoenix metro area was expected to continue for fifty years. Some estimates speculated a population in the metropolitan area of nearly seven million by 2050."[4] And ASU Law's inaugural graduating class of 1970 was there ready to do its part in advancing that stunning growth rate.

In 1970, the population of the Phoenix metropolitan area was 971,000. The urbanized area population was 863,357, four times what it had been in 1950 when Nick Udall was mayor and Barry Goldwater was a fledging city council member. The urbanized area spread over 387.5 square miles, resulting in a relatively low population density of 2,228 per square mile. By 1970, the Valley's population had spread beyond the city of Phoenix, but the city still was growing rapidly, and its 584,000 residents constituted 60 percent of the metro population. Mesa, the Valley's second most populous city through most of its existence, had a population in 1970 of 63,000, similar to that of Scottsdale and Tempe. Glendale and Chandler were the only other cities with over 10,000 residents.[5]

THE ARIZONA STATE BAR ASSOCIATION

The State Bar of Arizona in 1970 had less than 7,000 lawyers[6] with active licenses. ASU Law's graduating class of 1970 added another eighty-seven to the growing list of Arizona lawyers. They joined scores of law firms, prosecutorial agencies, public defender's offices, nonprofit law firms, and other legal entities. Chief Justice Lorna Lockwood and Justices Jesse Udall, Ernest McFarland, Jack Hays, and William Cameron presided over the swearing-in ceremony at the Arizona Supreme Court Building on the state capitol mall.[7]

Those newbie lawyers would take their place among Arizona's already rich lawyering and judicial history. The historic list already included Lorna Lockwood, the first female chief justice of any state supreme court; Valdamar Cordova, the first Hispanic federal district court judge; Thomas Tang, the first Chinese American federal judge; and Wing Ong, the first Asian American elected to state office.[8] Among the important legal issues of the day were fundamental immigration, civil rights, Fifth Amendment rights, Arizona's rights to Colorado River water, and female workers' rights to retirement benefits.[9] In a short time, the rights of lawyers to advertise their services and to practice law without regard to their political beliefs would take center stage nationally. ASU's first law graduates would be at the forefront of many of these cases.

Sandra Day O'Connor would come to play many roles in Arizona and America. When the Class of '70 graduated, she was the majority leader of the Arizona Senate. The next year, 1971, she wrote a letter to President Nixon, who was facing two U.S. Supreme Court vacancies. She urged him to consider a woman: "It is my belief that the citizens of this nation would warmly accept appointment of a woman to the Supreme Court."[10] Instead, Nixon appointed Lewis Powell, and William Rehnquist, a classmate of hers at Stanford. Many of ASU's law graduates tried cases or argued appeals before Sandra Day O'Connor here in the 1970s. She was a

Maricopa County Superior Court judge from 1975 to 1979, when Governor Bruce Babbitt appointed her to the Arizona Court of Appeals. She met President Reagan for the first time on July 1, 1981, in the Oval Office. He didn't interview anyone else after that meeting. He appointed her to the United States Supreme Court as an Associate Justice. She was confirmed by the U.S. Senate with a vote of 99–0 and took her seat as the first female U.S. Supreme Court Justice on September 25, 1981. She was then, as everyone in Arizona already knew, a "person for all seasons."[11]

Law schools reflect the visions and accomplishments of their deans. Willard Pedrick was the founding dean in 1965. Douglas Sylvester is the dean in 2020. Both were visionary. Dean Pedrick began with almost nothing—no faculty, students, building, or even a mission statement. But he had the vision and the strength of character to build what would become a top-25 American law school. He described himself in his first report to the ASU President as a "minister-without-portfolio commuting to Tempe from Northwestern Law School to work on a variety of matters." Dean Sylvester, fifty-five years later, had much more to say about the law school he built on the foundation laid by Dean Pedrick:

> *At ASU Law, we offer comprehensive curriculum, which includes more than 250 unique courses offered each year so students can tailor their education to their interests. We believe providing personalized and practical legal education is paramount. And therefore, we offer a number of programs and guaranteed externships that are led and supported by faculty, staff, and other experts who are passionately focused on students' success. And while we continue to increase the number of programs we offer and experience growing student interest, we continue to have one of the best student-to-faculty ratios in the country. ASU Law and its home in downtown Phoenix, the nation's fifth largest city, provide tremendous opportunities that range from exciting intellectual and practical academic experiences, to economic advantages that come from being the only law school within 100 miles and just steps away from law firms, government entities, and businesses. Opportunities also come in the form of rich cultural activities and an overall lifestyle that is enhanced by endless sunshine and the great outdoors. ASU Law also offers extensive programs beyond Phoenix, in key places like Washington, D.C., and Los Angeles.*[12]

There were no law school "rankings" in the sixties, but it's fair to guess that the ASU School of Law was an experiment in the making. In 2020, the school was ranked twenty-fourth in the nation, out of 206 ABA-accredited law schools. This book is the story of how that happened.

ABOR

The Arizona Board of Regents (ABOR) is a constitutional entity under Article 11, Section 5 of Arizona's constitution.[13] Article 11, Section 5 gives ABOR sole power to govern all three of our universities. "The legislature shall enact such laws as shall provide for the establishment and maintenance of a general and uniform public school system, which . . . include: . . . Universities . . ."[14] ABOR provides policy guidance to Arizona State University, Northern Arizona University, and the University of Arizona. It governs nine specific areas ranging from academic and student policies, construction plan, legal affairs, audit services, and the creation or dissolution of colleges, departments, centers and institutes. Creation of a new college on any university campus must first be approved by ABOR. On October 3, 1964, ABOR established two new colleges at Arizona State University—a College of Law and a College of Fine Arts.[15]

President G. Homer Durham spent a good deal of time over the next three years pushing, pulling, and nudging the new law school into existence. His first and unquestionably most important task was finding the right person to name as the inaugural dean. That turned out to be Willard H. Pedrick, JD. He was born in Ottumwa, Iowa, in 1914, received his BA from Parsons College in 1936 and his law degree from Northwestern University in 1939. He was first admitted to law practice in Iowa and secured a coveted one-year clerkship with Judge Frederick Moore Vinson at the U.S. Court of Appeals for the District of Columbia Circuit. He spent his first year in academia at the University of Cincinnati. In 1941, he joined the law faculty at the University of Texas at Austin. In 1942, he returned to Washington, DC, to work in the tax section of the Justice Department and subsequently in the Office of Economic Stabilization. In 1943, the U.S. Marine Corps commissioned him as a First Lieutenant and assigned him to the Intelligence Service. He left the Corps in 1945 to practice law in Iowa.

He joined the faculty at Northwestern University Law School in Chicago and moved steadily up the academic ladder for twenty years (1946 to 1966). He became the founding Dean of the College of Law at Arizona State University in 1965 and held the office until 1976, then continued to serve as a Professor of Law until his retirement in 1983. He was known all over America as a legal scholar and wrote many noted books and articles in his specialties, tort and tax law. He was well known as an expert on Australian law, a subject of great personal interest. That's his official, formal, new-dean reputation.

Dean Pedrick was, in his own words, "a kind of minister-without-portfolio commuting to Tempe from the Northwestern University School of Law to work on a variety of matters."[16] It was a busy commute. The "variety of matters" included extensive consultations with the architectural firm, Cartmell & Rossman, as they designed the new law-school building on the Tempe campus; preparation of the Federal Grant Application designed to secure federal funding for the building under the Higher Education Facilities Act of 1962[17]; and developing plans for the law library.[18]

Clarence Darrow famously said, "[t]he trouble with law and government is lawyers."[19] Dean Pedrick would come face-to-face with that reality as he worked to create a new law school with old government money. "Ped," as he liked to be called, was never without a deep thought, or a quick quip. He moved from Chicago to Tempe in July 1966 and met a pre-law student on the Tempe campus. He asked Ped, "What does a Dean do without faculty, students, or any instructional program in operation?" Ped's on-the-spot answer was that "he organizes."[20]

While he didn't keep a journal, it is likely that Ped spent some of his first summer on campus at ASU's Hayden Library. In 1966, when Hayden Library first opened, it had 205,000 square feet of space. Arizona State University was not yet a decade old—it had about 20,000 students. Today that iconic main library contains approximately 4.5 million volumes, and ASU's student population is four times what it was in 1966, including a growing segment of online students who may never step foot in an ASU library during their college career.[21]

PED'S PLAN

The law school officially opened in September of 1967, but not in its own building. The first classes were taught in 1967, pending completion of Armstrong Hall in 1968. Dean Pedrick's plan was traditionally ordered: "(1) faculty and staff recruitment, (2) development of the Law Library, (3) planning for the new physical plant, (4) development of the instructional program, (5) student enrollment and, finally (6) the organization and development of the Law Society of Arizona State University, a supporting arm for the new College."[22]

This five-part organizational plan (faculty—library—building—students—law society support) illustrates Dean Pedrick's priorities.[23] He knew that faculty had to come first because "the new school would rest heavily on the quality of the faculty recruited."[24] He aimed high "at the outset to attract not only able, but outstanding, nationally-known legal scholars."[25] He understood that "the attractions of the Phoenix area, the dynamic quality of Arizona State University and its mission for the future, together with reasonably competitive salaries and the excitement of helping to create a new law school would . . . attract some outstanding law teachers."[26]

PED'S FACULTY PICKS

Pedrick's first pick was an obvious one. He wanted someone who knew the job, had an international reputation, and was readily available. So, he picked his former dean at Northwestern. Professor Harold C. Havighurst[27] was sixty-eight years old, an unquestioned authority in the law of contracts and commerce, who "play[ed] a strong game of tennis, and his vitality in the classroom [was] legendary."[28]

His second pick was Professor Edward W. Cleary, who was then teaching at the University of Illinois College of Law. Cleary was a national authority on civil procedure and evidence, and Pedrick thought he might be looking for a more "attractive climate." He was fifty-nine years old and at "the peak of his productive powers as a scholar, a fact attested to by the circumstance that he [was] the Reporter on the Federal Rules of Evidence Project, appointed as such by the Supreme Court of the United States."[29]

With Havighurst and Cleary on board, Pedrick turned to the most difficult aspect of building a law school from scratch—the law librarian. He knew it would be the hardest position to fill because "[a] good law librarian must be professionally trained, preferably with a degree in library science, [and] additionally, be a qualified lawyer, with a law degree."[30]

In retrospect, this pick proved Pedrick understands what kind of law school he wanted to build. He wanted a law faculty that could teach law, but he also wanted one that included *qualified* lawyers. Then, as now, many law teachers were well versed in teaching the law, but not qualified to practice it. He found Professor

Richard D. Dahl, who at the time was the State Law Librarian for the State of Washington. Dahl was also the editor of the National Law Library Journal.

Just after persuading Professor Dahl to come to Arizona, he found University of Wisconsin's Professor Richard W. Effland. He'd been teaching law for twenty years and was an expert in property, trusts, and probate. Professor Effland was best known as one of the drafters of the new Uniform Probate Code. He had already decided to leave Wisconsin for a more moderate climate and was being courted by the University of Georgia, and Texas Tech. Pedrick persuaded him to come to Arizona. Twenty-five years later, Pedrick revealed just how he had won that competition. "[My] strategy was simple; I visited him in Madison Wisconsin, when it was 25 below zero. Then I had him come to Tempe in February when the orange trees were in bloom. Later I think he developed an allergy to orange blossoms. But by then he was here."[31]

Once he had a seasoned faculty core—Havighurst, Cleary, Dahl and Effland—Pedrick looked for a younger man for his founding faculty. He found Professor William C. Canby,[32] a 1956 graduate of the University of Minnesota, who had ranked number one in his class. Canby's first job out of law school had been a clerkship with United States Supreme Court Justice Charles E. Whittaker.[33] Then Canby spent three years practicing law with a distinguished St. Paul law firm. He rounded out his early career by spending four years with the Peace Corps in Africa. Those varied experiences made him one of the most highly sought-after young professors in the country. Pedrick entered the competition for him with UCLA, Washington, Texas, and Virginia. Pedrick prevailed and Canby became the fifth new faculty member in 1966.

With a strong faculty on board, Pedrick turned to recruiting key staff. He hired Kay Johnson as his secretary, knowing "she was an able executive, a skilled diplomat, and an expeditor—the ideal law dean's secretary."[34] Then he hired Mr. Shyam Hemrom-Maji as manager of Supporting Services, another import from Northwestern School of Law. He oversaw all administrative responsibilities. Pedrick said his "departure from Northwestern was cause for anguish on their part and rejoicing on ours."[35]

PED'S PRIMER ON LAW SCHOOL EDUCATION

Once he'd secured five excellent teachers, Pedrick turned his attention to what they'd teach. As he explained in his 1996 First Report to President Durham, the program of legal education was directly tied to faculty, building, and student body. "[T]he architecture of the new building is definitely affected by the nature of the [instructional] program . . . . Both the size and nature of the faculty are affected directly by the nature of the intended program . . . [Selecting] the student body will be affected by the nature of the school and its offerings."[36]

Ped came from a highly regarded and very traditional law school curriculum. He was thinking about what changes should be made from traditional to modern—*how* traditional should his new law school be. Just as there is a history about the study of math, biology, or politics, law study has its own historical predicate. Led by Ped, ASU Law's founding faculty in 1966 created a structural approach to the how, what, when, and why elements of the study of law at ASU. It varied slightly from a traditional model but felt quite familiar. Of course, there is no way of reading Dean Pedrick's mind given the half-century gap between what he said then and what he might say today. But Albert Einstein was not inhibited by time or distance. He said, "It is essential that the student acquire an understanding of and a lively feeling for values. He must acquire a vivid sense of the beautiful and of the morally good. Otherwise he—with his specialized knowledge—more closely resembles a well-trained dog than a harmoniously developed person."[37] Ped was likely an Einstein fan, and would have loved the well-trained dog metaphor.

LEGAL EDUCATION DEFINED

"Legal education . . . Instruction in law has been offered in universities since medieval times, but, since the advent of university-based law schools in the 18th and 19th centuries, legal education has faced the challenge of reconciling its aim of teaching law as one of the academic disciplines with its goal of preparing persons to become members of a profession. Most law schools have tried to find a middle path between being a mere trade school and being a citadel of pure theory."[38] True enough, but making lawyers was never a trade—it was a professional calling. Law schools, at least the ones in Arizona in the 1960s, made no pretense of being citadels of pure theory.

"Unfortunately, the criticism is sometimes made that these efforts result in a type of education that is not practical enough to be genuinely useful in resolving day-to-day legal problems but yet not as rigorously theoretical as a truly academic discipline ought to be."[39] Both Arizona law schools offered rigorous disciplines. The quality of their graduates proves that.

Perhaps the founding faculty knew that Rome, back in its glory days, had schools of rhetoric. They trained nascent Roman advocates who may have avoided death struggles in the Colosseum based on their words rather than their fighting skills. There was no systematic study of the law as such. During the third century BC, Tiberius Coruncanius,[40] the first plebeian Pontifex Maximus (chief of the priestly officials), gave public legal instruction, and a class of jurisprudentes (non-priestly legal consultants) emerged.[41] Pedrick may have been an early admirer of the Roman invention of law professors. Almost certainly, one of his second group of faculty picks, Professor Jonathan Rose, would come to be a genuine expert on the history of law teaching.

LAW STUDY

In Europe's medieval universities, including those in England, it was possible to study canon law and Roman law, but not the local or customary legal system, since the latter was understood as parochial—and therefore unworthy of university inclusion. English common law was indigenous. In medieval times education in the common law was provided for legal practitioners by the Inns of Court. They read the law and dined together. The American version of this, particularly in Phoenix, is represented by the Sandra Day O'Connor Inn of Court.[42]

The famous jurist, Sir William Blackstone,[43] lectured on English law at Oxford in the 1750s, but university teaching of the common law did not develop significantly until the nineteenth century. Since the late twentieth and early twenty-first century, several nations have adopted the United States model of legal education, providing university-based instruction in law as a profession rather than only as an academic discipline. In the early years of the United States, persons hoping to enter the law sought apprenticeships in the offices of leading lawyers, a method of training that provided an acceptable avenue to the bar well into the twentieth century. The Litchfield Law School,[44] founded in Litchfield, Connecticut, in 1784 by Tapping Reeve, was the first institution of its kind in the United States. By the late nineteenth century, Harvard had put in place several practices that eventually came to define American legal education, including the use of the "case method" of instruction, the requirement that students complete three years of training, and using a full-time faculty of scholars, rather than a part-time faculty of practicing lawyers as had been the case. As the number of law schools grew, so too did the proportion of the bar who were law school graduates. By the early twenty-first century, the United States had over 200 accredited law schools and the world's largest bar, numbering more than 1 million members.[45]

BABY BOOMERS GOING TO LAW SCHOOL

Fast-forward to the 1960s when Dean Pedrick envisioned a new college of law at Arizona State University. At least one scholar called those heady times, "The Rise of the LSAT and the Law School Application Boom—1960 to 1980."[46]

> *At the same time that affirmative action programs were taking root at American law schools, other demographic trends were transforming the structure of opportunity to attend law schools. Applications to ABA law schools increased sharply between 1960 and 1975, particularly between 1968 and 1973. [The Law School Admissions Council (LSAC)] indicates those LSAT administrations, a close proxy for application trends, jumped from 23,800 in 1960 to 133,316 in 1975, and a stunning increase of 460%. Total ABA first-year enrollments increased from 17,031 to 39,038 between 1960 and 1975, a more modest increase of 129%. In other words, the demand for legal education skyrocketed, even relative to increased supply. This jolt was most pronounced between the late 1960s and the early 1970s.*[47]

These trends would soon have a substantial impact on opportunities for students of color.

> *The baby boom—the dramatic increase in American birth rates following World War II—contributed significantly to the sharp increase in law school applications during the 1960s and 1970s. Besides the simple effect of increased numbers, baby boomers approached adulthood in an era when higher education was available to a much larger segment of society. A legal education was more attainable because of the G.I. Bill, Cold War educational competition, a strong economy for educated workers, and increased funding for state universities and student grant and loan programs. Further, in the*

late 1960s and early 1970s, many young men were motivated to apply to law school because they opposed the war in Vietnam and were seeking draft deferments.⁴⁸

WOMEN GOING TO LAW SCHOOL

A second factor driving the increased competition to law schools in the 1970s was the steady rise in applications from women. In the 1950s and 1960s, law schools adopted policies and practices that excluded women. In those days, it was not seen as contradictory for the legal education establishment to advocate racial desegregation yet support discrimination against women. One, now famous, female lawyer comes immediately to mind—Justice Ruth Bader Ginsberg. One of the most frequently told stories about her is the dinner she attended at Harvard Dean Erwin Griswold's home. He asked each of the female 1Ls to justify why they were taking up a spot that could have gone to a man.⁴⁹ She graduated in 1959 from Columbia Law School, first in her class.⁵⁰ Perhaps she took the slot to prove she excelled above the men at Harvard Law in 1959.

> *For example, in 1951, the AALS Special Committee on Racial Discrimination was able to get 85 of 102 member law schools to vote in favor of a resolution, without enforcement provisions, opposing racial discrimination in law school admissions. Yet the AALS Special Committee was careful to note:*
>
> *"The suggestion has been urged upon the committee that if the Association condemns discrimination in admission on ground of race, then it should go further and condemn discrimination on grounds of sex or religion. The committee does not believe this is so."*
>
> *. . .*
>
> *In 1968, ten ABA-accredited law schools, including Notre Dame, still had zero female students. Other schools in the mid-1960s, like Columbia, placed ceilings on the number of women who could enroll. In the 1960s and 1970s, feminism, the Civil Rights Movement, and other social forces put pressure on law schools to open their doors to women—that is at least White women*

from middle- to upper-class backgrounds. At the same time, these same forces contributed to the substantial expansion of the pool of female applicants. [There were] 1064 women first-year students at ABA law schools in 1965 (4% of total enrollments), compared to 3542 in 1970 (10%), 10,472 in 1975 (27%), and 15,272 in 1980 (36%). This trend has continued, with 18,592 women in 1990 (42%) and 21,499 in 2000 (49%).[51] In 2016, women outnumbered men in law school classrooms for the first time on record. Last year was similar, with 2017 data revealing that women's enrollment as law students once again outpaced that of their male colleagues. According to 2017 data, 56,490 women (51.27%) . . . were enrolled in law school.[52] Women are breaking barriers in the legal profession every day, and law school enrollment is no different.

THE "CORE" IN CORE CURRICULUM

Pedrick and his founding faculty decided on a program that would deliver a core curriculum in the first two years. By *core*, he meant those "basic skills and techniques of the legal profession could be adequately imparted to a selected student body over a two-year period."[53] This was contrary to the prevailing notion in American law schools it took three years to deliver legal knowledge and basic skills. Bar examiners and accrediting agencies assumed and required a three-year program of instruction. The founding faculty's novel approach meant that in the third year, it would be "possible to undertake a number of new, and to some extent experimental programs." As Dean Pedrick put it, "The world changes and with the world, so also does the legal profession change." His thesis was packed into a tightly scripted message:

> *Many see the prospect that the distribution of legal services will be enlarged. In such case, the profession will serve a much wider segment of our society, and the nature of the tasks entrusted to the profession may very well alter, to some extent, so that new skills and new techniques will be needed. The impact of science on so much of modern life is not likely to leave the legal profession unaffected. So, here again, new subject matter and new teaching methods may be in order. In a new school, like the College of Law at Arizona State University, a unique opportunity is presented to structure a program to meet the needs of the present and hopefully of the future. We have, accordingly a*

> *"core curriculum" program that packs and compresses into the first two years a basic, conventional legal program and leaves an opportunity for experimentation open to the third year, when faculty manpower (saved through a required two-year curriculum) will be available to support significant new endeavors in legal education.*[54]

FACULTY SIZE

This unconventional program of instruction impacted faculty size. He planned sixteen to twenty faculty over the first three years with a faculty-student ratio of "1 to 20 or 1 to 25." He foresaw "very real advantages in a faculty sufficiently small to remain in relatively intimate communication so that a sense of faculty cohesion and corporate responsibility can be a significant factor in the development of the new school."[55] In what would become a hallmark over time, he also envisioned "facilitating unstructured contacts between faculty and students, and thus, provide significant human relationships as a feature of our program of legal instruction."[56]

PED'S PICKS FOR THE FIRST CLASS

Enrolling the first student body would have been a challenge for most states, but Dean Pedrick saw Phoenix as ready for the picking.

> *The prime student recruitment area for the Arizona State University College of Law is clearly the metropolitan Phoenix urban population center with its nearly one million people.*[57] *To "get the word" to prospective law students in this area, the principal means employed were the conventional media of communication, the newspapers in particular.... the Dean made a very substantial number of appearances before the various Service Clubs explaining the nature of the new College and extolling its virtues.*[58]

They also produced an announcement in *The Bulletin* in the summer of 1966 advertising availability for the entering class in the fall of 1967.[59] By any measure, the recruiting succeeded: 1,600 inquiries were received; 320 formal applications were filed; 160 were admitted; 118 actually showed up on the first day of class, September 12, 1967. The faculty measured the quality of the applicants by selecting only those "whose undergraduate academic performances and level of achievement on the Law School Admission Test gave a substantial promise of success in demanding law courses. A qualitative admission standard . . . was developed in cooperation with the University of Arizona College of Law, and the administration of this standard was developed—an applicant must demonstrate a median LSAT score of 543 (and an average of 547) with a GPA on the four-point system of 2.71. These standards are not as stringent as those administered by the most select private law schools."[60]

The geographic distribution was 25 percent from out of state. Dean Pedrick reported "on an overall basis, the quality of the first entering class must be adjudged to be highly satisfactory, with a number of outstanding students in the group."[61] He expressed confidence in the school's new "Secretary to Admissions, Mrs. Olivia Birchett."[62] The inaugural class was not defined by ethnicity or gender, but most remember several women and persons of color in the first class.

---

1 Earl Zarbin, Skip Bryant, and Peggy Bryant, *The Bench and the Bar: A History of Maricopa County's Legal Profession* (Chatsworth, CA: Windsor Publications, 1991), 66.

2 Ibid., 66.

3 Ibid., 66–67.

4 Tom R. Rex, "Development of Metropolitan Phoenix: Historical, Current and Future Trends," ASU Digital Repository, Arizona State University, August 2000, https://repository.asu.edu/items/12471.

5 Ibid., 10.

6 I know that because my bar number is 2061.

7 "Judicial History," Arizona Judicial Branch, accessed January 29, 2020, https://www.azcourts.gov/meetthejustices/Judicial-History.

8 Stan Watts, *Images of America—A Legal History of Maricopa County* (Charleston, SC: Arcadia Publishing, 2007).

9 Ibid., 7.

10 Philip Y. Blue, review of *Sandra Day O'Connor: How the First Woman on the Supreme Court Became Its Most Influential Justice,* by Joan Biskpic, *Arizona State Law Journal* 130, no. 17 (2005): 63.

11 President Ronald Reagan, "Remarks Announcing the Intention To Nominate Sandra Day O'Connor To Be an Associate Justice of the Supreme Court of the United States," press briefing, White House, Washington, DC, July 7, (1981), https://www.reaganlibrary.gov/research/speeches/70781a.

12 "Dean's Message," Sandra Day O'Connor College of Law, accessed January 29, 2020, https://law.asu.edu/about/dean-message.

13 Ariz. Const. art. XI, § 5. It derives its authority to operate the university system from the Arizona Legislature: "The legislature shall enact such laws as shall provide for the establishment and maintenance of a general and uniform public school system." Ariz. Const. art. XI, § 1. *See generally, Kromko v. Ariz. Bd. of Regents,* 213 Ariz. 607, 613 (Ct. App. 2006); Commc'ns Workers of Am. v. Ariz. Bd. of Regents, 17 Ariz. App. 398, 399 (1972).

14 Ariz. Const. art. XI, § 1.

15 *See* Minutes—ABOR—October 3, 1964. Regent John G. Babbitt, then ABOR President, called the meeting to order. Regents Vivian Lahti Boysen, Elwood W. Bradford, George W. Chambers, Wesley P. Goss, Arthur B. Schellenburg, Governor Paul Fannin, and Superintendent W.W. were present. Regent Schellenburg, Chairman of the Budget Committee presented four new matters to the board for action;

item number four was a motion by the chair to establish "a College of Law and a College of Fine Arts at Arizona State University, with the Deans or administrative offices to be included in the 1965–66 budget." Regent Gross seconded the motion. ASU President G. Homer Durham led a discussion. Both motions carried unanimously.

16 Willard H. Pedrick, *Report of the Dean* (Arizona State University College of Law, 1967), 1.

17 "H.R. 6143 (88th): An Act to authorize assistance to public and other nonprofit institutions of higher education in financing the construction, rehabilitation, or improvement of needed academic and related facilities in undergraduate and graduate institutions." "H.R. 6143. Higher Education Facilities Act. Adoption of Conference Report. – House Vote #85 – Nov. 6, 1963." GovTrack.us. Accessed January 28, 2020, https://www.govtrack.us/congress/votes/88-1963/h85.

18 Pedrick, 1–2.

19 Tryon Edwards D.D. et al., eds., *The New Dictionary of Thoughts–A Cyclopedia of Quotations* (Standard Book Company), 1965.

20 Pedrick, 1.

21 Lewis, Britt, "50 Years In, Hayden Library Plans a Remake," ASU Now: Access, Excellence, Impact, ASU News, February 4, 2017, https://asunow.asu.edu/20161130-50-years-hayden-library-plans-remake.

22 Pedrick, 1–2.

23 Ibid., 2–3.

24 Ibid., 2.

25 Ibid.

26 Ibid.

27 "Harold Canfield Havighurst, a professor and dean of the Northwestern University School of Law for 35 years until his retirement in 1966, and a recognized authority on the law of contracts, died last Tuesday in Alexandria, Va., where he resided. A graduate of Ohio Wesleyan University and the Harvard Law School, Mr. Havighurst joined Northwestern's law faculty in 1930. He became dean in 1948 and served until 1957, when he taught at Cornell Law School for a year before returning to Northwestern. He moved to Arizona in 1967, where he taught at the College of Law at Arizona State University. He served on a number of professional bodies at the state and national level and was a longtime member of the National Conference of Commissioners on Uniform State Laws." Harold C. Havighurst obituary, 1981. *New York Times*, October 20, 31.

28 Pedrick, 2.

29 Ibid., 2–3.

30 Ibid.

31 *The Arizona Law Forum*, Special 25th Anniversary Issue—1992, Dean Pedrick Address, 20.

32 "William Cameron Canby Jr. (born May 22, 1931) is a Senior United States Circuit Judge of the United States Court of Appeals for the Ninth Circuit, sitting in Phoenix, Arizona. As both a professor at Arizona State University College of Law and a Circuit Judge of the United States Court of Appeals for the Ninth Circuit, Canby has become known as an authority on American Indian law. He has authored law review articles, a major textbook, and the West Nutshell Series primer on the subject. While still a professor at ASU, Canby successfully argued the case of Bates v. State Bar of Arizona, in which the Supreme Court held that the First Amendment allows lawyers to advertise in a manner that is not misleading to members of the general public." Wikipedia, s.v., "William Canby," last modified October 15, 2019, 00:42, https://en.wikipedia.org/wiki/William_Canby.

33 *See*, Wikipedia, s.v., "Charles Evans Whittaker," last modified December 4, 2019, 04:51, https://en.wikipedia.org/wiki/Charles_Evans_Whittaker. "Charles Evans Whittaker (February 22, 1901 – November 26, 1973) was an Associate Justice of the United States Supreme Court from 1957 to 1962. After working in private practice in Kansas City, Missouri, he was nominated for the United States District Court for the Western District of Missouri. In 1956, President Dwight D. Eisenhower nominated Whittaker to the United States Court of Appeals for the Eighth Circuit. In 1957, he won confirmation to the Supreme Court of the United States, thus becoming the first individual to serve as a judge on a federal district court, a federal court of appeals, and the United States Supreme Court. During his brief tenure on the Warren Court, Whittaker emerged as a swing vote. In 1962, he suffered a nervous breakdown and resigned from the Court. After leaving the Supreme Court, he served as chief counsel to General Motors and frequently criticized the Civil Rights Movement and the Warren Court." Ibid.

34 Pedrick, 5.

35 Ibid.

36 Ibid., 9.

37 Edwards, 164.

38 Glendon, Mary Ann, Lionel Astor Sheridan, and William P. Alford, *Encyclopaedia Britannica*, Xth ed., s.v. "Legal Education," Chicago: Encyclopaedia Britannica, 2012, https://www.britannica.com/topic/legal-education (accessed January 27, 2020).

39 Ibid.

40 Wikipedia, s.v., "Tiberius Coruncanius," last modified August 12, 2019, 22:48, https://en.wikipedia.org/wiki/Tiberius_Coruncanius. "Tiberius Coruncanius was a consul of the Roman Republic in 280 BC. As a military commander in that year and the following, he was known for the battles against Pyrrhus of Epirus that led to the expression 'Pyrrhic victory.' He was the first plebeian Pontifex Maximus, and possibly the first teacher of Roman law to offer public instruction." Ibid.

41 Ibid.

42 "The Sandra Day O'Connor American Inn of Court," American Inns of Court, accessed January 27, 2020, https://inns.innsofcourt.org/for-members/inns/the-sandra-day-oconnor-american-inn-of-court.aspx. The author is proud to have been a founding member of this Inn of Court. We were called Masters of the Bench, but mostly we were masters of the dinner table.

43 *Encyclopaedia Britannica*, s.v. "Sir William Blackstone," Chicago: Encyclopaedia Britannica, 2019. https://www.britannica.com/biography/William-Blackstone (accessed January 27, 2020). Sir William Blackstone SL KC was an English jurist, judge and Tory politician of the eighteenth century. He is most noted for writing the Commentaries on the Laws of England. Born into a middle-class family in London, Blackstone was educated at Charterhouse School before matriculating at Pembroke College, Oxford in 1738. After switching to and completing a Bachelor of Civil Law degree, he was made a Fellow of All Souls, Oxford on 2 November 1743, admitted to Middle Temple, and called to the Bar there in 1746.

44 Wikipedia, s.v., "Litchfield Law School," last modified January 6, 2020, 20:21, https://en.wikipedia.org/wiki/Litchfield_Law_School.

45 Glendon, "Legal Education."

46 Kidder, William C., "The Struggle for Access from Sweatt to Grutter: A History of African American, Latino, and American Indian Law School Admissions, 1950–2000," *Harvard Blackletter Law Journal* 19 (2003): 14.

47 Ibid.

48 Ibid.

49 Collins, Julia, "Celebration 45: The Alumnae of Harvard Law Return to Cambridge," Harvard Law Today, February 25, 1999, https://today.law.harvard.edu/feature/celebration-45-alumnae-harvard-law-return-cambridge/.

50 Rahnavardy, Kambiz, "RBG, The Documentary," Columbia Alumni Association, Washington, DC, accessed January 28, 2020, https://dc.alumni.columbia.edu/rbg.

51 Kidder, 15–17.

52 Zaretsky, Staci, "There Are Now More Women In Law School Than Ever Before," Above the Law, March 7, 2018, https://abovethelaw.com/2018/03/there-are-now-more-women-in-law-school-than-ever-before/.

53 Pedrick, 10.

54 Ibid., 10-11.

55 Ibid., 11. Dean Pedrick wisely predicted some resistance to what amounted to a two-year program of legal instruction. He said in his First Dean's report, in connection with the anticipated February 1968 opening of the new building that he was planning a conference on, "Needed Innovations in Legal Education, where the focus will be on definite, concrete curriculum proposals with the expectation that some 50 or 60 legal educators would come to the Phoenix area. They would give the new faculty the benefit of 'relatively searching examination of possible and needed innovations in the world of legal education.'"

56 Ibid.

57 Ibid. Dean Pedrick was a little off on estimating population. The Phoenix area was estimated to be 698,000 in 1965. "1965 Population Estimate for Phoenix, United States of America," accessed January 28, 2020, https://books.mongabay.com/population_estimates/1965/Phoenix-USA.html.

58 Ibid., 13. 59 Ibid.

60 Ibid., 14.

61 Ibid.

62 Ibid. Mrs. Birchett was a "dedicated and able administrator with an impressive record of experience in professional, educational, and businesses offices." Ibid. She was said to have "an intelligent understanding of the importance of dealing with inquiries and applications in a way that would make a favorable impression upon those who contact the school." Ibid.

CHAPTER 2

STUDYING AND TEACHING LAW IN THE 1960S

Every student in the 1967 first-year class took Constitutional Law from Professor Canby, learning firsthand about America's most important civil rights cases:[1] (1) *Dred Scott v. Sandford*[2] (1857)—Decreed a slave was his master's property and African Americans were not citizens; struck down the Missouri Compromise as unconstitutional. (2) *Plessy v. Ferguson*[3] (1896)—Decreed segregation was legal and constitutional as long as "facilities were equal." (3) *Powell v. Alabama*[4] (1932)—Decreed and overturned the *Scottsboro Boys* convictions and guaranteed counsel in state and federal courts. (4) *Shelley v. Kraemer*[5] (1948)—Decreed a court may not constitutionally enforce a "restrictive covenant" which prevents people of a certain race from owning or occupying property. (5) *Brown v. Board of Education of Topeka*[6] (1954)—Reversed *Plessy v. Ferguson*'s separate but equal ruling and decreed that segregation in public education is a denial of the equal protection of the laws. (6) *Loving v. Virginia*[7] (1967)—Decreed the prohibition on interracial marriage was unconstitutional. Sixteen states that still banned interracial marriage at the time were forced to revise their laws. Arizona was not one of the sixteen.

Just four years before ASU Law's 1Ls began their individual searches for legal meaning in 1967, the movement burst out into the open under the Johnson administration. They saw the 1963 March on Washington[8] as a loud roar for the nonviolent civil rights struggle. This at a time when war was raging in Vietnam.[9] The law students in the late 1960s studied law in the larger context of the Vietnam War *and* the civil rights movement. No doubt many had supported civil rights movements and protests and some would in just two more years make their way to Vietnam.

Five days after the Kennedy assassination,[10] President Johnson lobbied Congress for the earliest possible passage of the slain president's civil rights package. The Civil Rights Act of 1964 passed the House and was sent on to the Senate, where conservative Southerners conducted a forty-seven-day-long filibuster (delaying of legislative action by means of excessively long speechmaking), the longest in Senate history. In June, the Senate voted to cut off debate. The bill passed both houses, was signed into law by President Johnson, outlawed racial discrimination in public accommodations and gave the U.S. Justice Department increased powers to push for school desegregation.[11]

Its passage created another cottage industry for those who resisted civil rights and espoused state's rights. Voting rights became a weapon in the fight for civil rights. The Voting Rights Act of 1965 overcame legal barriers at the state and local levels that prevented African Americans from exercising their right to vote as guaranteed under the Fifteenth Amendment to the U.S. Constitution. In just two years, a committed president and a hardworking legislature enacted the two most far-reaching pieces of civil rights legislation in U.S. history.[12]

THE SEXUAL REVOLUTION—NOT IN LAW SCHOOL

Lest the study of the law in the 1960s be remembered only for the legal issues, mention must be made about social changes, including the so-called sexual revolution. If memory serves, that era evoked some thought, a little action, and a lot of noise. College students in particular thought they could wake up their elders by challenging the status quo. "Attitudes to a variety of issues changed, sometimes radically, throughout the decade. The urge to 'find oneself,' the activism of the 1960s, and the quest for autonomy were characterized by changes towards sexual attitudes at the time . . . often today referred to generally under the blanket metaphor of 'sexual revolution.'"[13]

POLICING

Along with war, racism, and sex, there was widespread angst about policing. ASU law students read law in class after reading the morning newspapers coverage about how some police forces treated thousands of young protestors. Some remember the era as one of peace and love, but law students took note that America's police forces were quick to attack civil protestors. "Police were supposed to simply uphold the law without getting personally attached to victims or suspects. However, while the police wanted people to see them as an unmovable force of justice, the public saw something different. They saw police attacking peaceful civil rights protesters with hoses and dogs in Birmingham, Alabama, in 1963. They saw college students protesting war or racism shot by police in Jacksonville, Mississippi, in 1970, just after national guardsmen killed college students protesting at Kent State in Ohio . . . . Police were not seen as impartial. Violent police actions damaged the reputation of police officers, greatly reducing the trust between police and citizens."[14]

Ped's handpicked law students were flooded with case law, statutory interpretation, and constitutional oversight, interests in real property, contractual obligations, and torts of all kinds every day. Perhaps it was best they were so busy. Maybe they paid less attention to the violence and monumental change that reshaped American culture, the political scene, and everyday life. Undoubtedly, they paid more attention to these changes when they graduated and began practicing law. Some became prosecutors and tried street crimes. Some leaned to the defense side and rose up with the protest movement. Others started careers in transactional law and ignored the cultural changes that blossomed outside office walls. A few became activists. All law students in the 1960s shared one thing in common when they graduated—a relief that they were not in class anymore and living proof that the rule of law was worth the fight.

While the new dean, his faculty, and their students were deeply engrossed in creating ASU's new law school, the rest of America muddled on, as though momentous things were not happening in Tempe, Arizona.[15] America withered under the Vietnam War, raging 584 air miles away. It suffered riots at home and cultural changes that woke up the sleepy 1950s. But for all the sensation and fear of death and destruction, there were happy, uplifting things popping up in America.

The Beatles gave their last public performance on top of the Apple Records building.[16] The first Boeing 747 Jumbo Jet came out of its hangar.[17] Woodstock drew over 350,000 rock and roll fans. The music came from groups including the Doors, Led Zeppelin, and Janis Joplin. The festival took place on a New York farm. They swayed back and forth with the Who, Jimi Hendrix, and Crosby Stills & Nash.[18]

PBS—APOLLO 11—THE DOW JONES 1000—35-CENT GAS

PBS enthralled much of America.[19] Apollo 11's heroes, Neil Armstrong and Edwin "Buzz" Aldrin, became the first humans to set foot on the moon. We saw it all on TV and heard those muffled, but still immortal words, "That's one small step for man, one giant leap for mankind." Buzz Aldrin described the view as "[m]agnificent desolation."[20]

The inflation rate was 5.46 percent.[21] The Dow Jones hit the unbelievable high of 1,000 in 1972.[22] New houses cost, on average, $15,550.00. Gas was 35 cents a gallon.[23] The Echo 2 satellite mission ended in June 1969. Echo 2 was a 135-foot satellite launched by NASA in January of 1964. It orbited the Earth in a near-polar orbit during its time in space and was visible to the naked eye across Earth's surface due to its large size and type of orbit. It performed passive communications experiments and measured the shape of the Earth. Then, making sky-watchers all over the Earth sad, it burned up upon re-entry into Earth's atmosphere.[24]

IN COLD BLOOD—THE BOSTON STRANGLER—RACE RIOTS— KENNEDY AND KING ASSASSINATIONS

Crime and punishment flourished in the 1960s. Cyclopedia writers were busy. Crime stories made headlines. In 1959, two petty criminals, Richard Hickock and Perry Smith, murdered four members of the Clutter family in their home outside Holcomb, Kansas. The killers were apprehended, tried, found guilty, and executed. What earned the crime and its aftermath lasting notoriety was a celebrated, best-selling book. Truman Capote wrote *In Cold Blood* in 1965. Arguably, the first nonfiction account written in crime-novel style.[25] In 1966, Charles Whitman, an architectural engineering student at the University of Texas at Austin, climbed to the top of a 307-foot tower in the middle of the campus. He used a long-range rifle to shoot pedestrians and police. Before police killed him, fourteen people lay dead and thirty-one injured.[26] The "Boston Strangler" murdered thirteen women between 1962 and 1964. Albert DeSalvo was eventually arrested. While in jail, he confessed to a fellow inmate, was tried, convicted, and sentenced to life in prison. Someone murdered him in his cell in 1973. The case went cold until 2013, when DNA evidence linked him only to the last victim, making the case there were other Boston Stranglers on the loose.[27]

Besides the war, riots, politics, free love, and very loud music, the sixties became known as the decade of student awareness. They rose up, demanded reform, and became activists like no other college-student generation in American history. On campuses from Berkeley to New York, they demanded desegregation, unrestricted free speech, and withdrawal from the war in Vietnam. Highly idealistic and inspired by periodic successes, the student activists believed they were creating a new America.

"During the 1960s, young Americans on and off campuses challenged conventional lifestyles and institutions. They protested the materialism, consumerism, and mania for success that drove American society. They urged people to explore alternative patterns of work and domesticity. They challenged traditions surrounding sex and marriage. And they argued that all paths to deeper fulfillment, even those involving illicit drugs, could be justified."[28]

Not every student marched systematic to the same progressive vision. In many places, above and below the Mason-Dixon Line, segregation was defended. President Johnson had signed the 1964 Civil Rights Act—legislation initiated by President John F. Kennedy before his assassination—into law on July 2 of that year.[29] "Violence reared its ugly head. *Bloody Sunday*—March 7, 1965—the civil rights movement in Alabama took an especially violent turn as 600 peaceful demonstrators participated in the Selma-to-Montgomery march to protest the killing of a black civil rights activist by a white police officer and encourage legislation to enforce the Fifteenth Amendment."[30] Law students and faculty all over the country were numbed by Bloody Sunday news coverage, but were hopeful that Washington would step in. Dean Pedrick was busy traveling back and forth between Chicago and Tempe planning ASU's new law school.[31]

> *Some citizens and conservative politicians opposed expanding government services, arguing against governmental dependency. New counterculture lifestyles were condemned as immoral. Student protestors were labeled self-indulgent children without the experience vital to making adult judgments. By the 1960s, decades of racial, economic, and political forces, which generated inner city poverty, resulted in "race riots" within minority areas in cities across the United States. The beating and rumored death of cab driver sparked the 1967 Newark riots. This event became, per capita, one of the deadliest civil disturbances of the 1960s. The long and short-term causes of*

the Newark riots are explored in depth in the documentary film **Revolution '67** *and many news reports of the times. The riots in Newark spread across the United States in most major cities and over 100 deaths were reported. Many inner city neighborhoods in these cities were destroyed. The assassinations of Rev. Martin Luther King, Jr. in Memphis, Tennessee and later of Robert Kennedy in Los Angeles in 1968 also led to nationwide rioting across the country with similar mass deaths. During the same time period, and since then, violent acts committed against African-American churches and their members have been commonplace.*[32]

While Arizona's law students knew about the Newark riots and the assassinations, and certainly had opinions about those tragic events, they had cases to read and tests to take. This was the state of affairs as the 1967 entering class at ASU Law matured into its first graduating class in 1970. Collectively and individually, the ASU Class of 1970 would face all of these issues as lawyers, not just citizens.

RACISM IN THE 1960S

Creating a new college of law in the 1960s was not done in isolation. Dean Pedrick and his intrepid start-up faculty were well aware of the cultural and legal challenges defining America. They knew all too well this new law school could not be created in an academic vacuum. It would have to be sensitive to the rage of the days—civil rights and their dismal place in large swaths of white America.[33] As we all know now, the civil rights protests and boycotts of the fifties were mere prelude to the explosions, deaths, and tragedies in the sixties. Well-established organizations were on point, and on fire. The National Association for the Advancement of Colored People (NAACP)[34] and newly established spears like Southern Christian Leadership Conference (SCLC)[35] struggled mightily to reduce, but still live with racism. They employed legal means and nonviolent resistance. The first faculty at ASU Law must have been acutely aware of their role as teachers in such a divided America.

Efforts to integrate public schools flooded school districts with lawsuits. African Americans seated themselves at "whites-only" lunch counters and refused to leave until served. "By the end of 1960, some 70,000 had participated in such demonstrations in 150 cities and towns. Over 3,600 had been arrested."[36] Joining them were the Freedom Riders: groups of black and white Americans who traveled by bus across the South and tested Supreme Court desegregation rulings and similar federal legislation.[37]

THE SIXTIES CIVIL RIGHTS LAWS

President John F. Kennedy[38] campaigned on a promise to push through additional civil rights initiatives. While the Democrats controlled Congress, those in power were *conservative* Southerners who detested every part of so-called civil rights legislation. Eventually, these Southern Democrats became Republicans. However, the mounting, often violent, resistance to civil rights laws spurred Kennedy into action.

On June 11, 1963, President Kennedy sent his civil rights message to Congress, urging it to pass a civil rights act. Alabama Governor George Wallace's immediate reaction to the message was predictable. He ordered the physical blocking of two African American students whom a federal judge had ordered admitted to the University of Alabama.[39] President Kennedy's words were to all Americans but directly aimed at Governor Wallace.

> *This afternoon, following a series of threats and defiant statements, the presence of Alabama National Guardsmen was required on the University of Alabama to carry out the final and unequivocal order of the United States District Court of the Northern District of Alabama. That order called for the admission of two clearly qualified young Alabama residents who happened to have been born Negro . . .*
>
> *I hope that every American, regardless of where he lives, will stop and examine his conscience about this and other related incidents. This Nation was founded by men of many nations and backgrounds. It was founded on the principle that all men are created equal, and that the rights of every man are diminished when the rights of one man are threatened.*
>
> *Today we are committed to a worldwide struggle to promote and protect the rights of all who wish to be free. And when Americans are sent to Viet Nam or West Berlin, we do not ask for whites only. It ought to be possible, therefore, for American students of any color to attend any public institution they select without having to be backed up by troops.*

It ought to be possible for American consumers of any color to receive equal service in places of public accommodation, such as hotels and restaurants and theaters and retail stores, without being forced to resort to demonstrations in the street, and it ought to be possible for American citizens of any color to register and to vote in a free election without interference or fear of reprisal.

It ought to be possible, in short, for every American to enjoy the privileges of being American without regard to his race or his color. In short, every American ought to have the right to be treated, as he would wish to be treated, as one would wish his children to be treated. But this is not the case . . . .

This is not a sectional issue. Difficulties over segregation and discrimination exist in every city, in every State of the Union, producing in many cities a rising tide of discontent that threatens the public safety. Nor is this a partisan issue. In a time of domestic crisis men of good will and generosity should be able to unite regardless of party or politics. This is not even a legal or legislative issue alone. It is better to settle these matters in the courts than on the streets, and new laws are needed at every level, but law alone cannot make men see right.

We are confronted primarily with a moral issue. It is as old as the scriptures and is as clear as the American Constitution. The heart of the question is whether all Americans are to be afforded equal rights and equal opportunities, whether we are going to treat our fellow Americans, as we want to be treated. If an American, because his skin is dark, cannot eat lunch in a restaurant open to the public, if he cannot send his children to the best public school available, if he cannot vote for the public officials who represent him, if, in short, he cannot enjoy the full and free life which all of us want, then who among us would be content to have the color of his skin changed and stand in his place?[40]

This spiraling speech deeply inspired millions of Americans. At the time, ASU's new College of Law was almost a secret, outside the university community. But ASU President Homer Durham, Dean Willard Pedrick, and his not-yet-formed band of law-school-builders listened and took heed. They were no doubt acutely aware their new college would be populated by teachers and students who themselves were living the divided life President Kennedy so eloquently described in June of 1963. The new college they would create would be framed by civil rights, defined by color-blind policies, and inspired by Americans who knew all too well the tragedy of racism.

Martin Luther King, Jr. (1929–1968) became the era's high-profile civil rights leader.[41] In 1963, he led a protest in Birmingham, Alabama, one of the most segregated cities in America. From 1957 through 1963, Birmingham was the site of fifty racially motivated bombing incidents; the city's police force had a reputation for harassment of the black community. During the protest, King was arrested and jailed. Police dogs and fire hoses were unleashed on demonstrators. In the following weeks, hundreds of civil rights demonstrations were mounted across the South. All culminated in August with a massive national "March on Washington," the purpose of which was to lobby Congress to support President Kennedy's civil rights initiatives.[42]

President Kennedy's haters were not limited to racists. Some hated him for cultural, political, and other reasons not yet on the national rearview mirror. He was assassinated on November 23, 1963.[43] The week after the Kennedy assassination, his successor, Lyndon Baines Johnson,[44] asked Congress for the earliest possible passage of the slain president's civil rights package.[45] The 1964 Civil Rights Act passed the House and was sent on to the Senate, where conservative Southerners conducted a fifty-seven-day-long filibuster (delaying of legislative action by means of excessively long speechmaking), the longest in Senate history. In June, the Senate voted to cut off debate. The bill passed and was signed into law. Among its provisions, it outlawed racial discrimination in public accommodations and gave the U.S. Justice Department increased powers to push for school desegregation.[46]

---

1 "Ten Important Supreme Court Decisions in Black History: From Dred Scott to Affirmative Action," Infoplease, accessed January 29, 2020, https://www.infoplease.com/ten-important-supreme-court-decisions-black-history.
2 60 U.S. (19 How.) 393 (1857).
3 163 U.S. 537 (1896).
4 287 U.S. 45 (1932).
5 334 U.S. 1 (1948).
6 347 U.S. 483 (1954).
7 388 U.S. 1 (1967).
8 The March on Washington was a massive protest march that occurred in August 1963, when some 250,000 people gathered in front of the Lincoln Memorial in Washington, DC. Also known as the March on Washington for Jobs and Freedom, the event aimed to draw attention to continuing challenges and inequalities faced by African Americans a century after emancipation. It was also the occasion of Martin

Luther King, Jr.'s now-iconic "I Have A Dream" speech. "March on Washington," History.com, October 29, 2009, https://www.history.com/topics/black-history/march-on-washington.

9   The Vietnam War was an undeclared war in Vietnam, Laos, and Cambodia that lasted from November 1, 1955 until the fall of Saigon on April 30, 1975. The Vietnam War was known as the Second Indochina War; and in Vietnam, the war was called the Resistance War Against America or simply the American War. The Vietnam War was the second of the Indochina Wars and was officially fought between North Vietnam and South Vietnam. North Vietnam was supported by the Soviet Union, China, and other communist allies; South Vietnam was supported by the United States, South Korea, the Philippines, Australia, Thailand and other anti-communist allies. From some US perspectives, the war is considered a Cold War-era proxy war that lasted some 19 years, with direct US involvement ending in 1973 following the Paris Peace Accords. The Vietnam War included the Laotian Civil War and the Cambodian Civil War, resulting in Vietnam, Laos, and Cambodia becoming communist states in 1975. Wikipedia, s.v., "Vietnam War," last modified January 29, 2020, https://en.wikipedia.org/wiki/Vietnam_War. The Vietnam War is the subject of scores of documented summaries, epilogues, and books. *See also* "Vietnam War: Causes, Facts & Impact," History.com, October 29, 2009, https://www.history.com/topics/vietnam-war/vietnam-war-history; Ronald H. Spector, "Vietnam War," in *Encyclopædia Britannica*, Encyclopædia Britannica, accessed January 29, 2020, https://www.britannica.com/event/Vietnam-War.

10   The Kennedy assassination took place on November 22, 1963. "Life of John F. Kennedy," JFK Library, accessed January 29, 2020, https://www.jfklibrary.org/learn/about-jfk/jfk-in-history/november-22-1963-death-of.

11   "Civil Rights Act of 1964," National Park Service, accessed January 29, 2020, https://www.nps.gov/articles/civil-rights-act.htm.

12   "Voting Rights Act of 1965," History.com, November 9, 2020, https://www.history.com/topics/black-history-voting-rights-act.

13   Wikipedia, s.v., "Sexual revolution in 1960s United States," last modified December 12, 2020, 18:48, https://en.wikipedia.org/wiki/Sexual_revolution_in_1960s_United_States.

14   Christopher Muscato, "U.S. Policing After 1960: Influences & Developments," Study.com, accessed January 29, 2020, https://study.com/academy/lesson/us-policing-after-1960-influences-developments.html.

15   In 1970, Tempe had 63,550 residents, up 155% over its 1960 census. Its largest employer was then, and is now, Arizona State University. What was once a sleepy little college town is now a wide-awake university town, bustling as the town surrounding America's largest public university. Wikipedia, s.v., "Tempe, Arizona: Demographics," last modified February 9, 2020, 7:45, https://en.wikipedia.org/wiki/Tempe,_Arizona#Demographics. *See also* "Mapping the Largest Public University in America," Concept3d.com, https://www.concept3d.com/case-studies/asu. *See also* Rob Berger, "The 10 Largest Universities in the United States," last modified December 3, 2019, https://www.doughroller.net/education/the-10-largest-universities-in-the-united-states/.

16   "30th January, 1969. The Last Public Performance by the Beatles," The Beatles.com, accessed February 9, 2020, https://www.thebeatles.com/feature/30th-january-1969-last-public-performance-beatles.

17   "747 Timeline: Boeing 747," Boeing 747, accessed February 9, 2020, http://www.boeing-747.com/747_timeline.php.

18   "Woodstock: About," Woodstock.com, accessed February 9, 2020, https://www.woodstock.com/.

19   "About PBS," PBS.org, accessed February 9, 2020, https://www.pbs.org/about/about-pbs/.

20   Wikipedia, s.v., "Apollo 11," last modified February 9, 2020, 8:32, https://en.wikipedia.org/wiki/Apollo_11.

21   The inflation rate in the United States in 1970 was 5.57%. That was 0.63 less than it was in the preceding 1969 and 2.30% more than in the following 1971. "United States Inflation Rate in 1970," Statbureau.org, last updated September 20, 2014, https://www.statbureau.org/en/united-states/inflation/1970.

22   Cheers rang out on the floor of the New York Stock Exchange when the Dow Jones Industrial Average crossed the 1000 mark on November 14, 1972. If ever there was a psychological barrier for the Dow Industrials, "Dow 1000" was it. The average had knocked on the door of 1000 repeatedly for six years but could never close above that "magic" level until November of 1972. "Dow Jones 1970–1979," last updated May 23, 2008, https://leduc998.wordpress.com/2008/05/23/dow-jones-1970-1979/.

23   "What Happened in 1969 Important News Events, Key Technology and Popular Culture: Cost of Living in 1969," The People History, accessed February 9, 2020, http://www.thepeoplehistory.com/1969.html.

24   Wikipedia, s.v., "Project Echo," last modified February 9, 2020, 11:32, https://en.wikipedia.org/wiki/Project_Echo.

25 "Truman Capote," Encyclopedia.com, last modified January 29, 2020, https://www.encyclopedia.com/people/literature-and-arts/american-literature-biographies/truman-capote.

26 Scott McMillin, "Charles Whitman, The Texas Bell Tower Sniper, Kills 14<" Wordhistoryproject.org, https://worldhistoryproject.org/1966/8/1/charles-whitman-the-texas-bell-tower-sniper-kills-14. *See also* Wikipedia, s.v., "University of Texas Tower Shooting," last modified February 9, 2020, 11:32, https://en.wikipedia.org/wiki/University_of_Texas_tower_shooting.

27 Wikipedia, s.v., "Boston Strangler," last updated January 15, 2021, 14:02, https://en.wikipedia.org/wiki/Boston_Strangler.

28 Shmoop Editorial Team, "The 1960s Summary & Analysis," *Shmoop University, Inc.*, last modified November 11, 2008, https://www.shmoop.com/1960s/summary.html.

29 "Civil Rights Movement: Civil Rights Act of 1964," History.com, last updated August 28, 2019, https://www.history.com/topics/black-history/civil-rights-movement#section_8.

30 "Civil Rights Movement: Bloody Sunday," History.com, last updated August 28, 2019, https://www.history.com/topics/black-history/civil-rights-movement#section_8.

31 Dean Smith—Interview with Dr. Willard Pedrick, April 2, 1987, page 1. ASU Law Archives.

32 Wikipedia, s.v., "Mass Racial Violence in the United States: Civil Rights Movement: 1955–1973," last modified February 9, 2020, 4:51, https://en.wikipedia.org/wiki/Mass_racial_violence_in_the_United_States#Civil_rights_movement:_1955–1973.

33 For example, *see* "The 1960s Government, Politics, and Law: Topics in the News," Encyclopedia.com, last updated December 29, 2019, https://www.encyclopedia.com/social-sciences/culture-magazines/1960s-government-politics-and-law-topics-news.

34 "The mission of the National Association for the Advancement of Colored People (NAACP) is to secure the political, educational, social, and economic equality of rights in order to eliminate race-based discrimination and ensure the health and well-being of all persons." "What is the mission of the NAACP?" NAACP, accessed February 9, 2020, https://www.naacp.org/about-us/.

35 "The Southern Christian Leadership Conference (SCLC) is an African-American civil rights organization. SCLC, which is closely associated with its first president, Martin Luther King Jr., had a large role in the American civil rights movement." Wikipedia, s.v., "Southern Christian Leadership Conference," last modified February 9, 2020, 9:19, https://en.wikipedia.org/wiki/Southern_Christian_Leadership_Conference.

36 David Farber, *The Age of Great Dreams: America in the* 1960s (New York: Hill and Wang, 1994), 67.

37 "Freedom Riders," History.com, last updated October 3, 2018, https://www.history.com/topics/black-history/freedom-rides.

38 John Fitzgerald "Jack" Kennedy, often referred to by his initials JFK, was an American politician who served as the 35th President of the United States from January 1961 until his assassination on November 22, 1963. He served at the height of the Cold War; the majority of his presidency dealt with managing relations with the Soviet Union. A member of the Democratic Party, Kennedy represented Massachusetts in the U.S. House of Representatives and Senate prior to becoming president. Wikipedia, s.v., "John F. Kennedy," last modified February 9, 2020, 1:37, https://en.wikipedia.org/wiki/John_F._Kennedy.

39 (1963) John F. Kennedy, "We Have a Moral Crisis: The Civil Rights Message to Congress, 1963," Blackpast.org, last updated June 11, 2010, https://www.blackpast.org/major_speeches/1963-john-f-kennedy-civil-rights-message-congress-3/.

40 Ibid.

41 Wikipedia, s.v., "Martin Luther King Jr.," last modified February 9, 2020, 4:39, https://en.wikipedia.org/wiki/Martin_Luther_King_Jr.

42 "The Birmingham campaign, or Birmingham movement, was a movement organized in early 1963 by the Southern Christian Leadership Conference (SCLC) to bring attention to the integration efforts of African Americans in Birmingham, Alabama.

"Led by Martin Luther King Jr., James Bevel, Fred Shuttlesworth and others, the campaign of nonviolent direct action culminated in widely publicized confrontations between young black students and white civic authorities, and eventually led the municipal government to change the city's discrimination laws.

"In the early 1960s, Birmingham was one of the most racially divided cities in the United States, both as enforced by law and culturally. Black citizens faced legal and economic disparities, and violent retribution when they attempted to draw attention to their problems. Martin Luther King Jr. called it the most segregated city in the country. Protests in Birmingham began with a boycott led by Shuttlesworth meant to pressure business leaders to open employment to people of all races, and end segregation in public facilities, restaurants, schools, and stores. When local business and governmental leaders resisted the boycott, SCLC agreed to assist. Organizer Wyatt Tee Walker joined Birmingham activist Shuttlesworth and began what they called Project C, a series of sit-ins and marches intended to provoke mass arrests.

"When the campaign ran low on adult volunteers, James Bevel, SCLC's Director of Direct Action, thought of the idea of having students become the main demonstrators in the Birmingham campaign. He then trained and directed high school, college, and elementary school students in nonviolence, and asked them to participate in the demonstrations by taking a peaceful walk fifty at a time from the 16th Street Baptist Church to City Hall in order to talk to the mayor about segregation. This resulted in over a thousand arrests, and, as the jails and holding areas filled with arrested students, the Birmingham Police Department, led by Eugene "Bull" Connor, used high-pressure water hoses and police attack dogs on the children and adult bystanders. Not all of the bystanders were peaceful, despite the avowed intentions of SCLC to hold a completely nonviolent walk, but the students held to the nonviolent premise. King and the SCLC drew both criticism and praise for allowing children to participate and put themselves in harm's way.

"The Birmingham campaign was a model of nonviolent direct action protest and, through the media, drew the world's attention to racial segregation in the South. It burnished King's reputation, ousted Connor from his job, forced desegregation in Birmingham, and directly paved the way for the Civil Rights Act of 1964 which prohibited racial discrimination in hiring practices and public services throughout the United States." Wikipedia, s.v., "Birmingham Campaign," last modified February 9, 2020, 14:56, https://en.wikipedia.org/wiki/Birmingham_campaign. *See also* Momodu, S., "The Birmingham Campaign (1963)" Blackpast.com, last updated August 31, 2016, https://blackpast.org/african-american-history/birmingham-campaign-1963/.

43 "November 22, 1963: Death of the President," John F. Kennedy Presidential Library, accessed February 9, 2020, https://www.jfklibrary.org/learn/about-jfk/jfk-in-history/november-22-1963-death-of-the-president.

44 Lyndon B. Johnson, often referred to as LBJ, was an American politician who served as the 36th President of the United States from 1963 to 1969. Formerly the 37th Vice President of the United States from 1961 to 1963, he assumed the presidency following the assassination and death of President John F. Kennedy. A Democrat from Texas, Johnson also served as a United States Representative and as the Majority Leader in the United States Senate, becoming one of only four people who have served in all four federally elected positions. Wikipedia, s.v., "Lyndon B. Johnson," last modified February 9, 2020, 17:41, https://en.wikipedia.org/wiki/Lyndon_B._Johnson.

45 "Civil Rights Act of 1964," National Park Service, last updated March 22, 2016, https://www.nps.gov/articles/civil-rights-act.htm.

46 Just three years later, Dean Pedrick's first class at the ASU College of Law would take their first class in Constitutional Law from Professor Canby. They would learn that although the 13th, 14th, and 15th Amendments outlawed slavery, provided for equal protection under the law, guaranteed citizenship, and protected the right to vote, individual states continued to allow unfair treatment of minorities and passed Jim Crow laws allowing segregation of public facilities. These were upheld by the Supreme Court in *Plessy v. Ferguson* (1895), which found state laws requiring racial segregation that were "separate but equal" to be constitutional. This finding helped continue legalized discrimination well into the 20th century. Following World War II, pressures to recognize, challenge, and change inequalities for minorities grew. One of the most notable challenges to the status quo was the 1954 landmark Supreme Court case *Brown v. Board of Education of Topeka, Kansas* which questioned the notion of "separate but equal" in public education. The Court found that "separate educational facilities are inherently unequal" and a violation of the 14th Amendment. This decision polarized Americans, fostered debate, and served as a catalyst to encourage federal action to protect civil rights. "Civil Rights Act of 1964," National Park Service, last updated March 22, 2016, https://www.nps.gov/articles/civil-rights-act.htm.

CHAPTER 3

WILLARD HIRAM PEDRICK— FOUNDING DEAN—1965

This is *not* a book about Willard H. Pedrick, known by everyone who knew him as "Ped." Or is it? By design, this is the story of ASU's College of Law from 1965 to 2020. It is long, filled with large characters, a great deal of success, a modicum of false starts, and the many thousands impacted by its very

existence. Even though this book is not about him, it raises the question—what would it have become without his birthing, his push, his sense of humor, wit, and delight in the law, law teaching, and lawyering at the highest levels? There would have been a college of law at ASU, had ABOR and President Homer Durham selected some other law professor to be the founding dean. But it would not have been the college this book is about. Ped was *sui generis*[1]—one of a kind.

Ped's role as the founding dean is not merely part of its history. His character and sense of time and place speaks volumes about its success and impact. From day one, his story became the college's story. His part of the story blends his biography with its history. History can be boring. Story is what makes history interesting. History includes facts and events, but story is about the people, successes, failures, feelings, motivations, and impact too often overlooked in mere history. Why read a biographical story when the information is available free on Wikipedia?[2] In ASU's College of Law story Ped is the answer. His story narrows the gap between what is assumed and what actually happened.

The larger context of Ped's story is his journey from Iowa, with stopovers in Illinois and Washington, DC, on the way to Arizona. On December 28, 1846, Iowa became the twenty-ninth state when President James K. Polk signed Iowa's admission bill into law.[3] In 1818, Illinois became the twenty-first U.S. state.[4] Arizona, known fondly as the baby state, was the forty-eighth state in 1912. While much younger, Arizona's history of the legal profession is rich and colorful. Ped's historic profile in Arizona law was detailed by his closest colleague, Alan Matheson, who later became dean. Matheson's twenty-eight-page interview of Ped on August 8, 1990 is a classy bit of history.[5]

FAMILY BACKGROUND & EDUCATION

Dean Matheson began Ped's oral history interview by asking, "Ped, if you will, tell us something about your family background and early education."[6]

Ped's answer was typically short and consistent with his reluctance to talk about himself. He loved to talk about his job and his profession, but he was always reluctant to discuss his origins. "I assume you want the short version."[7]

Matheson, a plain-speaking man himself, answered, "Yes."

Ped's sense of humor and his irreverent wit shows up early in this interview.

Willard Hiram Pedrick—Founding Dean—1965

If you've never been to New Jersey, you probably never have visited Pedricktown, New Jersey. But some element of the family came to the United States, before it was the United States, in colonial days. A branch of the family meandered to the Midwest. My grandfather, I think, was a farmer, a modest farmer in Iowa. My father was a travelling hardware salesman. And I had a brother and a sister and grew up in the little town of Fairfield, Iowa. And went to college there at a little school named Parsons College, which has since disappeared from the scene to be succeeded by Maharishi University, where they claim to not only meditate, but they claim to levitate as well. . . . Then I went on from college to the Northwestern Law School and graduated way back in 1939.[8]

Ped briefly mentioned his clerkship upon graduation from law school with Judge Frederick Moore Vinson, then on the United States Court of Appeals for the District of Columbia. He mentions casually, "Later of course, he became Chief Justice." He said nothing more in his own interview, even though there was much more to say about CJ Vinson.

In 1976, ten years after he founded the ASU Law School, Ped was interviewed for the "Fred M. Vinson Oral History Project, University of Kentucky."[9] In this interview, Ped told the story of how he became Judge Vinson's *first* law clerk, and much more than he shared in his Matheson interview. In it, he reminisced at some length about his initial impressions of the man who would become famous a few years later. He talked about Vinson moving from Congress to the Appeals Court, thanks to FDR. He talked about how Vinson organized his chambers, much as if he'd organized his congressional office. He talked about Vinson's philosophy of the law as they reflected on his earlier work for FDR on New Deal Legislation in Congress. He discussed Vinson's relationship with Judge Lawrence Groner,[10] also on the DC Circuit Court. He told stories about Vinson's enthusiasm for playing cards and social life in Washington. He relayed in small versions Vinson's opinions about A.B. Happy Chandler,[11] and Alben Parkley.[12]

In the Vinson interview, Ped talked about how he got a friend, Wilbur Lester, to take his place as Judge Vinson's law clerk, "because Vinson was reluctant to let him go." He recalled incidents about Vinson's role in FDR's cabinet and Vinson's philosophy on economic stabilization following FDR's "hold the line" order. He explained his desire to get into the military, as the war was on, and how Ed Prichard explained he'd get Lyndon Johnson to help him get into the Marines. He talked a good bit about the relationship between Vinson and Presidents Roosevelt and Truman. He recalled incidents about Vinson's service as Chief Justice of the United States after Truman appointed him to the highest court in 1946.[13] Had Ped stayed on as Vinson's law clerk, it is likely he would have gone to the Supreme Court with Vinson, instead of spending those two years in the U.S. Marine Corps.

FACULTY APPOINTMENTS

Ped's professional life after graduating from Northwestern University Law School in 1939 was as varied as it was enriching. He taught for one year at the University of Cincinnati (1940–41), and another year at the University of Texas (1941–42). He worked in the Justice Department in Washington (Tax Division) in 1942 and 1943, moved to the Office of Economic Stabilization from 1943 to 1944, followed by his clerkship with Judge Vinson, followed by two years in the military, and then back to Northwestern University College of Law from 1946 to 1966.

Ped told Matheson why he came to Arizona in 1966: "I think probably it was a midlife crisis of some sort. I was in my fifties . . . . I'd done a variety of things, been to a number of schools, I was ready to try my hand at a period of administration. Just a change of life. And the opportunity to work with others to put together a brand-new school was something that only a very few people in a generation today get a chance to do. So I really jumped at it when the opportunity came along."[14]

He credited ASU President Homer Durham for the opportunity.

> *Homer was a marvelous salesman, sang a siren song to perfection. We first met in Chicago . . . . I didn't think it was at all likely that I'd want to come to Arizona, and I didn't want to spend the school's money to come out for what might well be a fruitless visit. So I said, "You've got to be going through Chicago from time to time, all university presidents do that, and we can meet at the airport . . . ." So without any further conversation on the subject of how I would recognize him except that it was to be at the airport and I knew which flight he was coming on, I recognized him at once . . . . Then he told me about the marvels and wonders of Arizona and how this was the last big*

city without a law school, a university law school, and that the school could do great things for the university, the city, the state . . . so I said I'd better spend some of your money and come out and have a look.[15]

It was an amusing visit, he said. "For my first visit, Homer Durham drove me by some circuitous route from the airport to Tempe so that I never got a whiff of the stockyards, which were then located between the airport and Tempe. Of course they're gone now."[16]

Matheson asked him what kind of a law school he thought he could build here in Arizona.

Well I had a few, I thought, mildly innovative ideas. And I knew we would start with a relatively small faculty and of course, a relatively small student body too. But my idea was that, we felt in legal education generally, that the first year in law school was a resounding success. But the problem was with the third year, when students were sort of used to the system and bored and working in law offices, many of them, and not really giving the school a great lot of their time, interest and energy. And so the idea which I managed to persuade the new faculty to accept was that we would have a prescribed curriculum for two years, which was different a bit from other law schools, and then provide a third year of unrestricted electives, with a heavy emphasis on clinical education, seminars and a variety of experiences designed to make the third year as different as possible from the first two. And we thought that had real promise and I think, looking back on it, although we're now much more in the pattern of other law schools with a prescribed first year and electives in the second two years, still our modest experiment in legal education those early days of the school were very, I think, still were very successful. We ran a poll of our graduates eight years or so into the life of the school and the indication was the students who looked back on it felt it had been a good beginning.[17]

DEAN PEDRICK'S HANDPICKED FACULTY

Matheson was part of the accreditation team at ASU in 1967. He asked Ped to tell that part of the story.

> [What was] interesting about the accreditation was the fact that the American Bar Association, which is one of the accrediting groups, visited us early, and in the first year announced they were going to accredit us. Then another new law school, Texas Tech, heard about this, and approached the ABA and said, "If you're going to accredit ASU on the basis of the first year, you've got to do it for us too." Whereupon the ABA realized that they had sort of violated their own principles and, in a somewhat embarrassed fashion, gave me a call and said, "Well, you'll have to wait until you've graduated your first class." My bargaining position wasn't very good because they, after all, do it or don't. So, okay! But we were accredited at once on the graduation of our first class, which is as fast as is possible to do it.[18]

THE NEW LAW BUILDING AT ASU

Ped explained how the architects were selected for the new building on the Tempe campus.

> Homer Durham had already selected the architects. They were local architects, Cartmell and Rossman. One that was an Austrian by training and one was a graduate, as I recall, of the University of Southern California Architectural School. They found that I was interested in modern architecture because I had been chairman of the Cook County Zoning Board of Appeals for three years in the latter days of my stay at Northwestern.... I was open-minded and willing to think about new shapes and designs, they were off and running. I sent them around to visit several law schools that I thought had good features in their buildings. The result is the building that we have here now, the present building and I think it has worked over the twenty-one-year period of our life quite well. In the Great Hall I made a modest contribution because I came up with this idea of stadium seating, which enables you to put a rather large crowd in rather comfortable quarters for public lectures.[19]

THE PHOENIX BAR

Ped was worried about the job market for students in the first graduating class of 1970. So much so, that it made its way into his job interview with the ASU President.

> *Well, when I was negotiating with Homer Durham, I said, I'd like to find out whether the local profession will be supportive or whether it will not. So he arranged a luncheon of a good many—and there must have been eighteen or twenty—representing the legal profession and the bench and members of the Arizona Supreme Court. And they really promised in blood that they would really be supportive of the school. Directly on my sort of arrival in residence here, I set about sort of securing commitments to make good on their promises of support and we organized what we call the* Law Society of Arizona State University, *and a great many, in fact virtually all of the leading lawyers of the community, without regard to where they themselves had gone to law school, adopted this brand new orphan law school as worthy of their support. That, I think, was very, very helpful in securing opportunity for our graduates and financial support as well.*[20]

As it turned out, Ped had many contacts in the local bar. The managing partner of the Fennemore Craig law firm, Phil von Ammon, went to law school at Northwestern when Ped was there. They were a year apart and von Ammon edited one of Ped's notes while both were on the law review. He noted in his interview he and von Ammon "had very different political points of view, since Ped was 'a bleeding heart liberal and proud of it.'"[21]

He was warmly welcomed to Arizona by John D. Lyons, then the dean at the University of Arizona in Tucson. He told Dean Lyons he intended to build a law school in Tempe that would "reproduce Northwestern, quality-wise." That resonated with Dean Lyons and his faculty. Over the years Ped developed a close relationship with the faculty at the U of A; they said, "Well, if that's the kind of school you're going to set up, by all means come. We'll be helpful and friendly . . . Charles Ares, who later became dean of the school down there was a very good friend of mine. I split a tennis match with him. We played two sets. I won one. He won one. And it was so hot, even in Tucson I think it was about a hundred and five, we decided it was a good way to leave it."[22]

THE SCHOOL'S PROGRESS

When asked to reflect back over the last twenty years and assess the school's progress, Ped was, as always, positive. "Well, early in the life of the school . . . in operation five or six years . . . somebody queried deans and reported we were in the rank of the first thirty law schools in the United States and one with great prospects of significant improvement. Since there are about a hundred and seventy-five schools in the United States, we were very pleased . . . . My own notion with people who really know about the quality of law schools is we are very well regarded . . . our graduates are received by the profession both here and elsewhere . . . so I think's it's worked out."[23]

Ped, in 1990, knew that law schools were in a state of flux—he called them "cross-currents . . . you know, is law regarded as a classical avenue for a liberal education? On the other hand, the practice of law has its workaday world aspects, and so the question as to whether you're going to have a sort of classical liberal education in the law or whether you're going to have a sort of trade school approach is a never-ending source of tension. And every now and then, of course, a younger generation comes along and they have blinding new insights."[24]

Along with most of his founding faculty, he was "classically" educated in the law. They interacted with lawyers and disfavored the "trade" school perspective—that trained law students in how to practice, rather than acquiring a broad knowledge of law and legal remedies. He recognized the changes between his education in the thirties and the demands on his law school's curriculum in the nineties. "The law and practicing it has changed in our time . . . law schools have changed quite a lot in the half-century that I've been with it." He recognized a major shift between business lawyers advising large companies or the government and others who focused on problems of the individual. . . "[this accounts] for how far clinical education [in law schools] has come along as a new thing."[25]

THE PEDRICK FOLLIES

Matheson changed gears and moved away from law and toward music. Ped had for many years produced what he called the *follies*. He explained, in a roundabout way, how music and law blended in legal education.

> *One of the great scholars in the field of tort law was William Prosser. He taught several places, but wound up at Berkeley. And Prosser, as a student at Harvard, had done what I think is called the Hasty Pudding Show, which is a student musical. And he, in his later years, decided to do this for the law school*

world and in nineteen, I think it was 1956 produced what many think is his greatest show of all called My Share Brady, *which was based on the music of* My Fair Lady *and a story of a law school that got off the track because Prosser thought the foundations were unduly influencing law curriculum. Well, he invited me to be one of the cast and I enjoyed it. Then—he did three or four more shows over the years. Not every year but every other year or so. Then when he retired I did three or four shows.... I thought that it provided good fun . . . and enabled us in a light-hearted way sometimes to raise questions about whether legal education was going in the right direction or not.*[26]

TEACHING TORTS

Like most law teachers and students in the fifties and sixties, Ped greatly admired William Prosser.[27] Prosser was easily the most popular and most well-known torts teacher of his era. He authored several editions of *Prosser on Torts*, universally recognized as the leading work on the subject of tort law for a generation. It is still widely used today, now known as *Prosser and Keeton on Torts,* 5th edition. In the 1950s, Dean Prosser became Reporter for the *Second Restatement of Torts*. In a small exhibit about the Levering Act loyalty oath in the ground level of the Campanile at UC Berkeley, Prosser is quoted as saying, "If the authority exists to discharge a professor because he will not sign this oath on demand, then it exists to fire him because he will not sign an oath that he is not a Catholic, not a Mason, not a consumer of beer . . . there is no place to stop."[28]

Ped taught torts the way Prosser did. Both were disciples of the inestimable Leon Green.

[Leon Green] was my teacher and then my co-editor of the case book. His view of tort law was that the law is really shaped and affected greatly by the facts out of which the case arises. So instead of grouping the cases for study by doctrine: What is negligence? What is proximate cause? What is the duty problem? Et cetera. He grouped the cases into categories like fights, traffic cases, newspaper defamation, and a variety of other classifications such as railroad accidents and product liability. That approach has had a considerable impact on other casebooks and now many other casebooks in the field of tort law reflect that same sort of transactional approach. I surely believed in that

and was affected by his thinking in the field. Now of course, we're in an era where there are many ideas percolating in this area and many people, including one of my former students who is now on the Berkeley faculty, Professor Steven Sugarman, thinks that we ought to supplant tort law with various types of no-fault coverage. That would in effect substitute accident insurance for inquiry into the question of whether a particular individual defendant was or was not careless or negligent. But that controversy, I think, will rage for at least another twenty years before it's settled, if it's settled then.[29]

THE DEAN'S JOB

Ped loved being ASU's funding dean.

> *I have to admit that I had a marvelous time being dean. It was a change of life. And because everybody, the faculty and the staff and the university administration and the legal community was so supportive it was really a great experience. It was not a personal triumph, but an institutional triumph that this school has come along so well, so quickly. And it was just my good luck—and again I say, luck is better than planning—my good luck. I was under consideration for the deanship at Wisconsin and lost out to a local candidate. I was probably disappointed, but that's the best thing that happened to me because I wouldn't have been available for this post if I had taken that job. So it's been really a delight and the relationships we had in the early years when we were small, and knew the students personally was a marvelous period. We refer to it as the Camelot period. And it's not possible to recapture that, but I'm glad I had a chance to live through it.*[30]

Ped was also known for a very unusual teaching method—making his students stand up in class when responding to or asking a question. "Well, I'm a vanishing breed in one sense, in that as long as I was teaching torts, I had the student who was reciting stand. I would ask them to stand, and that meant that they knew that all the students in the class were focused on them and they felt a little pressure. I explained to the students, I thought this was good for them because that's the setting in which a lawyer does quite a bit of his or her work. So I was just helping them along. Although I'm not sure they all regarded it as really that helpful."[31]

Willard Hiram Pedrick—Founding Dean—1965

At the other law school in Tucson, none of the professors required students to stand before answering questions in class. But that may have been because none of them, except for Dean Ares, had been trial lawyers before moving to academia. Ped explained his thinking.

> [T]he law classroom, in a sense, is the training ground for advocacy and the students have the opportunity, not every day, but from time to time, to expound their own views in answer to questions. And their fellow students listen and evaluate and the teacher of course pursues with more questions still. The teacher may not have good answers himself or herself to the questions but has an inexhaustible store of questions. And this process of dialogue enables the students to see, hopefully, that the better forms of expression, the better ways of saying things distinguishes between the advocate who is effective and one who is simply not able to persuade others to his or her point of view. So the classroom design can facilitate this type of exchange. And in a good session you may have two, three, or four students entering in, some of them dragooned and some of them volunteering. I always like to call on students who hadn't volunteered, as well as some volunteers, so that they're all, I hope, at least in a state of readiness. My son, who is a lawyer now, would say, "Well, you try to keep them in a state of terror." But that's not really so. The object was to bring them along in this process of training advocates.[32]

TWO LAW SCHOOLS—ONE STATE

Ped's students all knew he was a lawyer, not just a law professor. He didn't just teach law; he was an accomplished advocate in his own right. And, unlike some law teachers, he understood instinctively that lawyers must get along with opposing counsel. He also understood the importance of law schools getting along with one another. Matheson asked him about the differences between ASU Law and the University of Arizona College of Law. "Well, in the early days when we had our core curriculum we were different. But I think the differences have ironed out a bit now, because we have gone more to a first-year program required, with rather fulsome electives in the last two years. Sometimes people ask me, 'What about the U. of A.? Is it a good school?' Well it is. It's an excellent school. And I think it's a better school because we're here, and we're a better school because they're there. And we know we've got to keep up to the mark. So do they."[33]

SUPREME COURT JUSTICE JOHN PAUL STEVENS

Over the years, Ped was credited, acknowledged, and recognized by many notable lawyers, teachers and judges. One shout-out that he likely enjoyed very much came during the Northwestern University School of Law's 151st Commencement Address, given by one of its most illustrious students, U.S. Supreme Court Justice John Paul Stevens.[34] He congratulated the student body and welcomed them to the proud group of Northwestern alumni. He said he'd conclude his address "with the obligatory giving of advice, including in this case advice he'd been given by one of his teachers at Northwestern—Professor Willard Pedrick . . . who taught both torts and federal taxation . . . [he] advised us that when planning our careers, we should not try to decide what we want to be doing at the end of our careers, but rather we should decide what to do *next*. The decision that Jack Barry, Ed Rothschild and I made in 1952 to form our own firm instead of climbing the ladder to partnership in the firm now known as Jenner & Block[35] was motivated, in part, by that sound advice."[36]

LEGAL IDEOLOGY & BIBLIOGRAPHY

In the early years Ped wrote many law review articles, but his 1970 article in the DePaul University law review stands out because his worldview and his legal ideology are so clearly articulated.

> *A great disappointment of our time has been the failure of those who make and change the social order to modify the system so as to provide opportunity to all segments of society for growth as individuals, for participation in creative productivity, for wellbeing and satisfaction. Any honest assessment will conclude that our spectacular success on the scientific and material level has been marked by an equally spectacular failure to use the new means available to better the real quality of life. Now, with riots in the cities and rebellion on the campus, some of it violent and some of it intellectual, there is general agreement that our society has simply not worked hard enough at the task of*

developing new social and economic frameworks, and particularly has not worked hard enough at producing leaders to help in the process of essential innovation, adjustment and accommodation. In this setting of general disaffection with the way in which we have been managing our stewardship of the system handed to us by our forebears, we increasingly hear concerned voices urging that the legal profession move into the void to provide a much larger share of the men who will be trained to give, and will give, much of their lives to the task of providing better direction for society.[37]

His prophetic words have special resonance at the time this book is being published. What would Ped think of today's lawyers and judges in the midst of attacks on the judiciary, the justice system and the freedom of the American press?

Ped was inducted into the Maricopa County Bar Association *Hall of Fame* posthumously, on October 28, 2009. The Hall of Fame was created in 2008 to honor Arizona lawyers and judges who had made an impact on the development of the Bar and the legal profession, made a unique contribution to the law and/or demonstrated significant leadership in the community and the profession. His award noted ". . . his national reputation as a great scholar and teacher and as an impresario whose musical presentations at the Association of American Law Schools' gatherings were legendary . . . After stepping down as Dean and returning to the faculty in 1976, Pedrick, through his statesmanship, teaching prowess, scholarly productivity, professional activities and decency—set an example of what a senior faculty member should be . . . although Pedrick retired from the faculty in 1983, he continued to teach at other law schools, including Iowa, UCLA, Colorado, Kansas, and Texas, to name a few—until 1992. He died in 1996."[38]

Ped's bibliography, attached to his ASU official November 12, 1976 resume, lists six books and twenty-four peer-reviewed legal articles published by fifteen law schools all over America. The titles on some articles reflect Ped's sense of humor even when tackling serious legal problems: "Injuries to Relations (with others)"; "Dollars, Delay, and the Automobile Victim"; "The Artful Dodger Trust Faces Life and Looks at Death"; "The Lunatic Driver"; "Taken for a Ride—The Automobile Guest and Assumption of Risk." Perhaps the most unusual part of his official ASU Resume is the section titled "Friends and Acquaintances who can commit on qualifications." This section identifies twenty-two individuals in four countries, many of whom are household names holding high office with great distinction.[39]

This short summary of Dean Pedrick's contributions to ASU and Arizona pales in comparison with his official written record. The *Arizona State University Archives* houses "The Willard Pedrick Papers." They are archived in thirty-three boxes, measuring 49.5 linear feet, divided into three series (accession #1996-01769, #1996-01779, and #1997-01812). Provenance was provided by JoAnn Pedrick, who donated the materials in 1996 and 1997.

---

1 Thesaurus.com, s.v. "sui generis," last modified 2013, https://www.thesaurus.com/browse/sui%20generis?s=t. Synonyms include alone, lone, one, one-off, only, singular, sole, solitary, special, unique. At the risk of overstatement, it might be said that Ped, among history's great law deans, is *sui generis*—a man of such stupendous ingenuity that the legal world may never see his like again.

2 *See,* for example, the following wikis: Wikipedia, s.v. "Arizona State University," last modified January 30, 2020, 18:37, https://en.wikipedia.org/wiki/Arizona_State_University; Wikipedia, s.v. "Sandra Day O'Connor College of Law," last modified February 23, 2020, 23:29, https://en.wikipedia.org/wiki/Sandra_Day_O%27Connor_College_of_Law; Wikipedia, s.v. "Law School," last modified January 19, 2020, 18:05, https://en.wikipedia.org/wiki/Law_school; Wikipedia, s.v. "Legal education," last modified January 17, 2020, 19:44, https://en.wikipedia.org/wiki/Legal_education; Wikipedia, s.v. "Bachelor of Law," last modified February 1, 2020, 6:15, https://en.wikipedia.org/wiki/Bachelor_of_Laws; Wikipedia, s.v. "Practice of law," last modified January 2, 2020, 12:00, https://en.wikipedia.org/wiki/Practice_of_law; Wikipedia, s.v. "Iowa," last modified February 9, 2020, 10:48 https://en.wikipedia.org/wiki/Iowa; Wikipedia, s.v. "Illinois," last modified February 11, 2020, 23:52, https://en.wikipedia.org/wiki/Illinois.

3 Wikipedia, s.v. "Iowa," last modified January 11, 2021, 21:42, https://en.wikipedia.org/wiki/Iowa.

4 Wikipedia, s.v. "Illinois," last modified January 16, 2021, 23:34, https://en.wikipedia.org/wiki/Illinois.

5 *See,* "Interview with Willard H. Pedrick," interview by Alan Matheson, Arizona Bar Foundation Oral History Project: Arizona Legal History (Arizona: Arizona Historical Society, 1990).

6 Ibid., 1.

7 Ibid.

8 Ibid.

9 "Interview with Willard H. Pedrick," *Fred M. Vinson Oral History Project,* by Terry Birdwhistell (Kentucky: University of Kentucky Libraries, 1976), audio https://kentuckyoralhistory.org/ark:/16417/xt7n8p5v9r7k.

10 Wikipedia, s.v. "Duncan Lawrence Groner," last modified March 13, 2019, https://en.wikipedia.org/wiki/Duncan_Lawrence_Groner. Duncan Lawrence Groner (September 6, 1873–July 17, 1957) was an Associate Justice and later Chief Justice of the United States Court of Appeals for the District of Columbia. Ibid.

11 Wikipedia, s.v. "Happy Chandler," last modified October 2 2019, 11:10, https://en.wikipedia.org/wiki/Happy_Chandler. Albert Benjamin "Happy" Chandler Sr. (July 14, 1898–June 15, 1991) was an American politician from the Commonwealth of Kentucky. He represented the Commonwealth in the U.S. Senate and served as its 44th and 49th governor. Aside from his political positions, he also served as the second Commissioner of Baseball from 1945 to 1951 and was inducted into the Baseball Hall of Fame in 1982. His grandson, Ben Chandler, later served as congressman for Kentucky's Sixth District. Ibid.

12 *Encyclopedia Britannica Online,* s.v. "Alben W. Barkley," last modified April 26, 2019, https://www.britannica.com/biography/Alben-W-Barkley. Alben William Barkley, November 24, 1877–April 30, 1956, was an American lawyer and politician from Kentucky who served in both houses of Congress and as the 35th vice president of the United States from 1949 to 1953. In 1905, he was elected county attorney for McCracken County, Kentucky. He was chosen County Judge/Executive in 1909 and U.S. Representative from Kentucky's First District in 1912. As a Representative, he was a liberal Democrat, supporting President Woodrow Wilson's New Freedom domestic agenda and foreign policy.

Endorsing Prohibition and denouncing pari-mutuel betting, Barkley narrowly lost the 1923 Democratic gubernatorial primary to fellow Representative J. Campbell Cantrill. In 1926, he unseated Republican Senator Richard P. Ernst. In the Senate, he supported the New Deal approach to addressing the Great Depression and was elected to succeed Senate Majority Leader Joseph T. Robinson upon Robinson's death in 1937. Ibid.

13 Wikipedia, s.v. "Vinson Court," last modified November 13, 2019, 00:55, https://en.wikipedia.org/wiki/Vinson_Court. The Vinson Court refers to the Supreme Court of the United States from 1946 to 1953, when Fred Vinson served as Chief Justice of the United States. Vinson succeeded Harlan F. Stone as Chief Justice after the latter's death, and Vinson served as Chief Justice until his death, at which point Earl Warren was nominated and confirmed to succeed Vinson. Ibid.

14 *See,* "Interview with Willard H. Pedrick," interview by Alan Matheson, *Arizona Bar Foundation Oral History Project: Arizona Legal History* (Arizona: Arizona Historical Society, 1990), at p. 3.

15 Ibid., 4.

16 Ibid., 4.

17 Ibid., 5.

18 Ibid., 8.

19 Ibid., 9.

20 Ibid., 11.

21 Ibid., 11.

22 Ibid., 12.

23 Ibid., 13.

24 Ibid., 14.

25 Ibid., 14.

26 Ibid., 15.

27 Wikipedia, s.v. "William Lloyd Prosser," last modified December 29, 2019, 16:54, https://en.wikipedia.org/wiki/William_Lloyd_Prosser. "William Lloyd Prosser was the Dean of the College of Law at UC Berkeley from 1948 to 1961. Prosser authored several editions of *Prosser on Torts,* universally recognized as the leading work on the subject of tort law for a generation. It is still widely used today, now known as *Prosser and Keeton on Torts,* 5th edition. Furthermore, in the 1950s, Dean Prosser became Reporter for the Second Restatement of Torts." Ibid.

28 Ibid.

29 "Interview with Willard H. Pedrick" by Matheson, at 17–18.

30 Ibid., 19–20.

31 Ibid., 21.

32 Ibid., 21.

33 Ibid., 21–22.

34 Wikipedia, s.v. "John Paul Stevens," last modified February 1, 2020, 16:35, https://en.wikipedia.org/wiki/John_Paul_Stevens. John Paul Stevens was an American lawyer and jurist who served as an Associate Justice of the United States Supreme Court from 1975 until his retirement in 2010. At the time of his retirement, he was the second-oldest serving justice in the history of the Court, the third-longest serving Supreme Court Justice in history. Stevens was considered to have been on the liberal side of the Court at the time of his retirement. Ibid.

35 Jenner & Block, "Overview," accessed November 19, 2019, https://jenner.com/about/chicago. "The Chicago office is Jenner & Block's first and largest office—the birthplace and center from which the firm has built its reputation and culture. The firm first opened its doors in 1914 as Newman, Poppenhusen & Stern, a three-person firm located in downtown Chicago in a building that was erected soon after the Great Chicago Fire of 1871. Today, Jenner & Block is one of the largest law firms in Chicago. Approximately 330 of the firm's lawyers are based in the firm's 1.1-million-square-foot office at 353 N. Clark, in a Class A, LEED-certified office tower." Ibid.

36 Justice John Paul Stevens, *Northwestern University School of Law's 151st Commencement Address*, 106 Nw. U. L. Rev. 851 (2012).

37 Willard H. Pedrick, *Collapsible Specialists*, 19 DePaul L. Rev. 699 (1970).

38 *See* ASU NOW: Access, Excellence, Impact, "Pedrick selected for Maricopa County Bar Association Hall of Fame," ASU online October 20, 2009, https://asunow.asu.edu/content/pedrick-selected-maricopa-county-bar-association-hall-fame.

39 Dean Pedrick's November 12, 1976 resume.

CHAPTER 4

WHAT IS NOTABLE—WHAT TO INCLUDE—WHAT TO EXCLUDE

The word *notable* is a truism, i.e., a person of note.[1] It has many synonyms: cause célèbre, celebrity, figure, icon, luminary, megastar, somebody, standout, star, superstar, VIP, astral, distinguished, eminent, illustrious, outstanding, preeminent, prestigious, redoubtable.

This book is about a college of law overflowing with notable students, faculty, leaders, clinics, centers, and programs. *The* Sandra Day O'Connor College of Law is itself notable; the proof of which is its Wikipedia page.[2] The site briefly states its history, and mentions its employees, costs, clinical programs, centers, notable lecturers and professors, law journals, notable alumni, references, and external links. But it does not explain why any of them are notable. The college has created a new Wikipedia-style website as both supplemental to and an integral part of this book. In HTML format, it digitally defines the individuals who most notably represent ASU Law's force and impact in Arizona and throughout the world.[3]

Identifying notable people is a fundamental challenge for biographers and history writers. It is our job to search public and private records to identify as many notable people as possible. It is, of course, an impossible task. When we list notable people, we risk comprehensiveness by leaving some out. When we list programs, centers, or events of any kind, we risk authenticity. At an elementary level, *writing* history is *making* history. The task is always daunting, to the point of absurdity. With a fifty-five-year-old law school, there is no way to encompass all of its affairs from 1965 to 2020. No author could possibly review all of the relevant records. This book cannot pretend complete inclusion or universal status. It can reference what the school itself has declared to be notable and worthy of inclusion. The school's Wikipedia page and its home page (law.asu.edu) list the following notable clinical programs, centers, lecturers, professors, journals, and alumni.

CLINICAL PROGRAMS

The Sandra Day O'Connor College of Law is rich in legal clinics. They are combined educational enterprises with skills training programs. Fundamentally, they supplement the "book" knowledge attained in the classroom by clinical "training" that allows students to receive law school credit as they work part-time in real legal service atmospheres. In addition to reading cases and statutes about torts, or real property, or criminal conduct, they engage the way licensed lawyers do. They do legal research, draft pleadings, motions and briefs and interview real clients. Arizona law permits students to appear in court on behalf of clients, with licensed lawyers at close hand. Legal clinics are generally *pro bono publico* offering free legal services to clients, and supervised by law professors.

In 2020, the college offered ten clinics: Civil Litigation Clinic; First Amendment Clinic; Immigration Clinic; Indian Legal Clinic; Innovation Advancement Program Clinic; Lodestar Mediation Clinic; Lisa Foundation Patent Law Clinic; Post-Conviction Clinic; Prosecution Clinic; Public Defender Clinic. Each clinic is separately presented in this book.

In academe, distinctions are drawn between clinics, centers, and programs. Academic centers are non-degree granting educational units. They are differentiated within the college by mission and scope. Centers have a substantial research/scholarship component to their mission, and offer both instruction and related services. Academic programs comprise the core, required and elective courses that lead to a certificate, rather than a degree.

In 2020, ASU Law had eight centers and programs: (1) Center for Law, Science and Innovation; (2) Center for Law & Global Affairs; (3) Indian Legal Program; (4) Barrett and O'Connor Center; (5) ASU California Center; (6) Center for Public Health Law and Policy; (7) Lodestar Dispute Resolution Center; (8) Academy for Justice. Each center and program is covered in separate chapters in this book.

What is Notable—What to Include—What to Exclude

LAW JOURNALS

A law journal, sometimes called a law review, is a student-run journal that publishes articles written by law professors, judges, and other legal professionals. They may also publish shorter pieces written by students, called "notes" or "comments." ASU Law has four separate journals: (1) *Arizona State Law Journal;* (2) *Jurimetrics: The Journal of Law, Science, and Technology;* (3) *Law Journal for Social Justice;* (4) *Sports and Entertainment Law Journal;* and (5), the *Corporate and Business Law Journal.* All are profiled in separate chapters in this book.

NOTABLE ALUMNI AND FACULTY

The college has identified the following thirty-two individuals as noted alumni on its Wikipedia site.[4] In addition, the new Wikipedia-style webpage created in conjunction with this book identifies an additional seventy-eight notable alumni and faculty.

1. Michael Daly Hawkins ('70) – Senior Judge, United States Court of Appeals for the Ninth Circuit
2. Roslyn O. Silver ('71) – Chief Judge, United States District Court for the District of Arizona
3. Harriet C. Babbitt ('72) – former U.S. Ambassador to the Organization of American States and Deputy Administrator of the U.S. Agency for International Development
4. Ruth McGregor ('74) – former Chief Justice, Arizona Supreme Court
5. Ed Pastor ('74) – U.S. Congressman, Arizona's 4th congressional district
6. Charles G. Case II ('75) – former Judge, United States Bankruptcy Court, District of Arizona
7. Barry G. Silverman ('76) – Judge, United States Court of Appeals for the Ninth Circuit
8. Terry Goddard ('76) – former Arizona Attorney General
9. Michael D. Ryan ('77) – former Justice, Arizona Supreme Court
10. Tena Campbell ('77) – Senior Judge, United States District Court for the District of Utah

THE SANDRA DAY O'CONNOR COLLEGE OF LAW

11. Phil Gordon (politician) ('78) – former Mayor of Phoenix, Arizona
12. Douglas L. Rayes ('78) – Judge, United States District Court for the District of Arizona
13. Grant Woods ('79) – former Arizona Attorney General
14. Rebecca White Berch ('79) – Chief Justice, Arizona Supreme Court
15. Richard D. Mahoney ('79) – former Arizona Secretary of State
16. Fred DuVal ('80) – chairman, Arizona Board of Regents
17. Rick Romley ('81) – former County Attorney for Maricopa County, Arizona
18. George McCaskey ('81) – chairman, Chicago Bears
19. Michael J. Ahearn ('82) – chairman and former CEO, First Solar
20. Steven E. Carr ('84) – first and only American ever elected to the highest governing body of the International Red Cross and Red Crescent Movement
21. David Yerushalmi ('84) – co-founder and Senior Counsel of the American Freedom Law Center
22. Ann Scott Timmer ('85) – Justice, Arizona Supreme Court
23. John Lopez, IV ('89) – Justice, Arizona Supreme Court
24. Joe Rogers ('89) – former Lieutenant Governor of Colorado
25. Bridget Shelton Bade ('90) – Judge, Ninth Circuit Court of Appeals, former United States Magistrate Judge for the District of Arizona.
26. Gloria Navarro ('92) – Judge, United States District Court for the District of Nevada
27. Rachel Mitchell ('92) – prosecutor who questioned Dr. Christine Blasey Ford during Brett Kavanaugh's hearing for confirmation to the United States Supreme Court
28. Diane Humetewa ('93) – Judge, United States District Court for the District of Arizona
29. James Hamm ('97) – private criminal justice consultant, qualified in courts as an expert on prison policy and procedure, time computations
30. Jerod E. Tufte ('02) – Justice, North Dakota Supreme Court
31. Kyrsten Sinema ('04) – U.S. Senator from Arizona, former U.S. Representative from Arizona's 9th congressional district
32. Courtney Ekmark (class of 2020) – played basketball on two NCAA championship teams at UConn before transferring to ASU in 2016;

What is Notable—What to Include—What to Exclude

enrolled in the O'Connor College in 2017 and played for ASU through her first two years of law school

EVEN MORE NOTABLE

The college has its own home page on asu.edu.[5] That site includes an important message from Dean Douglas Sylvester:[6]

> *Welcome to the Sandra Day O'Connor College of Law at Arizona State University where you will experience a higher degree of opportunity on your road to becoming a great lawyer or a master of legal principles in your industry. It is a privilege—and a great responsibility—to be entrusted with the name and legacy of former Supreme Court Justice Sandra Day O'Connor. We strive to honor her by committing ourselves, as she has, to advancing justice through education and public service.*
>
> *ASU Law and its home in downtown Phoenix, the nation's fifth largest city, provide tremendous opportunities that range from exciting intellectual and practical academic experiences, to economic advantages that come from being the only law school within 100 miles and just steps away from law firms, government entities, and businesses. Opportunities also come in the form of rich cultural activities and an overall lifestyle that is enhanced by endless sunshine and the great outdoors. ASU Law also offers extensive programs beyond Phoenix, in key places like Washington, D.C., and Los Angeles.*
>
> *With gainfully employed graduates, a dynamic and vibrant community, and an institution dedicated at every level to providing you with the finest educational experience possible, ASU Law is ideally suited to get you where you want to go.*[7]

Dean Sylvester is the voice, face, and muscle behind the law school's stunning climb up the notable ladder of American law schools. He has had many interactions with the school's namesake—Justice Sandra Day O'Connor. If anyone can define notable, she can. She knows the people, programs, and the output of the school that make it notable. She famously said, "We don't accomplish anything in this world alone . . . and whatever happens is the result of the whole tapestry of one's life and all the weavings of individual threads from one to another that creates something."

---

1 "Notable," Merriam-Webster, accessed February 12, 2020, https://www.merriam-webster.com/dictionary/notable.
2 Wikipedia, s.v., "Sandra Day O'Connor College of Law," last modified February 12, 2020, 14:52, https://en.wikipedia.org/wiki/Sandra_Day_O%27Connor_College_of_Law.
3 "50 Years of Impact," Sandra Day O'Connor College of Law, accessed February 12, 2020, https://law.asu.edu/50yearsofimpact.
4 Wikipedia, s.v., "Sandra Day O'Connor College of Law," last modified February 12, 2020, 14:52, https://en.wikipedia.org/wiki/Sandra_Day_O%27Connor_College_of_Law.
5 "Sandra Day O'Connor College of Law," Sandra Day O'Connor College of Law, accessed February 12, 2020, https://law.asu.edu/.
6 "Douglas Sylvester (Dean)," ASU.edu, accessed February 12, 2020, https://isearch.asu.edu/profile/504321.
7 "Dean's Message," Sandra Day O'Connor College of Law, accessed February 12, 2020, https://law.asu.edu/about/dean-message.

CHAPTER 5

BEGINNING THE STUDY OF LAW

Context is everything—even for 1Ls in a brand-new law school. In August 1967, the first class met the first dean and his handpicked inaugural faculty. The faculty was intensely focused on establishing that all-important teacher/student relationship. But they had to do it while the rest of America dealt with political chaos, the war raging in Vietnam, and auspicious people doing great and odd things. On August 1, just three weeks before that first meeting, race riots in the United States had spread to Washington, DC. Nine days later, U.S. Marines began a new operation in the Vietnam War, called Operation Cochise in the Que Son Valley.[1] On August 21, the People's Republic of China revealed it had shot down United States planes violating its airspace. On a lighter note, Jimi Hendrix's debut album, *Are You Experienced*, was released on August 23. On a grim note, the American Nazi Party leader, George Lincoln Rockwell, was assassinated two days later. Arguably the best day of the month, August 30, was the day Thurgood Marshall was confirmed as the first African American Justice of the United States Supreme Court. He was sworn in October 2, 1967, but it's doubtful the 1Ls watched the ceremony—they were deeply immersed in reading cases, experiencing the Socratic method for the first time, and wondering how it was possible to read multi-case assignments in four core courses.

RIOTS, ROILS, RECOURSE

There were no riots, roils, or recourse for the inaugural class at ASU Law. But at least one other law school was in deep turmoil that semester. Student unrest was the order of the day at Yale Law School. At Yale something called "legal realism" was screamed by students at faculty. "Yale gloried in its association with legal realism. In explaining why, person for person, Yale Law's graduates possibly occupied 'more seats of political power than the alumni of almost any other institution' and proved 'even more influential' in the academic world than in political life. A 1963 issue of *Newsweek* credited the school's realist roots: 'During the '20s and '30s, the legal realists on the Yale faculty preached and practiced the doctrine that law is not a self-contained set of unchanging rules, but a vital tool for structuring and restructuring society.' Realism transformed Yale, giving the school its identity as the anti-Harvard and laying the groundwork for its association with a liberal judiciary linked to the civil rights movement, even as it did not transform the classroom experience inside or outside Yale. The vision of its history that Yale promoted was designed to attract a certain kind of student during the late 1960s. At the same time, it helped to create a faculty certain of its own righteousness and liberalism—just as the attack on liberalism was gaining strength."[2]

No lesser a scholar than Robert Bork remembered when radicals first appeared in Yale's midst. "'The change at the Law School began abruptly with the class that entered in 1967.' To professors, it seemed that '[t]urmoil' had become 'the order of the day' as insurgents condemned their failure to display Yale's legendary innovativeness. The sixties came to the Law School, brought there by the Vietnam War and dissatisfaction with the classroom. In challenging the status quo, students hoped to become citizens of the school and transform it into a locus of democracy and community, pierce the smugness and elitism of its faculty, and redeem the lost promise of Yale in the 1930s."[3]

LAW STUDENT CHALLENGES TO
FACULTY LEADERSHIP & CONTROL

A Yale Law historian wrote about student challenge against Yale's curriculum and the faculty's pedagogy. "The Socratic method was cast as 'demeaning' while students viewed their professors as inquisitors bent on breaking them. For disaffected students, the grading system became an example of the Law School's problems with hierarchy and alienation from public interest. ASU Law only had first year students in the fall of 1967. They did not challenge curriculum. They did not yet have student organizations inside the school. At Yale, things were different, if for no other reason, Yale was then sixty-six years old. Affirmative action and sexism were also much-debated topics."[4] As the Black Law Students Union (BLSU) on the Yale campus was fighting for a louder voice on campus, so, too, were female students. Professor Laura Kalman wrote about Yale Law's activism in 1967. The activism so present among black and white students alike was "instrumental in laying 'the groundwork for a real expansion of clinical education.'"[5]

Of course, there was much more going on in America in the fall of 1967, while the 1Ls at ASU Law worked their way through Contracts, Torts, Criminal Law & Procedure, and Property Law. On September 4, the U.S. Marines engaged the Viet Cong in the four-day battle of Que Son—114 Americans and 376 North Vietnamese were killed.[6] One of the first outdoor shopping malls in California, Fashion Island, opened in Newport Beach. Jim Morrison and The Doors defied CBS censors on *The Ed Sullivan Show* when Morrison sings the word "higher" from their #1 hit "Light My Fire," despite having been asked not to.[7] On the first day of October, the Boston Red Sox clinched the American League pennant in one of the most memorable pennant races of all time with Boston (92–70) beating out the Minnesota Twins and Detroit Tigers by one game.[8] Joan Baez and thirty-nine of her fans were arrested on October 16 for blocking the entrance to Oakland California's military induction center.[9] *Hair* opened off-Broadway.[10] And, on October 26, U.S. Navy pilot John McCain was shot down over North Vietnam and made a POW. His capture was announced in the *New York Times* and *Washington Post* two days later.[11]

UNITING BEHIND THE WAR EFFORT

While no one knew it at the time, November 2, 1967 is memorable because President Lyndon B. Johnson held "a secret meeting with a group of the nation's most prestigious leaders ('the Wise Men') and asks them to suggest ways to unite the American people behind the war effort. They conclude that the American people should be given more optimistic reports on the progress of the war."[12] That same month saw the first issue of the magazine *Rolling Stone* in San Francisco.[13] It was not optimistic about the war.

While December was dominated by news, nearly all bad, of the Vietnam War, there were tidbits of good news. The Beatles *Magical Mystery Tour* came out.[14] Lonsdaleite, the rarest allotrope of carbon, was discovered in Arizona's Barringer

Crater. The Summer of Love was held in San Francisco,[15] and the Big Mac was introduced in Pittsburgh.[16]

---

1 "Que Son Valley," Vietnam War – A Memoir, accessed February 12, 2020, https://vwam.com/vets/queson.html.

2 Laura Kalman, *Yale Law School and the Sixties: Revolt and Revolution* (University of North Carolina Press, 2005), 44.

3 Ibid.

4 Ibid. The [Law] School began in the New Haven law office of Seth P. Staples in the 1800s, who began training lawyers. By 1810 he was operating a law school. He took on a former student, Samuel J. Hitchcock, as a law partner, and Hitchcock became the proprietor of the New Haven Law School, joined by David Daggett in 1824. (The Yale Law School shield, shown at the upper right of this page, shows staples and a rampant dog, representing Seth Staples and David Daggett.) The school's affiliation with Yale began in the mid-1820s, and in 1843, the school's students began receiving Yale degrees. Wikipedia, s.v., "Yale Law School," last modified February 12, 2020, 14:51, https://en.wikipedia.org/wiki/Yale_Law_School#History.

5 Kalman, *Yale Law School and the Sixties*, 44. Laura Kalman is a professor in the history department at the University of California, Santa Barbara, specializing in 20th-century American legal history. Kalman earned her J.D. from UCLA in 1977, Ph.D. from Yale University in 1982 and taught legal history at Yale Law School in 2001. Besides *Yale Law School and the Sixties*, Kalman has written three other books—all of which involve the history of Yale Law School. The books are: *Legal Realism at Yale, 1927–1960*; *The Strange Career of Legal Liberalism*; and *Abe Fortas: A Biography*.

6 "Que Son Valley," HistoryCentral.com, accessed February 12, 2020, https://www.historycentral.com/Vietnam/queson1.html.

7 "When The Doors Defied Ed Sullivan," Best Classic Bands, accessed February 12, 2020, https://bestclassicbands.com/doors-ed-sullivan-9-15-17/.

8 Wikipedia, s.v., "1967 Boston Red Sox Season," last modified February 12, 2020, https://en.wikipedia.org/wiki/1967_Boston_Red_Sox_season.

9 "On This Day: October 16, 1967: Joan Baez Arrested in Vietnam Protest," BBC, accessed on February 12, 2020, http://news.bbc.co.uk/onthisday/hi/dates/stories/october/16/newsid_2535000/2535301.stm.

10 Wikipedia, s.v., "*Hair* (musical)," last modified February 12, 2020, https://en.wikipedia.org/wiki/Hair_(musical).

11 Wikipedia, s.v., "John McCain," last modified February 12, 2020, https://en.wikipedia.org/wiki/John_McCain.

12 Wikipedia, s.v., "1967 in United States," last modified February 12, 2020, https://en.wikipedia.org/wiki/1967_in_the_United_States. *See also* "'Wise Men' Advise President Johnson to Negotiate Peace in Vietnam," History.com, accessed February 12, 2020, https://www.history.com/this-day-in-history/johnson-meets-with-the-wise-men-2.

13 Wikipedia, s.v., "1967 in United States," last modified February 12, 2020, https://en.wikipedia.org/wiki/1967_in_the_United_States.

14 "Magical Mystery Tour," The Beatles, accessed February 12, 2020, https://www.thebeatles.com/album/magical-mystery-tour.

15 "Summer of Love," The 60s Official Site: Where Music Is Our Middle Name, accessed February 12, 2020, http://www.the60sofficialsite.com/Summer-of-Love.html.

16 Wikipedia, s.v., "Big Mac," last modified February 12, 2020, https://en.wikipedia.org/wiki/Big_Mac.

CHAPTER 6

THE ASU LAW SOCIETY—1966 TO 1997

Dean Pedrick's first "Dean's Report," December 12, 1967, tackled the problem head on: "With no alumni, and with no prospect of any alumni for another three years, it seemed very important, indeed, to devise some organization through which sympathetic members of the legal profession and members of other professions and the business community might join together to provide both financial assistance and personal involvement to assist the new school. After an initial round of conversations with a number of the most respected members

of the legal profession in the Phoenix area, plans were made to establish a new organization to be known as *The Law Society of Arizona State University*...."[1]

That first year's class also knew the odds of getting jobs in good firms would be slim for two simple reasons: The University of Arizona College of Law had a lock on jobs with big firms for good reason—it had a fifty-five-year head start, and most of the big firms were managed by U of A Law graduates. Michael Gallagher, the 1970 class president, remembered it well: "A lot of us got jobs because Ped promised we would. He twisted arms in all the big firms and the public sector. Lots of us were employed because the firms hired us on his say-so."[2]

THE LAW SOCIETY'S INITIAL LEADERSHIP & STRUCTURAL GOALS

The Arizona State Corporation Commission certified the articles of incorporation for the Law Society on December 12, 1966.[3] The Founding Dinner was held at the Mountain Shadows Resort in Scottsdale on April 5, 1967. Dinner guests signed 185 enrollment cards and collectively pledged more than $31,000 in financial support for scholarships. The founding president, Riney B. Salmon of Jennings, Strouss, Salmon & Trask, gave a rousing speech followed by reassuring remarks by ASU President G. Homer Durham, Judge Walter E. Craig, Chief Justice Charles C. Bernstein, and Dean Charles E. Ares of the University of Arizona College of Law.

The Law Society amended and restated their bylaws on July 18, 1967. They refined the "General Purpose" section to define specific corporate purposes: (1) to provide scholarships and other financial assistance to law students; (2) to provide financial support for the educational program through contributions to the Law Library, legal research, increments to faculty salaries, and for a discretionary Dean's Fund to cover special needs relating to the operation of the law college, and generally to promote and assist the college.[4] They also set criteria for awarding student financial aid: "(a) Students must demonstrate need, or promise, or both. (b) There shall be no discrimination by reason of race, creed, or sex. (c) No awards for periods longer than three years and not for more than the cost of tuition, books, equipment, transportation, and a reasonable living allowance. (d) Selection shall be made by the Dean of the college, in consultation with the faculty. (e) Awards may be applied to benefit individuals, or paid directly to them."[5] Section 3 covered research grants. Section 4 dealt with library grants or gifts. Section 5 provided financial increments to faculty salaries with the approval of the Dean and the university President. Section 5 set the parameters for the Dean's Fund; on recommendation by the Dean the Society may make available funds for costs incurred in the proper administration of the affairs of the school and for which budgeted funds are not available.

In his 1967–1968 Report to the ASU President, Dean Pedrick outlined the school's relationship to the Law Society: "It is simply not possible to say too much by way of tribute to those members of the legal profession and others who have joined together to organize and develop the Law Society of Arizona State University. As a result of the dedicated service on the part of Mr. Riney B. Salmon, Sr., President of the Society, the members of the Board of Directors and others in the Society, the school has been supplied with financial assistance by way of scholarship funds, funds for assisting in meeting moving costs of new faculty members and for other purposes which have given to the school capabilities that were essential and could not have been supplied from any other source. A special word of appreciation ought to be given to the Richard Grand Foundation of Tucson[6] . . . [it] has been most generous in providing scholarship assistance to the school . . . At the end of the academic year 1967–68, the Law Society numbered 261 members, of whom 125 were Founding Members at the contribution rate of $250 each, or more. The Society had contributed to the school, its scholarship program and other needs, a total of $47,260.00 and had, in fact, underwritten a substantial scholarship program for the school."[7]

---

1 Willard H. Pedrick, *Annual Report of the Dean 1966–67* (Arizona State College of Law Archives, 1966–67), 15.

2 Michael Gallagher (1970 class president), interview with author, April 9, 2019.

3 *See*, Arizona Corporation Commission, *Articles of Incorporation The Law Society of Arizona State University*, (Arizona: eCorp, 1966), https://ecorp.azcc.gov/BusinessSearch/BusinessInfo?entityNumber=00701763. The articles were true to form—establishing the Society's right to buy, sell, hold, and use property to promote and assist in developing, supporting, and increasing the facilities, resources, and research programs. It was formed without capital stock as a charitable and educational nonprofit corporation. Riney B. Salmon was elected as the Society's first president. The list of other officers and directors was a veritable list of "Who's Who" in the Valley of the Sun's legal world at the time: Joseph S. Jenckes, Judge Jerry H. Glenn, Wayne E. Legg, Louis McClennen, Judge Charles C. Bernstein, Frank Haze Berch, C.A. Carson, III, Judge Walter E. Craig, Dr. G. Homer Durham, George R. Hill, Jarril F. Kaplan, Orme Lewis, Dean Willard H. Pedrick, Joseph P. Ralston, Nicholas Udall, Philip E. von Ammon, Mark Wilmer.

4 Sandra Day O'Connor College of Law, *By-laws Law Society of Arizona State University, Article I, Section 1*, Archives 1967.

5 Ibid., Section 2.

6 *See* "Richard Grand Foundation in San Francisco, California," NonProfitFacts.com, accessed February 12, 2020, http://www.nonprofitfacts.com/CA/Richard-Grand-Foundation.html. *See also* "Richard Grand," Legacy.com, April 14, 2013, https://www.legacy.com/obituaries/sfgate/obituary.aspx?pid=164188632.

7 Willard H. Pedrick, Annual Report of the Dean 1967–68 (Arizona State College of Law Archives, 1967–68), 13–14.

CHAPTER 7

ARMSTRONG HALL—1966 TO 1968

It didn't look like any other building on the ASU campus in Tempe, Arizona, in 1968. It didn't look like a college building at all. Some observers said it was "rather reminiscent of the British House of Commons . . . evokes the genuine spirit of the law . . . provides a dramatic setting for final arguments before a full bench."[1] It was asymmetrical. Hodgepodge, at first glance, but everyone warmed

to it quickly. Carmel & Rossman designed it. Del E. Webb built it. The Arizona Board of Regents paid for and owned it.[2] They built it on the corner of Orange Street and McAllister with crescent-shaped classrooms, offices, and a circular rotunda designed to offset the squeezed feeling that comes with smallish square rooms and narrow halls.

Two years earlier, on November 19, 1966, a groundbreaking ceremony had been held on the building site just east of the Women's Gymnasium. Five Arizona Supreme Court Justices (Chief Justice Fred C. Struckmeyer,[3] Vice-Chief Justice Charles Bernstein,[4] and Justices Jesse A. Udall,[5] Lorna E. Lockwood,[6] and Ernest W. McFarland[7]) and a young boy (John S. Armstrong, IV, age ten) whose great-grandfather, John Samuel Armstrong,[8] wrote the bill authorizing the Tempe Normal School, now ASU, wielded long-handled shovels to commemorate the historic occasion.[9] It was a day of fine speeches.

ASU President Homer Durham[10] said, "In the discourse of Arizona State University, we need the colleagueship and influence that legal scholarship can contribute . . . . In the long run, the college of law will assist freshman English, student journalism in the campus newspaper, debate in the faculty and student senates, the procedural and substantive work done in hundreds of committee meetings."[11]

Dean Charles Ares[12] of the University of Arizona College of Law in Tucson said, "Both schools will work imaginatively and wisely, sometimes together, sometimes separately, but both to the same end of playing leading roles in pushing forward the new frontiers of legal philosophy."[13]

Chief Justice Struckmeyer said, "The spirit of competition we create with the U of A will be healthy, producing not only more lawyers, but we will have better lawyers."[14] The groundbreaking ceremonies attracted many notable judges and lawyers: Dean Willard Pedrick; Williby E. Case, Jr.[15], President of the Arizona Bar Association; Chief Judge Henry S. Stevens[16] of the Arizona Court of Appeals; Judge James D. Hathaway,[17] Division Two of the Arizona Court of Appeals in Tucson; and Messrs. Cartmell and Rossman, designers.

The 1968 dedication ceremonies included, as a major part of the celebration, the unveiling of a monolinear[18] bust of John S. Armstrong and a bronze commemorative plaque describing the man for whom the building was designed. The bust was sculpted by John S. Armstrong, III, and a Paradise Valley artist.[19]

Other dignitaries at the 1968 dedication ceremonies included: Leon Levy,[20] President of the *Arizona Board of Regents*; Riney B. Salmon, President of the Law Society of Arizona State University and co-founder of Jennings, Strouss, Salmon & Trask[21] of Phoenix, Arizona; Earl F. Morris, President of the American Bar Association; Professor Joseph Sneed, Stanford School of Law and head of the Association of American Law Schools; H. Karl Mangum,[22] President of the Arizona State Bar Association; and Earnest W. McFarland, Chief Justice of the Arizona Supreme Court, who introduced the major speaker at the event—Chief Justice of the United States, Earl Warren.[23]

An overflow crowd of over 3,000 attended the dedication—held at ASU's Grady Gammage Auditorium—listened to Chief Justice Warren's speech and then marched, in "gowned elegance" to Armstrong Hall two blocks away. The Chief called for all law schools to equip lawyers for "service to country and mankind in addition to a profitable career."[24] He spoke about change.

> *The changing times in which we live call not only for a sharpening of the mind, but also for a broadening of it. This means the well-grounded lawyer should have a concept of past law and its interpretation to the present, but also face changed conditions and the necessity for the law to change with them . . . [they] must have a perception of the law as it should be as well as a knowledge of present law and of its application in the past . . . It is not fanciful to conclude that the legal profession may someday be split down the middle as it is in other countries, between lawyers advising private clients without regard to social interests and government-employed lawyers whose interest in the law is focused on innovations rather than its effects on the problems of individuals . . . there are likely 315,000 lawyers in this country with [only] 31,000 in governmental work (16,000 federal, 7,400 state, and 7,500 local governments) . . . lawyers should be qualified to work either in private or government areas . . . a polarization of these activities could lead to dividing the profession into three groups, as in many countries today—private, public, and judiciary . . . I submit such a system would not be consistent with our institutions, our free society, or the great challenge to young minds for an expanding and exciting legal career . . . such polarization in the law, it seems to me, that we must have greater integration of all the social sciences, as result of which our students will leave the law schools inspired by a knowledge of the*

history of our country . . . they will acquire an understanding of our institutions, an appreciation of how and why our people became protected by the Bill of Rights in our Constitution, by the danger of erosion of those rights.[25]

ABA President Earl F. Morris endorsed the Chief Justice's theme: "The legal profession has never faced more challenging issues—prevention and control of crime—continuing improvement of legal services to the poor—meeting the need for competent legal service to the middle-income bracket—increased legal research facilities."[26]

Arizona State Bar Association President Karl Mangum said Arizona lawyers had "weathered with pride" the new enthusiasm with which the new law building has developed. Arizona Supreme Court Chief Justice Ernest McFarland observed that the new law structure symbolized the faith Arizonans have in the legal profession. Professor Leon Green of the University of Texas Law School (Austin) emphasized that legal training must be expanded and deepened. He advised the crowd of young lawyers in the auditorium to "embrace the computer as a gracious gift of technology to help you master the factual details on which you must give advice and for which you must fashion appropriate law."[27]

ARMSTRONG HALL—REDEDICATION CEREMONY— FEBRUARY 26, 1997

From dedication in 1966 to rededication in 1997, Armstrong Hall was home to thousands of students, hundreds of teachers, and the kind of change that humanizes the law. Oral arguments before learned judges and justices were delivered in the Great Hall. Thousands of ping-pong games gave pause to the intensity of learning elsewhere in the building. Hundreds of thousands of law books were acquired, borrowed, used, reused, and discarded. Mock trials and appeals were won and lost by teams from schools all over the country. Five deans came and went and everything got bigger, better, more expensive and intensely visible.

From that august beginning on November 19, 1966, when Armstrong Hall was *dedicated* to February 26, 1997 when it was *rededicated*, the rule of law was advanced, an independent judiciary was strengthened, and students succeeded at the highest possible levels. On reflection, its lawyers and law teachers nurtured a dizzily growing body of law birthed in Armstrong Hall. It was a time to learn, apply, debate and resolve. In every corner of the state, and all over America, ASU lawyers made themselves known.

Time flashed by so fast that much of what happened is lost. But thousands of ASU law students became lawyers.[28] Hundreds of law professors earned tenure, and the law was much the better for it. Cases were filed, won, lost, appealed, and became common law out of arguments and weighty decisions reached in the rotunda, the Great Hall, and the classrooms. Businesses were formed, did well, or became insolvent. People were helped, causes advanced, elections monitored, justice handed down and out, all because of foundations laid, fortunes won and lost, and clients served—private, public, individually, and collectively in Armstrong Hall.

The *ASU Insight* magazine story by Sarah Auffret[29] captured the magic of the day. "Exactly 112 years after his grandfather helped create the school that became ASU, John S. Armstrong III of Scottsdale received the 1997 Distinguished Achievement Award from the College of Law. In a Feb. 26 ceremony at the southwest entrance of Armstrong Hall, the law building named after his grandfather, Armstrong unveiled a newly refurbished bronze sculpture of John Samuel Armstrong, Jr. In attendance were past winners of the Armstrong Prize, an award given each year to the most outstanding law graduate."

The large crowd gathered at the southwest entrance were thrilled to watch the unveiling of the bronze plaque on the door to the building.

In the Great Hall, three well-known speakers regaled the crowd with stories of Armstrong, its inhabitants, and its importance to legal education and the rule of law. In accordance with academic protocols for such occasions, ASU President Lattie F. Coor spoke first. Dean Richard J. Morgan followed, and the Hon. Ruth V. McGregor, then Chief Judge of the Arizona Court of Appeals, delivered the finale—a tribute to both the founder and all of the past winners of the coveted Armstrong Prize. Judge McGregor told the story as school history and personal history because she herself won the Armstrong Prize in 1974.

---

1 "College Has Unique Design," *Phoenix Gazette*, February 1, 1968, Special to the Gazette.

2 Under Arizona Law and ABOR's governance rules, all buildings on all three university campuses are titled in ABOR's name. ABOR ratified the award of a construction contract to the Del E. Webb Construction Company in the amount of $1,677,000.00 for 81,000 square feet at $20.40 per square feet at its November 26, 1966 meeting. E.L. Farmer Construction Company's losing bid came in at $1,689,000.00. *See* "Minutes" ABOR Minutes, 16. At its January 20, 1968 meeting, ASU President Durham informed the Regents the new law building, now named Armstrong Hall, would be dedicated on February 26, 1968 and expressed hope that all Regents and Governor Williams would attend. He also informed the Regents that Chief Justice Earl Warren would address the students and faculty. Prof. Jonathan Rose recalled that Gov. Williams refused to attend because CJ Warren would be on the platform. The Secretary of Labor, W. Willard Wirtz, was also present for the dedication.

3 Fred C. Struckmeyer Jr. (January 4, 1912–June 22, 1992) was a Justice of the Supreme Court of Arizona from January 3, 1955 to January 19, 1982. He served as Chief Justice of the Court on four occasions. Struckmeyer was the son of Fred Struckmeyer Sr., who served one term on the Superior Court in Maricopa County from 1923–1925. Wikipedia, s.v., "Fred C. Struckmeyer Jr.," last modified August 8, 2019, 03:40, https://en.wikipedia.org/wiki/Fred_C._Struckmeyer_Jr.

4 Charles C. Bernstein (June 2, 1904–April 29, 1976) was a Justice of the Supreme Court of Arizona from January 5, 1959 to January 4, 1969. He served as Chief Justice from January 1962 to December 1963 and from January 1967 to December 1967. Wikipedia, s.v., "Charles C. Bernstein," last modified December 25, 2020, 22:13, https://en.wikipedia.org/wiki/Charles_C._Bernstein.

5 Jesse Addison Udall (June 24, 1893 – April 18, 1980) was a member of the Udall political family who served as chief justice of the Arizona Supreme Court. Udall was born and raised in Arizona, he was the son of David King Udall and Ida Frances (Hunt) Udall and was named after Jesse Nathaniel Smith and Addison Pratt, his great-grandfather. Wikipedia, s.v., "Jesse Addison Udall," last modified August 26, 2019, 16:28, https://en.wikipedia.org/wiki/Jesse_Addison_Udall.

6 Lorna Elizabeth Lockwood was an American lawyer and judge who served as justice of the Arizona Supreme Court. Born in what was then Arizona Territory, Lockwood was the daughter of Alfred Collins Lockwood, who later served as chief justice of the Arizona Supreme Court. Lockwood attended the University of Arizona and the University of Arizona College of Law before entering private practice and serving several terms in the Arizona House of Representatives. Lockwood spent a decade on the bench of the Arizona Superior Court in Maricopa County, the first woman to serve in that role. In 1960, Lockwood was elected to the Arizona Supreme Court. She served as chief justice from 1965 to 1966 and 1970 to 1971, become the first female chief justice of a state supreme court in the United States. She retired from the court in 1975 and died three years later. Wikipedia, s.v., "Lorna E. Lockwood," last modified August 26, 2019, 16:29, https://en.wikipedia.org/wiki/Lorna_E._Lockwood.

7 Ernest William "Mac" McFarland (October 9, 1894 – June 8, 1984) was an American politician, jurist and, with Warren Atherton, one of the "Fathers of the G.I. Bill." He is the only Arizonan to serve in the highest office in all three branches of Arizona government, two at the state level, one at the federal level.

He was a Democratic Senator from Arizona from 1941 to 1953 (majority leader from 1951 to 1953) before he was the tenth governor of Arizona from 1955 to 1959. Finally, McFarland sat as Chief Justice on the Arizona Supreme Court in 1968. Wikipedia, s.v., "Ernest McFarland," last modified September 22, 2019, 15:28, https://en.wikipedia.org/wiki/Ernest_McFarland.

8   "The Founding of Arizona State University," ASU.edu, http://www.asu.edu/lib/archives/asustory/intro.htm.

9   *See*, Memorandum to President G. Homer Durham from Dean Willard Pedrick. "The Program for the College of Law groundbreaking ceremony scheduled for Saturday, November 19, 1966." ASU College of Law, Office of the Dean, Sandra Day O'Connor College of Law, Library Archives.

10   During the 1960s with the presidency of G. Homer Durham, Arizona State University began its academic maturing with the establishment of several new colleges, including the College of Fine Arts, the College of Law, the College of Nursing, the School of Social Work, and the reorganization of what became the College of Liberal Arts and Sciences and the College of Engineering and Applied Sciences. Perhaps most importantly, the university gained the authority to award the Doctor of Philosophy and other doctoral degrees. "Homer Durham: Eleventh President 1960–1969," ASU.edu, https://president.asu.edu/the-office/past-presidents/homer-durham. *See also* Wikipedia, s.v., "G. Homer Durham," last modified September 2, 2019, 03:14, https://en.wikipedia.org/wiki/G._Homer_Durham.

11   *The Arizona Republic*, Nov. 20, 1966. It is likely that some in the crowd wondered how a law school might assist "freshman English, and student journalism." But the fact that a college of law would cause debate in faculty and student senates was likely widely accepted. Wikipedia, s.v., "Ernest McFarland," last modified September 22, 2019, 15:28, https://en.wikipedia.org/wiki/Ernest_McFarland. *See also* "The Untold Story of an Arizona Legend," ewmcfarland.org, https://ewmcfarland.org/call-him-mac-2018.

12   Charles Edgar Ares was born September 11, 1926, in Tucson, Arizona. His Father, Albert Frederick Ares, was a cotton farmer in Marana. The family later farmed in the Flowing Wells area of Tucson, at Continental, and in Elfrida, where they worked on the Grizzly apple orchard. Ares attended elementary schools in Southern Arizona. He graduated from Tucson High School and joined the navy in 1944, when he was seventeen years old. In 1946, after two-and-a-half years in the navy, Ares enrolled at the University of Arizona where he majored in political science, and in 1949 became a student in the College of Law. He received his J.D. in 1952. Upon graduation from law school, Ares spent a year as law clerk to U.S. Supreme Court Justice William O. Douglas. He then returned to Tucson and entered private practice, first with Harry Ackerman and then with Morris and Stewart Udall. For the first three years he was also Deputy County Attorney. In 1961 Ares joined the New York University law faculty, returning to Tucson in 1966 to become Dean of the University of Arizona College of Law. After seven years he stepped down from the position of dean to become a full-time law professor. "Charles E. Ares," LegalLegacy.org, https://www.legallegacy.org/13-attorneys/28-charles-e-ares. *See also* "Charles E. Ares," University of Arizona, https://law.arizona.edu/charles-e-ares.

13   *The Arizona Republic*, Nov. 20, 1966. Looking back over the long history of ABOR's two law schools, Dean Ares was right—sometimes, *albeit* rarely, the schools worked together. More often than not, they progressed on different paths.

14   Ibid.

15   Born Kansas City, Missouri, 1928; brought to Phoenix 1933. Education: attended Stanford University; University of Arizona, LL.B. 1952. Experience: practiced Phoenix and Yuma; President, State Bar of Arizona, 1966–1967. Judge, Court of Appeals, 1971–1972. Judge, Superior Court, Maricopa County, 1973–1977. Died August 3, 1983. "Williby E. Case," AZcourts.gov, https://www.azcourts.gov/coa1/Former-Judges/WILLIBY-E-CASE.

16   Born Madison, Wisconsin, 1907. Education: University of Wisconsin, B.A. 1928; University of Arizona, J.D. 1931. Experience: practiced Phoenix; Assistant City Attorney, Phoenix, 1939–1942; Judge, Superior Court, Maricopa County, 1953–1965. Judge, Court of Appeals, 1965–1975. Died: October 8, 1993. "Henry S. Stevens," AZcourts.gov, https://www.azcourts.gov/coa1/Former-Judges/HENRY-S-STEVENS.

17   Arizona Court of Appeals, Division Two—Tucson Arizona. "James David Hathaway," Legacy.com, published on February 21, 2014, https://www.legacy.com/obituaries/tucson/obituary.aspx?pid=169785606.

18   A typeface having vertical and horizontal strokes of the same visual weight.

19   He was known for his philosophy of monolinearism, and his unique works of art. He is also said to have written the text of the bronze plaque. "In 1885, young John S. Armstrong introduced into the [Arizona] Territorial Legislature a bill to establish an institution of higher-education to teach among other things, the 'fundamental law of the United States and the responsibilities of citizens.' From this enabling legislation has come Arizona State University. To honor its legislative founder, the University has designated its College of Law as Armstrong Hall. February, 1968." *See*, Hal R. Moore, *The Arizonan*, February 2, 1968.

Armstrong Hall—1966 to 1968

20 Born in 1913 in Douglas, AZ, Leon Levy attended local schools including the University of Arizona where he was a member of the college football team. After college in 1934 he joined the family business. During 1943–1945 he served in the Navy and received training at the Naval Indoctrination Training Program on the campus of the University of Arizona in 1944–1945. In addition to work as Levy store treasurer, and later president, & chairman of the board, he maintained involvement with many Tucson and Arizona organizations and activities. Through the years Levy had a strong concern and association with higher education and the University of Arizona in particular. He served on the Arizona Board of Regents from 1960–1968 and became its chairman in 1968. "Leon Levy Collection," Arizona Historical Society, 2, http://www.arizonahistoricalsociety.org/wp-content/upLoads/library_Levy-Leon.pdf.

21 "Long recognized as one of Arizona's premier law firms, Jennings Strouss is one of the oldest, largest and most distinguished law firms based in Arizona. Since the firm was founded in 1942, Jennings Strouss has been deeply rooted in each of our locations' legal and business communities, and its attorneys have been instrumental in helping shape the dynamic growth of Arizona and many of its institutions. The firm's founders—Irving A. Jennings, Sr., Charles L. Strouss, Sr., Riney B. Salmon, Sr., and Ozell M. Trask—started practicing law in the 1920's when Arizona's economy was largely driven by agriculture and the mining industry. In 1942, the partnership began on the sixth floor of the Phoenix Title & Trust Building at First Avenue and Adams Street. Some of the first attorneys who came to the firm were: Richard Kleindienst, who helped build and energize the Republican Party in Arizona before becoming U.S. Attorney General under President Nixon; Rex Lee, former Solicitor General of the U.S.; Nicholas Udall, a former Phoenix Mayor who later became a Superior Court Judge; and Clarence Duncan, who was renowned for his precise legal mind and his teaching and mentoring of young attorneys." "History," Jennings Strouss Law Firm, https://jsslaw.com/about/history/.

22 Richard K. Mangum, "Harvey Karl Mangum: A Biography," Mangumwall.com, https://www.mangumwall.com/wp-content/uploads/sites/4452/2016/09/H-K-Mangum-biography.pdf.

23 "Earl Warren (March 19, 1891 – July 9, 1974) was an American jurist and politician who served as the 14th Chief Justice of the United States (1953–1969) and earlier as the 30th Governor of California (1943–1953). The Warren Court presided over a major shift in constitutional jurisprudence, with Warren writing the majority opinions in landmark cases such as Brown v. Board of Education, Reynolds v. Sims, and Miranda v. Arizona. Warren also led the Warren Commission, a presidential commission that investigated the 1963 assassination of President John F. Kennedy. He is as of 2019 the last Chief Justice to have served in an elected office. Warren was born in 1891 in Los Angeles and was raised in Bakersfield, California. After graduating from the law program at the University of California, Berkeley, he began a legal career in Oakland. He was hired as a deputy district attorney for Alameda County in 1920 and was appointed district attorney in 1925. He emerged as a leader of the state Republican Party and won election as the Attorney General of California in 1938. In that position, he played a role in the forced removal and internment of over 100,000 Japanese Americans during World War II. In the 1942 California gubernatorial election, Warren defeated incumbent Democratic governor Culbert Olson. He would serve as Governor of California until 1953, presiding over a period of major growth for the state. Warren served as Thomas E. Dewey's running mate in the 1948 presidential election, but Dewey lost the election to incumbent President Harry S. Truman. Warren sought the Republican nomination in the 1952 presidential election, but the party nominated General Dwight D. Eisenhower. After Eisenhower won election as president, he appointed Warren as Chief Justice. Warren helped arrange a unanimous decision in Brown v. Board of Education, which ruled that racial segregation in public schools was unconstitutional." Wikipedia, s.v., "Earl Warren," last modified October 20, 2019, 18:04, https://en.wikipedia.org/wiki/Earl_Warren.

24 John L. Carpenter, *Phoenix Gazette*, February 26, 1968.

25 Ibid.

26 Ibid.

27 Ibid.

28 As of 2020, the Sandra Day O'Connor has more than 8,000 law graduates. Every state has at least one ASU lawyer.

29 Sarah Auffret, *ASU Insight*, February 26, 1997, 3.

CHAPTER 8

INAUGURAL FACULTY—1967 TO 1970

*L*aw professors are like judges without gavels or robes. They make up hypothetical legal disputes, challenges, disputations, arguments, answers, and tricks of the trade. They know legal theory and jurisprudence, but not much about the essence of lawyering or what it takes to try a case. They don't decide, they grade. They don't practice, they teach. They write about the law, understand

its nuance, but spend no time with clients. They don't go to court, but know a great deal about what happens there. Some make tenure. Others make trouble for deans. All of them are central to everything that happens in a law school. Nothing good can come from a law school without good professors. Law schools are granite mountains of facts, laws, statutes, and cases, all hidden in clouds, cracks, crevices, caves, and bottomless pits. Law professors are the ropes, pulleys, crampons, oxygen, and Sherpas essential to reaching the top of the mountain, without falling off.

Nearly all law professors hold earned undergraduate degrees and juris doctorates. All went to accredited law schools. Many hold licenses to practice, but most are only occasionally put to use. All earned high grades, have mentoring skills, and write well. They publish scholarly papers to secure tenure and often engage other academics in interdisciplinary research and learning. Not surprisingly, they are vagabonds, change schools but not subjects, and are more introverted than practicing lawyers are. Importantly, all are skilled in the circumvention of simple law by making the answers the questions and turning solutions into problems. Like them or not, they will always make you think like a lawyer.

Dean Pedrick is profiled in Chapter 3. His seven successors were Dean Ernest Gellhorn[1] (1976 to 1978), Alan Matheson[2] (1978 to 1984), Dean Paul Bender[3] (1984 to 1989), Dean Richard Morgan[4] (1989 to 1997), Dean Patricia White[5] (1997 to 2007), Dean Paul Berman (2007 to 2010),[6] and Dean Douglas Sylvester[7] (2010 to present).[8]

ASU College of Law's inaugural faculty was handpicked by its inaugural dean, Willard Pedrick. His first hire, Richard Dahl, in 1966, was followed in 1967 by William Canby, Jr., Edward Cleary, Richard Effland, Harold Havighurst, and Alan Matheson.[9] In 1968 he hired Warren Cohen, George Dix, John P. Morris, and Jonathan Rose. Nineteen sixty-nine brought in Michael Berch, Arthur LeFrance, Stephen Lee, Milton Schroder, and Robert Strong, Jr. Nineteen seventy netted Leland Balder and Dale Furnish. These eighteen professors taught, mentored, and hand-carried the first three classes from knowing nothing to knowing it all. The graduating class of 1970 was their first production. Arizona law and practice were never the same again.

In 2020, of the original eighteen professors hired by Dean Pedrick between 1966 and 1970, only Alan Matheson, Jon Rose, Michael Berch, and Milt Schroder are occasionally "in the building."[10] By 1974, Dean Pedrick had added Harold Bruff, Gerald Caplan, Gilbert Venable, John LaSota, Jr., and Douglas Leslie. The first woman on the faculty was Susan Spivak, in 1972. The second woman, Beatrice Moulton, was hired in 1973. Richard Delgado and Donald Zimmerman came in 1974, bringing the total faculty to twenty-nine in just eight years. In 2019, one year away from the fiftieth anniversary of the first graduating class, the faculty count was fifty-six teaching and research faculty members and twenty-three professors of practice and lecturers in law. There were five Academic Professionals (law librarians who occasionally teach).[11]

Starting with Pedrick and Dahl, the inaugural faculty of eighteen professors moved the first class from 1L to 2L to 3L to alumni in just three years. Years of uncertainty but promise. Hope against challenge. And making much of it up as they went along. Alan Matheson, arguably the school's first historian, remembered the start:

> *The decision to have a law school was matched with a determination by the University and the State to launch the enterprise in grand fashion . . . . A distinguished founding faculty was assured when Dean Pedrick was able to persuade Edward W. Cleary of Illinois, Richard W. Effland of Wisconsin, Harold E. Havighurst of Northwestern, William C. Canby, and John P. Morris to come to Arizona. I was appointed Assistant Dean and joined the faculty at mid-year . . . . [We] greeted a charter class of 117 students . . . . The dedicatory address was given by late the Earl Warren, Chief Justice of the United States Supreme Court . . . a "well-grounded lawyer should have a concept, not only of what the law has been or how it has been interpreted up to the present time, but he must also be able to face change with them . . . . [H]e must have a perception of the law as it should be as well as knowledge of present law and of its application to the past." These words were a fitting description of the law program established by the new law school.*[12]

WILLARD H. PEDRICK

In many ways, Ped, as everyone who knew him addressed him, *was* ASU Law. It would have been created without him, had he declined President Homer Durham's offer, but it would not have become what it did—a law school on fire to make a name for itself, an experiment that worked—a place no one who was in the building ever forgot. He made it what is now a top-30 American law school.[13]

RICHARD C. DAHL

Perhaps the best description of Professor Dahl's contributions to ASU's Law School was written by Dean Patricia White after Professor Dahl died in Phoenix in 2007.[14] She said his contributions were invaluable. "He played an essential role in the remarkably quick move from idea to important institution that this school made. No law school can be a good law school without a highly effective library. Our library was good from day one. It's one of the hardest things to do when creating a law school."[15]

Inaugural Faculty—1967 to 1970

Professor Dahl was an old-school librarian even when he was a young man. His story is as true today as it was when Dean Pedrick picked him to build the school's first library in 1966. We all got the same *message* at about the same time. It wasn't just the sixties, or just ASU's brand-new law library, in a temporary building. Every law student, in every law school in America, gets the message, about the same time—the first week of classes as a 1L. *Every book you need to become a lawyer has already been written.* It's waiting for you. In the law library. Law libraries are apolitical—very democratic—never partisan—they open early and close late. The only entrance requirement is interest—in the law.

ASU's law library was designed, divined, devoured, and created by one man— Richard C. Dahl, BA, BLS, LLB. He theorized the library, sketched its dimensions on yellow legal pads, and hired every staff member for ten years.

His personal story is an essential part of how ASU Law maneuvered its way from not much in 1965—an unranked, untested, beginning law school—to a top-30 ranked law school when he died in 2007. He was a quiet man, as befits a lifelong librarian. His obituary in *The Arizona Republic* notes how his "acerbic wit could startle people, but inside he was soft as a marshmallow, with great love and loyalty for family and friends."

Professor Dahl was addicted to movies and other things.

> *Other addictions included books, walking, and the tying of complicated knots. [A WWII veteran, he enlisted and served] in France in the Army Quartermaster Corps from 1942–46 . . . . He served as the law librarian for the University of California, the University of Nebraska, the Office of the Judge Advocate General for the Navy, and Washington state. He also was Civil Division Librarian for the Department of Justice and the U.S. Treasury Department's librarian. He coauthored several law books. In 1966, Richard was recruited by Willard Pedrick, dean of the ASU College of Law, and was one of the school's founding faculty. He amassed the 60,000 volumes needed for accreditation and also taught legal research, ethics and government.*

After retiring, Professor of Law Emeritus Dahl earned a master's degree in history at ASU. Talk about life-long learning.[16]

In his December 1, 1967 report (the first year of classes in temporary quarters), Professor Dahl described the library as "in its formative stages . . . showed a volume count of 54,776 items, with expenditures and encumbrances of over $295,000.00." In his March 1, 1969 report, he counted "73,320 items, with additional expenditures and encumbrances of over $154,000.00." His descriptive voice was hesitant. "Initially buried under a tide of incoming material, we are starting to move slowly but surely from a level of frantic book-buying with little regard for bibliographic control, to a more sensible level of operation at which improved record-keeping procedures allow at least some measure of access to our growing collection."[17]

By second semester, 1969, Professor Dahl had hired six staff members. William R. Murray was the Assistant Law and Reference Librarian. He earned his LLB in 1967 from Memphis State University and his Masters in Law Library Science from the University of Washington in 1968. He was licensed to practice law in Tennessee. The Technical Services Librarian was James J. C. Taso from Taiwan. He earned his MALS at San Jose State College in 1967. The Technical Services Assistant was Carolyn S. Ream. She earned her AB at Monmouth College and MA at Northwestern University in Evanston, Illinois. The Admissions Clerk was Shirley Beck. Professor Dahl's secretary was Lorraine Knilans.[18]

Never known to discount challenges, Professor Dahl was direct in describing his law library's *problems*. He used the royal *we* with style.

> *Although we do not wish to play the role of* "**Prophet of Doom**," *we find ourselves necessarily crying the age-old lament of librarians for a larger staff and more money. We suspect the lament never ends for growing libraries. We will not belabor the obvious points that a growing collection requires an increasing staff and budget, and that even basic services are increasingly costly. We do, however, stress that our small staff causes us to slip further behind each day. Our staff of six persons is no larger now than it was at the time of our First Report, but our collection, in addition to being 34% larger (73,320 to 54,776 volumes) is much more varied. Essential library operations . . . remain distant dreams . . . . We have, of course, made some advancements, but certainly not enough to offset the slippage. In parallel with staff problems is our Staff-Student Assistant ratio . . . . utilization of their services has been, in effect, a welcoming of the Trojan Horse . . . . which can best be described as nerve-wracking. The fact that 64.4% of our total man-hours are expended by Student Assistants points out our excessive reliance on generally disinterested parties to maintain a complex operation . . . . The 15 months covered by this*

Inaugural Faculty—1967 to 1970

Report have been marked by a normal reduction from an initially hectic acquisitions rate, offset by an increased tempo of operational and administrative problem solving. We find the period to be productive, but not sufficiently productive to prevent backsliding. We feel our major advances have been the "straightening out" of our collection . . . , Though the College of Law Library is autonomous, we have maintained excellent relations with the University Library. It is fair to say that we receive much more assistance from that staff than we are able to give in return. We wish, therefore, to express our sincere appreciation to them.[19]

WILLIAM C. CANBY, JR.

William Canby was the only non-teacher on the inaugural faculty. After earning his bachelor's degree, he expected to go in the military because he'd been in the Air Force ROTC at Yale. But the Korean War had just ended. As he put it, "the

Air Force was having indigestion accepting all new people. And they said well if you had any reason to go to graduate school you could get a delay . . . . I always thought law would be interesting . . . . So that's what I did in Minnesota."[20] One of his classmates, Walter Mondale ("Fritz"),[21] later became President Carter's Vice President. Fritz and Bill married sisters. After graduating from the University of Minnesota Law School in 1956,[22] he practiced with the Oppenheimer Law Firm in St. Paul, before becoming a JAG officer in the Air Force. While stationed in Tacoma, Washington, he applied for and won a coveted clerkship with U.S. Supreme Court Justice Charles Evans Whittaker.[23] Then, he spent four years in Africa working for the Peace Corps.[24] When he left the Peace Corps, he came back to Minnesota and worked on Walter Mondale's first senatorial election campaign. After that campaign, he decided to look for a teaching job at a law school somewhere.

> *ASU was just in the planning stage [at that time] and [Pedrick] came out and visited [me] . . . and he had plans of the law school . . . . [H]e got all enthusiastic and engrossed and he was such a good salesman. After I interviewed a little bit more and came out to see ASU and everything I decided the idea of going with him and the new law school . . . . He's very down to earth but he's very enthusiastic and he's an incredible optimist and also it was a brand new law school and [he asked me] what would I like to teach well, how about constitutional law[,] well OK and then maybe conflict of laws, OK you can have that too. So, it was a rare chance to choose those and it just happened that he had assembled [a faculty]; I was the kid on the faculty. He had assembled a very prestigious faculty of older teachers. He had Ed Cleary, who had been the reporter for the Federal Rules of Evidence and had a casebook on evidence, very distinguished. He was probably the biggest catch that Pedrick made. Harold Havighurst, who had been Dean at Northwestern, came down to teach contracts. Dick Effland, who was a professor at Wisconsin and was the reporter for the Uniform Probate Code, came down to teach trusts, estates, and property. And there was Pedrick who himself had a torts casebook and was teaching torts as well as being Dean. And then myself, I hadn't taught. Dick Dahl was the librarian . . . . So, I was the only newcomer and everyone else was a very, very well established teacher.*[25]

Even though Canby had not taught, he recalled that first year, 1967:

Inaugural Faculty—1967 to 1970

Of course that first year, it's wonderful because we just had five or six of us there teaching [with an] entering class about 108 or 110 and we could have a faculty meeting almost in a closet. . . . we were all pretty much of the same mind . . . a pretty good idea of what we were trying to do. Pedrick's original idea was to economize on faculty for the first couple years, and we had a quite rigid curriculum. It was fixed for the first two years . . . . Just seminars in the third year. Now that got watered down and some of the classes got bigger and eventually electives were introduced . . . . at ASU, everybody in those first few classes took all their classes together for the first two years. And they got kind of a—it's such a common experience that they really had a real espirt d' coup . . . . they'd all had the same professors to appreciate, react against, make fun of, or whatever . . . . there were no upperclassmen . . . . it was pretty total experience . . . a really nice atmosphere . . . a lot of fun . . . some natural attrition . . . . my recollection is 108 in that first class and it was probably down slightly under 100 within a few months.[26]

EDWARD W. CLEARY

Professor Cleary was Dean Pedrick's third inaugural faculty member in the summer of 1967. He was, in the words of Chancellor John E. Cribbet,[27] "one of the

most distinguished graduates of the University of Illinois College of Law."[28] He graduated in 1932. He took a Yale JSD and practiced law in Jacksonville, Illinois, before joining the U.S. Navy in WWII. Over the next sixty years, he served as a revered law professor at ASU Law, and visited at Berkeley Boalt Hall College of Law, University of Colorado College of Law, and Stanford College of Law.[29]

He wrote many law review articles, but it was his *Handbook on Illinois Evidence*[30] that made him famous. Chancellor Cribbet said his book on evidence was "on the desk of each judge in the state." In addition, Cleary also was the general editor of *McCormick on Evidence*. Chief Justice Earl Warren appointed him as the reporter of the advisory committee to draft uniform rules of evidence for federal court.[31]

Cleary spent twenty-one years on the University of Illinois faculty and was said to be a "gentle but vigorous task master, one who taught both by precept and example." His writing style was "lean and polished. Purple prose and redundant phrases were stricken with a merciless pen. Even his committee reports were a pleasure to read and he could demolish a sloppy report by others with a twinkle in his eye and a witty remark to ease the pain."[32]

He won the 1974 Distinguished Teaching Award at ASU Law. At the time, ASU Law was driven by Socratic traditional teaching. In its law school incarnation, all of the inaugural faculty at ASU in the early 1970s used it in all classes. It theoretically drew answers leading to conclusions. In reality, it was a way to challenge student's premises, assumptions, and understanding of the law. "To Ed, life had more questions than answers and the classroom was a part of life. His job was to teach the students to think, not tell them what to think. The tools were there in the library and in the assigned materials, and he was a guide through the maze. The student must have the wit to follow. Of course, those who panted after black letter law and clear-cut answers to unanswerable questions were not always amused . . . . Although Ed was a great teacher in the Socratic tradition, he was also an experimenter in then new teaching techniques—practice court, appellate advocacy, etc."[33]

His colleagues at the University of Illinois College of Law were "sorry to lose him to the sandier pastures of Arizona in 1967, but [] tried to follow the lessons which he so ably taught and the Illinois ties were never severed."[34]

The *New York Times* obituary on January 22, 1990, confirmed he died at age eighty-two of congestive heart failure at Scottsdale Memorial Hospital in Scottsdale, Arizona.[35]

Inaugural Faculty—1967 to 1970

RICHARD W. EFFLAND

Professor Effland was another of Dean Pedrick's Midwestern faculty picks—he came to ASU Law to teach alongside Professors Canby, Cleary, Havighurst, and Matheson in the summer of 1967. That group of five taught every course to every student that first year. What made this small group *sui generis* was that this faculty had no Arizona connections and their students had no Midwestern connections. In what would become a remarkable Arizona State University feat, three of the five would win the highly coveted Faculty Research Award. The university, from 1964 to the present, picks one faculty member from among all the colleges at ASU to honor.

For example, Professor Keith Davis, from the College of Business, won it in 1964; in 1970 it went to Professor Carleton Moore, from the College of Chemistry & Geology; Professor Cleary was the first College of Law winner in 1974; Professor Pedrick won it in 1981; and Professor Richard Effland won it in 1984. Since 1984, only one other law professor has won ASU's most coveted faculty research award—Professor David Kaye, Regents Professor of Law, in 1999.[36] Prof. Michael Saks would become the second Regents Professor in 2006.

Walter B. Raushenbush[37] wrote an obituary titled "Memories of Dick Effland (1916–1989)."[38] He called his friend Dick "a star of the faculty at ASU, as he had been at UW."[39] ASU Law memorialized him on campus on January 21, 1989. Professor Rauschenbusch came to the ceremony to represent Dick's first faculty—the law faculty at the University of Wisconsin.

Professor Effland earned his BA degree in 1938 and his JD in 1940 at the University of Wisconsin, recording the third highest grade average in the history of the law school.[40] Later, he earned an LLM from Columbia, practiced law, and held several public sector positions.[41]

At ASU Law, he redrafted the Arizona probate code, and was by all accounts, "[a] moderate conservative, he relied not on ideology but on thoughtful examination and considered judgment as to the merits of any proposition."[42]

83

DALE B. FURNISH

Professor Furnish joined the ASU faculty in the fall of 1970, following a clerkship with Judge Martin D. Van Oosterhout[43] on the Eighth U.S. Circuit Court of Appeals. He served in Peru with the USAID,[44] and in Chile with the Ford Foundation.[45] He took a leave from ASU Law in 1987 and practiced law with the Molloy, Jones & Donahue firm in Tucson until 1992, when he returned to ASU Law.[46]

He is well known in the international law world "for his work in comparative law and international commercial and trade law, as well as US commercial law. Bilingual in Spanish, he has been invited to teach and speak in every country in South and Central America, and has served as Visiting Professor at the National Autonomous University of Mexico (UNAM) and the University of Sonora, Mexico (UNISON) and on two occasions at the Catholic University of Peru. [He] was elected a Supernumerary Member of the Mexican Academy of Private International and Comparative Law in 2003, one of only two US jurists so honored to date. . . . He is a roster member of the United States Panel of Arbitrators for NAFTA Chapter 19 disputes . . . [and] a Director at the National Law Center for Inter-American Free Trade (NLCIFT) . . . He has worked to reform secured transactions regimes in Mexico, El Salvador, Honduras and Tanzania since his retirement in 2004."[47]

His long and esteemed curriculum vitae lists scores of publications and many visits to foreign countries teaching and speaking about international law.[48]

HAROLD C. HAVIGHURST

When Dean Pedrick went about recruiting his inaugural faculty in 1966–67, he looked for both quality and energy. He wanted to recruit nationally prominent scholars who had the kind of energy it would take to both build a new law school and create a curriculum from scratch. He also needed teachers for a hundred law students with barely a half-dozen faculty members. Without question, Harold C. Havighurst met the quality standard, but it is probable that few thought he'd be

Inaugural Faculty—1967 to 1970

an energetic builder and a law school leader—he'd already done all that forty years earlier.

Professor Havighurst was born December 24, 1897, in Findlay, Ohio, fifteen years before Arizona became a state, sixty-one years before ASU Law was authorized by the Arizona Legislature, and seventy years before Dean Pedrick lured him to come west. He'd earned his BA in 1919 at Ohio Wesleyan University, his MA at Harvard in 1922, and his LLB at Harvard in 1926. He made full professor at Northwestern in 1932 and became dean of the Law School in 1948.[49] In fact, he was one of Pedrick's teachers at Northwestern. He stepped down from his deanship in 1957 to teach more and gave the famous Rosenthal Lecture in 1961 at Northwestern before anyone in Arizona even thought about starting a second law school. That lecture was later published as "The Nature of Private Contract," and is considered a national academic legal treasure today.[50] He retired in 1966. The next year, Dean Pedrick lured him out of retirement and back into the trenches teaching contract law to first-year law students.[51]

During his three years teaching at ASU Law, from 1967 to 1970, he also mentored seven other faculty members—professors Michael Berch, John Canby, Warren Cohen, George Dix, John Morris, Jon Rose, and Robert Strong—given that they had no experience teaching law.

He brought with him a nationally outstanding body of scholarship. His Hein Online[52] database includes thirty-one published works between 1931 and 1979. Three of his published law reviews came out while he was at ASU.[53]

Professor Havighurst's most important book, *Cases on Contracts*,[54] was published in 1934 and was unorthodox at the time. Daniel Schuyler, a colleague, explained, "It was not organized in terms of doctrine, such as consideration, estoppel, and fraud. Rather, it dealt with the law of contracts in terms of subject matter, such as employment, building and construction, loans, and even physicians. Few, if any, of us who were privileged to be students in Harold's Contracts course appreciated that the organization of his casebook was the product of his acute discernment of the function of law in society and a rejection of the illusion of certainty often fostered by a more doctrinaire approach. But most, if not all, of us, were keenly aware of the extraordinary quality of his teaching."55

Prof. Havighurst's October 20, 1981 obituary in the *New York Times* cited him as an "Authority on Contracts." It noted his death in Alexandria, Virginia, at eighty-three years of age.

ALAN A. MATHESON

Professor Alan A. Matheson graduated from the University of Utah three times. He earned his BA in 1953, Phi Beta Kappa. He earned his master of science in 1957, and his JD in 1959, Order of Coif. His first job out of law school was as a faculty associate at Columbia University Law School, doing research and teaching. Then he took a position in the President's office at Utah State University before coming to Arizona State University.

He is truly sui generis in the context of this book because he has "most institutional knowledge of the [ASU] college of law."[56] He served it in one capacity or another from 1967 to 1998. Almost everyone profiled in this book knew him well and worked either for him or with him. Professor David Kader wrote about his colleague, Dean Matheson, by referencing the book, *Pirkei Avot*,[57] and its seven qualities that characterize the wise man:

The wise man does not speak before him that is greater than he in wisdom; he does not break into his fellow's speech; he is not in a rush to reply; he asks what is relevant and replies to that point; he speaks of first things first and of last things last; of what he has not heard he says, "I have not heard"; and he acknowledges what is true.[58]

After the reference to an ancient text about wisdom, Prof. Kader said, "Some have neither intellectual nor moral virtues, some one but not the other. Only in a few are both developed—in the combination that makes for wisdom. Alan Matheson is one of those few. The College of Law has greatly benefited from his wisdom, and I have learned much of value from him."[59]

Dean Pedrick probably knew him better than most and certainly knew him first.

When I interviewed young Alan A. Matheson for a position on the founding faculty, I was struck by his extraordinary modesty. The quality of modesty among those in the ranks of law teaching is virtually unknown. . . For the period I served as Dean . . . Alan was my assistant, then my associate dean and my friend. . . . He became the inside dean and while I worked the outside world and joined with Alan and the faculty in developing the instructional program of the school. . . Alan was perfection itself . . . Alan brought to legal education a broad experience and insight into developing a sound and innovative program of legal education . . . It was during the turbulence of the 1960s, moderated in Arizona. . . Could the law school sustain a tradition of providing a forum for the expression of controversial ideas, expounded by controversial speakers, in the finest traditions of the First Amendment? At such times, it was providential that the school and the university had an associate dean who never wilted under pressure, who always had wise and restrained counsel to offer . . . He was our leader, the chairman of the board, and mediator of a talented, lively and sometimes rambunctious group of intellectuals of great talent who, by and large, are continually astonished at the genuine modesty of this able man who has served us so well.[60]

Dean Matheson is more fully detailed in Chapter 8, as one of ASU Law's eight deans from 1965 to 2020.

JOHN P. MORRIS

This book is about the past. But some parts of this story should be told in reverse chronological order. Everyone who lived this story and helped ASU Law become

the juggernaut it is now knew Professor Morris. Perhaps not personally, but they know what he did, and are much the better for it. They might know of him only by looking at the consequences of his rock-steady force on curriculum, capacity, choices, and consequences. With his direct involvement, it became the best it could possibly be. By starting his story in reverse from the time he died, and looking back on what he and his colleagues did together, mostly arm-in-arm, the impact is clear. The past streams back from the now, like legal education seen from a helium balloon slowly winding its way back down to earth.

Dean Willard Pedrick, Judge William C. Canby, Jr., Dean Alan Matheson and Dean Richard J. Morgan all worked closely with and tightly engaged Professor Morris at pivotal times. Together they built, remodeled, polished, and cultivated ASU Law from infancy to drinking age; that is from 1968 to 1989. He was hired by Dean Pedrick to work with Canby and Matheson, and eventually with Morgan. They all knew him well, *albeit* at different times, and under different educational postures.

He died in 1994. Willard Pedrick took it hard.

Inaugural Faculty—1967 to 1970

When I first heard the news of John Morris's death, I was literally heartsick—for some of the light, some rare insights, and some of the fun of life had gone out for me and for others. But then, I thought a bit and said to myself, "Pedrick pull up your socks. You have had the friendship of this truly remarkable man for 35 years." First, he was my student at Northwestern University Law School and then a colleague here at ASU for 25 years. He was my intimate friend and confidant. What more are we entitled to in this life? So I began to feel whole again because my memories of the grand person that was John Morris persist and will live on with me and with others. . . . I can just hear him saying "very commensurate," a favorite expression.[61]

Judge Canby remembered the little things that often make life great.

For a dozen years or so, John Morris and I were both full-time faculty members at the College of Law; for another ten, I was an adjunct and he remained full time. During that entire period, for me at least, to see John Morris was to be cheered up. It is hard to describe the ebullience, the smile, the bit of insightful information or the humorous twist that he seemed always eager to impart like a special favor. It became a bit of an addiction for me to wander next door into his office for my daily pick-me-up, which was nothing more than his greeting, his news for the day, and the joy that suffused both.[62]

Dean Alan Matheson remembered the month and year his twenty-six-year long relationship with John Morris began and how long it lasted and enriched both lives.

John Morris and I joined the faculty of the new Arizona State University College of Law at the same time in January 1968, and his friendship became an important part of my professional and personal life. A uniquely talented person, he had a dramatic influence upon the direction of the fledgling law school and helped to form and shape curriculum and policies. As a member of the founding faculty, John became the conscience of the law school, stressing the values of fairness, equality, and diversity in institutional choice and deliberation. His remarkable presence moved the law school community to be more thoughtful, more innovative, and more caring.[63]

Dean Richard Morgan credits Professor Morris with his own start at ASU, and much of his success during the nine years he and Morris worked together. Working hand-in-glove, they upgraded what Deans Pedrick and Matheson had started.

> *John Morris was the chair of the recruitment that year. Wonderful recruiter. Wonderfully optimistic guy. He picked us up at the airport in October of '79. He had a pretty nice car. As we descended the steps from the jet to the tarmac at old Terminal One in early October, 1979, Tina and I were nervous and apprehensive. Our landing at Phoenix's Sky Harbor Airport was a prelude to full-dress interviews at the Arizona State University College of Law, interviews that might well lead to a major career change and to our relocation from California where we had lived all of our lives. As we crossed the hot tarmac, I wondered if the interviewing trip to the desert might be a mistake.*[64]

One of the many things that made Prof. Morris so memorable was how deeply he affected colleagues like Dean Morgan, whom he met as part of ASU's effort to entice Dean Morgan to become the new dean when Dean Bender returned to a faculty position.

> *Upon entering the mercifully cool terminal, our doubts and fears began to dissipate. There to meet us was a smiling and obviously friendly representative of the law school, Professor John Peyton Morris, the Chair of the Faculty Appointments Committee and a member of the founding faculty. So engaging was Professor Morris that Tina and I were quickly put at ease. By the time we had claimed our bags, our nervousness had subsided. By the time we were in Professor Morris' car, headed north to Scottsdale, I concluded that the trip to the desert was not a mistake. The picture that John painted, as were rode north in his car and as we dined at his favorite Scottsdale restaurant, was a very attractive one, of a young and dynamic law school serving a growing and vibrant community in the beautiful Southwest. By the time we had finished that meal, Tina and I were convinced that the career-change and relocation, about which we had been worrying a couple of hours earlier, offered exciting and unique opportunities.*[65]

Inaugural Faculty—1967 to 1970

Pedrick remembered a John Morris that none of his colleagues knew—his student years at Northwestern, his war history, and his lawyering years in Chicago. As is the case with all lawyers, what happens in law school is the glue that binds lawyers to the profession, including academic law.

> *John did very well as an undergraduate student at Northwestern. Then the war came. He served with distinction as an officer in the Air Force in World War II but told me that when traveling cross-country by car in those days, with his then pregnant wife, they had to drive from Chicago to Texas non-stop because it was unlikely any motel would receive them. After the war, he entered the Northwestern University Law School as a scholarship student. His academic record there was superb—law review and Order of the Coif. Despite this, when he graduated from law school in 1959, no major Chicago law firm would interview him because of his color. A senior partner in one of the firms, Walker Smith, was so outraged he left the firm to form a partnership with John. That firm prospered, with John specializing in antitrust litigation and, among other things, opening some urban hospitals to black physicians.*[66]

Judge Canby remembered that John never avoided big problems. "This is not to say that John did not have a serious side; it is just that he did not play the game of life with his teeth clenched. His style was one of casual elegance. He had a good lawyer's preference for results over theory, and the results were there. To pick out a few: John's success, just before he joined the College of Law, in racially integrating the staffs of Chicago hospitals with the tool of antitrust law; his service in helping scores of minority athletes while serving, formally and informally, as the campus ombudsman for them; and his creation and management of his shipping company, which broke all precedent for minority ownership and employment."[67]

Dean Matheson recalled Professor Morris's generous nature, and many other personal characteristics known by everyone on the faculty. "John's enormous tangible contributions to the law school and its culture testify to his ability and generous nature. Perhaps even more significant, however, was the sheer force of his character and example—his vitality, his creativity, his inner strength, his integrity, and his compassion. He taught us all to be more sensitive, more appreciative of life, and more conscious of our obligations to others. Callimachus wrote, 'A good man never dies.' John Morris was a good man."[68]

Fortunately, Professor Morris wrote his own memoir in 1979—*The Way We Were*.[69] It is a word painting of the world-class institution now known as the Sandra Day O'Connor College of Law. "On the surface, legal education at Arizona State University appears to be orderly and complacent. The College of Law is successfully fulfilling its academic mission, which is, among other things, to train people to 'think like lawyers.' In the conduct of its research and scholarship it has proceeded in fits and starts, but generally reflects the faculty interest in publishing casebooks, articles, and assorted commentaries. It has absorbed the minorities and women into its legal education program and has persuaded these groups to accept the goals long associated with being successful in the profession. The students want, and many attain, that long sought after badge of success, being offered a $25,000 a year position in a private law firm or certain prestigious government jobs."[70]

Professor Morris's memoir is an eleven-year-look-back at the institution he helped build from day one. It had a right "to point with pride," he said "to all of these achievements."[71] Given the range of his many talents, he had more to say. "[E]leven years ago we were embarking on a path as an experimental institution. Unfortunately, that course has long since been subsumed in self-centered concerns of making the school fit the image of all truly great academic institutions."[72]

Understandably, the school—that is its founders, the university leaders, and new faculty—were self-centered, with a focus on growth, expansion, and better ratings. Professor Morris explained, "This means that we must recruit our faculty from the major law schools and thus be assured that our educational values and goals match theirs. One may analogize it to joining the student body at Linton Village College, Cambridge, England, and donning the uniform of the day: pale blue shirt, dark blue tie, and a dark blue blazer. Occasionally, a grey sweater is acceptable."[73]

Looking back at the most exciting thing imaginable for law faculty, the new eleven-year path was now less an experiment and more a transition to past models. Professor Morris was alternately sad and forward-looking. "The new legal unit at Arizona State had an unusual faculty, limited in number, and each for his own reasons prepared to re-examine the fundamental postulates of legal education. Should an academic institution respond to changes in the practice of law? To the deficiencies encountered in the delivery of legal service generally? To the poor? Should the university-connected institution deal with professional problems or confine itself to institutional requirements?"[74]

Some of the answers to these rhetorical questions are scattered throughout this text, but others were offered by Professor Morris.

> *These questions were asked and in the exchange of ideas, two separate problems were identified as matters, which the Langdell model did not solve. The first perceived deficiency was the standard third year curriculum. Third year programs in most law schools, we thought, were failures. Boredom is inevitable when that year is identical in form, content, and instructional method to the last two. Eventually, no dialogue exists between the student and the faculty member. Relying on sophisticated techniques and co-operative arrangements, the student muddles through. In large metropolitan areas the student seeks well-paid employment, which he hopes will lead to a permanent engagement. The instruction of the student is taken over by a practitioner who exploits this newfound source of cheap labor. The learning experience, at least in the academic sense, ceases and the direction and development of the student has passed from the faculty to the profession, who feel no educational responsibility for the student.*[75]

This point seems highly debatable. Most law firms, private and public, take pride in their role in expanding their newly minted lawyers' educations. Law schools teach students the law; law firms teach those students how to be lawyers. Over time, the transition from student to lawyer returns to center stage. All law professors were once students, most at least dabbled with law practice, and then returned to the front of the classroom, holding forth on the *law* as a subject rather than a practice.

Professor Morris was sure his faculty were up to the expansion needed after its decade-long experimentation. "Conceptually we were prepared to make the needed changes. The faculty was so small that it could operate as a committee of the whole. The students, the entering class, still recognized the superior intellect of all faculty members. They were malleable, receptive, and trusting."[76]

He knew all too well that some law schools veer off point into less than stellar status. He gave a small lecture in his memoir. "The point is that an institution cannot allow itself to be caught up in the day to day details of curriculum change, supervision of legal writing, and tenure requirements, and make those issues its *raison d'etre*. Once the faculty adopts that frame of reference the problems of the legal profession and the judiciary become phenomena for study, not for solution."[77]

Professor Morris's memoir is refreshing for another reason—he was candid about academe's well-known ambivalence about the actual practice of law. "The university law school has never believed that there is any particular connection between it and the practice of law. But law schools attract students only because they sell the ability to enter the profession. Chief Justice Warren E. Burger has been unrelenting in his criticism of the competence of lawyers. The press, the President, and the public have become increasingly critical of the delivery of legal services to the poor and persons of moderate income, and the quality of justice for all. These criticisms clearly encompass the law school as one of those responsible institutions. The legal profession is undergoing dramatic changes and legal education must respond."[78]

As was his habit for twenty-five years, Professor Morris didn't just identify problems—he offered solutions. "The university law college, and particularly Arizona State, need not give up its traditional academic role. It should re-examine its university commitments in light of the following modest proposal. The law college at Arizona State has a historical tradition and we should return to our roots, the core curriculum. When the student has completed the two year core curriculum, the Supreme Court of Arizona and the Arizona Bar Association should permit the student to take the bar examination. Upon successfully completing the examination, the student would be admitted to practice law in Arizona subject to completing a third year clinical internship program."[79]

This "modest proposal" was never implemented. Professor Morris was not only King Arthur; he had a little bit of Don Quixote in him. The legal profession in Arizona would have roundly supported his proposal then and now. Practicing lawyers rarely understand or have to face the reality of university budgets, especially those that fund professional schools. The plain fact of the matter is that universities cannot afford to give up that third year of tuition, even if it would advance Professor Morris's modest proposal.

His memoir said as much about the institution he helped build as it does about his role in it. He apparently worried about nostalgia superimposed over what actually happened.

This essay is not intended merely as a nostalgic reminiscence of the way we were. It is a modest effort to recall the strength that we have. We once accepted the philosophy that we in legal education should be responsible for and share in the solution of those myriad challenges buffeting the profession. We structured an academic program to meet certain of those perceived challenges. That structure remains in place. We should revitalize it and explore the many ways that we can adapt it to meet our needs and those of the profession. Most of all, we should not fritter away our time on such things as the normalization of grading, developing an adequate writing program, and the enormous detail which we involve ourselves in. These things must be done, but they are ancillary to our main function, which is to deal with the central questions raised by the critics: The competence of lawyers and the delivery of justice.[80]

Well said. At the Sandra Day O'Connor College of Law, it is still about *the competence of lawyers and the delivery of justice.*

JONATHAN ROSE

Professor Jonathan Rose was an Honors Graduate in English of the University of Pennsylvania in 1963. Three years later, he graduated from the University of Minnesota Law School, *magna cum laude*, and Order of the Coif. He has an impressive employment history. He was a professor of law at ASU Law from 1968 through 2012, when he retired as a Willard H. Pedrick Distinguished Research Scholar. He held an affiliate faculty appointment in ASU's Department of History from 2008 to the present. He spent eight consecutive summers (from 2009 to 2016) in England as a Visiting Member, Faculty of Law at the University of Cambridge. He was a Visiting Fellow at Clare Hall, and Visitor, Faculty of Laws, at the University of Oxford, in Spring 2002.[81]

His path to ASU was similar to that of the other seventeen professors in the inaugural years—Pedrick recruited him. He had spent 1963 to 1968 in the Antitrust Division of the Department of Justice. Over the course of his long and distinguished career he taught antitrust, contracts, legal ethics, English Legal History, law and economics, regulated industries, consumer protection, and legal writing.

He earned six awards: (1) Elected Life Member, Clare Hall, University of Cambridge, England; (2) Willard H. Pedrick Distinguished Research Scholar; (3) ASU Alumni Association Faculty Achievement Award for Teaching; (4) Maricopa County Bar Association, Outstanding Faculty Award; (5) Burlington Northern Award for Outstanding Teaching; (6) ASU College of Law Alumni Association Award—Outstanding Teacher.

He wrote a book, *Maintenance in Medieval England*.[82] And he edited the book titled *Laws, Lawyers, and Texts: Studies in Medieval Legal History in Honor of Paul Brand*.[83] He wrote chapters in seven other books.[84]

In a way, the connection between Dean Pedrick and Professor Rose was almost accidental. Pedrick was in Washington on other business. Professor Rose was there practicing law. Earlier, Professor Rose's dean at Minnesota had recommended ASU, a start-up law school, to his former student, Jon Rose. Professor Rose recalled it in his 2006 Oral History: "Willard Pedrick showed up in Washington one day at my office totally unannounced to tell me what a great opportunity this was and conduct a preliminary interview and he invited me to come out and interview and that led to me having a job offer which I accepted." He recalled the group as "[s]mall... I think there were six already here and three joined that year, so there were nine. It was very collegial; [we] generally ate lunch together.... There was a spirit of discovery.... three of the people here were very experienced law teachers [Pedrick, Cleary and Effland] ... Other than that no one else had any teaching experience." There were no women among the founding group, and only one minority who joined midyear. "Professor Morris was in the founding group. He and Alan Matheson... came in the second semester of the first year in January of 1968."[85]

Professor Rose spent forty-five years on the faculty. All of it teaching and much of it researching American law's roots in England. He is the only faculty member ever to have a room in the library dedicated solely to his or her passion. In his case it was English Legal History. He also had another first-and-only recognition in building the law school and its law library. He was so involved in the design and construction that they named the fire escape on the north side in his honor.[86]

By all accounts the dinner was a success and Professor Rose was "feted" in style and grace. The audience was told he was so deep into English Legal History that he taught himself both Medieval Latin and Law French. He is the only professor to get his own "bobblehead," which is now maintained in the school's archives.

Inaugural Faculty—1967 to 1970

The dinner celebrated the culmination of an endowed scholarship in his name, which raised $350,000.00.

Jennifer Wright, Class of 2008, likely speaking for many others at the dinner, said, "While he played the caricature of the law school professor in his first-year contracts course, Professor Rose treated students in his office with warm regard and mutual respect and always made himself available. Although some professors abandoned the Socratic Method, his use of it keenly developed both my legal analysis skills and my ability to hone in on important case details. No doubt the law school will need 10 new professors to replace one Jonathan Rose."[87]

"Jon Rose was a wonderful mentor to me," said Alastair Gamble, Class of 2007. "He pushed me when I needed to be pushed and softened when I needed a moment to remember why all the work was worth the effort. As a teacher, he is peerless. As a lawyer, he remains the standard by which I judge myself. As a friend, he is kind and generous. I am so fortunate to have known him in all three capacities."[88]

Gordon Campbell, class of 1972, capped the evening off. "I've never seen such a concentration of intellectual power as had been assembled at the law school. The one who stood out among the superstars . . . was the young guy, Jonathan Rose, who was just getting started. Perhaps it was that he was not far from me in age. Maybe it was that he seemed to have such intensity. Most likely, it was that, when it came to analytical thinking, he worked hard. And the things he thought, he could defend. He inspired me. On top of that, he was a good guy. He cared about us. I will always be grateful."[89]

MICHAEL A. BERCH

Professor Berch is almost certainly the most colorful, exaggerated, and exhausting law professor in ASU Law's history. There are many tales about him—some short, others tall, some funny, others not. By any measure, his is a fascinating story. He arrived in time to teach the entering class of 1969 and was on the dais when the first class, admitted in 1967, walked off the school's first graduation stage, diplomas in hand, waving goodbye to the faculty—all eleven of them. By the time he retired in 2019, the graduation ceremonies were much bigger, with scores of faculty and hundreds of students. But it is also the case that after fifty years, the year-end party was slightly less noisy, because Michael's full-throated classroom yell was gone.

He received his BA at Columbia College in 1956, and his JD at Columbia College of Law in 1959, with Honors, and was an editor on the *Columbia Law Review*. He spent 1959 to 1963 as an Assistant U.S. Attorney in the United States Department of Justice, Criminal Division, and in the Organized Crime and Appeals Sections for the Southern District of New York.

From 1963 to 1966, he was a lawyer at Townsend & Lewis in New York City. He spent another three years in New York in private practice before moving to Arizona in 1969.

His first classes were federal courts, civil procedure, conflict of laws, and law and the regulatory state. He was honored for his teaching skills and his classroom enthusiasm. He won "the ASU Alumni Association Distinguished Teacher Award in 1990, the Maricopa County Bar Association Outstanding Teacher of the Year Award for 1992–93, and the ASU Law Alumni Distinguished Professor of 2001. In April 2007, he was one of three recipients for the 12th Annual Last Lecturer Awards at ASU. In June 2007, he received the Arizona State Bar President's Award for outstanding services to the Bar's teaching mission, and he was a finalist for the 2008 Professor of the Year Award from the ASU Parents Association."[90]

Professor Berch's curriculum vitae[91] is age-appropriate for a man who practiced and taught law full-time for the last sixty years (1959 to 2019). In addition to teaching law at ASU, he was invited to teach at seven other law schools (Fordham, McGeorge, UC Davis, SMU, UC San Diego, Tennessee, and NYU). He coached ASU moot court teams from 1970 to retirement. He wrote or co-authored three books.[92] He also wrote seven law review articles, essays, and numerous briefs in federal and state courts.

There is no record of how many students he taught from 1969 to 2019. But given the school's steady growth, it is fair to assume he impacted the lives of at least 100 students every year, or 6,000 in his career.

MILTON R. SCHROEDER

Professor Schroeder graduated from Wesleyan University[93] in Middletown, Connecticut, in 1962, with honors and distinction. He was president of the student body, a Thorndike Scholar, and won the William Day Leadership Award. In 1965, he earned his JD from the University of Chicago Law School,[94] *cum laude,* Order of the Coif, and was Editor-in-Chief of the University of Chicago Law Review. He was the Weymouth Kirkland Scholar.[95]

He earned a coveted clerkship with Judge Carl McGowan[96] at the U.S. Circuit Court of Appeals for the District of Columbia in 1965. Following his clerkship, he joined one of America's premier law firms—Sidley & Austin,[97] in their Washington, DC, office.

He joined the ASU faculty in 1969, was on the dais in 1970 when the first class graduated, and was Associate Dean from 1978–1980. He held many positions over his long career at ASU Law. Many of them involved intercollegiate athletics. He represented ASU as the faculty athletic representative to the Pac-10 Athletic Conference and the National Collegiate Athletic Association (NCAA) and served for many years on the NCAA Committee on Infractions and as Chair of the NCAA Committee on Student Athlete Eligibility Appeals.

Like many other ASU Law professors, Professor Schroeder never forgot his first role in the profession—he was a lawyer. He wore many professional hats outside the confines of the law school[98]:

Member, American Law Institute.[99]

Member, American Bar Association.[100]

Member, American Society of International Law.[101]

Member, Arizona Bar Association.[102]

Member, District of Columbia Bar.

Member, Illinois Bar Association.

Judge Pro Tempore, Arizona Court of Appeals.

Arbitrator, Maricopa County Superior Court.

Consultant, State Bar of Arizona—Revised Article 9 of the Uniform Commercial Code.

Over the decades, he "taught Secured Transactions under the Uniform Commercial Code; Sales and Leases of Goods under the Uniform Commercial Code; Payment and Credit Systems; Banking Law and Regulation; and International Trade & Finance. He engaged in research in various topics related to banking and commercial law, such as the effort to prevent banking systems from being used to assist in financing terrorism."

He is the author of two book reviews, four books, and eleven peer-reviewed articles. He is best known for his three-volume national treatise, *The Law and Regulation of Financial Instruments*.[103] It was released in 1995, and updates were published annually until 2010. It is the definitive assessment of an enormously intricate set of statutes and regulations. Amazon sells the loose-leaf edition for $459.99 and promotes it: "Expert author Milton Schroeder provides an understanding of the extensive and often exceedingly technical body of law that is relevant to financial institutions transactions, and identifies the principal sources of statutory and other law bearing on particular issues. An excellent research tool for law practitioners who need a comprehensive and accessible resource on financial institutions law, this publication offers detailed descriptions of financial institution activities, key judicial decisions, statutes, legislative history, and regulations. It is also an excellent resource for law school students."[104]

Professor Schroeder gave a lengthy Oral History interview to ASU Reference Librarian Marianne Alcorn on July 8, 2006. Ms. Alcorn asked him about his famous book. "I hope the publisher will want to continue it. Actually its origins go back well before that time [1995]. It was originally the *Bank Officer's Handbook*."[105]

Milt is a scholar among scholars and a teacher of inestimable breadth.

---

1 *See* Chapter 17.
2 *See* Chapter 19.
3 *See* Chapter 24.
4 *See* Chapter 26.
5 *See* Chapter 28.
6 *See* Chapter 31.

Inaugural Faculty—1967 to 1970

7 *See* Chapter 32.

8 "50 Years of Impact," Sandra Day O'Connor College of Law, accessed February 16, 2020, https://law.asu.edu/50yearsofimpact.

9 Ibid.

10 The "new" building is in downtown Phoenix, at 111 East Taylor Street, not in downtown Tempe at 1100 S. McAllister Ave.

11 *See* "World-class Faculty," Sandra Day O'Connor College of Law, accessed February 16, 2020, https://law.asu.edu/faculty/faculty-directory?dept=1411&id=1.

12 Alan A. Matheson, *Arizona State University College of Law—A Brief History*, 1 Ariz. St. L. J. 3, 3–4 (1979).

13 "Best Law Schools," U.S. News & World Report: Education, accessed February 14, 2020, https://www.usnews.com/best-graduate-schools/top-law-schools/law-rankings.

14 "Richard Charles Dahl," *Arizona Republic* (Phoenix, AZ), April 16, 2007, https://www.legacy.com/obituaries/azcentral/obituary.aspx?n=richard-charles-dahl&pid=87673567. Professor White was serving as ASU Law's fifth dean when Professor Dahl died in 2007.

15 "Richard Charles Dahl," *Arizona Republic* (Phoenix, AZ), April 16, 2007, https://www.legacy.com/obituaries/azcentral/obituary.aspx?n=richard-charles-dahl&pid=87673567..

16 Ibid.

17 *See* Arizona State University College of Law Library—Second Report—December 1, 1967 to March 1, 1969, page 1.

18 Ibid., 8–10.

19 Ibid., 20–21.

20 William C. Canby, Jr. (Senior Judge, Ninth Circuit Court of Appeals), interview by Marianne Alcorn, August 18, 2006, Sandra Day O'Connor U.S. Courthouse, transcript, Sandra Day O'Connor College of Law, 1.

21 "Walter Frederick 'Fritz' Mondale is an American politician, diplomat and lawyer who served as the 42nd vice president of the United States from 1977 to 1981. A United States senator from Minnesota, he was the Democratic Party's nominee in the United States presidential election of 1984, but lost to Ronald Reagan in an Electoral College landslide. Reagan won 49 states while Mondale carried his home state of Minnesota and the District of Columbia. He became the oldest-living former U.S. vice president after the death of George H. W. Bush in 2018." Wikipedia, s.v., "Walter Mondale," last modified February 17, 2020, 4:29, https://en.wikipedia.org/wiki/Walter_Mondale.

22 Wikipedia, s.v., "William Canby," last modified February 17, 2020, 9:54, https://en.wikipedia.org/wiki/William_Canby.

23 Canby, interview. "Charles Evans Whittaker (February 22, 1901 – November 26, 1973) was an Associate Justice of the United States Supreme Court from 1957 to 1962. After working in private practice in Kansas City, Missouri, he was nominated for the United States District Court for the Western District of Missouri." Wikipedia, s.v., "Charles Evans Whittaker," last modified December 5, 2020, 10:18, https://en.wikipedia.org/wiki/Charles_Evans_Whittaker.

24 Canby, interview. "The Peace Corps is a volunteer program run by the United States government. Its official mission is to provide social and economic development abroad through technical assistance, while promoting mutual understanding between Americans and populations served. The program was established by Executive Order 10924, issued by President John F. Kennedy on March 1, 1961 and authorized by Congress on September 21, 1961 with passage of the Peace Corps Act (Pub.L. 87–293). Peace Corps Volunteers are American citizens, typically with a college degree, who work abroad for a period of two years after three months of training. Volunteers work with governments, schools, non-profit organizations, non-government organizations . . . and entrepreneurs in education, business, information technology, agriculture, and the environment. After 24 months of service, volunteers can request an extension of service. Since its inception, more than 235,000 Americans have joined the Peace Corps and served in 141 countries." Wikipedia, s.v., "Peace Corps," last modified February 17, 2020, 10:30, https://en.wikipedia.org/wiki/Peace_Corps. *See also* www.peacecorps.gov.

25 William C. Canby, Jr. (Senior Judge, Ninth Circuit Court of Appeals), interview by Marianne Alcorn, August 18, 2006, Sandra Day O'Connor U.S. Courthouse, transcript, Sandra Day O'Connor College of Law, 2–3.

26 Ibid., 4.

27 "John Edward Cribbet (February 21, 1918 – May 23, 2009) was a well-known legal scholar, dean of the University of Illinois College of Law, and chancellor of the University of Illinois." Wikipedia, s.v., "John E. Cribbet," last modified February 17, 2020, 10:11, https://en.wikipedia.org/wiki/John_E._Cribbet.

28 John E. Cribbet, *Tribute to Professor Edward W. Cleary*, 21 Ariz. St. L. J. 845, 845 (1989).

29 Ibid.

30 Edward W. Cleary and Michael H. Graham, *Cleary & Graham's Handbook of Illinois Evidence* (New York City: Aspen Publishers, 2008). Professor Graham is a professor at the University of Miami School of Law and also co-authored the 2004, 1999, 1994, 1990, and 1984 editions and all supplements.

31 Cribbet, *supra* note 234.

32 Ibid., 846.

33 Ibid.

34 Ibid., 847.

35 "Edward H. Cleary, 82, Lawyer and Professor," *New York Times* (New York, NY), January 22, 1990, https://www.nytimes.com/1990/01/22/obituaries/edward-h-cleary-82-lawyer-and-professor.html.

36 "Faculty Research Award Recipients," Alumni.asu.edu, accessed February 28, 2020, https://alumni.asu.edu/events/founders-day/faculty-research-award-recipients.

37 Walter B. Raushenbush, Emeritus Professor of Law, is a native of Madison. He graduated with high honors from Harvard College and the University of Wisconsin Law School. He joined the Law School Faculty in 1958, and taught Property, Real Estate, and Professional Responsibility. He served as a Visiting Professor of Law at the Universities of New Mexico, Arizona, Texas, Florida, and San Diego, and at Pepperdine and Arizona State Universities. He is a past-president of the national Law School Admission Council, and served on the Real Property question-drafting committee for the Multistate Bar Examination. "Walter B. Raushenbush," Prabook: World Biographical Encyclopedia, accessed February 28, 2020, https://prabook.com/web/walter_brandeis.raushenbush/797631.

38 Walter B. Raushenbush, *Memories of Dick Effland (1916–1989)*, XIX Wisc. L. Sch. F. 14 (1989), https://media.law.wisc.edu/m/ymjjn/gargoyle_19_4_4.pdf.

39 Ibid.

40 Ibid. In 1848, the University of Wisconsin authorized the Law department. In 1868, the Law department opens with the admission of fifteen students for a one-year course of study (twelve graduated). In 1889, the Law department becomes the College of Law and a second year is added to the curriculum. "Events in the History of the UW Law School," University of Wisconsin Law School, accessed February 18, 2020, https://law.wisc.edu/about/lore/events.html.

41 Raushenbush, *supra* note 244. Professor Effland's public sector positions include the State Department Liaison to the War Production Board (1941 to 1944); Secretary and Counsel for the Export-Import Bank (1944–1946). He joined the Wisconsin Law faculty in 1946 and taught there for twenty-one years. Ibid.

42 Ibid.

43 "Dale Furnish," iSearch, accessed February 18, 2020, https://isearch.asu.edu/profile/27299. Judge Van Oosterhout served on the Eight Circuit Court of Appeals from 1954 to 1979. Wikipedia, s.v., "Martin Donald Van Oosterhout," last modified February 18, 2020, 10:41, https://en.wikipedia.org/wiki/Martin_Donald_Van_Oosterhout.

44 "Dale Furnish," iSearch, accessed February 18, 2020, https://isearch.asu.edu/profile/27299. The United States Agency for International Development (USAID) is an independent agency of the United States federal government that is primarily responsible for administering civilian foreign aid and development assistance. "USAID," USAID.gov, accessed February 18, 2020, https://www.usaid.gov/.

45 The Ford Foundation is a "private foundation with the mission of advancing human welfare" throughout the US, Africa, Latin America, the Middle East, and Asia. Wikipedia, s.v., "Ford Foundation," last modified February 18, 2020, 10:29, https://en.wikipedia.org/wiki/Ford_Foundation.

46 "Dale Furnish," iSearch, accessed February 18, 2020, https://isearch.asu.edu/profile/27299.

47 Ibid.

48 *See* "Dale Beck Furnish," iSearch, accessed February 18, 2020, https://isearch.asu.edu/profile/27299/cv.html.

49 *Harold Canfield Havighurst: Biographical Resume*, 77 NW. U. L. Rev. 264, 264 (1982).

50 Michael L. Schwartz, *The Writings of Harold C. Havighurst*, 77 NW. U. L. Rev. 265, 265 (1982).

51 *Harold Canfield Havighurst: Biographical Resume*, 77 NW. U. L. Rev. 264, 264 (1982).

Inaugural Faculty—1967 to 1970

52 "Havighurst, Harold C.," HeinOnline, accessed February 18, 2020, http://hn3.giga-lib.com/HOL/AuthorProfile?action=edit&search_name=%20Havighurst,%20Harold%20C.&collection=journals.

53 These reviews include Harold C. Havighurst, *Doing Away with Presidential Impeachment: The Advantages of Parliamentary Government*, 1974 Ariz. St. L. J. 223 (1974); Harold C. Havighurst, *Settlement of Paternity Claims*, 1976 Ariz. St. L. J. 461 (1976); and Harold C. Havighurst, *Limitations Upon Freedom of Contract*, 1979 Ariz. St. L. J. 167 (1979).

54 Harold C. Havighurst, *Cases and Materials on the Law of Contracts*, (National Casebook Series, 1st ed. 1934; 2d ed. 1950).

55 Ibid.

56 "Alan Matheson," iSearch, accessed February 18, 2020, https://isearch.asu.edu/profile/274864.

57 Wikipedia, s.v., "Pirkei Avot," last modified February 18, 2020, https://en.wikipedia.org/wiki/Pirkei_Avot.

58 David Kader, "One of Those Few." 1984 Ariz. S. L.J. 419.

59 Ibid.

60 Willard H. Pedrick, "A Tribute from the Founding Dean," 1984 Ariz. St. L.J. 417 (1984).

61 William C. Canby, Jr., Richard J. Morgan, Willard H. Pedrick, Alan A. Matheson, *Tributes to John P. Morris*, 26 Ariz. St. L.J. 619, 623 (1994).

62 Ibid., 619.

63 Ibid., 627.

64 Ibid., 621.

65 Ibid.

66 Ibid., 624.

67 Ibid., 619.

68 Ibid., 628.

69 John P. Morris, *The Way We Were*, 1979 Ariz. St. L.J. 263 (1979).

70 Ibid., 263.

71 Ibid.

72 Ibid., 263–64.

73 Ibid., 264.

74 Ibid.

75 Ibid., 264–65.

76 Ibid., 265.

77 Ibid., 266 (emphasis added).

78 Ibid., 266–67.

79 Ibid., 267.

80 Ibid., 268.

81 "Resume: Jonathan Rose," iSearch, accessed February 19, 2020, https://isearch.asu.edu/profile/51225/cv.

82 Jonathan Rose, *Maintenance in Medieval England*, (Cambridge, MA: Cambridge University Press, 2017).

83 Susanne Jenks, Jonathan Rose, Christopher Whittick eds., *Laws, Lawyers, and Texts: Studies in Medieval Legal History in Honour of Paul Brand* (Leiden: Brill, 2012).

84 *See* Resume: Jonathan Rose, at 2–3.

85 Jonathan Rose (Professor, Sandra Day O'Connor College of Law), interview by Marianne Alcorn, June 14, 2006, Sandra Day O'Connor College of Law, transcript Sandra Day O'Connor College of Law, 1–2.

86 *See* Carrie Morales, "College of Law to Fete Longtime Professor at Annual Pedrick Society Dinner," Sandra Day O'Connor College of Law, accessed February 19, 2020, https://asunow.asu.edu/content/college-law-fete-longtime-professor-annual-pedrick-society-dinner.

87 Ibid.

88 Ibid.

89 Ibid.

90 "Michael Berch," iSearch, accessed February 19, 2020, https://isearch.asu.edu/profile/65771.

91 "Curriculum Vitae: Michael A. Berch," iSearch, accessed February 19, 2020, https://apps.law.asu.edu/files/faculty/cvs/michaelberch.pdf.

92 Ibid. His writings include a chapter in Arthur Hellman, ed., *The Bankruptcy Appellate Panel and its Implications for Adoption of Specialist Panels in the Courts of Appeals, Restructuring Justice* (Cornell Press, 1986); Michael A. Berch, Rebecca White Berch & Ralph S. Spritzer, *Introduction to Legal Method and Process*, 3rd ed. (West Publishing Co, 2002); and Michael A. Berch, *Handling Complex Litigation in Arizona* (CES, Inc. 1986).

93 The Wesleyan mission statement fits Professor Schroeder perfectly. "At Wesleyan, our open curriculum challenges and teaches you to think creatively, become intellectually agile, and take meaningful risks. This flexibility prepares you both for success and the inevitable setbacks along the path to discovery." "Welcome to Wesleyan University – Middletown, Connecticut," Wesleyan University, accessed February 19, 2020, https://www.wesleyan.edu/.

94 "Milton Schroeder," iSearch, accessed February 19, 2020, https://isearch.asu.edu/profile/44474. The University of Chicago College of Law's mission statement is equally apt. "UChicago Law aims to train well-rounded, critical, and socially conscious thinkers and doers. The cornerstones that provide the foundation for UChicago Law's educational mission are the life of the mind, participatory learning, interdisciplinary inquiry, and an education for generalists. What sets UChicago Law apart from other law schools is its unabashed enthusiasm for the life of the mind—the conviction that ideas matter, that they are worth discussing, and that legal education should devote itself to learning for learning's sake." "Mission of the Law School," University of Chicago Law School, accessed February 19, 2020, https://www.law.uchicago.edu/school/mission.

95 "Milton Schroeder," iSearch, accessed February 19, 2020, https://isearch.asu.edu/profile/44474.

96 Ibid. "On January 15, 1963, McGowan was nominated by President John F. Kennedy to a seat on the United States Court of Appeals for the District of Columbia Circuit vacated by Judge Henry White Edgerton. McGowan was confirmed by the United States Senate on March 15, 1963, and received his commission on March 27, 1963. He served as Chief Judge from January to May of 1981, assuming senior status on August 31, 1981. McGowan served in that capacity until his death on December 21, 1987, in Washington, D.C." Wikipedia, s.v., "Carl E. McGowan," last modified February 19, 2020, 12:59, https://en.wikipedia.org/wiki/Carl_E._McGowan.

97 "Milton Schroeder," iSearch, accessed February 19, 2020, https://isearch.asu.edu/profile/44474. "More than 150 years after the founding of our firm, Sidley today comprises a diverse group of legal professionals from many cultures who are dedicated to teamwork, collaboration and superior client service. Forging enduring relationships with the business community, while remaining attuned to the dynamic legal landscape, we understand and work to fulfill the needs of our global clients. We are proud to serve this varied and high-caliber group of market leaders, many of whom are pioneers in their respective industries and professions." "About Sidley," Sidley Austin LLP, accessed February 19, 2020, https://www.sidley.com/en/ourstory/aboutsidley.

98 "Milton Schroeder," iSearch, accessed February 19, 2020, https://isearch.asu.edu/profile/44474.

99 "The American Law Institute was founded in 1923 following a study conducted by a group of prominent American judges, lawyers, and teachers known as 'The Committee on the Establishment of a Permanent Organization for the Improvement of the Law.'" Today, it is the "leading independent organization in the United States producing scholarly work to clarify, modernize, and otherwise improve the law." "The election of an individual to The American Law Institute begins with a confidential nomination by an ALI member that is supported by two additional ALI members. Members are encouraged to propose individuals who have demonstrated excellence in the law, are of high character, will contribute to the work of the Institute, and are committed to its mission." "About ALI," American Law Institute, accessed February 19, 2020, https://www.ali.org/about-ali/; "Membership," American Law Institute, accessed February 19, 2020, https://www.ali.org/members/.

100 "The American Bar Association, founded August 21, 1878, is a voluntary bar association of lawyers and law students, which is not specific to any jurisdiction in the United States." Wikipedia, s.v., "American Bar Association," last modified February 19, 2020, 11:19, https://en.wikipedia.org/wiki/American_Bar_Association. *See also* https://www.americanbar.org/.

101 "The American Society of International Law (ASIL), founded in 1906, was chartered by the United States Congress in 1950 to foster the study of international law, and to promote the establishment and maintenance of international relations on the basis of law and justice." Wikipedia, s.v., "American Society of International Law," last modified February 19, 2020, 18:49, https://en.wikipedia.org/wiki/American_Society_of_International_Law. *See also* https://www.asil.org/.

102 "The State Bar of Arizona is a non-profit organization that operates under the supervision of the Arizona Supreme Court. The Bar regulates approximately 18,500 active attorneys and provides education

and development programs for the legal profession and the public. The Bar's mission states that it exists to serve and protect the public with respect to the provision of legal services and access to justice." "State Bar of Arizona: History and Structure—About Us," State Bar of Arizona, accessed February 19, 2020, https://www.azbar.org/AboutUs.

103 Milton R. Schroeder, *The Law and Regulation of Financial Institutions* (Warren, Gorham & Lamont, 1995).

104 "*The Law and Regulation of Financial Institutions,* 3-volume set," Amazon.com, accessed February 19, 2020, https://www.amazon.com/Law-Regulation-Financial-Institutions-set/dp/0769878792.

105 *See* Milton R. Schroeder (Professor, Sandra Day O'Connor College of Law), interview by Marianne Alcorn, July 6, 2006, Sandra Day O'Connor College of Law, transcript Sandra Day O'Connor College of Law, 6.

CHAPTER 9

DEAN WILLARD PEDRICK'S REPORT—1967 TO 1968

Dean Pedrick was a man of many talents, but timetables were not high on his list. He turned in his first obligatory report to President Durham on time. His second was not on time. These reports were common to most American law schools, and Pedrick had been reading them for years. Now that he had the chance to write them, something went awry.

SPRING WILL BE A LITTLE LATE THIS YEAR

His second report to the President of ASU was due on July 1, 1967; it would have covered the academic year 1967 to 1968. That was the pivotal first year for the school. While he was no doubt in regular communication with the President, his faculty and most assuredly his students, he was not tidy about deadlines.

> *In the words of a popular song of some years back, "Spring Will Be a Little Late This Year." That is a fair description of the Report of the Law School Dean for the academic year 1967–68. Here it is, December of 1969, and one might well question whether it is really worthwhile recalling early events of what must be regarded now as a bygone year in the life of the law school. Because the year in question was, in fact, the true beginning of the College of Law, for historical purposes, if for no other, it seems desirable to set down some of the events of consequence and to speculate a little about the developments to be anticipated in the future.*[1]

Without further ado, Dean Pedrick retreated to his first year as Dean, 1966–67, describing it as a year of organizational activity. Then, sliding effortlessly into the missing year, 1967–68, he described it as the year the College of Law "came to life."[2] He listed the components of the missing year—"our Founding Entering Class, an adventurous crew bold enough to cast their fortunes with the new untried and really unknown Law School, the faculty and staff, the physical plant, Armstrong Hall, including the library, and a corps of dedicated supporters within the University Administration and in the legal profession and business community."[3]

PED'S NUMBERS

With that, his report got down to business. The founding class was 118 students strong. The median LSAT score was 543 and the median GPA was 2.6. There were 14 women, which is about twice the national average for women in law school. There were "two American Indians, two Negroes, giving some representation to minority groups. One of the objects the school is determined to serve in light of the sad underrepresentation these groups presently have in the legal profession. There was a considerable age span (from 19 to 50), as a number of individuals in the Phoenix vicinity apparently had been waiting for some time the establishment of the new law school. . . . They were a frequent source of enrichment to the class discussions. . . ."[4]

Turning to the grading system, Dean Pedrick reported some difficulty. "In an established school," he said, "there are patterns and conventions which are commonly followed year after year without question. But, when one begins, every act, seemingly calls for a conscious decision as to whether it shall be done one way or the other. This occasioned extended faculty study and discussion. It finally was agreed upon [that we would use] the four-point system followed in the University generally."

STUDENT EXTRACURRICULAR ACTIVITIES

As for student activities, Dean Pedrick offered a "tribute to the spirit of enthusiasm and cooperation, which characterized this class. They seemed to be imbued with much the same spirit of excitement, which pervaded the faculty and accepted the difficulties of operation in makeshift quarters of the Matthews Center (the old

Dean Willard Pedrick's Report—1967 to 1968

Library Building) with high spirits . . . . Prof. Canby organized a Moot Court Program . . . . There was some attrition in the student body, as might be expected. When first semester grades were announced, several students were counseled to accept the adverse judgment on their promise for law study. They withdrew . . . . At the conclusion of the second semester the first-year class was about 100 students, of whom five were on academic probation. The survival rate was a good one."[5]

OUTSIDE FINANCIAL SUPPORT

Turning to a cheerier subject, Dean Pedrick reported on financial aid to students. "Thanks to the Law Society of Arizona State University . . . scholarship funds were provided for ten of the entering class of students. Loan funds administered through the University Office of Financial [sic] Aids were made available to a substantial number of students . . . with the net result that approximately one-third of the class enjoyed financial assistance, scholarships and/or loans. In a university where no State funds are provided for this purpose, the amount of financial assistance supplied was remarkable."[6]

Dean Pedrick reported that the founding faculty (Professors Havighurst, Effland, Canby and Dahl) were joined midyear by Prof. John Morris, "himself a member of a minority group." This brought "a new dimension to the law faculty and one greatly appreciated by our students."

LEAKS, BOOKS, AND BUILDINGS

Under the tab-heading Physical Facilities, Dean Pedrick made apologies. "We began our life in what might be described a 'leaking ship,' except that the Matthews Center Building was not a ship. It did leak, however, and somewhat disconcertingly, into the only classroom we had on those occasions when it did rain. The classroom . . . was big enough but that was its sole virtue. The acoustics were unfortunate, the seating in movable chairs was hard to organize in terms of reliable seating charts, the small platform on which the teacher perched, was not a happy situation for the 'pacing' type of law professor. In fact, if the truth be known, it was a better building than some law schools endure as permanent quarters. Among its other virtues is the fact that it had been a library, and accordingly we had adequate stack space for our rapidly growing collection. It had a spacious entryway, which served as a meeting place, or lounge for our students. It was an adequate physical plant for our beginning."⁷

The good news, Dean Pedrick said, was the "spectacular growth of the law library." The law librarian, Professor and Director of the Library, Richard Dahl, acquired "approximately 70,000 volumes, which surpassed more than half the law libraries of accredited law schools of the United States.

Dean Pedrick said the "big event" of the year was dedicating the new building. There is no mention in the Dean's Report about the costs or ABOR approval of the building. However, ABOR's minutes for its May 15, 1966 meeting document the financial issues succinctly. The capital outlay and ABOR approval confirms the base cost of the building at $1,902,000. Bonds would cover $884,847 in calendar 1966, with an additional bond issue in 1967 for $303,063. A Title II grant from the federal government covered the remaining $714,090 of the capital allocation.⁸ In its November 26, 1966 meeting, ABOR ratified a contract for Del E. Webb Corporation for $1,677,000 to build the law school. There were multiple change orders during the construction phase, which are documented in ABOR minutes.

THE GRAND OPENING

Dean Pedrick's second report to the ASU President spoke to the grand opening and the dedication of Armstrong Hall on February 26, 1968. He said, "the leading figures from the Bench, from the practicing profession, and from academic life joined to make this a most successful and auspicious celebration, marking not only the Dedication of the Law Building, but, in a very real sense, the intellectual dedication of the new school, itself.... Among the notable and principal speakers were Chief Justice Earl Warren of the Supreme Court of the United States, Chief Justice Ernest McFarland of the Arizona Supreme Court, US Secretary of Labor W. Willard Wirtz,⁹ Professors Norval Morris, Leon Green, Andrew S. Watson, John M. Ferren, Saul H. Mendlovitz, and A. Leo Levin. The Conference titled 'Needed Innovation in Legal Education,' was generously supported [by] law book publishers, brought to the ASU campus were deans and other representatives of approximately 60 law schools from all parts of the United States."¹⁰

Dean Pedrick estimated there were "approximately 900 people who joined in the final event of the building dedication proceedings." They moved into the building in March of 1968 and celebrated in what was initially called Moot Court

Hall. It was quickly changed to the Great Hall, when it was discovered that some were calling it "Mute" Court Hall.[11]

CHANGES IN THE PROGRAM

As expected, Dean Pedrick reported on Program Development. It followed the core curriculum drawn up the prior year, i.e., "in the first two years, would be those courses of instruction deemed essential by the faculty to adequate basic legal instruction." But, he also took the occasion to report on the problem of *legal writing*. "It is apparent that many law students, graduates though they be of undergraduate institutions, nevertheless are seriously deficient in their ability to write effective English. It shows up not only in moot court briefs and on examinations, but on other matters as well. This is a problem of very considerable dimensions. Every law school is sensitive to the problem and no one has a confident answer. We will have to marshal some additional strength, perhaps in the direction of utilization of graduate students drawn from the second and third-year classes to provide more personalized, intensive instruction in writing various types of material characteristic of the legal profession."

Next, he reported on "difficulties encountered by students with significantly different cultural backgrounds . . . a reasonably apt description of most of our minority-group students . . . . In its emphasis upon law relating to commerce and industry, and its emphasis upon facility in the effective use of English, the first-year program finds many of these culturally deprived students at a very serious disadvantage . . . . We offered tutorial assistance . . . this experiment was disappointing . . . . We have decided to approach this problem different in the future . . . This is a problem every major law school is engaging . . . . Those students are so badly under-represented in the profession at present."[12]

ACCREDITATION

Dean Pedrick was optimistic about the accreditation visit in "the winter of 1967." Dean John G. Hervey of the Oklahoma City University School of Law, representing the Section of Legal Education of the American Bar Association, was the visitor. He inspected the library, attended classes, reviewed all programs and "made it clear when he left us that he was enthusiastic about the quality of the legal program being developed here at ASU." Subsequently, he said, Dean Hervey "recommended that the school be extended provisional accreditation at once, and happily, the various agencies of the ABA have acted favorably on that recommendation . . . . The second accreditation agency, the Association of American Law Schools, will not visit us until the school year 1968–1969 . . . . Accordingly, on the accreditation front, we are in an excellent position to make good on our commitments to the Founding Class that they will graduate in June of 1970 as graduates of a fully-accredited Law School."

Dean Pedrick's report was, for the most part, delivered in informational style, not seemingly argumentative. But his passion for legal education came out in Section 11 of the report. It is essentially a critique on the way legal education was traditionally rendered in the 1960s, and an essay on what law schools should be doing.

LEGAL EDUCATION IN FERMENT

Dean Pedrick was a man of many words. His report, while long, deserves attention because he was confronted with making history, while at the same time, making new lawyers. It is apparent from this long statement that he was sensitive to how legal education was being delivered in other schools, while trying to advance an experiential focus in his "new" law school.

> *Because this report is largely concerned with preserving for historical purposes, some of the atmosphere of the first year of the school's life, it is not appropriate to expand at any length on problems of legal education as they are seen from the teaching side. It can be said, however, that if education generally is in ferment, that is certainly true, as well, of legal education. Our students are in a questioning frame of mind. They are not entirely persuaded that the old ways of studying appellate court cases in the traditional fields of Property, Torts, Criminal Law, Corporations, Constitutional Law, etc., are adequately relevant to the critical issues of the day. Although the first year of legal education is the only year experienced by this law school at this point, and that is a year of very great intellectual challenge and growth for most students, it is clear, even at the end of the first year, that many of the students have already begun to think in terms of the rather different kind*

of educational experience we have promised them for the third year of the program. This means, among other things, that there is a very real question whether the second year of the core curriculum will engage and hold the interest of the law student to the extent that we wish.... We will necessarily have to determine what changes, if any, are needed to make it more successful as an educational experience for the students.[13]

It is highly probable that Dean Pedrick was acutely aware of the virtual revolution in education taking place all over America at the same time he worried about curriculum and student expectations at ASU's new law school. The tepid fifties were history. The flame-throwing sixties were at large. The federal government became increasingly education-oriented. Presidents John F. Kennedy and Lyndon Johnson lobbied Congress for increased federal aid to education, leading to the creation of new programs. Their efforts displeased conservative politicians and Southern community leaders, particularly those who opposed school integration and who believed that education policy was strictly a local issue.[14] What all thinking Americans saw every night on TV were prime social movements. Everyone was involved at one level or another in the fight for equal rights for black Americans. Almost everyone was talking about the further desegregation of America's schools, as called for by the 1954 *Brown v. Board of Education of Topeka* case.[15] The government didn't offer funds to private and parochial schools, which incited heated debate throughout the decade. It wasn't just law students who began to question education writ large. As Ped had observed, legal education was "in ferment."

During the 1960s, students from grade school through university-level began studying old subjects in new ways. The civil rights movement challenged how American history was being taught. Social and cultural change were hand-in-hand and emphasized diversity. The struggles of black Americans and Native Americans were common fare at dinner tables. Education theorists insisted that teachers be empowered to develop their students' minds and encourage their intellectual curiosity, rather than merely stressing learning by rote. New scholastic disciplines found solace in social science, sociology, and theater arts to increasing numbers of foreign language classes. Bilingual education programs increased as immigrants began to insist on maintaining their native cultures and continuing to speak their native languages while simultaneously learning English.[16]

Dean Pedrick was a vibrant thinker, but not an activist in legal education circles. He expressed personal and likely faculty concerns in his report. "There is abroad in the land a kind of disorientation on the part of university students, who are confident, in some quarters at least, that life is not organized as it ought to be. This confidence about the inadequacies of the system is not matched by any agreement on the proper prescription. Nevertheless, the considerable concern on the part of university students with the nature and quality of life does not leave law students wholly untouched. Because the law has been a very significant instrument for social change in this country, the law schools have a special opportunity; it would appear, to use the student concern about society and its organization as the basis for enlisting student energies in constructive directions in terms of research and formulation of new prescriptions. In the third-year program planned for the Law School we particularly hope to capitalize on the interests of some of our students in engaging in some of the difficult problems of social organization."[17]

And with that middle-of-the-road stance, the dean closed his report as positively as he could under the circumstances. "The first year was a good year. We have grown in strength; we look to the future with confidence but with recognition that the demands to be made on us are substantial. The fact of our satisfactory progress to this point provides no basis at all for relaxation. Tomorrow's work is waiting."

---

1 Report of the Dean—College of Law—Arizona State University—July 1, 1967 – September 1, 1968.
2 Ibid., 1.
3 Ibid., 2.
4 Ibid., 3.
5 Ibid., 5.
6 Ibid., 5–6.
7 Ibid., 7–8.
8 ABOR Capital Outlay—Allocation for Arizona State University—May 15, 1966—ABOR Archival minutes and documents. The September 1, 1966 ABOR Meeting Minutes reflect unanimous approval of plans, authority to call for construction bids and the award of an ABOR contract, together with the approval of designating the new law building in memory of John Samuel Armstrong, member of the Territorial Legislature, who in March 1985, introduced and secured passage of the bill establishing the Territorial Normal School at Tempe, now Arizona State University. The estimated cost of the building was then estimated at $1,640,000. At 82,000 square feet, this produced a square foot cost of $20.00 per square foot, which ABOR approved.
9 William Willard Wirtz Jr. (March 14, 1912–April 24, 2010) was a U.S. administrator, cabinet officer, attorney, and law professor. He served as the Secretary of Labor between 1962 and 1969 under the administrations of Presidents John F. Kennedy and Lyndon B. Johnson. Wirtz was the last living member of Kennedy's cabinet. Wikipedia, s.v., "W. Willard Wirtz," last modified February 19, 2020, 11:46, https://en.wikipedia.org/wiki/W._Willard_Wirtz.
10 Report of the Dean—College of Law—Arizona State University—July 1, 1967–September 1, 1968, p. 10–12.
11 Ibid., 10.

12 Ibid., 11–12.

13 Ibid. 15.

14 "The 1960s Education: Overview," Encyclopedia, accessed February 19, 2020, https://www.encyclopedia.com/social-sciences/culture-magazines/1960s-education-overview.

15 *Brown v. Board of Education,* 347 U.S. 483 (1954).

16 "American History: The 1960s, a Decade That Changed a Nation," Learning English, accessed February 19, 2020, https://learningenglish.voanews.com/a/american-history-the-1960s-10-years-that-changed-a-nation-134041543/114624.html.

17 Report of the Dean—College of Law—Arizona State University—July 1, 1967–September 1, 1968, p. 16.

CHAPTER 10

INAUGURAL GRADUATES— 1970 THROUGH 1976

While an exact head count is unknowable, Dean Pedrick taught, mentored, pushed and regaled at least seven hundred students through the ASU College of Law from 1970 through 1976. Almost all went on to successful careers in the law. Picking a bare handful of those students to profile here is subjective, arbitrary and necessary. In a difficult search for brilliance among gemstones, the author took refuge in one of Shakespeare's many quotes about ability and achievement: "He hath born himself beyond the promise of his age, doing in the figure of a lamb, the feats of a lion."[1] The following lions and lionesses represent the reach, depth, and impact that the Sandra Day O'Connor College of Law has had on Arizona, America, and the world.

> 1970 – Mike Gallagher ... Mike Hawkins ... Joe Sims ... Jimmie Dee Smith
>
> 1971—Bob Blakey ... Cecil Patterson ... Roslyn Silver ... Les Schiefelbein
>
> 1972—Fritz Aspey ... Hattie Babbitt ... Lou Diesel ... Barry MacBan
>
> 1973—Tom Chauncey ... Bill Culbertson ... Marty Harper ... Terry Woods ... Harold Watkins
>
> 1974—H. Bartow Farr ... Ruth McGregor ... Ed Pastor ... Bill Sandweg ... Barry Silverman

1975—Bill Atkin … Michael Bailey … Chuck Case … James Allen Soto

1976 – Terry Goddard … Michael Grant … Doug Rayes

MICHAEL GALLAGHER, '70

The first-year law students in 1967 at ASU Law were a hearty bunch, eager, anxious, willing; then they discovered case law. Things would never be the same. They would live in strict accordance with the Socratic method. They'd come to know one another, not so much as family, but at least cousins-in-law. And all would remember those heady days they experimented as clueless, willing souls given to the law.

Forty years later Warren Brown would remember the leaky roof in Matthews Hall and playing chess with Professor Richard Dahl. Bob Cook would remember Dean Pedrick and Professor Michael Berch. He'd give a special message to his former classmates—"God bless you, for those of you still alive. Aren't you glad we quit?" Lee Davis was the first student to "be called on in Dean Pedrick's torts class, in a brand new school, completely unprepared, roasted for about an hour." Robert McConnell also remembered his teachers and his classmates. Forty years after their graduation in 1970, he would still remember Mike Gallagher. "I remember arriving early in the morning to Armstrong Hall to wake up Mike Gallagher, who routinely fell asleep in early morning hours after scouting baseball teams for the New York Mets." Les Weatherly, Jr., also remembered Gallagher forty years later. "Do not forget that Mike Gallagher started out to be a baseball pitcher, but somehow got sidetracked—and we are better off for the transition!"

Mike Gallagher would be the student body president by the time they graduated in 1970. Forty years later, he remembered his classmates as close-knit because

Inaugural Graduates—1970 through 1976

"there were no students in front of us to learn from. I'm guessing our experience was a bit unconventional."

His bio at the firm he co-founded is rich in detail, devoid of irony, and impressive by any measure. It begins at his birthplace (LeMars, Iowa, April 14, 1944), advances to high school (not named but located in Los Angeles, California). The next sentence (historic to Mike, but mere history to his firm) gives hint to what Mike Gallagher was like in his college years: "1962–1966 attended Arizona State University on a baseball scholarship; NCAA Champions 1965. B.A. 1966."

Mr. Gallagher spent four years earning a degree in history, on a baseball scholarship, as a pitcher, on a national championship team, under the tender glove and hand of ASU's legendary coach, Bobby Winkles. Winkles was Arizona State's first varsity baseball coach, from 1959 to 1971. He built Sun Devil baseball, and Mike was there to see most of it. His overall coaching record at ASU was 524–173, a winning percentage of .751. In his eleven years, Winkles coached ASU to its first three national titles (1965, 1967 and 1969). The ABCA Collegiate Baseball Hall of Fame inducted him in 1997. ASU's Packard Stadium was named in his honor. He coached many great players while he was at the helm of the Sun Devils, including Rick Monday, Sal Bando, Reggie Jackson, Sterling Slaughter, and Larry Gura. But for an injury, Mike Gallagher would have been on that list.

He spent four years as an associate at Snell & Wilmer (1970 to 1975), made partner and spent the next three years at the firm before leaving in 1975 to form a new two-lawyer firm with his close friend, Mike Kennedy. Their firm, Gallagher & Kennedy, grew to over a hundred lawyers in the next three decades. He retired as Chairman Emeritus from the law firm in 2016, but is still active in the business world.

HON. MICHAEL DALY HAWKINS, '70

Judge Hawkins has many claims to fame, but for this book, it's his membership in the historic first graduating class from ASU Law in 1970 that counts. The "Presentation Day" announcement on June 2, 1970, lists him as one of eighty-seven graduates, the Staff Editor of the *Law Journal,* a member of the Student Bar Association Council, and one of fifteen to graduate with honors. In his Class of 1979 Memory Book, distributed at the 40th Reunion in 2010, he remembered those

three pivotal years in law school: "Great teachers, good friends." Given his post-1970 record, it is certain he had many good friends then and now. He was what ASU called "through and through." Born in 1945 in Winslow, Arizona, he went to college and law school at ASU. Twenty-eight years later he went to the University of Virginia, where he earned a Masters' Degree in Law, writing his thesis on the antebellum slave trade.

Like many young men his age in the 1970s, he faced an important decision with the Vietnam War raging and big cities demonstrating. Upon graduation from law school, he chose the United States Marines and served with the rank of captain as a special courts military judge from 1970 to 1973. Then he joined Dushoff & Sacks. Later, he was a founding partner in Daughton, Hawkins, Brockleman, Buinan & Patterson. He was the U.S. Attorney in Arizona from 1977 to 1980, and then in private practice from 1980 to 1994. President Clinton nominated him the United States Court of Appeals for the Ninth Circuit on July 13, 1994, to fill the seat occupied by Judge Thomas Tang. He assumed senior status on February 12, 2010, but still hears cases in 2020.

President Carter appointed him in 1977 as the U.S. Attorney for the District of Arizona. He served until 1980, when he went back into private practice. He also served as a special prosecutor for the Navajo Nation from 1985 to 1989. And he was a visiting professor at the University of San Diego School of Law, teaching intellectual property.

He is widely known and respected for his work on the Ninth Circuit. "I think he's one of the best judges on the Ninth Circuit, and he's a complete moderate in the best sense of the word," said Hastings College of the Law Prof. Rory Little. "He is a careful, case by case, practical, pragmatic judge. He's not flashy; he doesn't write [Judge Alex] Kozinski-like flourishes. He's not histrionic in any particular direction like any number of other judges." Judge Kozinski, former Chief Judge of the Ninth Circuit said, "By all accounts, Judge Hawkins has come a long way from that corner in Winslow, but he's always made it back to Arizona . . . I'm honored to introduce this tribute to Judge Hawkins, an extraordinary jurist, a life-long Arizonan, a wonderful friend, and a real Mensch."

Inaugural Graduates—1970 through 1976

Dan Merkel, one of Judge Hawkins's law clerks, and later a law professor, wrote a long law review article focused largely on a strong dissent by Judge Hawkins. He said, "I take comfort knowing that we are blessed to have judges like Judge Hawkins—judges for justice—who remind us of the reasons that we adopt laws to guide officials as much as citizens: because they are the 'wise restraints that make men free.'"

He gave scores of speeches about the big issues in American and Arizona law. His January 28, 2011 speech to his fellow graduates from ASU Law explored "What 14 Lawyers Were Doing 100 Years Ago." It examined the 1910 Arizona Constitutional Convention.

While in private practice, he frequently served as a judge pro tempore of the Arizona Court of Appeals. A 1995 recipient of ASU's Alumni Achievement Award, he also was honored in 2003 by the State Bar of Arizona with its James Walsh Outstanding Jurist Award. In 2006, ASU's College of Law presented him with the John S. Lancy Award, recognizing him as an outstanding law journal alumnus. The Maricopa County Bar Association inducted him into the Hall of Fame in 2012.

In 2012, Hawkins joined Judge Stephen Reinhardt's majority ruling striking down California's gay marriage ban. It was the first federal appeals court ruling holding gay marriage bans were unconstitutional. The U.S. Supreme Court ruled similarly in another case three years later. Most recently, Judge Hawkins was one of three Ninth Circuit judges upholding Hawaii's denial of President Trump's travel ban targeting six predominantly Muslim countries.

Arguably, Judge Hawkins' most incisive judicial opinions revolved around his immigration decisions. Those decisions were chronicled by Lenni B. Benson (NYU School of Law) in a long law review article, entitled "The Search for Fair Agency Process: The Immigration Opinions of Judge Michael Daly Hawkins, 1994–2010." In her article, Professor Benson defined Judge Hawkins.

Judge Michael Daly Hawkins has been a member of the Ninth Circuit Court of Appeals since 1994; but he has been concerned with the forms and varieties of administrative or bureaucratic process his entire career. Perhaps because he spent several intense early years as a lawyer in the U.S. Marine Corps, or because he grew up in a small Arizona town on the edge of the Navajo nation, Judge Hawkins has been aware that due process guarantees and the quality of the adjudication within a bureaucratic system may be even more important than the procedure in general commercial or criminal litigation. Judge Hawkins has been a scholar and architect of reform in bureaucratic justice.[2]

In one of his most oft-cited cases, he said, "We review the work of government agencies with an understandable degree of deference. No amount of deference, however, can excuse the deliberate, calculated and cumulative unfairness which occurred here."[3]

Judge Hawkins can be fairly described as one of ASU's most celebrated graduates—smart, courageous, and honest to a fault.

JOE SIMS, '70

Sims earned a degree in finance from ASU, and joined the Arizona Department of Transportation. One of his co-workers, Neil Dessaint, '70, would become the Clerk of the Arizona Supreme Court. As Mr. Dessaint remembered it, "[Joe] kept up a running dialogue about the new venture planned at Arizona State University . . . all he could do was talk about law school." The jurisprudence drumbeat convinced Joe and Neil to take the LSAT. Sims, "nudged by Professor Rose, went to work at the Justice Department."[4] He graduated *magna cum laude* and was the Comments Editor on the *ASU Law Journal*.

"*Sing on Chairman of the Board.*" That's how the legal tribute to Joe Sims, class of 1970, labeled one of ASU's most famous lawyer-graduates.[5] Joe's profile, along with nine others,[6] validated ASU Law's "40 Years of Influence." The author, Dean Paul Berman, said it well: "It is impossible to measure influence with any kind of objective yardstick. But it is easy to see, perhaps easiest by imaging its absence. What would Arizona or the wider world have looked like without the College of Law at Arizona State University? If Joe Sims had continued to work at the Arizona Department of Transportation instead of heeding the College's siren call, maybe we wouldn't have SIRUS XM Radio to listen to." He posed the question about Joe forty years *after* Joe graduated. Influence? Indubitably.

Inaugural Graduates—1970 through 1976

Here is how his law firm, Jones Day,[7] describes him: "Joe Sims is one of the most recognized antitrust lawyers in the world. He is listed in *Chambers, Who's Who Legal, Legal 500, Best Lawyers of America*, and most other publications recognizing prominent antitrust lawyers. He is the only antitrust lawyer ever named by *The American Lawyer* as a 'Dealmaker of the Year' two times, in 2001 and 2009. In March 2010, he was recognized by *The National Law Journal* as one of 'The Decade's Most Influential Lawyers' and was most recently named the *Washington, DC Antitrust Lawyer of the Year* by Best Lawyers of America. He is one of four U.S. lawyers included in Expert Guides Best of the Best compilation of the 30 leading antitrust/competition law lawyers in the world." He has but a handful of peers in American law.

Before he migrated to Jones Day in 1978, he spent eight years in the U.S. Justice Department's Antitrust Division. After joining Jones Day, he became lead counsel on "some of the most significant transactions of recent years, and his clients include Apple, Chevron, Dell, General Motors, Procter & Gamble, and Sirius XM . . . At the top of the list for deals needing the most experienced antitrust counseling, just ask Abbott Laboratories, Time Warner, CBS Inc., Chevron and many others, states Lawdragon, where journalists, and lawyers list attorneys. Joe Sims is the foundation of Jones Day's antitrust practice and is regularly considered among the half-dozen best antitrust lawyers in the country."[8]

His tribute in the 2009–2010 Dean's Report summed up Joe's big win at Jones Day for SiriusXM. "If you're listening to Classic Vinyl or Siriusly Sinatra on an empty stretch of highway far beyond the reach of any land-based radio station, be grateful Joe Sims worked with a guy who just wouldn't shut up."[9]

JIMMIE DEE SMITH, '70

Smith might be a common name for a lawyer anywhere in America. But in Arizona, there is only one lawyer named Jimmie Dee Smith. He is a plainspoken man but certainly not "common." He is a small-town lawyer with a large reputation for leadership and public service, especially in terms of the State Bar Board of Governors. He is widely known in Arizona as the one-and-only *Jimmie Dee*.

Jimmie Dee's official Arizona State Bar listing reveals his educational history in his own words: "Mr. Smith earned his law degree from Arizona State University in 1970, where he was a member of the first graduating class of the College of Law.

He also attended Arizona Western College[10] in Yuma, received his business degree from Northern Arizona University.[11] Most importantly, Jimmie Smith attended grade school in Toltec,[12] Arizona."[13]

He is now, and has always been, a sole practitioner. He limits his practice to bankruptcy cases and representing clients in business matters and commercial disputes. "During his years of practice, he has represented many clients in criminal and civil cases in the Arizona State and Federal Trial and Appellate Courts. Mr. Smith has been sole lead counsel in over 100 Jury Trials and has handled many Appeals in the State and Federal Courts. He is certified by the State Bar of Arizona as a Specialist[14] in the field of Bankruptcy Law."[15]

Jimmie Dee served twice as president of the Yuma County Bar Association. He has served over twenty years on the State Bar of Arizona Board of Governors, representing Yuma and La Paz Counties. During his service on the State Bar Board of Governors, Jimmie served one-year terms in all of the State Bar Officer positions—secretary-treasurer, second vice president, first vice president, president-elect, and president (in 2006). Mr. Smith is also a member of the American Bar Association House of Delegates.[16]

ROBERT BLAKEY, JR., '71

Robert Blakey, Jr., likely had more fun than any other law student did in the four years he took to get through a three-year law school. He was known as "Bobby B" to friends, family, colleagues, clients, rugby players and other world adventurers. They knew him as a father, blindside flanker,[17] lawyer, and rock & roll drummer. He was a guy who never let anyone down, ever. He died in March 2014, as he might have put it, "just shy of seventy." By all accounts, he never looked or acted his age.

He earned his AB from Amherst College[18] in 1967 and his JD from ASU Law in 1971. He started law school with the inaugural class in 1967, finished his 1L year, and took a year off. He returned to law school in 1969 and graduated with the class that had been a year behind him. After passing the bar, he practiced law in Phoenix with the Arizona Attorney General's office filing and trying consumer fraud cases. He left the AG's office and moved to Prescott where he practiced real estate law. He retired from active practice in 2012. As expected, he continued to climb mountains and play his drums for the rest of his life.

After college and law school, he blended law, music, athletics, and world travel intermittently and exhaustively over the next forty-three years.[19] He played drums at Amherst, where he started his first band. He called it the *Flower and Vegetable Show*, after he saw that name on the marquee of the Boston Women's Club. He spent his year off law school surfing and playing in some of Hawaii's great nightspots. When he came back to Phoenix, and while studying law at ASU, his band, Motion, opened for big-name bands, including Buffalo Springfield,[20] the Beach Boys,[21] Gary Puckett[22] and Alice Cooper.[23] In 1995, he reconnected with his band, Lefty.

His obituary[24] captured the life of a man-in-full.

> *He was a stellar student and a dominate pitcher on the baseball team. The Arizona Republic referred to him as "Bullet Bob Blakey." After turning down an opportunity to play professional baseball for the Detroit Tigers, Bob attended Amherst College. . . . After four years of playing on the Amherst Rugby Club, Bob brought rugby back to Arizona in 1967. As the father of Arizona rugby, including women's rugby, he started the Arizona Rugby Union[25] and was its first President.[26] Bob Blakey arrived in Amherst from Phoenix in 1963 in the back of a Greyhound bus. He was the only member of our class to decline an offer to play professional sports for the promise of an Amherst education. Bob was a serious student, athlete and musician who entertained and engaged us with his wacky sense of humor, personal magnetism and vitality. After graduation, Bob returned to Phoenix to tour with area bands, to study law and to marry. . . From the moment he arrived at Amherst until his death last February, Bob engaged the people around him in an envelope of intimacy packed with humor rooted deeply in his Southwestern perspective. We were drawn to him knowing that the importance he attached to us was the reason for the strong attraction we felt. Bob made us laugh at his caricatures and the stories he told. His optimism highlighted the opportunity inherent*

in the next moment, and, when we took the chance, we found he was right, and had wonderful times with him.[27]

HON. CECIL B. PATTERSON, JR., '71

Judge Patterson was the first person in his class to become a trial judge, the first to serve on the Arizona Court of Appeals, and one of the first to have a scholarship named in his honor at his alma mater. "First Things First" could be his motto. First Things First "partners with families and communities to support the healthy development and learning of Arizona's young children."[28] He's on their Finance and Audit Committee.[29] Their website says, "His [Judge Patterson's] work at First Things First is one way he continues his distinguished career of public service."[30] He gave an Oral History interview in the Ross-Blakley Library in 2007. He talked about his firsts. "Every job that I had [from] clerking for legal services in 1969 through retiring in 2003, I was the first to do that job. Every single job I had."[31]

He was born in Newport News, Virginia, in 1941. He went to college at the Hampton Institute, now known as Hampton University,[32] where he earned his BA degree in 1963. The USAF engaged him for the next five years. His last duty station was Luke Air Force Base in Glendale, Arizona. That posting allowed him to join the first year class at ASU Law in 1968. He graduated with his JD in 1971 in the school's second graduating class.

Fresh out of law school, Patterson got a job clerking for Arizona's Chief Justice, Stanley Feldman. "He was Chief Justice and it was always good to have Stanley standing up there because I knew I had a friend there, not that other people weren't my friends, but he was personally."[33]

In sequence, he served as staff counsel with the Maricopa County Legal Aid Society, then the Phoenix Urban League, and then in private practice with Brush & Patterson. He was a judge on the Maricopa County Superior Court from 1980 to 1991. He left the trial bench after eleven years and served as chief counsel for the Human Services Division of the Arizona Attorney General's Office from 1991 to 1995. In 1995, Governor Fife Symington, III, appointed him to the Arizona Court of Appeals where served until 2011.[34]

Inaugural Graduates—1970 through 1976

His history of community engagement is legendary. His academic record, his judicial career, and his commitment to public service for his entire life resulted in the university's creation of a scholarship in his name on February 28, 2017. "A true trailblazer, The Honorable Cecil B. Patterson Jr. left behind a string of firsts, forever impacting the State of Arizona. His commitment to the community, mentoring young adults, and dedication to public service has made an impact on countless people, spanning beyond the legal community and into the general public. Join us as we celebrate the storied career of the Honorable Cecil B. Patterson, Jr., and announce the creation of an endowed Student Scholarship at ASU Law, named in his honor."[35]

While on the trial and appellate benches and while serving in public agencies, he found time to serve on the boards of the YMCA, United Way, Samaritan Health Services, the Red Cross, and the NAACP. Besides having an ASU Scholarship named in his honor, he won: (1) the City of Phoenix Martin Luther King, Jr., "Living the Dream Award,"[36] (2) the National Association of Attorneys General "Marvin Award,"[37] (3) the Arizona Black Lawyers Association "Trailblazer Award,"[38] and (3) the ASU College of Law "Distinguished Achievement Award."

In his Oral History interview at ASU in 2006 he reminisced about his classes and his teachers at ASU Law.

> *I remember Dean Pedrick shocked a bunch of people when he came in and started class that first day and asked a traditional question. . . . [I]t was a shock question . . . IDX versus WDX . . . he would call on somebody and just hammer them with questions . . . the Socratic method of teaching. People started shuddering and cowering and sliding down in the seat and whatever, but that was the way we were going to live for the next three years . . . . Mike Berch was very exuberant and in his exuberance, theatrical. . . . [Professor] Havighurst, he taught me commercial law. And he always had a pencil in his hand. And he would manipulate the pencil in his fingers, as he would talk to you and . . . man, and you could almost get transfixed on that rather than listening to the lecture. Professor Rose was always quite subdued and low key . . . . Professor Morris smiled a lot. He was very social, very bright. He was a very good mentor and confidante. In class, he was very positive and upbeat. He had, he brought some exuberance, but it was a demurred kind of exuberance to the class . . . he was the only African American on our faculty . . . he was just a wonderful man. I miss him.*[39]

Judge Patterson's work after law school and before his first judgeship says volumes about the kind of law he liked, and where he thought he'd go professionally. His first job at the Maricopa Legal Aid Society lasted a year. Then he did fair-housing work for the Urban League. "I'd gone to school so that I could work in a setting with minorities, African Americans principally. And people of less means poverty and in the Urban League it was all there. I said, hey I'm home. And then you know you still got to support family so I worked four jobs while I was there. I taught twice a semester, one of which was here at ASU in business school and taught [at] the community college—of course I had the full time job with them."[40]

As it turned out, he practiced law at the same time he was teaching as adjunct faculty in the ASU College of Business. "Actually some of the classes were early morning . . . I taught some business law for thirteen semesters. And only quit then because as judge I couldn't hold outside employment . . . . I loved teaching over there. I was trying cases so I'd go in and start teaching and say let me tell you what I did today and teach students. They loved it. I did too because it helped me think through a lot of things that I did."[41]

He spent eleven years (1980 to 1991) as a trial judge on the Maricopa County Superior Court. His longtime friend from the public defender's office, Grant Woods, class of '79, was Arizona's Attorney General. General Woods enticed Judge Patterson to step down from the Superior Court and join him at the AG's office.[42]

He went from the trial court to a policy position on the attorney general's leadership team. "I was one of [Grant Wood's] principle deputies . . . he had four principle deputies and I was one of those. . . . I ran a division, which was roughly a third of the office, about a hundred lawyers, about two hundred, two hundred fifty, support staff. It turned out to be highly political. I dabbled in politics and I wound up lobbying for five years at the legislature. Involving myself in things political all over the state. Grant would send me out talk to people about this, that, and the other. I'd take off and do it. And I suppose I was reasonable good at it."[43]

Judge Patterson may be best known, not for what he did, but what he did for others. He dug in early and fought long and hard for diversity and equal rights in Arizona. Because he was the first African American to serve on the Arizona Court of Appeals, he used that as a wedge point for others.

So, by the time I got to that role, I was accustomed to try and establish a standard and also pull people along, principally African American, but I brought a lot of Hispanics along. I brought a lot of them along. I have quite wide access to Hispanic bar and the Asian Pacific bar because of what I did . . . and of course, I brought more women in than minorities actually. Lot of the women were minorities of course. But I brought a lot of people in. It was an understanding that I had over time . . . somebody's got to plow the field. It just so happened that I wound up plowing every field that I went to. And I'd sit and talk to people and explain to them what my views of it were.[44]

Judge Patterson loved his law school.

The law school has been extraordinarily good to me. By virtue of the education I got here, the opportunities to serve through the law school, the people with whom I met and associated at the law school. . . . This is again a part of the giving back to something that has been as instrumental in your life as virtually anything, except you know your wife and kids and parents. I have extremely strong feelings about the now Sandra O'Day-Sandra Day O'Connor law school at Arizona State University. I think it's done extremely well, I'm extremely proud of it. . . . I could have gone to school back east, I was admitted to school back east, which was established, and had a reputation. . . . From the day I graduated, I started interacting with lawyers from some of the best schools across the country. I mean like within a month, six weeks after I graduated I was in training programs, national training programs. I honestly tell you, and I've told people this before I never once felt that I had come up short by going to a brand new law school. Not once. Period. . . . I have been able . . . [to] compete on equal footing. I mean they have more widely known named law schools, and when it comes down to skills, and the things that they teach, and the knowledge and abilities and what have you, no shortcoming whatsoever, period. That's my sales pitch for Arizona State.[45]

HON. ROSLYN SILVER, '71

The Honorable Roslyn O. Silver, Senior Judge of the United States District Court for the District of Arizona, is by every measure a lawyer of note, a judge of consequence, and a graduate known by every other ASU Law graduate in the 1970s. Of all the people profiled in this book, Judge Silver stands out as someone there at

the beginning, in close touch over the years, and now, fifty years later, still involved.

This book is history, both in the making, and on purpose. Judge Silver's history is the history of what the founding faculty hoped would happen. They wanted to make a difference in advancing the rule of law; she has done that. They wanted to teach law students in ways that prepared them for every legal turn in the road; she's seen them all. They picked students carefully, knowing that how those students turned out would reflect how well they were educated. She is that reflection.

She's a native Phoenician, grade school, middle school, and high school, but she went west to college—University of California, Santa Barbara. She earned her BA in 1968, just one year after Dean Pedrick and his happy band of new law professors taught their first classes at ASU Law. That put her a year behind the inaugural graduating class of 1970.

She was in the third graduating class—1972. She clerked for Arizona Supreme Court Justice Lorna Lockwood,[46] and was in private practice from 1972 to 1974. Then she joined the Navajo Nation's Native American Rights Fund (1974 to 1976). She worked as in-house counsel for Greyhound Corporation, doing labor and employment work, from 1976 to 1978. Back to private practice and working for the Equal Opportunity Commission in 1979. Still searching for the perfect job, she became an Assistant U.S. Attorney for the District of Arizona from 1980 to 1984. That prosecutorial experience positioned her for the move to the Arizona Attorney General's office from 1984 to 1986. She went back to the U.S. Attorney's office in 1986, and was promoted to Chief of the Criminal Division in 1989. She spent five years in that high office, until President Clinton nominated her to a seat on the United States District Court for the District of Arizona in 1994.[47] She became Chief Judge of the District Court in 2011 and took senior status in 2013.[48]

Tragically, her elevation to chief judge came about because the presiding chief judge, John Roll,[49] was murdered in Tucson, during the assassination attempt on Congresswoman Gabrielle Giffords.[50] Judge Silver said she was "shocked and devastated."[51] One of Judge Silver's former colleagues on the district court trial bench, Judge Mary Murguia,[52] now a Ninth Circuit Court appellate judge, said, "Judge Silver never lost her caring side. As good as she is about being prepared about the issues of law coming before her and the cases before her, she has a very compassionate side, and she's a very caring person . . . that side of her certainly served her well as chief judge and in other roles as well."[53]

From June 29, 1994, to December 4, 2019, Judge Silver resolved 1,399 cases at the district level.[54] In addition to formal published opinions and judgments, she wrote thirteen secondary materials, law review articles, essays, and other judicial offerings.[55] One particular article will reverberate with every lawyer who was a bit terrified when entering the pit of a courtroom for the first time, and faced a jury without a clear understanding of the process called *voir dire*. She explained:

> *It was early April 1980 at the Prescott, Arizona, federal courthouse, and I was trying my first jury trial as an assistant U.S. attorney. We were about to engage in the most mysterious of all trial processes:* **voir dire**. *I knew only that it was a deselection process whereby I was supposed to strike the jury panelists biased in favor of the accused, while attempting to retain those biased in favor of the government. In truth, the only certainty I had about this enterprise was the preferred pronunciation of it,* **vuwah-dear**. *When the judge belted out, "Counsel are you prepared for* **voredire**?" *I knew I was about to enter a tunnel without a light at the end of it.*[56]

As is often the case with senior Article III judges, it's best to listen to what they say as they reflect on a long career as lawyer and judge. "A judge must never forget the court belongs to the people, and that she is affecting the lives of every person who appears before her. We who wear the black robe have assumed a sacred trust to do our very best and to do what is right, even if many think it wrong."[57]

LES SCHIEFELBEIN, '71

Les Schiefelbein lives in rarified air only occupied by a small group of America's lawyers. They don't take garden-variety consumer, criminal or family law cases. They limit their skills to complex, multimillion-dollar commercial and government disputes. They don't try these cases. No one wants to litigate these disputes given the forum, venue, jurisdictional, and time issues. They are high-dollar mediators and arbitrators. They do their best work in conference rooms, not courtrooms. Their clients routinely see how mediating and arbitrating results in lower costs and

 quicker resolutions. Their clients preserve outcomes and sometimes improve relationships between opposing parties, a reality rare in litigating cases rather than arbitrating them.[58]

Mr. Schiefelbein earned two degrees at ASU (BA in 1967 and JD in 1971), a master's in law from the George Washington University Law School, and is a graduate of the Advanced Executive Program at the J.L. Kellogg Graduate School of Management at Northwestern University. In 2019, he completed the London School of Economics and Political Science course on Business, International Relations, and Political Economy. He is a retired colonel in the U.S. Air Force's Judge Advocate General Corps. He spent twenty-four years and nine months in the USAF, from 1971 to 1996.

Schiefelbein worked for the U.S. Department of Energy as senior procurement law attorney in the Office of General Counsel for five years, from 1978 to 1982. He spent thirty-one years at Lockheed Martin Space Systems Company,[59] serving as "Vice President and Deputy General Counsel, where he was a key advisor to senior management on a wide range of legal issues as counselor, commercial lawyer, litigator and business advisor. Schiefelbein has negotiated contracts and business agreements across the globe and has a deep understanding of commercial technologies and commercial and government business practices. His business acumen and extensive legal experience provides invaluable insight in resolution of disputed commercial matters. At Lockheed Martin, Schiefelbein developed a successful litigation and arbitration practice with a near perfect record of 156 cases won and only two lost. He acted as counsel and managed international arbitrations under the rules of the London Court of International Arbitration, the International Chamber of Commerce and the International Centre for Dispute Resolution of the American Arbitration Association. The arbitrations involved complex technical and novel legal issues in the design, construction, launch and performance of satellites and launch systems at a cost of up to $250 million. He defeated a plaintiff claim of $3 billion in a high profile Civil False Claims Act litigation. The case was twice featured on ABC's Nightline News."[60]

He has handled "over 300 cases in the course of his career, and has gained particular expertise as a sole, chair or panel arbitrator in commercial and government disputes to include aerospace, aviation, satellites, cybersecurity, national security, information technology, trade secrets, intellectual property, software licensing, energy and construction."[61]

He is the CEO of the Silicon Valley Arbitration & Mediation Center. "SVAMC serves the global technology sector by promoting business-practical dispute resolution. [It] works with leading technology companies, law firms, ADR institutions and universities in Silicon Valley and around the globe to provide educational programming and related resources regarding the effective and efficient resolution of technology-related disputes."[62]

In 2019, the Sandra Day O'Connor College of Law announced a major gift to the college to establish the Les Schiefelbein Global Dispute Resolution Program and Endowed Scholarship. It will provide students at ASU Law "an innovative and interactive environment to gain knowledge, experience and develop professional connections that will help prepare them for practice in international arbitration and mediation with global law firms, multinational corporations, governments and non-government organizations."[63]

> *"The generous gift from Les and Linda Schiefelbein to create the Global Dispute Resolution Program, at the Law School's Lodestar Dispute Resolution Center, will improve our ability to offer a world-class legal education to our students and prepare them for careers in the field of global dispute resolution," said Douglas Sylvester, dean of the Sandra Day O'Connor College of Law at Arizona State University. "Through this collaborative program, our students will have opportunities to interact with and learn from leading lawyers, arbitrators and mediators across multiple disciplines."*[64]

Mr. Schiefelbein said, "International dispute resolution is complex, constantly evolving due to the breadth of a global economy and the fast pace of technology innovation and the need for new practitioners, both men and women, is paramount. . . . The Sandra Day O'Connor College of Law has an impressive commitment to dispute resolution education, being ranked Number 7 in U.S. law schools for dispute resolution by U.S. News & World Report. It is the right place and this is the right time to provide a focused program to nurture the learning, talents, passion, and leadership skills for the next generation to be successful practitioners in global dispute resolution, especially where it is growing at a rapid pace in Asia, Europe and the United States."[65]

"The program will feature an annual International Arbitration Forum where top lawyers, counsel for global corporations, internationally recognized arbitrators and mediators, as well as leaders at arbitration institutions will engage in discussions on timely issues in international dispute resolution."[66]

ASPEY, WATKINS & DIESEL, PLLC

AWD LAW® is a Flagstaff Arizona law firm founded and managed by early ASU Law graduates Fritz Aspey, Harold Watkins, and Lou Diesel; classmates at ASU Law in the early 1970s. Today, they proudly claim to be "Northern Arizona's Law Firm."[67] Arguably, they are the largest Arizona private law firm north of Bell Road in Phoenix.

At their fortieth anniversary celebration in July 2015, *The Arizona Daily Sun* reported on how they built "a legal legacy" in Flagstaff. "In the last forty years Aspey Watkins & Diesel has grown from a three-man law firm tucked into the basement of the Masonic Temple in downtown Flagstaff to one of the largest firms in northern Arizona. . . We all went to school together, said Louis Diesel, Fritz had the genius to start our law firm. . . . They quit their jobs at other law firms to start their own firm but the bank wouldn't loan us money. We had to borrow based on our wives' salaries because they were the only ones who had jobs, according to the bank. . . One of their first clients was Coconino County. The trio locked in a contract with the county to handle every single public defense case for $40,000 per year. They handled 400 cases [in the first year]."[68]

The Hon. J. Thomas Brooks, a former Coconino County trial judge and an Arizona Court of Appeals judge, remembered those early days for the founding partners. "It is hard to believe that so many years have gone by since you [Fritz Aspey], Harold and Louis literally worked seven days and nights each week acting as the Public Defenders while also trying to start your own [private] practice. This was made even more difficult when the word got out to persons accused of crimes that the public defenders provided the best representation in the county!"[69]

FRITZ ASPEY, '72

Frederick M. "Fritz" Aspey founded the Flagstaff Arizona law firm *Aspey, Watkins & Diesel*[70] in 1975, with Harold Watkins, class of '73 and Lou Diesel, class of '73.

It grew to be Flagstaff's largest private law firm. He focuses his practice on business law, real estate, and mediation.

Mr. Aspey graduated from the ASU College of Law, earning his JD degree in 1972. He earned his BS degree at Northern Arizona University[71] in 1969. He is licensed to practice in these courts: U.S. Supreme Court, 1978; Supreme Court of Arizona, 1972; U.S. District Court – District of Arizona, 1973; U.S. Court of Appeals – Ninth Circuit, 1974; U.S. Court of Appeals – Federal Circuit, 1995; U.S. Claims Court, 1990; Navajo Nation, 1993 (inactive); and Hopi Tribal Court, 1988.

Mr. Aspey has served the Arizona Bar as president, Arizona State Bar Association,[72] 1990–1991; as a member of the Board of Governors from 1982 to 1992; and as a Judge Pro Tempore, Division One, 1985, 1992, 1995, Arizona Court of Appeals. He was president of the Coconino County Bar Association[73] in 1980. He is a member of many invited legal organizations, including Arizona Trial Lawyers Association;[74] American Association for Justice;[75] American Bar Association;[76] and the American Judicature Society.[77] He has been recognized by Martindale Hubbell® as an AV® lawyer and in the Preeminent category,[78] and is a trustee of, and a sustaining member of the Arizona Lawyers Foundation.[79] He has been both recognized and honored by the Arizona Bar Foundation, as a Founding Fellow;[80] ASU College of Law Alumni Association Outstanding Alumni Award, 1989; and he won the NAU Distinguished Alumnus Recognition Award, 1990, and the NAU Alumni Service Award, 1995.

HON. REDFIELD T. BAUM, '72

In 1970, Redfield T. Baum, then widely known as Tom, earned his bachelor's degree in history from Arizona State University, and his JD from what is now known as the Sandra Day O'Connor College of Law, in 1973. On graduation from law school, he was commissioned a second lieutenant in the U.S. Army and left the army as a captain in 1973.

From 1973 to 1990 he practiced law in Phoenix, focusing on commercial law, creditors' rights, bankruptcy, Chapter 11 reorganizations, and litigation.

Before becoming a federal judge, he was a partner at Rawlins, Ellis, Burris & Kiewit, and later at O'Connor, Cavanagh, Anderson, Westover, Killingsworth & Beshears.

In 1990, he was appointed to the federal bench as a bankruptcy court judge for the United States District of Arizona until 2013. In August 1996, Baum participated in the program "Reducing the Risk: Promoting Mutual Understanding in Insolvency Practices" given in San Jose, Costa Rica. The event was co-sponsored by the *Associacion Costarricense de Derecho Internacional* and the American Bankruptcy Institute. In 2000, he was chosen "one of the 10 outstanding bankruptcy judges" in the U.S. by *Turnarounds & Workouts,* a respected bankruptcy publication. Baum was also one of the original authors of the *Arizona Civil Remedies Book.* In 2005, Baum spoke at the International Bar Association's annual meeting in the Czech Republic.[81]

Four years later, in 2009, Baum and Judge Charles Case were invited to visit Prague and teach Czech insolvency judges, trustees, and practitioners how to write a good reorganization plan, how to value assets, and how to understand the dynamics of bankruptcy negotiation among various interest groups.[82]

He may be best known for his handling of the Phoenix Coyotes bankruptcy.[83] The holding company for the team filed Chapter 11 bankruptcy. It had agreed to sell the team for $212.5 million. The news was a surprise to the NHL. There was a dispute over whether the Coyotes would move to Chicago or stay in Phoenix.

The bankruptcy hearing was scheduled for May 7, 2009. The NHL argued that it had been in control of the team since November 2008. It argued that the holding company was barred from filing for bankruptcy. The holding company claimed that the agreement only gave the league voting rights, not outright control. Judge Baum had to decide who actually controlled the team.[84] On September 30, 2009, Judge Baum turned down existing offers saying, "In hockey parlance, the court is passing the puck to the NHL who can decide to take another shot at the sale net or it can pass off the puck."[85]

During his term on the U.S. Bankruptcy Court, he was on the Board of Governors for the National Conference of Bankruptcy Judges. He frequently served

Inaugural Graduates—1970 through 1976

as a judge pro tem on the Ninth Circuit Court Bankruptcy Appellate Panel. He was an instructor at the National Institute of Trial Bankruptcy Litigation Skills. He was one of three members of the U.S. Delegation to the Czech Republic, consulting on their insolvency law, and delivered a lecture the International Bar Association meeting in the Czech Republic in 2005.[86]

LOU DIESEL, '73

Louis M. Diesel is a founding partner at the Flagstaff law firm Aspey, Watkins & Diesel.[87] His practice focuses on personal injury, medical malpractice and wrongful death litigation. He represents clients in motor vehicle accidents, serious slip and fall incidents, and premises liability situations. Diesel has lectured throughout the state on personal injury litigation.[88]

Mr. Diesel earned his JD degree at Arizona State University College of Law in 1973, where he was a member of the *Law Journal*. He earned his master of science degree from ASU in 1975. His BS degree was awarded by Northern Arizona University, with high distinction (top 5 percent), in 1970.

He is admitted to practice law at the Supreme Court of Arizona, 1973; the U.S. District Court – District of Arizona, 1973; the U.S. Court of Appeals – Ninth Circuit, 1974; and the U.S. Supreme Court, 1978. He is a member of many legal organizations, including the Coconino County Bar Association, American Bar Association, and Arizona Trial Lawyers Association. He is a founding fellow of the Arizona Bar Foundation.[89] He is a co-author of the *Arizona Motor Vehicle Accident Deskbook*.[90]

Mr. Diesel has been recognized Martindale Hubbell® as an AV® lawyer in the Preeminent™ category, and by Southwest Super Lawyers.® He is a sustaining member of the Arizona Lawyers Foundation.[91]

HAROLD L. WATKINS, '73

Harold L. Watkins is a founding member of Aspey, Watkins, & Diesel, a Flagstaff, Arizona law firm, where he focuses on complex civil and commercial litigation. He was named as counsel in several class action matters of regional and statewide significance. He was also involved in the prosecution of numerous matters arising from operation of cities and towns throughout Arizona. He served as an appointed member to the first city council after the 1988 incorporation of Sedona, Arizona, and helped guide the city to its first elected council.

Mr. Watkins graduated from ASU Law School with a JD degree in 1973. He earned his BS degree at Northern Arizona University in 1970. He is admitted to practice law in these courts: U.S. Supreme Court, 1978; Supreme Court of Arizona, 1973; Supreme Court of California, 1980; U.S. District Court – District of Arizona, 1973; U.S. Court of Appeals – Ninth Circuit, 1974.

AMBASSADOR HATTIE C. BABBITT, '72

A woman of many titles. Law student—Lawyer—First Lady—Director—Chairperson—Administrator—Diplomat—Ambassador. From the time she was a first-year law student at what is now the Sandra Day O'Connor College of Law, she has excelled, challenged the status quo, and made a difference in Arizona, America, and across the world. She even has a railroad line, the "Hattie B," named after her.[92] Hattie later recalled her railroad line: "I loved the idea. It filled a hugely important need. . . . I mean, it was used so much it became the 'Sardine Express' because the cars were absolutely packed with people who would have otherwise spent, you know, eight or ten hours in traffic."[93]

Inaugural Graduates—1970 through 1976

She graduated from Arizona State University with a BA in Spanish (Spring 1969), and became a first-year law student in only the second year of the ASU Law School's existence (Fall 1969). She knew everyone in the school's inaugural 1970 graduating class. After law school, she clerked for Arizona Supreme Court Justice Jack D. Hays.[94] Twenty-three years later, she wrote about that experience, recalling Justice Hays fondly: "He was a generous and patient (if demanding) first boss who, by example, taught the fundamental value of fairness. In today's environment of attack lawyers, his gentlemanly demeanor and unerring radar for a just and impartial solution will be especially missed."[95]

Her first job as a lawyer was with the Phoenix firm of Robbins & Green, which eventually merged into Jennings, Strouss & Salmon.[96] She was an active trial lawyer for twenty years. She is an active lawyer/diplomat/public servant in Washington, DC.

Her current bio, as vice-chair of the National Democratic Institute,[97] is a study in public service and policy: "She provides counsel at the intersection of law, policy and public interest. Ms. Babbitt serves on a number of not-for-profit and for-profit boards. She is co-chair of the Global Water Challenge,[98] serves as vice-chair of the World Resource Institute,[99] and serves on the boards of NDI, The Water Initiative,[100] and the Institute for the Study of Diplomacy at Georgetown University.[101] She is also a member of the Council on Foreign Relations.[102] From 1997 to 2001, Ms. Babbitt served as deputy administrator of the U.S. Agency for International Development.[103] As the second most senior official for U.S. foreign assistance programs, she oversaw programs in the fields of democratization, humanitarian relief, women's empowerment, climate change, economic growth, education, health and the environment. Her responsibilities included oversight of USAID efforts to assist post-conflict reconstruction in the Balkans and East Timor.[104] Ms. Babbitt served at the Department of State[105] from 1993 to 1997 as U.S. Ambassador to the Organization of American States.[106] While in that role she led the U.S. negotiating effort to completion of the world's first anti-corruption convention and strengthened the Inter-American Human Rights Commission[107] and Inter-American cooperation against arms trafficking. Ms. Babbitt also served as a senior public policy scholar at the Woodrow Wilson International Center for Scholars.[108, 109]

She is senior vice president of Hunt Alternatives Fund,[110] has directed the Washington, DC, office of The Initiative for Inclusive Security[111] and the broader Hunt Alternatives Fund since early 2002.[112]

The *Notable Names Database*[113] site identifies a dozen more affiliations.[114] Looked at collectively, what these jobs and affiliations confirm is that Hattie Babbitt is arguably the busiest, most well-known, and most far-reaching diplomat to ever graduate from ASU Law.

BARRY MACBAN, '72

Barry MacBan is one of top trial lawyers in Arizona. He tried over three hundred jury trials in the last forty-five years.[115] That experience has put him on top of the Hallmark lists of American lawyers. He is an invited member of America's most prestigious lawyer organizations: Fellow, American College of Trial Lawyers;[116] Founding Fellow, Arizona Bar Foundation;[117] International Academy of Trial Lawyers;[118] American Board of Trial Advocates;[119] Arizona's Finest Lawyers Foundation;[120] Best Lawyers in America;[121] Board Certified Specialist, Arizona Board of Legal Specialization;[122] AV/5.0 Preeminent—Martindale Hubbell;[123] Inductee, Worldwide Lifetime Achievement;[124] Top Lawyers—Who's Who Publishers;[125] Top 100 Lawyers in America;[126] Founder, President, Delta Sigma Phi Legal Fraternity;[127] Founder, Ernest W. McFarland Lecture Series and Scholarship Fund;[128] President, Phi Delta Theta Fraternity.[129]

Mr. MacBan earned his BSBA degree at ASU in 1969, and his JD in 1972. He was in the second entering class of the new law school in 1968. During the last forty-five years of practice, Barry has tried over three hundred jury trials in every county within Arizona. These trials encompassed a wide range of medical malpractice, professional liability, product liability and other complex tort litigation cases.[130] His wife, Laura MacBan,[131] is his law partner. In 2015, he was recognized by *Continental Who's Who* among Pinnacle Professionals in the field of Legal Services as a result of his role as Managing Partner with MacBan Law.[132]

Inaugural Graduates—1970 through 1976

TOM CHAUNCEY, II, '73

Tom Chauncey, II, is a media lawyer with a prominent Phoenix law firm—Gust Rosenfeld, PLC.[133] Before joining the firm, Chauncey spent ten years as executive vice president, general counsel, and station manager for KOLD-TV[134] in Tucson, Arizona.[135] His firm bio confirms his unique talents in law and the media: "Tom Chauncey brings unique experience in media law to Gust Rosenfeld. He works with clients to resolve disputes involving libel, slander, access to records and privacy issues and frequently is involved in pre-publication issues for newspaper, television and radio clients. His experience in the communication field enables him to help clients work through the multiplicity of contractual, privacy, employment and access issues."[136]

Mr. Chauncey went to Northwestern University and earned a BA with Departmental Honors in 1970. He earned JD at the ASU College of Law in 1973, where he was a member of Phi Delta Phi[137] legal fraternity. He used his experience in both business and the Arabian horse world to deliver legal services to individual and corporate clients. He belongs to eleven professional groups.

1. American Bar Association (member, Communications Law Forum, Intellectual Property Section, Entertainment and Sports Industries Forum)
2. Arizona Supreme Court Task Force on Court Productivity (former member)
3. Cameras in the Courtroom Committee (former chairman)
4. Cronkite Foundation for Journalism and Telecommunications (board member and chair Nominations Committee)
5. Federal Communications Commission Bar Association[138]
6. First Amendment Coalition[139] (founding member and former president)
7. Lawyer-Pilots Bar Association[140]
8. Leadership Council on Legal Diversity[141] (member)
9. Maricopa County Bar Association (member, Corporate Counsel Division and Technology & Intellectual Property Law Section)

10. State Bar of Arizona (member, Business Law and Intellectual Property Law Sections)
11. The National Conference for Community and Justice[142] (former co-chairman)

As a widely known philanthropist, he is very involved with and has held leadership positions in many local, state and national foundations and nonprofits: Arizona Grantmakers Forum;[143] Arizona Pilots Association;[144] Arizona Historical Society;[145] Barrow Neurological Foundation;[146] Foundation for Blind Children;[147] Friendly House;[148] Fund for Central Arizona History; Homeward Bound;[149] Northwestern University Alumni Association of Phoenix;[150] Social Venture Partners of Arizona;[151] Soldier's Best Friend;[152] St. Joseph's Hospital and Medical Center.[153]

Mr. Chauncey won the 2017 Outstanding Alumnus Award from the Sandra Day O'Connor College of Law. The award defined him: "A problem solver, Tom successfully addresses issues in multiple forums simultaneously, such as zoning procedures, litigation and legislative action. He has implemented compliance programs in a proactive manner to help clients avoid the cost and adverse publicity of litigation. Tom's practice also includes acquisition and disposal of assets; legislative relations; employment issues (contracts, non-compete agreements, sexual harassment, termination); and the difficult environmental issues involved in buying, selling and financing real estate, including homes, commercial property and ranches."[154]

He accepted the award graciously and gave the audience good advice and shared memories. When asked about his fondest memory at ASU Law, he said, "I enjoyed jousting with Dean Pedrick's questions during torts class." He gave advice to ASU Law's future generation: "[J]oin a good study group and after graduation, associate with quality lawyers and do what you love, never forgetting ours is a profession based on service to others."[155] He closed his remarks to the assembled students, families and faculty by revealing something that most people would likely not know about him. "I can bake a cake without messing up the kitchen."[156]

WILLIAM K. "BILL" CULBERTSON, '73

Bill Culbertson spent thirty-seven years in Arizona courtrooms. He worked the pit as a prosecutor and defense lawyer and sat on the bench as a court commissioner and full-time judge pro tempore. Before his retirement in 2010, he was a high-profile

Inaugural Graduates—1970 through 1976

prosecutor in capital case prosecution in Maricopa and Yavapai counties. He graduated with a BSBA degree from ASU in 1970 and earned his JD from the ASU College of Law in 1973. He graduated from the National College of Judges in May 1984.

Mr. Culbertson served as a courtroom bailiff the year before he graduated from law school working for Judge Charles D. Roush[157] in the Maricopa County Superior Court in 1972. He was an associate attorney in private practice with Roush, Mori, Welch & Steiner, PLC, from September 1973 to January 1974.[158]

He spent the rest of his active career as a lawyer in public service. From 2008 to 2010 he was Chief of the Criminal Division—Yavapai County Public Defender's office. "In this assignment I represented defendants accused of the most serious crimes, including representing clients facing the death penalty, sex offense charges and kidnapping. I supervised more than a dozen employees, including 2 paralegals and 11 attorneys. I was tasked with heading up a training program to assist our staff and to assist the private criminal defense bar, supervision of these employees, personnel matters, heading up internal affair investigations and performing various other administrative tasks for the appointed official."[159]

In 2006 he worked for the State Bar of Arizona's Lawyer Regulation group "reviewing complaints of unethical activity by lawyers and I attended hearings in which I represented the interests of the Bar. I represented the Bar in contested disciplinary proceedings against Lourdes Lopez, a former Pima County prosecutor who was eventually disbarred for her role in a murder. I also represented the Bar in an investigation into a complex financial transaction in which a lawyer mishandled several hundreds of thousands of dollars belonging to his clients. I filed a petition for interim suspension with the Arizona Supreme Court, and the Respondent voluntarily resigned from the State Bar of Arizona shortly after I left employment at the Bar."[160]

In 2004 and 2005, he was a defense lawyer for the Maricopa Office of the Legal Defender. "While in this position I was responsible for representation of capital defendants, oversight of the Glendale Regional Court Center on behalf of the Legal Defender, and I was an advisor to the department head on various issues including long-term planning and personnel matters."[161]

From 1993 to 2003, Mr. Culbertson was Chief of the Major Crimes Division of the Maricopa County Attorney's Office. "While in this position, I was responsible for supervision of all capital murder cases, all organized crime/major drug cases and all wiretaps, as well as vehicular crimes, gang cases, family violence cases and sex crimes cases. I supervised six separate bureaus and up to seventy attorneys. I chaired the MCAO capital review committee, which reviewed every first-degree murder case to consider whether to file allegations of death penalty. I was also a member of the MCAO Incident Review team, as well as the MCAO Shooting Review team. I personally prosecuted several complex, high-profile cases, including the AZSCAM bribery case and several death penalty cases."[162]

In 1991 and 1992 he headed the MCAO's Criminal Trial Division: "I supervised the grand jury bureau, the preliminary hearing bureau, and the criminal trial bureaus of the Maricopa County Attorney's Office. The Criminal Trial Division handled the vast majority of felony cases not assigned to the Major Crimes Division. These cases were typically thefts, robberies, burglaries and drug cases."[163]

From 1989 to 1990 he was "assigned to a criminal trial bureau to prosecute felony cases. Part of this responsibility included charging decision, conducting preliminary hearings, and trying cases to juries. I conducted numerous jury trials on charges ranging from drug possession to aggravated assault."[164]

Before working as a prosecutor he was a pro tempore Maricopa County Juvenile Court judge from 1986 to 1989. "I was a full-time judge pro tempore of the juvenile division of the Maricopa County Superior Court, where I was assigned a staff consisting of a clerk, a bailiff and a court reporter. I heard and adjudicated delinquency hearings, transfer hearings, and contested dependency hearings. During this employment, I sat as the judge on hundreds of adjudication hearings and hundreds of disposition hearings."[165]

February 1984 to March 1986—Commissioner of the Superior Court of Maricopa County, Juvenile Division. "I heard uncontested matters in the juvenile court, including advisory hearings, adoption proceedings, uncontested dependency proceedings, and disposition hearings."[166]

Mr. Culbertson was lead counsel on six significant trials in Maricopa County Superior Court: *State of Arizona v. Walker and Tapp.*[167] *State of Arizona v. Djerf.*[168] *State of Arizona v. Osborn.*[169] *State of Arizona v. Harrod.*[170] *State of Arizona v. Sansing.*[171] *State v. Grell.*[172]

Inaugural Graduates—1970 through 1976

MARTY HARPER, '73

Mr. Harper earned his BA degree at Gonzaga University in 1965. He graduated from the ASU College of Law, *magna cum laude,* in 1973. He joined Lewis and Roca[173] in 1973 and practiced there for twenty-four years. In 1997, Mr. Harper left Lewis and Roca and thereafter helped several firms, including Polsinelli, start and build full-service practices in Arizona.[174]

At the end of October 2013, Mr. Harper retired from Polsinelli.[175] In December 2013, he became President and CEO of the ASU Alumni Law Group. "The Law Group is a unique not-for-profit teaching law firm dedicated to training recent graduates of the Sandra Day O'Connor College of Law how to practice law well. In addition, the Law Group is dedicated to providing quality legal services to an underserved segment of the Arizona community who are in need of quality legal services but at a reduced rate. Throughout his legal career, Mr. Harper has been involved in building and managing law firms. At various times, he was a practice group leader, office managing partner and a member of various firm executive committees and boards of directors."[176]

Mr. Harper represented a wide range of entities in a diverse array of large complex civil litigation matters. He is an AV® peer reviewed litigator[177] who has been included in Best Lawyers in America[178] for his experience in Commercial Litigation, Construction and Labor and Employment Law, and most recently is recognized as a "bet the company" litigator.

"From 2008 through the spring of 2012, Mr. Harper was the chair of Mackrell International,[179] a leading network of international law firms. In his role as chairman, Mr. Harper had a dynamic impact on the shape of the organization, adding over 20 quality law firms to its membership during his tenure as chair. Mr. Harper's position required him to chair meetings around the globe, from Hanoi, Vietnam, to Budapest, Hungary, Charleston, South Carolina, Athens, Greece and Sydney, Australia."[180]

He was managing partner of the ASU Alumni Law Group from 2011 to 2020.

TERRANCE P. "TERRY" WOODS, '73

Terry Woods, as his family, friends, colleagues, clients, and classmates called him, was truly unique in that he had another, more formal title during most of his career; *General Woods*. He graduated from ASU Law in 1970. Most of the male students were at risk given that America was at war in Vietnam. Many of his fellow students became notable for one reason or another. Lawyer Woods became Brigadier General Woods. During his student years, he served in the United States Air Force as a navigator. He also served in the Arizona Air National Guard as a navigator and JAG officer. His last military posting was chief judge of the Arizona Court of Military Appeals, from 1997 to 2013.

He graduated from the University of Arizona in 1966 with a BA. He graduated *cum laude* with his JD from ASU College of Law in 1973. He is admitted to practice in all Arizona courts and the U.S. Court of Appeals for the Ninth Circuit. He is a longstanding member of the Maricopa County Bar Association, the Arizona Association of Defense Counsel, and the National High School Baseball Coaches Association.

Mr. Woods was a founding member of the Broening Oberg Woods & Wilson law firm. His practice with the firm is in civil litigation, defending insurance carriers, insureds and representing injured plaintiffs. He also represents licensed professionals in disciplinary and regulatory matters. He is profiled in Best Lawyers, Southwest Super Lawyers and has its highest possible rating (A/V) on Martindale-Hubbell.

In 2018, a national controversy arose over whether the military should be sent to the U.S. border with Mexico. President Trump said the military should treat migrants with rocks as if they were armed with rifles. In Arizona, military experts were consulted for public comment. Gen. Terrance P. Woods was an expert consultant for NBC's *Channel 12 News*. They asked him whether President Trump's comments on the military using force [on the Mexican border] would be legal. Gen. Woods answered in crisp military fashion.

I could give you a scenario under which it will be allowed, but I don't think those will be the rules of engagement... Force is not always allowed. A border agent went on trial earlier this year for shooting a migrant who threw a rock over the border fence, though the agent was eventually acquitted of second-degree murder. He is now facing manslaughter and involuntary manslaughter charges in a retrial. Obviously, there was no immediate threat to him or the border, but if a mob of 1,000 people were to storm the fence and it starts to bend, then that certainly justifies a lot more action. "If we have a horde of a 1,000 people armed with rocks and other weapons, who all want to come at once and knock over the fence, we could legally meet that with military force[.]" ... So, we can verify that if the caravan becomes violent trying to overrun the border, it would be legal for the military to fight back. But [I] don't see this scenario playing out. I think that was exaggerated political talk.

H. BARTOW FARR, III, '74

Bart Farr was the 1973 Armstrong Prize[181] winner at the ASU College of Law. He is the consummate Washington, DC lawyer specializing in cases before the U.S. Supreme Court. Mr. Farr graduated in 1996 with an AB degree in English from Princeton University.[182] He earned his JD degree, *summa cum laude*, from the ASU College of Law in 1973, ranked first in his class, and served as Editor-In-Chief of the Journal of Law and Social Order.[183] Following graduation, he clerked for U.S. Supreme Court Chief Justice William H. Rehnquist.[184]

His first job after his Supreme Court clerkship was as an assistant U.S. Solicitor General.[185] Then he became one of the founding partners in the DC firm of Onek, Klein, & Farr. He also worked in successor firms, Klein, Farr, Smith & Taranto, then Farr & Taranto, from 1981 to 2013. He works for Kirkland & Ellis[186] in their Washington, DC office.

Mr. Farr's bio page on his firm's website confirms his elite focusing on U.S. Supreme Court. He has argued thirty-two cases before the U.S. Supreme Court. His law firm lists nine of his most representative cases: "Pennhurst State School v. Haldeman (Eleventh Amendment immunity); Browning Ferris v. Kelco[187] (punitive damages); Masson v. New Yorker Magazine[188] (First Amendment); Turner Broadcasting System v. FCC[189] (First Amendment); -Bruce Allied Terminix v. Dobson[190] (arbitration); PGA Tour v. Martin[191] (Americans with Disabilities Act); Olympic Airways v. Husain[192] (Warsaw Convention); Long Island Care at Home v. Coke[193] (Fair Labor Standards Act); NFIB v. Sebelius[194] (Affordable Care Act/severability)." https://www.kirkland.com/lawyers/f/farr-bartow

He is recognized by Chambers USA[195] for appellate law. He is licensed to practice before the U.S. Supreme Court and the United States Courts of Appeal for the Fourth, Sixth, Eighth, Ninth, and the District of Columbia circuits.

HON. RUTH MCGREGOR, '74

It is daunting to define Ruth McGregor because she has so many firsts, a wall covered with awards, an incalculable number of fans, friends, family, clients, students, clerks, and colleagues in so many places. She has no known enemies, loves animals, climbs mountains in Africa, leads nonprofits, sits on boards, writes extensively, and knows the law the way America's most distinguished legal scholars do.

Her Arizona Court of Appeals bio defines her sequentially: [**Born** LeMars, Iowa, 1943] [**Education**: University of Iowa, BA 1964, MA 1965, Arizona State University, JD 1974, University of Virginia, LLM, 1998] [**Teacher**, Central High School, 1966–67] [**Teacher**, Selma, Alabama Public High School, 1968–1969] [**Lawyer**, Fennemore Craig, 1974–1981 and 1982–1989] [**Law Clerk**, Justice Sandra Day O'Connor 1981–1982] [**Judge**, Court of Appeals, 1989–1998] [**Justice**, Arizona Supreme Court, 1998 to 2010]. She did it all while raising the bar in every job. She was great in the pit of trial courtrooms, at podiums in appellate courtrooms, at the front of the classroom as a teacher, at the lectern in graduate schools, and from the bench, grilling lawyers for over twenty years.

Inaugural Graduates—1970 through 1976

CREDENTIALS

The [**blocks**] in the prior paragraph do not do justice to Chief Justice McGregor. They inform as much as they mislead because there is much more to say about her professional life. Justice McGregor received a bachelor of arts degree, *summa cum laude*, and a master of arts degree from the University of Iowa. She received her doctor of jurisprudence degree, *summa cum laude*, from Arizona State University in Tempe, Arizona, and a master of laws in judicial process from the University of Virginia. Her long list of involvement, leadership, and impact in groups focusing on legal education, the discipline of lawyers and judges, and in organizations dedicated to assuring a fair and impartial judiciary is astounding:

- Officer and a member of the Board of Trustees for the American Inns of Court Foundation
- Officer and Board member for the National Association of Women Judges
- Board member of the Conference of Chief Justices
- Member of the Legal Council of the American Bar Association Section of Legal Education and Admission to the Bar (the accrediting body for American law schools)
- Recognized for her professional work by the State Bar of Arizona, the Arizona Women Lawyers Association, the American Inns of Court Foundation, the American Judicature Society, the United States Chamber of Commerce, the Arizona Women's Foundation, the University of Iowa, and the Sandra Day O'Connor College of Law at Arizona State University
- Special Master to resolve disputes in the state and federal court systems and as a special mediator during the 2012 and 2013 Phoenix-area transportation strikes
- Adjunct law faculty, teaching courses related to domestic violence and human trafficking
- Member of the Board of Directors of the Center for the Future of Arizona
- Member of Board of Directors of Justice At Stake
- Section delegate for the ABA Section of Legal Education and Admission to the Bar
- Special Advisor to the O'Connor Judicial Selection Initiative of the Institute for the Advancement of the American Legal System

- Member of Board, China International Legal Affairs & Culture Exchange Center

She graduated from the ASU College of Law in 1974, first in her class and winner of the Armstrong Award, given by the faculty to the student with the highest grade average. She was one of the few women hired by large law firms in Phoenix in the early 1970s. She tried cases and argued appeals for Fennemore Craig from 1974 to 1989. She was U.S. Supreme Court Justice Sandra Day O'Connor's first law clerk in 1981.

Justice McGregor is famous because fifteen local and national organizations sought her out for leadership positions. In each position, her intellect and experience are evident of her impact on Arizona and American law, writ large: *Arizona State Bar Association;*[196] *Arizona Women Lawyers Association;*[197] *American Inns of Court Foundation.*[198] *American Judicature Society;*[199] *Arizona Foundation for Women;*[200] *ABA Section of Legal Education and Admission to the Bar;*[201] *Conference of Chief Justices;*[202] *Center for the Future of Arizona;*[203] *Justice at Stake;*[204] *Legal Council of the American Bar Association Section of Legal Education and Admission to the Bar* (the accrediting body for American law schools);[205] *United States Chamber of Commerce;*[206] *Institute for the Advancement of the American Legal System;*[207] *The O'Connor Justice Prize.*[208]

For lawyers and judges, the ultimate honor comes from peers and colleagues who recognize your efforts, accomplishments, and impact. This short sketch is woefully short, compared to Justice McGregor's illustrious career. Who could say it better than one of her lifelong friends, her mentor, and America's first woman U.S. Supreme Court Justice, Sandra Day O'Connor? She wrote a tribute to honor Ruth's long service to the State of Arizona. The *Arizona State Law Journal* published it.[209] The *Journal* asked many of her friends, colleagues and former clerks to submit text. It is worth quoting at some length.

"In her nearly twenty years as an Arizona judge, Ruth McGregor authored more than two hundred published opinions, as well as hundreds of unpublished ones. The Chief Justice was undoubtedly influenced by her experience clerking for Justice O'Connor, for her professional style is exemplified by her straightforwardness in analyzing and writing about legal issues . . . . At oral argument, her approach was direct and to the point; she focused on the central issues and dissuaded the parties (and sometimes her colleagues on the Court) from diverting attention elsewhere.

Many attorneys learned a tough lesson while arguing before Chief Justice McGregor: The Court would not be distracted by weak arguments. Although her inquiries were demanding, the Chief's demeanor was not; she was always professional, fair, and respectful to others. The Chief Justice's writing, meanwhile, exemplified the analytical skill and directness society seeks in a jurist. She clearly and concisely explains complex legal issues. Her opinions also demonstrate a deep respect for the rule of law, while recognizing the practical implications of the Court's decisions.[210]

"Through her many opinions, the Chief Justice has left an indelible mark on Arizona law. Her influence is evident from the various honors that Chief Justice McGregor has received for her outstanding achievements as a jurist. The American Judicature Society selected her to receive the 2005 Dwight D. Opperman Award, given annually to one state court judge in recognition of a career of distinguished judicial service. The Chief also received the Distinguished Alumnus Award from both the University of Iowa and the Sandra Day O'Connor College of Law at Arizona State University. She will travel to Washington, D.C. in October 2009, to receive the A. Sherman Christensen Award for her outstanding service to the American Inns of Court. But the greatest tributes to the Chief Justice's achievements as a jurist are the law students, attorneys, and judges who attempt to emulate her incomparable style.[211]

"Under Chief Justice McGregor's stewardship, Arizona's judicial system has made improvements that benefit the State of Arizona, its courts, and its citizens. Her tenure as Chief Justice has lived up to the overarching goal she set forth in her strategic agenda: to transform the court system from '*Good to Great*.' The Chief Justice outlined five goals that she pursued throughout her term: (1) provide access to swift and fair justice; (2) protect children, families, and the community; (3) make the judiciary more accountable; (4) improve communication and cooperation with the community; and (5) serve the public by improving the legal profession."[212]

Sandra Day O'Connor closed her piece with this: "She [CJ McGregor] is the embodiment of all those qualities of professionalism and leadership that I think are important. She brings to every task she undertakes a positive, up-beat attitude along with a top-notch intellect and great interpersonal skills, and Arizona is fortunate indeed to have this woman serving the State's highest court, and Arizona State University Law School must cherish her as a law school graduate without peer."[213]

ED PASTOR, '74

Congressman Ed Pastor was born in Claypool, Arizona, in 1943, earned his undergraduate degree at ASU in chemistry in 1966, and then spent the next three years teaching chemistry at North High School in Phoenix. He came back to ASU in 1971 as a first-year law student, graduated in 1974, and became Arizona's first Latino elected to the U.S. House of Representatives in 1991.[214] He served the people of Arizona for more than forty years as a member of the U.S. Congress and a member of the Board of Supervisors for Maricopa County. How he did that is a great story for him, ASU, and Arizona.

He was the deputy director of the community service group Guadalupe Organization, Inc. He was an assistant to Arizona Governor Raúl Héctor Castro.[215] In 1976, Mr. Pastor was elected to the Maricopa County Board of Supervisors; he served three terms in that role as a county executive. In 1991, he was a candidate in a special election to succeed retiring twenty-eight-year incumbent Democrat Mo Udall in the U.S. Congress. Mo Udall's 2nd District comprised the southwestern part of Arizona including parts of Phoenix and half of Tucson. He defeated his closest challenger, Tucson mayor Tom Volgy, by 1,800 votes.[216] He then won the special election a month later with 55 percent of the vote to become the first Latino to represent Arizona in Congress. He was reelected four times without substantive Republican opposition, never dropping below 60 percent of the vote.[217]

Congressman Pastor's official Wikipedia page is rich in political detail. "In 1991, Pastor entered a special election to succeed retiring 28-year incumbent Democrat Mo Udall in the 2nd District, which then comprised the southwestern part of Arizona including parts of Phoenix and half of Tucson. Pastor won a narrow victory, defeating his closest challenger, Tucson mayor Tom Volgy, by 1,800 votes. He then won the special election a month later with 55 percent of the vote to become the first Latino to represent Arizona in Congress. He was reelected four times without substantive Republican opposition, never dropping below 60% of the vote. His former territory was renumbered as the 7th District following the 2000 census, but his home in Phoenix was drawn into the newly created 4th District.

Inaugural Graduates—1970 through 1976

Rather than move to the Phoenix portion of the reconfigured 7th, he opted to run in the 4th. The newly created district was heavily Democratic and majority-Latino, with Democrats having a nearly 2-to-1 advantage in registration, similar to his old district. He was reelected six times against nominal Republican opposition."[218] He served in Arizona's 7th Congressional District from 2013–2015, when he retired from Congress, and was succeeded by Ruben Gallego.[219]

By any measure, he was the dean of Arizona's House delegation. He was the state's first Hispanic elected to congress . . . [he] set many milestones during his career . . . But while he acknowledges the gains Hispanics have made in the House, Pastor keeps his focus on the task at hand. "The fact is I am Hispanic, the fact is there is a lot of pride in the Hispanic community . . . . I join the enthusiasm . . . but as an elected official you represent the entire community."[220]

He retired from Congress in 2015, saying, "I've been in public office for 39 years and it's been a pleasure to serve the people of Arizona. After 23 years in Congress, I feel it's time for me to seek out a new endeavor. It's been a great honor, a great experience and a great joy for me to serve in Congress. I think it's time for me to do something else."[221] The state's largest newspaper, *The Arizona Republic*, covered the story. "Alfredo Gutierrez,[222] a former state lawmaker who grew up with Pastor in the eastern Arizona mining town of Miami, said he believes there is a strong likelihood that Pastor's Congressional District 7 will be represented by a Latino candidate. . . . Gutierrez said that, as a Congressman, Pastor was a powerful member of the House Appropriations Committee. He added that Pastor also was a strong supporter of immigration reform . . . Shortly after Pastor made his announcement, House Minority Leader Nancy Pelosi issued a statement praising Pastor and his work in Congress. 'Congressman Ed Pastor is a trailblazer who has dedicated his life to serving the families of Arizona. Throughout his four decades in public service and his 12 terms in Congress, Ed Pastor never forgot his roots, and always worked to build a brighter future for the children of our nation, championing key investments in education, infrastructure, and small businesses. . . . His insight and passion will be missed by friends and colleagues on both sides of the aisle, and we wish him, his wife Verma, and the rest of his beautiful family all the best in their next steps.'"[223]

Congressman Pastor died at age seventy-five on November 27, 2018. Arizona Gov. Doug Ducey called Pastor "an Arizona trailblazer and true public servant" and said he ordered that flags be lowered statewide to half-staff to recognize "the long-lasting impact he will leave on Arizona."[224]

BILL SANDWEG, '74

Bill Sandweg belongs to an elite group of Arizona lawyers. He is an inducted Fellow and former Regent in the American College of Trial Lawyers.[225] As of 2018, only ninety-five[226] of the 24,551 lawyers in Arizona[227] are ACTL Fellows.

Mr. Sandweg graduated from Georgetown University, *magna cum laude,* with a BS degree in 1966. He majored in international affairs at the School of Foreign Service.[228] He got his JD at ASU Law in 1974, *magma cum laude,* where he was a senior editor of the *Arizona State Law Journal.*

Between college and law school, he served as an officer in the U.S. Air Force, flying jets and serving as a jet fighter instructor. He is licensed to practice in all Arizona courts, the U.S. District Court for the District of Arizona, and the United States Court of Appeals for the Ninth Circuit. He is a trial lawyer. "Bill's practice focuses on representing people who have been seriously injured or have lost loved ones as a result of medical malpractice and other negligent conduct."[229]

He also is an invited member of the American Board of Trial Advocates;[230] an Adjunct Professor of law at Arizona State University College of Law;[231] Arizona's Finest Lawyers;[232] Best Lawyers in America;[233] Maricopa County Superior Court, Judge Pro Tempore; Southwest Super Lawyers.[234]

Like all other ASU Law notable alumni profiled in this book, Bill Sandweg has a hard-earned reputation. His website defines it in terms everyone can understand: "A Reputation for Success—Over $100 Million in Verdicts and Settlements Recovered for Our Clients."[235]

HON. BARRY G. SILVERMAN, '76

Let us count the courts. First, Maricopa County Court Commissioner—1979 to 1984; second, Maricopa County Superior Court Judge—1984 to 1995; Third, United States Magistrate Judge—District of Arizona—1995 to 1997; Fourth, Appellate Judge—United States Court of Appeals for the Ninth Circuit—1997 to the present. Forty-one years and counting. On the bench, as a new judge, a seasoned judge, and now as senior status judge, he will always be an Article III judge. Always sticking his nose into other people's business. And at every level, Arizona lawyers knew they'd get a fair trial or hearing in his court, win or lose. We all knew he followed an old proverb: "A good judge conceives quickly, judges slowly."[236] He never played favorites, loose, or off the record.

Judge Silverman is and always was a "public citizen." He was educated in public schools, colleges, and universities. He's always worked in the public sector. A private citizen is, in general, a regular citizen, acting in the public interest. People become "public citizens" or "public servants" by publicly taking an oath to serve the greater good of the nation and the public or by accepting money from the public funds, paid out explicitly in the form of salary.[237] His first job out of law school was as a prosecutor for the City of Phoenix from 1976 until 1977. He joined the Maricopa County Attorney's Office as a line prosecutor from 1977 until 1979. He served as a Maricopa County Superior Court commissioner from 1979 until 1984. Arizona Governor Bruce Babbitt appointed him as a Maricopa County Superior Court judge in 1984. He was on that bench until 1995, when he was appointed a United States magistrate judge in Phoenix. President Bill Clinton nominated him on November 8, 1997, to a seat on the United States Court of Appeals for the Ninth Circuit vacated by Judge William Canby. He was confirmed by the United States Senate on January 28, 1998, and received his commission on February 4, 1998. Silverman, a registered Democrat, enjoyed bipartisan support, with backing from Republican Senator Jon Kyl, a key member of the Senate Judiciary Committee, and Senator John McCain.[238]

At all four levels of government, municipal, county, state and federal, he took oaths of office. All are substantially similar to the first oath he took, as a licensed lawyer in Arizona. At every level, he met his obligation "to employ for the purposes of maintaining causes confided to him such means only as are consistent with truth, and never seek to mislead the judges by any artifice or false statement of fact or law."[239] And it is certain he never forgot the lawyer's and judge's special obligation: "As a public citizen, a lawyer should seek improvement of the law, access to the legal system, the administration of justice and the quality of service rendered."[240] As a judge, he assumed additional obligations to the public. First, and foremost, he must meet a high standard. "The United States legal system is based upon the principle that an independent, impartial, and competent judiciary, composed of men and women of integrity, will interpret and apply the law that governs our society. Thus, the judiciary plays a central role in preserving the principles of justice and the rule of law."[241]

The Sandra Day O'Connor College of Law has produced a wealth of judicial officers over the last fifty years. Some were students, others faculty. Judge Silverman served during the judicial careers of seventeen other ASU Law graduates: Judge Bridget Shelton Bade, Judge William Canby, Justice Rebecca White, Judge Tina Campbell, Judge Charles Case, Judge Michael Hawkins, Judge Diane Humetewa, Justice John Lopez IV, Justice Clint Bolick, Justice Ruth McGregor, Judge Gloria Navarro, Judge Douglas Rayes, Justice Michael Ryan, Judge Alan Soto, Judge Roslyn Silver, Justice Ann Timmer, and Justice Jered Tufte.

Like each of his fellow ASU graduates, and his school's namesake, he has brought honor to their alma mater. Judge Silverman attended Phoenix's Central High School in the late 1960s. He earned his bachelor of arts degree, *summa cum laude*, from Arizona State University in 1973 and his juris doctor from the Arizona State University College of Law in 1976.

One way to think about him is to remember he was always a funny guy in a serious job. At least by the mid-1970s, every Maricopa County trial lawyer knew Judge Silverman had a great sense of humor. When handling a routine Monday morning arraignment calendar, he took pleas and assigned public defenders as necessary. As the judge called out their names, the manacled defendants in the orange jumpsuits arose. Some had lawyers in the back of the courtroom. One by one, he asked each defendant to stand. When they did, he read the charges and asked the routine question, "Are you represented by counsel?" One defendant stood up and said, "I am, your Honor. The Lord Jesus is my savior and my counsel." "Thank you sir," Judge Silverman said, "but I meant local counsel."[242]

He used humor as an asset. In 2007, he caught the attention of journalist Jill Redgage, then a reporter for the *East Valley Tribune*. She said, "Jokes tumble from Barry Silverman's mouth like children onto a playground. 'You know they say the definition of a lawyer is a Jewish boy who can't stand the sight of blood.'"[243] At ASU Law, he did freelancing for magazines, hosted a Sunday morning radio show, and later wrote a humor column for the *Arizona Attorney* magazine. Ms. Redgage reported on something he said about his nomination as a Democrat for the Ninth

Circuit job but supported by a Republican Senate. "'I guess they were looking for a registered Democrat that the Republicans would be able to stomach. . . . It just sort of fell in my lap, really.' A massive workload followed."

He also received a "Dishonorable Mention" for his entry in the 1988 Bulwer-Lytton Fiction Contest, a San Jose State University bad writing contest inspired by the author of the now infamous opening sentence, "It was a dark and stormy night . . . ."[244]

Writing for the majority in a 2005 decision, Judge Silverman summarized the dispute. "Defendant Michael Kremer was dissatisfied with the hair restoration services provided to him by the Bosley Medical Institute, Inc. In a bald-faced effort to get even . . . ." Who said judges could not pun their way to justice? Judge Silverman was kind to the defendant, but said he was "splitting hairs."[245] In a 2006 opinion, he said, "The Tillamook County Creamery Association, the maker of the Tillamook brand of cheese for nearly a hundred years, has a beef with a company called Tillamook Country Smoker, a purveyor of smoked meats and jerky."[246] He called the appellants the "cheese folks" and the appellees the "meat people."[247]

His Bloomberg page[248] confirms his non-judicial likes and memberships: Ring 55 of the Intl Brotherhood of Magicians;[249] the Psychic Entertainers Assn;[250] the American Association of Law Libraries;[251] the Gender Bias Task Force;[252] and the Society of American Magicians.[253]

In 1969, for a high school project, he learned about the 1966 landmark case, *Miranda v. Arizona*.[254] His interest inspired him to meet Miranda, whom he interviewed in jail. He told Ms. Redgage his parents "were a little bit horrified that I befriended Ernesto Miranda, a world-class rapist. . . . They were afraid I was going to bring him over to the house or something, which I never did."[255] He wrote a draft manuscript, which got to the "development stage" of a television movie and appeared in a feature 2006 story in *Phoenix Magazine*.

In his *Phoenix Magazine* story, he said Miranda was "A problem student in school . . . Ernie barely completed the eighth grade in 1955, a year that marked an important milestone in the young Miranda's life: his first felony arrest . . . Silverman, now a judge on the U.S. Court of Appeals for the 9th Circuit, interviewed Miranda several times and wrote an unpublished biography on the young inmate. In one of the meetings, Miranda said he would have preferred to remain at Leavenworth because it had a better library, but he was transferred to the Federal Correctional Institution at Lompoc, California. On the day before he was released, some friends visited Miranda . . . As he waved goodbye to them, the electric gate slammed shut, chopping off the top one-third of his right index finger.[256]

"He wrote about Miranda's legacy. While the inmates of Cellblock 2 were watching a police show, they heard a cop order his partner to read the 'Miranda rights' to a just-arrested car thief. Ernie told me that the entire cellblock burst into spontaneous applause. Although 'something of a celebrity in prison,' he was not universally liked . . . Rapists and child molesters often are singled out for ridicule and harassment, or worse."[257]

On the Ninth Circuit, he is known for writing the dissenting opinion for the 2-1 ruling in May 2002 that overturned a Sacramento federal district court's decision barring male prisoners the constitutional right to procreate and mail their sperm from jail.[258] Judge Silverman's dissent notes, "This is a seminal case in more ways than one. . . . With the upmost respect," he said complacently, "the majority's reading of the Constitution is as unprecedented as it is ill-conceived."[259] Giving the devil his due, Judge Silverman conceded that it was "true that the Eighth Amendment protects [prisoners] against forced surgical sterilization [citation omitted]. All of that, however, is a far cry from holding that inmates retain a constitutional right to procreate from prison via FedEx."[260] He proves in most of his opinions that humor is not a lost art in the judiciary.

Arguably, his biggest gift as a judge is his writing. He is not god-like, but he writes from on high, in a crisp hand, with Swiss-diamond clarity, and with the humor that made him famous as a lawyer and judge in Maricopa County. A serious man with a twinkle in his eye, Barry writes like few other circuit judges, all of whom are but one rung short on the ladder to the U.S. Supreme Court. He enjoys a well-deserved reputation for being right on the law most the time (unless you are on the losing side of the case). But it's that twinkle that most of us like in Barry's writing.[261]

Over the eighteen years he spent as a full-time appellate judge on the Ninth Circuit, he co-authored 189 opinions and sat on 1,218 oral arguments to the Court.[262] A simple LexisNexis Advance search run on June 26, 2019 identifies his name in 143 secondary articles, such as law reviews, op-ed pieces, and legal articles. At the risk of making an old friend smile, Judge Silverman's large body of work on the bench might be described thusly: "Jurisprudence, noun, the kind of prudence that keeps one inside the law."[263]

Inaugural Graduates—1970 through 1976

WILLIAM F. ATKIN, '75

Mr. Atkin is a proud and very productive member of the *J. Reuben Clark Law Society*.[264] In 2010, he won the *Franklin S. Richards Pro Bono Community Service Award*.[265] The citation read, "To an individual who has used his time, professional skills, experience, and leadership to enrich his community with positive, religious-anchored professional service." He is Associate General Counsel for The Church of Jesus Christ of Latter-day Saints and is responsible for the international legal affairs of the Church.

He grew up in Prescott, Arizona, just two hours away from ASU's Tempe campus, and planned to return to practice law after graduating *magna cum laude* in 1975. One of his professors, Dale Furnish,[266] gave him good advice in law school: "You can always go from New York City to Prescott, but you'll never be able to go from Prescott to New York City." Following that advice, Atkin spent three years with the U.S. Department of Justice, where he had major responsibilities in several antidumping actions, and international tariff cases.

He earned his BA degree from Bringham Young University in 1972. He received his JD from the ASU College of Law in 1975, *magna cum laude,* where he was Editor-in-Chief of the *Arizona State Law Journal.* He earned his LLM from Columbia University College of Law in 1979, with an emphasis on international and comparative law.

After law school, he clerked for Chief Judge David T. Lewis,[267] on the U.S. Court of Appeals for the Tenth Circuit. His first job was as a trial lawyer with the civil division of the U.S. Justice Department from 1976 to 1979, primarily representing the government in the Court of International Trade.

As a partner in the global firm of Baker & McKenzie[268]—the first law firm to employ 1,000 lawyers—Atkin did tours of duty in Caracas, Taipei, and Moscow. He learned to speak Spanish and Russian and taught at Moscow International University.[269] He spent seventeen years at Baker & McKenzie (1979 to 1996) and has been associate general counsel for the LDS Church since 1996. He specializes in international law, aiding the international mission of the Mormon Church.

While at Baker & McKenzie, he served as managing partner in Moscow, and as a founding member of the Board of Directors of the *American Chamber of Commerce in Moscow*.

In addition to the Franklin S. Richards Pro Bono Community Service Award, "he and his wife served as welfare service missionaries for Salt Lake's 'Inner City Project.' In that capacity, Bill worked closely with indigent people to address their legal and other temporal needs. After his welfare service mission, Bill was instrumental in establishing the framework for the [J. Ruben Clark] Society to provide legal services through the Inner City Project and to expand the existing program in the Salt Lake area. Bill then developed the Legal Guidelines for the J. Reuben Clark Law Society to be used to expand the Society's pro bono program beyond the Salt Lake Chapter. In addition, Bill has assisted those working with the Spanish-speaking community to address legal issues of common concern."[270]

Mr. Atkin's tribute page in Dean Berman's 2009–2010 Report captures the man's thirst for knowledge, a global life, and doing everything his way. "Bill Atkin didn't go to law school with the intent to see the world, but that's how things turned out." His response was pitch-perfect: "Seeing the world proved I didn't miss out by going to the law school closest to home. Other attorneys may be smarter than I am, but no one has a better legal education."

MICHAEL G. BAILEY, '75

Michael G. Bailey is the U.S. Attorney for the District of Arizona. On February 12, 2019, his nomination was sent to the United States Senate. Arizona Senator Martha McSally voiced her support of his nomination.[271] On May 2, 2019, his nomination was reported out of committee by voice vote. On May 24, 2019, Bailey's nomination was unanimously confirmed by the United States Senate.[272]

Mr. Bailey earned his BA degree from Westmont College[273] in 1987 and his JD from Arizona State University College of Law in 1990. He was a Maricopa County prosecutor and the chief deputy and chief of staff at the Arizona General's office from 2015 to 2019.[274]

Inaugural Graduates—1970 through 1976

HON. CHARLES G. CASE, JR., '75

Judge Charles G. Case, II, was a U.S. bankruptcy judge from 1994 to 2013.[275] Federal bankruptcy judges are judicial officers of a United States district court. He was appointed by the majority of judges of the U.S. Court of Appeals for the Ninth Circuit on January 5, 1994, and reappointed on January 5, 2009.

He graduated *cum laude* from Harvard University and earned a BA degree in 1969. In 1975, he took his juris doctorate, *magna cum laude*, from ASU College of Law. From 1975 to 1988, he practiced law with Lewis & Roca in Phoenix, Arizona.[276] He moved to the Phoenix firm of Meyer, Hendricks, Victor, Osborn & Maledon in 1988, where he concentrated on bankruptcy, Chapter 11 reorganizations, secured transactions, and commercial litigation.[277]

Judge Case is an invited member of six prestigious organizations: (1) American College of Bankruptcy;[278] (2) American Law Institute;[279] (3) International Insolvency Institute;[280] (4) International Exchange of Experience in Insolvency;[281] (5) American Bankruptcy Institute;[282] (5) National Conference of Bankruptcy Judges;[283] (6) Harvard Alumni Association.[284]

HON. JAMES ALAN SOTO, '75

Judge James Alan Soto is an Article III judge sitting on the U.S. District Court for the District of Arizona in Tucson, Arizona. "On December 19, 2013, President Obama nominated him to serve as a United States District Judge for the District of Arizona, to the seat vacated by Judge David C. Bury, who took senior status on December 31, 2012. On February 27 2014 his nomination was reported out of the committee. On May 13, 2014, Senate Majority Leader Harry Reid filed for cloture on his nomination. On May 15, 2014, The Senate voted 61–35 on the motion to invoke cloture on his nomination. Later that same day, the Senate voted 95–1 in favor of final confirmation. He received his judicial commission on June 9, 2014."[285]

Judge Soto earned his BS degree at ASU in 1971 and his JD from the ASU College of Law in 1975. He was a lawyer in the office of Nasib Karam from 1975 to 1976. From 1976 to 1979, he was a solo practitioner. From 1979 to 1992, he was associated with various law firms in Nogales, Arizona. From 1992 to 2001, he was a shareholder of Soto, Martin and Coogan, P.C.[286]

He served in the Arizona National Guard from 1971 to 1977.[287] Concurrently with his private practice, he held a number of public positions. "From 1975 to 1983, he worked as a part-time Deputy City Attorney in the Office of the Nogales City Attorney. He worked as a part-time Town Attorney in Patagonia, Arizona in from 1975 to 1992. He worked as a part-time Deputy County Attorney for the Santa Cruz County Attorney's Office in 1979. From 2001 to 2014, Soto served on the Superior Court in Santa Cruz County, where he also served as Presiding Superior Court Judge. Soto was elected to the bench as a Democrat."[288] Judge Soto was honored many times and was a member of several state and county entities.[289]

He is well known in Arizona for his courage as a judge and his sense of place and order. His most controversial case is a constant reminder of solid jurisprudence and indisputably fair rulings. The case involved a border shooting by a Customs & Border Patrol officer who shot a man named Jesus Castro Romo. He ordered the U.S. government on Friday to pay nearly $500,000 to Jesus Castro Romo, an undocumented migrant from Mexico who was shot and wounded by a Border Patrol agent on Nov. 16, 2010.[290]

"Government attorneys had argued that the shooting was justified because the former agent, Abel Canales, testified that Castro Romo was about to throw a rock when he shot him. . . Canales' credibility was undercut by the fact that he was convicted, in a separate case, of accepting bribes from drug dealers to let them run loads through his checkpoint. Canales' version of events also changed over time; initially, he'd told officials that he did not see Castro Romo pick up a rock just before he shot him. Soto found Castro Romo's testimony more credible. The judge found that he was not in the motion of throwing a rock at Canales, and that Canales' use of force was not justified or reasonable. In his ruling, Soto said that Canales committed an intentional battery against Castro. More broadly, Soto ruled that the possibility someone confronting an agent may have a rock in hand, 'as opposed to a much more lethal weapon, such as a gun, requires a greater level of certainty before deadly force can be justified as reasonable'. . . . Put more bluntly, the judge wrote, 'a rock is not as deadly an object as a gun and requires a greater degree of certainty that the object will be used than the threat or perceived threat of a gun.'"[291]

TERRY GODDARD, '76

Terry Goddard,[292] while at ASU Law in 1975, served an internship with the Arizona Attorney General's office. Three decades later, he was elected Arizona's twenty-fourth Attorney General.[293] Today, he is a member of Dentons'[294] public policy practice. As measured by the number of active lawyers, Dentons is the world's largest law firm.

He graduated from Harvard College in 1969 and from ASU College of Law in 1976. He served an active-duty tour in the U.S. Navy from 1970 to 1972, and was in the U.S. Navy Reserves for the next twenty-eight years, retiring in 1998 with the rank of Commander. He served as Mayor of Phoenix from 1984 to 1990, on the Central Arizona Water Conservation District board from 2001 to 2003.

His tribute page in the Sandra Day O'Connor College of Law's 2009–2010 Report validates what everyone who knows him thinks: He's spent his life in the law and has a unique vantage point to see what the law school has done for the Phoenix metropolitan area—"it kept talent in town." That was no small feat and Terry Goddard was in the middle of all of it. Since 2003, "Goddard has used his significant state power to fight cybercrime, identify theft, predatory lenders, consumer fraud, illegal drugs, and deceptive advertisers . . . he has served four terms as mayor, expanded and modernized the city's law enforcement, and set up nationally recognized programs in economic development, the arts, and historic preservation. The *National Leagues of Cities* elected him as President in 1989. City & County Magazine named 'Municipal Leader of the Year.' He also served seven years as Arizona Director for the US Department of Housing and Urban Development."[295]

His Dentons profile explains why the world's largest law firm invited him to join them. "Terry has a plethora of practical experience in the planning and management of major urban economic development programs, including the areas what it takes to achieve 'livability' in an urban context."

While urban development and water management are high on his skill set, it was his lawyering skills while serving multiple terms as Attorney General that makes ASU proud to claim him. Among many wins, his hallmark accomplishment as AG was the historic 2010 settlement with Western Union[296] over wire transfers involving smuggled human beings.[297] Western Union paid $94 million to settle a long-running battle with Arizona over whether the company "turned a blind eye to the use of its services in border-related crime. The company also agreed to provide border state prosecutors access to wire transfer records, something the company had resisted, but Arizona officials considered crucial to their cases."[298]

No one knows exactly how many ASU Law School graduates use their lawyering skills to better the lives and livelihoods of people in the cities, towns and states where they practice law. It is a safe bet that Terry Goddard's name would be on the top of most lists.

MICHAEL GRANT, '76

Michael Murray Grant received his bachelor's degree in English from Arizona State University in 1973 and his juris doctorate from ASU Law in 1976. He was there the year Dean Willard Pedrick stepped down from his deanship. His wiki page (2018) notes that "[h]e currently practices telecommunications and public utility law at Gallagher and Kennedy, PA,[299] in Phoenix."[300] While he still lives in Phoenix, he is retired from the practice of law.[301]

He worked in Arizona radio both as a disc jockey and an investigative reporter, most notably for KOY-AM.[302] Grant was widely known and admired for his TV weekly show, *Horizon*,[303] for a quarter century. His career-long affiliation with Arizona PBS and Arizona television began when he covered Sandra Day O'Connor's Senate confirmation[304] for KAET Channel 8 and PBS. He was a master interviewer and a solid voice on TV and radio. After Justice O'Connor's hearings, he was asked by KAET producers to start a new daily discussion show. "The special Friday edition was to be modeled after *Washington Week in Review*. Known as the roundtable discussion, local journalists would review the week's top news stories in an informal,

Inaugural Graduates—1970 through 1976

conversational format. Monday through Thursday's shows would focus on interviews with subjects close to a particular newsworthy event or issue."[305] There is no data confirming how many interviews he conducted in his twenty-five years on *Horizon*. Even so, it is surely the case that almost every noteworthy Arizonan made it to his show at least once.[306]

AMBASSADOR BARBARA BARRETT, '78

Ambassador Barrett is a 1978 graduate of the Sandra Day O'Connor College of Law. Without question, she is one of Arizona's most distinguished residents and one of Arizona State University's most accomplished and prestigious graduates. She has a stellar national and international reputation. Her bio at the Smithsonian Institute describes her in educational, business, civic, national, international, government, private sector, public sector, aeronautical, astronautical, legal, corporate executive, and leadership roles. She has dozens of biographical sketches on the internet. Her listing as a longtime member of the Smithsonian Board of Regents[307] is illustrative.

Biography: Barbara Barrett of Paradise Valley, Arizona, is CEO of Triple Creek Guest Ranch in Montana and serves on the boards of RAND, Sally Ride Science, and Aerospace corporations; the Horatio Alger Association; and the Lasker and Space foundations. Previously, she was Interim President of the Thunderbird School of Global Management, U.S. Ambassador to Finland, Senior Advisor to the U.S. Mission to the United Nations, CEO of the American Management Association, a teaching fellow at Harvard's Kennedy School, a partner in a large Phoenix law firm, and a member of the boards of Raytheon, Exponent, Piper Aircraft, Mayo Clinic, Hershey School and Trust, and Harvard's Institute of Politics. During the Reagan Administration, she served as the Deputy Administrator of the Federal Aviation Administration and Vice Chairman of the Civil Aeronautics Board. She was President of the International Women's Forum, Chairman of the Secretary of Commerce's Export Conference, and Chairman of the U.S. Advisory Commission on Public Diplomacy. Ambassador Barrett

participates with the Global Leadership Foundation, Club of Madrid, World Economic Forum, and Council on Foreign Relations. She is an instrument-rated pilot and certified astronaut. Barrett has a connection to the Smithsonian dating to the 1980s when she was a member of the National Air and Space Museum Board; she served on the Smithsonian National Board for most of the last decade and co-founded Smithsonian Gemstone Collectors in 2010. At the Smithsonian, she served on Advancement, Audit and Review, Compensation and Human Resources Committees.

Her long list of achievement and success in law, finance, education, aerospace, government, public service, and goodwill is stunning by any measure.

AERONAUTICAL AND AEROSPACE

She serves on the boards of RAND, Sally Ride Science, and Aerospace. *RAND Corporation* is an American nonprofit global policy think tank created in 1948 by Douglas Aircraft Company to offer research and analysis to the United States Armed Forces.[308] *Sally Ride Science* at UC San Diego is a nonprofit organization run by the University of California, San Diego. Sally Ride, America's first woman in space, founded it as a company in 2001.[309] The *Aerospace Corporation* is a California nonprofit corporation that operates a federally funded research and development center headquartered in El Segundo, California. It provides technical guidance and advice on all aspects of space missions to military, civil, and commercial customers.[310]

She is a distinguished lawyer, but that is not why she sits on so many aeronautical and astronautical boards. An instrument-rated pilot, Barrett was the first civilian woman to land in an F/A-18 Hornet on an aircraft carrier. The *Arizona Aviation Hall of Fame*[311] inducted her as a member in *2014*. She received the *Worcester Polytechnic Institute Presidential Medal*[312] from President Laurie Leshin.[313] She has trained as an astronaut, and was the backup spaceflight participant for the Soyuz TMA-16 flight to the International Space Station. Barrett was also deputy administrator of the *Federal Aviation Administration*[314] and vice chairman of the *U.S. Civil Aeronautics Board*.[315,316] And she "was reportedly the first civilian woman to land in an F/A-18 on an aircraft carrier. In 2009, she trained at the Gagarin Cosmonaut Training

Center, in Star City, Russia, and at the Baikonur Cosmodrome, in Kazakhstan, culminating in certification for spaceflight."[317]

In addition to the boards mentioned in her Smithsonian Institute bio, her *Wikipedia Page*[318] confirms, "she was the founding chair of the *Valley Bank of Arizona*,[319] a partner in a large Phoenix law firm and, before she was 30, an executive of two global Fortune 500 companies. In her community, Barrett was chair of the *Arizona District Export Council*,[320] *World Affairs Council*,[321] and *Economic Club of Phoenix*.[322] She also served on the boards of *Space Foundation*,[323] *Milton Hershey School*,[324] and *Hershey Trust Company*,[325] *Mayo Clinic*,[326] *Exponent Corporation*,[327] *Raytheon*,[328] and *Piper Aircraft*."[329]

EDUCATION AND ACADEMICS

She earned three degrees at ASU, and was honored with graduate degrees at six other universities.[330] She is a JFK Fellow, teaching leadership at Harvard University's *John F. Kennedy School of Government*.[331] In 2012 Barrett was interim president of *Thunderbird School of Global Management*,[332] now a unit of the *Arizona State University Knowledge Enterprise*.[333] She was CEO of the *American Management Association*.[334] As a member of the *U.S.-Afghan Women's Council*,[335] she founded *Project Artemis*, a program to train and mentor Afghan women entrepreneurs at Thunderbird.[336]

In 2000, Arizona State University renamed its Honors College "*The Craig and Barbara Barrett Honors College*"[337] or *Barrett, The Honors College* in recognition of Barbara and her husband, the then-CEO of Intel, Craig Barrett.[338]

GOVERNMENT SERVICE

In 1994, she was the first female Republican candidate for Governor of Arizona. She ran in the Republican primary against incumbent Governor Fife Symington, but failed to win her party's nomination.[339]

She was nominated by President George W. Bush on March 13, 2008, and unanimously confirmed by the United States Senate on April 29, 2008, to serve as *U.S. Ambassador Extraordinary and Plenipotentiary to the Republic of Finland*.[340] She was also a senior advisor to the *U.S. Mission to United Nations*.[341] While serving in

Helsinki, she bicycled 900 kilometers throughout the country. A year before moving to her diplomatic post in Finland, she climbed *Mt. Kilimanjaro*[342] in Africa.[343]

In May 2019, President Trump announced he would appoint her to be the next Secretary of the Air Force. "Mr. Trump announced Mrs. Barrett as his pick via Twitter on Tuesday, saying the former head of the Aerospace Corporation who also served as the deputy administrator for the Federal Aviation Administration will be an 'outstanding secretary!'"[344] The Secretary of the Air Force (SecAF, or SAF/OS) is the head of the Department of the Air Force, a military department within the United States Department of Defense. The Secretary is a civilian appointed by the President, by and with the advice and consent of the Senate. The Secretary reports to the Secretary of Defense and/or the Deputy Secretary of Defense, and is by statute responsible for and has the authority to conduct all the affairs of the Department of the Air Force.[345] The U.S. Senate confirmed her appointment to Secretary of the Air Force by a vote of 85 to 7 on October 16, 2019.[346] She was sworn in at the Pentagon on October 18, 2019, tweeting, "I'm conscious of the extraordinary privilege of working with the men & women of the @usairforce," she said in the tweet with her video. "We've got a lot to do & I'm ready to get to work!"[347]

AWARDS & RECOGNITION

Her wiki page[348] lists some of her Arizona and national awards: (1) Administrator's Award for Distinguished Service by the FAA; (2) Office of the Secretary of Defense Medal for Exceptional Public Service; (3) *Horatio Alger Award for Distinguished Americans*;[349] (4) *Woodrow Wilson Award for Corporate Citizenship*;[350] and (5) *Sandra Day O'Connor Board Excellence Award*.[351]

Barrett not only wins important American awards, she is active in entities that make awards. She is a member of the board of directors of the Lasker Foundation. The Lasker Awards have been awarded annually since 1945 to living persons who have contributed to medical science or who have performed public service on behalf of medicine. The Lasker Foundation, founded by Albert Lasker and his wife Mary Woodard Lasker, administers them. The awards are sometimes called "America's Nobels." Lasker Award has gained a reputation for identifying future winners of the Nobel Prize. Eighty-six Lasker laureates have received the Nobel Prize, including thirty-two in the last two decades.[352]

Inaugural Graduates—1970 through 1976

In 2008, Barrett was honored by the Arizona Historical League as its *"2008—Arizona Historymaker.™"* They aptly titled her videotaped Oral History as *"Arizona's Renaissance Woman."*[353] Barret responded to many questions that reveal the personal side of her life, and her journey from Pennsylvania to Arizona.

"I was born in Pennsylvania during a blizzard on Christmas evening and morning after Christmas. The doctor couldn't get there, so I was born at home. I grew up in southwestern Pennsylvania. My father considered himself an Arizonan . . . My father had been a cowboy in Arizona when he was young. He joined the service in Prescott, Arizona. He was hurt during the war. They put him in the hospital in Pennsylvania, which is where he met my mother. They married, settled down and raised six kids. He raised us telling us the great stories about Arizona . . . My father had grown up on a farm; he was a cattleman from birth, but Arizona was in his heart. He said he'd seen too many Westerns [movies], but he wanted to go see this place called Arizona. He rode the rails to come to Arizona when he was sixteen; ran away from home and came out West to be a cowboy."[354]

She came west at eighteen to attend Arizona State University in 1968. "When the time came to get serious about [college], I was a junior in high school . . . I took a look at the American College Dictionary which was on our shelves. In the back were listed all the colleges and they were listed in alphabetical order. My father's affection for Arizona and the alphabetical order listing of colleges had me strike upon the idea of going to Arizona to go to college; a combination of two things that my father had felt were both important . . . I [decided] to go to Arizona State University, though I'd never been West of Aliquippa, Pennsylvania at that time. I chose Arizona State University from the beauty of its catalog. Not the most scientific of reasons. But I was destined to come to Arizona."[355]

She explained how 1968 Arizona stirred her interest in government, public service, and her first interactions with Sandra Day O'Connor: "Well, I was a math major. I had scored very high on math exams . . . But when I got onto campus and was working at the state legislature, I also took a great interest in the political things that were going on. I ended up changing to Political Science, but I received a Bachelor of Science in Liberal Arts. I worked with state, county and municipal affairs committees in the Senate, which was chaired by Majority Leader Sandra Day O'Connor. It was an extraordinary privilege to work with and see in action such a wonderful woman, leader, Republican, jurist, and Arizonan."

Barrett's three years at the ASU College of Law were formative years. "I came back from Prescott and my life changed dramatically. I found a place to live by house-sitting on a ranch in Northern Scottsdale . . . I had a place to live that was free, caring for a small ranch for wonderful people who owned that ranch and several other properties around the country. I'd go to law school in the mornings, go downtown and work at law firms, or eventually at the Greyhound Corporation, which was head quartered here at the time. And then take care of the ranch at night . . . The first year was a very intense year that I enjoyed. I enjoyed new friends and a great challenge of studying law . . . I studied law out of defense."

Barrett has a worldview that grew over time once she got her law license. "I enjoyed very much first clerking at Greyhound and then serving as a lawyer on that floor. I did a lot of the international law, which was an extraordinary privilege. Greyhound Corporation had about two hundred subsidiaries all over the world. I had the privilege of doing a lot of that legal work. The lead lawyer for international law was Herb Nelson and he would travel all over the world. I was at home doing the research work and laying out some of the groundwork while he was negotiating contracts and agreements all over the world. Through his eyes, I had the privilege of working on legal issues in every corner of the globe . . . That was a huge exposure, and a stepping-stone to a lot of the international work that I've been doing since then."[356]

Her federal government work started when she quit practicing law with the Greyhound Corporation. "After practicing law in the corporate setting, I was asked to go back and be part of the Reagan administration in Washington, D.C. I was nominated by the President, confirmed by the Senate, sworn in, and became Vice Chairman of the five member Civil Aeronautics Board."

Barrett has a long history of involvement in higher education. She talked at length about that in her Oral History interview. "Education has always been a topic of great interest to me; as it was a high priority for my Arizona cowboy father, it is for his daughter. I consider education the ticket to opportunity. Naturally, I support educational institutions now and will in the future. Arizona State University was why I came here."

She is the proud recipient of the Horatio Alger Award.[357] "The *Horatio Alger Association* has a long history, a 60-year history of recognizing people who have come from humble means to achieve extraordinary success. That's what the award recognizes. What the association does that is most fulfilling is granting scholarships.

It seems that it's the largest provider of needs-based scholarships in America. It raises money to grant scholarships to young people who have faced severe adversity. I received the Horatio Alger Award in 1999. . . [the award ceremony] is an elaborate banquet. [in] the Chambers of the United States Supreme Court . . . for the Horatio Alger Association, the ten or so recipients of that award each year are brought into the courtroom itself. Justice Clarence Thomas draped a medal over my neck as though I were an Olympian, and spoke warmly and quite knowingly about the challenges that youth can involve. It was an unusual award because of the colleagues, the challenges, the pageantry, but most of all, because of the return to the students that received scholarships as a result of this recognition."[358]

HON. DOUGLAS L. RAYES, '78

Judge Douglas L. Rayes graduated from ASU with a BS in engineering, *summa cum laude*, in 1975, and from ASU's College of Law, JD, *cum laude*, in 1978. He joined the U.S. Army's Judge Advocate General Corps in 1979 and served until 1982. He graduated from the Army JAG School as a distinguished military graduate. He was assigned to the Third Armored Division in Frankfurt, Germany, where he prosecuted and later defended military personnel charged with major felonies before military jury panels.

He was an active trial lawyer in private practice from 1982 until 2000. For most of that period, he was a partner in the firm of McGroder, Tryon, Heller & Rayes, which later became Tryon, Heller & Rayes. His practice primarily involved personal injury and medical malpractice matters. He tried cases in many counties of Arizona and in New Mexico.[359]

In March 2000, Governor Jane Dee Hull[360] appointed him to the Maricopa County Superior Court, where he served until he was appointed to the United States District Court in 2014.[361] As a superior court judge, he presided over cases in family court, complex civil court, and criminal court. From March 2010 through December 2012, Judge Rayes served as the criminal presiding judge. Judge Rayes co-chaired the creation of the Veterans Court for the Maricopa County Superior Court.[362] He introduced the superior court to Phoenix's annual Homeless Veteran

Stand-Down,[363] which allowed homeless veterans to resolve outstanding criminal warrants, charges and fines.

Judge Rayes served on the Commission on Victims in the Courts,[364] which advises the Arizona Judicial Council on procedures to improve victim access and ensure fair treatment during their involvement in the criminal justice system. In conjunction with the Phoenix Police Department, he helped create an e-search warrant procedure. He served on the Capital Case Oversight Committee, established to examine the availability of resources for processing capital cases in Maricopa County and the Arizona appellate courts. He also served on the Court Leadership Institute of Arizona[365] and was a member of the Statewide Judicial Performance Review Commission.[366]

President Obama nominated him in 2013 to a seat on the U.S. District Court. The U.S. Senate confirmed him.[367] While on the District Court, he has sat by designation with the United States Court of Appeals for the Ninth Circuit. He is a member of the Ninth Circuit's Capital Case Committee.[368]

---

1 William Shakespeare, *Much Ado About Nothing*, Act 1, Scene 1, Line 12.

2 Lenni B. Benson, *The Search for Fair Agency Process: The Immigration Opinions of Judge Michael Daly Hawkins, 1994–2010*, 43 Ariz. St. L.J. 7, 7 (2011).

3 Ibid., citing *Circu v. Ashcroft*, 389 F.3d 938, 943 (9th Cir. 2004).

4 Ibid. Mr. Dessaint also joined the first-year class in 1967 and graduated with Joe in 1970. Both were high achievers and graduated with honors.

5 Legal Education in the Future Tense, Deans Report, 2009–2010, p. 13. Sandra Day O'Connor College of Law Library Archives.

6 Michael Gallagher, '70, Co-founder—Gallagher & Kennedy; Terry Goddard, '76, Phoenix Mayor and Arizona Attorney General; Rebecca Berch, '79, Chief Justice Arizona Supreme Court; Ed Pastor, '74, US Representative in Congress; Bill Atkin, '75, Associate General Counsel—Church of Jesus Christ of Latter-Day Saints; Michael Ahern, '82, Executive Chairman—First Solar, Inc.; Allison Binney, '00, Chief of Staff and Chief Counsel—US Senate Committee on Indian Affairs; Suzanne Barr, '03, Chief of Staff, US Immigration and Customs Enforcement.

7 "Joe Sims Biography," Department of Justice, accessed January 25, 2021, https://www.justice.gov/atr/joe-sims-biography.

8 Legal Education in the Future Tense, Deans Report, 2009–2010, p. 13. Sandra Day O'Connor College of Law Library Archives.

9 Ibid.

10 Arizona Western College is a public community college located in Yuma, Arizona, United States. It offers associate degrees, occupational certificates and transfer degrees. AWC also offers classes in Dateland, La Paz, San Luis, Somerton, and Wellton. "Arizona Western College," AZ Western, accessed February 19, 2020, https://www.azwestern.edu/.

11 Northern Arizona University is a public research university with its main campus in Flagstaff, Arizona. Governed by the Arizona Board of Regents and accredited by the Higher Learning Commission, the university offers 158 baccalaureate and graduate degree programs. Wikipedia, s.v., "Northern Arizona University," last modified February 19, 2020, https://en.wikipedia.org/wiki/Northern_Arizona_University. *See also* "About NAU," Northern Arizona University, accessed February 19, 2020, https://nau.edu/about/.

Inaugural Graduates—1970 through 1976

12 Toltec (GNIS FID: 12570) is a populated place located within the City of Eloy. In turn, the City of Eloy is located within Pinal County, Arizona. "Toltec Populated Place Profile," AZ HomeTownLocator, accessed February 19, 2020, https://arizona.hometownlocator.com/az/pinal/toltec.cfm.

13 "Jimmie Smith," State Bar of Arizona Legal Services Link, accessed February 19, 2020, https://azbar.legalserviceslink.com/attorneys-view/JimmieDeeSmith.

14 Ibid.

15 Ibid.

16 ABA House of Delegates: The control and administration of the American Bar Association is vested in the House of Delegates, the policy-making body of the association. The House meets twice each year, at ABA Annual and Midyear Meetings. "ABA House of Delegates," American Bar Association, accessed February 19, 2020, https://www.americanbar.org/groups/leadership/house_of_delegates/.

17 The blindside flanker on a rugby team is expected to cover the opposing team blindside at scrum and breakdown. The "Blindside" of the scrum is the side that the opposing scrum half is feeding the ball from. The Openside is the other side: "Open" in this situation means unimpeded. Wikipedia, s.v., "Glossary of rugby union terms," last modified February 19, 2020, 8:58, https://en.wikipedia.org/wiki/Glossary_of_rugby_union_terms.

18 Amherst College is a private liberal arts college in Amherst, Massachusetts. Founded in 1821 as an attempt to relocate Williams College by its then-president Zephaniah Swift Moore, Amherst is the third-oldest institution of higher education in Massachusetts. The institution was named after the town, which in turn had been named after Jeffery, Lord Amherst, Commander-in-Chief of British forces of North America during the French and Indian War. Originally established as a men's college, Amherst became coeducational in 1975. Wikipedia, s.v., "Amherst College," last modified February 19, 2020, 4:58, https://en.wikipedia.org/wiki/Amherst_College.

19 His life story is briefly summarized here based his 2014 obituary and interviews between the author and family members in 2019.

20 Buffalo Springfield was a Canadian-American rock band active from 1966 to 1968 whose most prominent members were Stephen Stills, Neil Young, and Richie Furay. The group released three albums and several singles, including "For What It's Worth." Wikipedia, s.v., "Buffalo Springfield," last modified January 25, 2021, 11:43, https://en.wikipedia.org/wiki/Buffalo_Springfield.

21 The Beach Boys is an American rock band formed in Hawthorne, California in 1961. The group's original lineup consisted of brothers Brian, Dennis, and Carl Wilson, their cousin Mike Love, and their friend Al Jardine. Wikipedia, s.v., "The Beach Boys," last modified February 19, 2020, 2:22, https://en.wikipedia.org/wiki/The_Beach_Boys.

22 Gary Puckett & The Union Gap was an American pop rock group active in the late 1960s. Their biggest hits were "Woman, Woman"; "Over You"; "Young Girl"; and "Lady Willpower." It was formed by Gary Puckett, Gary "Mutha" Withem, Dwight Bement, Kerry Chater and Paul Wheatbread, who eventually named it The Union Gap. Wikipedia, s.v., "Gary Puckett & The Union Gap," last modified December 9, 2020, 23:00, https://en.wikipedia.org/wiki/Gary_Puckett_%26_The_Union_Gap.

23 Alice Cooper (born Vincent Damon Furnier; February 4, 1948) is an American singer, songwriter, and actor whose career spans over 50 years. With his distinctive raspy voice and a stage show that features numerous props, including guillotines, electric chairs, fake blood, reptiles, baby dolls, and dueling swords, Cooper is considered by music journalists and peers alike to be "The Godfather of Shock Rock." Though sometimes also called "The Father of Shock Rock" (perhaps through muddling of the former via word-of-mouth), the former is Cooper's most commonly agreed-upon title. He has drawn equally from horror films, vaudeville, and garage rock to pioneer a macabre and theatrical brand of rock designed to shock people. Originating in Phoenix, Arizona, in the late 1960s after he moved from Detroit, Michigan, "Alice Cooper" was originally a band consisting of Furnier on vocals and harmonica, Glen Buxton on lead guitar, Michael Bruce on rhythm guitar, Dennis Dunaway on bass guitar, and Neal Smith on drums. The original Alice Cooper band released its first album in 1969. They broke into the international music mainstream with the 1971 hit song "I'm Eighteen" from their third studio album *Love It to Death*. Wikipedia, s.v., "Alice Cooper," last modified January 25, 2021, https://en.wikipedia.org/wiki/Alice_Cooper.

24 "Robert Blakey Jr. Obituary," *Arizona Republic,* accessed February 19, 2020, https://www.legacy.com/obituaries/azcentral/obituary.aspx?n=robert-blakey-jr&pid=170062399.

25 Wikipedia, s.v., "Arizona Rugby Union," last modified June 20, 2020, 16:58, https://en.wikipedia.org/wiki/Arizona_Rugby_Union.

26 Ibid.

27 "Robert Blakey '67," Amherst College, accessed February 19, 2020, https://www.amherst.edu/amherst-story/magazine/in_memory/1967/robertblakey.

28 The Arizona Early Childhood Development and Health Board consists of nine members appointed by the Governor and approved by the state Senate. The Board is responsible for ensuring that Arizona's early childhood funds are spent on services that help our state's young children be healthier and start kindergarten ready to succeed. "Members," First Things First, accessed February 19, 2020, https://www.firstthingsfirst.org/governance/board/members/.

29 "Finance and Audit Committee," First Things First, accessed February 19, 2020, https://www.firstthingsfirst.org/governance/board/committees/finance-audit-committee/.

30 Ibid.

31 ASU College of Law—Oral History Project—Marianne Alcorn—Ross-Blakley Law Library, 2006–2007, page 12.

32 Hampton University is a private historically black university in Hampton, Virginia. It was founded in 1868 by black and white leaders of the American Missionary Association after the American Civil War to provide education to freedmen. It is home to the Hampton University Museum, which is the oldest museum of the African diaspora in the United States, and the oldest museum in the commonwealth of Virginia. In 1878, it established a program for teaching Native Americans that lasted until 1923. "History," Hampton University, accessed February 19, 2020, http://www.hamptonu.edu/about/history.cfm.

33 ASU College of Law—Oral History Project—Marianne Alcorn—Ross-Blakley Law Library, 2006–2007, page 13.

34 Judge Patterson's judicial service is documented on the Arizona Court of Appeals (Division One). "Cecil B. Patterson Jr.," Arizona Court of Appeals – Division One, accessed February 19, 2020, https://www.azcourts.gov/coa1/Former-Judges/CECIL-B-PATTERSON-JR.

35 "The Honorable Cecil B. Patterson, Jr. Celebration & Scholarship Reception," ASU Events, accessed February 19, 2020, https://asuevents.asu.edu/content/honorable-cecil-b-patterson-jr-celebration-scholarship-reception.

36 The Phoenix Human Relations Commission, in collaboration with the Phoenix Equal Opportunity Department, recognizes the accomplishments of people who have made an impact on the quality of life of Phoenix residents and contributed significantly to creating a compassionate and socially just community with the Dr. Martin Luther King Jr. Living The Dream Awards and Calvin C. Goode Lifetime Achievement Award. "About," Arizona MLK.org, accessed February 19, 2020, https://arizonamlk.wixsite.com/azmlkorg/maintenance.

37 "About NAAG," National Association of Attorneys General, accessed February 19, 2020, https://www.naag.org/naag/about_naag/naag-history.php.

38 "Events," Arizona Black Bar Association, accessed February 19, 2020, https://arizonablackbar.com/events.

39 Ibid., 5–6.

40 Ibid., 10.

41 Ibid.

42 Ibid.

43 Ibid., 11–12.

44 Ibid., 12.

45 Ibid., 14–15.

46 Lorna Elizabeth Lockwood (March 24, 1903–September 23, 1977) was an American lawyer and judge who served as justice (and at times chief justice) of the Arizona Supreme Court. Born in what was then Arizona Territory, Lockwood was the daughter of Alfred Collins Lockwood, who later served as chief justice of the Arizona Supreme Court. Lockwood attended the University of Arizona and the University of Arizona College of Law before entering private practice and serving several terms in the Arizona House of Representatives. Lockwood spent a decade on the bench of the Arizona Superior Court in Maricopa County, the first woman to serve in that role. In 1960, Lockwood was elected to the Arizona Supreme Court. She served as chief justice from 1965 to 1966, and 1970 to 1971, become the first female chief justice of a state supreme court in the United States. She retired from the court in 1975 and died three years later. Wikipedia, s.v., "Lorna E. Lockwood," last modified October 4, 2020, 10:54, https://en.wikipedia.org/wiki/Lorna_E._Lockwood.

47 "Silver, Roslyn O.," Federal Judicial Center, accessed February 19, 2020, https://www.fjc.gov/history/judges/silver-roslyn-o.

Inaugural Graduates—1970 through 1976

48 Wikipedia, s.v., "Roslyn O. Silver," last modified September 10, 2020, 3:11, https://en.wikipedia.org/wiki/Roslyn_O._Silver.

49 John McCarthy Roll (February 8, 1947–January 8, 2011) was a United States District Judge who served on the United States District Court for the District of Arizona from 1991 until his murder in 2011, and as chief judge of that court from 2006 to 2011. With degrees from the University of Arizona College of Law and University of Virginia School of Law, Roll began his career as a court bailiff in Arizona and became an assistant city attorney of Tucson, Arizona in 1973. Later that year, Roll became a deputy county attorney for Pima County, Arizona until 1980, when he began serving as an Assistant United States Attorney for seven years. President George H. W. Bush appointed Roll to a federal judge seat in Arizona after Roll served four years as a state judge. Roll was killed in the 2011 Tucson shooting while attending a constituent outreach event held by United States Representative Gabrielle Giffords in Casas Adobes, near Tucson, Arizona. Wikipedia, s.v., "John Roll," last modified January 7, 2021, 23:20, https://en.wikipedia.org/wiki/John_Roll.

50 Wikipedia, s.v., "2011 Tucson Shooting," last modified January 24, 2021, 17:56, https://en.wikipedia.org/wiki/2011_Tucson_shooting.

51 Judicial Profile—Hon. Roslyn O. Silver, Andrea Marconi, 2013. http://www.fedbar.org/PDFs/Past-Judicial-Profiles/Ninth-Circuit_1/Silver-Hon-Roslyn.aspx.

52 Mary Helen Murguia (born September 6, 1960) is a United States Circuit Judge of the United States Court of Appeals for the Ninth Circuit, based in Phoenix, Arizona. Wikipedia, s.v., "Mary H. Murguia," last modified December 9, 2020, 6:10, https://en.wikipedia.org/wiki/Mary_H._Murguia.

53 Judicial Profile—Hon. Roslyn O. Silver, Andrea Marconi, 2013, 2-2. http://www.fedbar.org/PDFs/Past-Judicial-Profiles/Ninth-Circuit_1/Silver-Hon-Roslyn.aspx

54 LexisNexis Advance search by author December 7, 2019. https://advance.lexis.com/search/.

55 LexisNexis Advance search by author, December 7, 2019. https://advance.lexis.com/search/.

56 "From the Bench, Mind-Reading, Clairvoyance and Jury Questionnaires," 31 Litigation 3, (Fall 2004).

57 "Honorable Roslyn Silver," Federal Bar Association, accessed December 7, 2019, http://www.fedbar.org/PDFs/Past-Judicial-Profiles/Ninth-Circuit_1/Silver-Hon-Roslyn.aspx.

58 Todd B. Carver & Albert A. Vondra, "Alternative Dispute Resolution: Why It Doesn't Work and Why It Does," *Harvard Business Review*, May-June 1994, https://hbr.org/1994/05/alternative-dispute-resolution-why-it-doesnt-work-and-why-it-does.

59 Lockheed Martin Space is one of the four major business divisions of Lockheed Martin. It has its headquarters in Denver, Colorado with additional sites in Sunnyvale, California; Santa Cruz, California; Huntsville, Alabama; and elsewhere in the US and UK. The division currently employs about 16,000 people, and its most notable products are commercial and military satellites, space probes, missile defense systems, NASA's Orion Multi-Purpose Crew Vehicle, and the Space Shuttle External Tank. Wikipedia, s.v., "Lockheed Martin Space," last updated December 26, 2020, 19:22, https://en.wikipedia.org/wiki/Lockheed_Martin_Space_Systems.

60 "About – Les Schiefelbein ADR," Les Schiefelbein ADR, accessed December 7, 2019, https://schiefelbeinadr.wordpress.com/about/.

61 "Lester Schiefelbein," Silicon Valley Arbitration & Mediation Center, accessed December 7, 2019, https://svamc.org/member/Les/.

62 Ibid.

63 "Les Schiefelbein Endows Global Dispute Resolution And Scholarship Program At ASU's Sandra Day O'Connor College Of Law," Sandra Day O'Connor College of Law, accessed December 7, 2019, https://law.asu.edu/asulaw-newsletter/schiefelbein-endowment.

64 Ibid.

65 Ibid.

66 Ibid.

67 "Aspey Watkins & Diesel, PLLC – Northern AZ Lawyers," AWD Law, accessed December 7, 2019, https://www.awdlaw.com/.

68 "Building a Legal Legacy—Aspey Watkins & Diesel mark forty years in Flagstaff." Suzanne Adams-Occkrassa, Business Section, Section C2, Sunday, July 19, 2015.

69 Letter from J. Thomas Brooks to Frederick M. Aspey, December 6, 2005.

70 WD LAW® handles a broad range of matters. Civil and criminal. Business and personal. Disputes and dispute avoidance. Our attorneys represent clients in and out of court and before governmental entities. We have offices in Flagstaff and Sedona, but we've litigated cases from coast to coast, and we handle international

transactions. No client is too small, and no problem too large. "Aspey Watkins & Diesel, PLLC – Northern AZ Lawyers," AWD Law, accessed December 7, 2019, https://www.awdlaw.com/.

71 Northern Arizona University is a public research university with its main campus in Flagstaff, Arizona. Governed by the Arizona Board of Regents and accredited by the Higher Learning Commission, the university offers 158 baccalaureate and graduate degree programs. "Home," Northern Arizona University, accessed December 7, 2019, https://nau.edu/.

72 "Home," State Bar of Arizona, accessed December 7, 2019, https://www.azbar.org/.

73 "Home," Coconino County Bar Association, accessed December 7, 2019, http://coconinobar.com/.

74 Founded in 1964, originally as the Arizona Trial Lawyers Association, the core mission of the Arizona Association for Justice ("AzAJ") is strengthening and upholding our civil justice system and protecting the rights of Arizona citizens and consumers. Specifically, AzAJ is dedicated to promoting a fair, effective, and impartial justice system while supporting the work of attorneys in their efforts to ensure that any person who is injured by the misconduct or negligence of others can obtain justice in Arizona's courtrooms. "AzAJ," Arizona Association for Justice," accessed December 7, 2019, https://www.azaj.org/.

75 The American Association for Justice, formerly the Association of Trial Lawyers of America (ATLA®), provides trial attorneys with information, professional support and a nationwide network that enables them to most effectively and expertly represent clients. The mission of the American Association for Justice is to promote a fair and effective justice system—and to support the work of attorneys in their efforts to ensure that any person who is injured by the misconduct or negligence of others can obtain justice in America's courtrooms, even when taking on the most powerful interests. "Home," American Association for Justice, accessed December 7, 2019, https://www.justice.org.

76 The American Bar Association, founded August 21, 1878, is a voluntary bar association of lawyers and law students, which is not specific to any jurisdiction in the United States. The ABA's most important stated activities are the setting of academic standards for law schools, and the formulation of model ethical codes related to the legal profession. "American Bar Association," American Bar Association, accessed December 7, 2019, https://www.americanbar.org/.

77 The American Judicature Society is an independent, non-partisan membership organization working nationally to protect the integrity of the American justice system. AJS's membership—including judges, lawyers, and members of the public—promotes fair and impartial courts through research, publications, education, and advocacy for judicial reform. "Home," American Judicature Society, accessed December 7, 2019, http://americanjudicaturesociety.org/.

78 Martindale-Hubbell® Peer Review Ratings™, the gold standard in attorney ratings, have recognized lawyers for their strong legal ability and high ethical standards for more than a century. Attorneys looking to refer a client, as well as individuals researching lawyers for their own legal needs, use these ratings to identify, evaluate and select the most appropriate lawyer for their legal issue. "AV Peer Ratings & Client Review Awards," Martindale-Hubbell, accessed December 7, 2019, https://www.martindale.com/ratings-and-reviews/.

79 "Trustees – Leadership," Arizona Lawyers Foundation, accessed December 7, 2019, https://azlf.org/about/trustees-leadership/.

80 "Arizona Foundation for Legal Services and Education," Arizona Foundation for Legal Services and Education, accessed December 7, 2019, https://www.azflse.org/.

81 https://ballotpedia.org/Redfield_T._Baum

82 Ibid.

83 U.S. Bankruptcy Court, District of Arizona. In *Re Dewey Ranch Hockey, LLC*. 2:09-BK-09488-RTBP.

84 *The Arizona Republic*, "Coyotes, NHL to Battle in Court," May 7, 2009.

85 ESPN, "Judge Rejects Bids by Balsillie, NHL," October 1, 2009; *Sports Illustrated*, "Balsillie offers to buy off Glendale in bid for Coyotes," September 8, 2009.

86 https://20thannualsouthwestbankrupt2012.sched.com/speaker/redfieldt.baum.

87 AWD LAW® handles a broad range of matters. Civil and criminal. Business and personal. Disputes and dispute avoidance. Our attorneys represent clients in and out of court and before governmental entities. We have offices in Flagstaff and Sedona, but we've litigated cases from coast to coast, and we handle international transactions. No client is too small, and no problem too large. "Aspey Watkins & Diesel, PLLC – Northern AZ Lawyers," AWD Law, accessed December 7, 2019, https://www.awdlaw.com/.

88 "Louis M. Diesel," AWD Law, accessed December 7, 2019, https://www.awdlaw.com/attorney/louis-m-diesel.

Inaugural Graduates—1970 through 1976

89 The State Bar of Arizona created the Arizona Foundation for Legal Services & Education as a separate 501(c) 3 organization in 1978, charging it with the mission of promoting access to justice for all Arizonans. The Foundation strives to fulfill this mission by preparing Arizona youth for civic responsibility and providing access to justice for Arizonans most in need. Through the provision of technical and financial assistance to probation & resource officers, teachers & administrators, private attorneys & judges, and legal service attorneys & advocates, the Foundation works to level the playing field, so that all in Arizona have knowledge and access to the justice systems. "Mission," Arizona Foundation for Legal Services and Education, accessed December 7, 2019, https://azbf.org/mission.

90 *A Practical Desk Reference for the General Practitioner – Both Plaintiff and Defense*
This useful publication gives the general practitioner a quick reference guide to a number of areas likely to be encountered in the preparation of a motor vehicle accident case. *Arizona Motor Vehicle Accident Deskbook,* 2nd Ed. 2016, State Bar of Arizona, accessed December 7, 2019, https://azbar.inreachce.com/Details/Information/5e71ed8c-fc82-4d0f-9c98-e82a922d92a4.

91 "Home," Arizona Lawyers Foundation, accessed December 7, 2019, https://azlf.org/.

92 Phoenix Arizona had a series of storms that washed out several bridges over the Salt River from Mesa to Buckeye, through Phoenix, in February 1980. At the time, Ms. Babbitt was First Lady. Her husband, Bruce Babbitt, was governor. The city and state engineers, concerned about the stability of the bridges over the Salt River that had not been completely destroyed, decided to close most of the bridges, including the I-10 crossing. That caused a nightmare traffic jam in the metropolitan Phoenix area. The Valley of the Sun was divided in half. So, ADOT, Amtrak, and the Southern Pacific Transportation Company joined forces and developed a public rail transportation line, which they called the "Hattie B," after Hattie Babbitt because she had been a strong voice for action to solve a very difficult problem. The Hattie B ran from downtown Mesa over what is now Tempe Town Lake to Union Station in downtown Phoenix, making six or seven round trips, with five coaches and a locomotive at each end. Nadine Arroyo Rodriguez, "Did You Know: Hattie B. Rail Named After Arizona First Lady," KJZZ, March 6, 2015, http://kjzz.org/content/110531/did-you-know-hattie-b-rail-named-after-arizona-first-lady.

93 Ibid.

94 Jack D. H. Hays (February 17, 1917–June 18, 1995) was a Justice of the Supreme Court of Arizona from January 4, 1969 to February 23, 1987. He served as Chief Justice for three consecutive terms, from January 1972 to December 1974. At the time of his death, Hays still held the record for the most opinions authored by a justice in any single year (100). Wikipedia, s.v., "Jack D. H. Hays," last updated December 23, 2020, 4:29, https://en.wikipedia.org/wiki/Jack_D._H._Hays.

95 Harriet C. Babbitt, *Tribute to Jack D. H. Hays*, 27 Ariz. St. L.J. 771, 771 (1995).

96 Long recognized as one of Arizona's premier law firms, Jennings Strouss is one of the oldest, largest and most distinguished law firms based in Arizona. Since the firm was founded in 1942, Jennings Strouss has been deeply rooted in each of our locations' legal and business communities, and its attorneys have been instrumental in helping shape the dynamic growth of Arizona and many of its institutions.

The firm's founders—Irving A. Jennings, Sr., Charles L. Strouss, Sr., Riney B. Salmon, Sr., and Ozell M. Trask—started practicing law in the 1920's when Arizona's economy was largely driven by agriculture and the mining industry.

In 1942, the partnership began on the sixth floor of the Phoenix Title & Trust Building at First Avenue and Adams Street. Some of the first attorneys who came to the firm were: Richard Kleindienst, who helped build and energize the Republican Party in Arizona before becoming U.S. Attorney General under President Nixon; Rex Lee, former Solicitor General of the U.S.; Nicholas Udall, a former Phoenix Mayor who later became a Superior Court Judge; and Clarence Duncan, who was renowned for his precise legal mind and his teaching and mentoring of young attorneys. In 2006, Jennings Strouss merged with Robbins & Green adding several talented attorneys including Wayne Smith and Jack Rudel, to our Phoenix office, as well as the highly regarded *Harriet (Hattie) Babbitt*, the former U.S. Ambassador to the organization of American States (and wife of former Arizona Governor and the U.S. Interior Secretary Bruce Babbitt), to our Washington, D.C. office. "History," Jennings Strouss, accessed December 7, 2019, https://jsslaw.com/about/history/.

97 The National Democratic Institute, or National Democratic Institute for International Affairs, is a non-partisan, non-profit organization that works with partners in developing countries to increase the effectiveness of democratic institutions. NDI's core program areas include citizen participation, elections, debates, democratic governance, democracy and technology, political inclusion of marginalized groups, and gender, women and democracy, peace and security, political parties, and youth political participation. The organization's stated mission is to "support and strengthen democratic institutions worldwide through

citizen participation, openness and accountability in government." "Home," National Democratic Institute, accessed December 7, 2019, https://www.ndi.org/.

98 The Global Water Challenge is a non-profit organization to provide safe drinking water, sanitation, and hygiene education worldwide to people who lack these services. Launched by a diverse coalition of corporations, foundations, and aid organizations, the GWC is a unique partnership to build healthy communities and provide sustainable solutions to ensure the availability of potable water for those in need. The goal of the GWC is to bring safe water and sanitation to millions by identifying and multiplying the solutions that work. "Home," Global Water Challenge, accessed December 7, 2019, http://www.globalwaterchallenge.org/.

99 WRI is a global research organization that spans more than 50 countries, with offices in the United States, China, India, Brazil, Indonesia and more. Our more than 700 experts and staff work closely with leaders to turn big ideas into action to sustain our natural resources—the foundation of economic opportunity and human well-being. Our work focuses on six critical issues at the intersection of environment and development: climate, energy, food, forests, water, and cities and transport. "What We Do," World Resources Institute," accessed December 7, 2019, https://www.wri.org/our-work.

100 The Water Initiative (TWI) creates customized point-of-drinking (POD) water solutions and scales these solutions through micro-entrepreneurs, developers and government entities. The unique TWI process is to: DIAGNOSE the local unclean water conditions; DEVELOP affordable, convenient, effective, and trustworthy clean water solutions at the POD (Point-of-Drinking); and then DISTRIBUTE these solutions through local partners. TWI® is a team of leading global business executives and renowned scientists who develop and deploy "Point-of-Drinking" ("POD") water systems to fit local conditions. We engage local communities to co-create unique business development models to deliver customized and sustainable technology solutions which effectively remove water contaminants such as pathogens (bacteria and viruses), unsafe levels of inorganic materials (such as arsenic and fluorides) and harmful chemicals. http://thewaterintitative.com

101 Established in 1978, the Institute for the Study of Diplomacy is a research and teaching institute in the School of Foreign Service that seeks to bridge theory and practice in exploring global problems and the changing landscape of diplomatic engagement. "Global Database," Institute for the Study of Diplomacy, accessed December 10, 2019, https://global.georgetown.edu/georgetown_units/institute-for-the-study-of-diplomacy.

102 The Council on Foreign Relations, founded in 1921, is a United States nonprofit think tank specializing in U.S. foreign policy and international affairs. It is headquartered in New York City, with an additional office in Washington, D.C. Its membership, which numbers 4,900, has included senior politicians, more than a dozen secretaries of state, CIA directors, bankers, lawyers, professors and senior media figures. It is known for its neo-conservatism and neoliberalism leanings. "Home," Council on Foreign Relations, accessed December 10, 2019, https://www.cfr.org/.

103 The United States Agency for International Development is an independent agency of the United States federal government that is primarily responsible for administering civilian foreign aid and development assistance. With a budget of over $27 billion, USAID is one of the largest official aid agencies in the world, and accounts for more than half of all U.S. foreign assistance—the highest in the world in absolute dollar terms. "U.S. Agency for International Development," USAID, accessed December 10, 2019, https://www.usaid.gov/.

104 "Harriet C. Babbitt," National Democratic Institute, accessed December 10, 2019, https://www.ndi.org/people/harriet-c-babbitt.

105 The United States Department of State, commonly referred to as the State Department, is a federal executive department responsible for carrying out U.S. foreign policy and international relations. Established in 1789 as the nation's first executive department, its duties include advising the U.S. President, administering the nation's diplomatic missions, negotiating treaties and agreements with foreign entities, and representing the U.S. at the United Nations. "United States Department of State," U.S. Department of State, accessed December 10, 2019, https://www.state.gov/.

106 The Organization of American States, or the OAS or OEA, is a continental organization that was founded on 30 April 1948, for the purposes of regional solidarity and cooperation among its member states. Headquartered in the United States' capital Washington, D.C., the OAS's members are the 35 independent states of the Americas. "OAS," The Organization of American States, accessed December 10, 2019, http://www.oas.org/en/.

107 The Inter-American Commission on Human Rights is an autonomous organ of the Organization of American States. "OEA," Comisión Interamericana de Derechos Humanos, accessed December 10, 2019, http://www.oas.org/es/cidh/.

108 The Woodrow Wilson International Center for Scholars, located in Washington, D.C., is a United States Presidential Memorial that was established as part of the Smithsonian Institution by an act of Congress in 1968. It is also a highly recognized think tank, ranked among the top ten in the world. "Wilson Center," Wilson Center, accessed December 10, 2019, https://www.wilsoncenter.org/.

109 "Harriet C. Babbitt," National Democratic Institute, accessed December 10, 2019, https://www.ndi.org/people/harriet-c-babbitt.

110 Hunt Alternatives is a private family foundation located in Cambridge, Massachusetts. Founded by sisters Swanee Hunt and Helen LaKelly Hunt in 1981, Hunt Alternatives has contributed more than $80 million to social change worldwide. In 1992, the organization split into two entities: The Sister Fund, based in New York City, headed by Helen Hunt; and Hunt Alternatives, based in Denver, headed by Swanee Hunt. In 1997, after serving as ambassador to Austria for four years, Swanee Hunt returned to the United States, moving to Cambridge to found the Women and Public Policy Program at Harvard's JFK School of Government. Hunt Alternatives has operated out of Cambridge since 1997. With local, national, and international programs, Hunt Alternatives advances inclusive approaches to social change. Hunt Alternatives' international program is The Institute for Inclusive Security, which uses research, training, and advocacy to promote the inclusion of all stakeholders, especially women, in peace processes. FREEBASE. *See also* "Hunt Alternatives Fund," Alliance for Global Good, accessed December 10, 2019, http://afgg.org/?page_id=57.

111 According to their website, The Institute for Inclusive Security "advocates for the full participation of all stakeholders, especially women, in peace processes. Creating sustainable peace is achieved best by a diverse, citizen-driven approach. Of the many sectors of society currently excluded from peace processes, none is larger—or more critical to success—than women are. Since 1999, Inclusive Security has connected more than 400 women experts with over 3,000 policy shapers to collaborate on fresh, workable solutions to long-standing conflicts across the globe."

"Launched at Harvard's Kennedy School of Government, The Institute for Inclusive Security is currently an operating program of Hunt Alternatives Fund, which advances innovative and inclusive approaches to social change at local, national, and global levels." "The Initiative for Inclusive Security," SourceWatch, accessed December 10, 2019, https://www.sourcewatch.org/index.php?title=The_Initiative_for_Inclusive_Security.

112 "Harriet C. Babbitt," SourceWatch, accessed December 10, 2019, https://www.sourcewatch.org/index.php/Harriet_C._Babbitt.

113 Wikipedia, s.v., "NNDB," last updated January 7, 2021, 14:37, https://en.wikipedia.org/wiki/NNDB.

114 Baltic-American Partnership Fund Board of Directors; Campaign for American Leadership in the Middle East

Council on Foreign Relations; Dean for America; Friends of Hillary; Hillary Clinton for President; Hillary Rodham Clinton for US Senate Committee; International Women's Forum; John Kerry for President; Obama for America; National Democratic Institute for International Affairs Board of Directors; Planned Parenthood Central and Northern Arizona; Population Action International Board of Directors; Woodrow Wilson International Center for Scholars Senior Public Policy Scholar. "Harriet C. Babbitt," NNDB, accessed December 10, 2019, https://www.nndb.com/people/448/000119091/.

115 *See* bio at "Our Attorneys," Mac Ban Law Offices, accessed December 10, 2019, http://www.macban-lawoffices.com/our-attorneys/.

116 The American College of Trial Lawyers (ACTL) is composed of preeminent members of the Trial Bar from the United States and Canada and is recognized as the leading trial lawyers' organization in both countries. Fellowship is extended only by invitation, after careful investigation, to those experienced trial lawyers who have mastered the art of advocacy and whose professional careers have been marked by the highest standards of ethical conduct, professionalism, civility and collegiality. Although there are currently more than 5,800 Fellows across the U.S. and Canada, membership can never be more than 1% of the total lawyer population of any state or province. Qualified lawyers are called to Fellowship in the College from all branches of trial practice. They are selected from among advocates who represent plaintiffs or defendants in civil proceedings of all types, as well as prosecutors and criminal defense lawyers. The College is thus able to speak with a balanced voice on important issues affecting the administration of justice. "Membership," American College of Trial Lawyers, accessed December 13, 2019, https://www.actl.com/home/membership.

117 The State Bar of Arizona created the Arizona Foundation for Legal Services & Education as a separate 501(c) 3 organization in 1978, charging it with the mission of promoting access to justice for all Arizonans. The Foundation strives to fulfill this mission by preparing Arizona youth for civic responsibility and providing access to justice for Arizonans most in need. Through the provision of technical and financial assistance to probation & resource officers, teachers & administrators, private attorneys & judges, and legal service attorneys & advocates, the Foundation works to level the playing field, so that all in Arizona have knowledge

and access to the justice systems. "Mission," Arizona Foundation for Legal Services & Education, accessed December 13, 2019, https://azbf.org/mission.

118 The Academy is a group of truly elite trial lawyers representing both sides of the Bar: prosecutors and defense lawyers in criminal cases, and plaintiffs' and defense counsel in civil litigation. While the majority of the Fellows come from the U.S., the Academy includes lawyers from more than 30 countries. Fellowship is by invitation only, and trial lawyers are invited to become Fellows only after an extremely careful vetting process. The IATL PURPOSE—Promote Reforms in the Law—Facilitate the Administration of Justice—Promote the Rule of Law Internationally—Elevate the Standards of Integrity, Honor & Courtesy in the Legal Profession. "Home," International Academy of Trial Lawyers, accessed December 13, 2019, https://www.iatl.net.

119 Founded in 1958, ABOTA is a national association of experienced trial lawyers and judges. ABOTA and its members are dedicated to the preservation and promotion of the civil jury trial right provided by the Seventh Amendment to the U.S. Constitution. ABOTA membership consists of more than 7,600 lawyers—equally balanced between plaintiff and defense—and judges spread among 96 chapters in all 50 states and the District of Columbia. ABOTA is an invitation-only organization. Members must have at least five years of active experience as trial lawyers, have tried at least 10 civil jury trials to conclusion and possess additional litigation experience. Members must also exhibit the virtues of civility, integrity and professionalism by following our Code of Professionalism and Principles of Civility. The general purposes of this Association shall be to foster improvement in the ethical and technical standards of practice in the field of advocacy to the end that individual litigants may receive more effective representation and the general public be benefited by more efficient administration of justice consistent with time-tested and traditional principles of litigation. "Home," American Board of Trial Advocates, accessed December 13, 2019, https://www.abota.org/.

120 Sustaining Members of our predecessor, Arizona's Finest Lawyers LLC, enabled us to further the mission of "Identifying Lawyer Excellence and Informing Client Choice." As our goals and activities have shifted to mentoring, volunteering, professional development, community, service, and access to justice, the Arizona's Finest Lawyers Foundation, Inc. received its 501(c) (3) determination letter in early September 2017. We invite you to review our searchable directory for Arizona's Finest Lawyers in more than 40 practice areas. "Home," Arizona's Finest Lawyers, accessed December 13, 2019, https://www.azfinestlawyers.org/home.html.

121 Best Lawyers, LLC publishes peer-review and recommended lawyers guide for the global legal community. The company was founded in 1981 and is headquartered in Aiken, South Carolina. Recognition by Best Lawyers is based entirely on peer review. Our methodology is designed to capture, as accurately as possible, the consensus opinion of leading lawyers about the professional abilities of their colleagues within the same geographical area and legal practice area. Best Lawyers employs a sophisticated, conscientious, rational, and transparent survey process designed to elicit meaningful and substantive evaluations of the quality of legal services. Our belief has always been that the quality of a peer review survey is directly related to the quality of the voters. "A Purely Peer Review Methodology," Best Lawyers, accessed December 13, 2019, https://www.bestlawyers.com/methodology.

122 Applications are processed by the State Bar. Once ready for review, applications are submitted to the Advisory Commissions (AC). The AC reviews the applications and peer reviews. If favorable, the applicant is notified—typically by the end of January—that they have been approved to sit for the specialization examination. The examinations are usually scheduled in April. Exam results are submitted to the Bar and if the applicant receives a passing score, the AC will recommend certification to BLS who act upon the recommendation at the next available meeting. The application process, including the examination, may take up to twelve (12) months. "Become a Certified Legal Specialist," State Bar of Arizona, accessed December 13, 2019, https://www.azbar.org/for-lawyers/career-advancement/legal-specialization/.

123 Martindale-Hubbell is an information services company to the legal profession that was founded in 1868. The company publishes the Martindale-Hubbell Law Directory, which provides background information on lawyers and law firms in the United States and other countries. "Online Directory for Attorneys, Law Firms & Consumers," Martindale, accessed December 13, 2019, https://www.martindale.com/.

124 A Who's Who roster of prestigious Lifetime Achievement inductees. "A Who's Who Roster of Prestigious Lifetime Achievement Inductees," Who's Who Lifetime Achievement, accessed December 13, 2019, https://wwlifetimeachievement.com/.

125 The Marquis Who's Who Top Professionals series recognizes outstanding listees in their specific fields. Our features contain biographical details of professionals that have achieved a high level of recognition and achievement in their chosen profession.

The Marquis Who's Who Top Lawyers selection process is a comprehensive and detailed attempt to produce a list of professionals that have demonstrated achievement in the field of law. Our process involves

Inaugural Graduates—1970 through 1976

many factors, including an assessment of a professional's years of service and unique contributions. This, combined with a comprehensive interview of the professional, allows us to make an appropriate decision regarding inclusion in Top Lawyers. "Marquis Who's Who Top Lawyers," Marquis Top Lawyers, accessed December 13, 2019, https://marquistoplawyers.com/.

126 The National Trial Lawyers: Top 100 is an invitation-only organization composed of the premier trial lawyers from each state or region who meet stringent qualifications as civil plaintiff and/or criminal defense trial lawyers. Selection is based on a thorough multi-phase objective and uniformly applied process, which includes peer nominations combined with third-party research. Membership is extended only to the select few of the most qualified attorneys from each state or region who demonstrate superior qualifications of leadership, reputation, influence, stature and public profile measured by objective and uniformly applied standards in compliance with state bar and national Rule 4-7.

The National Trial Lawyers: Top 100 is an essential source of information, education and networking for the most accomplished trial lawyers throughout America. Through unique and professional networking opportunities, information and CLE programs, we continually strive to give our members a competitive edge in today's ever-changing legal profession. It is the mission of The National Trial Lawyers to provide networking opportunities, advocacy training, and the highest quality educational programs for the nation's leading trial lawyers. "The Top 100 Trial Lawyers," The National Trial Lawyers, accessed December 13, 2019, https://www.thenationaltriallawyers.org/ntl-groups/top-100-trial-lawyers/.

127 Delta Sigma Phi is a national, not-for-profit Fraternity that's helped young men become better for more than a century. Our great Fraternity helps and encourages our members to become better students, better leaders, better citizens, better professionals... better men. "Delta Sig at a Glance," Delta Sigma Phi, accessed December 13, 2019, https://www.deltasig.org/fraternity/delta-sig-at-a-glance/.

128 A new lecture series is being launched in the College of Education to commemorate former Arizona Gov. Ernest W. McFarland and to promote discussions about educational policy and reform. La Monica Everett-Haynes, "Education Launches New Lecture Series," University of Arizona News, October 28, 2009, https://uanews.arizona.edu/story/education-launches-new-lecture-series.

129 Phi Delta Theta, commonly known as Phi Delt, is an international social fraternity founded at Miami University in 1848 and headquartered in Oxford, Ohio. Phi Delta Theta, along with Beta Theta Pi and Sigma Chi, form the Miami Triad. The fraternity has about 185 active chapters and colonies in over 43 U.S. states and five Canadian provinces and has initiated more than 251,000 men between 1848 and 2014. There are over 160,000 living alumni. "Phi Delta Theta Fraternity: Become the Greatest Version of Yourself," Phi Delta Theta, accessed December 13, 2019, https://www.phideltatheta.org/.

130 "Our Attorneys," Mac Ban Law Offices, accessed December 10, 2019, http://www.macbanlawoffices.com/our-attorneys.

131 Laura MacBan is a graduate of the University of Arizona College of Law and has been in practice since 1988. Mac Ban Law Offices was selected as one of the "10 Best Law Firms" for client satisfaction in the practice area of Personal Injury Law in Arizona for 2016 by the American Institute of Personal Injury Attorneys. Since 2011, Laura Mac Ban has been selected Arizona's Finest Lawyers, Top 100 Litigation Lawyers in Arizona in 2014 to present by the American Society of Legal Advocates, America's Top 100 Civil Defense Litigators for 2018, The National Trial Lawyers: Top 100 for 2017 to present, Best Law Firms in Arizona—First-Tier Rankings for 2016 to present as published in *U.S. News & World Report,* Arizona Top Lawyers in 2014 to present as published by *The Arizona Republic,* selected Premier 100 Trial Attorneys for 2014–2016 by the National Academy of Jurisprudence fka American Academy of Trial Attorneys, and America's Top 100 High Stakes Litigators for 2018. She was also selected as a Woman of Outstanding Leadership by the International Women's Leadership Association for 2015. Ibid.

132 "Barry A. Mac Ban is recognized by Continental Who's Who among Pinnacle Professionals," PR Newswire, October 12, 2015, https://www.prnewswire.com/news-releases/barry-a-mac-ban-is-recognized-by-continental-whos-who-among-pinnacle-professionals-300157987.html.

133 "Gust Rosenfeld is a full service law firm established in 1921 with offices in Phoenix, Tucson, Wickenburg, Las Vegas, Los Angeles and Albuquerque. The firm is known for the quality of its lawyers and legal advice as well as its creative insights and practical solutions in business, public and civil law. Gust Rosenfeld is experienced in alternative dispute resolution, bankruptcy and creditors' rights, business and corporate law, commercial finance, education law, environmental law, franchises and franchising, insurance, intellectual property, labor and employment, litigation, natural resources, health care law, public finance, public law, real estate, taxation, and trusts and estates." "Home," Gust Rosenfeld PLC – Attorneys Since 1921," accessed December 10, 2019, https://www.gustlaw.com/.

134 "Home," KOLD News 13, accessed December 10, 2019, https://www.kold.com/.

135 "On November 13, 1952, the Federal Communications Commission (FCC) granted a construction permit to country singer Gene Autry for VHF channel 13 in Tucson. Two months later, on January 13, 1953, the Old Pueblo Television Company, owned by Autry, signed the station on the air as KOPO-TV, the second television station in Arizona, and first in Tucson."

136 "Tom Chauncey," Gust Rosenfeld, accessed December 10, 2019, https://www.gustlaw.com/attorneys3.tpl?GustLaw=Tom_Chauncey.

137 "Phi Delta Phi©® is the oldest legal organization in continuous existence in the United States, predating even the American Bar Association. It was founded in 1869 at the University of Michigan School of Law by four law students, who at the urging of their faculty, endeavored to create an association that would foster scholarship, civility, and ethical conduct in our profession. Since that time, Phi Delta Phi©® has grown beyond the borders of the United States to Canada, Latin America and Europe." "Home," The International Legal Honor Society of Phi Delta Phi, accessed December 15, 2019, https://www.phideltaphi.org/default.aspx.

138 "The Federal Communications Bar Association (FCBA) is a volunteer organization of attorneys, engineers, consultants, economists, government officials and law students involved in the study, development, interpretation and practice of communications and information technology law and policy. From broadband deployment to broadcast content, from emerging wireless technologies to emergency communications, from spectrum allocations to satellite broadcasting, the FCBA has something to offer nearly everyone involved in the communications industry. That's why the FCBA, more than two thousand members strong, has been the leading organization for communications lawyers and other professionals since 1936." "About the FCBA," FCBA, accessed December 15, 2019, http://www.fcba.org/about/about-the-fcba/.

139 "The First Amendment Coalition is an award-winning, nonprofit public interest organization dedicated to advancing free speech, more open and accountable government, and public participation in civic affairs. . . The mission of the First Amendment Coalition is to protect and promote freedom of expression and the people's right to know. The Coalition is a non-profit, nonpartisan educational and advocacy organization serving the public, public servants, and the media in all its forms. Its constituency reflects an increasingly diverse society. The Coalition is committed to the principle that government is accountable to the people, and strives through education, public advocacy, litigation, and other efforts to prevent unnecessary government secrecy and to resist censorship of all kinds. (Board of Directors, August 18, 2008)." "About Us," First Amendment Coalition, accessed December 15, 2019, https://firstamendmentcoalition.org/about/.

140 "Our natal day was the incorporation of the Legal Eagles Association on August 4, 1959, under the New Jersey Non-profit Corporation Act. Alfred Rathblott, our Association's first president, had the creative impulse to organize an association of flying lawyers. . . In 1965, when the name of our Association was changed a second time, the purposes of the cooperation were rewritten as follows: (a) to encourage the knowledge and understanding of aviation law; to promote spirit of fellowship within those of legal profession who have the interest of both lawyer and a pilot in the science or administration of aviation law; (b) to promote cooperation with governmental and other organizations so as to enhance general aviation safety and to offer to both governmental and civil agencies, the special knowledge and skill of its members so as to assist such agencies in the performance of their functions in the development of aviation law." "History," Lawyer-Pilots Bar Association, accessed December 15, 2019, https://www.lpba.org/History.asp.

141 "The Leadership Council on Legal Diversity is an organization of more than 300 corporate chief legal officers and law firm managing partners—the leadership of the profession—who have dedicated themselves to creating a truly diverse U.S. legal profession. Our action programs are designed to attract, inspire, and nurture the talent in society and within our organizations, thereby helping a new and more diverse generation of attorneys ascend to positions of leadership. By producing tangible results in the lives of talented individuals, we work to promote inclusiveness in our institutions, our circles of influence, and our society, with the ultimate goal of building a more open and diverse legal profession." "Our Mission," Leadership Council on Legal Diversity, accessed December 15, 2019, https://www.lcldnet.org/about/our-mission/.

142 "The National Conference for Community and Justice was an American social justice organization focused on fighting biases and promoting understanding between people of different races and cultures. The organization was founded in 1927 as the National Conference of Christians and Jews in response to anti-Catholic sentiment surrounding Al Smith's run for President. The national organization dissolved in 2005 following a diminishing of its endowment, but individual chapters around the country carry on the organization's mission." Wikipedia, s.v., "National Conference for Community and Justice," last updated January 25, 2021, 20:41, https://en.wikipedia.org/wiki/National_Conference_for_Community_and_Justice.

143 "Arizona Grantmakers Forum is the statewide network that connects, educates and advocates for Arizona philanthropy." "What We Do," Arizona Grantmakers Forum, accessed December 15, 2019, https://arizonagrantmakersforum.org/about-us/what-we-do/.

Inaugural Graduates—1970 through 1976

144 "The Arizona Pilot's Association (APA) was organized in 1978 to give Arizona's general aviation community a voice in aviation matters. Our mission remains much the same today as we continue to promote general aviation through advocacy at various levels of state and federal government, as well as through partnering with other aviation organizations in advocating our common interests: promoting aviation safety, pilot education, and public understanding of general aviation; preserving, maintaining, and even re-opening Arizona's backcountry and recreational airstrips; broadcasting Arizona aviation news; and connecting Arizona pilots through aviation events." "Why Join?" Arizona Pilot's Association, accessed December 15, 2019, https://azpilots.org/about-us/why-join.

145 "Established by an Act of the First Territorial Legislature on November 7, 1864, the Arizona Historical Society (AHS) is Arizona's oldest historical agency. Architects of the Territory's code of laws realized they were making history and that it was important to preserve a record of their activities. One of their earliest actions was to create the means for documenting the past and recording contemporary events as they unfolded. This became the Arizona Historical Society, formed to collect and preserve "all facts relating to the history of this Territory." "Who We Are," Arizona Historical Society, accessed December 15, 2019, https://arizonahistoricalsociety.org/about-ahs/ahs-history/.

146 "At Barrow Neurological Foundation our mission is simple: to be the catalyst for our donors' passion to provide the means necessary for the world's leading specialists at Barrow Neurological Institute to save lives. We provide philanthropic support of Barrow Neurological Institute, part of Dignity Health's St. Joseph's Hospital and Medical Center, in its mission to save human lives through innovative treatment, groundbreaking, curative research, and by educating the next generation of the world's leading neuro-clinicians and researchers. Barrow recruits the best clinical and research staff to pioneer answers to devastating neurological conditions, including Alzheimer's disease, brain tumors, Parkinson's disease, aneurysms, ALS and stroke." "Home," Barrow Neurological Foundation, accessed December 15, 2019, https://www.supportbarrow.org/.

147 "The Foundation for Blind Children was founded in 1952 by parents of blind children who wanted services for their blind children in Phoenix, instead of having to send them to the State Institution for the Blind in Tucson. The Foundation for Blind Children serves the blind and visually impaired of all ages, from birth to currently 102 years old. As the only agency of its kind in Arizona, the Foundation for Blind Children is an essential resource to families and children with blindness or low vision." "About Us," The Foundation for Blind Children, accessed December 15, 2019, https://www.seeitourway.org/about-us/.

148 "Friendly House is one of Arizona's pioneer social service agencies—first established in 1920 by the Phoenix Americanization Committee as part of a local initiative to assist immigrants in acquiring the citizenship, education and literacy skills necessary to acculturate into the United States. During the 1920's, an Americanization movement took hold to teach the language, customs, laws, and ideals of America to immigrants. Friendly House's origins emerged from both the Americanization and ongoing influence of the 'Settlement House' movements of the late 1980s (London, Chicago), where social reformers established houses in neighborhoods to provide education and social services directly to poor workers and immigrant populations who lived there. Now approaching a century as a charitable organization, Friendly House has evolved to address multiple social service needs in the community. For decades, the organization has remained true to the meaning of its mission." "History," Friendly House, accessed December 15, 2019, https://www.friendlyhouse.org/history.

149 "Homeward Bound creates pathways out of poverty for homeless families. Our values support our mission, shape our culture, and reflect the essence of Homeward Bound's operations." "About Us," Homeward Bound, accessed December 15, 2019, https://homewardboundaz.org/about/.

150 "The NU Club of Phoenix is your connection to your alma mater. Our events offer you the opportunity to meet fellow alumni, reconnect with friends and make new ones, and expand your professional and social networks. Our programming ranges from game watch parties and happy hours to family days at the park. Whether you're a recent graduate new to Phoenix or a part-time resident escaping the cold, we would love to see you at our next event!" "NU Club of Phoenix," Northwestern Alumni Association, accessed December 15, 2019, https://www.alumni.northwestern.edu/s/1479/02-naa/16/interior_lvls.aspx?sid=1479&gid=2&pgid=22722.

151 "Social Venture Partners is an international network of engaged philanthropists who invest time, money, and professional expertise in nonprofits, education, and social entrepreneurs. Our mission is to build the capacity of our Investees and strengthen their ability to accomplish their respective goals. Social Venture Partners Arizona is a partnership of more than 120 philanthropists, social entrepreneurs, impact investors, and business and community leaders. Our goal is to build stronger philanthropists who build stronger nonprofits, building a stronger community. Our Partners combine funds, making leveraged investments for increased impact. We also develop well-scoped volunteer opportunities so SVP Partners can deploy their

skills and expertise to strengthen Investee organizations." "Home," SVP Arizona, accessed December 15, 2019, https://www.socialventurepartners.org/arizona/.

152 "Soldier's Best Friend provides United States military veterans living with combat-related Post Traumatic Stress Disorder (PTSD) or Traumatic Brain Injury (TBI) with Service or Therapeutic Companion Dogs, most of which are rescued from local shelters. The veteran and dog train together to build a trusting relationship that saves two lives at once, and inspires countless others." "Home," Soldier's Best Friend, accessed December 15, 2019, https://soldiersbestfriend.org/.

153 "St. Joseph's is a nationally recognized center for quality tertiary care, medical education and research. It includes the internationally renowned Barrow Neurological Institute®, the Norton Thoracic Institute, Center for Women's Health, University of Arizona Cancer Center at St. Joseph's, and a Level I Trauma Center verified by the American College of Surgeons. The hospital is also a respected center for orthopedics, internal medicine, primary care and many other medical services. U.S. News & World Report routinely ranks St. Joseph's among the top hospitals in the United States for neurology and neurosurgery. Founded in 1895 by the Sisters of Mercy, St. Joseph's was the first hospital in the Phoenix area." "About Us | St. Joseph's Hospital & Medical Care," Dignity Health, accessed December 15, 2019, https://www.dignityhealth.org/arizona/locations/stjosephs/about-us.

154 "2017 Alumni Luncheon Outstanding Faculty and Alumni Award Recipients," Sandra Day O'Connor College of Law, March 1, 2017, https://law.asu.edu/asulaw-newsletter/outstanding-faculty-and-alumni.

155 Ibid.

156 Ibid.

157 Judge Roush served on the Maricopa County Superior Court bench from 1971 to 1976. "Judges of the Superior Court of Arizona in Maricopa County," Maricopa County Law Library, September 2004, http://www.superiorcourt.maricopa.gov/LawLibrary/docs/PDF/Judges/SuperiorCourtJudges3.pdf.

158 William K. Culbertson Resume, 1972 to 2010, page 3.

159 Ibid., 1.

160 Ibid.

161 Ibid., 2.

162 Ibid.

163 Ibid.

164 Ibid.

165 Ibid.

166 Ibid.

167 *State v. Walker,* 185 Ariz. 228 (1995).

168 *State v. Djerf,* 191 Ariz. 583 (1998).

169 *State of Arizona v. Osborn,* 220 Ariz. 174 (2009)

170 *State v. Harrod,* 204 Ariz. 567 (2003).

171 *State v. Sansing,* 206 Ariz. 232 (2003)

172 *State v. Grell,* 212 Ariz. 516 (2006)

173 "Lewis Roca Rothgerber Christie is a U.S. law firm, with approximately 300 attorneys in ten offices in Arizona, California, Colorado, Nevada and New Mexico. In 2015, The American Lawyer magazine ranked the firm number 179 in its annual Top 200 U.S. law firms list. Its administrative offices are located in Phoenix, where is it one of the top five law firms in Arizona. The firm has handled pro bono cases including Miranda v. Arizona, 384 U.S. 436 (1966), in which partners John P. Frank, John Flynn and others represented Ernesto Miranda in the landmark case US Supreme Court case, giving rise to *Miranda Rights*." Wikipedia, s.v., "Lewis Roca Rothgerber Christie," last updated December 13, 2020, 22:51,https://en.wikipedia.org/wiki/Lewis_Roca_Rothgerber_Christie.

See also "Home," Lewis Roca Rothgerber Christie LLP, accessed December 21, 2019, https://www.lrrc.com/.

174 "Marty Harper | Phoenix, AZ, Maricopa County Attorney," State Bar of Arizona Find a Lawyer, accessed December 21, 2019, https://azbar.legalserviceslink.com/attorneys-view/MartyHarper.

175 "Polsinelli is an Am Law 100 firm with 900 attorneys in 21 offices nationwide. Recognized by legal research firm BTI Consulting as one of the top firms for excellent client service and client relationships, the firm's attorneys provide value through practical legal counsel infused with business insight, and focus on health care, financial services, real estate, intellectual property, middle-market corporate, labor and

employment and business litigation." "Firm Overview," Polsinelli, accessed December 21, 2019, https://www.polsinelli.com/ourfirm/overview. *See also* "Phoenix | Office," Polsinelli, accessed December 21, 2019, https://www.polsinelli.com/offices/phoenix.

176 "Marty Harper Phoenix AZ," ASU Law Group, accessed December 21, 2019, https://asulawgroup.org/1-marty-harper/.

177 "Marty Harper Profile | Phoenix, AZ Lawyer," Martindale.com, accessed December 21, 2019, https://www.martindale.com/phoenix/arizona/marty-harper-50382-a/.

178 "Best Lawyers in America," Best Lawyers, accessed December 21, 2019, https://www.bestlawyers.com/America.

179 "Choosing an established international network for your business gives you the flexibility to create a legal team to suit your needs and value for money. Choosing Mackrell International gives you truly global coverage from a substantial team of worldwide lawyers committed to meeting the needs of any organisation working on a global scale whether through operations, sales, employment and labour and IP protection. This is a team with a track-record of helping clients deliver their goals thanks to a winning combination of global expertise and local influence." "Home," Mackrell International, accessed December 21, 2019, http://www.mackrell.net/.

180 "Marty Harper | Phoenix, AZ, Maricopa County Attorney," State Bar of Arizona Find an Lawyer, accessed December 21, 2019, https://azbar.legalserviceslink.com/attorneys-view/MartyHarper.

181 Awarded annually to the top-ranked student in the class. The award is named after John S. Armstrong, an Arizona Legislator who introduced the bill that established the Tempe Normal School in 1885, the forerunner to Arizona State University. It is the law school's highest honor. *See also* "Tempe Normal School Records 1884–1930," Arizona Archives Online, accessed December 21, 2019, http://www.azarchivesonline.org/xtf/view?docId=ead/asu/tnsrec.xml.

182 Princeton University is a private Ivy League research university in Princeton, New Jersey. Founded in 1746 in Elizabeth as the College of New Jersey, Princeton is the fourth-oldest institution of higher education in the United States and one of the nine colonial colleges chartered before the American Revolution. "Home," Princeton University, accessed January 2, 2020, https://www.princeton.edu/.

183 Established in 1969 and originally published under the title Law and the Social Order, the *Arizona State Law Journal* is a nationally recognized legal periodical that serves as the primary scholarly publication of the Sandra Day O'Connor College of Law at Arizona State University. The *Journal* is routinely cited in major textbooks, treatises, and opinions at all levels of the state and federal judiciary, including the United States Supreme Court. "Law Journals," Sandra Day O'Connor College of Law, accessed January 2, 2020, https://law.asu.edu/student-life/law-journals.

184 William Hubbs Rehnquist was an American jurist and lawyer who served on the Supreme Court of the United States for 33 years, first as an Associate Justice from 1972 to 1986, and then as the 16th Chief Justice of the United States from 1986 until his death in 2005. Wikipedia, s.v., "William Rehnquist," last updated January 24, 2021, 18:24, https://en.wikipedia.org/wiki/William_Rehnquist.

185 The Solicitor General of the United States is the fourth-highest-ranking official in the United States Department of Justice. The current Solicitor General, Noel Francisco, took office on September 19, 2017.[1]

The United States Solicitor General represents the federal government of the United States before the Supreme Court of the United States. The Solicitor General determines the legal position that the United States will take in the Supreme Court. In addition to supervising and conducting cases in which the government is a party, the office of the Solicitor General also files amicus curiae briefs in cases in which the federal government has a significant interest in the legal issue. The Office of the Solicitor General argues on behalf of the government in virtually every case in which the United States is a party, and also argues in most of the cases in which the government has filed an amicus brief. In the federal courts of appeal, the Office of the Solicitor General reviews cases decided against the United States and determines whether the government will seek review in the Supreme Court. The Solicitor General's office also reviews cases decided against the United States in the federal district courts and approves every case in which the government files an appeal. Wikipedia, s.v., "Solicitor General of the United States," last updated January 21, 2021, 22:43, https://en.wikipedia.org/wiki/Solicitor_General_of_the_United_States.

186 Kirkland & Ellis's "Philosophy—Our principal goals are to provide the highest quality legal services available anywhere; to be an instrumental part of each client's success; and to recruit, retain and advance the brightest legal talent. We seek long-term, partnering relationships with clients, to the end of providing the best total solution to their legal needs." "Services," Kirkland & Ellis LLP, accessed January 2, 2020, https://www.kirkland.com/services.

187 *Browning-Ferris Industries v. Kelco Disposal,* 492 U.S. 257 (1989), was a case in which the Supreme Court of the United States held that the Eighth Amendment's prohibition of unreasonable fines does not apply to punitive-damage awards in civil cases when the United States is not a party. Wikipedia, s.v., "Browning-Ferris Industries of Vermont, Inc. v. Kelco Disposal, Inc.," last updated December 12, 2020, 15:00, https://en.wikipedia.org/wiki/Browning-Ferris_Industries_of_Vermont,_Inc._v._Kelco_Disposal,_Inc.

188 "The U.S. Const. amend. I limits California's libel law in various respects. When the plaintiff is a public figure, he cannot recover unless he proves by clear and convincing evidence that the defendant published the defamatory statement with actual malice, meaning with knowledge that it was false or with reckless disregard of whether it was false or not." 501 U.S. 496, 111 S. Ct. 2419 (1991).

189 "In reviewing the constitutionality of a statute, courts must accord substantial deference to the predictive judgments of Congress. The Supreme Court's sole obligation is to assure that, in formulating its judgments; Congress has drawn reasonable inferences based on substantial evidence. Substantiality is to be measured in this context by a standard more deferential than the Supreme Court accords to judgments of an administrative agency." 520 U.S. 180, 117 S. Ct. 1174 (1997).

190 "Appellant companies challenged the judgment from the Baldwin Circuit Court (Alabama), which denied its motion to compel arbitration under the Federal Arbitration Act, 9 U.S.C.S. § 1 et seq., in a tort and breach of contract action filed by appellee customers. . . The court affirmed in part and reversed and remanded in part. The court held that the customers' claims, based on the companies' clearance letter, were not subject to arbitration. The court determined that the breach of contract claims were inherently related to the party's agreement and that those claims were subject to arbitration." 684 So. 2d 102 (1995).

191 "On writ of certiorari to the United States Court of Appeals for the Ninth Circuit, petitioner professional golf tournament sponsor challenged a judgment affirming entry of a permanent injunction ordering petitioner to suspend its "walking rule" and allow respondent to use a golf cart in its tournaments under the Americans with Disabilities Act of 1990 (ADA), 42 U.S.C.S. § 12101 et seq. The court found that golf courses were specifically identified as a public accommodation. 42 U.S.C.S. § 12181(7) (L). Petitioner could not discriminate against either spectators or competitors on the basis of disability. The court found that a waiver of the walking rule for respondent would not work a fundamental alteration of the game." 532 U.S. 661 (2001).

192 "Respondents, a passenger's wife and others, filed a wrongful-death suit concerning the death of the passenger on an international flight. The district court found petitioner airline liable. The United States Court of Appeals for the Ninth Circuit affirmed, and held that a flight attendant's refusal to reseat the passenger was clearly external to the passenger, and it was unexpected and unusual. The Supreme Court granted certiorari. The judgment of the court of appeals was affirmed." 540 U.S. 644 (2004).

193 "The Fair Labor Standards Act exempts from the statute's minimum wage and maximum hours rules any employee employed in domestic service employment to provide companionship services for individuals who (because of age or infirmity) are unable to care for themselves. This includes those 'companionship' workers who are employed by an employer or agency other than the family or household using their services." 551 U.S. 158.

194 "*National Federation of Independent Business v. Sebelius,* 567 U.S. 519, was a landmark United States Supreme Court decision in which the Court upheld Congress' power to enact most provisions of the Patient Protection and Affordable Care Act, commonly called Obamacare, and the Health Care and Education Reconciliation Act, including a requirement for most Americans to have health insurance by 2014. The Acts represented a major set of changes to the American health care system that had been the subject of highly contentious debate, largely divided on political party lines." Wikipedia, s.v., "National Federation of Independent Business v. Sebelius," last updated December 19, 2020, 6:38, https://en.wikipedia.org/wiki/National_Federation_of_Independent_Business_v._Sebelius.

195 "Bartow Farr, USA," Chambers, accessed January 2, 2020, https://chambers.com/lawyer/bartow-farr-usa-5:160766.

196 "Mission, Vision, & Core Values," State Bar of Arizona, accessed January 2, 2020, https://www.azbar.org/about-us/mission-vision-core-values/.

197 "Home," Arizona Women Lawyers Association, accessed January 2, 2020, https://awla.clubexpress.com/content.aspx?sl=1038329608.

198 "AIC Home," American Inns of Court, accessed January 2, 2020, http://home.innsofcourt.org/.

199 "Home," American Judicature Society, accessed January 2, 2020, http://americanjudicaturesociety.org/.

200 "Vision and Mission," Arizona Foundation for Women, accessed January 2, 2020, https://www.azfw.org/vision-mission.

Inaugural Graduates—1970 through 1976

201 "ABA Mission and Goals," American Bar Association, accessed January 2, 2020, https://www.americanbar.org/about_the_aba/aba-mission-goals/.

202 "Home," CCJ, accessed January 2, 2020, https://ccj.ncsc.org/.

203 "Our Mission," Center for the Future of Arizona, accessed January 2, 2020, https://www.arizonafuture.org/who-we-are/mission/.

204 "Resources from Justice at Stake," Brennan Center for Justice, accessed January 25, 2020, https://www.brennancenter.org/resources-justice-stake.

205 "About Us," American Bar Association Section of Legal Education and Admission to the Bar, accessed January 29, 2020, https://www.americanbar.org/groups/legal_education/about_us/.

206 "About the U.S. Chamber of Commerce," U.S. Chamber of Commerce, accessed January 29, 2020, https://www.uschamber.com/about/about-the-us-chamber.

207 "About," IAALS, accessed January 29, 2020, https://iaals.du.edu/about.

208 "About," O'Connor Justice Prize, accessed January 29, 2020, http://oconnorjusticeprize.org/about/.

209 Sandra Day O'Connor, *A Tribute to Chief Justice Ruth McGregor: Foreword*, 42 Ariz. St. L.J. 339 (Summer 2010).

210 Ibid., 345–46.

211 Ibid., 349–50.

212 Ibid., 350–51.

213 Ibid., 340.

214 Wikipedia, s.v., "Ed Pastor," last updated December 23, 2020, 18:32, https://en.wikipedia.org/wiki/Ed_Pastor.

215 Raúl Héctor Castro was a Mexican American politician, diplomat and judge. In 1964, Castro was selected to be U.S. Ambassador to El Salvador, a position he held until 1968 when he was appointed U.S. Ambassador to Bolivia. In 1974, Castro was elected to serve as the 14th governor of Arizona and resigned two years into his term to become U.S. Ambassador to Argentina. Prior to his entry into public service, Castro was a lawyer and a judge for Pima County, Arizona. He was a member of the Democratic Party. Wikipedia, s.v., "Raúl Hector Castro," last updated December 26, 2020, 2:08, https://en.wikipedia.org/wiki/Raúl_Héctor_Castro.

216 Wikipedia, s.v., "Ed Pastor," last updated December 23, 2020, 18:32, https://en.wikipedia.org/wiki/Ed_Pastor.

217 Ibid.

218 Wikipedia, s.v., "Ed Pastor," last updated December 23, 2020, 18:32, https://en.wikipedia.org/wiki/Ed_Pastor.

219 Ruben Marinelarena Gallego (born November 20, 1979) is an American politician who is the U.S. Representative for Arizona's 7th congressional district. A Democrat, he previously served as a member of the Arizona House of Representatives, serving as assistant minority leader in the Arizona House of Representatives from 2012 until his resignation to run for Congress. Gallego was elected to Congress in the 2014 midterm congressional elections. His district includes most of southern, western, and downtown Phoenix, along with a portion of Glendale. Wikipedia, s.v., "Ruben Gallego," last updated January 18, 2021, 00:13, https://en.wikipedia.org/wiki/Ruben_Gallego.

220 "Ed Pastor: Current Hispanic-American Members," GPO, https://www.govinfo.gov/content/pkg/GPO-CDOC-108hdoc225/pdf/GPO-CDOC-108hdoc225-3-15.pdf.

221 Rebekah L. Sanders, "Congressman Ed Pastor Announces Retirement," *Arizona Republic*, February 27, 2014, https://www.azcentral.com/story/news/politics/2014/02/27/congressman-ed-pastor-announces-retirement/5866219/.

222 In 1972, Gutierrez was elected to the Arizona State Senate, and he was selected to serve as the majority leader in the Senate in 1974. He served in a leadership position until 1986, when he declined to run for re-election. Gutierrez was also the Democratic candidate for governor of Arizona in 2002. In 2014, Gutierrez was appointed to the Maricopa County Community College board after the death of board member Ben Miranda. He ran unopposed and was re-elected in 2016. "Alfredo Gutierrez," Ballotpedia, accessed February 4, 2020, https://ballotpedia.org/Alfredo_Gutierrez.

223 Ibid.

224 Fox 10 Web Staff, "Ed Pastor, Arizona's 1st Hispanic Congressman, Dies," *Fox 10 Phoenix*, November 29, 2018, http://www.fox10phoenix.com/news/arizona-news/former-arizona-congressman-ed-pastor-dies-at-75.

225 "The American College of Trial Lawyers is an invitation only fellowship of exceptional trial lawyers of diverse backgrounds from the United States and Canada. The College thoroughly investigates each nominee for admission and selects only those who have demonstrated the very highest standards of trial advocacy, ethical conduct, integrity, professionalism and collegiality. The College maintains and seeks to improve the standards of trial practice, professionalism, ethics, and the administration of justice through education and public statements on important legal issues relating to its mission. The College strongly supports the independence of the judiciary, trial by jury, respect for the rule of law, access to justice, and fair and just representation of all parties to legal proceedings. . . Although there are currently more than 5,800 Fellows across the U.S. and Canada, membership can never be more than 1% of the total lawyer population of any state or province." "Membership," American College of Trial Lawyers, accessed January 28, 2020, https://www.actl.com/home/membership.

226 https://online.actl.com/actlssa/censsacustlkup.nav_page.

227 https://www.azbar.org/media/1945050/2018annualreportfinal.pdf 228 "Homepage," Walsh School of Foreign Service, accessed January 28, 2020, https://sfs.georgetown.edu/.

229 "Bill Sandweg and John Ager are both Certified Specialists in Personal Injury and Wrongful Death Litigation by the State Bar of Arizona Board of Legal Specialization. We have been litigating cases in Phoenix and throughout Arizona for over 70 years combined. . . Our full-time professional staff includes a nurse consultant and a personal injury paralegal who also have more than 60 years combined experience. . . We have tried over 75 civil cases in Arizona state and federal courts." "Bill Sandweg," Sandweg & Ager: Medical Malpractice & Serious Injury Lawyer, accessed January 16, 2020, https://www.sandwegandager.net/attorney-profiles/bill-sandweg/.

230 "Founded in 1958, ABOTA is a national association of experienced trial lawyers and judges. ABOTA and its members are dedicated to the preservation and promotion of the civil jury trial right provided by the Seventh Amendment to the U.S. Constitution. ABOTA membership consists of more than 7,600 lawyers—equally balanced between plaintiff and defense—and judges spread among 96 chapters in all 50 states and the District of Columbia. ABOTA is an invitation-only organization. Members must have at least five years of active experience as trial lawyers, have tried at least 10 civil jury trials to conclusion and possess additional litigation experience. Members must also exhibit the virtues of civility, integrity and professionalism by following our Code of Professionalism and Principles of Civility." "Home," American Board of Trial Advocates, accessed January 16, 2020, https://www.abota.org/.

231 "William Sandweg," iSearch, accessed January 16, 2020, https://isearch.asu.edu/profile/1809623.

232 "Home," Arizona's Finest Lawyers, accessed January 16, 2020, https://azlf.org/site-closing/.

233 "Best Lawyers in America," Best Lawyers, accessed January 16, 2020, https://www.bestlawyers.com/America.

234 "Lawyer and Attorney Ratings," Super Lawyers, accessed January 16, 2020, https://www.superlawyers.com.

235 "Phoenix Medical Malpractice Lawyers," Sandweg & Ager, P.C., accessed January 16, 2020, https://www.sandwegandager.net/.

236 *The Quotable Lawyer*, David S. Shrager and Elizabeth Frost, New England Publishing Associates, Inc., 1986, Quote 68.1, page 141.

237 "What is the difference between a private citizen and a public citizen?" Quora, accessed January 18, 2020, https://www.quora.com/What-is-the-difference-between-a-private-citizen-and-a-public-citizen.

238 "Barry G. Silverman," Alchetron, accessed January 18, 2020, https://alchetron.com/Barry-G-Silverman.

239 ARSC 41(a) (e).

240 ARSC 42, Preamble, Comment [6].

241 ARSC 81, Preamble.

242 Personal recollection of the author.

243 Jill Redgage, "Federal Judge's Humor Just One Key Asset," *East Valley Tribune*, August 31, 2007, https://www.eastvalleytribune.com/news/federal-judge-s-humor-just-one-key-asset/article_915e500d-6f84-595c-a77b-6a570f7fc0e7.html.

244 "Ninth Circuit Judge Barry G. Silverman to Assume Senior Status," Ninth Circuit Court of Appeals, October 15, 2015, http://cdn.ca9.uscourts.gov/datastore/ce9/2015/10/15/Silverman_Senior_Status.pdf.

245 *Bosley Med. Inst., Inc. v. Kremer*, 403 F.3d 672 (9th Cir. 2005).

246 *Tillamook Country Smoker, Inc. v. Tillamook Cty. Creamery Ass'n*, 465 F.3d 1102, 1105 (9th Cir. 2006).

247 Gary L. Stuart, "The Legal Word: Writing & Appellate Judges," 45 *AZ Attorney* 12, July/August, 2009.

248 "Barry G. Silverman, United States Court of Appeals for the Ninth Circuit" Bloomberg Markets, accessed January 18, 2020, https://www.bloomberg.com/profile/person/3028728.

249 "Home," The International Brotherhood of Magicians, accessed January 18, 2020, https://www.magician.org/.

250 "Home," Psychic Entertainers Association, accessed January 18, 2020, https://www.p-e-a.org/.

251 "Homepage," AALL, accessed January 18, 2020, https://www.aallnet.org/.

252 Lynn Hecht Schafran & Norma Juliet Wikler, The Foundation for Women Judges, "Operating a Task Force on Gender in the Courts: A Manual for Action," http://womenlaw.stanford.edu/pdf/gender-bias.pdf.

253 "Home," The Society of American Magicians, accessed January 18, 2020, https://www.magicsam.com/default.aspx.

254 *Miranda v. Arizona*, 384 U.S. 436 (1966), was a landmark decision of the United States Supreme Court. In a 5–4 majority, the Court held that both inculpatory and exculpatory statements made in response to interrogation by a defendant in police custody will be admissible at trial only if the prosecution can show that the defendant was informed of the right to consult with an attorney before and during questioning and of the right against self-incrimination before police questioning, and that the defendant not only understood these rights, but voluntarily waived them. Wikipedia, s.v., "Miranda v. Arizona," last updated January 25, 2021, 18:08, https://en.wikipedia.org/wiki/Miranda_v._Arizona. Full disclosure—the author has interviewed Judge Silverman several times over the years about the Miranda case. *See also* http://miranda-vs-arizona.com/.

255 *See* FN7 above.

256 Ron Dungan, "Miranda and the Right to Remain Silent: The Phoenix Story," *Arizona Republic*, June 11, 2016, https://www.azcentral.com/story/news/local/phoenix/2016/06/11/miranda-and-right-remain-silent-phoenix-story/85206416/.

257 Ibid.

258 William Glaberson, "Skepticism Follows Court Ruling In Favor of Inmate Procreation," *The New York Times*, September 8, 2001, https://query.nytimes.com/gst/fullpage.html. *See also* "Prison procreation lawsuit reinstated," *BBC News*, September 6, 2001, http://news.bbc.co.uk/1/hi/world/americas/1529425.stm.

259 *Gerber v. Hickman*, 264 F.3d 882, 893 (9th Cir.), reh'g en banc granted, opinion vacated, 273 F.3d 843 (9th Cir. 2001), and on reh'g en banc, 291 F.3d 617 (9th Cir. 2002).

260 Ibid.

261 Gary L. Stuart, "The Legal Word: Writing & Appellate Judges," 45 *AZ Attorney* 12, July/August, 2009.

262 "Barry G. Silverman (Ninth Circuit)," Court Listener, accessed January 18, 2020, https://www.courtlistener.com/person/2968/barry-g-silverman/.

263 *The Enlarged Devil's Dictionary,* by Ambrose Bierce (1842–1914?), research and editing by Ernest Jerome Hopkins, Professor Emeritus of Journalism, Arizona State University, Doubleday & Company, Inc. Garden City, New York, 1967, at page 168.

264 The J. Reuben Clark Law Society is an organization of lawyers and law school students consisting of over 65 professional and 125 student chapters throughout the world. Named in honor of J. Reuben Clark, a former United States Ambassador to Mexico and Under Secretary of State, the society's membership is primarily composed of members of The Church of Jesus Christ of Latter-day Saints (LDS Church), although there is no requirement that those in the society be church members. Alumni and students of the J. Reuben Clark Law School at Brigham Young University (BYU) are de facto members of the society. The organization currently claims as members 14 circuit court of appeals judges, 18 U.S. district court judges, four United States Attorneys, six U.S. Senators, including erstwhile President Pro Tempore Orrin Hatch, nine U.S. Representatives, 17 Fortune 500 corporate counselors, more than 85 state judges (including of state supreme courts), and thousands of practicing attorneys and law students. Wikipedia, s.v., "J. Reuben Clark Law Society," last updated November 23, 2020, 19:01, https://en.wikipedia.org/wiki/J._Reuben_Clark_Law_Society.

265 Through The Franklin S. Richards Public Service Award, the Law Society honors those whose selfless service epitomizes the virtues the Society espouses. These virtues include service to the poor, needy, and disadvantaged, community outreach, which fosters greater understanding of, and compliance with, the rule of law and actions and influence that improve the legal community's ability to provide justice for all. Franklin Snyder Richards, the award's namesake, was the very first general counsel for the Church of Jesus Christ of Latter-Day Saints. "Franklin S. Richards Public Service Award," J. Reuben Clark Law Society, accessed February 19, 2020, http://www.jrcls.org/?folder=pro_bono&page=franklin_richards.

266 "Dale Furnish," iSearch, accessed February 18, 2020, https://isearch.asu.edu/profile/27299.

267 David Thomas Lewis (April 25, 1912 – September 28, 1983) was a United States Circuit Judge of the United States Court of Appeals for the Tenth Circuit. Wikipedia, s.v., "David Thomas Lewis," last updated December 7, 2020, 3:41, https://en.wikipedia.org/wiki/David_Thomas_Lewis.

268 "The New Lawyers for the New World—As the original global law firm, we bring the right talent to every client issue, regardless of where the client is. We partner with our clients to deliver solutions in the world's largest economies as well as newly opening markets. We are global citizens, industry savvy, diverse and have a thirst for innovation. Our strength is our ability to adopt a new type of thinking and use cutting-edge legal technologies to help clients overcome the challenges of competing in today's new world economic order. "About Us," Baker McKenzie, accessed February 19, 2020, https://www.bakermckenzie.com/en/aboutus.

269 Sandra Day O'Connor College of Law, Ross-Blakley Law Library Archives, "Legal Education in the Future Tense—2009–2010 Report."

270 "Service Outreach Committee," J. Reuben Clark Law Society, accessed February 19, 2020, http://www.jrcls.org/history/content/service_outreach_committee/2010%20-%20William%20F.%20Atkin.pdf.

271 "Today, U.S. Senator Martha McSally commended President Trump on the nomination of Michael Bailey for U.S. Attorney for the District of Arizona. 'I would like to thank President Trump for nominating Michael Bailey to be U.S. Attorney for the District of Arizona,' Sen. McSally said. 'Mr. Bailey currently serves as chief deputy and chief of staff in the Arizona Attorney General's Office. He has decades of experience as a prosecutor and in private practice and is highly qualified for the position. Arizona has been without a U.S. Attorney for far too long. Filling this position is needed to keep the people of our state safe. I will work to ensure that Mr. Bailey is confirmed without delay.'" Martha McSally, "McSally Commends President's Nomination of Michael Bailey for U.S. Attorney for the District of Arizona," Senator Martha McSally, February 12, 2019, https://www.mcsally.senate.gov/mcsally-commends-presidents-nomination-michael-bailey-us-attorney-district-arizona.

272 "Results of Executive Business Meeting 05-02-2019," Senate Judiciary Committee, accessed February 19, 2020, https://www.judiciary.senate.gov/imo/media/doc/05-02-2019%20Results%20of%20Executive%20Business%20Meeting.pdf.

273 Westmont College, founded in 1937, is an interdenominational Christian liberal arts college in Montecito near Santa Barbara, Santa Barbara County, California. "Westmont College | Deeper Thinking. Wider Impact," Westmont College, accessed February 19, 2020, https://www.westmont.edu/.

274 Wikipedia, s.v., "Michael G. Bailey," last updated January 25, 2021, 17:23, https://en.wikipedia.org/wiki/Michael_G._Bailey.

275 Wikipedia, s.v., "Charles G. Case II," last updated May 28, 2020, 4:01, https://en.wikipedia.org/wiki/Charles_G._Case_II; https://www.uscourts.gov/judicial-milestones/charles-g-case-ii.

276 "Firm Overview," Lewis Roca Rothgerber Christie, accessed February 19, 2020, https://www.lrrc.com/firm-overview.

277 "Charles G. Case II," People's Pill, accessed February 19, 2020, https://peoplepill.com/people/charles-g-case-ii/.

278 The American College of Bankruptcy (hereinafter the "College" or "ACB") is an honorary public service association of United States and international insolvency professionals who are invited to join as Fellows based on a proven record of the highest standards of expertise, leadership, integrity, professionalism, scholarship, and service to the bankruptcy practice and to their communities. In recognizing distinguished professionals from every area of bankruptcy and insolvency practice, the College highlights qualities, values, and achievements to which others in the field aspire. "About," American College of Bankruptcy, accessed February 19, 2020, https://www.americancollegeofbankruptcy.com/about/.

279 About ALI: The American Law Institute is the leading independent organization in the United States producing scholarly work to clarify, modernize, and otherwise improve the law.
ALI drafts, discusses, revises, and publishes Restatements of the Law, Model Codes, and Principles of Law that are enormously influential in the courts and legislatures, as well as in legal scholarship and education.

By participating in the Institute's work, its distinguished members have the opportunity to influence the development of the law in both existing and emerging areas, to work with other eminent lawyers, judges, and academics, to give back to a profession to which they are deeply dedicated, and to contribute to the public good. "Visionaries Documentary," The American Law Institute, accessed February 17, 2021, https://www.ali.org/about-ali/ali-documentary/.

280 A non-profit, limited membership organization. An invitation-only membership of the most senior, experienced and respected practitioners, academics, judges and financial industry professionals in the world. Dedicated to improving international cooperation in the insolvency field. Focused on promoting greater

Inaugural Graduates—1970 through 1976

international cooperation and coordination through improvements in the law and in legal procedures. Continually studying, analyzing and providing solutions to problems in cross-border insolvencies and reorganizations. Awarded special consultative status to United Nations Agencies. "Home," International Insolvency Institute, accessed February 17, 2021, https://www.iiiglobal.org/.

281 NSOL International is a worldwide federation of national associations of accountants and lawyers who specialize in turnaround and insolvency. There are currently over 44 Member Associations with over 10,500 professionals participating as members of INSOL International. Individuals who are not members of a member association join as individual members. INSOL also has ancillary groups that represent the judiciary, regulators, lenders and academics. These groups play an invaluable role within INSOL and provide valuable forums for discussions of mutual problems. "Home," INSOL International, accessed February 17, 2021, https://www.insol.org/.

282 The American Bankruptcy Institute is an organization of over 13,000 bankruptcy and insolvency professionals, including attorneys, judges, law professors, accountants, investment bankers and turnaround specialists. It bills itself as the "largest multi-disciplinary, non-partisan organization dedicated to research and education on matters related to insolvency." "ABI," American Bankruptcy Institute, accessed February 17, 2021, https://www.abi.org/.

283 Membership in the National Conference of Bankruptcy Judges is restricted to actively serving United States Bankruptcy Judges (including recall judges), retired U.S. Bankruptcy Judges, and former U.S. Bankruptcy Judges not eligible for retirement, and qualifying international judges. "Home," NCBJ National Conference of Bankruptcy Judges, accessed February 17, 2021, https://www.ncbj.org/.

284 "Harvard Alumni," Harvard.edu, accessed February 17, 2021, https://alumni.harvard.edu/.

285 Wikipedia, s.v., "James Alan Soto," last updated December 3, 2020, 14:07, https://en.wikipedia.org/wiki/James_Alan_Soto.

286 "Dan Coogan and Kip Martin began their careers in Nogales, Arizona as associates in the firm of Larson, Soto & Arana. Kip began at the firm in February 1987. Dan arrived in 1989. As new lawyers, Dan and Kip had the opportunity to learn from the excellent and experienced partners E. Leigh Larson, James A. Soto and Kimberly H. Arana. In 1993, after the departure of Mrs. Arana and the unfortunate death of Mr. Larson, Dan, Kip and Mr. Soto formed the firm of Soto, Martin and Coogan, P.C. Dan, Kip and Mr. Soto practiced together until 2001 when Mr. Soto was appointed Presiding Judge of the Santa Cruz County Superior Court. From 2001 to the present, Dan and Kip through the firm of Coogan & Martin, P.C. have continued the firm's tradition of hard work and bringing the highest technical and ethical standards to the representation of their clients." "History of the Practice," Coogan & Martin, P.C., accessed February 17, 2021,http://www.nogaleslaw.com/nogales_law_firm_history.html.

287 Federal Questionnaire, Feb. 6 2014, Page 3. https://www.judiciary.senate.gov/imo/media/doc/James-Soto-Senate-Questionnaire.pdf.

288 Wikipedia, s.v., "James Alan Soto," last updated December 3, 2020, 14:07, https://en.wikipedia.org/wiki/James_Alan_Soto.

289 "James A. Soto," Ballotpedia, accessed February 17, 2021, https://ballotpedia.org/James_A._Soto.

290 *Romo v. United States,* 2015 U.S. Dist. LEXIS 180221.

291 "James A. Soto," Ballotpedia, accessed February 17, 2021, https://ballotpedia.org/James_A._Soto#cite_note-Questions-5. *See also* https://www.usatoday.com/story/news/nation/2015/02/11/border-patrol-shooting-unreasonable-lawsuit/23252269/.

292 Formally, Samuel Pearson "Terry" Goddard III.

293 Goddard served as AG from 2003 to 2011. *See* Wikipedia, s.v., "Terry Goddard," last updated January 23, 2021, 20:02, https://en.wikipedia.org/wiki/Terry_Goddard.

294 Dentons is a multinational law firm. In 2015 it was ranked as 8th-largest law firm in the world by revenue and the world's largest law firm by number of lawyers. The firm is called Dentons in all languages other than Chinese, in which it is called 大成. Dentons, accessed February 17, 2021, https://www.dentons.com/en.

295 ASU College of Law, "Legal Education in the Future Sense," Dean's Report 2009–2010, p. 16.

296 The Western Union Company is an American worldwide financial services and communications company. Up until it discontinued the service in 2006, Western Union was globally the best-known American company in the business of exchanging telegrams. "Western Union," Western Union Holdings, accessed February 17, 2021, https://www.westernunion.com/us/en/home.html.

297 Randal C. Archibold, Western Union to Pay in Border-Crime Deal, *The New York Times,* February 11, 2020, https://nytimes.com/2010/02/12/us/12arizona.html.

298 Ibid.

299 Gallagher & Kennedy, accessed February 17, 2021, https://gknet.com/.

300 Wikipedia, s.v., "Michael Grant (television)," last updated March 11, 2020, 13:00, https://en.wikipedia.org/wiki/Michael_Grant_(television).

301 "Michael M. Grant," Find a Lawyer, accessed February 21, 2021, https://azbar.legalserviceslink.com/attorneys-view/MichaelMGrant.

302 "KOY was the first radio station in the state of Arizona, signing on in 1921 as Amateur Radio station 6BBH on 360 meters (833 kHz). Earl Nielsen was the holder of the 6BBH call sign (there were no country prefixes for hams prior to 1928). At that time, broadcasting by ham radio operators was legal. KOY (1230 AM) in Phoenix is the oldest radio station in the state of Arizona. It is owned and operated by iHeartMedia. The station is currently branded as '93.7 El Patrón.' Its studios are located in Phoenix near Sky Harbor International Airport and its transmitter is located southwest of downtown Phoenix near the intersection of Interstate 17 and Buckeye Road. Wikipedia, s.v., "KOY," last updated January 22, 2021, 5:12, https://en.wikipedia.org/wiki/KOY.

303 "For more than 35 years, viewers have relied on *Arizona Horizon* for in-depth coverage of issues of concern to Arizonans. From state politics to national news that impacts our state, *Arizona Horizon* has consistently provided unprecedented, insightful public affairs programming." "About the Show," Arizona PBS, accessed February 21, 2021, https://azpbs.org/news/horizon/about-arizona-horizon/.

Unlike conventional newscasts, *Arizona Horizon* goes beyond headlines and sound bites. The program's format of pre-taped reports and studio discussion offers viewers an opportunity to explore all sides of each issue. *Arizona Horizon* reports examine a wide range of subjects including politics, consumer affairs, the environment, business, health concerns and social and legal issues.

304 O'Connor, a former state lawmaker who had begun working as a judge only seven years before, had no experience in the federal courts at the time. But polling found the public overwhelmingly welcomed a woman to the Supreme Court and specifically considered O'Connor qualified. Behind the scenes, Reagan helped dissipate concerns about his nominee's conservative credentials. She was confirmed 99-0. Ronald J. Hansen, "Spectacle of Sandra O'Connor's 1981 Confirmation Hearing Foreshadowed Today's Politics," *Arizona Republic*, March 15, 2019, https://www.azcentral.com/story/news/local/phoenix/2019/03/15/sandra-day-oconnor-senate-confirmation-hearings-1981-were-spectacle-barry-goldwater-ted-kennedy/2722312002/.

305 Wikipedia, s.v., "Michael Grant (television)," last updated March 11, 2020, 13:00, https://en.wikipedia.org/wiki/Michael_Grant_(television).

306 Based on the author's small number of appearances on the show and the hundreds of *Horizon* shows he watched in those twenty-five years.

307 Congress vested responsibility for the administration of the Smithsonian in a 17-member Board of Regents.

As specified in the Smithsonian's charter, the Chief Justice of the United States and the Vice President of the United States are ex officio members of the Board, meaning that they serve as a duty of their office. The Chief Justice also serves as the Chancellor of the Smithsonian. There are six congressional Regents: Three Senators are appointed by the President pro tempore of the United States Senate and three Representatives are appointed by the Speaker of the United States House of Representatives. Their terms on the Board coincide with their elected terms in Congress, and they may be reappointed to the Board if reelected. Nine Regents are from the general public, two of whom must reside in the District of Columbia and seven of whom must be inhabitants of the 50 states (but no two from the same state). Each is nominated by the Board of Regents and appointed for a statutory term of six years by a Joint Resolution of the Congress, which is then signed into law by the President. In accordance with the Bylaws adopted by the Board of Regents in 1979, citizen members may not serve more than two successive terms. The members of the Board of Regents are: Chief Justice John G. Roberts, Jr.; Vice President Michael R. Pence (ex officio); Senator John Boozman; Senator Patrick Leahy; Senator David Perdue; Representative Doris Matsui; Representative Lucille Roybal-Allard; Representative John Shimkus; Barbara M. Barrett (Arizona); Steve Case (Virginia), Vice Chair; John Fahey (Washington, D.C.); Roger W. Ferguson, Jr. (Washington, D.C.); Michael Govan (California); Risa J. Lavizzo-Mourey (Pennsylvania); Michael M. Lynton (New York); John W. McCarter, Jr. (Illinois); David M. Rubenstein (Maryland), Chair. https://www.si.edu/regents/members.

308 https://www.rand.org/.

309 https://sallyridescience.ucsd.edu/about/.

310 https://aerospace.org/.

311 https://en.wikipedia.org/wiki/Arizona_Aviation_Hall_of_Fame.

312 https://www.wpi.edu/.

Inaugural Graduates—1970 through 1976

313 Dr. Laurie Leshin is the 16th President of Worcester Polytechnic Institute, and is the first female president in the Institution's 150-year history. Leshin is an accomplished academic and administrative leader, geochemist, and space scientist. https://en.wikipedia.org/wiki/Laurie_Leshin.

314 https://www.faa.gov/.

315 The Civil Aeronautics Board was an agency of the federal government of the United States, formed in 1938 and abolished in 1985, that regulated aviation services including scheduled passenger airline service and provided air accident investigation https://en.wikipedia.org/wiki/Civil_Aeronautics_Board.

316 https://en.wikipedia.org/wiki/Barbara_Barrett.

317 https://www.caltech.edu/about/news/barbara-mcconnell-barrett-elected-new-trustee-42336.

318 https://en.wikipedia.org/wiki/Barbara_Barrett.

319 Valley National Bank of Arizona was a bank based in Phoenix, Arizona, founded in 1900 and acquired by Bank One in 1992. The bank was one of Arizona's leading financial institutions during the 20th century and the last major independent bank in Arizona at the time of its acquisition. https://en.wikipedia.org/wiki/Valley_National_Bank_of_Arizona.

320 The Arizona District Export Council provides local leadership in international trade through its 30+ member council of international trade veterans and experts, all appointed by the U.S. Secretary of Commerce. https://www.exportaz.org/.

321 The World Affairs Councils of America is a network of 93 autonomous and nonpartisan councils across 40 states. https://www.worldaffairscouncils.org/.

322 The Economic Club of Phoenix (ECP), the premier luncheon speaker series in the Valley, hosts leaders from some of the best-known and most influential companies in the world. It was founded in January 1985 by the Dean's Council, a group of prominent business executives, in conjunction with Arizona State University's W. P. Carey School of Business. https://wpcarey.asu.edu/economic-club/purpose.

323 Space Foundation is an American nonprofit organization that advocates for all sectors of the global space industry through space awareness activities, educational programs and major industry events. Founded in 1983, the Space Foundation vision is to inspire, educate, connect, and advocate on behalf of the global space community. https://www.spacefoundation.org/.

324 The Milton Hershey School is a private philanthropic (pre-K through 12) boarding school in Hershey, Pennsylvania. Originally named the Hershey Industrial School, the institution was founded and funded by chocolate industrialist Milton Snavely Hershey and his wife, Catherine Sweeney Hershey. https://www.mhskids.org/.

325 The Hershey Trust Company is a United States corporation incorporated on April 28, 1905, by Milton S. Hershey, Harry Lebkicher and John E. Snyder. The company is majority owner of The Hershey Company and sole private owner of Hershey Entertainment and Resorts Company and administrator of the 2,000-student Milton Hershey School. It manages the $13.751 billion USD endowment of the Milton Hershey School and School Trust. http://www.hersheytrust.com/.

326 *U.S. News & World Report* has recognized Mayo Clinic as the No. 1 hospital overall and top ranked in twelve specialties. https://www.mayoclinic.org/about-mayo-clinic/quality/top-ranked.

327 Exponent is a fifty-year old, multi-disciplinary engineering and scientific consulting firm that brings together more than 90 different disciplines to solve engineering, science, regulatory, and business issues facing our clients. https://www.exponent.com/.

328 The Raytheon Company is a major U.S. defense contractor and industrial corporation with core manufacturing concentrations in weapons and military and commercial electronics. It was previously involved in corporate and special-mission aircraft until early 2007. Raytheon is the world's largest producer of guided missiles. On June 9, 2019, Raytheon announced a merger of equals with the aerospace companies of United Technologies. https://www.raytheon.com/.

329 Piper Aircraft, Inc. is a manufacturer of general aviation aircraft, located at the Vero Beach Municipal Airport in Vero Beach, Florida, United States and owned since 2009 by the Government of Brunei. In the late 20th century, it was considered to be one of the "Big Three" in the field of general aviation manufacturing, along with Beechcraft and Cessna. https://www.piper.com/.

330 ASU, Embry-Riddle Aeronautical University, Thunderbird School of Global Management, University of South Carolina, Pepperdine University, and Finlanda University.

331 The John F. Kennedy School of Government at Harvard University is a public policy and public administration school of Harvard University in Cambridge, Massachusetts, United States. The school offers master's degrees in public policy, public administration, and international development, grants several doctoral degrees, and many executive education programs. It conducts research in subjects relating to

politics, government, international affairs, and economics. Since 1970, the school has graduated 17 heads of state, the most of any educational institution. https://www.hks.harvard.edu/.

332 Thunderbird School of Global Management at Arizona State University is a global management school located in Phoenix, Arizona. Founded 1946 as an independent, private institution, it was acquired by Arizona State University in 2014. The school derives its name from Thunderbird Field No. 1, a decommissioned World War II-era US Army Air Force base that served as its campus for over 70 years. https://thunderbird.asu.edu/.

333 Knowledge Enterprise Development is part of ASU's research enterprise. It trains and supports entrepreneurs, leads the university's economic development activities, engages with corporate partners and international development agencies, and facilitates technology transfer. https://research.asu.edu/ked-units.

334 The American Management Association is an American non-profit educational membership organization for the promotion of management, based in New York City. The association has its headquarters in New York City, and has local head-offices throughout the world. https://www.amanet.org/.

335 The U.S.-Afghan Women's Council (USAWC) is a non-partisan public-private partnership that convenes governments, civil society and the private sector around the goal of supporting Afghan women and girls' education, healthcare, economic empowerment and leadership. The Council leverages public and private resources to advance member-driven initiatives and highlights the experiences and needs of Afghan women and girls. https://gucchd.georgetown.edu/USAWC/.

336 https://thunderbird.asu.edu/global-impact/project-artemis-afghanistan.

337 Barrett, The Honors College at Arizona State University is a program that provides over 5,400 students with a residential experience that is similar to that which one might find at a smaller college or university, while still giving access to the resources of a major research institution. https://barretthonors.asu.edu/.

338 Craig R. Barrett (born August 29, 1939) is an American business executive who served as the chairman of the board of Intel Corporation until May 2009. He became CEO of Intel in 1998, a position he held for seven years. After retiring from Intel, Barrett joined the faculty at Thunderbird School of Global Management in Phoenix, Arizona. https://en.wikipedia.org/wiki/Craig_Barrett_(chief_executive).

339 https://en.wikipedia.org/wiki/1994_Arizona_gubernatorial_election.

340 https://www.bushcenter.org/people/barbara-m-barrett-.html.

341 The U.S. Mission to the United Nations (USUN) serves as the United States' delegation to the United Nations. USUN is responsible for carrying out the nation's participation in the world body. In 1947, the United States Mission was created by an act of Congress to assist the President and the Department of State in conducting United States policy at the United Nations. Since that time, USUN has served a vital role as the Department of State's UN branch. Today, USUN has approximately 150 people on staff who serve to represent the United States' political, economic and social, legal, military, public diplomacy and management interests at the United Nations. https://usun.usmission.gov/mission/.

342 Mount Kilimanjaro or just Kilimanjaro, with its three volcanic cones, Kibo, Mawenzi, and Shira, is a dormant volcano in Tanzania. It is the highest mountain in Africa, with its summit about 4,900 meters (16,100 ft) from its base, and 5,895 meters (19,341 ft) above sea level. https://en.wikipedia.org/wiki/Mount_Kilimanjaro.

343 https://en.wikipedia.org/wiki/Barbara_Barrett.

344 https://www.washingtontimes.com/news/2019/may/21/barbara-barrett-nominated-be-air-force-secretary-t/.

345 https://en.wikipedia.org/wiki/United_States_Secretary_of_the_Air_Force.

346 *Arizona Republic*, Yvonne Wingett Sanchez, Friday, October 18, 2019, page 13A.

347 https://www.airforcetimes.com/news/your-air-force/2019/10/18/the-air-force-has-a-new-secretary-barbara-barrett-sworn-in/.

348 https://en.wikipedia.org/wiki/Barbara_Barrett.

349 Lifetime membership in the Horatio Alger Association is conferred on 10 to 12 individuals each year with the presentation of the Horatio Alger Award. The Award symbolizes the Association's values, including personal initiative and perseverance, leadership and commitment to excellence, belief in the free-enterprise system and the importance of higher education, community service, and the vision and determination to achieve a better future. https://horatioalger.org/horatio-alger-award/.

350 Woodrow Wilson Awards are given out in multiple countries each year by the Woodrow Wilson International Center for Scholars of the Smithsonian Institution to individuals in both the public sphere and business who have shown an outstanding commitment to President of the United States Woodrow

Wilson's dream of integrating politics, scholarship, and policy for the common good. Created in 1999 as a local Award for leadership in Washington, DC, the Awards were expanded in 2001 to recognize great leaders and thinkers throughout the world. Funding from the Awards supports additional research, scholars, and programs in Washington and the home community of the recipients. https://en.wikipedia.org/wiki/Woodrow_Wilson_Awards.

351 The Sandra Day O'Connor Board Excellence Award is presented to women lawyers who have served with distinction as independent directors of public companies and exemplify the manner in which Sandra Day O'Connor leads her life, paving new paths for the women who come after her. https://www.directwomen.org/sandra-day-oconnor-board-excellence-award.

352 http://www.laskerfoundation.org/.

353 Oral History interview with Barbara Barrett (BB) conducted by Pam Stevenson (PS) for the Historical League, Inc. and videotaped by Bill Stevenson on June 18, 2007 at the Barretts' Paradise Valley home. Barbara Barrett photograph by Mike Paulson. Transcripts for website edited by members of Historical League, Inc.

354 Id at p 3.

355 Id at p 7.

356 Id at p 18.

357 See footnote 42, infra.

358 Id at p 38.

359 "Douglas Rayes,"iSearch, accessed February 21, 2021, https://isearch.asu.edu/profile/849917.

360 Jane Dee Hull is a former American politician and educator. In 1997, she ascended to the office of governor of Arizona following the resignation of Fife Symington, becoming the state's 20th governor. Hull was elected in her own right the following year, and served until 2003. Wikipedia, s.v., "Jane Dee Hull," last updated January 18, 2021, 9:09, https://en.wikipedia.org/wiki/Jane_Dee_Hull.

361 Ibid.

362 As more and more veterans return from military service, the courts are seeing an increasing number of offenders with service-related trauma. Such trauma has resulted in higher rates of divorce, drug and alcohol abuse, and in some cases, incarceration and suicide in veterans. Without appropriate treatment, these veterans are at risk of harming themselves or others. Veterans Court is based on a collaborative initiative between several agencies: Maricopa County Adult Probation Department, Veterans Service Outreach Specialist, Carl Hayden Veterans Hospital, The Veterans Administration Regional Office, Mercy Maricopa Integrated Care, Maricopa County Attorney, Maricopa County Public Defender, Terros Veteran Peer Navigator, Correctional Health Services, and Behavioral Health Provider Networks. Veterans Court works with high-risk veterans who are currently on probation with Maricopa County Adult Probation. "Veterans Court," The Judicial Branch of Arizona, accessed February 21, 2021, https://superiorcourt.maricopa.gov/criminal/veterans-court/.

363 Stand-Downs are typically one- to three-day events providing supplies and services to homeless Veterans, such as food, shelter, clothing, health screenings and VA Social Security benefits counseling. Veterans can also receive referrals to other assistance such as health care, housing solutions, employment, substance use treatment and mental health counseling. They are collaborative events, coordinated between local VA Medical Centers, other government agencies and community-based homeless service providers. "Veterans Experiencing Homelessness," U.S. Department of Veterans Affairs, accessed February 21, 2021, https://www.va.gov/homeless/events.asp.

364 The Commission is charged with: Advising the AJC on matters affecting victims' rights and the administration of justice; Making recommendations to the Committee on Continuing Education and Training (COJET) and the AJC regarding training and education for judges and court personnel on victims' rights and appropriate treatment of victims; Working with the Committee on Probation (COP) and other court committees and entities as necessary to promote the improved collection and disbursement of victim restitution; Serving as the Judicial Branch liaison to other established victims' advocacy organizations; and Making other recommendations to the AJC that preserve the rights afforded to victims in Arizona Constitution, Article II, Section 2.1 and ACJA § 5-204. "Commission on Victims in the Courts, Arizona Judicial Branch, accessed February 21, 2021, https://www.azcourts.gov/cscommittees/Commission-on-Victims-in-the-Courts.

365 "Leadership Institute," Arizona Judicial Branch, accessed February 21, 2021, https://www.azcourts.gov/clia/.

366 Arizona has developed a process to evaluate each judge's work and report back to you. Judicial evaluations collect input from everyone who has contact with a judge including litigants, witnesses, jurors and lawyers. This input is then used to rate key aspects of each judge's performance including whether they

can apply the law fairly, treat people with respect and manage a courtroom. "Arizona Judicial Performance Review," Arizona Judicial Branch, accessed February 21, 2021, https://www.azcourts.gov/jpr/.

367 Judge Rayes is a Republican. http://whiterhouse.gof/the-press-office/20130927114047.

368 http://cdn.ca9.uscourts.gov/datastore/uploads/general/Circuit%20CJA%20Policies%20Effective%2010-20-16.pdf.

CHAPTER 11

THE STARSKY SAGA—1968 TO 1970

The 1968–1970 academic years at ASU Law were volitant, to say the least. The first entering class was now on the cusp of lawyer-hood. They had one last semester in a public university, surrounded by large public issues, and were almost ready to enter the fray. Enter Morris Joseph Starsky.[1] He was an Assistant Professor of Philosophy at ASU, and taught his philosophy classes in the Matthews Center in the middle of the Tempe campus. All law school classes were taught in the Matthews Center, pending completion of their new building on the east side of the campus.

These upperclassmen and women in ASU Law had studied law for two full years, nonstop, in a core curriculum deep into "law," with only slight references to "philosophy." The relationship between law and philosophy runs deep in the veins of lawyers and philosophers. The body public uses the word "law" primarily in terms of law enforcement. It's often a cold association. "Legal," or its reciprocal "illegal," suggest more than just enforcement; they carry the hot blood of accusation and guilt.

"Law has been built on the backbones of some of the greatest thinkers of our time. Many of them were once philosophers who questioned anything and everything. In this effect, law and philosophy are deeply intertwined and inherently related."[2] In softer, older, slower times, the world's greatest philosophers questioned things such as, "What is law? What constitutes a just law?" and much more.[3]

The 3Ls at ASU Law in January 1970 were about to get an on-campus, front-row seat at a small battle of wits between law, philosophy, and free speech. It would gush right out of the Matthews Center into the entrance to the Great Hall at Armstrong Hall, the new law school building. ASU accused Starsky of "[failing] to exercise appropriate restraint or to exercise critical self-discipline and judgment using, extending, and transmitting knowledge."[4] It was one of eight charges ultimately filed against Starsky. The charges arose out of a series of incidents from 1968 to 1970.

STARSKY AT ARMSTRONG HALL

In May 1968, Starsky showed up at the new law school building and handed out mimeographed copies of a letter to everyone on the doorsteps. It was a letter to the President of Columbia University, apparently from a student. It was not remotely connected to anything going on at ASU. But it contained a quote, then in the news cycle by an activist—LeRoi Jones[5]: "Up against the wall, m-----f-----" that would later be used to prove that Starsky's intent was "to promote disaffection and disloyalty . . . between the faculty and the Administration at Arizona State University."[6]

Starsky and other activists were demonstrating frequently on campus in 1968, 1969, and 1970 at ASU and the University of Arizona. Students and faculty engaged in brisk dialogue about free speech, due process of law, and politics. ASU's law students would soon be witness to enriching and enraging lessons about what it meant to represent someone in a court of law, a board of inquiry, or a university faced with the political conflicts of the era.

When lawyers defend clients, they do not think about whether the *thing* a client is being prosecuted for is moral, right, wrong, good, or bad. Morality, right, wrong and other philosophical tests are not the issue. Lawyers focus instead on how and whether existing law flows with, or circumvents, regulatory reality. Law and philosophy were about to become a bombshell on ASU's Tempe campus in January of 1970.

Starsky was a philosopher and a self-described political and social activist.[7] By all accounts, he avoided politicizing his class lectures. Nonetheless, he became a "controversial and outspoken opponent of the Vietnam War, a vigorous support of organized labor, and an active participant in the Socialist Workers Party. . . .

[At ASU,] he was the faculty coordinator for the ASU Chapter of Students for a Democratic Society.[8] His aggressive and at times profane commentary landed him several radio and television news appearances."[9]

ANTI-RACISM RALLIES

The Starsky confrontation/saga started on January 14, 1970, when he requested and was granted permission by his ASU department chair to dismiss a class early so he could attend an anti-racism rally in Tucson.[10] He appeared in support of eight University of Arizona students arrested while demonstrating against the U of A's participation in sports competitions with Brigham Young University, which did not allow black athletes. Starsky was not arrested, but his presence in Tucson, occasioned by cutting his ASU class to attend the scheduled demonstration at the University of Arizona, generated several actions at Arizona State University.[11]

The Arizona Board of Regents[12] under Arizona law is the "employer" of all faculty and staff at all three Arizona public universities.[13] Two weeks after the highly publicized demonstration at the U of A, ABOR held its regularly scheduled meeting at ASU in Tempe. Regent Gordon Paris told the board he had prepared a proposed resolution and wished it to be incorporated in the minutes of the meeting:

> *The Arizona Board of Regents recognizes and supports the principle that when a faculty member speaks or writes as a private citizen, he should be free from institutional censorship or discipline. The Board is mindful, however, that a faculty member's special position in the community imposes upon him the particular obligations and serious responsibilities of conducting his behavior and activities in the best interests of the university and his profession. The Board instructs the President of Arizona State University to institute proceedings in accordance with due process and university procedures to recommend what appropriate disciplinary action, if any, should be taken in regard to Assistant Professor Morris J. Starsky including whether his appointment be renewed or terminated.*

After reading his resolution, Regent Gordon D. Paris moved for its adoption. Regent Jack Williams (Arizona's Governor) seconded it. It unanimously carried.[14] Lawyers and law professors for both universities were present—Assistant Dean of the College of Law Alan Matheson represented ASU and Professor Thomas L. Hall represented the University of Arizona.

With that January 31, 1970 resolution, ABOR addressed both the political and the legal issues extant in most American college campuses in the raging seventies. Just three months later, on May 4, 1970, twenty-eight Ohio National guardsmen fired approximately sixty-seven rounds in thirteen seconds, killing four Kent State University students, and wounding nine others. The students were engaged in a nonviolent protest of the bombing of Cambodia by U.S. military forces. Hundreds of universities, colleges, and high schools closed throughout the U.S.; four million students went on strike.[15]

ABOR FIRES STARSKY

Starsky's battle had just begun. It would be nonviolent; he would fight it vigorously. He would lose the war while winning the battle. The battle was about free speech, but the war was about employment. A month after the Kent State massacre, ABOR held its June 10, 1970 meeting on the ASU campus.[16] The sole issue before the board was Professor Starsky. Board President Goss read a prepared statement, summarizing the board's position regarding Starsky's employment at ASU.

> *On February 21, 1970 this Board, having theretofore been apprised of charges of improper and unprofessional conduct against Assistant Professor Morris J. Starsky . . . directed that such charges be explored. On March 4, 1970, the [ASU President] instituted a formal hearing . . . in accord with the Faculty Constitution and By-Laws . . . Written charges were lodged against Dr. Starsky by President Newburn . . . [the charges were] periodically heard by the Committee on Academic Freedom and Tenure . . . beginning March 24, 1970, and ending April 29, 1970 . . . Dr. Starsky was personally present and represented by legal counsel . . . both of them saw, confronted and cross-examined all witnesses against Dr. Starsky, who was furnished with copies of all exhibits offered in evidence by the University . . . Dr. Starsky and his counsel offered and examined witnesses in behalf of the former and submitted evidence in his behalf; freely argued and commented upon testimony and evidence; and both sides made concluding summations . . . Dr.*

The Starsky Saga—1968 to 1970

Harry K. Newburn, President of the University, has submitted to this Board a report . . . with relevant recommendations . . . [17]

ABOR unanimously found that "Dr. Starsky [was] guilty of substantial, wrongful, and prejudicial acts" "and deeds with which he was charged (except as to three specified activities as to which no evidence was offered, and except that instead of iniating [sic], urging, and encouraging the incident of November 20, 1968, Dr. Starsky supported and participated in such incident in violation of Regents ordinance)." ABOR specifically found that "Dr. Starsky, by his own testimony, would not consider himself bound in the future to obey or enforce the rules and regulations of the University and this Board . . . . It is therefore the judgment of the Board that the interests of education in the State of Arizona require that Dr. Stansky no longer be permitted to teach on the campuses under the jurisdiction of this Board."[18]

By June of 1970, Starsky had applied for a sabbatical leave. The Board gave him "the opportunity to take a terminal sabbatical leave for the full academic year, 1970–71."[19] If he chose not to accept the sabbatical leave terms, his contractual relationship with ASU would be terminated as the end of the 1969–70 academic year and no new contract would be tendered to him.[20]

In the ABOR July 11, 1970 meeting, Regent Singer told the board that Dr. Starsky's lawyer, Alan M. Kyman,[21] had written to President Newburn[22] and made "various allegations . . . as well as counter-proposals to the action taken by" the Board at the June 10, 1970 meeting. After discussion, the Board voted to maintain the position taken in the June 10 meeting.[23] Mr. Kyman's June 25, 1970 letter to ASU President Newburn is categorical. He said his client applied for a one-semester sabbatical, not two. ABOR had publicly stated he was entitled to a sabbatical, unconditionally, and then attached new conditions to it. Dr. Starsky was not willing to accept a conditional sabbatical. Kyman also reminded ABOR and President Newburn there was a pending lawsuit, which may cause Starsky's reinstatement.[24] Richard G. Landini, ASU President Newburn's assistant, responded to Kyman's letter on June 30, 1970. He said Newburn was out of the state but would respond on his return. He also said, "Although I have no authority in the matter, I might conjecture that only the Arizona Board of Regents itself can make changes in the action it has taken regarding Dr. Starsky." This was no longer an ASU issue; it was now an ABOR issue.[25]

THE SANDRA DAY O'CONNOR COLLEGE OF LAW

STARSKY FILES CIVIL RIGHTS CASE IN
U.S. DISTRICT COURT FOR ARIZONA

Starsky filed a multi-count civil rights action against ABOR in 1970. He named two ASU presidents and each regent individually,[26] claiming they violated his First and Fourteenth Amendment rights under 42 U.S.C. §§ 1981–1985.[27] Starsky's federal complaint took legal aim primarily at ABOR's June 10, 1970 decision.[28] Judge Carl Muecke[29] resolved the case in December of 1972 by ruling in Starsky's favor. His ninety-page opinion is a mini-seminar in constitutional litigation where teachers are dismissed in violation of their constitutional rights.

> *The public employee, [Starsky] a college professor, was discharged after he spoke at a protest rally during the time of his regularly scheduled class. The employee filed a civil rights action contending that his discharge was based on an impermissible restrictive view of his First Amendment rights. The employer and board members argued that the board of regents acted within its lawful discretion in dismissing the employee for a series of unprofessional acts. They argued that the speech lost constitutional protection in that it amounted to verbal act or lacked professional restraint and accuracy. The court granted the employee's motion for summary judgment because (1) all of the public communications took place off campus and all dealt with matters of public interest; (2) the board of regents, in discharging the public employee, violated its own standards not to discipline a teacher for speaking or writing as a citizen, and violated the employee's rights to freedom of speech by applying constitutionally impermissible standards to speech made as a citizen; and (3) there was no evidence of detriment to the employer's interest in the speeches.*[30]

To salt ABOR's wound, Judge Muecke declared that ABOR had to reinstate Starsky to his position as an ASU professor. In ruling for Starsky against ABOR, Judge Muecke relied on three points of law: (1) "Undifferentiated fear or apprehension of disturbance is not enough to overcome the right of free expression;" (2) "A teacher's public criticism may be constitutionally protected and may, therefore, be an impermissible basis for termination of employment"; (3) "A teacher has the same First Amendment rights as any other citizen. The employer cannot restrict this right although it may balance the interests of the teacher, as a citizen, in commenting upon matters of public concern and the interests of the state, as an employer, in promoting the efficiency of the public services it performs through its employees."[31]

ABOR APPEALS TO THE NINTH CIRCUIT COURT OF APPEALS

ABOR appealed the trial court's decision to the United States Court of Appeals for the Ninth Circuit. On February 26, 1975, the Ninth Circuit panel affirmed in part the district court's entry of summary judgment in Starsky's favor, holding that on the stipulated facts, the court was "not in error" under the prevailing standard of review in appellate cases.[32] It ruled for Starsky on procedural grounds, rather than on "the merits" because it was reviewing the entry of summary judgment by a trial judge, rather than a verdict rendered by a trial jury. In bench cases, the judge may resolve all factual issues. On appeal, the reviewing court must apply the "clearly erroneous standard, meaning that unless the lower court's findings were clearly erroneous, they would not altered by the appellate court."[33] The trial court's central findings were that the Arizona Board of Regents violated Starsky's First Amendment rights and improperly predicted the decision not to renew his yearly contract at ASU. The Ninth Circuit noted that the trial court had decided the merits of Starsky's claims based on a written record by the faculty committee at ASU.

The Ninth Circuit opinion dealt with eight incidents—the first being his cancellation of a class at ASU to attend and participate in a protest rally at the University of Arizona. Seven other incidents were resolved at the trial court level. The disciplinary proceedings were instituted by the Board of Regents, not ASU's faculty Committee on Academic Freedom and Tenure. That was important because, although ASU did not have a formal tenure system, Starsky had attained a "stability of employment" which entitled him to a hearing before any decision was made not to renew his contract of employment.[34]

That committee compiled nearly 1,200 pages of transcript and made detailed findings regarding the eight specific incidents. Although it did not condone all of Starsky's conduct, it concluded that the incident did not warrant dismissal. ASU's president forwarded the committee's findings and recommended to ABOR sanctions short of dismissal. "Nonetheless . . . the Board, as it had the power to do, decided not to renew Starsky's yearly contract and thus terminated his employment. In making this decision, the regents relied on all eight incidents without assigning particular significance to any of them."³⁵ The trial court had held on the merits "that the evidence did not support some of the factual findings of the Board and held that, of the eight incidents for which Starsky was discharged, six involved constitutionally protected speech under applicable Supreme Court precedents" and that canceling the class was not constitutionally protected. The Ninth Circuit said, "Applying the clearly erroneous rule . . . we sustain the district judge's findings of fact, which were based on his exhaustive review of the evidence. Furthermore, we agree with his careful application of the law to each of the eight incidents."³⁶

To the extent there was any message for Arizona's public university system, it was this: The Board of Regents is a governance entity, not a court of law. It did not evaluate the evidence; it made a governance decision, not a legal one.

Starsky's view of the facts in the trial court is there was "a conspiracy among the regents to punish him for his unpopular views." Neither court dealt with that issue. Starsky's theory was that his First Amendment rights had been infringed. The regents' theory was that one valid ground for dismissal validated their action.³⁷ The Ninth Circuit allowed the trial court's judgment to stand.³⁸ Ultimately, the Ninth Circuit upheld the lower court's ruling in Starsky's favor and remanded the case back to the court to determine "(1) whether the regents waived the defense based on the terminal sabbatical agreement, and (2) if they did not, whether by accepting the terminal sabbatical agreement, Starsky relinquished his claims against the university arising from his termination."³⁹ Starsky, as of the end of the legal case, got no damages and was never again employed by ASU, or any other major university.⁴⁰

No one knew it at the time, but Starsky was the subject of an ongoing FBI investigation in 1970. In 1975, he became one of the first U.S. citizens to receive federal records under the newly created Freedom of Information Act.⁴¹ It gives citizens "the right to request access to federal agency records or information except to the extent the records are protected from disclosure by any of nine exemptions contained in the law or by one of three special law enforcement record exclusions."⁴² The documents he received under his FOIA request "revealed he was the subject of illegal wiretap and surveillance activities, and that the FBI attempted to facilitate his dismissal from ASU by sending an anonymous letter to university officials accusing Starsky of fomenting violence. He was one of the first people targeted by the FBI program known as COINTELPRO."⁴³

The Starsky Saga—1968 to 1970

In 1981, the new ASU President, J. Russell Nelson,[44] agreed to a settlement "for a small portion of back wages," which Starsky accepted because of declining health.[45] He died at eighty-five in 1989. Thirty-three years after his termination, his son attended ASU as a student. ASU provided financial assistance to allow him to enroll at ASU. The decision to give financial aid was not based on his father's history, the ASU Provost said, but was well within the "bounds of normal decision-making on [financial] aid."[46] ASU Provost Milton Glick[47] said, "I think the whole incident thirty years ago was quite unfortunate."[48]

---

1 Starsky earned a BA degree from the University of Rochester in 1955, an MA in 1958, and his PhD in 1967, in philosophy from the University of Michigan. He was hired by ASU as an Assistant Professor of Philosophy in 1964, while completing his thesis for his doctoral degree. Wikipedia, s.v., "Morris Starsky," last modified February 19, 2020, 12:49, https://en.wikipedia.org/wiki/Morris_Starsky.

2 "The Relationship Between Law, Philosophy and Morality," Van Norman Law, accessed February 19, 2020, https://www.vannormanlaw.com/relationship-law-philosophy-morality/.

3 "The Relationship Between Law, Philosophy and Morality," Van Norman Law, accessed February 19, 2020, https://www.vannormanlaw.com/relationship-law-philosophy-morality/.

4 *Starsky v. Williams*, 353 F. Supp 900, 907 (D. Ariz. 1972).

5 "Amiri Baraka (born Everett LeRoi Jones; October 7, 1934 – January 9, 2014), previously known as LeRoi Jones and Imamu Amear Baraka, was an American writer of poetry, drama, fiction, essays and music criticism. He was the author of numerous books of poetry and taught at several universities, including the State University of New York at Buffalo and the State University of New York at Stony Brook. He received the PEN/Beyond Margins Award, in 2008 for *Tales of the Out and the Gone*. Baraka's career spanned nearly 50 years, and his themes range from black liberation to white racism. Some poems that are always associated with him are 'The Music: Reflection on Jazz and Blues,' 'The Book of Monk,' and 'New Music, New Poetry,' works that draw on topics from the worlds of society, music, and literature. Baraka's poetry and writing have attracted both high praise and condemnation. In the African-American community, some compare Baraka to James Baldwin and recognize him as one of the most respected and most widely published black writers of his generation. Others have said his work is an expression of violence, misogyny, and homophobia. Regardless of viewpoint, Baraka's plays, poetry, and essays have been defining texts for African-American culture. Baraka's brief tenure as Poet Laureate of New Jersey (2002–2003) involved controversy over a public reading of his poem 'Somebody Blew Up America?' which resulted in accusations of anti-Semitism and negative attention from critics and politicians." Wikipedia, s.v., "Amiri Baraka," last modified February 19, 2020, 11:01, https://en.wikipedia.org/wiki/Amiri_Baraka.

6 Starsky, 353 F. Supp at 907.

7 Wikipedia, s.v., "Morris Starsky," last modified February 19, 2020, 12:49, https://en.wikipedia.org/wiki/Morris_Starsky.

8 Ibid. "Students for a Democratic Society (SDS), American student organization that flourished in the mid-to-late 1960s and was known for its activism against the Vietnam War. SDS, founded in 1959, had its origins in the student branch of the League for Industrial Democracy, a social democratic educational organization. An organizational meeting was held in Ann Arbor, Michigan, in 1960, and Robert Alan Haber was elected president of SDS. Initially, SDS chapters throughout the nation were involved in the civil rights movement. Operating under the principles of the 'Port Huron Statement,' a manifesto written by Tom Hayden and Haber and issued in 1962, the organization grew slowly until the escalation of U.S. involvement in Vietnam (1965). SDS organized a national march on Washington, D.C., in April 1965, and, from about that period, SDS grew increasingly militant, especially about issues relating to the war, such as the drafting of students. Tactics included the occupation of university and college administration buildings on campuses across the country." "Students for a Democratic Society" in *Encyclopedia Britannica*. Encyclopedia Britannica, accessed February 19, 2020 https://www.britannica.com/topic/Students-for-a-Democratic-Society.

9 Ibid.

10 Wikipedia, s.v., "Morris Starsky," last modified February 19, 2020, 12:49, https://en.wikipedia.org/wiki/Morris_Starsky. *See also* Morris J. Starsky Papers, Arizona Archives Online, accessed February 24, 2020, http://www.azarchivesonline.org/xtf/view?docId=ead/asu/starsky.xml;query=morris%20starsky;brand=default.

11 Ibid.

12 "The Arizona Board of Regents (ABOR) is the governing body of Arizona's public university system, providing policy guidance to Arizona State University, Northern Arizona University, the University of Arizona and their branch campuses. . . . In 1885, the Territorial Legislature authorized the establishment of the University of Arizona and provided for the management, direction, governance, and control by a Board of Regents. The state colleges, one in Tempe and one in Flagstaff, were governed by a three-member State Board of Education that included the Superintendent of Public Instruction and two members appointed by the Governor.

"In March 1945, the Governor signed a law uniting the governing boards of the university and state colleges of Arizona. The authority of the Board of Regents expanded to include the Arizona State Teachers College at Tempe (since 1958 Arizona State University), and Arizona State Teachers College at Flagstaff (since 1966 Northern Arizona University)." Wikipedia, s.v., "Arizona Board of Regents," last modified February 19, 2020, 00:51, https://en.wikipedia.org/wiki/Arizona_Board_of_Regents.

13 *See* Ariz. Rev. Stat. Ann. §15-725 (which has since been repealed and replaced by Ariz. Rev. Stat. Ann. § 15-1626 [2020]), which gives ABOR the legal right to remove faculty or staff "when the interests of education in this state so require."

14 *See* ABOR Minutes of a Meeting, January 31, 1970, at 72.

15 The most significant battle against students would occur just a few months after the UofA nonviolent demonstration at issue in the Starsky saga. "The Kent State shootings (also known as the May 4 massacre or the Kent State massacre) were the shootings on May 4, 1970, of unarmed college students by members of the Ohio National Guard at Kent State University in Kent, Ohio, during a mass protest against the bombing of Cambodia by United States military forces. Twenty-eight guardsmen fired approximately 67 rounds over a period of 13 seconds, killing four students and wounding nine others, one of whom suffered permanent paralysis. Some of the students who were shot had been protesting against the Cambodian Campaign, which President Richard Nixon announced during a television address on April 30 of that year. Other students who were shot had been walking nearby or observing the protest from a distance. There was a significant national response to the shootings: hundreds of universities, colleges, and high schools closed throughout the United States due to a student strike of 4 million students, and the event further affected public opinion, at an already socially contentious time, over the role of the United States in the Vietnam War." Wikipedia, s.v., "Kent State shootings," last modified February 19, 2020, 4:44, https://en.wikipedia.org/wiki/Kent_State_shootings.

16 *See* ABOR Minutes of a Meeting, June 10, 1970. ABOR President Goss called the meeting to order at 3:00 PM in the Regents Room at ASU. Regents Elwood Bradford, Margaret Christy, Wesley Goss, Gordon Paris, Norman Sharber, Paul Singer, W.P. Shofstall, and Regent Governor Jack Williams were present. President Goss informed the audience that the Board would "dispense with the usual [board] agenda matters . . . and proceed with the matter of Assistant Professor Morris J. Starsky."

17 Ibid., 134.

18 Ibid.

19 By accepting a terminal leave, Starsky would be paid 60% of his regular salary, would have to absent himself from the ASU campus while on sabbatical leave, and would have his contract not renewed at the close of the 1970–71 academic year. Nor would he be required to return to campus following his sabbatical. Ibid., 134–135.

20 Ibid., 134–35.

21 Kyman was a respected member of the Arizona Bar Association. He died March 29, 2019. "[H]e attended Stanford University, graduating in 1952. He graduated from the University of Arizona School of Law in 1955 and opened a solo practice in Phoenix that year. Alan practiced law in Phoenix for over 55 years; defending civil liberties and helping real people solve real problems with compassion and respect." "Alan Kyman Obituary – Phoenix, AZ" Legacy.com, accessed February 19, 2020, https://www.legacy.com/obituaries/azcentral/obituary.aspx?pid=192026032.

22 Harry K. Newburn was ASU's twelfth president, serving from 1969 to 1971. "Harry K. Newburn," ASU Office of the President, accessed February 19, 2020, https://president.asu.edu/the-office/past-presidents/harry-k-newburn.

23 *See* ABOR Minutes of a Meeting, July 11, 1970, 1970 Minutes Book, Volume XXIV, 139.

24 See Alan Kyman to Harry Newburn, Documents File, Meeting of July 11, 1970 Volume XXIV.

25 See Richard Landini to Alan Kyman, Documents File, Meeting of July 11, 1970 Volume XXIV.

26 *Starsky v. Williams,* 353 F. Supp. 900 (D. Ariz. 1972). Morris J. Starsky v. Jack R. Williams; H.K. Newburn; Elwood W. Bradford; James Elliot Dunsheath; Wesley P. Goss; Gordon D. Paris; Margaret M. Christy; Norman G. Sharber; Paul L. Singer; Kenneth G. Bentson; Weldon P. Shofstall; Sidney S. Woods; John A. Lentz; Betty Riggle; Hartford Accident & Indemnity Company; Western Surety Company; Pacific Insurance Company; Fireman's Fund; American Insurance Companies; The Fidelity & Casualty Company of New York; Great American Insurance Company; Board of Regents of the Universities and State College of Arizona; and John W. Schwada. Dr. Newburn was ASU's President when ABOR terminated Dr. Starsky. Dr. Schwada succeeded him when he became ASU's 13th President in 1971.

27 42 U.S.C. § 1983 provides that "[e]very person who, under color of any statute, ordinance, regulation, custom, or usage, of any State of Territory or the District of Columbia, subjects . . . any citizen of the United States . . . to the deprivation of any rights, privileges, or immunities secured by the Constitution and laws, shall be liable to the party injured in an action at law, suit in equity, or other proper proceeding for redress . . . ."

28 Starsky, 353 F. Supp at 904.

29 "Born in New York City, New York, Muecke received a Bachelor of Arts degree from the College of William & Mary in 1941 and a Bachelor of Laws from the James E. Rogers College of Law at the University of Arizona in 1953. He was a United States Marine Corps Major during World War II, from 1942 to 1946, and remained at that rank in the United States Marine Corps Reserve until 1950. Because of his excellent German, he was tapped by the Office of Strategic Services (the precursor to the Central Intelligence Agency) to go to France, where he worked with German defectors to return to Germany to spy on the Nazi regime. He was in private practice in Phoenix, Arizona from 1953 to 1961, becoming the United States Attorney for the District of Arizona from 1961 to 1964. On August 17, 1964, Muecke was nominated by President Lyndon B. Johnson to a seat on the United States District Court for the District of Arizona vacated by Judge David W. Ling. Muecke was confirmed by the United States Senate on September 29, 1964, and received his commission on October 1, 1964. He served as Chief Judge from 1979 to 1984, assuming senior status on November 30, 1984. He continued to serve in that capacity until his death on September 21, 2007, in Flagstaff, Arizona." Wikipedia, s.v., "Charles Andrew Muecke," last modified February 19, 2020, 18:33, https://en.wikipedia.org/wiki/Charles_Andrew_Muecke.

30 *Starsky v. Williams,* 353 F. Supp. 900 (D. Ariz. 1972).

31 *Starsky,* 353 F. Supp. at 918–19, 921 (citations omitted).

32 *Starsky v. Williams,* 512 F. 2d 109 (9th Cir. 1975).

33 Wikipedia, s.v., "Standard of Review," last modified February 19, 2020, 22:31, https://en.wikipedia.org/wiki/Standard_of_review. "In law, the standard of review is the amount of deference given by one court in reviewing a decision of a lower court or tribunal. A low standard of review means that the decision under review will be varied or overturned if the reviewing court considers there is any error at all in the lower court's decision. A high standard of review means that deference is accorded to the decision under review, so that it will not be disturbed just because the reviewing court might have decided the matter differently."

34 *Starsky,* 512 F. 2d at 110.

35 Ibid.

36 Ibid., 111.

37 Ibid., 112.

38 The regents also raised an argument in both courts that Starsky and the university had raised a contractual settlement of the dispute, which was an "accord and satisfaction" which bars the action in both courts. It was based on a terminal sabbatical agreement offered by the regents and accepted by Starsky not long after the inception of the lawsuit. In its opinion, at page 114, the Ninth Circuit openly wondered why the regents or the parties did not mention the pending lawsuit in the settlement agreement. On appeal, the regents urged the Ninth Circuit to hold, as a matter of law, that Starsky's claim was barred by the putative settlement reflected by the sabbatical agreement. It declined "to do because the record indicates that the court below did not rule on the issue and because there appeared to be material issues of fact." The Ninth Circuit offered some solace in saying, "[a]lthough the sabbatical agreement seems to us to establish, prima facie, a contractual settlement that would bar this action, we cannot ignore the fact that the regents did not preserve this issue as effectively as they should have to the trial judge and therefore failed to secure a ruling on it. Moreover, the fact that this action was pending, but is not mentioned in the papers relied on by the regents, raises doubts as to the parties' intentions." *Starsky,* 512 F. 2d at 114. "Arguably, therefore,

the regents might be deemed to have abandoned the issue. Indeed we think they came perilously close to doing so." Ibid., 115. Ultimately, the issue was resolved at the lower court in favor of the regents because it avoided damages on the basis of Starsky's acceptance of a terminal sabbatical leave.

39 Ibid., 117.

40 Lorraine Starsky, "After the Blacklist: Starsky Remembered," *The Arizona Republic,* June 11, 2000; Bill Hart, "Family Asks ASU to Fix Torn Legacy," *The Arizona Republic,* February 11, 2003.

41 "Freedom of Information Act," United States Department of State, accessed February 19, 2020, https://foia.state.gov/Learn/FOIA.aspx.

42 Ibid. The nine exemption categories that authorize government agencies to withhold information are: (1) classified information for national defense or foreign policy; (2) internal personnel rules and practices; (3) information that is exempt under other laws; (4) trade secrets and confidential business information; (5) inter-agency or intra-agency memoranda or letters that are protected by legal privileges; (6) personnel and medical files; (7) law enforcement records or information; (8) information concerning bank supervision; (9) geological and geophysical information.

43 Wikipedia, s.v., "Morris Starsky," last modified February 19, 2020, 12:49, https://en.wikipedia.org/wiki/Morris_Starsky.

44 "J. Russell Nelson," ASU Office of the President, accessed February 19, 2020, www.president.asu.edu/the-office/past-presidents/j-russell-nelson. "J. Russell Nelson served as ASU's president from 1981 to 1989. He believed that the educational mission was the most important part of the university, and that everything else was subordinate to that, including athletics. Although his administration was marked by disharmony with the athletic department, he worked to make athletics a source of pride for the university." Ibid.

45 Wikipedia, s.v., "Morris Starsky," last modified February 19, 2020, 12:49, https://en.wikipedia.org/wiki/Morris_Starsky.

46 Bill Hart, "Ex-Prof's Son Receives Aid, ASU Denies Financial Agreement Linked to Family's History," *The Arizona Republic,* April 21, 2003.

47 Dr. Milton Glick "served as senior vice president in 1991, and then as executive vice president and provost at Arizona State University (ASU). During his 15 year-tenure with ASU, the school experienced unprecedented success, with a doubling number of minorities enrollment, a 20-percent improvement in freshman retention rate, and a 15-percent improvement in graduation rate. Funding for sponsored research tripled, and ASU recruited 10 faculty with prestigious national academy memberships, and one Nobel Laureate. The number of National Merit Scholars rose from about a dozen to more than 500 and the Tempe campus became the largest in the United States in terms of enrollment." Wikipedia, s.v., "Milton Glick," last modified February 19, 2020, 19:49, https://en.wikipedia.org/wiki/Milton_Glick.

48 Bill Hart, "Ex-Prof's Son Receives Aid, ASU Denies Financial Agreement Linked to Family's History," *The Arizona Republic,* April 21, 2003.

CHAPTER

THE FIRST TWO YEARS—1967 TO 1969

The first year of law school is nothing like the last year of college. That simple fact deludes some into thinking that if they were good at college they will be good at law school. They suffer from delusions of continuing good. Law schools are to colleges what high schools are to middle school. There is no recess. They do not allow you leisure time, which so often accompanied traditional undergraduate lecture classes. College professors are in your brain. Law school professors are in your face. The cosmic distance between college students and their professors is replaced by relentless interaction between law students and law professors. All law professors, especially in *Year One*, use the vaunted Socratic method. They ask open-ended questions before they lecture. They expect answers now, not after you've thought about it for thirty seconds. They assume you've actually read the cases in the syllabus. Not even God can help those who don't. While the cases are cold and old, the law professor stalking the front of the room is about to apply them to real-life situations. Cases, like everyday problems, are messy, disturbing, ambiguous, and deadly serious. That's why professors use them and students live with them, day-to-day. Going to class was more or less optional in college. Showing up for class, on time, eyes up, on guard, fully prepared was an everyday ritual at the ASU School of Law in 1967. Grades were based on preparation, attendance, classroom performance, and a final exam. No quizzes or midterms. Just a final exam. You're in or out based on that one three-hour ordeal. It was blue-book everlasting life, or crucifixion. That first year, 1967 had 118 students. Three years later, 87 graduated. They came in as soft intellectuals and left as hardened advocates.

FIRST CLASSES AND FIRST LAW SCHOOL PROFESSORS

In college, most students never have a class taught by a college dean. In law school, all students take classes from deans, assistant deans, associate deans, and deans-in-waiting. They manage the business and educational sides of the college, but they are all teachers first, and deans on the side.

ASU's first class in 1967 learned quickly, or they didn't learn at all. They got Dean Pedrick's penchant for folly and follies, notwithstanding his stellar rep from Northwestern School of Law. A few might have known about his time at the DOJ, his stint as Chair at the Cook County Zoning Board of Appeals, and that year he spent as a visiting professor in Western Australia. They knew Professor Canby had a one-of-a-kind history, as in, Did you know he was a U.S. Supreme Court clerk and *then* scooted off to Africa for four years! He was the deputy director of the Peace Corps in Ethiopia and the Director in Uganda. He even was a special assistant to a state university in New York, called Old Westbury. They knew Professor Cleary and were scared to death—the Reporter for the Joint Committee on Illinois Practice and the current Reporter for the Committee of Rules of Evidence in the federal courts. Holy moly, he's the real deal. And what about their librarian, Professor Richard Dahl, with the huge brain—he'd been the librarian for the University of Nebraska, the Judge Advocate General's office, the U.S. Department of the Navy, and the library up in the state of Washington. He even co-authored the legal dictionary and was Editor of the *Law Library Journal*. How'd Ped get him here? And what about Prof. Havighurst—four degrees including an LLD?[1] How many books can one man write? Professor Effland—not a guy to mess with—knows about export banks, taught at Wisconsin, Stanford, NYU, UC Berkley—and is a big deal in the ABA—uniform laws and the *Reporter for the Uniform Probate Code*. Professor Alan Matheson is Ped's assistant dean and is listed in *Encyclopedia Americana*. Professor John Morris—the youngest and most fun guy in the building—a real lawyer too—practiced with a big Chicago firm—specialized in labor relations and anti-trust cases, and was the director of the Chicago Chapter of the ACLU—he's for real—lawyer and law professor. And all of them, except Canby, wear glasses—from reading cases late at night by flashlight, no doubt.

The First Two Years—1967 to 1969

THE CORE CURRICULUM

The 1L class in the fall of 1967 took the same courses, taught by the same professors, more or less in tandem. They took Contracts 501 from Professor Rose. The catalog understated the complexity.

> *The Study of contract doctrines and their role in judicial process. The judicial doctrines and where applicable the Uniform Commercial Code are studied in the context of contracts covering employment, personal family arrangements, building and construction, the sale of goods, loans; assignment of wages and accounts receivable. Also examined are statutes of limitations; payment and settlement; remedies and measure of damages; problems of advocacy and counseling.*[2]

They took Procedure 505 from Prof. Cleary. He would explain in class, repeatedly, the manner in which the substantive law would be nourished, limited, or confused by its remedial context.

> *An introduction to the common procedural steps in litigation as an aid to understating the terminology and concepts of procedure. Common law remedies, equitable relief, the extraordinary remedies and the problems arising from the abolition of the forms of action and the union of law and equity are studied. The approach is essentially historical and explores her manner in which the substantive law has been at once nourished, limited and confused by its remedial context.*[3]

Property 507 was taught by Prof. Effland, a national expert on the subject. As in all law schools, property law had little to do with selling houses, or large tracts of land to developers. It was all about equitable estates, remainders, executory interests, and other fascinating things, like Blackacre and Whiteacre. Who knew there even was a rule against perpetuities?[4] Poor baby perpetuities—who will take care of them.

> *Introduction to the law of real and personal property various legal and equitable estates in land, life estates, remainders, concurrent interests, executory interests, limitations on creation of future interests. Modern concepts of property and an introduction to the modern efforts to define the public interest in relationship of property.*[5]

Legal Writing and Research was not so much a course as it was a redefining of looking for and writing things down. It was very different from how legal writing was taught at other law schools. Everyone in the first-year class came to the building four class-days a week prior to the start of formal classes. They listened to various teachers orient them to the study of law. They had intensive assignments designed to introduce the "neophyte" law student to research tools used to "find the law." That would give them a "store of well-founded confidence that he can find reported cases referred to in class." They were told that the upcoming class in Legislation would require writing exercises to "sharpen the legal research tools developed in elemental fashion during orientation." Then, as a reminder of the importance of legal writing (not to be confused with English writing, or literature), they would be assigned a "series of legal problems to be researched and then to write an acceptable solution thereto." Those assignments would take the form of office memorandums, opinion letters, or briefs." That would be, they were assured, "an intensive, supervised experience in researching and writing legal papers."[6]

The fourth substantive class in the first semester of the first year was Torts 505, taught by Dean Pedrick. It is almost certain that he explained what a "tort" was on the first day of class. Most tort teachers did it this way. A contract is a contract, a crime is a crime, property can be real, or personal, and procedure is not substantive. Everything else in law is a tort.[7] The official class description was:

> *Protection of person, property and relational interests against physical, appropriational, and defamatory harms. Doctrines of trespass, nuisance, negligence, conversion, deceit, privacy, slander, libel, seduction, alienation of affections, malicious prosecution, inducement of breach of contract, and unfair competition are studied in a variety of factual settings. The focus is on the operation of the judicial process as it is revealed in the disposition of tort cases.*[8]

The last of the five substantive courses in that seminal year was Constitutional Law 510, taught by Professor Canby. Who better than a man who'd served a coveted U.S. Supreme Court clerkship, and eventually found his way to a seat on the U.S. Circuit Court of Appeals for the Ninth Circuit? That syllabus read:

> *The role of the courts in the Federal system, the distribution of powers between state and federal governments, the role of procedure in litigation in constitutional questions, fundamental protection for personal, property and social rights.*

The second semester of the first year was a continuum for Contracts, Torts, and Property. Those were six-unit courses spread out over two semesters. One new four-unit course was added in the second semester of that first year, Criminal Law and Procedure 509:

> *A study of legislative and judicial formulations designed to deal with anti-social activity, the substantive elements of particular crimes, problems in the administration of criminal law and the penal system generally. The problems of criminal procedure as effected by constitutional requirements are examined. Emphasis is placed on the role and the responsibilities of the legal profession in the administration and improvement of our system of criminal justice.*

There were no electives. There would be no electives in the second year either. These were foundation courses "which nearly everyone agrees should be encountered by every law student."[9] The expectation was that, under the core-curriculum approach, all students for two years would "study and sit together in all of their courses . . . . That will generate an awareness of individual identity, a sense of cohesion, and responsibility of the group of student lawyers, an appreciation of shared experiences and the maximum opportunity for student contribution to the educational processes in a teaching system that depends for its success on the student input . . . . Drawing on the experience of the leading law schools, a modern program of legal education should provide challenge and opportunity for every serious and able student."[10] It would be the case that every survivor of those first three pivotal years at ASU Law was indeed "serious and able."

THE SECOND-YEAR CURRICULUM—A HINT AT LAWYERING

Year Two, 1968 to 1969, would be a sequel. Because it was a law school, not an undergraduate academic walk, it was also a breathing year—everybody takes a deep breath, some from exhaustion, others from expectation. It would be more cases, more easily read, now that legal jargon was no longer a mystery. *Res ipsa loquitur* for that.[11] It would be the same faculty, but now the students knew what to expect, how to slope and shape, and when to duck.

ASU Law School's second year jumped from basics to real law, from scribbling on yellow pads to actual legal documents, and analytical papers. From lightning-speed learning, to in-depth and endless explorations of legal nuance driven by insatiable curiosity. And like moving from elementary school to high school (skipping junior high), everyone's behavior is up a notch. No more coddling, picky questions, negativity, separation anxiety, and temper tantrums in torts. Now they moved from questions to solutions, comprehensive assessments, even a little glimpse of what lawyers actually do all day, every day.

The second-year course list added ten new courses and the excitement of Moot Court. ASU Law's approach to moot court varied from moot court programs in other law schools. In most other schools it was an elective to be chosen or declined based on student choice. At ASU Law, the faculty divided the entire class into "law firms" of two students each. They all used an appellate case for both briefing and argument based on the lower court trial record. Faculty supervised the briefs. The moot court arguments were held in the Great Hall before judges drawn from state and federal courts, the local bar, and law faculty. For those who liked mooting court cases, the second semester of the second year was continued on a voluntary basis with the winning team advancing in the third year to the National Moot Court competition.[12]

The course list for the first semester of the second year required all students to take nine new courses: Administrative Law 550, taught by Professor Matheson; Corporations 554, taught by Professor Morris; Federal Income Taxation 556, Procedure 557, taught by Prof. Cleary; Trusts and Estates 559, taught by Professor Effland; Antitrust Law 551, taught by Professor Morris; Commercial Law 552, taught by Prof. Havighurst; Conflict of Laws 553, taught by Prof. Canby; and Evidence 555, taught by Prof. Cleary.

The First Two Years—1967 to 1969

In its second year, ASU Law admitted another 100+ students. The new 2Ls, survivors of Year One, got a grade of 70 or better in every 1L class. A dozen or so didn't make the cut. The second-year students wondered when they would actually *do* law rather than just *study* it.

LEGAL CLINICS—INTERNSHIPS—SEMINARS

Clinics, internships, seminars, and third-year courses were on the drawing board halfway through the second semester of Year Two. A smorgasbord of some twenty-two classes was included in the student's manual for 1969–70.[13] However, the second-year class was urged not to get overly excited about taking "all" those courses.

> *A full third-year academic load will be 12–15 course credit hours per semester, so it should be evident that no single student will be able to take all the courses, seminars, and other credit-carrying activities offered by the school. Nor need the student be limited to selection from the law school smorgasbord. He may undertake independent research and study projects of his own suggestion, with appropriate credit to be arranged.*[14]

The school manual encouraged all students to live on or near campus "if at all possible." You can't read cases while driving, right? The 2L cost was up but just a notch. The general fees were $143.00 plus a special Law fee of $32.00. Non-residents paid $407.50 extra.[15] They "discouraged" part-time work off campus: "It is difficult for the law student to carry part-time employment while in law school—difficult, though not impossible. The rigors of the law school course are such that the law student should expect to devote 50 to 60 hours per week on preparation, class attendance and written work. Acceptance of admission carries a commitment on the part of the applicant for law student. The law student is simply not a part of the *leisure* society. It will be well to remember that class sessions will be scheduled throughout the day."[16] No kidding. We're not in college anymore, are we?

The 2Ls naturally thought about the kind of law they wanted to practice. That was discouraged, in writing. "For most students while in law school, it is not sensible to arrive at any firm decision to practice as a specialist in criminal law, corporate law, taxation, personal injury law, or any of the other emerging specialties. Specialization in the legal profession is a fact of life in the larger cities, but for the most part, specialization takes place after the student leaves and enters the practice. Few students indeed have any basis for knowing when they are in law school what kinds of opportunities will come their way later."[17]

THIRD-YEAR PACKING VS. THIRD-YEAR SLACKING

The third year at ASU Law's new law school likely looked like any other state law school's third year. While there is little documentary proof, Dean Pedrick and his inaugural faculty had their hands full. Most students were counting down the days. The end was in sight. Some shifted into fifth gear, others coasted, and some put everything in neutral. Said differently, the choice was to pack or slack.

All 3Ls face the same question—another year of high cost—another year of low income. And some no doubt took matters into their own hands—they worked downtown more than they studied on campus.

But most ASU 3Ls in the fall of 1969 likely took advantage of the clinics, seminar courses, and work opportunities for the same reason. The third year was easier, and a chance to reflect on what to do in year four—the first year of lawyering. The year every law student thinks about the end game. Will my end game, my employment opportunities, blossom if I take law and literature, or should I dig deeper into trusts and estate planning? It was always a rhetorical question. In Property 101 just two short years ago, the question was whether the conveying of Blackacre was conveyed was burdened by . . .

As the end of the third year became reality, a much different burden appeared. The looming bar exam. Then, as now, the bar exam was not a given—you had to work for it just like you passed the first semester courses in law school. Law graduates quickly learned the bar exam was like final exams in law school, only on steroids. Bar review teachers were real lawyers, not just law professors. They hurled seemingly easy situations at you—A hit B. Now you had three years of law school under your belt you should immediately think about what that simple statement meant. What is a hit? Merely a tap? A gut punch? In self-defense? On a football field? A boxing ring? What about implied consent? Battery, but not assault? You had to *think* while you read the questions—for two and a half days. Your ability to apply the law to simple situations would mean passing or failing the bar. The questions, answers, and analysis would get you not just a passing grade; it would get you a license to practice law. That was always the goal, right?

The First Two Years—1967 to 1969

1 The LL.D. is the Doctor of Laws, a doctorate-level academic degree in law. It is the highest level of law degree awarded in the profession. Wikipedia, s.v., "Doctor of Law," last updated December 18, 2020, 13:26, https://en.wikipedia.org/wiki/Doctor_of_Law#United_States.

2 Ibid., 30.

3 Ibid., 31.

4 *Black's Law Dictionary* defines the rule against perpetuities as "[t]he common-law rule prohibiting a grant of an estate unless the interest must vest, if at all, no later than 21 years (plus a period of gestation to cover a posthumous birth) after the death of some person alive when the interest was created." Henry Campbell Black, M.A., Fourth Edition, West Publishing Co., 1957, page 1299.

5 Ibid., 31.

6 Ibid., 32–33.

7 At least that's the way the author's torts teacher put it.

8 Ibid., 30.

9 Bulletin—ASU College of Law—1968–1969, Bureau of Publications, Arizona State University, 1967. Page 29.

10 Ibid.

11 "The Thing Speaks for Itself." Wikipedia, s.v., "Res ipsa loquitur," last updated December 23, 2020, 6:06, https://en.wikipedia.org/wiki/Res_ipsa_loquitur.

12 Bulletin—ASU College of Law—1968–1969, Bureau of Publications, Arizona State University, 1967. Page 34.

13 The list included: Business Tax Planning; Comparative Law; Corporate Finance; Creditors and Debtors; Current Constitutional Issues; Estate Planning; Family Law; Federal Estate and Gift Taxation; Federal Practice; International Law; Jurisprudence; Labor Law; Land Use Controls; Law and Social Change; The Lawyer as Counselor; Legal Problems of Indians; Modern Urban Problems; Natural Resources; Poverty Law—Legal Aid Clinic; Professional Responsibilities; State and Local Taxation; Trial Practice.

14 Bulletin—ASU College of Law—1968–1969, Bureau of Publications, Arizona State University, 1967. Page 37.

15 Ibid., 11.

16 Ibid., 18.

17 Ibid., 22.

CHAPTER 13

THE INDIAN LAW PROGRAM—1967

The term Indian Law, with a capital "I," is too often seen through either an identity lens or a cultural assessment. "It's not the law of India, or American law applicable to some Americans, but not others. We don't have Mexican Law, or African-American Law. In US Law, the term 'Indians' refers generally to the indigenous peoples of the continent at the time of European colonization.[1] 'Alaska Natives' and 'Native Hawaiians' refer to peoples indigenous to the areas occupied by those named states. The terms 'tribe' or 'band' designate a group of Indians of the same or similar heritage united in a community under one leadership or government, and inhabiting a particular territory. Because Indians have increasingly preferred 'nation' or 'people,' the term 'tribe' has become controversial. The terms used may vary from statute to statute and case to case as well."[2]

Federal Indian policy establishes the relationship between the United States government and Indian tribes within its borders. The Constitution gives the federal government primary responsibility for dealing with tribes. Law and U.S. public policy related to Native Americans have evolved continuously since the founding of the United States.[3]

THE HISTORY OF ASU'S INDIAN LEGAL PROGRAM
(1967 TO 2020)

There is an official start date (1988) and an actual start date (1967). Dean Paul Bender gets the credit for the official start. Professor Bill Canby gets it for the actual start date. At the outset, it was a great idea, unofficially recognized and underfunded. Canby gave it a great deal of his time and talent. Twenty-one years later, Dean Bender made it official, got it properly funded and, like his friend and colleague, Bill Canby, gave it a great deal of his time and talent. Here's how that happened.

ASU's ILP came about almost accidentally in the summer of 1967. The story, told twenty-five years later at the 25th Anniversary of the ILP, is extensively repeated here.[4]

The founding dean, Willard Pedrick, asked Professor Bill Canby to serve as acting dean for a month. Within two weeks, Canby received a request from the regional office of the U.S. Bureau of Indian Affairs asking for a law professor to meet once a month to instruct tribal judges from across the state. Canby said yes and took on the project himself. Canby and the judges met eight or nine times a year for several years. Then Warren Cohen joined the faculty and, with Canby, the duo created the informal Office of Indian Law. Under this name, they increased outreach and fostered relationships with tribes, usually funding their activities from their own pockets. The relationship grew and tribes sought advice and guidance from the program.

In the fall of 1969, Canby created the first Indian law course, an elective available only to third-year students. His first class had eleven enrolled students, including Native students Kent Ware and Bob Melvin. Canby continued to teach the class, and it became so popular that by 1980, the last year he taught it, there were forty-four students enrolled. The College of Law has offered a federal Indian law class every year since 1971. In 1971, Canby and Cohen traveled to Indian country, visiting the tribal courts to give legal presentations and to provide legal training. They also recruited students, and Canby attended the Pre-Law Summer Institute in New Mexico to tell Native students about the opportunities at the Arizona College of Law. Those opportunities expanded. Students started to observe tribal courts. They began to meet with tribal communities to discuss code reform. They assisted with tribal legislative activity.

When Paul Bender became dean, the law school added more staff, and the faculty recognized the growing need for an official program. Dean Bender was instrumental in nurturing the idea and was the driving force in founding the formal Indian Legal Program.

THE ILP GAINS MOMENTUM—1984 TO 2019

Prof. Canby did most of the work in the program until 1985 when Leigh Price came to Tempe as a visiting professor. Canby asked him how the law school could better serve the needs of the Indian community. In 1987, Professors Michael Berch and Jeffery Murphy intensified recruitment of Indian students. And Bender asked Canby to pitch the idea of an official program at a meeting of the faculty. "I knew from the beginning that this was exactly the kind of thing that the University should be doing," Canby said. He made the presentation that the Program was a worthy scholarly pursuit and a way to serve the community and build a stronger, more developed and cohesive state.

In August 1987, Professor Rick Brown chaired a roundtable meeting to discuss whether there was a need for an Indian Legal Program at the law school. ASU faculty, Indian law practitioners, tribal judges and national and local Indian law organization personnel shared their experiences, vision and strategies for encouraging Indian students to pursue a law degree, to educate the general student body about Indian law, and to provide support to students who enter into law school. Twenty-two committed teachers and lawyers laid the template for the ILP: Rick Brown, Fred Ragsdale, Delfred Leslie, Steve Trtla, Ray Austin, William C. Canby, Jr., Rennard Strickland, Carol Lujan, Jay Abby, Brian Murphy, John Leshy, Steven Heeley, John Echohawk, Linus Everling, Leigh Price, Michael Berch, James Weinstein, Jane Aiken, LynDee Wells, Rod Lewis, Laurence Winer, and Gloria Kindig.

In October 1987, ASU's law professors met with tribal members to discuss mutually beneficial effects of ILP. Canby invited the Inter-Tribal Council of Arizona,[5] the Southwest Indian Court Judges Association,[6] the ASU School of Justice Studies,[7] and the National Indian Justice Center[8] to work with the law school. The group expanded to include Arizona superior court judges and tribal court judges of many of the Arizona Native American tribes.

The final step was to create an ad hoc planning committee (Professors Laurence Winer, Rick Brown, Jane Aiken, James Weinstein, Michael Berch, Leigh Price, and non-voting student members LynDee Wells, and Gloria Kindig). That committee produced a detailed report that today serves as the foundation for the ILP.

A young student, Autumn Monteau-Nabors[9] of the Three Affiliated Tribes of Fort Berthold,[10] captured the ILP's impact in the Native American community.

> *I honestly feel that I grew up in the Indian Legal Program, especially because I decided to go to law school at a young age, right after my undergraduate study. The folks at the ILP not only forced you to grow, they instilled in you a desire to grow into a professional who would contribute to our Indian communities. I owe a great deal of gratitude to the ILP, the college of law, and my colleagues for the effort they put into my professional development and the confidence they had, and still have in my abilities. Because these are individuals I greatly respect and look up to, their encouragement has helped me to develop much-needed confidence in myself. I will always fondly remember my law school experience and will be forever grateful to the ILP.*

Monteau-Nabors's 2013 statement is a recurring sentiment for one of America's first efforts to train Native American lawyers, educate all its graduates about Indian Law and promote an understanding of the difference between the legal systems of Indian Nations and the United States. It matches squarely with a state that boasts twenty-two recognized Indian tribes that occupy and govern 27 percent of the land in Arizona. Over 250 students from tribes across North America have earned law degrees and certificates through the ILP. They come from 100 tribes. Faculty leadership accounts for much of the ILP's success.

The ILP's consistent timeline for growth and success bears noting here.

> 1969—Professor William Canby taught the first Federal Indian Law seminar.

> 1971—ASU Law instituted an informal "Office of Indian Programs" with Canby and Professor Warren Cohen.

> 1985—Professor Lee Price joins as visiting faculty.

> 1987—Maricopa County Superior Court judges meet with Tribal Court Judges.

The Indian Law Program—1967

1988—The ILP is accredited by ASU President J. Russell Nelson.[11]

1993—ASU Librarian Alison Ewing begins active ILP support of faculty and students.

1994—Prof. Rebecca Tsosie[12] joins ASU Faculty and is appointed in 1996 as ILP's first faculty executive director.

1998—ILP certificate program initiated.

2001—Robert N. Clinton[13] joins ASU Law faculty as Goldwater Chair.

2002—ASU President Michael Crow[14] formally endorses creation of the Indian Legal Clinic.

2003—Professor Kevin Grover[15] joins the ILP Faculty.

2003—First Indian Law CLE offered by ILP.

2004—Mary Wynne becomes Director of the Indian Law Clinic.

2005—LLM in Tribal Law, Policy & Government initiated at Sandra Day O'Connor College of Law.

2005—Indian Legal Clinic launched, and Clinic hosts first Tribal Court Skills College.

2007—Professor Kevin Grover takes leave to serve as Director of the Smithsonian Institution's National Museum of the American Indian.

2007—Patty Ferguson-Bohnee[16] appointed Director, Indian Legal Clinic.

2008—16th Annual National Native American Students Association Moot Court Competition; Ross-Blakley Law Library develops Indian Law Portal; Indian Country's Winning Hand—20 Years of IGRA—CLE; ILP begins coordinating Arizona Native Vote Collection Protection Project; Inaugural William C. Canby Lecture: "Indians, Crime, and the Law," by Kevin Washburn,[17] Professor of Law, University of Minnesota.

2009—Indian Legal Clinic awarded ASU President's Social Embeddedness Award; Carl Artman[18] joins ILP as Professor of Practice; Second Annual Canby Lecture: "Tribal Governance and Individual Rights—the Delicate Balance of Power and Alarm," by Diane Enos,[19] President Salt River Pima-Maricopa Indian Community.

2010—Third Annual Canby Lecture: "Will the White Man's Indian Ever Die?" by Kevin Grover, Director, Smithsonian Institutions' National Museum of the American Indian; Repatriation at Twenty—Self-Determination and Human Rights CLE Conference.

MEASURING OUTCOMES OF THE ILP

There are many ways to measure achievement in academic and clinical programs—dollars spent—jobs secured—successes—accomplishments, and disappointments. For the ILP, what counts is that graduates of their program work throughout *Indian country*. That's not just a catchy phrase used in old novels and new marketing programs. The term Indian country is defined in 18 U.S.C. § 1151 and 40 C.F.R. § 171.3. In law, it means "all land within the limits of any Indian reservation under the jurisdiction of the United States Government, notwithstanding the issuance of any patent, and, including rights-of-way running through the reservation; all dependent Indian communities within the borders of the United States whether within the original or subsequently acquired territory thereof, and whether within or without the limits of a state; and all Indian allotments, the Indian titles to which have not been extinguished, including rights-of-way running through the same." Consistent with the statutory definition of Indian country, and federal case law interpreting this statutory language, lands held by the federal government in trust for Indian tribes that exist outside of formal reservations are informal reservations and, thus, are Indian country.[20]

As of 2013, ASU's ILP graduates serve as judges, tribal leaders, department directors, tribal liaisons, in-house tribal counsel, and as many other types of legal representative. Four graduates serve as chief justices of their respective tribal court systems, one is the president of her tribe, others have been elected to serve in the state legislature, some have started their own law firms focusing on representation of Indian tribes and peoples, and some have become partners in major law firms.

Their graduates impact Indian country daily, whether it is by assisting individual Indian clients, developing codes for tribes, representing tribal businesses to promote economic development, advocating for state or national policy, educating the public about Indian law and jurisdiction, or promoting tribal justice systems.

Whether in English or the hundred different Indian languages they speak, the best measurement of ASU's ILP is simple: "Look who their graduates have become. Look where they work. They practice Indian law, mostly on Indian reservations. Today, the ILP is one of the most robust focused law programs in America. The ILP delivers well-defined incentives and outcomes:[21]

1. Indian Law Certificates for students who finish 21 hours of relevant curriculum, write a substantial paper, and complete practical work in the Indian Legal Clinic.
2. Rosette LLP, American Indian Economic Development Program provides an innovative and challenging curriculum for students; hosts annual conferences that focus on tribal economic development for students, attorneys, tribal leaders, tribal citizens, policymakers, entrepreneurs, developers, and financial advisers; and is creating a community outreach component.
3. National conferences and lectures that invite top scholars and attorneys to present contemporary legal issues in Indian country.
4. Native Vote Election Protection Project allows students to assist voters and tribal communities to prevent voter disenfranchisement.
5. Tribal Court Trial Skills College provides three days of training for tribal court advocates.
6. Native American Pipeline to Law Initiative invites students and attorneys to assist in community outreach, mentorship, and pre-law advising to help improve access to justice in tribal communities."

---

1 "American Indian Law," Wex Legal Dictionary/Encyclopedia LII, accessed February 28, 2020, https://www.law.cornell.edu/wex/American_Indian_law.

2 Ibid., Overview, 1.

3 Wikipedia, s.v., "Outline of United States federal Indian law and policy," last updated January 23, 2021, 7:30, https://en.wikipedia.org/wiki/Outline_of_United_States_federal_Indian_law_and_policy.

4 The detailed explanation for the ILP's start is extensively copied here from the brochure titled "The Indian Legal Program—25 Years of History—Celebrating the Past, Looking toward the Future." It is archived in the Ross-Blakley Library in the Sandra Day O'Connor College of Law.

5 The Inter Tribal Council of Arizona was established in 1952 to provide a united voice for tribal governments located in the State of Arizona to address common issues of concerns. On July 9, 1975, the council established a private, non-profit corporation, Inter Tribal Council of Arizona, Inc. (ITCA), under the laws

of the State of Arizona to promote Indian self-reliance through public policy development. ITCA provides an independent capacity to obtain, analyze and disseminate information vital to Indian community self-development. "Home," Inter Tribal Council of Arizona, accessed February 28, 2020, http://itcaonline.com/.

6   NAICJA is a national association comprised of tribal justice personnel & others devoted to supporting and strengthening tribal justice systems through education, information sharing, and advocacy. NAICJA is a non-profit corporation established in 1969 as a corporation in the state of Delaware following the enactment of the federal Indian Civil Rights Act of 1968. The Act required tribes to follow certain requirements similar to those in the Bill of Rights in the U.S. Constitution. Tribal courts are the forums where those rights are enforced. NAICJA's early goal was to provide education to tribal judges so that they could conduct proceedings in compliance with ICRA.

As a national representative membership organization, NAICJA's mission is to strengthen and enhance tribal justice systems. "Home," National American Indian Court Judges Association – NAICJA, accessed February 28, 2020, http://www.naicja.org/.

7   ASU's School of Social Transformation and its Justice Studies degree program is an innovative social science program examining current social justice issues such as human rights, domestic violence and immigration, against a backdrop of legal systems, law and culture. Students enrolled in the BA program in justice studies also have the opportunity to explore other languages and cultures, giving them the tools needed to communicate and work effectively with people both within and outside the U.S. As so many social justice issues occur across countries and cultures, this equips students with a dynamic knowledge of the world's justice systems and gives them the skills to create meaningful, real-world change. "BA Justice Studies," School of Social Transformation, accessed February 2020, https://dev-sst20.ws.asu.edu/degree/undergrad/ba-justice-studies.

8   The National Indian Justice Center, Inc., (NIJC) is an Indian owned and operated non-profit corporation with principal offices in Santa Rosa, California. NIJC was established in 1983 through the collective efforts of the National American Indian Court Judges Association, the American Indian Lawyer Training Program, and the Bureau of Indian Affairs in order to establish an independent national resource for Native communities and tribal government. The goals of NIJC are to design and deliver legal education, research, and technical assistance programs which seek to improve the quality of life for Native communities and the administration of justice in Indian country. "About the National Indian Justice Center," National Indian Justice Center, accessed February 2020, http://www.nijc.org/about_us.html.

9   Autumn Monteau-Nabors is a New Mexico lawyer and served two terms (2013 and 2014) as Chair of the State Bar of New Mexico's Indian Law Section. Monteau-Nabors' statement is contained in the ILP's 25-year history brochure archived in the Ross-Blakley Law Library at the Sandra Day O'Connor College of Law.

10   The Mandan, Hidatsa and Arikara Nation, also known as the Three Affiliated Tribes, is located on the Fort Berthold Indian Reservation in central North Dakota. The reservation is located on the Missouri River in McLean, Mountrail, Dunn, McKenzie, Mercer and Ward counties. The reservation consists of 988,000 acres, of which 457,837 acres are owned by Native Americans, either as individual allotments or communally by the tribe.

The Tribal headquarters is located 4 miles west of New Town, ND. "Home," MHA Nation, accessed February 2020, https://www.mhanation.com/.

11   Jack Russell Nelson (December 18, 1929 – March 23, 2016) was an American educator who served as a chancellor/president of the University of Colorado Boulder and Arizona State University in Tempe, Arizona. He was ASU's 14th President, serving from 1981 to 1989. Wikipedia, s.v., "J. Russell Nelson," last modified January 28, 2020, 9:06, https://en.wikipedia.org/wiki/J._Russell_Nelson.

12   Rebecca Tsosie is a Regents Professor at the James E. Rogers College of Law at the University of Arizona and also serves as Special Advisor to the Provost for Diversity and Inclusion. Professor Tsosie, who is of Yaqui descent, is a faculty member for the Indigenous Peoples' Law and Policy Program at the University of Arizona, and she is widely known for her work in the fields of federal Indian law and indigenous peoples' human rights. Prior to joining the UA faculty, Professor Tsosie was a Regents' Professor and Vice Provost for Inclusion and Community Engagement at Arizona State University. Professor Tsosie was the first faculty Executive Director for ASU's Indian Legal Program and served in that position for 15 years. "Rebecca Tsosie," University of Arizona Law, accessed January 2020, https://law.arizona.edu/rebecca-tsosie.

13   Prior to his retirement, Professor Clinton served as the Foundation Professor of Law at the Sandra Day O'Connor College of Law at Arizona State University and was an Affiliated Faculty member of the ASU American Indian Studies Program. He was also a Faculty Fellow in the Center for Law Science & Innovation. He also was an Affiliated Faculty member of the ASU Center on the Future of War. "Basic Bio," Office of Robert N. Clinton, accessed January 2020, http://robert-clinton.com/.

The Indian Law Program—1967

14 Michael M. Crow (born October 11, 1955) is an American academic and university administrator. He is the 16th and current president of Arizona State University, having succeeded Lattie F. Coor on July 1, 2002. He was previously Executive Vice-Provost of Columbia University, where he was also Professor of Science and Technology Policy in the School of International and Public Affairs. He is also chairman of the board for In-Q-Tel, the Central Intelligence Agency's venture capital firm. Wikipedia, s.v., "Michael M. Crow," last modified October 15, 2020, 20:48, https://en.wikipedia.org/wiki/Michael_M._Crow.

15 Kevin Gover is an author, educator, policy specialist, and an administrator in the public, private, and academic realms. Since 2007, Gover has served as director of the Smithsonian Institution's National Museum of the American Indian. He has also been Professor of Law at Sandra Day O'Connor College of Law at Arizona State University, Tempe. Kevin Glover is a member of the Pawnee Tribe of Oklahoma. Gover received his J.D. degree *(cum laude)* from the University of New Mexico School of Law in 1981, and his A.B. in Public and International Affairs from Princeton University in 1978. After graduation, he clerked for United States District Judge Juan Burciaga. Gover then entered private practice and then started work with a large firm in Washington, DC. In 1986, Kevin Gover formed a firm in New Mexico with two other highly regarded tribal attorneys. The firm grew into one of the largest Indian-owned law firms in the country. In 1997, Kevin Gover was selected by President Clinton to serve as Assistant Secretary of the Interior for Indian Affairs under Interior Secretary and former Arizona Governor, Bruce Babbitt. He served as Assistant Secretary until January 2001. His service was notable for his work on upgrading Indian law enforcement, rebuilding decrepit Indian schools, reforming trust services and overhauling the Bureau of Indian Affairs' management systems. Assistant Secretary Gover won wide praise for these reform efforts, but also for the apology he crafted on behalf of the Bureau of Indian Affairs to the nation's Indian communities for the history of wrongs done to them. Since 2007, Professor Gover has served as director of the Smithsonian Institution's National Museum of the American Indian. He also serves as a Judge for the Tonto Apache Tribal Court of Appeals, and the San Carlos Apache Tribal Court of Appeals, as well as on the governing boards of several non-profit educational institutions. "Kevin Gover: Life and Work, World Wisdom, accessed January 2020, http://www.worldwisdom.com/public/authors/Kevin-Gover.aspx.

16 Patty Ferguson-Bohnee has substantial experience in Indian law, election law and policy matters, voting rights, and status clarification of tribes. She is a clinical professor of law, the faculty director of the Indian Legal Program and the director of the Indian Legal Clinic at ASU. Professor Ferguson-Bohnee has testified before the United States Senate Committee on Indian Affairs and the Louisiana State Legislature regarding tribal recognition, and has successfully assisted four Louisiana tribes in obtaining state recognition. Professor Ferguson-Bohnee has represented tribal clients in administrative, state, federal, and tribal courts, as well as before state and local governing bodies and proposed revisions to the Real Estate Disclosure Reports to include tribal provisions. She has assisted in complex voting rights litigation on behalf of tribes, and she has drafted state legislative and congressional testimony on behalf of tribes with respect to voting rights' issues. Before joining ASU in 2008, Professor Ferguson-Bohnee clerked for Judge Betty Binns Fletcher of the 9th U.S. Circuit Court of Appeals and was an associate in the Indian Law and Tribal Relations Practice Group at Sacks Tierney P.A. in Phoenix. As a Fulbright Scholar to France, she researched French colonial relations with Louisiana Indians in the 17th and 18th centuries.

Professor Ferguson-Bohnee, a member of the Pointe-au-Chien Indian tribe, serves as the Native Vote Election Protection Coordinator for the State of Arizona. "Patty Ferguson Bohnee," iSearch, accessed January 2020, https://isearch.asu.edu/profile/1101447.

17 Kevin K. Washburn is an American law professor, former dean of the University of New Mexico School of Law, and current Dean of the University of Iowa College of Law. He served in the administration of President Barack Obama as Assistant Secretary for Indian Affairs at the U.S. Department of the Interior from 2012 to 2016. Washburn has also been a federal prosecutor, a trial attorney at the U.S. Department of Justice, and the General Counsel of the National Indian Gaming Commission. Washburn is a member of the Chickasaw Nation of Oklahoma, a federally recognized Indian tribe. Wikipedia, s.v., "Kevin K. Washburn," last modified January 21, 2021, 3:03, https://en.wikipedia.org/wiki/Kevin_K._Washburn.

18 Carl J. Artman served as the United States Assistant Secretary of the Interior for Indian Affairs with jurisdiction over the Office of Indian Affairs, Bureau of Indian Affairs and the Bureau of Indian Education from 2007 to 2008, and he served as the Associate Solicitor for Indian Affairs at the Department of the Interior from 2005 to 2007. He received a B.A. from Columbia College in Columbia, Missouri, an M.B.A. from the University of Wisconsin-Madison School of Business, J.D. from Washington University in St. Louis, and an L.L.M. from University of Denver College of Law. Wikipedia, s.v., "Carl J. Artman," last modified December 12, 2020, 23:22, https://en.wikipedia.org/wiki/Carl_J._Artman.

19 Diane Enos is the 23rd President of the Salt River Pima-Maricopa Indian Community and the second woman elected to this office, sworn into office in December 2006. She is the daughter of Naomi and

Johnson Enos, and the great-granddaughter of Jose Anton, one of the leaders for the Pima communities at the time of the Indian Reorganization Act. "Diane Enos," ASU College of Law, accessed January 2020, http://conferences.asucollegeoflaw.com/tribaleconomies/diane-enos/.

20 "Definition of Indian Country," US EPA, accessed January 2020, https://www.epa.gov/pesticide-applicator-certification-indian-country/definition-indian-country.

21 "Indian Legal Program," Sandra Day O'Connor College of Law, accessed January 2020, https://law.asu.edu/focus-areas/indian-law.

CHAPTER 14

DEAN PEDRICK'S 1971–72 REPORT

*D*ean Pedrick called the academic year of 1971–72 a "milestone year of sorts."[1] He was obviously proud of graduating the law school's third class, sending 281 law graduates into the profession. He reported that the entering class of 1971 was the most highly selected, meaning their undergraduate credentials were higher than the first three classes had been. He also hired "four distinguished law teachers."[2] The *Oliver Wendell Holmes Devise Lecture Series* was presented by Prof. Philip Kurland. And he was particularly happy to tell President Durham about the "appearance at the close of the academic year by the Court's newest justice and the first justice from Arizona, Mr. Justice William H. Rehnquist."[3]

APPLICATIONS & STUDENT LEADERSHIP

Applications came in at a dizzy pace—1,333 applications for an entering class targeted at 121 but growing to 141 by the time admissions closed. Pedrick was happy to report applications up 2 to 1 from non-residents; the balance was 99 Arizona residents and 42 non-residents. They were better credentialed, as well; median GPAs were up to the 3.0 level and the LSAT went up to the 590s—the 75th percentile nationwide. He expressed "growing concern on the emphasis of grades and testing . . . to the exclusion of personal qualities such as personality, pertinacity, judgment, maturity, background experience, interest in public service, etc."[4] The total enrollment capped out at 404—"the real capacity of the school."

Pedrick singled out second-year student Ted Jarvi for his Student Bar Association leadership, and Gloria Aguilar for her leadership in the Mexican-American Law

Student Association. He praised the efforts of students committed to open membership policies for women, minority groups such as the Yaqui Indian community and migrant farm workers. He noted that four issues of the *Devil's Advocate*, the law student's newspaper, had been published.

FACULTY ACCOMPLISHMENTS

He praised his faculty as a "remarkable group of legal scholars . . . which virtually everyone was a Law Review Editor . . . with five who were Editors-In-Chief."[5] He regretted the loss "to competition. . . when Prof. George Dix . . . was appointed to the faculty at the University of Texas Law School at the rank of full Professor, at a very substantial increase in salary."[6] He appeared worried that "Prof. Stephen E. Lee [was serving] as a Visiting Professor at Cornell . . . . [and that] four other faculty members were approached by other [law] schools . . . . [It's] flattering but, at the same time, distressing."[7]

By 1971, ASU Law had eighteen "law teachers," fourteen of which taught courses; the other four performed "administrative assignments." Visiting on campus were Judge Eduardo Jimenez de Arechaga of Chile, teaching International Law; Professor Nathaniel Nathanson of Northwestern University teaching "current cases in the Supreme Court"; and Professor Derek Mendes de Costa, from the University of Toronto School of Law, who taught Family Law and a seminar in Problems of Negligence Law. Faculty research and publication was up, particularly in terms of "the practical completion of the Evidence Rules project of the [U.S.] Supreme Court . . . under the distinguished direction of Prof. Edward Cleary."[8]

EXPERIMENTING WITH CLINICAL EDUCATION

Clinical education was "still in its experimental stage." The problem, Pedrick said, was "how to insure that the clinic experience is maximized as a learning experience in terms of professional standards and intellectual stimulation."[9] The clinic professors, Arthur La France and Gerald Caplan, had "genuine [interest] and . . . [were] resourceful and imaginative."[10] This was attributed to the "perennial feature of the relationship between the practicing profession and the world of legal education is the somewhat nervous attitude which some elements of the bar have in viewing legal education."[11] Dean Pedrick may have been alluding to the tension between practicing lawyers and law professors embraced in the adage "Those who can, practice law. Those who cannot, teach law." ASU was experimenting with "bringing into legal education the teaching of professional skills such as drafting, negotiating, interviewing, etc. One might think that this new emphasis on the practical and the professional would find favor with the practicing profession.... There are some, however, who moan the introduction of skills instruction in the belief that something of great value must have been lost in the process."[12] Pedrick noted some basic metrics. In 1971, 94,000 law students were enrolled in accredited schools in America. There were 300,000 practicing lawyers. Pedrick pondered that apparent conundrum: "[I]n the course of the next five years, Law Schools will be graduating perhaps twice as many as the conventional openings for law graduates seem to require. The result is likely to be a very considerable increase in the number of young lawyers just out of law school establishing their own offices. Because the Law Schools have not to this point represented that they were training people to be finished, or even medium-finished practitioners, we are now forced to consider whether we may not necessarily have to give some greater attention to the matter of instructing on the mundane subject of a law practice."[13]

Unfortunately, Dean Pedrick's report confirms the view held by many Arizona lawyers at the time. Law professors actually thought law practice was "mundane." There are hundreds of lawyers who graduated from ASU and would never have traded in their shingles for an academic title in the 1970s. Most found law practice exciting, intellectually stimulating, and much more lucrative than law teaching. Litigating a complex case in a challenging court before a jury of confirmed doubters will always trump reading about it in class. Everything is relative.

> Some professors were good at both teaching and practicing. Dean Pedrick singled Professor Michael Berch out in his 1971–72 Report. *"Dean Charles Ares of the University of Arizona . . . with Professors Caplan and LaSota on our faculty [have] contribut[ed] many hours [to the revision of Arizona's Rules of Criminal Procedure].... Prof. Michel Berch ... is working with the State Bar of Arizona and the Supreme Court of the State to develop improved jury instructions.... [T]he Police Foundation (a Ford Foundation grantee) [supports] Professor Caplan's project for development of guidelines for police practice.... [along with] Mr. Andis Kaulins, a graduate of the Stanford University Law School. Prof. John Morris [won a National Science Foundation*

grant] to study legal problems associated with professional sports . . . . the University transferred to [our] Legal Resources Institute a substantial sum to enable [us] to undertake research projects not otherwise funded but with respect to which there is prospect of outside funding once the project is launched."[14]

PROBLEMS

Not surprisingly, Dean Pedrick reported on problems as well as successes. The Operations Budget was too low. The Faculty Salary Scale was not competitive. The Guadalupe Project, a student legal services project in the Guadalupe community, was appreciated but not adequately supervised, suffered from inadequate funding and professional supervision. The size of the faculty was a problem; they needed "modest increments to the faculty." They wanted two new faculty members for the budget year of 1973–74. The current faculty ratio was 1-22; the classes were large—130 to 140 students per core class. Dean Pedrick pointed out that the ratio at the University of Arizona was about 1-16. The working student was a "matter of concern . . . [with] an increasing number of our students . . . working part-time in law offices . . . . [S]ome [faculty] regard such law employment as a most unwise diversion of the student's time and energy from the academic study of law . . . Others take the view that the part-time law office experience may, indeed, be positively educational and a useful supplement to the academic instruction."[15] The fact was that "many third-year students in metropolitan centers [were] engaged in part-time [work]."[16]

THANKS TO THE LAW SOCIETY OF ARIZONA STATE UNIVERSITY

Dean Pedrick closed his report by expressing his continuing appreciation for the support provided by the Law Society of Arizona State University. The Sixth Annual Dinner featured Justice Rehnquist as principal speaker. Five hundred members attended in the Thunderbird Room of the Western Ho Hotel. As was his habit, Dean Pedrick concluded with humor. "We look back on our five years in violation of Satchel Page's dictum that one ought not to look back because someone might be gaining. We believe that our short past entitles us to feel that a good beginning has been made."[17]

Dean Pedrick's 1971–72 Report

1 Willard H. Pedrick, *Annual Report of the Dean, 1971–72* (Arizona State University College of Law Archives), 1.
2 Ibid.
3 Ibid.
4 Ibid., 3.
5 Ibid., 5.
6 Ibid.
7 Ibid., 5–6.
8 Ibid., 8.
9 Ibid., 10.
10 Ibid.
11 Ibid.
12 Ibid., 11.
13 Ibid., 12.
14 Ibid., 16.
15 Ibid., 21.
16 Ibid., 21.
17 Ibid., 22.

CHAPTER 15

ASU LAW'S FIRST GRADUATING CLASS—1970

The inaugural class took center stage at the inaugural graduation ceremony in 1970. Every seat in the auditorium had a small booklet containing the names of the graduates, in alphabetical order.

Joe Vance Anderson; Bruce Gaillard Arnold (Staff Editor, Journal); Mary Alice Bass; Arby R. Beardslee; Francis John Bently (cum laude); John Darryl Betha (cum laude, Law Journal & Constitution Drafting Committee); Charles Ray Brooks; Warren Raymond Brown (Law Journal); John Edmund Burke; Timothy John Burke (cum laude, Articles Editor, Law Journal); Joshua Brush

Jr. (Student Bar Association Council); Kirk Alan Burtch (cum laude); Irby K. Cain; Roger Nelson Cheney; Robert McConnell Cook (President Student Bar Association, Chairman, Moot Court Board, Captain, National Moot Court Team); James Leo Cowley; Lee Harry Davis; Noel Kenneth Dessaint (cum laude, Managing Editor Law Journal); Peter Stanley Fairman (Law Journal); Robert Jay Farrer; Herbert Spencer Fibel (Vice President, Treasurer, Student Bar Association); Ronald Brown Fineberg; Ruth Geiger Finn (summa cum laude, Civil Rights Board); Smith Gibbons Frost; Michael Lantaff Gallagher (President Student Bar Association); Jack Attlee Grady; Sarah Dickinson Grant; Donald B. Guthrie; Allen Adley Haggard; Richard William Harris; Michael Daly Hawkins (cum laude, Staff Editor, Law Journal, Student Bar Council); John Douglas Helm (Law Journal); J. Willie Henderson (Student Bar Council, Constitution Drafting Committee); John Edward Herrick (Chairman Moot Court Board); Ralph Dale Hobart (Constitution Drafting Committee, Student Legal Services); Robert Leon Hungerford, Jr. (Student Bar Association Council, Moot Court Board, National Moot Court Team); Richard Anthony Johnson; Richard Gordon Johnson, Jr. (Law Journal); Ward Seyfarth Johnson (cum laude, Chairman, Student Placement Committee); Richard Allen Jones (summa cum laude); Robert Elijah Jones; Gerald Ervin Kriehn; Elliot Kurzman; Theodore Lee Kyle; Albert Lagman; John Stewart Lancy (magna cum laude, Editor-in-Chief, Law Journal); John Webster Matlock; John Robert Moore (cum laude, Staff Editor, Law Journal, Treasurer Student Bar Association); George Bourges Mount (cum laude); Charles Samuel Murry (Co-Chairman, Civil Rights Research Board); Peter Michael Napier (Moot Court Board); Thomas Delbert Nelson (Moot Court Board); Daniel Field Norton, Jr.; Daniel John Oehler; Thomas Lee Palmer (magna cum laude, Comment Editor, Law Journal); Harry Pappas (Chairman Constitution Drafting Committee); Gary Lee Patten; Gary Ray Pope (Placement Committee); Paul John Prato (Law Journal); John Arthur Propsta (President, Vice President, Student Bar Association); John Joseph Relihan, Jr.; Murray Rosen; Robert Leslie Schaefer (Student Bar Association, Chairman Graduation Committee); David Karl Schatz; Ronald A. Schlosser; Duane William Schulz (Constitution Drafting Committee); Rodney Bacchus Shields; Warren B. Siegal; Joe Sims (magna cum laude, Comment Editor, Law Journal); Jimmie Dee Smith (cum laude); William Marshall Spence

ASU Law's First Graduating Class—1970

(Placement Committee); Craig Scott Stanlis; Stuart Jesse Susser (Graduation Committee); Charles Malen Thomas; Richard Jesus Trujillo; Kent Carnes Ware, II; Monny Lester Weatherly, Jr.; Robert James Weber (Graduation Committee); Cecil Peter Whitmer; Kathy Morgan Whittaker; Galen Harvey Wilkes (Law Journal); Karl Edward Wochner (Student Bar Council, Placement Committee, Constitution Drafting).

Graduate, *noun*: A person who has successfully completed a course of study or training.[1] Like everything else remotely related to "the law," graduating from law school is at once an argument, a status, a relief, and a shaky start. The argument is whether law school teaches law or trains lawyers. The former is an academic endeavor, the latter a profession. One is not the other. There is no consensus—only argument. The cynic might say most law professors teach the law because they failed to practice it. The peacemaker would respond that most lawyers are not good teachers. The compromiser would say, before you can practice law you must learn it, so shut up and listen. The truth, at least speaking for my people, *lawyers*, is that the only way to learn how to be a lawyer is to be a lawyer. Almost everyone who graduated from law school in the last half century knows the bad joke—Those who get As in law school make full professor; those who make Bs make judge; those who make Cs make money. There's an ounce of truth in that old saw. But for every top 10-percenter in most law school classes, there's a B- student who became a law school dean.

The word is useful as an adjective—as in a graduated cup, tube, flask, or measuring glass, used especially by chemists and pharmacists. It's a verb, as in successfully completing an academic degree, course of training, or high school—as in I graduated from Gallup High in 1957. Graduation is also the ceremony sometimes associated with it, in which students become graduates. Before graduation, candidates are referred to as graduands. The date of graduation is often called graduation day. The graduation ceremony itself is also called commencement, convocation, or invocation. When ceremonies are associated, they mandate a procession of academic staff and candidates—gowned and capped, with a valedictorian in tow. At the university level, the faculty dons formal academic dress, as will the regents, trustees, senior academic officers, and validated degree candidates. It's pomp and ceremony at its most decadent. It is often accompanied by exhaustion, surprise, glee, and revenge.

The ASU College of Law's First Graduating Ceremony on June 2, 1970, was all of that. All eighty-seven members of the class were there, dressed for the occasion, facing a stage full of capped and gowned faculty, deans, regents, and honored guests.[2] Erwin N. Griswold, then Solicitor General of the United States, gave the inaugural commencement address.[3]

His title, "Being a Lawyer," was perfect. He was speaking to eighty-seven graduates who were unique that year. When they were 1Ls, there were no students ahead of them—no one to talk to—no one to ask about courses, professors, outlines, class notes, hiding places, what not to do, or how to do it. They were not only newbie students; they were taking first-year classes from several almost-newbie professors. There were no guardrails, safety nets, or time-outs. Griswold knew that. He was an experienced appellate lawyer, an accomplished dean at Harvard Law, and a grand toastmaster. "You must have had a remarkable experience here, pioneering as first year students, and now presenting yourselves as the first graduating class. Everything you have done has set a new tradition."[4]

Former Dean Griswold took pity on ASU Law's new dean. "Dean Pedrick has been without alumni for the last three years. But you will now remedy that situation and I know your growing alumni body will be a great source of strength over the years. I know from my own experience that most of you will be playing important roles of leadership over the next forty or fifty years." Of course there was no way of knowing that then.

The Class of 1970 held a forty-year reunion on April 9, 2010. Mike Gallagher ('70) was the Master of Ceremonies at the reunion and the founder of a large Phoenix law firm, Gallagher & Kennedy.[5] His "special memory" of his three years in the entering class was clear: "We were a close-knit group with no students in front to learn from. Our experience was a bit unconventional." He had advice for the 1Ls at ASU Law in 2010—"If you want a job someday, worry about those first year grades. I didn't, but it's much tougher today."

Solicitor General Griswold told the 1970 graduates, "At the present time, there is among many students a considerable disdain for the private law firm and for the private practice of law. This is a new development in an ancient profession, new even in this country, which has always set its own standards and made its own traditions. Private practice is sometimes depicted today as something rather reprehensible as a means by which able minds are organized to represent the interests, or the establishment, and thus to enhance the entrenchment of privilege and power. I know too, that some legal work can be rather dreary. Divorces, title searches, and the aftermath of automobile accidents. But there is always some person for whom the work is important."

The passage of fifty years since those remarks were made to the class of 1970 means that no one can say today how Griswold's dreary assessment of private law practice felt. But the vast majority of the members of that first graduating class became practicing lawyers, many in public practice but many more in private practice. That year, 1970, saw over 200 new lawyers take the 1970 summer bar. Most became working lawyers. It's fair to guess there was little of the "disdain" Griswold saw in Washington, DC, law graduates. Griswold told the students about the current issue of *Harvard Law Review,* May 1970. He talked about an article by Lloyd Cutler,[6] "a fine and public spirted lawyer in Washington today." He said the article was a "very effective presentation of the role of private law firm in American life today and its opportunities for public service and constructive activity which is available for lawyers in private practice." His audience was largely lawyers about to engage in public and private practice in Phoenix. The private bar greatly outnumbered the public bar in Phoenix in 1970, so part of Griswold's message may have fallen on deaf ears.

Point two in Griswold's three-point address concerned new law graduates making "significant contributions to law development and reform." This was likely a more welcome topic. As a sun-belt state, Arizona in 1970 was growth-oriented and an important border state. There were opportunities for young lawyers to do what Griswold called "legal and social reform." But then again, we were at the height of the Vietnam War and Watergate was on the horizon. Those issues were more relevant than seeking opportunity for law reform or development. Griswold called out the late John P. Frank, a Phoenix lawyer at the time with Lewis & Roca. He said Mr. Frank was a leader in law development and reform and commended one of John P. Frank's recent books. He quoted Justice Stone: "You are now entering the public profession of the law." Once the bar results were released, more than half the room would go into the private profession of the law.

Griswold's third point was something he called "organic social life." He argued the law was one instrument to reach the civilized goal of an "organic social life." He urged the audience, "As men of the law, one of your primary functions is to work ceaselessly for the orderly and rational resolution of all disputes through the processes of law." There were eighty-seven graduates there that day; five were women.[7] It is unclear whether Griswold would have agreed that women ought to have a larger presence in the legal profession.[8]

Given the uproar of protests about civil rights and the Vietnam War, it was understandable, even predictable, that the Solicitor General would raise student activism, free speech, and racism. He said, "You are young and that is a great asset... As Chancellor Heard[9] recently said of the University, its 'obligation is not to protect students from ideas, but rather to expose them to ideas and make them capable of handling and hopefully having ideas...' We must help our youth shun moral postures and be willing to understand the difficulties and obstacles, and then to undertake the gritty, difficult work of urgent reform in a highly diverse, pluralistic nation. We must get away from the outbursts of emotional and spiritual malaise, and instead find ways to work steadily to gain an end to discrimination, peace without isolationism, better schools, less pollution, and the continued production of political leaders of vision and high caliber, many of whom will in likelihood be lawyers—very likely some of you."

Solicitor General Griswold ended his address by referring the new graduates to Sir Frederick Pollock[10] who wrote of the *fabric of the law*.

> *The least of us is happy who hereafter may point to so much as one stone thereof and say, "the work of my hands is there." I have no doubt that the work of your hands will soon be evidenced in this state and this nation. It is a privilege to salute you as the first alumni of this law school.*

It was a lofty address, given as though it had been delivered from a pulpit. It's entirely possible that the audience knew nothing about the work of Sir Frederick Pollock.

The Class of 1970 had many that would become "notable" over time. By 2020 that class and the forty-nine that would follow would include more than 7,600 newly minted lawyers. It is not possible to profile all of them here, but the following graduates are exemplars of what ASU Law would ultimately produce.

ASU Law's First Graduating Class—1970

1 *Merriam-Webster*, s.v. "graduate," accessed November 18, 2019, https://www.merriam-webster.com/dictionary/graduate.

2 Dean Willard Pedrick presided; John S. Armstrong III presented the Armstrong Award to _____; Harry K. Newburn was the ASU President; Joseph S. Jencks, Jr. was the vice-president of the Law Society of Arizona State University; G. Homer Durham, former ASU President and current Utah Commissioner of Higher Education.

3 Wikipedia, s.v. "Erwin Griswold," last modified October 2, 2019, 23:49, https://en.wikipedia.org/wiki/Erwin_Griswold. Erwin Nathaniel Griswold was an appellate attorney who argued many cases before the U.S. Supreme Court. Griswold served as Solicitor General of the United States under Presidents Lyndon B. Johnson and Richard M. Nixon. He also served as Dean of Harvard Law School for 21 years. Several times, he was considered for appointment to the U.S. Supreme Court. During a career that spanned more than six decades, he served as member of the U.S. Commission on Civil Rights and as President of the American Bar Foundation.

4 *See* Solicitor General Erwin N. Griswold: First Commencement of the School of Law of Arizona State University, Tempe, Arizona June 2, 1970 at 10:00, archived at Sandra Day O'Connor College of Law at Arizona State University.

5 Gallagher & Kennedy, "G&K Co-Founders" accessed November 18, 2019, https://gknet.com/about/history/. "The law firm of Gallagher & Kennedy was founded in 1978, when Mike Kennedy and Mike Gallagher decided to open their own law firm in Phoenix. Just 40 years later, the law firm is the sixth largest law firm in Arizona. History has shown Gallagher & Kennedy to be a classic American success story, built on the vision of two optimistic and tenacious young attorneys. Though lacking deep pockets, the two Mikes were rich in ambition and determination. Kennedy quips, 'The lender's collateral for a modest business loan consisted of "seconds" on our Country Squire and Monte Carlo.' In the early days, the firm's work primarily focused on insurance and litigation. While the start-up quarters and earliest client list were modest, the young firm was on its way. At the 10-year mark, Gallagher & Kennedy had begun to expand from primarily a litigation-based firm to include more business law services. Weathering the economic turbulence of the 80s, the firm was well-positioned to participate in Arizona's explosive growth of the 90s. With a mounting track record of success and growing reputation in the community, the firm was able to attract top talent to fuel its growth and expansion into the practice areas of Environmental Law, Personal Injury & Wrongful Death, Bankruptcy & Creditors Rights, Intellectual Property and Criminal Law."

6 Wikipedia, s.v. "Lloyd Cutler," last modified June 13, 2019, 23:43, https://en.wikipedia.org/wiki/Lloyd_Cutler. "Lloyd Norton Cutler (November 10, 1917–May 8, 2005) was an American attorney, who served as White House Counsel during the Democratic administrations of Presidents Carter and Clinton."

7 Mary Alice Bass, Ruth Geiger Finn *(summa cum laude)*, Sarah Dickinson Grant, S. Debra Miller, and Kathy Morgan Whittaker.

8 Questia, Sheryl Sandberg's Can Do Feminism: Why She's a Reformer in the Church of Meritocracy and not a Heretic, accessed November 18, 2019, https://www.questia.com/magazine/1G1-334178430/sheryl-sandberg-s-can-do-feminism-why-she-s-a-reformer. "The Harvard Law School held out until 1950. And even then I think they acted very reluctantly. One of the women admitted to Harvard in the 1950s tells the story of being invited, along with the eight other women in her class, to Dean Griswold's home for dinner. She was very pleased with the invitation, thinking the Dean wanted to make them feel welcome. Instead, after dinner, the Dean required each woman in turn to justify why she was occupying a place in the class that could be held by a man. Not until 1972 were women admitted to all law schools approved by the A.B.A."

9 Mr. Griswold's reference to Chancellor Heard is unclear. Chancellor Heard served as Vanderbilt University's fifth Chancellor from 1963–1982 and oversaw many changes in the campus.

10 Wikipedia, s.v. "Sir Frederick Pollock, 3rd Baronet," last modified September 5, 2019, 14:34. https://en.wikipedia.org/wiki/Sir_Frederick_Pollock,_3rd_Baronet. Sir Frederick Pollock, 3rd Baronet PC, FBA was an English jurist best known for his History of English Law before the Time of Edward I, written with F.W. Maitland, and his lifelong correspondence with US Supreme Court Justice Oliver Wendell Holmes. He was a Cambridge Apostle.

CHAPTER 16

DEAN PEDRICK'S LAST REPORT 1974 TO 1975

"This is a Dean's Report to end *this* law Dean's Reports—for a very good reason."[1] He began it as he customarily did—he announced it as both an ending and a beginning, in that order. "This is the last Dean's Report by the present incumbent prior to his ascension here at Arizona State University to the post of full-time Professor of Law."[2]

He called it his *Last Hurrah*, and warned its intended reader (President Schwada) that he'd be taking a "few liberties." His words display the genius and fun the inventor of legal education at Arizona State University had. It is his longest because he took the liberty of talking not just about the 1974–75 academic year; he offered "some persiflage." For nonlawyer readers, that means frivolous bantering talk. Law professors are even better at it than lawyers are. Pedrick was as down-to-earth as any law dean was at either of Arizona's two law schools. He knew "[l]aw dean's annual reports tend to present law deans at their worst."[3] Perhaps that explains why only one of his successors (Ernest Gellhorn) followed his lead and actually wrote a Dean's Report.[4]

Pedrick thought law deans reflected "[b]y and large . . . an all-too-serious view of the world and legal education and an altogether-too-serious view of the function and importance of the law dean."[5] To prove his point, he focused the July 1975 report on three events he'd experienced "this past year." These events, he said, "demonstrate[e] that this law school is not completely and unremittingly serious."[6]

PED'S NUMBER ONE PROBLEM

Number one on his list was the "troublesome, indeed agonizing, problem . . . the Law Building, splendid as it is, was not planned with sufficient foresight to anticipate the coming of large numbers of women law students. The result was the overtaxing of facilities for physical relief . . . . what was needed . . . on this score were "separate but equal facilities" . . . . women students declined to sit tight and adopt a policy of "watchful waiting." They commissioned bargaining representatives to wait upon the Dean. The upshot of the not-too-extended bargaining session was an agreement that if moderate male law student support could be secured, one of the "relief facilities" would be converted from its designation as a male haven to become, thereafter, a refuge for females . . . . The text of the notice posted to signal this earthshaking event was phrased as follows . . . "Subject: Restroom (Who's Tired) Facilities—Reassignment."[7]

His Memorandum to Students, edited for space, reads:

> *To alleviate physical suffering, preserve public health and provide for the common defense . . . I, Dean Pedrick the First, exercising all my authority under the Constitution as Commander of Something . . . proclaim . . . Whereas, Armstrong Hall . . . was planned without that prudence or foresight . . . with the result that facilities for the relief of physical suffering (. . . FFRPS . . .) are grossly inadequate for the Ms's now comprising a substantial part of the student enrollment . . . and Whereas, Hell hath no fury like women scorned (actually, they have been quite decent) . . . . the signs on the basement restrooms will be exchanged so the larger room will be for WOMEN and the smaller room will be for MEN . . . . Further improvement . . . will be undertaken subject to advice from that most learned profession – the plumbers . . .*[8]

PED'S LAW REVUE

Number two on his list dealt with his favorite college tradition, the annual law school musical, known as the "Law Revue." It featured a "motley assortment of students . . . [and] faculty."⁹ This year's musical was centered on the "search for a successor dean and was appropriately entitled, 'Dean for A Day.'"¹⁰ Doubting both the musical and his not-yet-revealed successor, he said, "The solo and chorus offerings of both the music and dance set the musical art form back a conservative twenty years – to the occasional delight of a full house. The shortest run musical of the Western United States was adjudged to be a great success . . . featuring the retiring Dean singing plaintively, 'Please Release Me, Let me Go.'"¹¹

THIRD-YEAR GRADING

Number three, was the school's third-year grading system, a product of his own invention. The system was, he said, "[a]fflicted, perhaps, by the cynicism that comes from being too long in the office . . . the third-year pass/fail grading system could be improved by the addition of two additional tiers, representing honors and high honors to provide additional incentive to the sometimes lagging third-year student."[12] He underestimated the first and second year students, who, unbeknownst to him, actually liked the system the way it was. "Thus, the 'Pedrick' grading proposal brought the students of the College of Law together in a monolithic mass of opposition to any change in the third-year grading system. In terms of unifying the constituency, the grading proposal can only be compared with President Nixon's Watergate gambit. At an open forum session given over to the 'Pedrick' grading proposal, student attendance was high. Minds were as sharp as steel traps and just as closed. Consistency of argument was not prized. Student opponents . . . argued on the one hand that grading tends to discourage students from taking difficult courses to which they, nevertheless, apply themselves with zeal in their great desire to learn. Other students argued that the present credit/no-credit system accommodated, in happy fashion, to the circumstance that [more than half of the third-year class] carry substantial part-time employment as law clerks in downtown law offices . . . any action designed to secure more time, and attention for their academic pursuits would prejudice the good life . . . . At a subsequent faculty meeting, the majority of the faculty voted to shelve the grading proposal . . . [which] was later hailed in the student newspaper as a great stroke of statesmanship."[13]

QUALITY AND PROGRESS

The last thirty-page Dean's report began with six pages of classic Pedrick humor. The ensuing twenty-four pages were as eloquent as they were substantive. In those pages he took time to "cast up the balance to assess the quality of the operation and progress toward goals."[14] The report has an appendix longer than the actual report, including what Dean Pedrick called The Philosophy of the College of Law. It is included in the appendices to this book. He summarized it in the body of the report:

> *. . . the philosophy of the College of Law can be stated in disarmingly simple terms. That philosophy has simply been to have the College of Law serve our society and all of its elements by (1) providing opportunity for a rigorous legal education in preparation for the profession, (2) by conducting research to improve the law and its administration and (3) by public service, such as participating in provision of legal services to the poor, participating in programs of continuing education to update and upgrade the skills of the practicing profession and in providing a forum for consideration of law-related public issues.*[15]

All law schools, whether new or vintage, face a common problem—applications. The top law schools take single-digit percentages of each year's applications. The majority of law schools take less than half of their applicants. The ASU College of Law, as summarized in Dean Pedrick's final report, had a "veritable flood" of applications. In 1975, it had "not yet abated nor [was] relief in sight . . . an entering class of 145 [students came from] 1,500 applications . . . . it included members from the principal minority groups in the Arizona population and the largest number of women in an entering law class to date—one third . . . from the distaff side."[16] The class was, "in terms of its paper credentials, [] fully comparable to the entering classes of the best State University Law Schools."[17] At 400, the size of the school was "ideal." He was pleased to announce that last year's bar pass rate was 66 percent but this year's pass rate was 95 percent. Dean Pedrick noted the school seemed to have matured over his ten-year tenure in its organized co-curricular activities, notably, the Law Journal, the Moot Court Program, the Student Bar Association, and the school's newspaper, *The Devil's Advocate*.[18] There were many "[s]pecial interest groups, such as Women in Law, El Grupo, the Black Student's Association, the Indian Law Student's Association and the Legal Fraternities."[19]

He was proud of his faculty, calling it "one of the great law faculties in the United States."[20] Admitting it was a large claim, he said the proof was in the "healthy and active interest other Law Schools have taken in our faculty, particularly the younger members who might be subject to enticement."[21] He noted a first for Arizona law schools—the first Arizona professor to visit at the other Arizona law school. Prof. Junius Hoffman of the University of Arizona College of Law taught the Securities Regulation course at ASU that year.[22]

AN EVOLVING LAW SCHOOL

Dean Pedrick dedicated six pages to the educational program, noting that a "considerable evolution has taken place," over the course of ten years. They were, he said, "paddl[ing] upstream as respects our philosophy of legal education . . . . offer[ing], in our beginning years, . . . a core curriculum, encompassing both the first and the second year of Law School, in distinction to the program of most law schools where only the first year is prescribed . . . . We have moved at this stage to a partially elective second year."[23] He noted an experiment in '74–'75 called "the 'Stanford Plan,' giving each first-year student one course in a small section of about 25 students (with all other courses taken in a large section of 120)."[24] He implied that the early plan using quadrants in the third year was unworkable, that the early legal clinics did not function efficiently. He said, "our third-year program has become a hybrid with some instruction offered in eight-week segments and other instruction offered in the conventional semester-long program."[25]

Apparently, in the '70s, all law schools were troubled by the inability to engage a major share of student's time and interest against competition, and particularly the competition of part-time, law-related employment in law offices. It's a problem of major dimensions and "occupies attention of the law faculties throughout the country."[26] Consequently, Dean Pedrick created a task force charged, "in the most far-reaching fashion, with responsibility for evaluating the third-year program and recommending measures to secure its improvement."[27]

Many practicing lawyers in Arizona during that era might have respectfully suggested that the emphasis on a third year of traditional law school education was misplaced. If the essential purpose of a school of law is "providing opportunity for a rigorous legal education in preparation for the profession,"[28] as stated in ASU's *Philosophy of Legal Education*, perhaps consulting the profession would have helped. Most working lawyers of the era knew full well the only way to "be" a lawyer, was to "be" a lawyer. Law school, from a lawyer's perspective, is limited to learning how to find and interpret the law. It is of little value in learning how to "be" effective in practicing law. The necessity for a three-year school of law says more about the availability of tuition dollars than it does about better lawyering.

SKILLS TRAINING

Closely related to the third-year debate within law schools, the longtime issue of "skills training" was on Pedrick's mind in July 1975. Technically, law schools see the issue in terms of using law school resources on aspiring lawyers to be practical or skillful. This conflicts with how law professors see their jobs. Mostly, they are much more interested in theoretical or jurisprudential approaches to law study. That's why they profess rather than practice. It's always a balancing act. Pedrick was uniquely tuned in on the difference. "How that balance is to be struck will probably never be resolved in wholly satisfying fashion, at least in terms that would satisfy the individual practitioner or the individual law teacher. At the moment, in 1974–75, a considerable public debate on the subject is underway, sparked, to some extent, by the action of the Second Circuit Court of Appeals, responding to Circuit Judge Kaufman in appointing a special committee to recommend qualifications for practice in the Second Circuit."[29]

Dean Pedrick was right. The mid-seventies saw many debates about whether law schools could turn out court-ready lawyers. "If the weakness of the apprentice system was to produce advocates without scholarship, the weakness of the law school system is to turn out scholars with no skill at advocacy."[30] The most visible critic of trial lawyer competency during the peak of the controversy was Chief Justice Warren E. Burger. "As a measure of trial lawyer competency, the Chief Justice estimated that from one-third to one-half of the lawyers who appeared in serious cases were not really qualified."[31] While the Chief's observations were not universal, most lawyers and law professors agreed that changes were needed to secure quality representation in American courtrooms.

Dean Pedrick's Last Report 1974 to 1975

As Pedrick reported, Chief Judge Irving R. Kaufman of the United States Court of Appeals for the Second Circuit sounded the alarm. "[In 1973] Chief Justice Burger and I began questioning the quality of trial advocacy in our courts. Since then we have not been alone. The Federal Judicial Center in a survey of federal judges found that 41 per cent of those responding regarded lawyer's performances as a 'serious problem.' The Chief Judge then issued a call for improvement in advocacy offerings and asked for innovation in instructional methodology: 'Langdell's theory of legal education was a brilliant innovation for its time, an era when far fewer demands were made on lawyers and on the law . . . . This concept of legal education, even if valid in 1871, is certainly now fundamentally flawed.'"[32]

Pedrick laid out, for his faculty, and for the ASU President, how he saw the dichotomy in 1975: "By and large, the law school world is opposed to requiring particular courses as a prerequisite to practice in the Federal Courts . . . . to look back to the law school courses to correct a present problem of sub-standard professional performance on the part of the existing Bar is, at best, a long-term solution to an immediate problem . . . . importantly, the law school world is concerned with the narrowing of the law school curriculum and in the direction of requiring some types of instruction of a high-cost nature, i.e., Trial Advocacy."[33] While his thoughts resonated with many, the plain fact was that law schools were ill-equipped then to teach trial advocacy. Today's law schools are well-equipped to deal with the issue with legal clinics managed by working lawyers as adjunct faculty, and Professors of Practice in-house, full-time at most schools.

Pedrick was also correct to point out that "[a] relatively small part of the practicing profession is actually involved in trial work, perhaps not more than 10–15% of the profession go to court with any regularity."[34] It is likely those percentages are too high today, since fewer lawyers ever try a case. ADR and arbitration are to today's lawyers what jury trials were to the 1970s lawyers, at least in Arizona. Pedrick, while decidedly on the side of law professors, recognized the need for change. "Hopefully . . . the ensuing public debate will [result in] remit[ting] most of the problem to the universities and their law schools for resolution . . . . in struggling with the hard question of resource allocation as between instruction in legal theory in basic fields as against practice-oriented skills training, the providers of legal education ought to be entrusted with striking the balance."[35]

ARE LAW SCHOOLS FULL UP?

Pedrick also focused his last report on the existential question facing law schools in the mid-seventies. Were they full? He said, "It is widely known that virtually all of the Law Schools of the United States are full to overflowing. In 1974–75 . . . the [ABA] . . . reported that the accredited Law Schools . . . were full. This means, in concrete terms, that the Law Schools of this country are now graduating approximately 30,000 law students per year . . . in a country where the total profession now numbers more than 350,000 . . . . we may [] be overproducing law graduates . . . . [will there] be jobs or placements for the law graduates in the years ahead."[36]

He knew the raw data. The Labor Department was reporting for the 1980s economic growth that would require 15,000 to 20,000 graduates per year, whereas all the law schools combined would be graduating 30,000 to 35,000 graduates per year.[37] That could have meant serious unemployment problem for law graduates. But he was optimistic in his report.

> *"[T]here is a growing appreciation of the fact that a major segment of our society does not presently use legal services at all, though their need for legal service is established. As society is presently organized, the business community and property owners utilize a large part of the legal talent of the country . . . . the poor are beginning to receive some legal service . . . . there is a very large market for legal services not presently being served at all. But the winds of change are blowing . . . . prepaid, insured systems, sometimes providing a full range of legal service . . . . The College of Law . . . is happily situated in one of the rapidly growing population centers of this country . . . . our placement experience . . . has been a very satisfactory experience to date . . ."*[38]

In what he called the Epilogue to his report, he said, "serving as the Founding Dean . . . has been the most satisfying professional experience of my life . . . . I would pay special tribute to Dr. G. Homer Durham . . . and to President John W. Schwada for his continuing support . . . . To the faculty . . . and to the students . . . it has been a splendid experience to work with you . . . . To my Associate Dean Alan A. Matheson, I owe, and the Law School owes, more than I can measure."[39]

Dean Pedrick's Last Report 1974 to 1975

THE PHILOSOPHY OF THE ASU COLLEGE OF LAW

Dean Pedrick's five-page "Philosophy of the ASU College of Law," is a road map for how, in just ten short years, the ASU College of Law went from an idea to a reality. Reading it, you can tick off most of what he and his founding faculty accomplished in a single decade. He defined its core function: "to provide the basic educational training to convert the aspiring, beginning law student into an aspiring beginning lawyer . . ."[40] He defined how it was done: "through unique instructional methods including the so-called 'case system,' problem-centered teaching, seminars and clinical experience . . ."[41] He clarified what the students needed to succeed: "an ability to use and to understand legal method."[42] He told them what they needed most. "The law student does learn to 'think like a lawyer' and this involves developing analytical skills, acquisition of legal concepts and vocabulary, appreciation of legal procedure, facility in more precise use of language and an appreciation of the intellectual discipline and heritage of the profession and its role in society."[43] Most important, he carefully explained what they were about to do. "[I]t is recognized that the educational experience of the law student is simply the basic beginning education for the lawyer—an education which necessarily must continue throughout the life of the practicing professional."[44]

In retrospect, it's a good thing he did not write this and distribute it to all applicants for law school in 1966. Many would have opted out and looked to medical school for an alternative career.

He also left markers for all future deans and professors at the ASU College of Law. "[T]he ongoing development of the educational and the service functions of the Law School rests ultimately with the law faculty . . . . [they must] provide leadership, [] develop proposals and [] focus the collective judgment . . . on issues as they arise."[45] He also left warnings. "The philosophy of service to society . . . is, of course, an 'impossible dream' in the sense that we will never be satisfied with our performance . . . . If we aim for the unattainable, we can hope in the course of the struggle to achieve most of what can be done by mortals. Soon, under new leadership, we must assess the work of the first decade of the life of the Law School. We believe that judgment will be that we have made great progress towards serving the philosophy on which the Law School has been based."[46]

Great progress, indeed.

1 Willard H. Pedrick, *Annual Report of the Dean, 1974–75* (Arizona State University College of Law Archives), 1.

2 Ibid.

3 Ibid.

4 The seven deans at ASU Law who followed Pedrick from 1965 to 2019 are Ernest Gellhorn, Alan Matheson, Paul Bender, Richard Morgan, Patricia White, Paul Berman and Douglas Sylvester. With the exception of one report by Dean Gellhorn, none of the others sent formal reports to their respective presidents of Arizona State University.

5 Pedrick, at 1–2.

6 Ibid., 2.

7 Ibid., 2–3.

8 Ibid., 3.

9 Ibid., 4.

10 Ibid.

11 Ibid.

12 Ibid.

13 Ibid., 5–6.

14 Ibid., 6.

15 Ibid., 7.

16 Ibid., 7–8.

17 Ibid., 8.

18 Ibid., 9.

19 Ibid.

20 Ibid.

21 Ibid., 9–10.

22 Ibid., 11.

23 Ibid., 14–15.

24 Ibid., 15.

25 Ibid.

26 Ibid., 16.

27 Ibid.

28 Ibid., 15.

29 Ibid., 18–19.

30 Ronald L. Carlson, *Competency and Professionalism in Modern Litigation: The Role of the Law Schools*, 23 Ga. L. Rev. 689, 689, *quoting* Robert H. Jackson, *Training the Trial Lawyer: A Neglected Area of Legal Education*, 3 Stan. L. Rev. 48, 57 (1950).

31 Carlson, 692.

32 Ibid., 692, *quoting* Irving R. Kaufman, *Continuing the Call for Courtroom Competence*, 64 A.B.A. J. 1626, 1626 (1978).

33 Pedrick, at 19–20.

34 Ibid., 20.

35 Ibid., 23.

36 Ibid., 23–24.

37 Ibid., 24.

38 Ibid., 25–27.

39 Ibid., 28–29.

40 Ibid., Appendix 1, 1.

41 Ibid.

42 Ibid., Appendix 1, 1–2.

43 Ibid., Appendix 1, 2.
44 Ibid.
45 Ibid., Appendix 1, 3–4.
46 Ibid., Appendix 1, 5.

PART TWO

The Growth Years: 1976 to 2000

1980 Law Journal Luncheon

CHAPTER 17

DEAN ERNEST GELHORN, 1976 TO 1978

Dean Ernest Gellhorn's impressive bio and experience garnered his selection as Dean Pedrick's successor. He was a legal scholar, an expert in anti-trust law and a Guggenheim Fellow.[1] He earned two degrees at the University of Minnesota, and held deanships in three law schools: Arizona State University, Case Western Reserve University, and the University of Washington. He also earned tenured professorships at the University of Virginia, George Mason University, and a faculty professorship at Duke University.[2] He died in 2005 at seventy.

Dean Gellhorn succeeded Dean Pedrick in mid-December 1975, inheriting an experimental seven-year-old law school. Despite the glow that always surrounds succession, he surely knew it wouldn't be easy to manage the swirling mass of young professors, younger students, and formative classes arrayed in a curriculum that changed with the weather. There were unmet goals, boundaries not yet set, and an exceptionally tough act to follow in the inestimable Willard Homer Pedrick. On the upside, he inherited unquestioned success, five years of graduated lawyers, and a cohesion rarely seen in a new school in such a short period of time.

THE SANDRA DAY O'CONNOR COLLEGE OF LAW

REPORT TO ASU UNIVERSITY PRESIDENT SCHWADA

While his tenure would be short, he stayed true to the Pedrick dogma by writing his first report to President Schwada for the 1975–1976 academic year. It was not remotely similar to the previous reports submitted by Dean Pedrick. His sixty-six-page report was single-spaced, written in flawless grammar, styled academically, and in a formal tone befitting a lesser writing to a superior. The narrative summation was a modest sixteen pages, very unlike his predecessor's reports. Absent were the easy-breezy tones, self-deprecating jokes, and wit so ably penned by Dean Pedrick. He attached a daunting appendix, chock-full of charts, graphs, data points, budgetary assessments and projections of projections. It is a historical masterpiece written in TIMES NEW ROMAN font chronicling the progress and successes made by Dean Pedrick and his merry band of law-school builders. Gellhorn steered the ship, and added needed ballast, but would leave the deanship a year later.

FOCUS

He began by defining his goal. "Rather than just report what has occurred within the college, my focus is wider than the law school because it is not an island within itself . . . . Law schools are intimately affected by developments outside the classroom. What happens in the community, and especially in the legal profession, is likely to be reflected in the educational program of a law school."[3] He paraphrased Justice Holmes: "The law is a thinking person's profession." He tied that quote to his report by saying, "The education of the mind involves an exploration of the meaning of ideas as well as their implementation . . . . Law is the mechanism through which social order is maintained, economic progress is sought, and community development is achieved."[4]

During the first few pages, Dean Gellhorn addressed several changes in legal education and the practice of law he thought important. While recognizing the leadership role of lawyers in seeking racial equality in public education and the plight of the poor, he thought lawyers had spread their activities over too wide an area, and so were not "overwhelmingly successful, with lasting reforms difficult to achieve."[5] He expressed hope that "attention is now focused in two directions. On the one hand, government is no longer immediately assumed to be the solver of all problems . . . . We need less rather than more government . . . . The primary task of law is to allow people to solve their own problems.... The profession is turning inward and examining its record and performance."⁶

Gellhorn knew legal trends had counterparts in law schools. He recommended, "law schools take a more modest view of what government aided by law can do." And he connected this thought to what lawyers were doing.

> *This has not resulted, however, in a decline in the number of lawyers "needed" (as determined by the availability of jobs) today. The demand for lawyers is still increasing faster than population growth. And this is due, at least in part, to the second trend: law's inward focus. That is, the profession is now paying increased attention to the preparation and competence of lawyers, to the availability of legal services for all segments of the community and to the kind of justice provided by the legal system. Concern about the quality of legal services underlies the current controversy in many states (including Arizona) over proposals for mandatory continuing legal education. In the same vein, lawyer advertising has become a major topic of dispute and reflects widespread worry about the limited availability of legal services to the middle class and the poor.*⁷

TRENDS IN LEGAL EDUCATION

Without doubt, Dean Pedrick knew the trends in lawyering and legal education in the mid-1970s. But he and his founding faculty were inventing legal education as they went along. They did not contemplate dramatic change and tackling the changing trends expressed by Dean Gellhorn. "[F]ocusing on the limits of law and on the profession itself, and their spirit of questioning established programs and views have *invaded* the law schools, including the Arizona State University College of Law.... These developments are likely to continue and spread.... They will impact students, faculty and budget."⁸

Dean Gellhorn dwelled at some length on not just the names of the classes but also on the substance of what was being taught. He encouraged additions to the curriculum, especially "non-law school subjects—sociology, psychiatry, computer science and allied fields. He questioned whether sound policy meant questioning the value of large classes taught through the Socratic method. He compared trends in legal education—when once all a law teacher needed was a library of appellate case reports—the legal scholar now requires "travel funds, computer time, research assistants, and library materials from other disciplines." He insisted teaching in these areas requires smaller classes, more individualized instruction, and lower teacher/student ratios. He may have sounded slightly heretical by calling for "student preparation in interviewing, negotiating, litigating, appellate arguing, instrument drafting and in what is increasingly called *lawyering skills*." He was writing to the president of his university, but he sounded like a lawyer's lawyer, not a traditional law school dean.

He likely had the ear of younger faculty members, especially those who either had been lawyers themselves or believed in skills training when he said the school was paying attention to Professor Francis Allen,[9] who argued for improving the "art of communication which is basic to an education in the law." Dean Gellhorn supported the new effort at ASU to teach communication "in separate, identifiable courses not part of a substantive class such as Contracts or Criminal Law . . . moreover these courses are taught in service-connected programs where all law students deal with and serve clients."

Dean Gellhorn, like every ASU dean who would follow him, focused on the essence—the goals and methods of legal education. He questioned the "assumptions of our curricula, of teaching approaches, of writing requirements—even of three-year programs." He said they were "undergoing increased scrutiny." He reminded President Schwada that a critical self-study must be prepared as "part of the law school's periodic inspection for accreditation."

He minimized his takeover as dean. "On the surface that may seem to have been an important change, and even the most significant event of the academic year. I think not. What Dean Pedrick built since the school's founding a decade ago is not a personal monument, but a sound and sensitive program with an able and productive faculty and student body. It is a solid foundation on which to build."

THE 1975–76 ACADEMIC YEAR

The balance of his report explained the names, dates, events, costs, wins, and losses during the 1975–76 academic year. He broke it up into subcategories.

A. *The Curriculum.* A great deal of change under a task force headed by Professor Milton Schroder. A new administrative reorganization. New clinics.

B. ***The Student Body.*** Three hundred ninety students in the building; 26 percent women. Minority students remained constant at 11 percent. Applications up to 1,400 for 140 seats. Four-fifths were Arizona residents—well within the Regent's policy of 75 percent. Bar exam passage rate—85 percent. Employment 95 percent obtained. "It was a good year for students, but this does not mean they are a self-satisfied lot. They seek improvement in faculty-student relations, vending machine service, curriculum, admissions standards, grading policies, academic policies, speaker's programs, campus security, etc. They are articulate and forthright—working with them requires candor and sensitivity. The confrontation approach of the early 1970s no longer holds sway for most of them."[10]

C. ***The Faculty.*** During 1975–76, thirty-one professorial appointees in the building, including ten visiting or part-time faculty members. New members—Associate Professor Robert L. Misner. Visitors—Professor Eric Edwards, Professor David Jackson, Professor Nathaniel Nathanson. Adjuncts—John P. Frank, Wendell P. Kay, John A. LaSota, Jr., Louis McClennen, Judge Mary M. Schroeder, Samuel J. Sutton and John P. Todd. Clinical—Raimundo Montes de Oca, Victor A. Aronow. Promotions—Douglas Leslie and Beatrice Moulton promoted to the rank of Professor of Law, tenured. Losses—Associate Professor Gilbert T. Venable returned to the practice of law. Interdisciplinary Studies—four faculty members (Professors Canby, Furnish, Morris, and Zillman) accepted at the Economics Institute for Law Professors.

D. ***The Law Library.*** Added 4,500 volumes bringing the total to 133,102 volumes. Major problem—rise in book losses. Trying to increase library security has failed.

E. ***External Relations.*** Eight hundred graduates in practice in Arizona and the nation. We can no longer meet our commitment to the alumni on an *ad hoc* basis. Increasing pressure on the administrative office from the practicing bar, governmental bodies, and the judiciary. So, we are reorganizing the administrative staff, adding a separate staff office for Law School Relations, and CLE. Fifty thousand dollars raised this year from private sources—goal is to raise $100,000 annually over the next five years. It is evident we need to develop further and stronger ties to the legal community.

Dean Gellhorn's Appendix Number 1 covered his faculty's activity outside the classroom for the year.[11]

FACULTY ACHIEVEMENTS

Professor Michael L. Altman. Addressed the National Advisory Committee on Criminal Justice, Standards and Goals. Addressed the White House Domestic Council Committee on Privacy. He is a board member of the ACLU, is on the executive committee of the ASU Chapter of the AAUP, and is a delegate to the ASU Faculty Senate.

Professor Michael A. Berch. Spoke before the Tri-State Bar Association on securities litigation.

Associate Professor Harold H. Bruff. Wrote proposal to the Administrative Conference of the United States regarding exempting members of the independent regulatory commissions from mandatory retirement. Testified before the U.S. Senate on legislative veto of administrative regulation.

Professor William C. Canby, Jr. On sabbatical leave this fall in Washington, DC, studying content regulation and the First Amendment in broadcasting. Attended National American Indian Court Judges Conference. Was a panelist on ACLU seminar on Indian Civil Liberties. Evaluated the Colorado and Connecticut state humanities programs for the National Endowment for the Humanities. Appointed to the Arizona Legal Services Council. Serves as a board member of the Arizona Center for Law in the Public Interest. Served as counsel for the respondents in ***In Re Bates and O'Steen,*** which will decide the question of lawyer advertising in Arizona.

Professor Edward W. Cleary. Testified on the "lower courts" bill to reorganize courts of limited jurisdiction in Arizona. Also addressed the New Mexico State Bar Association on evidence techniques of trial advocacy.

Professor Richard C. Dahl. Lectured on legal research at the State Prison in Florence. Taught a course on Introduction to Law for paralegals at Scottsdale Community College.

Professor Richard W. Effland. Drafted House Bill 2316 to amend the Arizona Probate Code. Lectured on the Probate Code at the Fifth National Conference of the Probate Code in Salt Lake City. Spoke to the New Mexico Bar Association. Participated in a "Prime Time Show" on public television. Served as a visiting professor of law at the University of Wisconsin.

Professor Dale B. Furnish. Participated in CLE programs on the UCC. Consulted with the Judiciary Committee of the Arizona Senate relating to provisional remedies for satisfaction of debts. Spoke at several high schools on legal subjects. Lectured on present and future legal responses to Mexico economic development on the Future of Mexico meeting held in Tempe.

Dean Ernest Gellhorn. Testified before U.S. House and Senate committees on regulatory reform. Spoke on control of the intelligence agencies in Phoenix, Durham, Charlottesville, NYC and Washington. Presented bicentennial addresses in Phoenix and Sun City. Lectured on constitutional limitations on law school admissions policies at the Homestead and in New York, San Francisco and East Lansing. Served as a moot court judge at BYU Law School. Appointed as ex officio board member of the Arizona Board of Governors. Is a member of the Board of Advisors for the American University and the Duke University Law Journals, and of the FTC Committee on anti-trust regulation, and of the FTC Committee on anti-trust regulation.

Professor Stephen E. Lee. Elected to membership in the American Law Institute. Appeared on public television to discuss income taxes, campaign finance laws. Lectured in CLE program. Organized the ASU Law Student participation program in an IRS-sponsored program. Served as officer of the ACLU.

Associate Dean Alan A. Matheson. Spoke on law school admissions at ASU and NAU, lectured on the federal Privacy Act to the Arizona Welfare Rights Organization and discussed public education and the law with the Ocotillo Teachers Association. He attended the Institute of International Education, served on its screening committee for Fulbright scholarships to Great Britain, and participated in the Services Committee of the Law School Admissions Council. At the University he has served on these committees: Ad Hoc Faculty Salary Committee, Ad Hoc Committee for Criteria for Retention beyond Age 65, Retirement Appeals Committee, and the Affirmative Action Officer Screening Committee. He continues to serve as a member of the board of directors of the Tri-City Mental Health Association.

Associate Professor Robert L. Misner. Served as the reporter for the Speedy Trial Act Planning Committee of the United States District Courts of Arizona and California and attended the Ninth Circuit Conference on its implementation. Gave lectures at the ASU College of Nursing and for the Bureau of Land Management's training program for paralegals in Phoenix. Served on two University Committees: the Ad Hoc Committee on the Elderly and the Interdisciplinary Committee on Human Experimentation.

Professor John P. Morris. Served as a Council Member of the Association of American University Professors and was selected as a permanent fellow of Clare Hall, Cambridge University, England. He taught a continuing legal education course for practicing attorneys in Phoenix on antitrust law, participated in a Bureau of Land Management training program for paralegals and served on the ASU Personnel and Fundraising committees.

Professor Beatrice A. Moulton. Served as Chairman of the Committee on Clinical Education of the American Bar Association Section on Legal Education and Admissions to the Bar, on the board of the Arizona Center for Law in the Public Interest and on the Community Program Advisory Committee of KAET. Also produced a set of prototype teaching materials including videotaped lawyer performances, addressed the Tri-City Bar on teaching negotiation in law school, and participated as an instructor in a new lawyer-training program for the Legal Services Corporation.

Professor Willard H. Pedrick. Taught as a visiting professor at the UCLA Law School during the spring semester and was honored by a tribute in the 1975 *Arizona State Law Journal* (issue no. 2). Addressed an Association of American Law Schools Section—Why Law Deans Quit, and gave class-day addresses at the ASU and Ohio State University law schools. Also spoke on estate planning at continuing legal education forums in Chicago and Springfield, Missouri, and participated in the Multi-State Bar Exam Committee on Torts Questions in San Francisco. Was elected president of the Phoenix Executives Club for 1976–77. Served on the ASU Ad Hoc Committee on the President's Advisory Council on Off-Campus Teaching.

Professor Jonathan Rose. Spent the second semester on sabbatical leave at Southampton University, England, and lectured there and on the Continent. Also was appointed as a member of the Committee on Legal Specialization of the State Bar of Arizona.

Professor Milton R. Schroeder. Testified frequently before Arizona legislative committees on legislation to reform real estate subdividing regulation and was the principal draftsman for Senate Bill 2168 on Subdivision Land Fraud. Lectured on land fraud and on state land planning before several groups in Phoenix. Spoke on the Uniform Commercial Code to Arizona county recorders in Phoenix and the State Bar of Arizona's continuing legal education forums in Tucson and Tempe. Taught in the Bureau of Land Management training program for paralegals. Chaired (and authored) a major Law School task force report on the curriculum.

Served as a trustee of the Rocky Mountain Mineral Law Foundation as a consultant to the Secretary of State of Arizona, as chairman of the State Bar of Arizona Committee on Land Fraud, and as a member of the Imagineering Task Force of the City of Scottsdale.

Associate Professor Robert E. Strong, Jr. Lectured on will drafting in Tucson and Tempe in a continuing legal education program for the State Bar of Arizona. Served on the Appeal Committee on Tuition Status for the University.

Associate Professor Gilbert T. Venable. Lectured to nine groups meeting in or near Phoenix on legal rights of children, the disabled, and Indian water rights.

Associate Professor Donald N. Zillman. Taught summer CLE institutes at the University of Utah last summer and ASU this summer, and in the U.S. Army's Judge Advocate General School in Virginia. Served as co-chairman and moderator of the ASU-American Society of International Law regional meeting on Mexican-American law. Serves ASU as a member of the Faculty Senate and chairman of the University Trial Board.

Dean Gellhorn's second and last report to ASU President was submitted to ASU President John W. Schwada on July 1, 1977. When he was chairman of the Association of American Law Schools Committee on Special Admissions, that committee advised the AALS Executive Committee on Bakke and aided in preparation of its amicus brief submitted to the United States Supreme Court. He gave President Schwada a short brief of Bakke because this case is likely to "affect legal education in the future. . . . and, indeed of the legal profession. It is the decision of the California Supreme Court announced on September 16, 1976, in Bakke v. Regents of University of California[12] holding that the University of California at Davis medical school's practice of relying upon race as a factor in making admissions decisions violated the Equal Protection Clause of the Fourteenth Amendment to the United States Constitution."[13] As most lawyers will recall, the California court's opinion was about a medical school. However, the admissions process at most, if not all, public and private law schools at the time was similar. That meant that the U.S. Supreme Court's review of the case would substantially affect law schools. In the mid-seventies they all had some form of special program that admits minority students with lower numerical credentials in order to increase the number of qualified members of racial minorities in professional schools.

He gave President Schwada a short brief on the importance of Bakke. "The success of minority admissions programs and their importance is underscored when one examines what would occur if they were prohibited by an affirmance of the California court's decision in Bakke. The unpleasant but unalterable reality is that the California decision would mean a return to the virtually-all white law school student bodies that existed prior to the mid-1960s."[14]

The U.S. Supreme Court affirmed the holding that the University's special admissions program was unlawful and the order that the respondent, Bakke, be admitted to the medical school. The Court reversed that part of the judgment enjoining the University from any consideration of race in its admissions process. Race could be considered in admissions if it was factored in with other characteristics in a competitive process.[15]

Dean Gellhorn brought President Schwada up to date on ASU Law's admissions. "Last year I reported that over 1,300 applicants had sought the 140 places in our first-year class. This year the law faculty sought to relieve that pressure slightly by enlarging the first year class to 150, clearly the maximum number our current facilities will support. Yet despite a nationwide decline of over 10 percent in law school applications for the 1977 entering class, our pool increased by over 20 percent to more than 1,600."[16] And he explained the special admission standards for minority applicants in 1977. "Similarly, we have kept our commitment of resources to specially-admitted students within reasonable and manageable limits. Minority admissions on a special basis have not exceeded 12 percent of the entering class, and in 1977 such admissions will include only 5 percent of available spaces."[17]

Besides the challenge presented by *Bakke* in California, he also informed President Schwada about important changes in the law school's curriculum.

He said it had been "enriched on several fronts. The appellate advocacy seminar, in which both law students and lawyers participated, was offered for a second time on an experimental basis. We are currently evaluating both the experience and cost of the program to determine whether it should (and can) be continued. Our offerings in professional responsibility were expanded when two Phoenix lawyers, Larry Hammond and Andy Hurwitz, whose backgrounds include clerkships to justices of the Supreme Court of the United States, taught a seminar on the legal profession—including topics such as lawyer advertising and the effective delivery of legal services."[18]

As always, the student body was part of every dean's annual report to the ASU president. Dean Gellhorn's report was very good news at ASU; 392 full-time students were on campus; 14 special students took courses in the Law School. Of the regular students, 128 (or 33 percent) were women, an increase of 8 percent from the previous year. And 33 (or 8 percent) of the student body were members of minority groups. The quality of the student body, as measured by numerical credentials and reflected in previous honors and achievements, continues to improve. The median LSAT for the entering class was 629, and its median undergraduate grade average was 3.52 (on a 4.0 scale). Eighty-five percent of the entering class were residents of Arizona, and two-thirds were twenty-six years or younger. Political science, history, accounting, or business was the undergraduate field of study for half the class, but others ranged over a wide field, including English, mathematics, engineering, nursing, and anthropology. The largest group, again about half, were graduates of either ASU or the University of Arizona, while the others were spread from Antioch and Barnard through Virginia and Yale.[19]

He reported on salaries. "Initial salaries paid to our graduates range widely from $10,000 to $22,000, with the median salary being $14,000. And new faculty. Lowenthal graduated from the University of Chicago Law School in 1969 after being Comments and Topics editor of the University of Chicago Law Review and served as an Associate in Law on the faculty of Boalt Hall. In addition, he practiced law for six years in the Bay Area. And visiting faculty. Professors John J. Barcelo of Cornell, David A Binder of UCLA, and C. Douglas Miller of Florida. Former Harvard Law School Dean Erwin N. Griswold, James W. Mercer, an attorney with the Securities and Exchange Commission, and Professors Walter B. Raushenbush of Wisconsin and David A. Rice of Boston University. In addition, several practitioners and judges were relied upon on an adjunct basis to meet particular curricular needs and to cement the bridge between the law school and the bench and bar."[20]

External relations were always an issue for the Law School. Dean Gellhorn brought President Schwada up on that topic. "Continuing efforts are made to maintain close relations with the legislature, bench, bar, and alumni of the Law School. Each has extended generous support to the school during the past year. We plan to continue and expand these efforts. The Law Alumni Association has expanded its scope and operations this past year and now includes over 900 graduates. Its President was Timothy H. Barnes, a 1973 graduate. It sponsored legal seminars, which have thus far raised $1,000 for a law student loan fund, and held several social events seeking to continue ties among alumni and with the law School. The law Society grew in size during the past year and held an annual dinner, co-sponsored for the first time with our burgeoning Alumni Association, attended by over 500 guests including Governor Raul H. Castro, and the speaker was Mr. Justice Byron R. White. The Law Society's Board of Directors met four times, reviewed plans and programs of the law school, and gave generously of its time and experience."

He closed his report by saying, "The past year has seen the College of Law make real strides in its effort to achieve excellence in the education provided all students, in its contribution to legal scholarship, and in the service given the bar and community. The students and faculty have honestly sought to understand and respond to the many challenges facing legal education. We are grateful for your continuing support and understanding."

Soon after he penned his second report he became the new dean at Case Western Reserve College of law. He was succeeded at ASU Law by Dean Alan Matheson in 1977.

---

1 Wikipedia, s.v., "Guggenheim Fellowship," last modified January 11, 2021, 22:51, https://en.wikipedia.org/wiki/Guggenheim_Fellowship. Guggenheim Fellowships are grants that have been awarded annually since 1925 by the John Simon Guggenheim Memorial Foundation to those "who have demonstrated exceptional capacity for productive scholarship or exceptional creative ability in the arts." The roll of Fellows includes numerous Nobel Laureates, Pulitzer, and other prizewinners.
2 Wikipedia, s.v., "Ernest Gellhorn," last modified December 25, 2020, 22:27, https://en.wikipedia.org/wiki/Ernest_Gellhorn.
3 College of Law—Arizona State University—Report of the Dean—Ernest Gellhorn, 1975–1976, at p. 1.
4 Ibid.
5 Ibid., 2.
6 Ibid., 3.
7 Ibid. 3–4. It is worth noting that Dean Gellhorn's concern about legal advertising in 1976 did not mention the overarching role the ASU Law School would play in the monumental change about to happen when two ASU students, John Bates and Van O'Steen, and their ASU Professor, William C. Canby, successfully challenged the age-old ban on lawyer advertising. *See* Chapter 18, *supra*.
8 College of Law—Arizona State University—Report of the Dean—Ernest Gellhorn, 1975–1976, Section II, p 4.
9 At the time, the former dean of the University of Michigan Law School, and the current president of the Association of American Law Schools.
10 College of Law—Arizona State University—Report of the Dean—Ernest Gellhorn, 1975–1976, p 10–11.
11 College of Law—Arizona State University—Report of the Dean—Ernest Gellhorn, 1975–1976, pages 17 to 20.
12 *Bakke v. Regents of University of Cal.*, 18 Cal. 3d 34, 553 P.2d 1152 (1976).
13 Arizona State Law Forum, Volume 1, Number 1, Winter 1977. At page 2.
14 Ibid., 4.
15 Regents of *Univ. of Cal. v. Bakke*, 438 U.S. 265, 1978.
16 Arizona State Law Forum, Volume 1, Number 1, Winter 1977, at page 6.

17 Ibid., 7.
18 Ibid., 7.
19 Ibid., 8.
20 Ibid., 9.

CHAPTER 18

JOHN R. BATES & VAN O'STEEN—LEGAL ADVERTISING—1976

This chapter is about two exceptional law students from the Class of 1972—John R. Bates and Van O'Steen. Their fame started inauspiciously with a disciplinary case explicitly designed to test a historic legal barrier to practicing lawyers—the ban on legal advertising.[1]

For most lawyers, the dread and despair that comes with bar discipline is gut-wrenching because it is often career ending. When disaster strikes, most lawyers don invisibility cloaks, and dread the oncoming scourge of their colleagues. Members of the bar never want to see their names in the caption of a supreme court disciplinary decision. But as all lawyers know, for every rule there is an exception.

John R. Bates and Van O'Steen were the ultimate exception. They didn't glory in the discipline handed down, but they didn't fear it either. They intentionally violated the Arizona Supreme Court's rule banning legal advertising, welcoming the chance to explain their case to the court, their colleagues, and lawyers all over America. They were smart, courageous lawyers. Their case forced the bar to change its mind and were proud of it. It made American legal history and affected the practice of law in every state. They virtually invented lawyer advertising, although not nearly as slick or deceptive[2] as today's lawyer ads often are.

LAWYER ADVERTISING

The professional conduct rule they violated was a simple one—lawyers must not advertise their services.[3] The original anti-advertising rule was sixty-eight years old. The American Bar Association's *Canons of Professional Ethics* in American law from 1908 to 1937 forbade all manner of crass conduct by lawyers.[4] Canon 27 said, "The most worthy and effective advertisement possible, even for a young lawyer, and especially with his brother lawyers, is the establishment of a well-merited reputation for professional capacity and fidelity to trust . . . [S]olicitation of business by circulars or advertisements, or by personal communications or interviews, not warranted by personal relations, is unprofessional. It is equally unprofessional to procure business by indirection through touters[5] of any kind."[6]

THE ARIZONA SUPREME COURT CASE—1976

The legal world faced by John Bates and Van O'Steen in 1976 bore no relationship to the one in which lawyer advertising was unthinkable. That world, in what are now called the "early days of the bar," which was populated by young men who "came to the Inns of Court to study and eat the requisite dinners there in order to become barristers, [they] were the sons of well-to-do parents, who did not have to worry about earning their keep, and who traditionally looked down on all forms of trade and the competitive spirit characteristic thereof . . . The profession of the law hence acquired a certain traditional dignity."[7]

John Bates and Van O'Steen are notable graduates of ASU. They were in the 1972 graduating class, took classes from famous professors, including Dean Willard Pedrick (in Torts) and Professor Canby (in Constitutional Law). Bates was first in the class and won the Armstrong Award.[8] O'Steen graduated *cum laude*. Both were highly regarded by the faculty and their fellow students. They likely could have landed jobs at one of the top law firms in Phoenix but chose instead to work for the Maricopa County Legal Aid Society. That was a pro bono legal clinic, representing people unable to pay normal legal fees.

In 1974, they started their own law firm, a clinic, in Phoenix. They concentrated on low-cost legal services offered to poorer clients, the first one in Arizona. "We wanted," Bates said, "to change the existing system, which favored existing law firms, who did not seek clients among the underserved. In the provision of legal services, a huge number of people were turned away because of lack of financial resources. We wanted to offer affordable legal services."[9]

Their new law firm/clinic struggled to secure a viable base of clients. "After two years, we concluded that the clinic would not succeed if we did not advertise. Because our fees were so low, we needed a greater volume of clients than could be obtained by simply hanging out our shingle and waiting."[10] They placed an ad in *The Arizona Republic*. O'Steen said, "We knew we would get a strong reaction from the state bar for our price-list ad."[11] The February 22, 1976 ad shouted in small cap lettering:

> DO YOU NEED A LAWYER? LEGAL SERVICES AT VERY REASONABLE RATES.
>
> *DIVORCE OR LEGAL SEPARATION—UNCONTESTED—BOTH SPOUSES SIGN PAPERS--$175.00 PLUS $20.00 COURT FILING FEE.
>
> *PREPARATION OF ALL COURT PAPERS AND INSTRUCTIONS ON HOW TO DO YOUR OWN SIMPLE UNCONTESTED DIVORCE--$100.00.
>
> *ADOPTION—UNCONTESTED SEVERANCE PROCEEDING--$225.00 PLUS APPROXIMATELY $10.00 PUBLICATION COST.
>
> *BANKRUPTCY—NON BUSINESS, NO CONTESTED PROCEEDINGS—INDIVIDUAL $250.00 PLUS $55.00 COURT FILING FEE. WIFE AND HUSBAND--$300.00 PLUS $110.00 COURT FILING FEE.
>
> *CHANGE OF NAME--$95.00 PLUS $20 COURT FILING FEE. *INFORMATION REGARDING OTHER TYPES OF CASES FURNISHED ON REQUEST.
>
> **LEGAL CLINIC OF BATES & O'STEEN—617 N. 3RD STREET, PHOENIX, ARIZONA 85004.**[12]

JOHN BATES, VAN O'STEEN, AND BILL CANBY

The day they ran the ad, knowing full well the likely response, Bates and O'Steen did another smart thing. They took their former constitutional law professor out to lunch.[13] O'Steen said, "[w]e thought the prudent thing to do was to speak with Bill Canby, our constitutional law professor at Arizona State University. He is a brilliant lawyer, law professor and jurist." Bates added, "I selected Bill Canby for several reasons; first he has a brilliant legal mind. Second, he was sympathetic to our cause. Third, he had a deep background in constitutional law."[14] They picked the perfect lawyer to handle their case.

Professor Canby[15] recalled that first meeting: "They told me they had placed an ad in a local newspaper advertising the price for their legal services. I knew how the bar would react. They said they needed an attorney. I agreed on two conditions: (1) I could control the litigation, and (2) I would charge no fee."[16]

The President of the State Bar[17] filed a complaint against Bates and O'Steen for violating the anti-advertising rule. The State Bar's hearing panel made only one finding and recommended that each be suspended from the practice of law for six months.[18] The State Bar Board of Governors, reviewing that recommendation, reduced the punishment to a one-week suspension.[19] That recommendation was transferred to the Arizona Supreme Court.

The Court identified five questions on review: "1. Does DR 2–101(B) violate either the federal or state antitrust laws? 2. Does [it] violate the First and Fourteenth Amendments of the United States Constitution? 3. Does [it] violate the Fourteenth Amendment right of equal protection of the law? 4. Is [the rule] void for vagueness? 5. Does the State Bar Disciplinary procedure violate due process?"[20]

The Court made short work of the first question. Respondents contend that the disciplinary rule violates the federal and Arizona antitrust statutes.[21] They relied heavily on *Goldfarb v. Virginia State Bar*.[22] The Court held that "[w]e do not believe that the holding of *Goldfarb* applies to the facts of this case. *Goldfarb* . . . was concerned with a minimum fee schedule . . . The control of advertising . . . is far different than price fixing by a local bar association . . . . The Sherman Act does not apply to state action . . . The regulation of the State Bar by the Supreme Court is an activity of the State of Arizona acting as sovereign and exempt [from] the Sherman Act."

The second argument was almost as easy. The Arizona Supreme Court found no First Amendment violation. The third argument—Equal Protection—called for an explanation. "Respondents contend that since advertising is permitted by qualified legal assistance programs, they are being denied equal protection of the law by not being allowed to advertise . . . . We disagree . . . the purpose of allowing legal assistance organizations a limited amount of advertising is to bring to the attention of those of limited finances . . . of the fact that such services are available. The attorney himself may not advertise but only the legal assistance organization. We do not believe that [the disciplinary rule] violates the equal protection provisions of the United States Constitutions or the Arizona Constitution."[23]

The Supreme Court found the disciplinary rule clear, and not overbroad. Attorneys or non-attorneys should have no difficulty reading this rule as prohibiting a lawyer from publicizing himself through "newspaper or magazine advertisements."[24]

The Court gave some credence to the respondents' due process argument. "Admittedly, there is a question when members of a profession attempt to self-regulate their profession and impose discipline for violations of what may be at times technical and complex standards. While there is a necessity for fair and impartial hearings, there is also the necessity that the persons who must hear the allegations of professional misconduct have the required knowledge of the standards and needs of the profession. Non-professionals alone could not bring to the hearings a sufficient knowledge and understanding of professional standards or a compulsion to enforce them. The most the non-professional would bring to such a hearing is business ethics, and business ethics, while adequate for the commercial world, are not sufficient as a standard for professional conduct. We must then balance the need for an informed and concerned Board with the degree of pecuniary interest, however slight or minimal, which may exist when attorneys sit in judgment of other attorneys. In the instant case, we do not find a sufficient pecuniary interest by the Committee or the Board to require that they be disqualified because of interest."[25]

And with that, the Arizona Supreme Court found Bates and O'Steen in violation of the disciplinary rule, but since "the act was done in good faith to test the constitutionality of [the rule]. We believe that the respondents should be censured only."

Justice Frank Gordon issued a special concurring opinion: "Whether a blanket ban on certain forms of advertisement is unconstitutional as violative of the First

Amendment is a far weightier question which I am not yet prepared to resolve in the negative. I am concerned, however, that to impulsively discard the regulations leaving few if any guidelines in their wake, might well initiate a flood of media combat for legal business which would serve neither the best interests of the public nor the bar."[26] As was often the case, Justice Gordon was fortune-teller. His metaphor about leaving things in their "wake" and initiating a "flood" were about to happen.

Justice Jack Hays wrote a dissent. While technically it was a "dissent" for legal reasons, it was actually a suggestion that his colleagues on the high bench were not as harsh as he thought they should be. "I cannot go along with the punishment imposed. It appears to me that the 'watered down' version of punishment adopted by the majority invites more and better testing of all the provisions of the Code of Professional Ethics. Admittedly, the Respondents violated the Code in order to secure clients for their legal clinic. The testing of an allegedly questionable provision was incidental and the method of testing was the one calculated to attain the monetary advantage sought. I would adopt the penalty recommended . . . suspension for not less than six (6) months."[27]

Justice William Holohan dissented on the merits.

> *Despite my own personal dislike of the concept of advertising by attorneys, I have concluded that the advertising ban . . . is unconstitutional. . . . [T]he time has arrived for us to review that ban in light of the fact that such action is in fact contrary to the national public policy. It may be that we have the power to exempt attorneys from the Sherman Act, but should we continue such a position in the face of national public policy to the contrary . . . What is at stake in this case is more than regulation of a profession or the discipline of two lawyers. More fundamentally there is involved the right of the public as consumers and citizens to know about the activities of the legal profession. Obviously the information of what lawyers charge is important for private economic decisions by those in need of legal services. Such information is also helpful, perhaps indispensable, to the formation of an intelligent opinion by the public on how well the legal system is working and whether it should be regulated or even altered. This Court's power to regulate the profession of law comes from the people, and what the people give they can also take away. The rule at issue prevents access to such information by the public . . . In summary, the ban on advertising . . . is contrary to national policy, is a*

denial of First Amendment rights, and violates the equal protection provision of the Fourteenth Amendment. This Court should forthrightly declare the rule unconstitutional. We can then attempt to write rules, which provide for public access to information about attorneys.[28]

It is absurd to think, especially retroactively, that one Arizona Supreme Court justice could have foreseen what was about to happen in the highest court of the land. However, it must have been soothing music to John Bates and Van O'Steen as they dealt with the censure they got from the full court for doing something one justice thought unconstitutional.

THE UNITED STATES SUPREME COURT CASE—1977

Bates and O'Steen persevered. With style, grace, and suburb lawyering by Professor Canby. They were innovators, and ahead of their time, but there would be much more to come. They would not just rewrite lawyer advertising; they became a key to a lock on professionalism. The prevailing view, particularly in senior lawyers of the day, was a deep-seated fear that price advertising would morph into rank commercialization. That would diminish the profession's sense of dignity. We'd become the hustle and bustle that would destroy our service orientation and irreparably damage the delicate balance between lawyer's fees and the profession's reputation for selflessly service. Their petition for certiorari in the U.S. Supreme Court was granted. Professor Canby argued their case on January 18, 1977. John P. Frank argued for the State Bar of Arizona. Justices Burger, Brennan, Stewart, White, Marshall, Blackmun, Powell, Rehnquist, and Stevens heard the arguments.

The Court ruled 5 to 4 in favor of Bates & O'Steen on June 27, 1977. Rehearing was denied on October 3, 1977. The opinion is fifty-four pages long, not counting footnotes. As he had in the *Virginia Pharmacy*[29] case, Justice Blackmun wrote the majority opinion. Chief Justice Burger concurred in part and dissented in part. Justice Powell concurred in part and dissented in part. Justice Rehnquist dissented in part. When the judicial dust settled, Justice Powell may have written the real legacy of what John Bates and Van O'Steen started with their small ad in the *Arizona Republic* offering modest fees for simple legal work. Justice Powell said, "[I]t is clear that within undefined limits today's decision will effect profound changes in the practice of law, viewed for centuries as a learned profession. The supervisory power of the courts over members of the bar, as officers of the courts, and the authority of the respective States to oversee the regulation of the profession have been weakened."[30]

The Court's unofficial summary was dispositive. It affirmed that part of the Arizona Supreme Court's decision dealing with the Sherman Act because the disciplinary rule was the activity of the state acting as sovereign. It reversed that part of the judgment dealing with the First Amendment, holding that advertising by attorneys could not be subject to blanket suppression. In addition, it found the truthful advertisement placed by Bates and O'Steen to be constitutionally protected.

While *Bates v. State Bar of Arizona* is the seminal American case on lawyer advertising, its core ruling was often forgotten over the years in two important aspects. The *Bates* decision did not address the larger problems associated with legal advertising about the *quality* of legal services. It did not resolve problems associated with *solicitation* of clients. In fact, it ignored the "basic factual content" of legal advertising. Rather, the heart of the *Bates* dispute was whether lawyers could constitutionally advertise the prices at which routine legal services would be performed.[31]

BATES, O'STEEN, CANBY, AND JOHN P. FRANK—THOUGHTS ON LAWYER ADVERTISING.

In 2004, the principals, Bates, O'Steen, Canby, and John P. Frank, looked back on their historic battle at the U.S. Supreme Court.[32] Judge Canby said, "I thought the case was a natural for the U.S. Supreme Court, particularly since in *Virginia Pharmacy* the Court had broken ground on commercial speech. It wasn't too hard to make the connection to attorneys." He continued, "the case stands for the idea that commercial speech is something that offers vitally important information to consumers just as other types of speech, and the speech is important because it leads to economic decisions that govern our lives. Abraham Lincoln advertised his services when he practiced law."

John P. Frank,[33] who had briefed and argued the case for the State Bar of Arizona, said, "My skin crawls and my stomach screams when I see ads for lawyers who promise to fight like tigers and at very low cost. I believe that advertising has become so sufficiently promiscuous that it is a profound change in the practice of law."[34]

Van O'Steen[35] said in 2004, "The case was the high-water mark of my legal career as a party, not a lawyer. I see it as a great consumer victory. It led to reduced costs of legal services."[36]

John Bates[37] said, "I think the decision was a victory for the public in general. When I look back at the case and what we accomplished, I have a feeling of satisfaction."[38]

In a nationwide response throughout the '70s, '80s and '90s, bar associations worked tirelessly to keep the advertising tiger at bay. Collectively, bar associations in every state fashioned suppression not as a blanket, but rather as thin sheets that didn't quite cover the body of the profession. Anti-advertising for lawyers smoldered as long as it was an analog world. The digital legal world would disrobe the profession so everyone could see. That would come after Yellow Page ads, posters at bus stops, and grainy TV ads. The internet would perpetuate a virtual explosion in lawyer ads and self-promotion that almost matched Hollywood.

Bates v. State Bar of Arizona is unquestionably the seminal American case on lawyer advertising. It has been cited in 1,017 other American cases, cussed, discussed, honored, maligned, and otherwise revisited in approximately 2,868 times in the last forty-two years, and written-up in at least eighty-six treatises.[39] It is a First Amendment decision about advertising lawyer's fees in a newspaper. Today's trial lawyers should remember that it did not deal with advertising claims about the *quality* of legal services, nor did it resolve the problems associated with in-person *solicitation* of clients. It did not deal with basic factual content in lawyer advertising on either a general or a particular basis. The heart of the *Bates* dispute was whether lawyers could constitutionally advertise the prices they charged for routine legal services.[40]

THE FUTURE OF LAWYER ADVERTISING

What's next for lawyer advertising? How will technology and social media impact it? Is it still a direct threat to the profession? It's naïve to believe that *Bates v. State Bar of Arizona* provides any answers today. It's a forty-two-year-old case. The profession's questions for the decade include who the legal innovators are and how the profession will respond to systemic changes. Are there other constitutional dimensions in how, when, and why lawyers engage putative clients?

How about high-volume, mega law firms with global offices and thousands of lawyers? The shakeout period is over. Advertising is not just here to stay; it's here to change legal services at every level. One writer said, "It's like going from mom-and-pop grocery stores to supermarkets. We are seeing the emergence of regional and international law firms: Jacoby & Meyers, Hyatt Legal Services (in 20 states)—law firms could not grow that way without advertising." And other restrictions? "Statutes prohibiting the unauthorized practice of law should be abolished. State legislatures, bar associations, and supreme courts have no business restricting the buyer's choice to licensed lawyers. Legal Luddites, look out."[41]

On January 1, 2021, legal advertising for Arizona lawyers changed dramatically. Vice-Chief Justice Ann Timmer led the Legal Services Task Force for two years. Under her leadership, the Arizona Supreme Court significantly amended advertising rules to account for technological advances in the delivery of legal services as cross-border marketing of legal services. The changes simplified and accommodated multijurisdictional advertising.[42] Unquestionably, the change from regulating how lawyers advertised to commentary about legal advertising was earthshaking to the Arizona bar.

The 2021 Arizona Supreme Court rules eliminated ER 7.2 in its entirety, including the historic prohibition against giving anything of "value" for client referrals. All of the former prohibitions in ER 7.2 were vacated because "they serve no productive regulatory purpose as no quantifiable data suggests that paying for referrals confuses or harms consumers."[43]

---

1 *In the Matter of Members of the State Bar of Arizona,* John R. Bates and Van O'Steen, 113 Ariz. 394 (Ariz. 1976).

2 Lawyers are well advised to avoid ads that are misleading, i.e. language or portrayals about (1) fees, including what prospective clients are and are not responsible for, (2) statements that can be construed to predict success, and (3) the use of actors to portray lawyers or events leading to lawsuits. Sarah Andropoulos, "Three Examples of 'Misleading' Content in Attorney Advertising," *Justia,* last modified November 4, 2015, https://onward.justia.com/2015/11/04/three-examples-of-misleading-content-in-attorney-advertising/.

3 Ariz. Rev. Stat. Sup. Ct. R. 29(a). Disciplinary Rule 2-101(B) was the relevant rule in 1976. "A lawyer shall not publicize himself, or his partner, or associate or any other lawyer affiliated with him or his firm, as a lawyer through newspaper or magazine advertisements, radio or television announcements, display advertisements in the city or telephone directories or other means of commercial publicity, nor shall he authorize or permit others to do so in his behalf."

4 American Bar Association, *Canons of Professional Ethics* (1908), http://minnesotalegalhistoryproject.org/assets/ABA%20Canons%20(1908).pdf.

5 *See ABA Opinion* 284 (1951).

6 American Bar Association, *Canons of Professional Ethics* (1908), http://minnesotalegalhistoryproject.org/assets/ABA%20Canons%20(1908).pdf. *See also* Henry S. Drinker, *Legal Ethics* (New York: Columbia University Press, 1953), 215. Henry S. Drinker was a member of the Philadelphia Bar and the Chairman of the Standing Committee on Professional Ethics and Grievances of the American Bar Association.

7 Ibid., 210.

8 The top honor at the Sandra Day O'Connor College of Law is the John S. Armstrong Award, which "honors Armstrong, an Arizona legislator who introduced the bill that established Arizona's first institution of higher learning, the Tempe Normal School (forerunner of ASU)." Staci McCabe, "2 Law Students to Receive Armstrong Award," Sandra Day O'Connor College of Law, last modified May 15, 2011, https://law.asu.edu/content/2-law-students-receive-armstrong-award-0.

9 David L. Hudson, Jr., "Bates Participants Reflect on Landmark Case," Freedom Forum Institute, last modified November 18, 2004, https://www.freedomforuminstitute.org/2004/11/18/bates-participants-reflect-on-landmark-case/.

10 Ibid.

11 Ibid.

12 Wikipedia, s.v., "*Bates v. State Bar of Arizona*," last modified January 2, 2020, 00:43, https://en.wikipedia.org/wiki/Bates_v._State_Bar_of_Arizona.

13 David L. Hudson, Jr., "Bates Participants Reflect on Landmark Case," Freedom Forum Institute, last modified November 18, 2004, https://www.freedomforuminstitute.org/2004/11/18/bates-participants-reflect-on-landmark-case/.

14 Ibid.

15 "William Cameron Canby Jr. is a Senior United States Circuit Judge of the United States Court of Appeals for the Ninth Circuit. As both a professor at Arizona State University College of Law and a Circuit Judge of the United States Court of Appeals for the Ninth Circuit, Canby has become known as an authority on American Indian law. He has authored law review articles, a major textbook, and the West Nutshell Series primer on the subject." Wikipedia, s.v., "William Canby," last modified February 28, 2020, 00:22, https://en.wikipedia.org/wiki/William_Canby.

16 Hudson, Jr., *supra* note 889.

17 Mark I. Harrison was the President of the State Bar of Arizona at the time. *In Re Bates*, 113 Ariz. 394, 396 (Ariz. 1976).

18 The Special Administrative Committee held a hearing on April 7, 1976, before Ivan Robinette, Carl W. Divelbiss, and Philip E. vonAmmon, Chairman. Ibid., 395.

19 "The act of the Respondents was on one hand a deliberate and knowing violation of the Rule, but on the other hand was undertaken as an earnest challenge to the validity of a rule they conscientiously believe to be invalid. We therefore recommend a penalty of one-week suspension from the practice of law for each of them, the weeks to run consecutively and not simultaneously, so as to avoid the closing down of their practice. We further recommend that the enforcement of this discipline be suspended until 30 days after a final decision has been made concerning the validity of the rule in the highest court to which it is presented. The foregoing Findings of Fact, Conclusions of Law, and Recommendations are issued by the Board of Governors this 30th day of April, 1976, pursuant to Rule 36(d) of the Rules of the Supreme Court of the State of Arizona. /s/ Mark I. Harrison, President State Bar of Arizona." Ibid., 396.

20 Ibid., 395.

21 Ibid. Specifically, the respondents contend that the federal antitrust statutes that were violated were Sections 1 and 2 of the Sherman Act and the Arizona antitrust statutes that were violated were Ariz. Rev. Stat. §§44–1401 through 44–1413.

22 421 U.S. 773 (1975). In *Goldfarb,* the court held that a county bar's publication of a minimum fee schedule was anticompetitive activity, which the Sherman Act was clearly meant to proscribe.

23 In *Re Bates*, 113 Ariz. at 399.

24 Ibid., 400.

25 Ibid.

26 Ibid., 402.

27 Ibid., 402.

28 Ibid., 403–04.

29 *Virginia St. Pharmacy Bd. v. Virginia Consumer Counsel, Inc.,* 425 U.S. 748 (1976). *See also Bigelow v. Virginia,* 421 U.S. 809 (1975). Both cases were precedent in the *Bates* case as both held that commercial speech was entitled to certain protection under the First Amendment.

30 *Bates v. State Bar of Arizona,* 433 U.S. 350, 389 (1977).

31 Gary L. Stuart, "The Ethical Trial Lawyer," State Bar of Arizona, 1994 at 74–75.

32 Hudson, Jr., *supra* note 889.

33 "John Paul Frank (November 10, 1917–September 7, 2002) was an American lawyer and scholar involved in landmark civil rights, school desegregation, and criminal procedure cases before the United States Supreme Court." He earned his bachelor's, master's and law degrees from the University of Wisconsin. "He clerked for Justice Hugo Black of the U.S. Supreme Court from 1942 to 1943. Frank spent the next two years as the assistant to the Secretary of the Interior and then to the U.S. Attorney General. He studied at Yale Law School and obtained a S.J.D. in 1947. In 1946, he joined the faculty of the Indiana University, Bloomington School of Law. He returned to Yale Law School to teach from 1949 to 1954, when he joined the law firm of Lewis & Roca in Phoenix, Arizona.

Frank helped then-Chief Counsel for the NAACP Legal Defense and Educational Fund, Thurgood Marshall, formulate strategy in the school desegregation case of *Brown v. Board of Education of Topeka* (1954). Frank argued the case of *Miranda v. Arizona* (1966), which required that police inform criminal suspects of their rights. In *Bates v. State Bar of Arizona* (1977), Frank unsuccessfully argued before the U.S. Supreme Court that state bar limits on attorney advertising were consistent with the right to free speech under the First Amendment.

Frank's papers are held at the Library of Congress." Wikipedia, s.v. "John Paul Frank," last modified February 28, 2020, 9:28, https://en.wikipedia.org/wiki/John_Paul_Frank.

34 Hudson, Jr., *supra* note 889.

35 O'Steen is a highly respected lawyer in Phoenix, Arizona. He was inducted into the Maricopa Bar Association *Hall of Fame* in 2017. He is the managing partner of his new firm, O'Steen & Harrison. His website ad reads, "Phoenix Personal Injury and Car Accident Lawyers. If you or a loved one has been injured in an accident, we would like to help you. It is important that you get expert advice from a personal injury lawyer as soon as possible following an accident. Prompt investigations and preservation of evidence may be critical to the success of your personal injury claim. We will handle everything for you, eliminating the hassles associated with the legal and insurance aspects of your personal injury case in order to best represent you. The Law Firm You Choose Does Make a Difference!" *See* "Phoenix Personal Injury Lawyers," O'Steen & Harrison, PLC, accessed February 28, 2020, https://www.vanosteen.com/.

36 Hudson, Jr., *supra* note 889.

37 John Bates earned an advanced degree in law from ASU Law, was a law teacher, and moved to Ohio to work for the Southeastern Ohio Legal Services office. He lives and practices law in Ohio. His website ad says, "We are Attorney John R. Bates, experienced and nationally known bankruptcy attorney and Attorney James F. Hausen, experienced bankruptcy attorney. Together we have a combined 55 years of legal experience. We do only consumer bankruptcies and have filed thousands of them for residents of Northeast Ohio." Under "Why Choose Us?" the website says that "We offer free initial consultations by phone or in person and in the evening (by phone) if you prefer. Our fees are highly competitive and we offer special fee arrangements in appropriate cases. Call and we will be happy to tell you what your case would cost. You can retain us with only a small payment and you can make payments on the rest of the fee before the case is filed. YOU choose the amount and timing of the payments." *See* "Bankruptcy Attorneys for Akron, Canton, Wooster and New Philadelphia," Akron Bankruptcy Attorneys Bates & Hausen, LLC, accessed February 28, 2020, https://www.akroncantonbankruptcyattorney.com/.

38 Hudson, Jr., *supra* note 889.

39 *See* "Shepard's® Report for Bates v. State Bar of Arizona," LexisNexis, accessed February 28, 2020, https://advance.lexis.com/shepards/shepardspreviewpod/?pdmfid=1000516&crid=5fb935e3-732c-48a6-8ac4-9b3c01e8cb97&pdshepid=urn%3AcontentItem%3A7XW4-F561-2NSF-C0HV-00000-00&pdshepcat=initial&ecomp=73h9k&prid=747fa54a-571f-47eb-9415-f7d065afe7b3.

40 Gary L. Stuart, *The Ethical Trial Lawyer* (State Bar of Arizona Publishing, 1994), 74–75.

41 John Dentinger, "Spotlight: Lawyers' Ad Man," *Reason* (1987), https://reason.com/archives/1987/03/01/lawyers-ad-man.

42 Hon. Ann A. Scott Timmer, "Task Force On the Delivery of Legal Services: An Overview." *Arizona Attorney Magazine*, Vol. 56, Number 8, April 2020 at 20–21.

43 Ibid. at 20.

CHAPTER 19

DEAN ALAN MATHESON 1978 TO 1984

Dean Matheson graduated from the University of Utah three times. He earned his BA in 1953, Phi Beta Kappa. He earned his master of science in 1957, and his JD in 1959, Order of Coif. His first job out of law school was as a faculty associate at Columbia University Law School, doing research and teaching. Then he took a position in the President's office at Utah State University before coming to Arizona State University. His selection as a founding professor at ASU's fledging college of law took a different path, as relayed in his 2006 Oral History.

> *Both my father and my older brothers were lawyers . . . . I had taken the examination to be a Foreign Service Officer and I passed fortunately, but there were no positions. And so they said wait and we'll notify you when a position is available. So, in the interim I started law school [University of Utah College of Law]. By the time they contacted me I had finished two years of law school and I had made the investment and decided to continue . . . . I had no idea that I would ever be a teacher . . . . The then President of Arizona State was Homer Durham who said I'd like you to come down and visit me . . . . I came down and had the luncheon with him and Dean Pedrick [in the summer of 1967]. They offered me the position of legal advisor to the*

president of the university and Assistant Dean or Associate Dean of the Law School, a dual position. . . . I had to finish out my job at Utah State and came back to Arizona in the middle of December [1968]." . . . The law school had started. . . . [I met] the original faculty [in September] . . . Pedrick, Canby, Cleary, Effland, Dahl, Havighurst.

Professor Matheson wrote at length about the school's strength and maturing as it entered the mainstream of legal education in 1979.

> *From the beginning, the law school was committed to the best in traditional legal education, but special features of the curriculum marked the school as innovative in its approach. Believing that the third year of law study—often met with apathy by students—could be rejuvenated, the faculty adopted a program which provided a conventional required first-year, a prescribed second-year of ten "core" courses, and an elective third-year devoted to small courses, seminars, internships, and independent study. The theory of the program was that students would gain a solid foundation from conventional courses in the first two years and then enter an entirely different educational setting during the final period. . . . The new program, initially quite successful, did not survive in its original form. After experimenting with the core curriculum for four years, the school began to move away from the required core. . . . The faculty modified the program in 1972 by adding additional courses to the second-year listing and allowing students to pick from among the increased offerings.*[1]

As it turned out, Alan Matheson was in and out of the dean's office at ASU College of Law for the next forty years. He served either as dean or as interim dean five times—1972, 1978–79, 1979–1984, 1989, and 1997–98.[2] He started as *the* associate dean, under Founding Dean Willard Pedrick. He served as dean from 1977 to 1984. Then again as dean in 1990, then again in 1997–98. Dean Pedrick left the deanship in 1976. Dean Ernest A. E. Gellhorn served for a year and a half; Alan Matheson began his deanship in 1977 and served until 1984. His recollections of Dean Pedrick, the original faculty, and those early years are priceless.

He began his deanship feeling "overwhelmed."[3] That's because he had to follow the inaugural dean, with whom he'd worked closely for ten years.

Dean Alan Matheson 1978 to 1984

I had such great respect for Willard Pedrick and he was the ideal person to be the founding dean. He was an entrepreneur, he was an optimist . . . he was creative, had great ideas, some not so great, but he had ideas and presented them and kept things moving along at a high pitch, a high pace. Just an amazing human being. . . . [T]he role of dean has evolved considerably. . . . Ped's was the challenge of creating something from nothing, an enormous task, in all fronts. . . . It was really something and he thrived on it, he just absolutely loved it, that was his role.[4]

Dean Matheson made important changes when he became Dean in 1977.

"I attended some of the dean's conferences, read their reports, and read the literature sent forward by other law schools. . . . Some of the things I wanted to incorporate included expanded programs, pro bono activities for the students, expanded curriculum, the development of some specialized study areas, those kinds of things. An expanded student body with better relationships with the community." He supported expanded journals and law reviews because they give "more opportunity to students particularly with the larger law schools. One journal can only use so many personnel and the multiple journals expand the opportunity here."[5]

He described the growth of the clinic program.

When the law school opened we had a clinic which was an arm of Community Legal Services for Maricopa County. We had an employee from Community Legal Services there and used some students for assistance there but we didn't have an organized clinical program. As time went on, we received a grant [from the American Bar Foundation] to expand the clinic. . . . And we went from there and we started the in-house civil law clinic, and then as time went on there was an interest in criminal law so we then had a defender clinic and a prosecutor's clinic. . . . [T]here was some opposition from faculty members. . . . They thought it was deleterious to the educational program— they wanted [just] the academic side. My opinion . . . was that the clinical work was a wonderful complement to the academic and that together those training areas would create better lawyers and alum.[6]

Dean Matheson's term as dean included a significant controversy related to his mentor, Dean Pedrick. Under his leadership, a major change in curriculum was made.

> *Pedrick and the charter faculty agreed on a curriculum that involved courses for both first and second year students and that was very different from other schools. Most had a required first year but none had a required second year.... [Pedrick's] plan was everyone would take the required courses and then after two years they would have covered the courses that are highly important, many of which are on bar exams and so on. Then in the third year they'd have complete freedom to choose whether it be externships or clinics or specialized courses. And as part of that package the law school had adopted a grading system for the third year that was different from the others. The grading system for the third year was pass/fail for all courses. During my administration, the faculty reconsidered the pass/fail and thought it was not a good policy. The students were not working as hard as they should be when they knew the pass/fail system was in effect. So they changed it. The mistake the faculty made was in not grandfathering it. So it went into effect right away and the class that was coming up next (second year students) but were then third year resented this change considerable and they did not forgive us. And evidence of that is in the alumni contributions over the years from that class—lack of contributions.[7]*

Over time, the faculty's failure to grandfather the pass/fail grading system for third-year students softened.

> *As we added new faculty members after the charter group, usually younger people who were just getting into teaching, they were chafing with this system because they wanted to have our law school similar to other law schools. I don't think they caught the spirt of the innovative law school that Ped had. And so, the faculty in its wisdom started to slice off things, adding some electives to the second year, reducing the number of required courses . . . to take sometime during their law school career, beyond the first year. Course[s] such as professional responsibility . . . by the American Bar Association. And constitutional law, individual rights . . . . [I]t was a matter of attrition . . . .*

Dean Alan Matheson 1978 to 1984

> *[T]he students ... were very concerned. They felt that their adult judgment was being neglected and they wanted to take [these] courses ... after the first year. So the pressure from the students and the pressure from the new faculty members moved the school to change back to the traditional system. And I think with some loss. It was very interesting but did not have faculty support.*[8]

The early years, 1967 and 1968, were not without controversy. Dean Matheson recalled it well.

> *The law school class that started in the old Matthews Library on the mall and we had a couple of classrooms on the second floor where the museum is now located. And that was my first office at the law school. I had no ceiling on this office—it was a cubicle between two classrooms. On one side was Herald Havighurst, the distinguished former dean from Northwestern, teaching contracts. On the other side of me was a philosophy class taught by Morris Starsky, this firebrand who was fired by the university. So I had this stately, urbane, respected figure on one side and a person chomping at the bit—very emotional, loud presentation of the other so I got a very liberal education there.*[9]

Matheson's 2006 Oral History is important because he so clearly recalls events that might otherwise be lost.

> *I came in December [1968] and the new building was under construction [and] nearly completed. So basically Ped planned the building with the architects.... [He] sent them around and he himself went to other law schools all over the country. He said his happiest year as Dean was the first year because he had no faculty, no students, and no alumni, so he made all the decisions on his own. The rest of us came in after the fact.... [A]t mid-year we moved the law school over.... The library over there, such as it was, was moved here by fire line, passing the books along lines into the new library [at Armstrong Hall]. There were lots of offices unoccupied [in the new building] and the students discovered that ... so they took over the offices that were not housing faculty members and laid claim to them. And for that first year or year and a half ... we didn't need the space. But*

sometimes we'd go into a room and there would be clothing and books and sleeping bags and so on.[10]

Dean Matheson put the 1968 Dedicatory of Armstrong Hall into political perspective.

[A]t that time of the dedication, we had a national conference.... We brought in wonderful, wonderful people and a response from all over the country... so as we were dedicating the building we had the dedicatory over at Gammage.... Chief Justice [Earl Warren][11] *was the speaker. It was kind of touching because as we came into the building there were trucks moving around the curve of Gammage with big signs "Impeach Earl Warren"*[12] *back and forth. I was planning the dedication activities and got a threatening call [against] the law school if we allowed Earl Warren to speak. But he ignored the distraction, came in and gave a wonderful speech to a packed audience, 3,000 people gave him a rousing ovation. Arizona's governor, Jack Williams,*[13] *refused to sit on the stage with him and sent a substitute.*[14]

Dean Pedrick had planned what was then, and still is now, the longest academic procession in history. "After that speech then... we lined up with Earl Warren, the guests, members of the judiciary, other academics at ASU with JD degrees and the students and we marched from Gammage in a line all the way across campus to the new building and then had a ceremony in the Great Hall where [President] Homer Durham[15] gave Ped an object... to pass the ownership from the university to the law school."[16]

Dean Matheson, as the successor [17] to Dean Pedrick, had to deal with funding issues not faced by the founding dean.

These were very lean years... we had a pulp free budget given to us in the fall and then we always had a mid-year adjustment where the university because of pressures had to take back a portion of what we had been given, so we in our minds just planned that we would not have what was given to us in the fall. It was very difficult, very difficult and I remember one year the appropriation for salary increases was so slight that the largest amount we could give to staff members was fifty dollars.... The award of that fifty

Dean Alan Matheson 1978 to 1984

dollars caused more consternation and unhappiness than if we had been giving a thousand. Cause it was a recognition of a difference but we just didn't have the money to do what we needed to do, and we survived in large part when faculty members went on leave or we had an unfilled line. We used the so-called salary savings just for operational expenses. It was a very bleak financial time ... we did not have a special tuition for law students or special fee as we have now, which makes quite a difference.[18]

Dean Matheson was on the inaugural faculty and became the dean eight years later. One of the things he inherited as dean was the curriculum. He played a significant role in how the curriculum changed over those eight years. He recalled those years when giving his Oral History to Marianne Alcorn twenty-eight years later in 2006.

Pedrick and the charter faculty agreed on a curriculum that involved required courses for both first and second years and that was very different from other law schools. . . . And as part of that package the law school had adopted a grading system for the third year different from the others. During my administration the faculty reconsidered the pass/fail and thought it was not a good policy because they felt the students were not working as hard as they should when they knew the pass/fail system was in effect. So they changed it. The mistake the faculty made was in not grandfathering it. So it went into effect right away and the class that was coming up next—second year students who were then third year resented this change considerably. They did not forgive us. [The] evidence of that is in the alumni contributions over the years from that class, or the lack of contributions.[19]

---

1 Ibid., 5.
2 "Alan Matheson," iSearch, accessed February 2020, https://isearch.asu.edu/profile/274864.
3 Alan Matheson, interview by Marianne Alcorn, Arizona State University College of Law, June 27, 2006.
4 Ibid., 5–6.
5 Ibid., 7.
6 Ibid., 7.
7 Ibid., 8–9.
8 Ibid., 9.
9 Ibid., 10.
10 Alan Matheson, interview by Marianne Alcorn, Arizona State University College of Law, June 27, 2006.

11 Wikipedia, s.v. "Earl Warren," last modified February 29, 2020, 18:17, https://en.wikipedia.org/wiki/Earl_Warren. Earl Warren (March 19, 1891–July 9, 1974) was an American jurist and politician who served as the 14th Chief Justice of the United States (1953–1969) and earlier as the 30th Governor of California (1943–1953). The Warren Court presided over a major shift in constitutional jurisprudence, with Warren writing the majority opinions in landmark cases such as *Brown v. Board of Education, Reynolds v. Sims,* and *Miranda v. Arizona.* Warren also led the Warren Commission, a presidential commission that investigated the 1963 assassination of President John F. Kennedy. He is as of 2019 the last Chief Justice to have served in an elected office.

12 David Von Drehle, "Conservatives have trained for this moment for decades," *The Washington Post,* June 29, 2018, https://www.washingtonpost.com/opinions/conservatives-have-trained-for-this-moment-for-decades/2018/06/29/a10cae78-7bb6-11e8-80be-6d32e182a3bc_story.html. "During the bitter presidential campaign of 1968, half a century ago, Richard M. Nixon tapped anger over the liberalism of the so-called Warren Court—the Supreme Court led by Nixon's longtime rival, Chief Justice Earl Warren. Even then, the anger was nothing new. For years, billboards demanding "Impeach Earl Warren" had dotted the byways of the South and Midwest, put there by conservatives outraged by the court's landmark decisions regarding civil rights, voting rights, religion, free speech, sexual liberation, protections for accused criminals and more."

13 Wikipedia, s.v. "Jack Williams (American politician)," last modified February 24, 2020, 02:37, https://en.wikipedia.org/wiki/Jack_Williams_(American_politician). John Richard "Jack" Williams (October 29, 1909–August 24, 1998) was an American radio announcer and politician. After gaining public recognition throughout Arizona because of his work in radio, he went on to become a two-term Mayor of Phoenix, Arizona and a three-term Governor of Arizona.

14 Professor Jonathan Rose confirmed Dean Matheson's recollection about Gov. Williams' refusal to attend the Earl Warren speech in an interview with the author, March 2019.

15 "Homer Durham," Office of the President, Arizona State University, accessed March 1, 2020, https://president.asu.edu/the-office/past-presidents/homer-durham. During the 1960s with the presidency of G. Homer Durham, Arizona State University began its academic maturing with the establishment of several new colleges, including the College of Fine Arts, the College of Law, the College of Nursing, the School of Social Work, and the reorganization of what became the College of Liberal Arts and Sciences and the College of Engineering and Applied Sciences. Perhaps most importantly, the university gained the authority to award the Doctor of Philosophy and other doctoral degrees. President Durham came to the fledgling university with its 10,000 students in 1960, and before the end of his tenure in 1969, Durham developed it into a university with national status and 23,000 students. President Durham also brought many cultural activities to Arizona State University, including performances and exhibitions of music and the arts. *See also* Wikipedia, s.v. "G. Homer Durham," last modified December 23, 2019, 01:59, https://en.wikipedia.org/wiki/G._Homer_Durham.

16 A fine gesture, for sure. However, all property on the ASU, U of A, and NAU campuses is vested in ABOR, not in individual universities. *See* A.R.S. § 15–1625; https://www.azleg.gov/ars/15/01625.htm.

17 When Dean Pedrick retired in 1976, his replacement was Ernest Gellhorn. Gellhorn's tenure was short—18 months. He was replaced by Alan Matheson, Pedrick's handpicked associate dean.

18 Alan Matheson, interview by Marianne Alcorn, Arizona State University College of Law, June 27, 2006, at pages 11–12.

19 Ibid., 24.

CHAPTER 20

COACH FRANK KUSH—THE LEGEND—THE SAGA—1978 TO 2000

Frank Kush died on June 22, 2017, with his legacy intact. Three decades earlier, he boosted ASU football into a national powerhouse.[1] His saga is intertwined with ASU Law's story because so many law students, faculty, and alumni were involved. Even more watched him as undergrads, and countless alumni cheered him on and off the field. They held strong opinions about Coach Kush's twenty-two-year saga *against* ASU. And everyone in and out of the law school had an opinion. Did Coach Kush really slug a player for muffing a punt? ASU Law alumni took sides. Thousands debated the core elements—justice—fair dealing—football. When the legal dust finally settled, ABOR, ASU leadership, and ASU Law had made headlines no one wanted.

He is arguably the most debated personality ever employed at ASU; his firing as head football coach in October 1978 made nationwide news.[2] His story is the stuff of legends, and like most legends, most of his is true. The rest of it will never be settled, just as his death didn't settle whether he punched Kevin Rutledge for muffing a punt and losing a football game. That punch, given or imagined, is not his legend, or his legacy. His legacy is winning, in preseason practices, before, during and after the game, and before, during, and after the trials. He was tried on the field, in the locker room, in the courtroom, and in the court of public opinion. For Kush it was never a game; it was *blitzkrieg*.[3] For him football was never a contact sport; it was a collision sport. You didn't just block the other guy; you slammed him to the ground and hoped he couldn't get up. And most of all, you did what he said. Every time. All season long.

His was a remarkable record—a lifetime of achievement on the field. "All-American guard at Michigan State; his Spartans were national champions his senior year. His first coaching assignment was with an Army team at Fort Benning, Georgia. He earned the head coach job with the ASU Sun Devils at the age of 29. His teams won 76% of their games and nine conference titles. ASU finished ranked in the Associated Press Top 10 poll four times: 1970, 1971, 1973 and 1975. Quite incidentally, those were also the Ped years. Kush won twenty-one consecutive victories over three seasons (1969–71), with winning streaks of thirteen games (twice) and twelve games (twice). He posted a 6–1 record in post-season bowl games. He coached thirty All-Americans, including QB Danny White, DBs Mike Haynes and John Harris, WR John Jefferson, LBs Ron Pritchard, Bob Breuning, and Larry Gordon, DE Al Harris and RB Woody Green. At least 129 of his players went on to play professionally. He was named Coach of the Year in 1975, the year Ped stepped down as dean but stayed as faculty. Kush was the 19th winningest Division 1 coach and had a better record than Woody Hayes, Earl Blaik, Darrel Royal, Dan Devine, Ara Parseghian and Pop Warner. He ranks 22nd in number of coaching victories and 7th in most victories at one school."[4]

Only one player, among the hundreds he coached, sued him. Kevin Rutledge. And true to form, the coach won and the player lost—big time.[5] When the lawsuit was filed, football was king in American sports and every fan read America's leading sports magazine, *Sports Illustrated*. Its lead story followed the other newspapers and media outlets that were "on" the story. *Sports Illustrated's* Ron Reid laid it out with a catchy headline (There's the Devil to Pay).[6]

> There have been many college football scandals[7] over the years, some involving widespread subversion of the rulebook. But few of them have caused as much of an uproar as the unseemly succession of events that culminated on Oct. 28, 1978[8] in the sacking of Arizona State Coach Frank Kush. It is a sorry epic, a kind of Cactus Horror Yahoo Show, that raises urgent—and

all too familiar—questions about college football in general. Is any coach bigger than his school's athletic program? Should backers dictate policy to a university as a condition of their financial contributions? And for whose benefit is intercollegiate football played anyway?[9]

More than one reporter mixed up the dates. The on-the-field incident (Kush allegedly slugging Rutledge on the sidelines) occurred on October 28, 1978, at an away game in Washington. Kush's actual suspension occurred on October 13, 1979, before a home game against the same team in Arizona.[10]

THE TIMELINE, ACCUSATIONS, AND OUTCOMES IN *RUTLEDGE VS KUSH ET. AL.*

The timeline, accusations, and outcomes for the *Rutledge vs. Kush* saga were restated for clarity twenty years later by Paola Boivin in the *Arizona Republic*.

> *Kush was fired by ASU on Oct. 28, 1978, hours before a home-field Pac10 game against the University of Washington. The punch he allegedly threw at Kevin Rutledge occurred a year earlier at an away game against the University of Washington. On Sept. 29, 1979, Rutledge filed two lawsuits against Kush charging he was harassed into quitting the team. A month later, on Oct. 9, 1979, the* State Press, *ASU's student newspaper, quotes an unidentified player saying he saw Kush hit Rutledge. On Oct. 10, 1979, several players tell Athletic Director Fred Miller that they saw Kush hit Rutledge. On Oct. 12, 1979, Kush is suspended. On Oct. 13, 1979, Kush held a news conference, and announced his impending dismissal. Uninvited, Kush shows up at Sun Devil Stadium and coaches ASU to 12–7 upset over No. 6 Washington. On Oct. 15, 1979 [ASU Athletic Director] Miller explains that Kush now is officially fired, accuses Kush of cover-up in Rutledge incident. On Oct. 16, 1979, the Sun Angel Foundation calls for reinstatement of Kush and announces plan to suspend $1.2 million funding for golf course. On Jan. 3, 1980, AD Miller fired. On Dec. 31, 1980, the NCAA places ASU on probation for two years for 30 rules violations that took place during Kush's tenure. On Oct. 1, 1986, after seven years in and out of courts, Rutledge lawsuit dismissed by federal judge. On Oct.*

> *14, 1988, Federal Appeals Court [Ninth Circuit] in San Francisco upholds dismissal of lawsuit. Legendary coach Frank Kush has a bronze statue of him outside Sun Devil Stadium. [In 1979] Sun Devil players responded to the firing of Frank Kush with an emotional 12–7 upset of the sixth-ranked Washington Huskies, then carried Kush off the field. Signs supporting Frank Kush were everywhere on the Tempe campus when the coach was fired over Kevin Rutledge's allegations that Kush had punched him. Rutledge never won his lawsuit. He moved to Tucson to get out of Kush's shadow and to this day won't talk to reporters about the controversy.*[11]

The contemporaneous 1979 *Sports Illustrated*[12] story dug deeper.

> *Kush, the 50-year-old taskmaster who is at the center of the storm, compiled a 176-54-1 record during 21½ years at Arizona State and became, in the manner of successful football coaches everywhere, a folk hero in Sun Devil country. One of 15 children of a Pennsylvania coal miner, Kush made All-America as a scrappy 170-pound defensive guard on Michigan State's 1952 national champions, and as a coach he tried to instill the same combativeness in his players. He slapped helmets, kicked butts, yanked facemasks, doled out punishment laps up a 500-foot hillock known as Mount Kush and, according to what a former player, Mike Tomco, once told a reporter, stomped on players' hands. A former Arizona State player, Steve Chambers, has told TIME, "He's hit me with pipes, boards and a ship's rope." Through it all, Kush said, "My job is to win football games, put people in the stadium, and make money for the university."*[13]

THE TRIAL AND APPEAL—
RUTLEDGE V. KUSH—1979 TO 1985

Kevin Rutledge's lawyer, Robert Hing,[14] filed two lawsuits against Kush—one in the Maricopa County Superior Court[15]—the other in the U.S. District Court for the District of Arizona. In the state case, filed on October 22, 1979, he named the Arizona Board of Regents, Arizona State University, Frank Kush, William Maskill, Gary Horton, Fred Miller, and John Schwada. His case alleged, among other trial theories, violating federally protected civil rights under 42 U.S.C. §§ 1983 and

1985(2). Those claims were dismissed by the court on May 30, 1980.[16] Hing filed his second amended complaint, setting forth nine claims against the defendants.[17] He sued Head Coach Kush for assault and battery, intentional interference with contractual relations, defamation, and misrepresentation. He sued Assistant Coach Maskill for intentional interference with contractual relations. He sued the Board of Regents for breach of contract and for liability under the doctrine of respondeat superior for the actions of Kush and Maskill. He sued Athletic Director Miller, Provost Hamm, and President Schwada for negligent supervision of Kush and Maskill.[18] ASU Law graduate Mike Gallagher was retained to represent ABOR. Warren Platt, a graduate of the UofA Law School, represented Kush.

Before trial, Judge Kleinschmidt[19] dismissed the conspiracy counts for breach of contract and intentional infliction of emotional distress against Kush and Maskill. The Board of Regents was granted summary judgment on the negligent supervision theory. And AD Miller was dismissed from the lawsuit on December 9, 1980.[20]

The jury trial started on January 26, 1981. It would be a long, bitter, and widely followed case. Local and national media representatives crowded the courtroom. Robert Hing, Rutledge's lawyer, made a powerful opening statement.

> *[Rutledge] was stunned [by the punch] . . . [and by the] coaches driving [him] off the football team despite his football scholarship, misrepresentation by the school when Rutledge was offered the scholarship, and negligence by Mr. Hamm and Mr. Schwada in their ability to control Kush and Maskill . . . [Kush] was dissatisfied with Rutledge's punting, approached him after his last punt . . . called him "gutless" and cursed at him . . . he grabbed him by the face mask, shook him from side to side and slugged him in the mouth . . . he wasn't seriously injured by the punch . . . but the mental suffering and humiliation was something else again.*[21]

Warren Platt,[22] Kush's lawyer, told the jury in his opening statement that the case "was brought by his [Kevin Rutledge's] father, Gordon, and a drag-strip operator, Rick Lynch, [who] were bound and determined that Frank Kush was going to be fired by Arizona State University." Platt said that [Lynch] was a "'football groupie' . . . who 'got his kicks' out of developing relationships with football players and had a 'paranoid obsession' to see Kush dismissed . . . ." Mr. Platt questioned why the damage suit was not filed until a year after an incident where Kush allegedly punched the younger Rutledge, and asked why the suit was filed just before the opening of the 1979 football season.[23]

Platt's argument was very factual. He held a gold-colored football helmet while making his statement, and told the jury, "[I]t's physically impossible with his helmet on Kevin Rutledge's head and the chin strap buckled for Coach Kush to hit him where he said he was hit . . . . This football helmet is designed to be a very, very tight fit." Platt added that Rutledge had testified at his deposition that the chinstrap was tightly buckled when Kush approached him.[24] Gallagher argued the law, which heavily favored ABOR.

On February 12, 1982, Judge Kleinschmidt ordered that the claims of assault and battery, defamation against Kush and ABOR would be tried *first*. The remaining issues (intentional interference with contract, breach of contract, and negligent supervision would be tried *after* the jury resolved the first set of issues. On March 17, 1981, Judge Kleinschmidt granted Kush's motion for directed verdict on the defamation claim. Three days later, the case went to the jury.

After several days of deliberation, the jury informed the Court it had reached a verdict—a seven to five verdict—but the jury's note did not say which way the jury split—for Rutledge, or for Kush. The judge informed counsel of the split and asked if both sides would accept the split verdict, without knowing which way the majority vote would go. Both lawyers agreed. The Court called the jury into the courtroom and the seven-to-five verdict was announced—in favor of all defendants. With that verdict in hand, the trial resumed to resolve the remaining issue of intentional interference with contract, breach of contract, and negligent supervision.[25] After two days, the jury went back into deliberation; and after a short deliberation, the jury returned the same seven-to-five verdict on the last count for the defendants. It returned verdicts for Kush and ABOR on assault, battery, and misrepresentation.[26]

After six weeks of trial, Judge Kleinschmidt granted Kush's motion for a directed verdict on the defamation claim. On March 20, 1981, the jury returned verdicts for Kush and ABOR on the assault and misrepresentation claims. Then the trial continued before the same jury on the remaining claims. The jury also found for Kush and ABOR on all remaining matters on March 29, 1981.

It would take four more years, but finally, on May 23, 1985, the Arizona Court of Appeals sustained all lower court rulings and the jury's bifurcated verdicts in Kush and ABOR's favor.[27] In what was an unusual comment from an appellate court, the court not only agreed with Judge Kleinschmidt's rulings and orders, it complimented him: "This was a long, bitter, and hard-fought trial. The record indicates the trial court did an admirable job of controlling the proceedings and ensuring that all parties obtained a fair trial. Based upon our resolution of the issues raised on appeal, the judgment of the trial court is affirmed."[28]

THE ARIZONA SUPREME COURT

The appellate court made short work out of the argument that the jury's verdict should be reversed because Rutledge was forced to present Lynch's testimony via videotape rather than in person. "The trial court has great discretion in controlling the conduct of a trial. Rutledge was allowed to 'present his case' by presenting the testimony of Rick Lynch. Given the comments of counsel the trial court was faced with the likely prospect of having a long and grueling trial, which had already gone five weeks, mistried if Lynch were to testify in open court.... [W]e find no abuse of discretion in ordering that Rich Lynch's testimony be presented by way of videotape."[29]

Rutledge also sought reversal because the Court allowed nine witnesses to testify by giving "hearsay" evidence. Hearsay is defined as an out-of-court statement, made in court, to prove the truth of the matter asserted.[30] The rule against hearsay was designed to prevent gossip from being offered to convict someone. It's fair to say that Phoenix, Arizona, was full of gossip about Frank Kush in 1979.

Most of the testimony which Rutledge claims was hearsay arises from a coaches' meeting held by Kush on October 3, 1979. Rutledge took the position that Kush, in discussing the Rutledge incident, told his assistant coaches that "they had to stick together, even if it meant lying or perjuring themselves, or else they would all be fired" ... Rutledge maintained that the meeting corroborated Rutledge's allegation that Kush had punched Rutledge. Kush took the position that he was not discussing Rutledge at the meeting but that he was discussing Rick Lynch and Lynch's adverse effect on the team due primarily to his telephoning and speaking to players and their families in attempts to coerce players into stating that they had seen Kush punch Rutledge. Consequently, most of the testimony that Rutledge claims constituted hearsay pertains to statements to the effect that Lynch was telephoning players and to what was purportedly said by Lynch to the players.[31]

The existence of audio tapes allegedly recorded by Lynch was debated often during the trial. One player, Gary Bouck, testified that he'd "telephoned Rick Lynch," and that, at some time after the conversation, Lynch informed Bouck that he had recorded their telephone conversation. Bouck stated that he and Lynch had several subsequent telephone conversations and on each occasion, Lynch would inform Bouck beforehand that the conversation would be recorded and that Bouck agreed to the recordings. Bouck was then asked if Lynch had told him to whom the recorded tapes were given. Bouck testified that he could not remember if Lynch ever told him who was given the tapes, "but somewhere down the line it's been told to me that the tapes were given to Mr. Hing [Rutledge's counsel]."[32]

Closing arguments in hotly contested trials are often fertile ground for reversible error. The Kush trial was vigorously argued by all three lead counsel—Hing for Rutledge—Gallagher for ABOR—and Platt for Kush. In particular, Mr. Platt's closing argument was extensively based on much of the hearsay evidence produced in the seven weeks of trial. Rutledge argued on appeal that Platt's trial court argument was reversible error because it was given "without any regard for the extremely limited purpose for which the testimony had been admitted."[33]

While closing arguments are often debated at the appellate level years after the trial, the debate is often limited to whether an argument was objected to *at the time of trial*. In *Kush,* especially considering Warren Platt's highly effective argument on behalf of Kush, the timing was everything.

The Court of Appeals read the briefs and the trial transcript of the closing arguments. It easily disposed of Rutledge's claims of error.[34]

THE FEDERAL CASE

Kevin Rutledge also filed a federal case in the U.S. District Court for the District of Arizona against the same defendants he sued in state court. His federal claims asserted violations of the federal Civil Rights Act, 42 U.S.C.S §§ 1983 and 1985. The district court dismissed all claims on dispositive motions soon after filing. He appealed the dismissal to the United States Circuit Court of Appeals for the Ninth Circuit. That court affirmed in part, reversed in part, and remanded in part. It held ABOR and ASU were immune from suit in federal court under the 11th Amendment to the U.S. Constitution[35] on his claims that ASU's athletic director failed to supervise Kush. It also held that while Rutledge's claims for common law torts against his coaches were not barred by immunity, he had failed to state a justiciable claim because he had not been deprived of any right secured by the United States Constitution. The court found Rutledge had no legal right to maintain his position on the state university football team. However, he had sufficiently alleged a private conspiracy to obstruct justice claim under part one of Section 1985, at least well enough to escape a motion to dismiss.[36]

Later, the district court resolved the case in an unpublished order. Meanwhile, an important legal question made its way to the United States Supreme Court. Because the Ninth Circuit had ruled in ABOR's and Kush's favor on all but one claim, the defendants sought a writ of certiorari. It was granted and the case was argued in the U.S. Supreme Court on January 12, 1983. The issue was fundamental access to federal courts in America for civil rights violations.

Because Rutledge won this issue at the Ninth Circuit, ABOR took the case to the Supreme Court, via a writ of certiorari. Once the writ was granted, ABOR's Mike Gallagher argued Rutledge had "asserted a variety of common-law and statutory claims . . . and that ASU officials violated 42 U.S.C.S. § 1985(2) by engaging in a 'conspiracy to intimidate and threaten various potential material witnesses in order to prevent them from testifying freely, fully and truthfully in his lawsuit in federal court." On certiorari, the Supreme Court ruled that the appellate court properly reinstated the § 1985(2) claim. The Court rejected ABOR's contention that dismissal was required because there was no claim that the conspiracy was motivated by the kind of racial, or perhaps otherwise class-based, invidiously discriminatory animus that was required in an action under § 1985(3). No allegations of class-based invidiously discriminatory animus were required under the first part of § 1985(2), which proscribed intimidation of witnesses in the federal courts.[37]

THE MEDIA COVERAGE—KUSH—RUTLEDGE—ASU—ABOR

The media coverage about Kush, his fans, detractors, and coaching style was gigantic, by any measurement. Lexis.Nexis.advance's database, as of May 2019, included 305 articles written under several hundred bylines from scores of media providers, connecting two names—Frank Kush and Kevin Rutledge.[38] The digital record indicates wide Arizona coverage in addition to articles from *The Washington Post, The Globe, The Mail, Newsweek, World News Digest*, UPI, AP, *Information Bank Abstracts, NY Times, Facts on File—World News, LA Times,* and the *Chicago*

Tribune. There are doubtless many more resting peacefully in morgue files all over the football world in Canada and the U.S. And there are now scores of digital websites, blogsites, and resources on the Kush saga. Amazon.com advertises one book (*Frank Kush—The Incredible Life Story of a Coaching Legend in His Own Words*, by Frank Kush and Jeffrey Jay Ellish, December 31, 2014). A Google search on April 26, 2019 for "Frank Kush" produced "About 92,000 results (0.48 seconds)."[39]

The Frank Kush Wikipedia page[40] covers his life, coaching career, and a succinct statement about his dismissal from ASU:

> *In September 1979 former Sun Devil punter Kevin Rutledge filed a $1.1 million lawsuit against the school, accusing Kush and his staff of mental and physical harassment that forced him to transfer. The most dramatic charge was that Kush had punched Rutledge in the mouth after a bad punt in the October 28, 1978, game against the Washington Huskies. During the next few weeks, overzealous fans turned things ugly when the insurance office of Rutledge's father suffered a fire and the family's attorney received two death threats. On October 13, 1979, Kush was fired as head coach for interfering with the school's internal investigation into Rutledge's allegations. Athletic director Fred Miller cited Kush's alleged attempts to pressure players and coaches into keeping quiet. The decision came just three hours before the team's home game against Washington. Kush was allowed to coach the game, with the Sun Devils pulling off an emotional 12–7 upset of the sixth-ranked Huskies, fueled by the angry crowd incensed by the decision. After the game ended, Kush was carried off the field by his team. The win gave him a 3–2 record on the season, but all three victories were later forfeited when it was determined that Arizona State had used ineligible players. After nearly two years, Kush would be found not liable in the case, but remained absent from the sideline throughout 1980, the first time in more than 30 years that he had been away from the game. Litigation related to the Rutledge incident continued until 1986.*

FRANK KUSH, THE ASU STUDENT BODY, AND THE SUN ANGLES

Like all universities in the Pac-10 Athletic Conference, football was for some an obsession, and for others a distraction. ASU's students were not as agitated by Kush's ouster as its alumni were.

> *While the students certainly like it when the Sun Devils win, they are often less vociferous about the victories than the team's adult boosters. And the seats allocated to undergraduates, most of which are in the north end zone, indicate that Arizona State's program is more closely geared to fulfilling the wishes of the Sun Angels and other Phoenix-area businessmen, who, among them, lay claim to most of the good seats. This may explain why a pep rally the night before last Saturday's Washington State game, the first such event at Tempe in many years, was attended by no more than 100 of the school's 37,122 students. A TV newsman covering the rally asked students their opinions of the Kush case and was told by one them, "This school has an athletic reputation, but there are a lot of people here who take pride in their academics, too—students and professors alike. And I think what they say is true: you wouldn't get the same kind of publicity if a professor was let go. And I don't think that is too cool."*[41]

The Sun Angel Foundation, ASU's booster club, got a share of the notoriety and some of the blame for the Kush saga. "The influence wielded by the Sun Angel Foundation is another matter. A booster club is an independent organization, and it exercises only the clout that its school allows it to. Under NCAA regulations, a university is responsible for the activities of its boosters. While many of those activities—attending road games, throwing appreciation dinners and the like—are innocuous enough, it has long been clear that when booster clubs become deeply involved in recruiting or make a practice of contributing money with strings attached, rules violations and other problems can—and too often do—arise . . ."[42]

THE SANDRA DAY O'CONNOR COLLEGE OF LAW

FRANK KUSH & ASU TWENTY YEARS LATER

While it could hardly be called *Kiss & Make-Up Time*, in 2000 Frank Kush returned to Sun Devil Stadium at ASU. He accepted a job at ASU to work with the athletic director. The *Arizona Republic*'s Don Ketchum put it this way:

> It's been nearly 21 years since Frank Kush was voted off Arizona State's island and set adrift in a sea of controversy. Now the football coaching legend has become the ultimate survivor. He has washed up on the shore of Tempe Town Lake and is ready to begin life anew as a Sun Devil. Kush, 71, has been hired to a full-time position as a special assistant to the athletic director, according to an announcement by interim AD Christine Wilkinson on Tuesday. "It's great that he can come home and be part of the ICA (intercollegiate athletics) family," Wilkinson said. Wilkinson received the stamp of approval from ASU President Lattie Coor.... "The school needs to bring former players and alumni together and let them know how great an institution ASU is," said Kush.... "You need somebody to develop a camaraderie, and this is a great opportunity for me to be that somebody." According to Wilkinson, Kush will be an ambassador for the department, "not just one sport. He will work with the corporate and local community levels, strengthen ties with the former student-athletes and help the athletic director with special projects."[43]

THE LEGACY AND THE SETTLEMENT

It bears repetition that Kush was not fired for slugging Kevin Rutledge, and that Kush won in both state and federal courts. His legal wins may have come because juries and judges believed Kush's denial he hit Rutledge. Or that Rutledge failed to make his case for any of a number of legal reasons. What should be remembered is ASU dismissed him for "trying to cover up the incident by persuading staff members and players to change their stories. An NCAA investigation found Arizona State guilty of numerous other violations.... [ASU] was put on probation, eliminated from television and bowl games for two years... As time tends to soften transgressions, there eventually was a move afoot to restore Kush to idolatry. On Sept. 21, 1996, during halftime ceremonies at the Arizona State-Nebraska game, the field at Sun Devil Stadium was renamed Frank Kush Field. More than 300 former players attended."[44]

Kush received a $200,000 settlement after suing ABOR and ASU for $2.4 Million. And he consistently denied he ever struck Rutledge.

---

1 "Remembering Sun Devil legend Frank Kush," ASU Now: Access, Excellence, Impact, Arizona State University, accessed May 6, 2019, https://asunow.asu.edu/20170622-sun-devil-life-remembering-asu-legend-frank-kush-football-coach.

2 Wikipedia, s.v. "Arizona State Sun Devils football," last modified February 28, 2020, 05:50, https://en.wikipedia.org/wiki/Arizona_State_Sun_Devils_football#Frank_Kush_era_(1958–1979). *See also Sports Illustrated*, October 29, 1979, https://www.si.com/vault/issue/70854/31.

3 "Blitzkrieg," Bing, accessed March 1, 2020, https://www.bing.com/search?q=blitzkrieg&form=EDGTCT&q-s=SC&cvid=373d50f8df5e4ff9bf6ac505cbe42c98&cc=US&setlang=en-US. blitz·krieg, (plural noun)—an intense military campaign intended to bring about a swift victory. Synonyms: bombardment · battery · bombing · onslaught · barrage · sally · attack · assault · raid · offensive · strike · blitzkrieg · razzia.

4 "About Frank," Frank Kush Youth Foundation, accessed March 1, 2020, http://frankkush.org/.

5 *See Rutledge v. Arizona Bd. of Regents*, 147 Ariz. 534 (1985).

6 Ron Reid, "There's the Devil to Pay," *Sports Illustrated*, October 29, 1979, https://www.si.com/vault/1979/10/29/106774479/theres-the-devil-to-pay. The subtitle for Mr. Reid's story was: "The heat was on at Arizona State when Coach Frank Kush was canned, baring big-time college football's seamy side."

7 Chelena Goldman, "The Biggest Scandals in College Football History," Sportscasting.com, September 25, 2019, https://www.sportscasting.com/sports/the-biggest-scandals-in-college-football-history/. ASU had one other football scandal. It is briefly covered at this website, "the Loren Wade case." It did not implicate the coach, or the football team, but it did "cast a cloud over the Sun Devils. Tailback Loren Wade, a junior, had already been accused of threatening two female athletes—one of which had been his girlfriend—and of possibly carrying a firearm. Then in spring 2005, Wade shot and killed former Sun Devils player Brandon Falkner in the parking lot of a Scottsdale nightclub. Wade is currently serving a 20-year jail sentence for killing Falkner."

8 The incident that led to Kush's suspension by the Arizona Board of Regents in 1979 occurred on October 28, 1978 during an away-game at the University of Washington. The firing occurred a year later on October 13, 1979.

9 Ron Reid, "There's the Devil to Pay," *Sports Illustrated*, October 29, 1979, https://www.si.com/vault/1979/10/29/106774479/theres-the-devil-to-pay.

10 Wikipedia, s.v. "Frank Kush," last modified February 8, 2020, 03:55, https://en.wikipedia.org/wiki/Frank_Kush. On October 13, 1979, Kush was fired as head coach for interfering with the school's internal investigation into Rutledge's allegations. Athletic Director Fred Miller cited Kush's alleged attempts to pressure players and coaches into keeping quiet. The decision came just three hours before the team's home game against Washington. Kush was allowed to coach the game, with the Sun Devils pulling off an emotional 12–7 upset of the sixth-ranked Huskies, fueled by the angry crowd incensed by the decision. After the game ended, Kush was carried off the field by his team. The win gave him a 3–2 record on the season, but all three victories were later forfeited when it was determined that Arizona State had used ineligible players.

11 Paola Boivin, "20 Years After Kush Firing Split Community, Changed Coaching," *The Arizona Republic*, October 15, 1999, Friday Final Chaser Edition.

12 Ron Reid, "There's the Devil to Pay," *Sports Illustrated*, October 29, 1979, https://www.si.com/vault/1979/10/29/106774479/theres-the-devil-to-pay.

13 Ibid.

14 Robert Ong Hing is an active member of the State Bar of Arizona, employed by Stockton & Hing, Scottsdale, Arizona.

15 Filed, October 22, 1979, Superior Court of Maricopa County, The Hon. Thomas C. Kleinschmidt, presiding.

16 *Rutledge v. Arizona Bd. of Regents*, 147 Ariz. 534 (1985).

17 *See Rutledge v. Arizona Bd. of Regents,* 147 Ariz. 534, 539 (1985). (I) assault & battery by Kush; (II) intentional interference with contractual and advantageous business and educational relationship with ASU; (III) a conspiracy by Kush and Maskill to interfere with Rutledge's contractual and educational relationships with ASU; (IV) Kush misrepresented the availability of football scholarships during the 1977–1978 school year; (V) claim for defamation against Kush; (VI) Kush and Maskill were liable for intentional infliction of emotional distress; (VII) respondeat superior liability asserted against A.S.U., the Board of Regents, Miller, Hamm and Schwada for the actions of Kush and Maskill; (VIII) alleged that the Board of Regents breached its contract with Rutledge by allowing Kush and Maskill to coerce Rutledge into leaving A.S.U., thereby forfeiting his scholarship; (IX) against the Board of Regents, Miller, Schwada and Hamm for negligent supervision of Kush. Rutledge sought compensatory and punitive damages under all counts except Counts VII (respondeat superior), VIII (breach of contract), and IX (negligent supervision), in which he sought only compensatory damages.

18 Ibid.

19 Judge Kleinschmidt is a retired judge and a member of the Phoenix law firm, Schneider & Onofry.

20 *Rutledge v. Arizona Bd. of Regents,* 147 Ariz. 534, 539 (1985).

21 Ibid.

22 Mr. Platt is an active member of the Arizona State Bar Association and is employed by Snell & Wilmer in their Irvine, California office.

23 *Rutledge v. Arizona Bd. of Regents,* 147 Ariz. 534 (1985).

24 UPI, "Kush Lawyer Questions Motive in Suit," *New York Times,* January 27, 1981, https://www.nytimes.com/1981/01/27/sports/kush-lawyer-questions-motive-in-suit.html.

25 *Rutledge,* 147 Ariz. at 540.

26 Author Interviews with Mr. Gallagher on _____, and Mr. Platt on _____.

27 The decision by Judges Jack Ogg, Robert Corcoran, and Donald Froeb was unanimous.

28 *Rutledge,* 147 Ariz. at 558.

29 Ibid., 543.

30 "Hearsay Evidence," FindLaw, accesses March 1, 2020, https://criminal.findlaw.com/criminal-procedure/hearsay-evidence.html. *See also* Arizona Rules of Evidence, Rule 801.

31 *Rutledge,* 147 Ariz. at 544.

32 Ibid., 548.

33 Ibid., 549.

34 Ibid.

35 The Eleventh Amendment (Amendment XI) to the United States Constitution was passed by Congress on March 4, 1794, and ratified by the states on February 7, 1795. It restricts the ability of individuals to bring suit against states in federal court. It was adopted to overrule the U.S. Supreme Court's decision in *Chisholm v. Georgia* (1793). In that case, the Supreme Court had held that states did not enjoy sovereign immunity from suits made by citizens of other states in federal court. Thus, the Eleventh Amendment established that federal courts do not have the authority to hear cases brought by private citizens against states. ABOR is a constitutionally created body of the State of Arizona. ASU is governed by ABOR. Both are immune from suits in federal court, but not state court. However, federal courts can enjoin state officials from violating federal law.

36 *Rutledge v. Arizona Bd. of Regents,* 660 F.2d 1345 (1981).

37 *Kush v. Rutledge,* 460 U.S. 719, 727 (1983).

38 LexisNexis Advance, s.v. "Frank Kush and Kevin Rutledge," accessed April and May 2019, https://advance.lexis.com/firsttime?crid=3929ee7c-11d7-440b-ae5c-1af2fe7743b4.

39 "Frank Kush," Google, accessed April 26, 2019, https://www.google.com/search?q=%22Frank+Kush%22&rlz=1C1SQJL_en__807__807&oq=%22Frank+Kush%22+&aqs=chrome..69i57j0l5.7717j1j8&sourceid=chrome&ie=UTF-8.

40 Wikipedia, s.v. "Frank Kush," last modified February 8, 2020, 03:55, https://en.wikipedia.org/wiki/Frank_Kush.

41 Ron Reid, "There's the Devil to Pay," *Sports Illustrated,* October 29, 1979, https://www.si.com/vault/1979/10/29/106774479/theres-the-devil-to-pay.

42 Ibid.

43 Don Ketchum, "ASU Hires Kush to Work with AD," *The Arizona Republic*, July 26, 2000, Wednesday Final Chaser Edition.

44 Chris Dufrense, "The New Camp Kush," *LA Times*, November 14, 1996.

CHAPTER 21

ASU LAW SKILLS TRAINING—
1970S

*L*egal education seems simple enough to define. "Legal education is the education of individuals in the principles, practices, and theory of law. It may be undertaken for several reasons, including to provide the knowledge and skills necessary for admission to legal practice in a particular jurisdiction, to provide a greater breadth of knowledge to those working in other professions such as politics or business . . . ."[1]

However, that broad, benign definition was meant for "traditional" American law schools, like legal education in the 1950s. True, they educated individuals in principles, practices, and theories about the law. It is also the case that traditional law school education enabled students to acquire enough legal knowledge for admission to legal practice. But that's where traditional legal education often stopped, even in the best of American law schools. The difference from the 30,000-foot level was traditional law school's disdain for also training students to practice law, or giving them the necessary skills to be good at law practice. It was enough in traditional law schools to provide knowledge and theory. Skills training could be safely left to the legal profession—at least to law firms that provided skills training as part of the path to partnership. The difference at ground level was how law schools taught students to find and understand the law. Law firms trained law graduates how to use the law to advance clients' objectives. The difference is between the theory of the law and its application.

THE EPITHET "TRADE SCHOOL"

At least by the 1970s, law schools were moving toward clinical programs and away from a purely traditional education—theory mostly, no advocacy or skills training. To the surprise of some, law schools were not part of a traditional university system in the nineteenth century. Whether law schools should be part of a university was doubtful. True scholars tut-tutted the sense that law schools trained students rather than educating them. "The epithet 'trade school' floats in and out of the variegated criticisms, and always a certain amount of tension exists between the law school and the rest of the university . . . some of it is the more or less separate status of the law school as a professional college, and some of it is the belief that all law schools do is *train* (an epithet in itself) a largely parasitic class of technicians devoted to serving the rich and powerful in American society."[2] Thorstein Veblen[3] said, "law schools belong in the modern university no more than a school of fencing or dancing."[4]

In the first half of the twentieth century, there were two schools of thought about law schools. One version, the traditional notion, focused on the "teaching" part of legal education.

> *If a legal education is designed solely to prepare the student to pass a bar examination, to know the rules (whatever that may mean), and to learn "the tricks of the trade," then the law school does* not *belong in the modern university. These things can be handled outside the academy and with far less of an expenditure of time, money, and energy. Such a design would also result in an unlearned bar and in lawyers ill equipped to serve the needs of a complex, democratic society. Nonetheless, it is this view of the legal education that leads to the argument that law schools have no place in the academy. To the extent that law schools see themselves in such a narrow role, they are sowing the seeds of their own destruction. But no law school worthy of the name sets so narrow a goal for its graduates. Rather, it understands that lawyers are being educated, "(1) to assume direction of all phases of the areas of personal conduct inherent in a complex society and economy; (2) to provide a very large proportion of national leadership at all levels of authority; and (3) to serve, at little or no compensation, the needs of indigent criminal defendants and to participate, so far as a lawyer can, in the 'war on poverty . . . .'"*[5]

RAISON D'ETRE

Beyond teaching the law, there is an equally compelling justification for law schools embedded in universities. "The second and higher level is less obvious both to the teacher and the taught. It is the silent *raison d'etre* of legal education and the lasting claim for public and private support of the law schools. At this level, the faculty seeks to guide the student toward an understanding of, and respect for, the rule of law, without which a free society cannot long endure."[6]

The first and second arguments just noted are pertinent to law *teaching*. But a third component advances skills training in law schools. Kellis E. Parker,[7] a noted law professor, was a lifetime advocate for clinical legal programs in American law schools. His views stem from neither the theoretical side nor the practical side of the equation. His view is informed by the constitutional mandate for it.

> *At least two constitutional provisions are involved when the poor are denied access to legal representation. Advocacy and petition for redress of grievances are rights protected by the first amendment. The fourteenth amendment's equal protection clause extends equal justice to the poor in both civil and criminal proceedings. Demands for equal access to the courts and equal justice by the poor have not gone unanswered. In* **Gideon v. Wainwright**,[8] *the Supreme Court of the United States held that the poor are entitled to counsel in serious criminal cases in state courts. In* **Douglas v. California**,[9] *the Court held that counsel is required on appeal. In re* **Gault**[10] *established the principle that lawyers are required in juvenile court proceedings. Finally,* **United States v. Wade**[11] *held that counsel is required at lineups. Yet, lawyer shortages throughout the United States have robbed these decisions of significance for millions of America's poor.*[12]

ADVOCACY TRAINING AS A SUBSET OF SKILLS TRAINING

The early arguments favoring adding skills training to legal education focused on differentiating legal theory from legal practice. There is another component, one layer below merely differentiating how law professors educated law students—trial advocacy. Lawyers educated in the fifties, sixties, and seventies had little or no trial advocacy training. Adding advocacy was a logical addition to law school curriculum throughout the seventies and eighties. Professor Ronald L. Carlson[13] was an early advocate for advocacy training in law schools.

> *"If the weakness of the apprentice system was to produce advocates without scholarship, the weakness of the law school system is to turn out scholars with no skill at advocacy"*.... *In the 1970s, a remarkable dialogue occurred among judges, lawyers, and legal educators. Occasionally, acrimony marked the discussions. At issue was the question of lawyer competency and the responsibility for alleged deficiencies in the trial performance of practicing attorneys. No other contemporary controversy over curriculum has generated such attention outside of the law school world. One source observed:* "For much of the past decade the key point of contention in legal education has been whether law schools are doing all they can or should to produce competent lawyers. Critics ranging from Chief Justice Warren E. Burger[14] to the man on the street have complained loudly that, whatever else the schools may be teaching their students, they aren't providing adequate training in practical legal skills."[15]

Judge Malcolm R. Wilkey[16] advanced the argument. He explained it to a group of bar examiners in 1981.

> *[L]aw schools needed to undertake a "thoughtful, coherent reorganization of the whole curriculum." Questions were asked about the allocation of resources. Many law schools were accustomed to the large class/single instructor model. In the face of hesitancy to adopt a different pattern*.... "Most law schools are not noted for a devotion to teaching or sponsoring research about the litigation process. Historically, adjunct professors have taught trial advocacy courses and have relied upon war stories instead of rigorous analysis.... Whatever the validity of these and other more complex reasons, there is little doubt that litigation instruction and research in law school has been neglected and that this neglect has contributed to public dissatisfaction with our litigation system."[17]

At the ASU College of Law, practical skills and advocacy training became hallmarks of Deans Bender, Morgan, White, and Sylvester. They recognized the obvious. Their law students, from the early eighties to the present, demanded more than lectures *on* the law. Those students knew that to be a good lawyer they would have to acquire practice skills before they got a job. They knew, from internships, externships, and summer law clerking experiences, that success at lawyering was infinitely more demanding. They would have to know how to ask good questions—that would not come from just reading appellate briefs and opinions. They knew split-second decision-making was vital—that can't come from the Socratic method of remembering what a judge had ruled. They needed to know, before taking the bar exam, the difference between tort law and ambulance chasing. Most important, they sensed the difference between professors who had practiced and those who had not. ASU Law, on their watch, hired very few teachers who shunned the thought of engaging clients, and keeping time and billing records. ASU Law deans knew the essential difference. As a group, they subscribed to the basic notion that if teaching the law does not come with a practical knowledge of it, it's nearly impossible to become both a legal scholar and a good teacher.

Starting in the early 1970s ASU Law aspired to teach its students how to "think like a lawyer." By the 1980s the school had progressed to skills training for law practice in addition to thinking like lawyers. Over the next two decades, advancements were made in advocacy training and good practice skills.

But the changing marketplace for lawyers in 2020 and beyond will call for significant skills training and much more attention to what many call "new lawyering." *Forbes Magazine* ran an op-ed piece by Mark A. Cohen[18] in 2019 aptly titled, "What Are Law Schools Training Students For?"

> *The marketplace has changed markedly, particularly during the past decade. Legal delivery is now a three-legged stool supported by legal, business, and technical expertise. Law is no longer solely about lawyers; law firms are not the default provider of legal services; legal practice is no longer synonymous with legal delivery; the legal buy/sell balance of power has shifted from lawyers to legal buyers; lawyers do not control both sides of legal buy/sell; and the function and role of most lawyers is changing as digital transformation has made legal consumers—not lawyers—the arbiters of value. These changes are affecting what it means to "think like a lawyer" and, more importantly, what skills "legal" skills are required in today's marketplace.*[19]

1 "Legal education," The Free Dictionary by Farlex, accessed March 1, 2020, https://encyclopedia.thefreedictionary.com/Legal+Education.

2 John E. Cribbet, *Changeless, Ever-Changing University: The Role of the Law School*, 26 Ariz. L. Rev. 241, 250 (1984) (emphasis in original).

3 Thorstein Veblen was a Norwegian-American economist and sociologist who became famous as a witty critic of capitalism. Wikipedia, s.v., "Thorstein Veblen," last modified March 2, 2020, 16:43, https://en.wikipedia.org/wiki/Thorstein_Veblen.

4 Ibid., citing Stevens, *Two Cheers for 1870: The American Law School*, 5 Persp. in Am, Hist. 405, 427 n.12 (1971).

5 Cribbet, *supra* note 985, at 250–51, citing A. Casner & W. Leach, Cases and Text on Property 3, 4 (2d ed. 1969).

6 Cribbet, *supra* note 985, at 252.

7 Kellis E. Parker was a noted legal scholar and civil rights activist who embraced jazz as a framework for understanding the law. In 1972, became the first full-time black law professor at Columbia University. "Parker, Kellis E. 1942–2000," Encyclopedia.com, accessed March 1, 2020, https://www.encyclopedia.com/education/news-wires-white-papers-and-books/parker-kellis-e-1942-2000.

8 "*Gideon v. Wainwright*, 372 U.S. 335 (1963), is a landmark case in United States Supreme Court history. In it, the Supreme Court unanimously ruled that states are required under the Sixth Amendment of the U.S. Constitution to provide an attorney to defendants in criminal cases who are unable to afford their own attorneys. The case extended the right to counsel, which had been found under the Fifth and Sixth Amendments to impose requirements on the federal government, by imposing those requirements upon the states as well." Wikipedia, s.v., "*Gideon v. Wainwright*," last modified March 3, 2020, 18:34, https://en.wikipedia.org/wiki/Gideon_v._Wainwright.

9 "*Douglas v. California*, 372 U.S. 353 (1963), is famous for requiring that counsel be appointed to indigent defendants on appeal in state court if state law permits an appeal as a matter of right." Wikipedia, s.v., "*Douglas v. California*," last modified May 7, 2019, 5:15, https://en.wikipedia.org/wiki/Douglas_v._California.

10 "*In re Gault*, 387 U.S. 1 (1967), was a landmark U.S. Supreme Court decision in which the Primary Holding was that the Due Process Clause of the 14th Amendment applies to juvenile defendants as well as to adult defendants. Juveniles accused of crimes in a delinquency proceeding must be afforded many of the same due process rights as adults, such as the right to timely notification of the charges, the right to confront witnesses, the right against self-incrimination, and the right to counsel. The court's opinion was written by Justice Abe Fortas, a noted proponent of children's rights." Wikipedia, s.v., "*In re Gault*," last modified December 4, 2019, 15:23, https://en.wikipedia.org/wiki/In_re_Gault.

11 "*United States v. Wade*, 388 U.S. 218 (1967), was a case decided by the Supreme Court of the United States that held that a criminal defendant has a Sixth Amendment right to counsel at a lineup held after indictment." Wikipedia, s.v., "*United States v. Wade*," last modified July 31, 2019, 8:32, https://en.wikipedia.org/wiki/United_States_v._Wade.

12 Kellis E. Parker, *A New Approach to Clinical Legal Education*, 8 Cal. W. L. Rev. 146, 146 (1971).

13 Fuller E. Callaway Chair of Law Emeritus, University of Georgia. B.A. 1956, Augustana College; J.D. 1959, Northwestern University (Clarion DeWitt Hardy Scholar); LL.M. 1961, Georgetown University (E. Barrett Prettyman Fellow in Trial Advocacy). In 1987 Professor Carlson was the recipient of the Richard S. Jacobson Award from the Roscoe Pound Foundation. The Jacobson Award was established to recognize excellence in teaching principles of trial advocacy. "Fuller E. Callaway Chair of Law Emeritus Ronald L. Carlson has been a member of the University of Georgia School of Law faculty since 1984. A prolific scholar, Carlson began writing about and analyzing evidentiary rules during the early stages of the Federal Rules of Evidence. In December 2000, when Federal Rule of Evidence 703 was amended, the Federal Rules Advisory Committee relied upon Carlson's Vanderbilt article on expert witnesses in the official Federal Advisory Committee Notes.... Additionally, he is the author of 18 books on evidence, trial practice and criminal procedure, and his law school course book on the law of evidence, published with Carolina Academic Press Publishing Company, will go into its eighth edition in the fall of 2018." His most recent scholarship includes three books plus a book supplement, which were all published during the 2017–18 academic year. "Ronald L. Carlson," School of Law, University of Georgia, accessed March 1, 2020, https://www.law.uga.edu/profile/ronald-l-carlson.

14 "Warren Earl Burger was the 15th Chief Justice of the United States, serving from 1969 to 1986. Born in Saint Paul, Minnesota, Burger graduated from the St. Paul College of Law in 1931. He helped secure the Minnesota delegation's support for Dwight D. Eisenhower at the 1952 Republican National Convention. After Eisenhower won the 1952 presidential election, he appointed Burger to the position of Assistant

Attorney General in charge of the Civil Division. In 1956, Eisenhower appointed Burger to the United States Court of Appeals for the District of Columbia Circuit. Burger served on this court until 1969 and became known as a critic of the Warren Court." Wikipedia, s.v., "Warren E. Burger," last modified February 29, 2020, 4:21, https://en.wikipedia.org/wiki/Warren_E._Burger.

15 Ronald L. Carlson, *Competency and Professionalism in Modern Litigation: The Role of the Law Schools*, 23 Ga. L. Rev. 689, 689–91 (Spring 1989), citing Jackson, *Training the Trial Lawyer: A Neglected Area of Legal Education*, 3 Stan. L. Rev. 48, 57 (1950); Jacobson, *The Great Debate Over Legal Education: Who's to Blame for Incompetent Lawyers?* Chronicle of Higher Ed., Sept. 9, 1981, at 5, col. 1.

16 "Malcolm Richard Wilkey (December 6, 1918–August 15, 2009) was a United States Circuit Judge of the United States Court of Appeals for the District of Columbia Circuit and United States Ambassador to Uruguay." Wikipedia, s.v., "Malcolm Richard Wilkey," last modified March 3, 2020, 22:56, https://en.wikipedia.org/wiki/Malcolm_Richard_Wilkey.

17 Carlson, *supra* note 998, at 694.

18 Professor Mark A. Cohen is the CEO of Legalmosaic (www.legalmosaic.com), a legal business consulting company. He is widely regarded as a global thought leader in the legal vertical. "Mark A. Cohen," Georgetown Law University Center, accessed December 2019, https://www.law.georgetown.edu/faculty/mark-a-cohen/.

19 Mark A. Cohen, "What Are Law Schools Training Students For?" *Forbes,* November 19, 2018, https://www.forbes.com/sites/markcohen1/2018/11/19/what-are-law-schools-training-students-for/#4f6753df64f2.

CHAPTER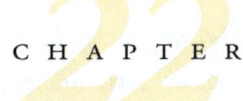

ASU LAW JOURNALS 1970 TO 2020

THE ARIZONA STATE LAW JOURNAL

Arizona State Law Journal, published from 1969[1] to 1973[2] as *Law and the Social Order* at Arizona State University's law school, is the primary scholarly publication at Sandra Day O'Connor College of Law.[3] The *Journal* features a blog featuring emerging Arizona legal issues.[4] "The *Journal* is routinely cited in major textbooks, treatises, and opinions at all levels of the state and federal judiciary, including the United States Supreme Court."[5] The *Journal* was ranked 48th in the nation by the TaxProf Blog[6] and 86th in the nation by Washington & Lee.[7] The *Journal* selects members based on high achievement in law school classes and an exam testing writing and citation skills.[8]

JURIMETRICS

Jurimetrics (originally *M.U.L.L.*, or *Modern Uses of Logic in Law*), was founded in 1959 and adopted its current name in 1966. It began under the auspices of the American Bar Association's Electronic Data Retrieval Committee.[9] The journal awards a $1,000 prize to the author published in its pages who makes the strongest contribution to the field. The first issue included analysis of the promise and limitations of machines in helping solve legal and logical problems, with founder Layman E. Allen discussing propositional calculi and logic.[10] The journal remains focused on the relationships between law, science, and technology, and is published at Arizona State University's Sandra Day O'Connor College of Law, with a staff comprised of students.

LAW JOURNAL FOR SOCIAL JUSTICE

The student-founded *Law Journal for Social Justice* began in 2011 with a symposium issue concerning recently passed Arizona legislation, with Professor Zachary Kramer serving as the faculty adviser since the beginning.[11] Two controversial pieces of legislation spawned the symposium issue: S.B. 1070, a law that made failure to carry immigration documentation a misdemeanor offense, and H.B. 2525, a criminal sentencing reform proposal. Its mission from the beginning was to build "solution-driven dialog" to rectify injustices.[12] The first issue included analysis of S.B. 1070's disparate racial impact[13]; challenges related to achieving permanent U.S. residency[14]; review of criminal judgments[15]; as well as racial profiling.[16]

ARIZONA STATE SPORTS AND ENTERTAINMENT LAW JOURNAL

Arizona State Sports and Entertainment Law Journal also published its first issue in 2011. Sandra Day O'Connor College of Law students built the *SELJ* from a blog originally devoted to sports and performing arts law.[17] A conference to introduce the *SELJ* drew over two hundred guests including lawyers, educators, and sports and entertainment professionals.[18] It has addressed issues such as pay for college athletes,[19] copyright and antitrust,[20] and liabilities for sports injuries.[21] The founding editor-in-chief of *SELJ*, Samuel Renaut, has remained connected to the Sandra Day O'Connor College of Law and serves as the director of its Sports Law and Business Program.

CORPORATE AND BUSINESS LAW JOURNAL

ASU's *Corporate and Business Law Journal*, or *CABLJ*, launched in 2019, to expand the opportunity to exchange ideas about business matters in which East Coast institutions have been historically dominant.[22] It includes discussions of corporate governance, securities, markets, employment law, and mergers and acquisitions.[23]

---

1 See "Law and the Social Order 1969 Law & Soc. Order (1969)," HeinOnline, accessed January 2020, https://heinonline.org/HOL/Page?handle=hein.journals/arzjl1969&id=1&collection=journals&index=journals/arzjl.

2 See "Law and the Social Order 1973 Law & Soc. Order (1973)," HeinOnline, accessed January 2020, https://heinonline.org/HOL/Page?handle=hein.journals/arzjl1973&id=1&collection=journals&index=journals/arzjl.

3 "Law Journals," Sandra Day O'Connor College of Law, accessed January 2020, https://law.asu.edu/student-life/law-journals.

4 "Arizona State Law Journal," *Arizona State Law Journal,* accessed January 2020, http://arizonastatelawjournal.org/.

5 "Law Journals," Sandra Day O'Connor College of Law, accessed January 2020, https://law.asu.edu/student-life/law-journals.

6 Paul Caron, "2019 Meta ranking of Flagship of U.S. Law Reviews," TaxProf Blog, July 25, 2019, https://taxprof.typepad.com/taxprof_blog/2019/07/2019-meta-ranking-of-flagship-us-law-reviews.html.

7 "Law Journals," Washington and Lee University, accessed December 2019, https://managementtools4.wlu.edu/LawJournals/.

8 "Membership Selection," *Arizona State Law Journal,* accessed January 2020, http://arizonastatelawjournal.org/members/membership-selection/.

9 1 M.U.L.L. Mod. Uses Log. L. 1 (1959), https://heinonline.org/HOL/Print?handle=hein.journals/juraba1&collection=journals&id=7&errormessage=Subject%20issue%20to%20the%20terms%20of%20the%20license%20agreement,%20you%20are%20not%20permitted%20to%20download%20an%20entire%20volume%20or%20issue&startid=&endid=33&email_addr=&email=.

10 Ibid.

11 1 L.J. Soc. Justice 1, 1 (2011), https://ljsj.files.wordpress.com/2011/08/ljsj-finished-vol-1-1-2011.pdf.

12 Ibid., 2.

13 Kevin R. Johnson, *A Case Study of Color-Blind Rhetoric: The Racially Disparate Impacts of Arizona's S.B. 1070 and the Failure of Comprehensive Immigration Reform*, 1 L.J. Soc. Justice 3, 3 (2011).

14 Evelyn H. Cruz & Sean Carpenter, *We Want You When We Need You, Otherwise Get Out: The Historical Struggle of Mexican Immigrants to Obtain Lawful Permanent Residency in the United States*, 1 L.J. Soc. Justice 50 (2011).

15 Sigmund G. Popko, *Putting Finality in Perspective: Collateral Review of Criminal Judgments in the DNA Era*, 1 L.J. Soc. Justice 75 (2011).

16 Mary Romero, *Keeping Citizenship Rights White: Arizona's Racial Profiling Practices in Immigration Law Enforcement*, 1 L.J. Soc. Justice 97 (2011).

17 1 Ariz. St. U. Sports & Ent. L.J. (2011), https://heinonline.org/HOL/Page?handle=hein.journals/selj1&id=9&collection=journals&index=journals/selj.

18 Ibid.

19 2 Ariz. St. U. Sports & Ent. L.J. (2012), https://heinonline.org/HOL/Page?handle=hein.journals/selj2&id=1&size=2&collection=journals&index=journals/selj.

20 3 Ariz. St. U. Sports & Ent. L.J. (2013–2014), https://heinonline.org/HOL/Page?handle=hein.journals/selj3&id=1&size=2&collection=journals&index=journals/selj.

21 4 Ariz. St. U. Sports & Ent. L.J. (2014–2015), https://heinonline.org/HOL/Page?handle=hein.journals/selj4&id=1&size=2&collection=journals&index=journals/selj.

22 "Corporate and Business Journal," Sandra Day O'Connor College of Law, accessed November 2019, https://law.asu.edu/student-life/corporate-and-business-journal.

23 Ibid.

CHAPTER 23

ASU LAW CENTER FOR LAW, SCIENCE, & TECHNOLOGY, 1984

The legendary Jack Brown[1] was a central figure in establishing *The Center for the Study of Law, Science, & Technology* at Arizona State University College of Law. He said, "The center was conceived as a major resource to encourage and assist scholarship concerning the needs and demands of the intersecting areas of law, science and technology. ASU's Law School faculty is uniquely qualified to carry out that mission. The Center can gain additional recognition of Arizona as a progenitor of learning and deserves the broadest community."[2]

From its 1984 inception, bold ambitions and striking talents merged to create a center unlike any other in Arizona or the rest of the country. As part of a Research 1 institution, its founders and academic affiliates believed in its mission: "To anticipate issues raised by new knowledge, stimulate dialogue between legal and scientific scholars, and conduct research that helps ensure the legal system's sound treatment, management and accommodation of scientific and technical developments."[3]

Over its first twenty years, through *interdisciplinary research*, the Center has examined, both legally and scientifically, the interplay of law *and* science. To do that it engaged scholars vested in scientific evidence, statistics and mathematical methods, intellectual property and computer software, environmental law, health care and bioethics, evolutionary biology, and information and communication technologies.[4]

In time, it became a robust engine for growth as the Phoenix metro business community offered one of the nation's highest concentrations of high technology resources. With the Sandra Day O'Connor College of Law now centered in downtown Phoenix, the opportunities for collaborative studies in law, science, and technology rapidly increased. Five distinct offerings connect law to science at the Center: (1) interdisciplinary research conferences, (2) service to the legal profession, (3) scholarly publications, (4) student activities, and (5) specialized curriculum. A prominent scientist[5] said it best: "The rapid advances in biological technology have profound implications, and the legal issues raised by this new knowledge need to be addressed by experts. The Center is a pioneer in integrating the ideas of lawyers, ethicists, geneticists and philosophers. I have attended three meetings at ASU, and I found the discussions among legal and scientific scholars to bridge a large knowledge gap. It is critical that this mission be continued."[6]

SCHOLARLY PUBLICATIONS

The Center created and edited the ASU College of Law *Jurimetrics Journal of Law, Science, and Technology*, which became an internationally recognized and referred journal, co-published with the American Bar Association Section of Science and Technology. It is today the oldest and most widely circulated journal in the field of law and science.[7] It offers scholarly works by law faculty, scientists, and lawyers on subjects of national and international importance. Special issues are often published in conjunction with Center conferences. Francisco Ayala, PhD,[8] said, "Science and the law are inextricably related. Technological change and scientific discoveries often force the law to develop in new directions, and the law is often instrumental in fostering and protecting research and invention."[9]

STUDENT ACTIVITIES

The Sandra Day O'Connor College of Law attracts many students with educational and professional backgrounds in science and technology. Other students acquire such interests during law school. Conferences, workshops and periodic student meetings sponsored by the Center provide opportunities for students to meet with distinguished experts from law, industry, and the science disciplines. The college offers special courses designed to expose law students to the legal and public policy challenges raised by new scientific knowledge. Courses are offered in environmental law, evolutionary biology, health care law and bioethics, information and communications technology, intellectual property and computer software, scientific evidence, statistics, and mathematical methods.

INTERDISCIPLINARY RESEARCH CONFERENCES

The keystone offerings at the Center are the interdisciplinary research conferences because they explore significant legal problems of compelling national interest. In chronological order, the Center explored five legal constructs: (1) The 1988 "Baby Doe" Symposium explored the legal and ethical issues in depriving newborns of life-sustaining treatment. (2) The 1989 Conference on Copyright Protection of Computer Software considered the application of copyright law to computer programs and interfaces. (3) The 1991 NIH-sponsored Workshop on the Human Genome Initiative produced a detailed research agenda for the legal and social policy issues raised by worldwide attempts to map and sequence the human genome. (4) The 1993 Second International Conference on Forensic Statistics addressed the issue of probability theory and statistics in legislative, administrative, and judicial proceedings. (5) The 1995 Workshop on Medical Futility looked at legal and ethical issues that arise when consumers seek medical care that health care providers believe is medically or ethically unjustifiable.[10]

FACULTY AFFILIATES

The Center is driven by research expertise from affiliates at ASU in the fields of chemical engineering, economics, exercise science, geology, philosophy, physical education, zoology and law. Over the last thirty-five years, the list has reflected a diversity of law and science. Over its twenty-five year history, scores of lawyer-scientists, lawyer-engineers, lawyer-philosophers and other multi-disciplinary, interdisciplinary scholars worked, in, for, and around the Center's many buildings, sidewalks, and gathering places.

The original scholars were Daniel S. Strouse,[11] Karjala Dennis,[12] Ira Ellman,[13] Owen Jones,[14] David H. Kaye,[15] John D. Leshey,[16] Jonathan H. Rose,[17] Laurence H. Winer,[18] Milton R. Wessel,[19] Jane H. Aiken,[20] Richard L. Brown,[21] Joseph M. Feller,[22] Mark A. Hall,[23] and Fernando R. Teson.[24]

Besides adding new scholars, programs, disciplines, and workshops over its thirty-plus years, the Center renamed itself. It is now ASU Law's *Center for Law, Science and Innovation*.[25] It still advances science and technology law and policy, but it now focuses not *just* on technology; it focuses on *innovation*. That's because as technologies emerge, they rapidly transform substantive law in many areas. In a word, they innovate.[26] Its refocus and reach are clear: "Artificial intelligence, precision medicine, big data, autonomous systems, blockchain, 3D printers, drones and mobile apps are just some of the developments that raise novel legal issues with regard to regulation, liability, privacy, intellectual property, individual rights, and how lawyers and professionals practice every day. ASU Law is dedicated to training 21st-century lawyers who will have unique expertise and competitive advantage in today's legal world." "As science and technology assume central roles in our lives, economy, and legal system, the Center for Law, Science and Innovation is uniquely positioned as an innovator in teaching and applying science, technology and law. From robotics to genetics, neuroscience to nanotech, LSI's innovative projects and programs constantly evolve to address challenging governance and policy issues through cutting-edge curriculum, practical experience, conferences and workshops, research projects, and scholarship."[27]

The challenge to all authors writing about large institutions is producing content that is both relevant *and* current. CLS&I's relevant work and legal scholarship in 2018 might not be current in 2020. Innovation often trumps relevancy. Writing about ASU Law's Center for Law, Science and Innovation in draft might not be relevant in the final manuscript. It might not be current when it morphs into a book. The effort feels like tapping letters on a keyboard that blur as time streaks by the monitor. CLS&I's ideas, scholarship, and impact change almost daily. It's never static, always dynamic. It is an engine in its own right. Lawyers have always had to live with changes in the law, changes in rules, customs, standards, judges, and jobs. But deep down, we are advocates, not scientists. That's why the CLS&I is so vital to ASU Law. Faculty and students don't just adapt, they must innovate and imagine a legal system inside technology and wrapped around science.

As of October 20, 2019, the primary website's home page says,

> *The Center for Law, Science and Innovation in Arizona State University's Sandra Day O'Connor College of Law is the first and largest academic center focused on the intersection of law with science and technology. Its 26 faculty fellows work with students and research fellows to explore innovations in law and policy for a world of rapidly changing technologies, through leading-edge scholarship, education, and policy dialogue. The center engages research focusing on regulatory, governance, legal, policy, social and ethical aspects of emerging technologies, including (but not limited to) nanotechnology, synthetic biology, biotechnology, genomics, personalized medicine, stem cell and regenerative medicine, human enhancement technologies, geoengineering, neuroscience, and robotics.*[28]

"It is a resource to support and connect our students with unique content, contacts, skills, and resources to prepare them for modern legal practice. ASU Law offers more than 50 law, science, and technology related courses, supported and taught by our 50+ faculty fellows. Programs and projects include annual conferences, workshops and speakers, individual and group research activities, and sci-tech externships and clinical work."[29]

"At ASU Law, LSI is home to intellectual property, life sciences and biotechnology, governance of emerging technologies focus areas, and our newest addition—data, privacy, and security. In each area, LSI offers a specialized graduation certificate with robust coursework, student cohorts with attorney and faculty mentorship, and presentation and publication opportunities. In addition, LSI collaborates with five ASU Law student organizations, programs in health law, international law, and sustainability law, and other ASU partners to create an interdisciplinary understanding of the issues driven by science and technology that span all areas of law, policy, and practice."[30]

Law schools are institutional engines whose core function produces lawyers. But ASU Law is supplementary. "JD students can supplement and enhance their degree with the Certificate in Law, Science and Technology. The certificate program includes focused coursework, mentorship, and extracurricular educational opportunities for preparing 21st century lawyers. Students can choose to earn a general LST certificate, or focus in one or more of the following: Intellectual Property, Life Sciences, Data, Privacy and Security."[31]

CURRENT CLS&I LEADERSHIP

Gary Marchant is a Regents' Professor of Law[32] and director of the Center for Law, Science and Innovation. "His research interests include legal aspects of genomics and personalized medicine, the use of genetic information in environmental regulation, risk and the precautionary principle, and governance of emerging technologies such as nanotechnology, neuroscience, biotechnology and artificial intelligence. He teaches courses in Law, Science and Technology, Genetics and the Law, Biotechnology: Science, Law and Policy, Health Technologies and Innovation, Privacy, Big Data and Emerging Technologies, and Artificial Intelligence: Law and Ethics. [ABOR named him] a Regents' Professor in 2011 and also is a professor in ASU's School of Life Sciences, a Distinguished Sustainability Scientist in ASU's Julie Ann Wrigley Global Institute of Sustainability, and is a Lincoln Professor of Emerging Technologies Law and Ethics with the Lincoln Center for Applied Ethics at ASU. Prior to joining ASU in 1999, Professor Marchant was a partner at the Washington, D.C., office of Kirkland & Ellis, where his practice focused on environmental and administrative law. During law school, he was Editor-in-Chief of the Harvard Journal of Law & Technology and editor of the Harvard Environmental Law Review and was awarded the Fay Diploma (awarded to top graduating student at Harvard Law School). Professor Marchant frequently lectures about the intersection of law and science at national and international conferences. He has authored more than 150 articles and book chapters on various issues relating to emerging technologies. Among other activities, he has served on five National Academy of Sciences committees, has been the principal investigator on several major grants, and organized numerous academic conferences on law and science issues."[33]

Joshua Abbott[34] is the Center Director and a tenured professor in ASU's School of Life Sciences. The CSKI Executive council has eighteen members: Michael Arkfeld,[35] Arnie Calica,[36] Dan Christensen, Larry Cohen,[37] Kirk T. Hartley,[38] James (Jim) Hennessy, Gerard (Jerry) Lewis, Keith Lindor,[39] Dawn Marchant,[40]

Robert (Bob) J. Milligan,[41] Roger N. Morris,[42] Dr. George Poste,[43] K Royal,[44] John Shufeldt,[45] Judge Roslyn O. Silver,[46] Yvonne Stevens,[47] and Cory Tyszka.[48]

2019 CLSI CONFERENCE "GOVERNANCE OF EMERGING TECHNOLOGIES & SCIENCE (GETS)—MAY 2019

In May 2019, the CLSI presented its seventh national conference. As was the case for the prior six conferences, its reach was wide, content deep, and impact serious. As has become its signature, it addressed ethical, legal, regulatory, and policy issues invested in the emergence of new technologies and scientific advances. Drawing on the combined expertise of leaders in academia, industry, and government, it focused on finding governance solutions for rapidly changing technologies. The dual challenge of any governance system is to encourage research, investment, and development while guarding against potential risks to health, safety, environment, and society. Accordingly, CLSI 2019 confronted the challenge by creating a forum for cross-disciplinary discussion involving experts in law, engineering, science, business, medicine, ethics, and other fields.[49]

To put the 2019 Conference in context, it is helpful to recall what preceded it: "The broadest possible range of technologies and scientific study, including nanotechnology, artificial intelligence, robotics, autonomous vehicles, the internet of things, human-machine interfaces, neuroscience, synthetic biology, genomics, personalized medicine, telemedicine, human enhancement, gene editing, surveillance, national security, virtual and augmented reality, blockchain, and autonomous weapons. The value-added proposition was governance strategies and lessons learned in one field can often be applied to others in ways that generate new breakthroughs. The 2019 Conference was *the* go-to event for forward-looking policy makers, technologists, and business leaders at the forefront of a changing world."[50]

The keynote speakers were eclectic and roundly applauded: Sheila Hayman, award-winning documentary filmmaker;[51] Rachel Mushahwar, Vice President, General Manager, U.S. Enterprise, Government, and Cloud Industries, Intel.[52]

MERGING LAW WITH TECHNOLOGY

ASU is not alone in the "insistent call for analytics and other technology experts in all sorts of fields. Some are integrating tech training with the coursework for other advanced degrees, such as MBAs, nursing degrees and J.D.s. Others are rolling out niche degrees in hot specialties such as medical informatics, digital forensics and cybersecurity. 'Savvy students know that jobs of the future will rely on technology,' argues Tim Westerbeck, president of Chicago-based consulting firm Eduvantis. 'So higher education institutions are working hard to create these programs.'"[53]

States are also active in the legal side of technology. The New York Department of Financial Services has a new regulatory scheme mandating new cybersecurity requirements similar to those already in existence for banks, insurance companies and other financial services institutions. Their rules "underscore that cybersecurity is not solely a technology or information security team matter. Each new requirement—and implementing new governance, policies, technology and personnel—likely presents risk created by *the intersection between law and technology*."[54]

A January 2019 law review article approaches the morphing of law into technology at some length. The author explores "the impending conflict between the protection of civil rights and artificial intelligence (AI). While both areas of law have amassed rich and well-developed areas of scholarly work and doctrinal support, a growing body of scholars are interrogating the *intersection between them*. [They] argue[] that the issues surrounding algorithmic accountability demonstrate a deeper, more structural tension within a new generation of disputes regarding law and technology . . . the true promise of AI does not lie in the information we reveal to one another, but rather in the questions it raises about the interaction of technology, property, and civil rights."[55]

The important name change (from the *Center for Law, Science, and Technology* to the *Center for Law, Science and Innovation*) is noteworthy for a different reason than was likely envisioned by the Center's leaders. A 2015 law review article, "Innovation Experimentalism in the Age of the Sharing Economy," challenges the existing definition of innovation.[56]

> *Conventional wisdom says that innovation is fundamentally at odds with the regulatory state: It is a gift of a handful of lonely geniuses that need to be unchained from state control and its rigid and obsolete regulations. The "innovation state" is "no country" for old rules. More recently, this claim has been heard in the debate on the regulation of sharing-economy platforms that defy, for example, existing hotel and transportation regulations with an allegedly new concept of shared services. However, few scholars would seriously*

argue that the state should completely abdicate all responsibility for regulating innovation. Therefore, this Article suggests that the heart of the matter is not whether the state should be "in" or "out" of the innovation game, but rather when and how it should be involved. Drawing on examples from the sharing economy and the literature in law and technology, this Article addresses the timing of this state intervention, suggesting the use of experimental and sunrise regulations. When regulators are unable to make informed predictions about innovative products, they should consider limiting the territorial scope of application of a new rule, timing its duration, or delaying its commencement date. This can be achieved with temporary and experimental rules, which can be tested and reviewed on a systematic basis, or sunrise clauses, which delay the coming-into-effect of certain regulatory dispositions.[57]

PEERS

Duke's law school offers two degrees, the JD/LLM and LLM in Law and Entrepreneurship. Its program "integrates rigorous course work, real-world experience, and high-level networking opportunities to position [students] to advise, create, and lead the innovative ventures that will drive tomorrow's global economy."[58] Harvard's Law, Science, and Technology Program of Study "seeks to guide students on how to best take advantage of Harvard's unparalleled resources in this field, and to build a community of students and professors interested in the intersections between law and technology." A Massachusetts Institute of Technology scholar wrote a lengthy essay on the subject. "The ascendance of both modern law and science has been achieved in competition against traditional institutions, especially religious interpretations of nature and human relations; their cultural dominion signifies a radical transformation in the sources of human agency and authority. Both law and science are deeply and noticeably marked by formal rationality."[59]

IMPACT

By any measurement the impact of ASU's CLS&I is great. By merging scientific theories, technological change, and innovative ways to better the human condition, the Center helps everyone understand the connection between what were once disparate disciplines. It aids in developing laws essential to "good" technology. By combining the energies of all three disciplines, we can do many great things more efficiently and legally. What engineers and scientists don't know about the law equals what lawyers don't understand about science and technology. They went to different colleges. Put them in the same room, or center, and wonders happen.

Fast-forward to February 2020. Faculty Director Gary Marchant received the honor of becoming a fellow of the American Association for the Advancement of Science, after being elected in by his peers. AAAS has stated its mission to "advance science engineering and innovation throughout the world for the benefit of all people."[60]

> *There were 443 honorees this year, across 24 categories, with Marchant selected to be one of eight fellows named in the Societal Impacts of Science and Engineering sector. "AAAS is the world's largest scientific organization, so it's a nice honor to be recognized by such a prestigious group," Marchant said in his ASU Now interview. Marchant has led the Center for more than 20 years, with ASU Law Dean Douglas Sylvester saying, "Professor Marchant is the reason ASU Law has been at the forefront of law, science and innovation. He has long been recognized as one of the preeminent scholars in his field, and this well-deserved recognition reflects that."*[61]

---

1 "Jack E. Brown, a lawyer prominent in several early cases concerning the computer industry and intellectual property . . . Brown & Bain, the Phoenix law firm that Mr. Brown founded 40 years ago. [Brown & Bain eventually merged into Perkins Coie.] Mr. Brown's specialty was high-technology litigation, particularly copyright violations. Most notably, he represented Apple Computer in its unsuccessful 'look and feel' case in 1989 against Microsoft's Windows operating system. A United States District Court judge ruled against Apple, holding that an element of an interface, like the recycle bin on the Windows screen, infringed on a copyright only if it looked exactly the same as another interface, in this example, Apple's trash basket. Mr. Brown was more successful keeping the Franklin Computer Corporation from cloning the Apple II personal computer in 1983. He also represented I.B.M., Intel, Unisys and United Technologies, among other companies. He was listed [] in the *National Law Journal* as one of the 100 most influential lawyers in the United States . . . He received a bachelor's degree from Northwestern University and a law degree from Harvard." Nick Ravo, *Jack E. Brown, 72, a Computer Industry Lawyer*, N.Y. Times, Jan. 14, 2020, https://www.nytimes.com/2000/01/14/business/jack-e-brown-72-a-computer-industry-lawyer.html.
2 See The Center for the Study of Law, Science, & Technology, Arizona State University, Sandra Day O'Connor College of Law Archives, 1984, page 2.
3 Ibid., 5.
4 Ibid., 2.
5 P. Michael Conneally, Ph.D., was a Distinguished Professor of Medical and Molecular Genetics and Neurology at the Indiana University School of Medicine and Medical Center. Wikipedia, s.v., "P. Michael Conneally," last updated January 22, 2020, 15:43, https://en.wikipedia.org/wiki/P._Michael_Conneally.
6 The Center for the Study of Law, Science, & Technology, Arizona State University, Sandra Day O'Connor College of Law Archives, 1984, page 3.

7 "About Jurimetrics," Sandra Day O'Connor College of Law, last visited March 4, 2020, https://law.asu.edu/jurimetrics/. "*Jurimetrics* was first published in 1959 under the leadership of Layman Allen as Modern Uses of Logic in Law (MULL). The current name was adopted in 1966. *Jurimetrics* is the oldest journal of law and science in the United States, and it enjoys a circulation of more than 8,000, which includes all members of the ABA Section of Science & Technology Law." "*Jurimetrics, The Journal of Law, Science, and Technology* (ISSN 0897-1277), published quarterly, is the journal of the American Bar Association Section of Science & Technology Law and the Center for Law, Science & Innovation. *Jurimetrics* is a forum for the publication and exchange of ideas and information about the relationships between law, science and technology" in life, and the empirical social, and behavioral sciences; engineering, aerospace, communications and computers; logic, mathematics, statistics, and quantitative methods; use of science and technology in law practice, litigation, adjudication, legislation, and court and agency administration; legal regulation and policy implications of science and technology.

8 "Francisco José Ayala Pereda is a Spanish-American evolutionary biologist and philosopher who was a longtime faculty member at the University of California, Irvine and University of California, Davis. He is a former Dominican priest, ordained in 1960, but left the priesthood that same year. After graduating from the University of Salamanca, he moved to the United States in 1961 to study for a PhD at Columbia University. There, he studied for his doctorate under Theodosius Dobzhansky, graduating in 1964. He became a US citizen in 1971." Wikipedia, s.v., "Francisco J. Ayala," last modified March 3, 2020, 2:46, https://en.wikipedia.org/wiki/Francisco_J._Ayala.

9 The Center for the Study of Law, Science, & Technology, Arizona State University, Sandra Day O'Connor College of Law Archives, 1984, page 3.

10 Ibid., 2.

11 "Daniel Stanton Strouse," AZ Central Obituaries Powered by Legacy.com, accessed March 4, 2020, https://www.legacy.com/obituaries/azcentral/obituary.aspx?n=daniel-stanton-strouse&pid=92446440.

12 Wikipedia, s.v., "Dennis Karjala," last modified November 26, 2019, 1:55, https://en.wikipedia.org/wiki/Dennis_Karjala.

13 "Ira Mark Ellman," Sandra Day O'Connor College of Law, accessed March 4, 2020, http://homepages.law.asu.edu/~ira01/.

14 "Owen D. Jones," Vanderbilt Law School, accessed March 4, 2020, https://law.vanderbilt.edu/bio/owen-jones.

15 "David H. Kaye," PennState Law, University Park, PA, accessed March 4, 2020, https://pennstatelaw.psu.edu/faculty/kaye.

16 "John Leshy, Professor of Law," UC Hastings College of the Law, accessed March 4, 2020, https://www.uchastings.edu/people/john-leshy/.

17 "Jonathan Rose, Professor of Law," Sandra Day O'Connor College of Law, accessed March 4, 2020, http://homepages.law.asu.edu/~jonrose/.

18 "Laurence H. Winer: CV," Sandra Day O'Connor College of Law, accessed March 4, 2020, http://apps.law.asu.edu/files/faculty/cvs/laurencehwiner.pdf.

19 "Milton R. Wessel," Prabook, accessed March 4, 2020, https://prabook.com/web/milton_r.wessel/391386.

20 "Jane H. Aiken," Georgetown Law, accessed March 4, 2020, https://www.law.georgetown.edu/faculty/jane-h-aiken/.

21 "Richard L. Brown," UNLV – William S. Boyd School of Law, accessed March 4, 2020, https://law.unlv.edu/content/richard-l-brown.

22 "Joseph M. Feller: CV," Sandra Day O'Connor College of Law, accessed March 4, 2020, https://apps.law.asu.edu/files/faculty/cvs/fellerjoseph.pdf.

23 "Mark Hall," Faculty | Wake Forest Law, accessed March 4, 2020, http://web.law.wfu.edu/faculty/profile/hallma/.

24 "Fernando Tesón," College of Law, Florida State University, accessed March 4, 2020, https://law.fsu.edu/faculty-staff/fernando-teson.

25 "Science and Technology Law," Sandra Day O'Connor College of Law, accessed March 4, 2020, https://law.asu.edu/focus-areas/law-technology.

26 Innovation is a new idea, or more-effective device or process. Innovation can be viewed as the application of better solutions that meet new requirements, unarticulated needs, or existing market needs. This is accomplished through more-effective products, processes, services, technologies, or business models that are

readily available to markets, governments and society. Wikipedia, s.v., "Innovation," last modified March 4, 2020, 00:37, https://en.wikipedia.org/wiki/Innovation.

27 *See* "Center for Law, Science and Innovation," Sandra Day O'Connor College of Law, accessed March 4, 2020, https://law.asu.edu/centers/law-science-innovation.

28 "Center for Law, Science and Innovation," Science@ASU, accessed March 4, 2020, https://science.asu.edu/center-law-science-and-innovation.

29 Ibid.

30 "Science and Technology Law: Student Opportunities," Sandra Day O'Connor College of Law, accessed March 4, 2020, https://law.asu.edu/focus-areas/law-technology.

31 "JD Certificates: Law, Science and Technology Certificate," Sandra Day O'Connor College of Law, accessed March 4, 2020, https://law.asu.edu/degree-programs/jd/certificates/lst-certificate.

32 The Arizona Board of Regents (ABOR) "Policy 6-208 permits the rank of Regents Professor to be awarded only to full professors with exceptional achievements that have brought them national or international distinction. This highest of faculty ranks may be awarded to no more than three (3) percent of the total tenured and tenure-track faculty members." Arizona Board of Regents, "Executive Summary Action Item #32: Appointment of Regents Professors," (meeting, Arizona Board of Regents, Tucson, AZ, January 22–23, 2004), https://public.azregents.edu/Board/Item-32-2004-01-UA-Regents-Professor.pdf.

33 "Gary Marchant," ASU iSearch, accessed March 4, 2020, https://isearch.asu.edu/profile/228973.

34 "Joshua K. Abbott: CV," Sandra Day O'Connor College of Law, accessed March 4, 2020, https://isearch.asu.edu/sites/default/files/cv/AbbottCV_Long.pdf.

35 "About Michael Arkfeld," Arkfeld eDiscovery Education Center, accessed March 4, 2020, http://www.ediscoveryeducationcenter.com/about-michael-arkfeld.

36 https://health.usnews.com/doctors/arnold-calica-291533 *See also* Yvonne Stevens, "LSI Study Group Kicks Off 2016 With Big Data," *Bits, Bots & Biomakers* (blog), Center for Law, Science & Innovation at ASU's Sandra Day O'Connor College of Law, January 15, 2016, http://blogs.asucollegeoflaw.com/lsi/tag/arnie-calica-big-data/.

37 "Larry Cohen," Cronus Law, PLLC, accessed March 4, 2020, https://www.cronuslaw.com/attorneys/larry-cohen.

38 "Hartley, Kirt T.," GNARUS Advisors, LLC, accessed March 4, 2020, http://gnarusllc.com/expert/hartley-kirk-t/.

39 "Keith Lindor," ASU iSearch, accessed March 4, 2020, https://isearch.asu.edu/profile/1861421.

40 "Dawn Marchant," LinkedIn, accessed March 4, 2020, https://www.linkedin.com/in/dawn-marchant-1b428515/.

41 "Robert J. Milligan," Milligan Lawless, accessed March 4, 2020, https://milliganlawless.com/prof/robert-j-milligan/.

42 "Roger N. Morris, R.Ph, Phoenix Health Law Attorney," Quarles & Brady, LLP, accessed March 4, 2020, https://www.quarles.com/roger-n-morris/.

43 Wikipedia, s.v., "George Poste," last modified February 16, 2020, 21:44, https://en.wikipedia.org/wiki/George_Poste.

44 "K Royal, FIP, CIPP/E / US, CIPM," LinkedIn, accessed March 4, 2020, https://www.linkedin.com/in/kroyal/.

45 "Dr. John Shufeldt," John Shufeldt MD, accessed March 4, 2020, http://www.drjohnshufeldt.com/bio/.

46 Wikipedia, s.v., "Roslyn O. Silver," last modified April 10, 2019, 18:06, https://en.wikipedia.org/wiki/Roslyn_O._Silver.

47 "Yvonne Stevens," ASU iSearch, accessed March 4, 2020, https://isearch.asu.edu/profile/1619270.

48 "Cory Tyszka," Jones, Skelton & Hochuli, PLC, accessed March 4, 2020, https://www.jshfirm.com/attorneys/ctyszka/.

49 "Conference on Governance of Emerging Technologies and Science," ASU Sandra Day O'Connor College of Law, accessed March 4, 2020, https://events.asucollegeoflaw.com/gets/.

50 *See* registration materials and documents in CLSI archives in the law library at Sandra Day O'Connor College of Law, 111 E. Taylor St., Phoenix, AZ 85004.

51 Sheila Hayman has written, produced and directed dozens of documentary films all over the world. She has won a BAFTA, a BAFTA Fulbright Fellowship, and Time Out "Documentary Series of the Year."

As a writer, she has been Young Journalist of the Year and a Hodder Headline Lead Title novelist. She has written for most of the major UK newspapers and been a columnist for *The Guardian.*
"Sheila Hayman: About," Sheila Hayman, accessed March 4, 2020, https://www.sheilahayman.com/.

52 Rachel Mushahwar is a global executive with 23+ years of experience in a variety of industries where she has consistently delivered significant and measurable bottom-line results and has been continuously rewarded with new challenges and opportunities. An expert in aligning strategy with organizational vision and objectives, she leads new initiatives with C-suite executives to help them shape and refine their strategic objectives and achieve business goals through implementation of strategic roadmaps, solid technology foundations, and standardized process management. Mushahwar is the Vice President and General Manager of US Business Consumption Enterprise, Government, and Cloud Industries at Intel and leads nine different industry verticals in the US (Cloud, Retail, Transportation, Manufacturing, Energy, Financial Services, Government/SLED, Media/Entertainment, and Health Life Sciences) and is accountable for about $4B in sales. Her focus is on enabling companies to realize the value of innovative offerings and delivering end-to-end innovative solutions to the industry that solve real-world business problems. She was recently named as "US Business Woman of the Year" by Insight Success and named by ChainStoreAge as one of the "Top Ten Women in Technology" in January 2017, and *Women's Wear Daily* listed her among the "Top Industry Transformers" in December 2016. She has been on *Wall Street Journal Live,* and most recently *NBC Press.*

Mushahwar holds a bachelor's degree in computer science and an MBA in international business (both *summa cum laude*) and is an alumna of Columbia's Graduate School of Business in New York. She is an active supporter of STEM (science, technology, engineering, and math) education and programs. "Rachel Mushahwar," LinkedIn, accessed March 4, 2020, https://www.linkedin.com/in/rachelmushahwar/.

53 Arlene Weintraub, "Taking the Tech Track," USNEWS.com, March 26, 2015, https://www.usnews.com/news/college-of-tomorrow/articles/2015/03/26/taking-the-tech-track

54 Holland & Knight LLP, "New York Department of Financial Services Revises Proposed Cybersecurity Rule," Lexology, January 13, 2017, https://www.lexology.com/library/detail.aspx?g=fcc3c1f5-f340-4313-a284-88f67354e827.

55 Sonia K. Katyal, *Private Accountability in the Age of Artificial Intelligence*, 66 UCLA L. Rev. 54, 54 (emphasis added).

56 Sofia Ranchordas, *Innovation Experimentalism in the Age of the Sharing Economy*, 19 Lewis & Clark L. Rev. 871, 871–72 (2015).

57 Ibid.

58 "Law & Entrepreneurship," Duke Law, accessed March 11, 2020, https://law.duke.edu/llmle/.

59 Massachusetts Institute of Technology, USA, *Law and Science, Volume I: Epistemological, Evidentiary and Relational Engagements*, ed. Susan S. Silbey (Hampshire: Ashgate Publishing Company, 2008), xi.

60 http://blogs.asucollegeoflaw.com/lsi/ February 5, 2020 blog post by Claire Chandler.

61 Ibid.

CHAPTER 24

DEAN PAUL BENDER, 1984 TO 1989

From 1965 to 2020, the ASU College of Law had eight deans[1] and employed more than 100 professors of law, professors of practice, and adjunct professors. All were legal overachievers, most published erudite articles and books, several were accomplished lawyers, and all served with distinction. A remarkable number achieved national reputations. A handful were routinely sought out for comment on important state and national legal, business, and intellectual issues. It is difficult to identify just one individual who clearly stands out among a peer group of outstanding people. However, there is one who truly stands out—Paul Bender. His listing on *The Federalist Society's* website[2] bears repeating here:

> *Paul Bender is professor of law and dean emeritus for the Sandra Day O'Connor College of Law. He teaches courses on U.S. and Arizona constitutional law. He has written extensively about constitutional law, intellectual property and Indian law, and is coauthor of the two-volume casebook/treatise, Political and Civil Rights in the United States. Professor Bender has argued more than 20 cases before the U.S. Supreme Court, and actively participates in constitutional litigation in federal and state courts. Professor Bender served as dean of the College of Law from 1984–1989, during which time he*

was instrumental in starting its Indian Legal Program. Prior to joining the College faculty, he was law clerk to 2nd U.S. Circuit Court of Appeals Judge Learned Hand and to U.S. Supreme Court Justice Felix Frankfurter, and spent 24 years as a faculty member at the University of Pennsylvania Law School. Professor Bender served as Principal Deputy Solicitor General of the United States from 1993–1997, with responsibility for Supreme Court and federal appellate litigation in the areas of civil rights, race and sex discrimination, freedom of speech and religion, and tort claims against the federal government. Professor Bender has served as a member of the Hopi Tribe's Court of Appeals, and is currently Chief Justice of the Fort McDowell Nation Supreme Court, and the San Carlos Apache Court of Appeals.

ACADEMIC CREDENTIALS

His academic accomplishments are peerless. He earned his AB degree at Harvard College, *cum laude,* in physics in 1954. He earned his law degree at Harvard Law School in 1957, *magna cum laude,* with a class rank of third out of 505. He made the Editorial Board of the *Harvard Law Review,* served as Research Assistant to Professor Benjamin Kaplan, earned a Frederick Sheldon Training Fellowship at Harvard Law and won two of the most prestigious law clerkships in America. He was an associate at Paul, Weiss, Rifkind, Wharton, & Garrison in 1957. He was Judge Learned Hand's law clerk from 1958 to 1959 at the United States Court of Appeals for the Second Circuit. And he was Justice Felix Frankfurter's law clerk from 1959 to 1960 on the United States Supreme Court. Following his clerkship with Justice Frankfurter, he became an Assistant Professor at the University of Pennsylvania Law School in 1960, and a Visiting Assistant Professor at Stanford Law School in the summer of 1962. He went back to Penn in 1963, made full professor in 1966 and stayed there until he moved to Arizona in 1984 to become ASU Law's fourth dean. He held the deanship from 1984 to 1989.

Over his long career as lawyer, law professor, and dean, he served two universities: University of Pennsylvania (1960 to 1984) and Arizona State University (1984 to 1989). He was in and out of government service over the years; as Assistant to the Solicitor General of the United States, U.S. Department of Justice in the 1960s, and as Principal Deputy Solicitor General of the United States from 1993 to 1996. He held ten major advisory positions from 1967 through 1998.[3] Perhaps most importantly, he wrote four books (with other scholars),[4] four student notes,[5] twenty-eight articles, book chapters, and reviews,[6] and fourteen "other writings."[7] With all that, he also gave forty-nine scholarly lectures and presentations.[8] In his spare time, he testified nine times before the U.S. Senate, the U.S. House of Representatives, and the Arizona Senate Committee on the Judiciary.[9]

His official CV lists several dozen (too many to footnote) faculty, community, and professional service committees over the sixty-three years since he graduated from law school. However, his academic record clarifies the distinction between being "just" a law professor and becoming a "legal scholar." In academia,[10] the distinction is important. Dean Bender belongs to that small group of law teachers in America who seek and acquire tenure and spend as much time writing and researching as they teach. In that rarefied air, there is another distinction "between those with the goal of a professorship only, and those who strive to become scholars of law. The latter category includes the professor whose work will be read and valued by those who do valuable work in her field and the professor whom other faculties would be eager to have present her work at their schools, perhaps visit for a semester or a year, or even hire laterally."[11] By any measure, Paul Bender is a legal scholar.

He participated in the law school's Oral History project, managed by Marianne Alcorn of the Ross-Blakley Law Library in 2006. It turned out to be a twenty-page, single-spaced chronicle of his life from the 1950s. He said he "really enjoyed the first year of law school because it was a lot of fun—really challenging, really interesting, liked everything about it, my classmates were interesting."[12]

CLERKSHIPS AND FELLOWSHIPS

Much to his surprise, his first semester grades put him number three in his class. He gave the credit to the other two guys in his study group—Dave Shapiro, who came in first, and Bob Monheim, who was sixth in the class. Their grades got them all onto the law review. That meant they would get better jobs. In his 3L year, he was awarded a Sheldon Fellowship, which gave him a stipend to travel anywhere he wanted. When he got out of law school, he worked for the New York firm of Paul, Weiss, Rifkin & Morgan, doing copyright and entertainment law. Then in the fall of 1957 he used the Sheldon Fellowship to go to Europe with his wife. They went to Poland, Yugoslavia, Spain, Portugal, France, Switzerland and England. While in England, he got a call from the associate dean at Harvard saying he could get a clerkship in U.S. Circuit Court with either Judge Magruder[13] on the First Circuit, or Judge Learned Hand,[14] on the Second Circuit. He'd intended on going back to the Paul, Weiss firm when his clerkship finished with Judge Hand, but he got a call from Al Saks, who'd been a clerk for Justice Felix Frankfurter on the U.S. Supreme Court. He offered him the move up to the U.S. Supreme Court and clerk for Justice Frankfurter. That turned out to be a singular point in his career.

> As he explained it to Ms. Alcorn, Justice Frankfurter altered his career path. "One day I was in the office.... [Justice Frankfurter] said 'Paul you have an academic mind... you should think about going into academics... you don't want to go back to Paul Weiss.... do you want to be a rich Park Avenue lawyer and have eight bathrooms in your house and stuff like that? You know academics is really the thing you want to do'... So the law schools came around to interview and somebody from Michigan came and someone from Penn and they offered me a job and so I said what the hell and I decided to do that rather than go back to Paul Weiss.... Philadelphia seemed like a nice place and Margie got a job... teaching at [a] Friend Select school there, which was right downtown... so we went to [Penn]."[15]

Dean Bender also told Ms. Alcorn about clerking for famous judges.

> You know Hand was a senior judge and didn't sit on many cases. He wrote his own opinions and wouldn't let me write anything, not even a memo... your job was to read the cases, read the briefs, talk to him about it, and he would write a draft and go over it and talk about it, sort of a cooperative thing... and you sort of got to share his life during that time.... He was very nice... a wonderful man.... Then I went down to clerk for Frankfurter and that was quite a different thing.... He'd had a heart attack, but was back working full time.... That was a year when it was really a full time job, but it was not a year when the Supreme Court was terribly interesting in what it did... Brown v. Board had been decided in 1954, but I was there in '59 to '60.... The court was very quiet basically... not very liberal or very conservative... Earl Warren had joined the court as Chief Justice, Brenan was probably the most liberal member... Black and Douglas were still there... Frankfurter and Stewart and Harlan were sort of the middle

of the court . . . Whitaker and Clark were very much under Frankfurter's influence . . . he was such a dominating intellect and so persistent in his arguments . . . he held the court . . . as soon as he left almost all the cases he wrote were overruled or ignored . . . .[16]

MAPP V. OHIO

Mapp v. Ohio[17] was a 1961 landmark case in criminal procedure, in which the United States Supreme Court decided that evidence obtained in violation of the Fourth Amendment, which protects against "unreasonable searches and seizures," may not be used in state law criminal prosecutions in state courts, and in federal criminal law prosecutions in federal courts, as had been the law. The U.S. Supreme Court voted 6–3 in favor of *Mapp*. Five Justices held that the states were bound to exclude evidence seized in violation of the Fourth Amendment. This majority decision applied the exclusionary rule to the states. The three dissenting Justices would have adhered to the Court's contrary prior holding in *Wolf v. Colorado*,[18] which declined to apply the exclusionary rule to the states. *Wolf* was a Frankfurter decision.

Dean Bender's Oral History transcript with Ms. Alcorn reveals an interesting piece of history about that famous case. When Justice Frankfurter retired from the court in 1961, President Kennedy nominated Goldberg in 1962 to fill Frankfurter's seat. Goldberg was a liberal justice, but he was replaced by Abe Fortas. Dean Bender was teaching at Penn when the famous decision in *Mapp v. Ohio* came down. He told Ms. Alcorn what happened.

> *I was teaching at Penn and I got a call one day from Frankfurter, he said you'll never believe what they just did . . . . They had just had the conference about* **Mapp v. Ohio** *and overruled a Frankfurter decision [Wolf v. Colorado], which held that the exclusionary rule did not apply in the states. The states were free to have exclusionary rule or not . . . . It was an opinion Frankfurter had written and was very proud of . . . . He starts telling me that Stewart was going to write the opinion, and he said you know when I talked to them for forty-five minutes at the conference, I could just see him pacing up and down in the conference room, lecturing them about how they must not do this . . . but it wasn't working anymore because there was Brennan and*

Warren who weren't going to get pushed around by that and they had their own ideas of what should happen . . . I think they were right, I'm sure if I had still been a law clerk I would have told them they were right and he would have told me I was wrong and he would have done the same thing. But they were beginning; I mean he saw these things as issues about the competence of courts. Frankfurter is a great believer in the democratic system. He really meant the democratic system. He was willing to go along with democratic decisions even when he thought they were really wrong because that was the best system. And he was a great admirer of the British system where there is no written constitution, still isn't. I'm sure he would have probably voted too, if it was up to him, and he was on a state court.[19]

Mapp v. Ohio is one of a handful of landmark Supreme Court cases in America. Writing the majority opinion, Justice Clark said, "our holding that the exclusionary rule is an essential part of both the Fourth and 14th Amendments is not only the logical dictate of prior cases, but it also makes very good sense. There is no war between the Constitution and common sense."[20] It stands for one of the great principles of constitutional law—every state must observe the exclusionary rule. It prohibits the use of evidence or testimony obtained in violation of civil liberties and rights protected by the U.S. Constitution.[21]

Rudolph Abel v. United States

The most famous case Dean Bender worked on while he was Justice Frankfurter's law clerk was *Abel v. United States*.[22] Like most famous cases, the *Abel* case has a Wikipedia page, summarizing the essential facts and ruling.[23] The FBI suspected Rudolph Abel of being a spy for the Soviet Union and entering the U.S. illegally. The INS arrested Abel for being in the United States illegally but agreed to allow the FBI to try to flip Abel into becoming a double agent against the Soviet Union before carrying out the arrest. When he was arrested, the INS searched his hotel room. The evidence turned up by the INS and FBI searches was used in Abel's trial, in which he was convicted and sentenced to thirty years' imprisonment. Abel appealed to the Supreme Court arguing the searches violated the Fourth Amendment and the evidence should not have been used at his trial. The Supreme Court affirmed Abel's conviction in a 5–4 decision. Justice Felix Frankfurter wrote the majority opinion, joined by Justices Tom C. Clark, John Harlan, Potter Stewart and Charles Evans Whittaker. While noting that the government must not be permitted to circumvent the Fourth Amendment by invoking an administrative procedure, the Court accepted the lower courts' findings that the FBI's interaction with the INS in this case was in good faith. It found the INS searches were made under a valid arrest, and thus the evidence was discovered appropriately.

Dean Bender's recollection was succinct.

Frankfurter thought the role of the courts was to let the democratic system work except in situations which were really outrageous . . . so his approach . . . was basically a due process approach. He would look at each case and if he thought it was an outrage it was unconstitutional. If it wasn't an outrage he'd let the democratic process work. That to him was basically what the court's role was . . . . The biggest case I worked on, most famous case I worked on was a case called Abel *against the United States, which involved a federal prosecution . . . . The exclusionary rule applied . . . it involved the legality of a search that produced evidence against Rudolph Abel who was a Soviet spy . . . . The opinion by Frankfurter affirmed the conviction and held that there hadn't been a violation of the fourth amendment . . . Abel was a few years later traded for Francis Gary Powers, the U-2 pilot, so we accomplished something . . . We got Gary Powers back by putting Abel in jail.*[24]

ASU COLLEGE OF LAW DEAN

Ms. Alcorn changed the subject, asked why he left Penn and came to Arizona as a new dean.

I'd been teaching for a lot of years and it was getting to be the same thing over and over . . . . They asked if I would like to come out and talked about being dean . . . . The university provost at that time, Jack Kinsinger,[25] *was very interested in the law school and wanted to do everything he could to make the law school a better place including diversifying student population, diversifying the faculty, stuff like that . . . . His views and mine about what a law school ought to be were very similar . . . a lot of support there . . . . So I said I would come out . . . . He was very supportive and it enabled us to start doing a lot of things that I think have turned out to be good for the school. He had a real interest in making the school a better place and more creative, a more diverse place, a place with a lot more opportunities for minorities . . . the fact that we got the Indian Law program going was in part due to that support.*[26]

POLITICS AND LAW FIRMS

The 1980s were growth years for ASU, its law school and metropolitan Phoenix. The downtown Phoenix law firms[27] were growing, but not particularly involved in or supportive of the law school in Tempe. Bender told Ms. Alcorn about his efforts to change that dynamic:

A lot of [the people we were trying to connect with] were with big law firms, so we started trying to get [them] to think of making significant contributions to the law school on a regular basis. And I spent a lot of time trying to do that. And then I got involved in current events around here. [Governor Evan] Mecham[28] *was getting impeached at the time. I got asked to help the senate here work out the procedures, [Chief Justice] Frank Gordon*[29] *was presiding, I got to know people on the Supreme Court. [They were] very welcoming and let me get involved in a whole lot of stuff. I got involved with the senate there and then I started doing stuff on television which was fun and that got me involved in other issues . . . . [Governor] Rose Mofford*[30] *appointed me chairman of a task force to try to deal with a medical malpractice insurance crisis. [Chief Justice] Frank Gordon asked me to be the chairman of a commission on trying to get more minorities into the judiciary . . . . I was asked to draft [and chair] the committee that drafted the rules for the victims' rights amendment to the Arizona Constitution.*[31]

DEAN BENDER AT THE STATE LEGISLATURE

Dean Bender not only took it upon himself to become involved in state legislative matters, he moved his faculty to become activists as well:

I felt that I was being useful there and I did whatever I could to try and encourage faculty members to get involved with the legislature [with] some

> *success in that although there was, a lot of faculty members are really reluctant to get involved in things that they are not in complete control of. And the legislature is someplace you're not in complete control . . . . at that time interest rates were high and the bar had a lot of money because of lawyer's trust fund accounts which they are required to set up . . . in the aggregate these [] funds . . . are too small [and] it's just a couple of days that lawyers had a trust account . . . . So all the states set up these statewide trust fund accounts and they produce a lot of money and the bar used them for public interest things [and] to support legal services for the poor . . . . The legislature was constantly trying to take that money away and use it for something else. So we would go down to the legislature and try to persuade them to do the right thing. And it was hard for them to understand that it was good to use this money to provide lawyers for people accused of capital crimes that it was important that they have representation if they didn't they would just have more and more problems . . . . I think we succeeded in persuading them that, to let us, let the bar use the money for legal services for the poor.*[32]

ASU LEGAL CLINICS—CAPITAL PUNISHMENT—STUDENT PARTICIPATION

Experiential learning is a fundamental way the Sandra Day O'Connor College of Law trains law students to become effective, ethical lawyers. But it wasn't always that way. When Dean Bender came to ASU in 1984, he pushed the concept:

> *When I first came here the leaders of the legislature, Burton Barr*[33] *and Alfredo Gutierrez*[34] *were really good people who worked together and were interested in doing good stuff so that was a fun part of the job. We got a capital punishment clinic that we got started and would help represent people. I remember one time our clinic . . . won a judgment against the state because of the way they treated prisoners, strip searches and stuff like that. That was furor in the legislature . . . . The state law school is suing the state and getting money. So we had to persuade them that it was a . . . good way of getting students educated in how to represent clients . . . they shouldn't see it as the law school against the state, they should see it as the law school helping to enforce the law properly.*[35]

DEAN BENDER AND DIVERSITY

Before 1965 and up to 1980, diversity on public state universities was narrowly focused on redressing historical wrongs against black Americans and including more women in education and the work force. Title IX[36] was passed in 1972, outlawing discrimination based on sex in educational programs or in activities that receive federal assistance. Different entities and communities looked at diversity in terms of their constituencies. Dean Bender's community was the law school and its obligations to diversify.

> *It remained a major thing to try to diversify the school . . . in a number of ways. The way the ABA thought about racial diversity and they were talking about blacks and Hispanics but I was interested in geographical diversity trying to get some students from other parts of the country and also intellectual diversity trying to get as many high-ranking students, really outstanding students who would come here and might stay, might not, but if they stayed they would really be good lawyers, they could get jobs in New York and Washington and Los Angeles and the school's influence would spread. . . . [Provost] Kinsinger was very supportive . . . and [tried] to free up scholarship money to get . . . [outstanding] students who wouldn't otherwise come here . . . because we were giving them [] a good education [and] financial assistance for that and also using scholarship money to get minority students because it became clear that that was the key to a minority population that so many minority students especially the ones who we could attract had great financial need and if you couldn't give them enough financial support they couldn't come. And by having scholarship money available to them we were able to dramatically increase the number of minority students and also get students from out of state, really good students to upgrade the student body.*[37]

INTERACTIONS WITH THE JUDICIARY

Dean Bender had always interacted with the judiciary and felt comfortable in judicial circles, debates, and advocated for judicial independence. In return, the judiciary frequently called on him on issues of common interest. But as a dean in a Western state, he had limited knowledge of the legal and judicial issues facing Native Americans. That changed in the mid-1980s.

> *I got involved with Frank Gordon who was then Chief Justice . . . he was really interested in Indian stuff. He had been a judge in Kingman . . . . He invited me up to the Hopi reservation one weekend . . . [to meet] the Hopi Tribal Judge Delford Leslie[38] [he] thought it would be interesting if I got to know him, he was a young guy not a lawyer. And so I went up there and I met Delford and we formed a relationship that was really interesting. And the Hopis asked me to come up and do a survey of their court system to see what changes should be made because there was a lot of controversy within the tribe about whether they should have a full-time chief judge, or [even] whether he should be Hopi . . . . I did a report for them about that and that got me involved in Indian affairs and we started a relationship with the Navajos we started sending them summer law clerks . . . Indian students and I got to work with the Navajo Supreme Court on a bunch of things and that led us into really adopting this very aggressive Indian Law program [at the law school]. Lee Price who had been involved in Indian stuff with the EPA spent a sabbatical here and just at the time when we started doing that and he was very helpful in recruiting our first class of Indian students, we had five Indian students we recruited and then that just blossomed and we got a director of the program who did a lot of time recruiting students, really invested in that. We started teaching more stuff, Bill Canby had done that while he was here, but when he left to go on the Ninth Circuit there was really nobody, but John Leshy taught Indian Law occasionally but there was no strong presence so we tried to hire people who were really into Indian law and we tried to get more Indian students . . . we tried to build relationships with the tribe that we could offer them legal services and send externs out there we started running classes for tribal judges and things like that took off.[39]*

ASU LAW'S CLINICAL EDUCATION PROGRAMS

Ms. Alcorn pivoted and asked Dean Bender about his efforts to build clinics at ASU.

> *Well, we brought people here . . . who were really interested in clinical education . . . this is a big issue, remains a big issue on the faculty . . . my view of that was that people who teach clinical courses are at the same level of prestige, power, or whatever authority as any faculty member. It's just as important, and so we tried to get people who were of good quality that they would suffice as regular faculty members teaching regular courses. [It] wasn't that they were second-class people who weren't good enough to teach regular [law school classes]. We tried to attract people who were really good, tenure track faculty members who would give the clinical programs the same status as the other programs had and I think we were somewhat . . . successful in doing that. And like Cathy O'Grady now who is directing the programs this year . . . . She's always had an interest in clinical education and she's really smart and she's a full time tenured faculty member. And you know that didn't used to happen . . . . Bob Bartels and Gary Lowenthal would do some stuff in the clinic but they were regular faculty members doing clinical stuff. People who just did clinical stuff were of a lower category. And we tried to upgrade that and attract better people here and expand the programs. I think that's been somewhat successful although it could be more successful in my view.*[40]

MINORITY RECRUITMENT OF STUDENTS AND FACULTY

Minority recruitment of both students and faculty was a focus, but, in his words, "less successful." He explained it to Ms. Alcorn:

> *Yeah, I think we were, somewhat less successful maybe because there is more competition. But yeah we significantly increased the black population and the Hispanic population and we've had some outstanding students in both of those areas. We've been not so good about Hispanic faculty and it's been hard to keep black faculty here. It's not a great, there's not a great black community here and so it's hard to get people to think of this, black people who grew up in the east for example, to think of this as a place they want to come and that's still our problem. But we've done, we've made some progress in that area.*[41]

Dean Paul Bender, 1984 to 1989

CURRICULUM CHANGES—INTERDISCIPLINARY PROGRAMS

By the turn of the twenty-first century interdisciplinary education in law schools was the "new thing." A long, comprehensive law review article by Prof. Kim Diana Connolly aptly defined the wide scale effort by law schools to become *interdisciplinary*.

> *Legal problems are like elephants: examining them from only one perspective gives a distorted image of the whole. In order to understand legal problems, lawyers often need to examine them from the perspective of multiple disciplines. Likewise, successful legal problem solving sometimes means that lawyers need to be able to collaborate with other professionals in order to address a client's problems. Yet traditional legal education does little to provide law students with the skills relevant to working with non-legal ideas and the professionals who are trained in those ideas. The typical law school graduate is ill prepared, in other words, to assess the elephant.*[42]

LEAVING ASU FROM 1994 TO 1997 TO SERVE IN THE U.S. JUSTICE DEPARTMENT IN WASHINGTON

Professors and deans sometimes leave academia for public or private practice. When they do, most don't come back. ASU was lucky. Dean Bender came back.

> *I had worked in the Solicitor General's office in the mid-sixties when I was [at] Penn. Some of my classmates were there ... I had met Ralph Spritzer who was then the senior person in the office and Archie Cox was the Solicitor General and Ralph said well why don't you come here for a summer ... during summer vacation and work in the office ... Archie thought that was a great idea being an academic and they started bringing people in I think I was the second one to come from a law school to spend some time in the office. And that was really interesting stuff and then I spent about a year and a half in the office. I took a leave and I did argue some cases and I came very close to staying there at that time in the office. But instead I went back to Penn. And so when Clinton got elected ... he appointed Drew Days a Yale faculty*

member to be Solicitor General. And I had known Drew for years because he was in charge of a program that the Legal Defense Fund holds every fall where they bring their cooperating lawyers from all over the country to come and do a three-day update on civil rights law . . . . They had asked me to do a session every year on the Supreme Court and I've been doing that for a number of years and Drew was in charge of that program. [When] Drew got to be Solicitor General out of the blue he called me and said would I come and be his Principal Deputy which was what they now called the job of the senior person in the office other than the Solicitor General . . . . by that time it was a political appointment it wasn't something you got through seniority. So he could appoint somebody with the president's approval to that job. And it was so tempting . . . because I knew it was a wonderful job and got you to argue before the [Supreme Court] which I love to do and be involved in a whole range of interesting issues, the Principal Deputy had traditionally done civil rights related work. And so with some reluctance because we were enjoying ourselves here [in Arizona] we decided we'd go to Washington so I did that for three plus years and then Drew had to go back to Yale and somebody else came in and they wanted to have their own Principal Deputy so I came back here . . . . There were a lot of frustrations also because I was not happy with a number of positions that the Clinton administration was taking for example gays in the military, those restrictions but overall it was a rewarding thing to do, I really enjoyed it.[43]

UNITED STATES SUPREME COURT ORAL ARGUMENTS

So far, Dean Bender has argued "twenty-plus" cases before SCOTUS. Ms. Alcorn asked him about those cases.

> *[In the three years I spent as the Principal Deputy Solicitor General (1994–97)] I argued about five cases a year . . . . Basically about one case a month. And then supervised a whole lot of briefs and other people supervised other people arguing. So, yeah it was a lot of fun . . . . The court at that time still [was] really interesting [] to argue before because they're very active they all ask questions except for Thomas . . . John Roberts who had that job as Principal Deputy before I did, has been very active . . . . in some ways*

it's like you are running a seminar with nine obnoxious students who just keep interrupting you and asking questions. But they're good questions and its challenging. And it's very conversational and really comfortable. More comfortable to argue there than anywhere else because you're on a level with them physically you are speaking straight at them they're not above you, and you're on a level with them intellectually. They treat you as an equal most of the time and they're interested in what you have to say and . . . you're interested in what they have to say and there is a back and forth and some of it is open minded and it's just, a lot of them are academics . . . [Justice] Breyer . . . obviously has teaching experience . . . [Justice] Ruth Ginsburg[44] *is also a long time academic.*

STUDENT LEADERSHIP AND AFFIRMATIVE ACTION ADMISSIONS

Dean Bender's views and preferences on politically sensitive issues were well known at ASU. He told Ms. Alcorn:

It's a big issue on the faculty about the status of clinical people and the tension [it created.] Some wanted [clinical people] relegated to a second-class status and wanted . . . clinical education to that second class status . . . I was in the camp of people who wanted [first-class status for clinical teachers]. I also was interested in having more student involvement in the governing of the law school, [but] there was not a lot of faculty enthusiasm for that . . . . The affirmative action stuff was controversial and a number of members of the faculty then and still who were not really in favor of an aggressive affirmative action program. Who think that when you recruit a lot of Indian students or black students or Hispanic students whose LSAT scores are lower than the general population of the school that that drags the school down in ratings . . . and hurts the prestige of the school and so there's a lot of tension . . . . same thing with recruiting faculty . . . some people who think it is important to have some racial diversity on the faculty and there's some people who think it's not important, why do you care about that? . . . . Here I think we've been somewhat successful although not as successful as I would like to be in diversifying the faculty.[45]

THE SANDRA DAY O'CONNOR COLLEGE OF LAW

WHERE IS THE SCHOOL GOING?

Marianne Alcorn's long interview with Dean Bender took place August 14, 2006. They had been discussing his deanship, from 1984 to 1989, and his life in Washington, DC, from 1994 to 1997. She closed the interview by asking for a closing comment.

> *I haven't really paid attention recently to the directions the school is going [as of 2006]. The faculty has gotten a lot bigger I know. I've been, again this is just impressionistic because I don't know enough about it, but I don't think I'm really happy about the direction the whole university is going towards more commercial interest and more interest in affiliations with corporations and aiding the corporate world and stuff like that. I mean some of that stuff is good, but I think that a university—and this is happening at universities all over the country—should not become too dominated by the corporate world, the financial world, and I think some of that probably is happening at the law school. I think the president of the university has a real interest in us being part of that movement toward more business related curriculum and courses. So, I would like . . . to have more emphasis on teaching people how to think about problems, analyze problems. More emphasis on exposing people to the good they can do in other areas representing the poor, representing ordinary kinds of clients, helping to draft legislation to help the masses of people as well as to help corporations and interests like that. So I'm not sure that the school is entirely, the whole university is entirely going in the right direction in that regard. A lot of the additions to the faculty have been in business law and international law. We [were weak] in some of that stuff and it's good to expand it, but I think we may be leaning a little too much in that direction.*[46]

Trish White was dean when Ms. Alcorn took Dean Bender's Oral History. She was succeeded by Paul Berman, who in 2011 was succeeded by Douglas Sylvester. Whether Deans White, Berman, or Sylvester considered Dean Bender's closing thoughts is not readily apparent. But there has been a noticeable increase in distinguished faculty whose scholarly interests are in business and international law.

Dean Paul Bender, 1984 to 1989

1 Willard Pedrick (1965 to 1976); Ernest Gellhorn (1976 to 1978); Alan Matheson (1978 to 1984); Paul Bender (1984 to 1989); Richard Morgan (1989 to 1997); Patricia White (1997 to 2007); Paul Berman (2007 to 2010); Douglas Sylvester (2010 to date).

2 "Prof. Paul Bender," The Federalist Society, accessed March 12, 2020, https://fedsoc.org/contributors/paul-bender.

3 Project Director, Study of Criminal Justice Reform in Philadelphia, Greater Philadelphia Movement, 1967–1968; General Counsel, United States Commission on Obscenity and Pornography, 1968–1970; Senior Advisor and Reporter, Panel on Human Rights and United States Foreign Policy, United Nations Association of the USA, 1978–1979; Consultant, Canadian Department of Justice, Charter Litigation and Issues Relating to Free Expression and Equality Rights, 1984; Chair, Governor's Task Force on Medical Malpractice Insurance, State of Arizona, 1988–89; Facilitator, National Dialogue Between the Museum Community and Indian Tribes Regarding Repatriation of Human Remains and Religious and Cultural Items, Heard Museum, Phoenix, AZ, 1989–90; Chair, State Bar of Arizona Committee on Implementation of Victims' Rights Amendment to Arizona Constitution, 1990–91; Chair, Arizona Supreme Court Commission on Minorities in the Judiciary, 1991–93. Arbitrator for Gila River Indian Community in arbitration with State of Arizona regarding Indian Gaming, 1998; Neutral Arbitrator in arbitration between New Mexico Indian Tribes and the State of New Mexico regarding Indian Gaming, 1998. "Resume: Paul Bender," Arizona State University, accessed March 12, 2020, https://isearch.asu.edu/profile/274462/cv.

4 *Cases and Materials on the Arizona Constitution* (1997) with annual updates; Volume I, Political and Civil Rights in the United States, 4th ed. (with N. Dorsen and B. Neuborne), Little Brown & Co., 1976 (primary responsibility for chapters on Privacy, Defamation, Obscenity, Commercial Speech, the Right to Travel and the Rights of Mental Patients, Prisoners and Military Personnel); Volume II, Political and Civil Rights in the United States, 4th ed. (with N. Dorsen, B. Neuborne, and S. Law), Little Brown & Co., 1979 (primary responsibility for chapters on Equal Protection, State Action, Congressional Power, Post Civil War Legislation and Title VI of the 1964 Civil Rights Act); Supplements to Volumes I and II, Political and Civil Rights in the United States, 4th ed. (with N. Dorsen, B. Neuborne, S. Law and J. Gora), 1978, 1980, 1981, 1982; Materials on Litigation, Reginald Heber Smith Community Lawyer Fellowship Program (with A. Amsterdam, 1968), (with A. Amsterdam and R. Sobel, 1969). "Resume: Paul Bender."

5 Developments in the Law. Defamation, 69 Harv. L. Rev. 875 (1956) (group note); Book Note: Professional Negligence, 69 Harv. L. Rev. 790 (1956); The Supreme Court. 1955 Term, 70 Harv. L. Rev. 95 (1956) (supervising editor); Developments in the Law. Remedies Against the United States and Its Officials. 70 Harv. L. Rev. 827 (1957) (supervising editor). "Resume: Paul Bender."

6 The Retroactive Effect of an Overruling Constitutional Decision, 110 U. Pa. L. Rev. 650 (1962); Product Simulation, 64 Colum. L. Rev. 1228 (1964); The Definition of "Obscene" Under Existing Law, in Vol. II, Technical Report of the Commission on Obscenity and Pornography (1970); Implications of *Stanley v. Georgia,* in Vol. II, Technical Report of the Commission on Obscenity and Pornography (1970); The Techniques of Subtle Erosion: The Nixon Court, *Harper's Magazine,* December, 1972 (winner of American Bar Association Gavel Award, 1973); The Obscenity Muddle, *Harper's Magazine,* February, 1973; The Privacies of Life, *Harper's Magazine,* April, 1974; The Reluctant Court, Civil Liberties Review, Fall, 1975; Constitutional Law, in Society of American Law Teachers, Looking at Law School (Taplinger, 1977, 1984, 1996 revised ed.); Book Review: The Brethren (by Woodward & Armstrong), 128 U. Pa. L. Rev. 716 (1980); The Judicial Protection of Rights, in The U.S. Bill of Rights and the Canadian Charter of Rights and Freedoms, W. R. McKercher, ed. (Ontario Economic Council, 1983); Justifications for Limiting Constitutionally Guaranteed Rights and Freedoms: The Proper Role of Section One of the Canadian Charter, 13 Manitoba L. J. 669(1983); Book Review: Is the Burger Court Really Like the Warren Court?, Review of "The Burger Court: The Counter-Revolution That Wasn't" (Blasi, ed.), U. Mich. L. Rev. 635 (1984); *Privacy, in Our Endangered Rights* (Dorsen, ed.) (Pantheon Books, 1984); The Canadian Charter of Rights and Freedoms and the United States Bill of Rights: A Comparison, 28 McGill L.J. 811 (1983); The Obscenity and Pornography Report, in The Media. *Social Science and Social Policy for Children: Different Paths to a Common Goal,* Rubinstein & Brown, eds. (Ablex Publ. Corp., 1985); *Free Expression, in The Limitation of Human Rights in Comparative Constitutional Law* (Maestral, et al., eds.) (Les Editions Yvon Blais, Inc., 1986); Judicial Activism Under State Constitutions, 21 Rutgers L.J. 1113 (1990) (with E.M. Maltz); Constitutional Doctrines Relevant to Ethnic and Cultural Diversity in the United States, in Harmonizing Arizona's Ethnic & Cultural Diversity, Background Report for 60th Arizona Town Hall (1992); 1990 Arizona Repatriation Legislation, 24 Az. St. L.J. 391 (1992); Community and the First Amendment, 29 Az. St. L.J. 485 (1997); The Arizona Supreme Court. Its 1997–1998 Decisions, 31 Az. St. L.J. 1 (1999); Foreword: The School Tax

Credit Case-A Study in Constitutional Misinterpretation, 32 AZ. St. L.J. 1 (2000); Does Copyright Violate the First Amendment? In Kaplan, An Unhurried View of Copyright Republished with Contributions from Friends (Matthew Bender 2005); The Constitutionality of Proposed Federal Database Protection Legislation, 28 Dayton L.R. 143 (2003); Justice Stanley Feldman: An Extraordinary Judicial Career, 66 Albany L.R. 593 (2003); The Constitutionality of Campaign Finance Legislation After *Buckley v. Valeo*, 34 Az.St.L.J. 1106 (2002); Some Thoughts on the Interpretation of Arizona Constitutional Rights, 35 Az.St.L.J. 295 (2003). "Resume: Paul Bender."

7 Conversation with Learned Hand (with L. Henkin) (unpublished, 1961); Police Brutality in Chester, Pennsylvania, March-April 1964, Report prepared for the Greater Philadelphia Branch of the American Civil Liberties Union, 1964; The 24-Hour Magistrate's Court in Philadelphia, Report prepared for the Philadelphia District Attorney and the Greater Philadelphia Movement, 1968; Obscenity Controls, Consultant's report for the National Commission on Reform of Federal Criminal Laws, (in Working Papers of the Commission, pp. 1203 et. seg., GPO 1970); Legal Considerations Relating to Erotica, Legal Panel Report of the Commission on Obscenity and Pornography (in Report of the Commission, pp. 293, et. seq., 1980 (reporter and principal draftsperson); Legislative Recommendations and Drafts of Proposed Legislation, in Report of the Commission on Obscenity and Pornography, 1970, pp. 51 et. seg., 1980 (reporter and principal draftsperson); Cases and Materials on Federal Civil Rights Legislation (unpublished teaching materials, 1971); Cases and Materials on Prisoner's Rights (unpublished teaching materials, 1972); Materials for Law School 1: Contemporary Legal Issues (unpublished teaching materials for undergraduate course in constitutional law, Univ. of Pa., 1972); *Encyclopedia Americana,* "Obscenity," (Vol. 20, p. 595, 1980); Report on the Deliberations of the Committee on Maintenance of Revolutionary Values, Bicentennial Conference on the United States Constitution (with M. Field) (American Academy of Political and Social Science, 1980; also in The Annals, July 1976); United States Foreign Policy and Human Rights: Principles. Priorities. Practice, United Nations Association of the USA, National Policy Panel Report, 1979 (reporter and principal draftsperson); *Encyclopedia of American Constitutional Law,* (Levy & Karst, eds.), Retroactivity of Judicial Decisions (1985); Report of the Panel for a National Dialogue on Museum/Native American Relations, Heard Museum, Phoenix, Arizona, 1990; Frequent Op-Ed. articles on State and National Legal Issues, *Arizona Republic* and other newspapers, 1990–1997. "Resume: Paul Bender."

8 Annual Lectures on Current U.S. Supreme Court Decisions and Developments, Earl Warren Legal Training Program, NAACP Legal Defense Fund, Airlie House, VA, 1976–1992; 1997–present; Lectures on The American Bill of Rights, Annual Human Rights Seminar, Canadian Human Rights Foundation, University of Prince Edward Island, Charlottetown, P.E.I., 1980–1987; Lectures on Recent U.S. Supreme Court Decisions, Pennsylvania Superior Court Judges Seminar, Philadelphia, PA, (1981–1983). Six Lectures: The Supreme Court and the Resolution of Current Political Controversies, Continuum Program, College of General Studies, University of Pennsylvania, Philadelphia, 1978; Constitutionality of Bar Examinations, Address to the Annual Meeting of the National Conference of Bar Examiners, San Francisco, CA, August 1972 (reprinted in 42 The Bar Examiner 55 (1973); The Impact of *Griswold v. Connecticut,* Address to the 10th Anniversary Seminar in Celebration of the Griswold Decision, Planned Parenthood League of Connecticut, New Haven, CN, 1975; Colloquium on Obscenity, Annenberg School, University of Pennsylvania, 1976; Challenging Professional Authority: Socratic Dialogue and Discussion, Annenberg School; Conference on the Media and the Professions, University of Pennsylvania, 1979; Judicial Disciplinary Proceedings and The Separation of Powers, Second Circuit Judicial Conference, 1979; Responding to a "Wrong" Decision of the Supreme Court, Address to the Annual Meeting of the St. Thomas More Society, Philadelphia, PA, 1979; The Burger Court and the First Amendment, Saturday Morning Forum, Alumni Society of the University of Pennsylvania Law School, March, 1980; The First Amendment and the Conduct of Judicial Business, American Bar Association, Appellate Judges' Seminar, Philadelphia, October, 1981; The Equal Protection Clause, ABA Appellate Judges Seminar, Palm Beach, FL, March 1982; The Canadian Charter of Rights and the Limits of the Criminal Sanction, Dalhousie Law School, Halifax, Canada, March 1982; The Judicial Protection of Rights, Conference on the U.S. Bill of Rights, Implications for Canada, University of Western Ontario, Canada, March 1982; Distinguished Guest Lecturer, University of Alberta Law School, Edmonton, Canada, January 1983 (Lectures on the U.S. Bill of Rights and the Canadian Charter of Rights and Freedoms); The First Amendment, Feminism and Pornography, Lecture and Panel Discussion (University of Michigan Law School, April 1983); Keynote speaker, The Charter After 18 Months, National Conference of the Canadian Institute for the Administration of Justice, Winnipeg, Canada, October, 1983; European, United States and International Law Relevant to the Canadian Charter of Rights and Freedoms, Canadian Institute for the Administration of Justice, Winnipeg, Canada, October, 1983; The Canadian Charter and the U.S. Bill of Rights, Dalhousie University Law School, Halifax, Canada, July, 1984; Enforcement of Charter Rights, Judge's Day Program, Canadian Bar Association Convention, Winnipeg, Canada, August, 1984; An American Constitutional Lawyer Looks at the Canadian Charter, University of Toronto Law

Dean Paul Bender, 1984 to 1989

School, Toronto, Canada, September, 1984; The Canadian Charter and the U.S. Bill of Rights, McGill University Law School, Montreal, Canada, 1985; Free Expression Rights, paper presented at Conference on Human Rights in Comparative Constitutional Law, Institute of Comparative Law, McGill University, Montreal, Canada, 1985; Judicial Control of the Press, the U.S. Experience, Conference on the Courts and the Media, Canadian Institute for the Administration of Justice, Montreal, Canada, 1987; Censorship in the U.S., Conference on the Suppression of Knowledge, Philadelphia Library Consortium, Library Company of Philadelphia, 1988; The Equal Protection Clause, Federal Judicial Center Lectures for Federal District and Circuit Judges, Berkeley, CA, 1986, 1987; Recent Supreme Court Civil Rights and Civil Liberties Decisions, Federal Judicial Center Lectures for Federal District and Circuit Judges: 9th Circuit, Monterey, CA, 1988, 1989; 6th Circuit, Cincinnati, OH, 1988; 8th and 10th Circuits, San Diego, CA, 1989; Understanding the Executive, Legislative and Judicial Branches, 5th Annual Arizona Legislators' Institute, Morrison Institute for Public Policy, 1988; Distinguished guest lecturer, University of Manitoba Law School, The U.S. Supreme Court (1996); Distinguished guest lecturer, University of Victoria Law School, The First Five Years of the Canadian Charter of Rights and Freedoms (1989); The Solicitor General's Office, 11th Circuit Judicial Conference (1995); The Supreme Court Today, State Bar of Arizona (1997); Qualified Immunity and The Prison Litigation Reform Act, Federal Judicial Center, Lectures for federal district judges (1997); Lying in Newsgathering, ABA Media Law Section, 1998; Recent U.S. Supreme Court Developments in Individual Rights, Wisconsin State Bar, 1998. Public Interest Litigation: Counsel for applicants to the Pennsylvania Bar challenging the racially discriminatory impact of the Pennsylvania bar examination (1970–1972); Co-Special Counsel for the United States Federal Elections Commission in *Buckley v. Valeo* (D.C. Cir. and U.S. Supreme Ct., 1975–1976); Special Counsel for U.S. Senator Robert Morgan and the U.S. Senate regarding Speech and Debate Clause issues in the Japanese Electronics Antitrust Litigation (E.D. Pa., 1978); Co-Special Counsel for the Supreme Court of Pennsylvania in *Philadelphia Newspapers v. Jerome* (U.S. Sup. Ct. 1979) (press access to judicial suppression hearings); Special Counsel for the Pennsylvania Judicial Inquiry and Review Board in *First Amendment Coalition v. Judicial Inquiry and Review Board* (E.D. Pa., 1983) (press access to proceedings of judicial disciplinary board); Counsel for the American Civil Liberties Union in challenges to conditions of confinement at Dallas institution for Defective Delinquents (E.D. Pa., 1965); the constitutionality of Mayor's proclamation banning outdoor meetings in Philadelphia (U.S. Sup. Ct., 1970); vagrancy arrests in Aspen, CO (D. Colo. 1968); Pennsylvania abortion funding legislation (3rd Cir. 1980); Arizona Individual Tax Credit Program for Private and Religious School Scholarships (U.S. Sup.Ct., D. Az 9t1i Cir. U.S. Sup.Ct. (2000–present); Az. Corporate Tax Credit Program (Az.Sup. Ct. 2006–present). *Ad-World v. Township of Doylestown,* (3rd Cir. 1982) (challenge to ordinance banning unauthorized distribution of free community newspapers); *Price v. Cohen* (E.D. Pa. 1982; 3rd Cir. 1982) (challenge to constitutionality of 1982 PA Welfare Reform Act); Paul Bender Page 11 *Arizona State Senate v. Arizonans for Fair Representation,* U.S. Supreme Court (1992); As Principal Deputy Solicitor General of the United States from 1993–1996, argued on behalf of the United States in 15 cases in the U.S. Supreme Court and had principal responsibility for the United States, briefs in about 60 U.S. Supreme Court cases, including the equal protection cases in which the U.S. was involved, cases under federal civil rights statutes and cases involving freedom of expression and freedom of religion; Counsel for respondent in *Stewart v. Martinez-Villareal,* 66 U.S.L.W. 4352 (U.S. Sup. Ct. 1998); Counsel for respondent in *South Dakota v. Yankton Sioux Tribe,* 66 U.S.L.W. 4092 (U.S. Sup. Ct. 1998); Amicus Curiae at the Court's invitation in *Beeles v. Offset Corp.,* Ariz. Supreme Ct., 1998. "Resume: Paul Bender."

9 Hearings before Constitution Subcommittee, Committee on the Judiciary, U.S. Senate, Proposed Constitutional Amendment on School Prayer (June 27, 1983); Hearing before the Subcommittee on Oversight and Management, Committee on Governmental Affairs, U.S. Senate, Social Security Disability Reviews (S. Hrg. 98–296, pp. 100, 140, 98th Cong. 1st Sess. June 8, 1983); Hearings before the Committee on the Judiciary, U.S. Senate, Proposed Constitutional Amendment to Permit Voluntary School Prayer, (S. J. Res. 199, Sept. 16, 1982; pp. 385,454); Hearings before the Subcommittees on Judicial Machinery and Constitution of the Committee on the Judiciary U.S. Senate, on Judicial Discipline and Tenure (96th Cong., 1st Sess., June 25, 1979, p. 118); Hearings before the Subcommittee on Civil and Constitutional Rights, of the Committee on the Judiciary, U.S. House of Rep., Proposed Constitutional Amendments on Abortion (94th Cong. 2nd Sess., Feb. 5, 1976, p. 113); Public Hearing on House Bill No. 1725, Pa. House of Representatives Committee on Health and Welfare, Proposed 1981 Abortion Control Act (Sept., 1981); Hearing on Proposal to Modify Funding of IOLTA (Interest on Lawyers Trust Accounts) Program, Judiciary Committee of Arizona State Senate, 1988; Hearing Before the Select Committee on Indian Affairs, U.S. Senate, Native American Grave and Reburial Protection Act, (101st Cong. 2nd Sess) (1990); Hearing Before the Select Committee on Indian Affairs, U.S. Senate, the 9th Circuit's Kennewick Man decision. "Resume: Paul Bender."

10 Sometimes formalized as "The Academy." It refers to the worldwide human group composed of professors and researchers at institutes of higher learning. The name traces back to Plato's school of philosophy, founded approximately 385 BC at Akademia, a sanctuary of Athena, the goddess of wisdom and skill, north of Athens, Greece. *See* Wikipedia, s.v., "Academy," last modified February 25, 2020, 5:28, https://en.wikipedia.org/wiki/Academy.

11 *See* Buell, Samuel W. "Becoming a Legal Scholar." *Michigan Law Review* 110, no. 6 (April 2012), 1175–90—.

12 Paul Bender, interview by Marianne Alcorn, August 14, 2006, ASU Law Oral History Project, at 1.

13 Calvert Magruder (December 26, 1893–May 22, 1968) was a United States Circuit Judge of the United States Court of Appeals for the First Circuit. Wikipedia, s.v. "Calvert Magruder," last modified October 28, 2019, 12:05, https://en.wikipedia.org/wiki/Calvert_Magruder.

14 Billings Learned Hand was an American judge and judicial philosopher. He served on the United States District Court for the Southern District of New York and later the United States Court of Appeals for the Second Circuit. Hand has been quoted more often by legal scholars and by the Supreme Court of the United States than any other lower-court judge. Wikipedia, s.v. "Learned Hand," last modified March 3, 2020, 20:50, https://en.wikipedia.org/wiki/Learned_Hand.

15 Paul Bender, interview, at 3–4.

16 Ibid., 4–5.

17 367 U.S. 643 (1961).

18 338 U.S. 25 (1949).

19 Paul Bender, interview, at 5–6.

20 "*Mapp v. Ohio:* Key Excerpts from the Majority Opinion." Landmark Supreme Court Cases. Accessed March 13, 2020. https://www.landmarkcases.org/mapp-v-ohio/mapp-v-ohio-key-excerpts-from-the-majority-opinion.

21 "What Was the Significance of *Mapp v. Ohio?*" enotes.com, accessed March 13, 2020, https://www.enotes.com/homework-help/what-would-significance-law-case-mapp-v-ohio-least-219135.

22 362 U.S. 217 (1960).

23 Wikipedia, s.v. *"Abel v. United States,"* last modified February 19. 2020, 11:28, https://en.wikipedia.org/wiki/Abel_v._United_States.

24 Paul Bender, interview, at 6.

25 Jack Kinsinger was Vice President for Academic Affairs from 1982–1987. *See* Jack Kinsinger, interview by Ted Humphrey, December 4, 2009, ASU Retirees, https://asura.asu.edu/KinsingerVideoClip.

26 Paul Bender, interview, at 6.

27 The four largest Phoenix firms in the early 1980s were Jennings, Strouss, & Salmon, Fennemore Craig, Snell & Wilmer, and Lewis & Roca.

28 "As governor, Mecham was plagued by controversy . . . and became the first U.S. governor to simultaneously face removal from office through impeachment, a scheduled recall election, and a felony indictment. He was the first Arizona governor to be impeached. Mecham served one term as a state senator before beginning a string of unsuccessful runs for public office." Wikipedia, s.v., "Evan Mecham," last modified March 11, 2020, 00:22, https://en.wikipedia.org/wiki/Evan_Mecham.

29 "Frank X. Gordon Jr. (January 9, 1929 – January 6, 2020) was a Justice of the Supreme Court of Arizona from September 16, 1975 to February 3, 1992. He served as Chief Justice from January 1987 to December 1992. Gordon was the first Supreme Court appointment under the new merit selection system, he was appointed by Governor Raul Castro." Wikipedia, s.v., "Frank Gordon Jr.," last modified January 13, 2020, 23:03, https://en.wikipedia.org/wiki/Frank_Gordon_Jr.

30 Rose Perica Mofford was an American civil servant and politician who led a 51-year career in state government. "Beginning her career with the State of Arizona as a secretary, Mofford worked her way up the ranks to become the state's first female secretary of state and first female governor." Wikipedia, s.v., "Rose Mofford," last modified December 18, 2019, 03:58, https://en.wikipedia.org/wiki/Rose_Mofford.

31 Paul Bender, interview, at 7–8.

32 Ibid., 8.

33 "Burton Barr (1917–1997) was an American Colonel, businessman and politician. He served as a Republican member of the Arizona House of Representatives from 1964 to 1986, and as its Republican Majority Leader from 1966 to 1986." Wikipedia, s.v., "Burton Barr," last modified February 18, 2020, 05:11, https://en.wikipedia.org/wiki/Burton_Barr.

34 "Alfredo Gutierrez was the District 5 representative on the governing board of the Maricopa County Community College District in Arizona. Gutierrez won a new term in the general election on November 8, 2016. In addition to his role on the board, Gutierrez [was] an immigration reform advocate, author, and former majority leader in the Arizona State Senate." "Alfredo Gutierrez," Ballotpedia, https://ballotpedia.org/Alfredo_Gutierrez.

35 Paul Bender, interview, at 8.

36 Title IX is a federal civil rights law in the United States of America that was passed as part of the Education Amendments of 1972. This is Public Law No. 92-318, 86 Stat. 235, codified at 20 U.S.C. §§ 1681–1688.

37 Paul Bender, interview, at 8–9.

38 Delford Leslie was a Hopi Tribal Judge. The Hopi are a Native American tribe, who primarily live on the 2,531,773 sq mi (6,557.26 km²) Hopi Reservation in northeastern Arizona. As of the 2010 census, there were 19,338 Hopi in the United States. The Hopi language is one of the 30 of the Uto-Aztecan language family. Wikipedia, s.v., "Hopi," last modified February 22, 2020, 1:32, https://en.wikipedia.org/wiki/Hopi.

39 Paul Bender, interview, at 9.

40 Ibid., 12.

41 Ibid., 13.

42 Kim Diana Connolly. "Elucidating the Elephant: Interdisciplinary Law School Classes." *Washington University Journal of Law & Policy* 11, no. 1 (2003): 11–61, at 13–14.

43 Ibid., 14–15.

44 Ruth Bader Ginsburg, born Joan Ruth Bader; March 15, 1933, is an American lawyer and jurist who is an Associate Justice of the U.S. Supreme Court. Ginsburg was appointed by President Bill Clinton and took the oath of office on August 10, 1993. She is the second female justice (after Sandra Day O'Connor) of four to be confirmed to the court (along with Sonia Sotomayor and Elena Kagan, who are still serving). Following O'Connor's retirement, and until Sotomayor joined the court, Ginsburg was the only female justice on the Supreme Court. During that time, Ginsburg became more forceful with her dissents, which were noted by legal observers and in popular culture. She is generally viewed as belonging to the liberal wing of the court. Ginsburg has authored notable majority opinions, including *United States v. Virginia*, *Olmstead v. L.C.*, and *Friends of the Earth, Inc. v. Laidlaw Environmental Services, Inc.* Wikipedia, s.v., "Ruth Bader Ginsburg," last modified March 13, 2020, 16:37, https://en.wikipedia.org/wiki/Ruth_Bader_Ginsburg.

45 Paul Bender, interview, at 16–17.

46 Ibid., 19.

CHAPTER 25

THE JAMES HAMM SAGA 1993 TO 2005

Getting into a good law school is hard. Getting out with a JD is harder. Passing the bar examination is exceptionally hard. And for some, getting a license to practice law is impossible. James Joseph Hamm is living proof of that. He had a compelling story, a solid record, a bright and engaging mind, a purpose in life, a law degree, and he passed the bar examination. It wasn't enough. He did not prove he was of sufficient moral character to practice law in Arizona.

Some stories are best told like horse races—starting with the outcome and finishing at the starting gate. Mr. Hamm's story is one of those. The LexisNexis "overview" crisply defines the outcome.

> *Some 30 years earlier, the applicant [James Hamm], was convicted of a murder. The applicant spent time in prison, and before his release, he earned a bachelor's degree. After his release, but while he was on parole, the applicant was accepted to law school, which he successfully completed. He then took and passed the Bar examination. The supreme court, here, rejected the applicant's request to be admitted to the Bar because the applicant failed show he was of good moral character . . . . The supreme court noted the applicant demonstrated a lack of candor before the Committee [on Character and Fitness] and*

355

the supreme court. The supreme court further noted the applicant's failure to accept full responsibility for his serious criminal misconduct. Also, the applicant failed to accept responsibility for parental financial obligations to his son, who was born before the applicant went to prison. The supreme court concluded that the applicant had not met the stringent standard that applied to an applicant in his position who sought to show his present good moral character. Finally, the supreme court noted that the applicant had received a full opportunity to be heard.[1]

CHARACTER & FITNESS TO PRACTICE

Hamm's case was resolved under Arizona Supreme Court Rules 34, 35 and 36. They establish process and procedure for all admissions to licensure in Arizona courts. The initial assessment of whether the applicant is of "good moral character"[2] and fit to practice law is done by the Committee on Character and Fitness. It evaluates all applicants for licensure and "may recommend an applicant for admission *only* if that applicant, in addition to meeting other requirements, satisfies the Committee that he or she is of good moral character."[3] The applicant bears the burden of establishing his or her good moral character.[4] If in the screening process, there is any conduct that might call into question the applicant's moral fitness to practice law, the Committee on Character and Fitness (CC&F) takes these factors into account:

> *(a) The applicant's age, experience and general level of sophistication at the time of the conduct; (b) The recency of the conduct; (c) The reliability of the information concerning the conduct; (d) The seriousness of the conduct; (e) Consideration given by the applicant to relevant laws, rules and responsibilities at the time of the conduct; (f) The factors underlying the conduct; (g) The cumulative effect of the conduct (h) The evidence of rehabilitation; (i) The applicant's positive social contributions since the conduct; (j) The applicant's candor in the admissions process (k) The materiality of any omissions or misrepresentations by the applicant.*[5]

When conduct of an applicant involves the commission of a violent crime,[6] CC&F must hold an informal hearing.[7] Under Arizona law, "[t]here is a presumption, rebuttable by clear and convincing evidence presented at a proceeding, that an applicant who has been convicted of a misdemeanor involving a serious crime or of any felony must be denied admission."[8] "If three or more Committee members who attended the hearing or who have read the entire record do not recommend admission of an applicant, the Committee must hold a formal hearing to consider whether to recommend the applicant for admission to the Bar. If the applicant fails to convince the Committee of his or her good moral character, the Committee has a *duty not to recommend* that person to this Court."[9]

On receiving a CC&F report not recommending an applicant for licensure, the Court independently determines whether the applicant possesses good moral character and, based upon that determination, grants or denies the candidate's application. Although the Court gives serious consideration to the facts, as found by and its CC&F, the ultimate decision rests with the Supreme Court. The ultimate question is whether the applicant has established good moral character.[10]

The Court considers each case on its own merits. "Upright character" is something more than an absence of bad character. It means that an applicant for admission "must have conducted himself as a man of upright character ordinarily would, should, or does. Such character expresses itself not in negatives nor in following the line of least resistance, but quite often in the will to do the unpleasant thing if it is right, and the resolve not to do the pleasant thing if it is wrong."[11]

The Court's concern must be with an applicant's "present moral character."[12] Past misconduct and bad acts may relate to an applicant's current character. Where an applicant for admission to the bar has a criminal record, his or her burden of establishing present good moral character takes on the added weight of proving full and complete rehabilitation after conviction. Although a prior conviction is not conclusive of a lack of present good moral character, it adds to his burden of establishing present good character by requiring convincing proof of full and complete rehabilitation.[13]

An applicant for initial admission attempting to overcome the negative implications of a serious felony on his moral character likewise must overcome a greater burden for more serious crimes. In the case of extremely damning past misconduct, showing rehabilitation may be virtually impossible to make. The Arizona Supreme Court does not have a *per se* rule excluding an applicant whose past includes serious criminal misconduct. However, its opinion in *In re Hamm* confirms that no other jurisdiction has admitted to practice "a person convicted of first-degree murder."[14] It generally agrees with those other jurisdictions that hold any applicant with serious criminal misconduct in his background must make "extraordinary showing of rehabilitation, and present good moral character to be admitted to the practice of law."[15]

The Arizona Supreme Court's lengthy opinion describes the 1974 murders, Hamm's role in them, a summary of Hamm's prison experience, his efforts toward rehabilitation, and relevant parts of his personal life once he was released from prison in 1992.

THE 1974 MURDERS

The relevant personal and criminal history is set out in the Arizona Supreme Court's Opinion denying his admission to practice. He was twenty-six years old and living on the streets of Tucson. Although he had attended divinity school and worked as a part-time pastor, Hamm describes his life in 1974 as reflecting personal and social failures. In 1973, he had separated from his wife, with whom he had a son. Although he had no criminal record, he supported himself by selling small quantities of marijuana. He used marijuana and other drugs and abused alcohol.

> *On September 6, 1974, Hamm met two young men who identified themselves as college students from Missouri. The two, Willard Morley and Zane Staples, came to Tucson to buy twenty pounds of marijuana. Hamm agreed to sell it to them, but apparently could not acquire that quantity of marijuana. Rather than call off the transaction, Hamm and two accomplices, Garland Wells and Bill Reeser, agreed to rob Staples and Morley of the money intended for the purchase. On September 7, Wells gave Hamm a gun to use during the robbery. Later that day, Wells and Hamm directed Morley and Staples to drive to the outskirts of Tucson, purportedly to complete the drug transaction; Reeser followed in another vehicle. Both Wells and Hamm carried guns; Morley and Staples were unarmed. Hamm sat behind Morley, the driver, and Wells sat behind Staples. At some point, Hamm detected that Staples was becoming suspicious. As Morley stopped the car, and without making any demand on the victims for money, Hamm shot Morley in the back of the head, killing him. At the same time, Wells shot Staples. Hamm then shot Staples in the back as he tried to escape and shot Morley again. Wells*

also shot Morley, then pursued Staples, whom he ultimately killed outside of the car. Hamm and Wells took $1,400.00 from the glove compartment and fled the scene in the van driven by Reeser. They left the bodies of Morley and Staples lying in the desert.

Hamm took his share of the money and visited his sister in California. At the hearing held to consider his application to the Bar, he told the Committee he "was compelled to come back to Tucson," despite knowing he probably would be caught. Police officers arrested Hamm shortly after his return. While in custody, he told the police that Morley and Staples were killed in a gun battle during the drug deal. Initially charged with two counts of first-degree murder and two counts of armed robbery, Hamm pled guilty to one count of first-degree murder and was sentenced to life in prison, with no possibility of parole for twenty-five years. [16]

HAMM'S EFFORTS AT REHABILITATION IN AND OUT OF PRISON

Once in prison, Hamm began taking steps toward rehabilitation and became a model prisoner. After spending one year in maximum security, he applied for and received a job in a computer-training program that allowed him to be transferred to medium security. Once in medium security, Hamm apparently took advantage of any and every educational opportunity the prison system offered. He completed certificates in yoga and meditation and, on his own, studied Jungian psychology. He helped fellow inmates learn to read and write and to take responsibility for their actions. He obtained a bachelor's degree in applied sociology, summa cum laude, *from Northern Arizona University through a prison study program.*

While in prison, he met and married Donna Leone. She and Hamm founded Middle Ground Prison Reform (Middle Ground), a prisoner and prisoner family advocacy organization involved in lobbying for laws related to the criminal justice system and prisons. Middle Ground also provides public education about those topics.

> *In 1989, the Governor, acting on the recommendation of the Arizona Board of Pardons and Parole (the Board), commuted Hamm's sentence. When he had served nearly seventeen years, in July 1992, the Board released Hamm on parole, conditioned upon his abstention from alcohol or drugs, drug and alcohol testing, and fifteen hours of community service each month. In December 2001, the Arizona Board of Executive Clemency granted his third application for absolute discharge.*
>
> *Between his release in August 1992 and his absolute discharge in December 2001, Hamm performed thousands of hours of community service. He advocated for prisoners' rights in various forums by writing position papers, appearing on radio programs, testifying in legislative hearings, and speaking at churches, schools, and civic organizations. He also appeared in a public service video encouraging children not to do drugs or join gangs. Hamm now works as the Director of Advocacy Services at Middle Ground Prison Reform.*[17]

He applied for and was admitted to Arizona State University's College of Law for the fall semester of 1993. While there is no written confirmation of his post-law school intentions, there is a record of his first-year acceptance as a 1L student. The Arizona Board of Regents was aware, as was the general student body, that Hamm was on campus and in the law school. ABOR board minutes, September 23, 1993, confirm that over 60 percent of the students in the Student Senate support the decision of the law school to admit James Hamm.[18]

Following the specific discussion about Hamm, the regents were given an update by ASU President Lattie Coor on the ASU Law School admissions process.

> *He reported his meeting with the Provost [Dr. Milton Glick] and the Dean of the Law College [Professor Paul Bender] and they reviewed the admissions process for the law school as there had been considerable attention to the process as a result of the publicity surrounding the admission of James Hamm . . . The law school and its admissions committee had acted properly and thoughtfully within the policies of the State of Arizona and the University . . . The faculty is currently reviewing its admissions process. Dr. Coor has requested that the Dean and the law school faculty make sure that there is full thoughtfulness in future admissions decisions when a candidate*

> *reveals criminal background at the level of felony and when a felon is recommended by the law school admissions committee, the concurrence of the Dean be made a part of the process.*[19]

While on parole, Hamm graduated from the Arizona State University College of Law in 1996. Three years later, in July 1999, Hamm took and passed the Arizona Bar Examination. He waited until 2003 to file his Character and Fitness Report with the Committee. The Committee recommended to the Court he not be admitted to practice because he had not proved he was of sufficient moral character to be a lawyer. The Committee highlighted candor issues, accused him of practicing law without a license, and noted facts concerning his failure to pay child support in their report to the Supreme Court.[20]

THE ARIZONA SUPREME COURT OPINION

The Court's opinion recognizes that Hamm did not just commit a serious felony and that his past criminal conduct was beyond dispute.[21] It noted that Hamm acknowledges that no more serious criminal conduct exists than committing first-degree murder. It said murder is the most serious crime known to the law.[22] Most important, the Court said, "Indeed, we are aware of no instance in which a person convicted of first-degree murder has been admitted to the practice of law."[23]

If no other person in American history has ever been admitted to practice law after being convicted of first-degree murder, the question Hamm must have asked himself is *what* is my chance? He was on the wrong side of history—no one had ever done what he was trying to do. He must have known that. He had to prove by clear and convincing evidence that he *was* of good moral character. To do that before a large panel of lawyers on the CC&F and the five justices of Arizona's Supreme Court, he faced an enormous legal challenge—overcoming the precedential *Greenberg* case.[24]

> *[Greenberg] was involved in selling marihuana during his early years in law school.... He denied the allegations.... [He] had not filed a tax return ... because the only income he had was from the sale of marihuana and had ignored the inquiries of the Internal Revenue Services. Eventually he filed the tax return and admitted involvement in the marihuana (sic)*

> transactions. *The court concluded that the applicant had not sustained his burden of showing good and moral character. It noted that his decision to make a full disclosure came in slow stages, that he had recently told bar counsel that his position of noninvolvement was unchanged, and he answered a [CC&F] question regarding incidents that had a bearing on his character for admission to the bar in an unresponsive way.*[25]

The *Greenberg* case was routinely cited as precedent in nearly every case for admission to practice that involved any doubtful character issues. Hamm's burden was staggering—he had to somehow convince a seasoned supreme court that his case was the one-in-a-million and that *Greenberg* was not binding precedent.

THE PUBLIC REACTION TO THE HAMM CASE

The Arizona Republic's headline the week after the oral argument in the Arizona Supreme Court screamed "Freed Killer Wants OK to Practice Law."[26] Michael Kiefer quoted Hamm's argument to the Court: "I stand before this court having admitted a violent crime in 1974."[27] Kiefer reported Hamm's argument admitting shame, grief, and remorse for shooting two men during a robbery and that "one of them died before my eyes, at my hand, an innocent man."[28] Hamm represented himself. The CC&F was represented by Lawrence McDonough. He said Hamm was "stuck with candor problems."[29] Kiefer noted Justice Andrew Hurwitz saying in open court that his research suggested no one convicted of first-degree murder has ever been admitted to practice.

The president of the State Bar noted the bar's position: "We think there should be a bright-line on premeditated first-degree murder; [they] should not be licensed to practice law."[30] Defense lawyer Ulises Ferragut countered, "I think the man borders on genius.... I think James Hamm is the poster child for rehabilitation, and if we can't see fit to admit him to practice law based on his years of rehabilitation and service to the community, then is there really system by which someone can be rehabilitated?"[31]

Kiefer also reported on Hamm's courthouse steps remarks, just after the arguments concluded. "The horror of that crime is so significant that I think it overwhelms people.... It won't change the burden I carry.... When I wake up tomorrow morning I'm going to have the same burden on my back that I had 31 years ago when I shot that man to death. That's not going to change."[32]

Hamm's application was so unusual it made the *New York Times* in December 2001.[33] It posed Hamm's quest as more a debt he owed to himself than one the State of Arizona owed him. "But for Mr. Hamm, the status of murderer-turned-lawyer specializing in prisoners' rights would not so much answer the age-old question of what rights should accrue to a man who has paid his debt to society as fulfill a commitment he made upon sentencing: that he would accept full responsibility for what he did and make the best of his situation."[34]

The *New York Times* reported "noisy outrage" directed at Arizona State University School of Law for accepting him as a student in 1993, and by lawyers and lawmakers who contended "a man with such a background was not fit for the profession . . . . 'To view the photos of the men who died at [his] hands would make one vomit,' said Dan Cracchiolo, a Phoenix lawyer who for years has expressed outrage at Mr. Hamm's efforts to become a lawyer. 'To think that a noble profession like ours would admit someone who did this is so contrary to the notion of fairness and fair play . . . you lower the bar. What's next, letting in a rapist or child molester?'"[35]

The 2001 President of the Arizona State Senate was also quoted in the *Times* article. "He is winning support in some quarters . . . '[I have moved from] mildly objecting to ambivalent . . . . I'm at the Capitol every day . . . nobody ever brings it up.'"[36] The *Times* closed the article with Hamm's say on the matter. "'I'm someone who started out with a psychological breakdown . . . . Now, I believe a lot of people can identify with me—not because I committed a crime but because I've dealt with something difficult and struggled to do the right thing. I will abide with whatever they decide.'"[37]

THE 2019 VIEW OF REHABILITATION, LAW SCHOOL ADMISSIONS, & LICENSURE

Time is a great teacher, but unfortunately it kills all its pupils.[38] "Time is said to be eternal. It is said that it has neither a beginning nor an end. Yet men are able to measure it as years, months, days, hours, minutes and seconds. They have also given meanings to the words—past, present and future. True, time has a meaning. It moves. What was yesterday is *not* today. What is today will not be tomorrow.

Yesterday is gone. Today is and tomorrow is yet to come. Yet time is said to have no holiday. It exists always."[39]

The Arizona Supreme Court denied Hamm's application for licensure on December 7, 2005. As of 2019, no one in America convicted of first-degree premeditated murder has been licensed to practice law. But time erodes the sense of right and wrong—even in the legal profession.

Twenty-three years after Hamm graduated from the ASU College of Law, the *New York Times* brought the subject back up—this time in an article about the Tulane College of Law. The February 1, 2019 headline screamed murder again. "He Committed Murder—Then He Graduated From an Elite Law School—Would You Hire Him as Your Attorney?"[40] This article is not about James Hamm. It's about a man named Bruce Reilly, a speaker at a 2019 Princeton University conference. The subject was artificial intelligence in public policy, specifically decisions about releasing prison inmates on bail or parole. Mr. Reilly said, "'Statistically . . . the safest person to let out of prison is a murderer.'"[41] He argued, "a person convicted of lesser crimes often cycles in and out of prison, while someone serving a long sentence for murder has typically matured out of crime by the time he is released."[42]

Mr. Reilly knew what he was talking about. He killed a man in 1992 with a fireplace poker, pled guilty to second-degree murder and was sentenced to twenty years in prison. In prison, he became a legal adviser to fellow inmates, studied case law, and wrote dozens of court briefs. He was paroled in 2005, enrolled in a small college, took the law school admissions test, and was accepted to the Tulane College of Law in 2011. He got his JD, but not his license to practice.

It is likely that neither James Hamm nor Bruce Reilly can ever practice law. And there is at least one more graduate of a top law school to hold a JD, pass a bar exam, and never become a lawyer. Hamm was not the only convicted murderer to graduate from ASU Law. In the spring of 1994, a man named Michael Davis finished his three years and passed all his courses. However, he had hidden his conviction on his admission records. Once the school found out, they withheld his diploma.[43]

Statistically, the odds against convicted murderers are insurmountable. All states have character and fitness committees. All have rules similar to Arizona. All are unlikely to find as a matter of law that post-crime rehabilitation can restore the level of moral fitness and character we expect from lawyers. The rules are rigid because they are designed solely to protect clients, not to advance the careers of lawyers.

These rules are not predicated on forgiveness. They are predicated on protecting the public. And they recognize what the *New York Times* called "the sheer hysteria of a murder conviction."[44] But it's not just "murder." It's premeditated, first-degree, with malice aforethought, murder that creates sheer hysteria.[45]

Courts have long distinguished between immorality and murder. "This court does not sit as a court of morality. [It sits] to inflict punishment against those who offend the social law."[46]

"Gentlemen of the jury, the charge against the prisoner is murder, and the punishment of murder is death; and that simple statement is sufficient to suggest to us the awful solemnity of the occasion which brings you and me face to face."[47]

American courts will likely come face to face with other convicted murderers seeking a license to practice law and trying to overcome disallowing committees on character and fitness. Petitioners in those cases would do well to remember what Anne Hocking, the famous British mystery writer said: "Other sins only speak, murder cries out."[48]

---

1 *In re Hamm*, 211 Ariz. 458 (2005).

2 "No applicant will be recommended for admission to the practice of law in Arizona by the Committee on Character and Fitness unless the Committee is satisfied that the applicant is of good moral character." Ariz. Supreme Ct. R. 34(b) (1) (B) [hereinafter "R. ___"].

3 *Hamm*, 211 Ariz. at 462 (citing R. 34(a)).

4 *In re Greenberg*, 126 Ariz. 290, 292 (1980) (citing *In re Levine*, 97 Ariz. 88 (1964)).

5 *Hamm*, 211 Ariz. at 462 (citing R. 36(a) 3).

6 "The Committee on Character & Fitness is authorized to receive criminal history information regarding any applicant . . . from any law enforcement agency in conjunction with the admission process." R. 38(b) (3) (B).

7 R. 36(d) (4) (A).

8 R. 36(b) (2)—Conviction of a Crime.

9 *Hamm*, 211 Ariz. at 462 (citing *In re Klahr*, 102 Ariz. 529, 531 (1967); *Levine*, 97 Ariz. at 91 ("If the proof of good moral character falls short of convincing the Committee on Examinations and Admissions, it is its duty not to recommend admission."); *In re Courtney*, 83 Ariz. 231, 233, (1957)).

10 *In re Kiser*, 107 Ariz. 326 (1971) (holding applicant possessed good moral character); *see also Levine*, 97 Ariz. at 92 (holding the Court must, "using our independent judgment, *de novo* determine whether the necessary qualifications have been shown"). The court does not limit its independent review to matters of law; it has "the ultimate responsibility for determination of fact and law." *In re Ronwin*, 139 Ariz. 576, 579 (1983); *see also In re Walker*, 112 Ariz. 134, 137 (1975) (making a finding regarding the credibility of testimony, although in agreement with the Committee).

11 *Greenberg*, 126 Ariz. at 292 (quoting *In re Farmer*, 191 N.C. 235, 238 (N.C. 1926)).

12 *Hamm*, 126 Ariz. at 463.

13 *Greenberg*, 126 Ariz. at 292.

14 *Hamm*, 211 Ariz. at 464.

15 "We agree with the New Jersey Supreme Court, which recognized that 'in the case of extremely damning past misconduct, a showing of rehabilitation may be virtually impossible to make.' *In re Matthews*, 94 N.J. 59 (1983). Indeed, we are aware of no instance in which a person convicted of first-degree murder has been admitted to the practice of law." *Hamm*, 211 Ariz. at 464.

16 *Hamm*, 211 Ariz. at 460–61.

17 Ibid., 461.

18 *See* ABOR Minutes of a Meeting, September 23, 1993, ABOR Docs file. ABOR President Douglas Wall convened the meeting. Regents John Munger (Tucson), Andrew Hurwitz (Phoenix), and Donald Pitt (Tucson), along with ABOR Board Counsel Joel Sideman were present and participated in the discussion. All were prominent lawyers.

19 Ibid.

20 *Hamm*, 211 Ariz. 458; *see also* Michael Kiefer, "Freed Killer Wants OK to Practice Law," *The Arizona Republic*, October 4, 2005.

21 *Hamm*, 211 Ariz. at 463.

22 Ibid., citing *Tucson Rapid Transit Co. v. Rubiaz,* 21 Ariz. 221, 231 (1920).

23 Ibid., 464. There is an article apparently published by Mother Jones; https://www.motherjones.com/politics/2014/07/robert-dowlut-nra-murder-mystery/. This short story contains no sources or citations. It alleges, "Maybe the only person convicted of 1st degree murder to eventually become a licensed lawyer is Robert Dowlut." The article describes Dowlut as the general counsel for the National Rifle Association. Author attempted to confirm Mother Jones' assertions, but could find no legal citations, or other publicity about this "maybe" claim. Author independently researched whether anyone was ever licensed to practice law after conviction of first-degree murder. No such case was found. There is no apparent support for, or news coverage about the Mother Jones claim about Mr. Dowlut.

24 *Greenberg*, 126 Ariz. 290 (1980).

25 Ibid. (quote from LexisNexis "Overview").

26 Michael Kiefer, "Freed Killer Wants OK to Practice Law," *Arizona Republic*, October 4, 2005.

27 Ibid.

28 Ibid.

29 Ibid.

30 Ibid.

31 Ibid.

32 Ibid.

33 Michael Janofsky, "A Rare Legal Quest: From Murderer to Lawyer," *New York Times*, December 27, 2001, National Edition.

34 Ibid.

35 Ibid.

36 Ibid.

37 Ibid.

38 Quote by Hector Berlioz, taken from Richard Kehl, ed., *Breathing on Your Own: Quotations for Independent Thinkers,*" (Seattle: Darling & Company, 2001), 199. Belioz was a French romantic composer. *See* Wikipedia, s.v. "Hector Berlioz," last modified March 4, 2020, 04:08, https://en.wikipedia.org/wiki/Hector_Berlioz.

39 M. Sanjeeta, "Essay on the Importance of Time," *Preserve Articles*, http://www.preservearticles.com/201104095181/importance-of-time.html.

40 Noam Scheiber, "He Committed Murder—Then He Graduated From an Elite Law School—Would You Hire Him As Your Attorney?" *New York Times*, February 2, 2019.

41 Ibid.

42 Ibid.

43 William H. Carlile, "Criminal Records Become a Big Issue on College Campus," *Christian Science Monitor,* November 17, 1995, https://www.csmonitor.com/1995/1117/17031.html.

44 Scheiber, *supra* note 1172.

45 Wikipedia, s.v. "Murder," last modified March 19, 2020, 12:48, https://en.wikipedia.org/wiki/Murder.

46 *Evans v. Evans* [1899] 68 AC 71 (PC) 74.

47 John Inglis, "A Complete Report on the Trial of Miss Madeline Smith," 1857, quoted in David Shrager and Elizabeth Frost, eds., *The Quotable Lawyer* (New York: Facts On File, Inc., 1986), 225.

48 Ibid. *See* Wikipedia, s.v. "Anne Hocking," last modified July 14, 2019, 19:27, https://en.wikipedia.org/wiki/Anne_Hocking.

CHAPTER 26

DEAN RICHARD MORGAN, 1989 TO 1997

Dean Morgan's career path from law school differed greatly from the other deans at ASU Law. Many of them had only practiced law for short periods of time before they entered the academy and began teaching and writing in law schools. Morgan graduated from the University of California at Berkeley, with a BA in political science in 1967. He took his JD degree at the University of California at Los Angeles, Order of the Coif, in May 1971, and practiced law for eight years before moving to academia.

He joined Feldman, Waldman & Klein in their San Francisco office in June 1971 for six months. Then he moved to Nossaman, Krueger & Marsh[1] in Los Angeles in January 1972 as an associate attorney. He made partner in April 1977 and stayed with the firm until June 1980.

LAW PROFESSOR AND SEQUENTIAL DEANSHIPS— WYOMING TO ARIZONA TO NEVADA

His start in academia was with the ASU College of Law in June 1980. He was an associate professor of law until August 1983 when he was promoted to full professor and Associate Dean under Dean Alan Matheson. He taught at ASU until July 1987 when he left to become Dean of the University of Wyoming College of Law in Laramie, Wyoming.[2] In January 1990, he returned to ASU as its fifth dean and as a tenured professor of law. He spent the next seven years at ASU before accepting an appointment as the inaugural dean at the new William S. Boyd School of Law at the University of Nevada, Law Vegas.

He had anticipated taking a sabbatical for the 1997–98 academic year. Accordingly, ASU had already appointed former Dean Alan Matheson as acting dean during Morgan's sabbatical year.[3]

The headline in the *Arizona Journal* on July 21, 1997, gave Richard Morgan a new name, a new claim to fame, and a rare chance to do something very few law professors ever get. "Morgan Named 'Founding Dean' of UNLV Law School."[4] Jodi Weisberg,[5] a lawyer turned newspaper reporter, interviewed Dick, as he was known to colleagues and students, and captured the essence of Dick's roll of the dice. "A gambler could roll the dice a million times and not hit the jackpot won by Richard Morgan, until recently the dean of the Arizona State University College of Law. Morgan, 52, was recently chosen to be the founding dean of the University of Nevada at Las Vegas (UNLV). 'This type of opportunity only comes up about every 50 years,' said Morgan. 'It's going to be fun.'" The front-page article included a photo smiling over the caption: "One of the reasons Richard Morgan, the new dean of UNLV's College of Law is so happy is that it will allow him to emulate his mentor, Willard Pedrick, founding dean of the ASU Law School."[6]

A cliché might have captured that move—their loss was ASU's gain. Then to burnish the cliché, ASU's provost, Milt Glick said, "Clearly, UNLV's gain is ASU's loss."[7]

Morgan said he was "following in the footsteps of his friend and mentor, Willard H. Pedrick, who founded the ASU College of law . . . I enjoyed his description of the excitement of founding ASU's Law School . . . and I have the opportunity to follow in Ped's footsteps and start a first-rate law school in a community that wants and needs one."[8]

Dick Morgan's departure was lamented by many. University of Arizona Dean Joe Seligman agreed that being a founding dean "is an unusual opportunity. Dick has both a wealth of experience and imagination and he will be a great asset to UNLV."[9] Arizona Supreme Court Chief Justice Thomas Zlaket said, "We'll miss him. Dick has been an outstanding dean and a great friend of the legal community in Arizona. We hate to lose him to Nevada but it is a great opportunity and I wish him well."[10] ASU Professor Gary Lowenthal said, "I'm really sad. He was a wonderful dean . . . he was the best."[11] Robert Van Wyck, president of the State Bar of Arizona said, "I congratulate him on his courageous move . . . . I'll miss his counsel and advice and I'll also miss jogging with him on the morning of board meetings." Maricopa County Presiding Judge Robert Myers summed Morgan up: "I've worked with him frequently and he's a terrific guy. Dick will do a good job wherever he is. He's energetic, bright, and has the ability to make friends and influence people."[12]

The Business Journal noted the unique nature of starting a new law school in Nevada. "Until now, Nevada and Alaska were the only two states without law schools . . . it has been studied for quite some time—in fact it has been in the works for about 20 years—but has never been approved by the state legislature . . . Nevada finally has reached a level of growth and maturity to support a program."[13]

That's one clear differentiation between Nevada and Arizona. In Arizona, the legislature has no say in what colleges can be created by its public universities. The Arizona Board of Regents is a constitutional body and empowered to create or close colleges.

Morgan put it into context, saying, "My wife and I are going to spend a month in Alaska and visit family in California and Washington . . . . Ped was very special, and it's a dream come true to follow his footsteps . . . . If everything goes smoothly, we'll have full accreditation in five years . . . . I'm so excited . . . this is going to be fun!!"[14] He started his deanship in Las Vegas on September 1, 1997.

IN HIS OWN WORDS

Before he left ASU, and after he had accepted the deanship at ASU, he gave a lengthy interview to Associate Librarian Marianne Alcorn in the Ross-Blakley Law Library. The single-spaced transcript is eighteen pages long and details the ups, downs, and stalls during his fourteen years[15] at ASU.

Ms. Alcorn asked Dean Morgan in 1997 about his transition from law practice to law school. Morgan told her the 1980 ASU job started with two telephone conversations.

> *Paul Markus who was a classmate of mine from the UCLA law school was already in legal education. . . . at the University of Illinois. He called me and told me that he'd been talking with a friend of his on the Arizona State*

> *faculty; I think it was Dale Furnish. He had heard from his friend that ASU was looking for a corporate type for their faculty . . . and that he had given his friend . . . my name . . . And so I said fine, thank you for that. And then Milt Schroeder who was then the Associate Dean in 1979 . . . called me up and asked if I was indeed interested . . . And I said let me think about it, so I went home and talked to my wife Tina about it . . . I'd been talking about this for years and this is an opportunity to go interview at a school like this doesn't fall into your lap every day. . . . I told Milt I'd be willing to interview.*[16]

ASU Law was only twelve years old when they interviewed Morgan for an associate professor position. Professor John Morris was the chair of recruitment at the time and arranged Morgan's visit to the Tempe campus. "Alan Matheson was the dean and he has us to dinner at his house . . . we really liked the people, we liked the school, the weather was beautiful, the place was clearly up and coming . . . it had a real excitement about it."[17]

Professor Morris called Morgan a few months later "to say things were looking good and wanted to know if I would take it if it were extended. And I said yeah I probably would, depends on the terms. And then Alan Matheson called to say the offer was there and we negotiated the terms. [We] moved to ASU in June 1980 and was there for the better part of fifteen years."[18]

In the fall of 1979, ASU Law was advancing on all fronts. Prof. Morgan remembered it clearly in his Oral History project.

> *I came in with a large influx of new faculty. There were six or seven people who joined the faculty the year that I did, and they included women and minorities. Ann Stanton joined the faculty that year. Karen Zander, an African American woman, who was at the law school for a few years and has since moved to North Carolina I believe, the state of North Carolina, joined the faculty that year. Charles Calleros was scheduled to join the faculty that year, but he deferred for a year because he was clerking for Judge Hug of the Ninth Circuit and wanted to stay on for another year. . . . Victor Gold was in that group, a very successful faculty member at ASU for four years and then moved to Loyola where he still is. . . . John Leshy was in that group, as you well know Leshy was on the ASU faculty for a decade, then left to become Solicitor of the Department of Interior under Bill Clinton, and now is on*

the Hastings faculty and running a foundation as well. . . . That year there was a large number of people who were hired and it was a fairly diverse large number of people.[19]

Nineteen seventy-nine was a pivotal year for ASU Law. It was the start of an era in which the inaugural faculty was well past the experiment of starting a new law school. The curriculum had been expanded and there were many new faces on the faculty. Morgan explained how classes worked in the early eighties.

I started out teaching business associations [in] the corporations' class. The first semester I taught I only had one class. It was a four-unit business associations class. I apparently did something to anger the powers that be because I wound up teaching this four-unit class from four until five o'clock in the afternoon Monday, Tuesday, Thursday, and Friday. I had 150 students in the class. It hadn't been taught for a while. And teaching 150 students business associations from 4–5 on Friday afternoons was a bit of a challenge indeed, but I survived it. And after that in subsequent semesters, I taught commercial law and legal ethics, so I had two business associations' courses in my repertoire, two commercial law classes, and legal ethics. I also taught on occasion corporate reorganization class, specialized class in reorganizing corporations. I really only taught a full load and participated a full time faculty member for three years, 1980–1983, because in 1983 Alan Matheson asked me to move into administration as Associate Dean. Well I expected that would be only a brief sojourn to help Alan out. It turned out that from 1983 forward I have been more of an administrator than anything else. And so my full time teaching ended in 1983. I went to a partial load at that point. I've never had a full time teaching load since for the last 22 years.[20]

In July 1992, the ABA released the long-awaited Macerate Report known as the "*Task Force on Law Schools and the Profession: Narrowing the Gap.*"[21] Robert Macerate, Esq., was the chair. This title was carefully picked, as noted in the Introduction. "At its birth this Task Force acquired a name that projects a distorted image of a legal education community separated from the 'profession' by a 'gap' that requires narrowing. As the Task Force proceeded to fulfill the mission suggested by its name and to narrow the 'gap,' it recognized that the image was false. Thus, the title of this Report attempts to correct the distortion and suggests a different and more accurate vision of the relationship between legal education and the practicing bar."²²

Ms. Alcorn asked Dean Morgan about the conflicting views about skills training in law schools as opposed to its traditional role as must teachers *of* the law.

> *Another area is we are doing a lot more with is professionalism and skills training... In the early '90s, the Macerate report came out, report that Bob Macerate of the ABA authored with a committee that talked about the fundamental skills and values that a lawyer needs to learn and understand to be a professional. A lot of law schools have generally taken that report pretty seriously and are trying to do more with instilling professionalism in their students. Either through skills training classes or augmented ethics classes.... There are a greater array of those courses now than there was twenty years ago. And that reflects not only the Macerate Report and the emphasis that the bar is putting on those kinds of skills, but also reflects the fact that a lot of law students, a lot of law graduates these days are not going into law offices where they're going to get excellent mentorship for five years. In the good old days thirty years ago, the expectation was that law school just began the process of legal education. Teach the students the theory, teach them how to read the law, how to do research, how to self-educate, and then send them out into a quality law office to gain the practical experience and practical mentoring to be a lawyer.*²³

At the time of his interview with Ms. Alcorn, Morgan had served as dean at three law schools. That experience gave him a solid platform from which to offer an insider's opinion on the job.

> *The role of the dean I think has evolved.... Back in the days when ASU was founded by Willard Pedrick... The dean's job was much different than it is today. There wasn't nearly the fundraising public relations element that the dean has today. Administrative staffs were much smaller in those days. Law schools didn't purport to provide nearly the range of services to the students that they do today. Pedrick presided over an administration that probably had three of four professionals working for him... it wasn't as big*

of a management chore in those days. There wasn't the fundraising aspect to it . . . the dean's job in those days was to be the intellectual leader of the law school and Pedrick was. I mean he was in the classroom he was writing books, he was writing articles, and he was showing the faculty the way on how one is a scholar. He was showing the students the way on how excellent teaching ought to be done. . . . He built an excellent law school.[24]

Morgan spoke at some length about the central difference between deans in the seventies and deans in the nineties. He explained how deans became managers of the enterprise, which had grown exponentially over two decades.

Over the years the dean's role generally has evolved to be much more of a management role; law schools have very large staffs these days. They have to be managed by somebody, the dean or somebody else. Secondly, the modem dean has to do a lot of fundraising, a lot of interaction with the legislature, regents, and central administration, be the public face of the law school. The dean also has to be very good at faculty governance, that is dealing with faculties in ways that are effective and efficient. . . Deans interface with faculty inappropriately in my opinion on admissions matters, curricular matters, hiring matters, tenure and promotion matters. Those areas are the province of the faculty and the dean is the leader in those areas, but has to work effectively with the faculty on decision making in those areas. . . In some respects [it is] a more demanding job.[25]

REHABILITATION AND JAMES HAMM

The James Hamm saga had tested almost everyone on the faculty and had angered many more in the legal community. All of it happened on Dean Morgan's watch. Hamm had been admitted as a student in 1993, under a loose assumption he only wanted to learn the law, not practice it. That assumption created what Dean Morgan would call a "firestorm."[26] The James Hamm saga is summarized in Chapter 12, *infra*. The embers and the ignition of the firestorm is part of Dean Morgan's detailed interview by Marianne Alcorn after he left ASU and was building what would become the William S. Boyd College of Law[27] at UNLV.

Let me just start with the James Hamm situation. James Hamm . . . was admitted by the admissions committee to start in the class that entered in the class of 1993. . . . He was a convicted murderer who had served the prior 18 years I think in state prison in Arizona. . . . Some kind of a drug connected transaction that went wrong and he killed a couple of people. . . he was sentenced to death actually, but along the way he had his sentence commuted to life in prison and while he was in prison he got an education at the tax payer's expense. Northern Arizona University gave him a college education from which he profited immensely. He graduated with a degree in sociology and a 4.0 GPA. He became a model prisoner and tutored other students in academic work. Anyway, he became in the words of the people in the prison system the poster boy for rehabilitation. . . . The people that are in charge of keeping the public safe decided that he was no longer a threat to society and let him out of prison where upon he applied to go to law school. And he applied only at ASU, no other place, so we were the only one who got to be in the barrel with him to have all this fun. . . . [Some people] in the university system knew him well . . . a guy of real quality, if we believe in rehabilitation at all . . . he ought to be admitted to law school and make something . . . allowed to pursue that education and do good for society in part as penance for the bad that he'd done to society . . . he had tremendously high LSAT score, 4.0 GPA, letters of recommendation from prison officials. . .[28]

Today, the Sandra Day O'Connor College of Law admits students through its admissions committee. The factors that influence its decisions are stated on the school's website. "LSAT performance, undergraduate grade point average, quality and grading patterns of undergraduate institutions, previous graduate education, demonstrated commitment to public service, work and leadership experience, extracurricular or community activities, history of overcoming economic or other disadvantages, uniqueness of experience and background, maturity, ability to communicate, foreign language proficiency, honors and awards, service in the armed forces, and publications."[29]

The admissions committee does not interview applicants. It relies "solely upon the information the applicant chooses to share in their application to make an informed decision. ASU Law is committed to a more sustainable and resilient future and requires applicants to apply electronically through the Law School Admissions Council (LSAC) website at LSAC.org."[30]

In 1993, Hamm was admitted after consultation with Dean Morgan.

> *I was approached by Doug Blaze, the chair of the admissions committee in the summer or the spring of '93 I think it was saying that they wanted to admit this guy, and he had this criminal record and would I support the committee if they admitted him. I looked at his file, and the letters, and all the stuff I've just described and I said yes I will support you. Probably will set off a firestorm, but I will support you, and I have all kinds of reasons I could go into if we had hours for why I decided to do that. I think they're good reasons. So, he was admitted. And later on when a prominent attorney in town found out that we had admitted a murderer to the law school and started raising hell about it, it became quite a furor. Although not an entirely unproductive one, we had a good conversation with legislators and good conversation in the Phoenix Newspapers and on local and national television shows about such things as do we as a society believe in rehabilitation? Is there a place for redemption and mercy in our society?*[31]

There was another convicted murderer, Michael Davis, who graduated the following year, 1994, from ASU Law. Dean Morgan remembered that episode well.

> *In contrast Walter Waldington also known as Michael Davis was a different sort of situation. He too had been convicted of murder and had served time in a Texas prison, but he had no one arguing that he was rehabilitated or that he was a poster child for anything. When he applied to the ASU law school the school, this was before my deanship, the school did not require the disclosure of prior criminal records and so he didn't disclose his prior criminal record. Indeed his application went to some lengths to conceal a good chunk of his life. And that was a chunk in which he had been in the Texas State Penitentiary for some heinous killings. The admissions committee that considered his application didn't pick up on that chunk and there were things in there that could have raised red flags but when an admissions committee is looking at 2000 applications, you're not going to see every red flag. Anyway,*

he was a murderer who, unlike Mr. Hamm, we had admitted unknowingly. And he came forth after the Hamm controversy started, he came forth and said "I've got a little criminal trouble in my life too, I'm not going to tell you what it is because you didn't ask about it, but you should be aware that when I apply for admission to the bar there may be a little dust up; but everything is really ok in my life." And when he applied for admission to the bar, the bar authorities called to tell me that we had a triple murderer in our midst that we knew nothing about. And as I say, there was nothing to suggest if there was anything particularly positive about Mr. Davis's, or Walter Walthauser, I think was his real name. Anyway, let's call him Davis for this purpose. There wasn't anything particularly wholesome about him. We hadn't known about any of this. Again, we hadn't asked, as a law school, what his criminal record was. And had his application been at all respects complete we wouldn't have had any choice but to have said ok we graduate you. We're going to give you a degree. But his application wasn't complete; it omitted key information of things that were going on during the nine years that he was in the slammer in Texas. And so on that basis I started a disciplinary proceeding against him and we expelled him from the law school and did not grant him a degree.[32]

Dean Morgan closed his interview by connecting the wonderful experience he had at ASU Law and his mentor Willard Pedrick to the new opportunity in his life—inaugural dean at UNLV's Boyd School of Law. Ms. Alcorn prefaced her question to Dean Morgan by reminding him what Dean Pedrick had said in his interview about the "chance to be a dean in a brand new law school in a big city—[it] was my good fortune to be on hand to get that chance. . . . Do you feel the same way about being the founding dean at UNLV?"[33]

Dean Morgan's was a shout-out for Pedrick and an important statement about Ped's legacy at ASU.

Absolutely. That's why I'm here [UNLV]. I'm here because of Pedrick. I loved the guy; he was so joyful about the years the years he had spent as the founding dean at ASU. Talked so happily about all of that, how satisfied he was, how much fun it had been, how he felt about it even years later. And he said to me on more than one occasion, I don't know if you'll ever get a chance to do what I did, because I didn't think there would be anymore state law schools that would open up. But if one ever opens up you ought to try to do it. And low and behold, not only did UNLV open up, when UNLV started making noises about a law school, I thought it would probably be the only new state law school in a long time. . . But I was lucky enough, as Pedrick was, to get in on the ground floor of this one. That's why I'm here. If it weren't for Pedrick's advice and example, I might very well still be at ASU. I was perfectly happy with the job down there, aside from the fact that I managed to attract crisis after crisis after crisis, but I was still doing ok, I think. But when this came up, I just thought it was a unique opportunity.[34]

And it was. Dean Morgan retired in 2007, after building and running the William S. Boyd School of Law for ten years.

---

1 "Firm History," Nossaman LLP, accessed March 4, 2020, https://www.nossaman.com/about-firm-history. Better known since the 1970s as Nossaman, Gunther, Knox & Elliot.
2 Wikipedia, s.v. "University of Wyoming College of Law," last modified September 25, 2019, 12:34, https://en.wikipedia.org/wiki/University_of_Wyoming_College_of_Law. The University of Wyoming College of Law was founded in 1920. *See also* "UW College of Law," University of Wyoming, http://www.uwyo.edu/law/.
3 Stephanie Balzer, "ASU Law School Dean Picked for Vegas Role," *Phoenix Business Journal*, July 13, 1997:7, https://www.bizjournals.com/phoenix/stories/1997/07/14/story8.html?s=print.
4 Jodi Weisberg, *Morgan Named Founding Dean of UNLV Law School*, 3 Ariz. J. 4, July 21, 1997.
5 Jodi Weisberg was a University of Arizona College of Law graduate. She was admitted to the Arizona Bar on May 19, 1983 and resigned in good standing many years later to pursue law teaching, writing, and stand-up comedy.
6 Weisberg, *supra* note 1184.
7 Judith Smith, *ASU Insight*, July 11, 1997: 2.
8 Ibid.
9 Weisberg, *supra* note 1184.
10 Ibid., 12.
11 Ibid.
12 Ibid.
13 Stephanie Balzer, "ASU Law School Dean Picked for Vegas Role," *Phoenix Business Journal*, July 13, 1997:7, https://www.bizjournals.com/phoenix/stories/1997/07/14/story8.html?s=print.
14 Ibid.
15 Seven years as a law professor and seven more as dean.
16 Dean Richard Morgan, interview by Marianne Alcorn, *Oral History Project*, ASU College of Law: 3.
17 Ibid., 4.
18 Ibid.
19 Ibid., 6.
20 Ibid., 7.
21 American Bar Association, Legal Education and Professional Development—An Educational Continuum, July 1992, https://www.americanbar.org/content/dam/aba/publications/misc/legal_education/2013_legal_education_and_professional_development_maccrate_report).authcheckdam.pdf.
22 Ibid., 3.
23 Dean Richard Morgan, interview by Marianne Alcorn, *Oral History Project*, ASU College of Law: 8.

24 Ibid., 8–9.
25 Ibid., 10.
26 Ibid., 14.
27 UNLV, "Richard J. Morgan," accessed March 4, 2020, https://law.unlv.edu/content/richard-j-morgan.
28 Dean Richard Morgan, interview by Marianne Alcorn, *Oral History Project*, ASU College of Law: 13.
29 "JD Admissions," Arizona State University, accessed March 4, 2020, https://law.asu.edu/admissions/apply/jd.
30 Ibid.
31 Dean Richard Morgan, interview by Marianne Alcorn, *Oral History Project*, ASU College of Law: 14.
32 Dean Richard Morgan, interview by Marianne Alcorn, *Oral History Project*, ASU College of Law: 14–15.
33 Ibid., 15.
34 Ibid., 16.

CHAPTER 27

ASU LAW SCHOOL CELEBRATES ITS 25TH ANNIVERSARY, 1970 TO 1992

The "twenty-fifth anniversary" was celebrated as though 1992 was actually the twenty-fifth year of its existence. The school was twenty-five years old in 1992, but only twenty-three years after 1970, the year that the first graduates marched across the Gammage Auditorium stage. And the school itself was by then five years old. ABOR granted ASU's request to build a law school in 1965. President Homer Durham hired Willard Pedrick to build it in 1966, and Ped and his inaugural faculty taught the first courses in September 1967.

Anniversaries are mandated celebrations, but this particular anniversary—the founding of a law school—was celebrated in grand style, as though it were its hundredth. Everyone at the big dinner celebration was a law student, practicing lawyer, law professor, or a relative of someone fixated on the law. Neither Shakespeare nor Oscar Wilde were fond of the law. Shakespeare said, "The Law is past depth to those who, without heed, plunge into it."[1] Oscar Wilde was blunt: "Lawyers always argue and they always win—the bastards." The room was full of deep legal thinkers and argumentative lawyers. ASU Law's twenty-fifth anniversary of its founding was best described by Paul Eckstein,[2] then the president of the ASU Law Society. "It hardly seems possible that 25 years have passed since the University of Arizona got its medical school and Arizona State University got the best of the deal—what a glorious 25 years it has been."[3]

GOLF AND A BLACK-TIE DINNER

As was the common practice for law schools of that era, the two-day celebration started on Friday with a day-long, Continuing Legal Education seminar, picked up Saturday morning with a golf tournament, and culminated Saturday night with a black-tie dinner at the Arizona Biltmore. Approximately 750 ASU alumni, friends, judges, clients, and students started the evening with cocktails, celebrating the classes of '72, '77, '82 and '87. Michael Grant[4] ('76), then famous for KAET-TV's *Horizon* nightly news show, was master of ceremonies. Paul Eckstein chaired the 25th Anniversary Celebration Committee. Joe Sims[5] ('70), the first Student Body Chair in 1967–68, greeted guests in the obligatory reception line with David Ortiz, the 1992–93 Student Body Chair.

Richard Mahoney[6] ('80), then-Arizona Secretary of State, presented the crowd with a State of Arizona Proclamation making that day "Arizona State University College of Law Day." The quick-witted speakers included Grant Woods[7] ('79), then-Arizona Attorney General, Dean Richard Morgan, and ASU President Lattie Coor,[8] who presented founding Dean Willard Pedrick with the ASU Distinguished Achievement Award. The Honorable William C. Canby, Jr.,[9] introduced a video retrospective on the first twenty-five years of the college. And then, Justice O'Connor[10] was introduced by Justice Ruth McGregor[11] ('74), her first law clerk.

The golf tournament was organized by Randy Nussbaum[12] ('80). Randy didn't win—he was better at law than golf. Most lawyers paired with clients. The CLE, conducted the day before the dinner, addressed "Recent Decisional Trends of the United States Supreme Court."

Of great interest were the comments by a former faculty member and current sitting judge on the Ninth Circuit Court of Appeals, the Honorable William C. Canby. Judge Canby talked about "the astonishing depth and diversity of Supreme Court case law in reversing my opinions."[13] The CLE moderator, Judge Barry Silverman[14] ('76), offered a good many quips and kept the program moving at the speed of light rail. Judge Ruth McGregor ('74) spoke on First Amendment issues[15] and contributed her appellate law perspective.[16] Given the importance of the occasion, the CLE topics included matters in which ASU Law had become a leader: Freedom of Speech, Freedom of Religion,[17] Indian Law, Labor Law and Access to Courts,[18] Procedural Due Process,[19] Eighth Amendment—Death Penalty,[20] Eighth

Amendment—Excessive Force,[21] Fourth Amendment—Search & Seizure,[22] Sixth Amendment—Speedy Trial.[23]

At most ASU events in the 1990s, ASU President Lattie F. Coor[24] either presided or spoke. At the law school's big night, he sparkled and roused the big crowd. "I join you with great enthusiasm on behalf of the entire university in celebrating your twenty-fifth birthday. Enthusiastic, not so much for the fact that it's twenty-five years, but because of what you've done. To have earned a reputation as academically as strong as yours in as brief a period of time sets you apart *from any college of any kind anywhere.*" Coming from the effervescent Lattie Coor, these comments no doubt made every law student and lawyer in the room beam. He was one of those rare public speakers that John Andrew Holmes had in mind when he said, "Speech is conveniently located midway between thought and action, where it often substitutes for both."[25] President Coor didn't just speak to groups; he activated them.

Continuing his presentation, Lattie explained, "Before coming here to ASU, I was at a university that had just celebrated its 200th anniversary in New England, where time is viewed in a little different perspective. I can tell you no one in any of those universities could ever imagine such stature in such a brief period of time. As well, the fact that you as a college are such an integral part of the entire legal community in the Valley and in Arizona and that you have done it with such style and with a clear sense that the future will only get better is a reflection of the college's rapid rise to the forefront . . . I salute you for your accomplishments, for everyone on the faculty who has been involved, for every member of the community who has given time and support to this law school. You are a model for the rest of ASU. What you have done in twenty-five years sets the standard that will allow the rest of this young, vibrant, promising university to put no boundaries on its standards for the future. Happy Birthday, College of Law."[26]

Other parts of this book will more fully cover how Dean Willard Pedrick, the keynote speaker at the grand dinner that evening, came to be the inaugural dean. Lattie Coor briefly noted in his presentation of Dean Pedrick a small piece of that fascinating tale. "I get to do double-duty this evening . . . to tell you the real reason you got started the way you did. I had a chance to read the papers of Homer Durham . . . He [Durham] tells the tale of when he and a few others asked around the country for the very best people in the country to start a new law school . . . [an associate dean at Harvard] gave them a list of names. Durham said they didn't want an "A list," they wanted the *very best* people in the country to do this. Pedrick was on that short list . . . His name cropped up time and again . . . the Harvard associated dean said, 'you'll never get him—he is unmovable—he is sufficiently distinguished and established—you can never bring him to you.'"[27]

ASU DISTINGUISHED ACHIEVEMENT AWARD

Dean Pedrick accepted the most important award that Arizona State University could bestow that evening—The ASU Distinguished Achievement Award. His address to the crowd was typical—plain spoken—moving—and funny. "President Coor, Dean Morgan, Mike Grant, Justice O'Connor, alumni, students, friends of the law school. *What a crowd!* I'm just glad I stayed alive to be here. It wasn't that easy, either. After twenty-five years, I'm finally going to come clean. I admit I was not qualified to be a founding dean. Absolutely none! Actually, in 1965, I don't think there was anybody alive in the U.S. who had started a law school.[28] Despite my lack of experience, I was willing to have a go at it. What made me think I could do it? Well, the answer is an unshakable belief that every lawyer, and spouses will attest to this, every lawyer thinks that she or he can do anything."[29]

Dean Pedrick told the audience how he recruited his stellar faculty. He said a mutual alcoholic friend told him Ed Cleary, the pride of the University of Illinois law school, was interested. Pedrick offered him everything but money as an inducement.[30] Pedrick secured Dick Effland with a simple strategy—he visited him in Madison, Wisconsin, when it was 25 degrees below zero—then brought him to Tempe in February when the orange trees were in blossom. He also said Professor Effland developed an allergy to orange blossoms.

He snagged Harold Havighurst, his former professor and dean at Northwestern, who came to Tempe "to watch over me and see to it, as a Northwestern graduate, that I didn't let the side down."[31]

Pedrick talked about many other early faculty members and noted they were now "gone." So now, "I come to the living," he said. "Still going strong those for whom breathing has become a habit, I recruited Bill Canby by promising him we'd have him appointed to the Ninth Circuit Court of Appeals if he would teach here at least ten years. He did and we did. We made that promise to another prospective faculty member, Milt Schroder,[32] except that we said to him if you teach here for at least ten years we'll get you or your spouse appointed to the Ninth Circuit Court of Appeals, and we delivered![33] John Morris[34] was my student at Northwestern and I accordingly knew he'd been well taught. I also knew he'd been a superlative student there."[35] He got Dick Dahl,[36] the organizing founder of the law library, because he liked the way he thought. At their first meeting, Dahl's first sentence was, "I suppose you wonder how a Dahl like me happens to be in a court library." For Pedrick, that was a perfect start. Alan Matheson, he said, "is evidence of the fact that as founding dean, I led a charmed life. Had I been on the Titanic, I would have turned into a dolphin. Alan was actually recruited by President Homer Durham, but when I learned he'd been offered a faculty position at the University of Iowa Law School, I knew he would be a great addition. After all, Iowa had not seen fit when I was available as a beginning law teacher to make *me* an offer."

Always the master of metaphor, Pedrick told the happy crowd how he recruited the first students. "Well you know the line from the movie *Field of Dreams*—'if you build it, they will come.' Well, we did and they did. A rather motley crew, but spirited, even when sober. And able, I must admit."

He talked about the serious subject of law curriculum. "The curriculum, mildly innovative, must have been sound. Look at that class and what it's done. Will the founding class stand?"

They did, got a rapturous round of applause, sat, and let Pedrick salute them. "You had the courage to come to a brand-new law school. I've said before and I'll say it again: I enjoy getting more credit than I deserve. The enterprise has had great support from this university. President Durham, and now President Lattie Coor in particular, my successors in the deanship, all five of us, including that indefatigable Dick Morgan, the founding faculty and the splendid additions thereto, the students, and in the intervening years and now, together with our friends from the legal profession and the business community."

Dean Pedrick gave special recognition to Dean Chuck Ares, former dean of the University of Arizona College of Law. "They were helpful to us at every turn from the very beginning, and in my own view, we've been good for them too." [37] He said funny things about Bob Hope, a man he was a fan of for fifty years. He closed his keynote speech with a melodic line, "Thanks for the Memories."

---

1 Tryon Edwards, D.D., *The New Dictionary of Thoughts,* revised by C.N. Catrevas, A.B., Jonathan Edwards, A.M., and Ralph Emerson Browns, A.M., originally compiled by Standard Book Company, 1965.

2 Perkins Coie, "Professionals," accessed March 4, 2020, https://www.perkinscoie.com/en/professionals/paul-f-eckstein.html. Paul Eckstein's practice is focused on civil litigation (including appellate matters) involving commercial, legal malpractice, constitutional, Indian law and political law issues. He also frequently serves as a mediator and arbitrator. He also teaches Constitutional Law at the Sandra Day O'Connor College of Law at Arizona State University.

3 "Letter to Dean Richard Morgan from Eckstein," *The Law Forum,* Special 25th Anniversary Issue (1992). It's also worth noting that the founding Dean, Willard Pedrick, was Emeriti Faculty in 1992. In this same issue of the *Arizona Law Forum,* he guaranteed the faculty and students that he'd be back for the 50th Anniversary, and "if I'm not here for any reason, sue me!"

4 Wikipedia, s.v "Michael Grant," last modified January 27, 2018, 20:51, https://en.wikipedia.org/wiki/Michael_Grant_(television). Michael Murray Grant (born July 16, 1951 in Hutchinson, Kansas) is an attorney and former host of the long-running Arizona Public Television program *Horizon*. Before his work on *Horizon,* Grant worked in Arizona radio both as a disc jockey and as an investigative reporter, most notably for KOY-AM. Grant received his Bachelor's degree in English from Arizona State University in 1973 and his Juris Doctorate from ASU in 1976. He currently practices telecommunications and public utility law at Gallagher and Kennedy, PA, in Phoenix.

5 Jones Day, "Lawyers," accessed March 4, 2020, https://www.jonesday.com/jsims/ (site discontinued). Joe Sims is one of the most recognized antitrust lawyers in the world. He is listed in *Chambers, Who's Who Legal, Legal 500, Best Lawyers of America,* and most other publications recognizing prominent antitrust lawyers. He is the only antitrust lawyer ever named by The American Lawyer as a "Dealmaker of the Year" two separate times, in 2001 and 2009.

6 Richard D. Mahoney (born May 28, 1951) was the Secretary of State of Arizona from 1991 until 1995. He is currently the director of the School of Public and International Affairs at North Carolina State University, effective July 1, 2012. SPIA is part of NC State's College of Humanities and Social Sciences. Mahoney was educated at Brophy College Preparatory, Princeton University, Johns Hopkins University and Arizona State University. Mahoney has lectured as a visiting professor at Templeton College (Oxford University), The JFK School of Government (Harvard University), the Beijing Institute of Foreign Trade, and the Universidad Del Pacifico—Ecuador (Quito campus). He was also professor emeritus at the Thunderbird School of Global Management. Mahoney is the author of three books, two of which are about the John F. Kennedy administration: *JFK: Ordeal in Africa* (1983) and *Sons and Brothers: The Days of Jack and Bobby Kennedy* (1999). His latest book is entitled *Getting Away with Murder: The Real Story Behind American Taliban John Walker Lindh and What the U.S. Government Had to Hide* (2004). Mahoney has also authored numerous articles and monographs on presidential history, foreign policy, international trade, and political risk; and a volume of poetry in Spanish, entitled *Pétalos* (1995). Wikipedia, s.v., "Richard Mahoney," last modified January 8, 2021, 8:13, https://en.wikipedia.org/wiki/Richard_Mahoney.

7 Grant Woods (born May 19, 1954) served as Attorney General of Arizona from 1991 until 1999. He was a supporter of John McCain in his race for the Republican U.S. Senate nomination against J. D. Hayworth in 2010. Grant Woods is the son of Arizona developer Joe Woods. He was the first congressional chief of staff for the late U.S. Sen. John McCain, R-Ariz. Grant has been elected to the International Academy of Trial Lawyers, which is limited to the top 500 trial lawyers in the world. Wikipedia, s.v., "Grant Woods," last modified January 8, 2021: 8:08, https://en.wikipedia.org/wiki/Grant_Woods.

8 Wikipedia, s.v. "Lattie F. Coor," last modified November 24, 2019, 04:41, https://en.wikipedia.org/wiki/Lattie_F._Coor. Lattie Finch Coor Jr. is an American academic specializing in public policy and the past president of two universities. He was the 15th President of Arizona State University and the 21st President of the University of Vermont. Coor graduated from Northern Arizona University in 1958 with a BA in Political Science. He received his MA and PhD from Washington University in St. Louis where his 1964 doctoral dissertation was titled The Increasing Vulnerability of the American Governor. He remained at Washington University for the next ten years as a faculty member and eventually as its Vice Chancellor. He left in 1976 when he became the 21st President of the University of Vermont. He served in that capacity until 1989 and then moved to Arizona State University where he became its 15th President. After his retirement from the presidency of ASU in 2002 he stayed on as professor and Ernest W. McFarland Chair in Leadership and Public Policy in the university's School of Public Affairs. In 2002 he also co-founded a "do tank," Center for the Future of Arizona, and serves as Chairman and Founding Director.

9 Wikipedia, s.v. "William Canby," last modified October 25, 2019, 00:42, https://en.wikipedia.org/wiki/William_Canby. William Cameron Canby Jr. (born May 22, 1931) is a Senior United States Circuit Judge of the United States Court of Appeals for the Ninth Circuit, sitting in Phoenix, Arizona. As both a professor at Arizona State University College of Law and a Circuit Judge of the United States Court of Appeals for the Ninth Circuit, Canby has become known as an authority on American Indian law. He has

authored law review articles, a major textbook, and the West Nutshell Series primer on the subject. While still a professor at ASU, Canby successfully argued the case of *Bates v. State Bar of Arizona,* in which the Supreme Court held that the First Amendment allows lawyers to advertise in a manner that is not misleading to members of the general public.

10 Wikipedia, s.v. "Sandra Day O'Connor," last modified February 25, 2020, 22:40, https://en.wikipedia.org/wiki/Sandra_Day_O%27Connor. Sandra Day O'Connor (born March 26, 1930) is a retired Associate Justice of the Supreme Court of the United States, who served from her appointment in 1981 by President Ronald Reagan until her retirement in 2006. She was the first woman to serve on the Court. *See also* Britannica, Sandra Day O'Connor, https://www.britannica.com/biography/Sandra-Day-OConnor. On April 5, 2006, ASU Law was officially renamed the Sandra Day O'Connor College of Law at Arizona State University. This was, and still is, the only law school to be named after a woman. Seven months later on November 17, Justice O'Connor was the honored guest at a renaming celebration at Armstrong Hall in Tempe, Arizona. Under the banner of the Sandra Day O'Connor College of Law, ASU has jumped to No. 25 among all law schools and—like its namesake—has continued to increase its efforts to serve the community. "Celebrating 10 Years as the Sandra Day O'Connor College of Law," Sandra Day O'Connor College of Law, accessed March 3, 2020, https://law.asu.edu/asulaw-newsletter/oconnor-renaming.

11 Wikipedia, s.v. "Ruth McGregor," last modified January 22, 2020, 08:54, https://en.wikipedia.org/wiki/Ruth_McGregor. Ruth V. McGregor (born 1943) is a former justice of the Arizona Supreme Court. McGregor was a justice of the state's highest court from 1998, when she was appointed to the court by Republican Governor of Arizona Jane Dee Hull until her retirement in 2009. She was retained in 2000 and 2006. She served a term as Chief Justice that ended with her retirement from the court. She retired from the court on June 30, 2009. McGregor received a B.A. degree from the University of Iowa in 1964, an M.A. from the University of Iowa in 1965, and her law degree from the Sandra Day O'Connor College of Law at Arizona State University in 1974.

12 Sacks Tierney, "Attorneys," accessed March 4, 2020, https://www.sackstierney.com/attorneys/nussbaum.htm. Mr. Nussbaum is a Certified Bankruptcy Specialist (Arizona Board of Legal Specialization) and a Certified Business Bankruptcy Specialist (American Board of Certification). His peers have honored him with multiple peer rankings for his professional, civic and charitable achievements. Randy has been named to Super Lawyers' "Top 50 Arizona" list of attorneys multiple times and has been selected by The Best Lawyers in America® every year since 2010. Best Lawyers also selected Randy as its 2019 "Lawyer of the Year" (Scottsdale) in Bankruptcy and Creditor Debtor Rights. J.D., Arizona State University, 1980. B.A., *cum laude,* Arizona State University, 1977.

13 Ibid., 7.

14 Wikipedia, s.v. "Barry G. Silverman," last modified November 17, 2019, 17:04, https://en.wikipedia.org/wiki/Barry_G._Silverman. Barry G. Silverman is a federal judge on senior status with the United States Court of Appeals for the Ninth Circuit. He joined the court in 1998 after being nominated by President Bill Clinton. Silverman assumed senior status on October 11, 2016. Born in The Bronx, New York, Silverman attended Phoenix's Central High School in the late 1960s. Silverman earned his Bachelor of Arts degree from Arizona State University in 1973 and his Juris Doctor from the Sandra Day O'Connor College of Law at Arizona State University in 1976. Silverman served as assistant city prosecutor for the city of Phoenix from 1976 until 1977 and was the deputy county attorney from 1977 until 1979, being assigned to the courtroom of future United States Supreme Court Justice Sandra Day O'Connor, who at that time was an Arizona jurist. Silverman was a Maricopa County superior court commissioner from 1979 until 1984. Then-Arizona Governor Bruce Babbitt appointed Silverman a state superior court judge in 1984. In 1995, Silverman was appointed a United States Magistrate Judge in Phoenix.

15 *US v. Albertini,* 472 U.S. 675 (1985), rev'g 710 F.2d 1410 (9th Cir. 1983).

16 Judge McGregor would eventually be elevated to the Arizona Supreme Court and serve as its Chief Justice from 1998 to 2009.

17 *Lying v. Northwest Indian Cemetery Protective Ass'n v. Peterson,* 795 F.2d 688 (9th Cir. 1986).

18 *Bill Johnson Restaurants, Inc. v. NLRB,* 461 U.S. 731 (1983), rev'g 660 F. 2d 1335 (9th Cir. 1981).

19 *Olim v. Wakinekona,* 461 U.S. 238 (1883), rev'g 664 F.2d 708 (9th Cir. 1981).

20 *Lewis v. Jeffers,* 110 S.Ct. 3092 (1990).

21 *Whitley v. Albers,* 475 U.S. 312 (1986), rev'g 743 F.2d 1372, (9th Cir. 1984).

22 *United States v. Johns,* 469 U.S. 478 (1985), rev'g 707 F.2d 1093 (1983).

23 *United States v. Loud Hawk,* 474 U.S. 302 (1986), rev'g 741 F.2d 1184 (9th Cir. 1984).

24 Wikipedia, s.v. "Lattie F. Coor," last modified November 24, 2019, 04:41, https://en.wikipedia.org/wiki/Lattie_F._Coor. "Lattie Finch Coor Jr. (born September 26, 1936) is an American academic specializing in public policy and the past president of two universities. He was the 15th President of Arizona State University (1990–2002) and the 21st President of the University of Vermont (1976–1989)."

25 Edward Murphy, *Webster's Treasury of Relevant Quotations,* (Gramercy Books, Random House, 1978), 540. John Andres Holmes (March 14, 1773–July 7, 1843) was an American politician. He served as a U.S. Representative from Massachusetts and was one of the first two U.S. Senators from Maine. Holmes was noted for his involvement in the Treaty of Ghent. Wikipedia, s.v., "John Holmes (Maine politician)," last updated January 7, 2021, 6:05, https://en.wikipedia.org/wiki/John_Holmes_ (Maine politician).

26 At the risk of taking advantage of personal privilege, the author recalls fondly the way President Coor introduced him to a large crowd on the ASU campus when he was appointed to the Arizona Board of Regents in 2000. "Here is a recovering lawyer and an emerging author."

27 "Special 25th Anniversary Issue," *The Law Forum* (1992): 18.

28 While that was the case in 1965, Rex E. Lee, a Jennings, Strouss & Salmon lawyer in Phoenix, became the founding dean at the J. Reuben Clark Law School at Brigham Young University in 1971, a year after ASU Law's first graduating class. Wikipedia, s.v., "Rex E. Lee," last updated February 17, 2021, 7:57, https://en.wikipedia.org/wiki/Rex_E._Lee.

29 Dean Pedrick told the audience a good deal more about this essential lawyer trait. "First, you analyze the problem. What do you need to start a law school? A building. You need a faculty, students, a few ideas about curriculum . . . what about the old Matthews Center building . . . apart from leaking like a sieve, only when it rained, I wanted to have the exhilaration of spending two to three million dollars, so we were promised a new building . . . How to recruit a faculty? Be lucky. Planning is good but luck is better . . ."

30 "Ed, we'll even give you an eight o'clock in the morning class. Well, he doubted that any honest folk were up and about at that hour."

31 Ibid., 20.

32 Milton Schroeder. Emeritus Professor of Law. Arizona State University Sandra Day O'Connor College of Law. Emeritus Professor, May 2010. Professor, 1972–2010. Associate Professor, 1969–71. Associate Dean, 1978–1980.

    Sidley and Austin, Washington, D.C., Associate Attorney, 1966–69. Hon. Carl McGowan, United States Court of Appeals for the District of Columbia Circuit, Washington, D.C., Law Clerk, 1965–1966.

    Education. The University of Chicago Law School, Chicago, Illinois. J.D., *cum laude,* Coif, Editor-in-Chief University of Chicago Law Review, Weymouth Kirkland Scholar (1965). Wesleyan University, Middletown, Connecticut. B.A. with honors and distinction; College Body President; Thorndike Scholar; William Day Leonard leadership award (1962). "Milton Schroeder: Emeritus Professor of Law," Sandra Day O'Connor College of Law, accessed February 2020, https://apps.law.asu.edu/files/faculty/cvs/schroedermilt.pdf.

33 "Members," American Law Institute website, accessed March 10, 2020, https://www.ali.org/members/member/10067 (site discontinued). Mary M. Schroeder has served on the U.S. Court of Appeals for the Ninth Circuit since 1979, and was its Chief Judge from December 2000 to 2007, the first woman to hold that position. Prior to that, she served as a judge on the Arizona Court of Appeals from 1975 to 1979, and formerly she was a partner in the law firm of Lewis and Roca.

34 John Morris was a law professor from 1968 to 1993, was committed to the principles of justice and equal opportunity and worked tirelessly throughout his life to foster diversity. The College gives an annual lecture in his honor; the John P. Morris Black Law Student Association at the ASU College of Law. *See also* Chapter 8 *infra*.

35 Pedrick also said, "While I was talking to him at his Chicago home, his then twelve-year old daughter Robin, now a respected law teacher herself, turned to me, and at twelve, shyly asked, 'would you comment on the political situation in Arizona?' I evaded but talked about the subject for at least ten minutes and it must have been pretty good. I wish I could remember what I said. To our great good fortune, we got John."

36 "ASU Retirees Association," Arizona State University, accessed March 10, 2020, https://asura.asu.edu. Richard Charles Dahl, professor emeritus of the Sandra Day O'Connor College of Law at ASU and its founding librarian. He majored in philosophy at University of California (Berkeley), and then attended the Harvard Graduate School of Business Administration. He earned his Bachelor of Library Science from UC Berkeley School of Librarianship (1951), and a J.D. from Catholic University (1958). He served as the law librarian for the University of California, the University of Nebraska, the Office of the Judge Advocate General for the Navy, and Washington State. He also was Civil Division Librarian for the Department of Justice and the U.S. Treasury Department's librarian. In 1966, Richard was recruited by Willard Pedrick,

dean of the ASU College of Law, and was one of the school's founding faculty. He amassed the 60,000 volumes needed for accreditation and also taught legal research, ethics and government.

37   Dean Ares became the Dean at the University of Arizona law school when the author was a 3L there—I can still remember him speaking very positively about the entering class of 1967, my graduation year. He was right—I practiced with many graduates of both law schools before becoming adjunct faculty at ASU Law in 1994.

PART THREE

The Success Years: 2000 to 2020

CHAPTER 28

DEAN PATRICIA WHITE, 1997 TO 2007

Dean White, known by everyone as Trish, became the dean at the Sandra Day O'Connor College of Law on January 1, 1999. She said she was ready to be a dean and everyone who met her said it was about time. She majored in philosophy at the University of Michigan in 1971 and earned her MA in philosophy and her JD in 1974. While in law school, she continued her graduate studies for a PhD in philosophy, while simultaneously serving as editor of the *Michigan Law Review*. She gave law practice a serious try in 1974 at Steptoe & Johnson[1] in Washington, DC, and then moved on to Caplin & Drysdale.[2] She joined the Georgetown University Law School[3] faculty in 1979 and moved to her alma matter in 1988. While at Michigan Law, she became "of counsel" to the Detroit firm of Bodman, Longley & Darling, now Bodman.com.[4] She served for a year as a tax advisor to the Economic Study Committee of Major League Baseball. In 1994, she moved to Utah and joined the law faculty at the University of Utah, while also serving as counsel to Parsons, Behle & Latimer.[5] Along the way she was admitted to practice in DC, Michigan, and Utah. The American College of Tax Counsel[6] inducted her as a fellow. By the mid-1990s she was widely considered an expert in tax, torts, bioethics, philosophy of law, and trusts and estates and was a widely published author in both law and bioethical journals.

EDUCATED

She may be the most well educated dean in ASU Law's fifty-five-year history.[7] She earned three degrees at the University of Michigan; her BA in 1971, her MA in 1974, and her JD in 1974. She became an "ABD"[8] at the University of Michigan. She explained that in September 2006 as part of her Oral History Project at ASU.

> *I wanted to become a philosophy professor and I was interested in the philosophy of law. I was married to a philosophy professor, there weren't many jobs in philosophy and so I thought that the best way to be able to become a professor was to be better qualified to teach philosophy of law than anyone was, there weren't people with joint degrees at that point and so I went to the University of Michigan where my husband was on the philosophy faculty . . . . I simultaneously entered the PhD program in philosophy and the law school and embarked upon doing both degrees simultaneously.*[9]

She thought Michigan was the second or third best law school in the country and the second or third best philosophy department in the country. "I did it because I was going to become a philosophy professor and that I thought that having a law degree would differentiate me from everybody else."[10]

Arguably, she may also have been the hardest-working graduate student to join ASU's faculty in its history. "Well, so in law school I did all the normal things in law school as well as, I took full loads in both philosophy and law and I was a graduate teaching assistant in philosophy so I was doing both things, just doing twice as much work as other people which was one of the reasons I had so little sympathy for law students who complained about [] their workload."[11]

STUDY. WORK. LEARN. SUCCEED

While Dean White was over-achieving at the University of Michigan in 1974, the ASU Law School was just eight years old. It prohibited its students from working at outside jobs during the 1L and 2L years, much less serving as a graduate teaching assistant and taking a full course load in a PhD program in another college on the same campus. Eventually she made a choice.

> *I enjoyed both my graduate education [in philosophy] and my law education, but I found that I really enjoyed the law. . . . I took a tax course a basic tax course my third year . . . and I really liked it. . . . Thought I was really pretty good at it and thought it would be fun to practice law for a year . . . [but] [t]hought I would be better doing philosophical theoretical[] stuff if I actually had some, some context to put it in. And my husband was able in that year to have a leave and get a grant from the Center for Hellenic Studies which is in DC. And so we went to DC for the year with the idea was that I would practice law for a year and he would be writing.*[12]

LAW AND PHILOSOPHY

This is the intersection where law students become lawyers by taking a bar exam and earning a law license. Dean White did that by taking the Michigan *and* the DC bars *and* practicing with a prestigious law firm, so, as she put it, to put "context into her philosophical theoretical stuff." Some might have wondered whether there was anything philosophical about tax law. Academics won out. When her husband's one-year leave of absence was up, she left Steptoe & Johnson. They went back to Michigan—he to Ann Arbor and the University of Michigan, and she to Ohio and the University of Toledo Law School. She said it was a "fifty-minute commute" from one campus to the other. That lasted a year.

> *And then my husband and I hit upon this great idea, which was that I could, we would move to Washington and I would practice law in Washington and he would commute to Ann Arbor. And so we moved to Washington and I began practicing with [Caplin] & Drysdale, which is a boutique tax firm in Washington. . . . I got a call midway through my second year from Georgetown out of the blue saying that . . . they had a real crisis of needing somebody to come and teach [income tax law] and my name had been given to them by one of my professors at Michigan as being a really talented young tax person who had had an interest in teaching and who was in DC. And so they called me and asked me if I'd like to come and visit and teach for a year.*[13]

PHD—ABD—ASU

The year as a visiting professor turned into a tenure-track position on the Georgetown Law faculty. The cost was not finishing her PhD at Michigan. "I did not finish my PhD, because when we went to Washington for that first time I had assumed that in my spare time I would write my thesis . . . . I had done everything else . . . all my course work, all the preliminary exams . . . my thesis prospective had been accepted . . . [but] that first year I had an infant, and I was a new associate at Steptoe & Johnson and I discovered the reality of law practice which was that you don't, on top of that, have time to write a PhD thesis . . . . So I didn't, so I'm an ABD."

She spent the next eight years at Georgetown, then moved back to Ann Arbor and taught at the University of Michigan Law School for seven years, from 1988 to 1995. She accepted a faculty appointment at the University of Utah and taught there from 1995 until 1999. Her journey to ASU Law was unexpected.

> *I got a call out of the blue from Charles Calleros[14] saying that [they were] looking for a dean and embarked on a national search and my name had been given . . . and would I be interested? I said well no, I wouldn't be interested. I have no intention of being Dean. As luck would have had it, Charles called me in December, and my son and I had—my son is a golfer and he was fifteen—and we had spent Thanksgiving just before Charles happened to call on our very first trip to Arizona, and we went to The Boulders . . . it was our very first trip to Arizona and we had a lovely time and we thought of course it was very beautiful. So that's what we thought Arizona was like and that's all we saw . . . . A week later, Charles calls . . . he says well I'm going to send you the stuff about the school anyway and give it, give it some thought . . . and . . . my son . . . says, "well of course you're interested. The Boulders, we could live at the Boulders! . . . . I saw houses and condos around The Boulders; I could play golf . . . that's Arizona."[15]*

TEACHING LAW & PRACTICING LAW—YIN AND YANG

To ASU's benefit, Trish White had a different take on the relationship between law faculty and law practitioners.

> *[A]ll the time I was a law professor, sort of my part of my penchant in life was always doing two things at the same time . . . . I was also a lawyer and I always practiced law. I always had this sort of pointy-head side, and this practical side. So I was always "of counsel" to a law firm for years, different law firms in each of the places that I had, I had taught. And really did a lot of legal practice as well as being a full-time law professor. And you're not supposed to do that sort of thing, but I always thought the difference or the line that's drawn between practice and the academy was most unfortunate and that I was protected in some sense because I'm deeply theoretical . . . the sort of way that law professors look down at people who are practical didn't kind of apply to me because I was a philosopher and I was very interested in meta-theory. But I always felt that my meta-theory was far better served by really knowing something about law, and context, and law and practice. So I really led a dual life all the time I was a law professor. And so the thought of coming to a place where there weren't a lot of law schools and it's a big and sophisticated legal community on the one hand, but on the other hand the one good law school was not tarred and precluded from having anything to do with practice, struck me as very appealing and would allow for doing something that other schools didn't do.[16]*

A DECISION CAREFULLY MADE

As is always the case, the faculty is involved in the search for a new dean, but they do not make the hiring decision. New deans are hired by presidents and provosts. In this case, Lattie Coor was ASU's president and Milt Glick was the provost. Trish White met them both.

> *I was very impressed and spent time with Milt Glick that first interview and with Lattie Coor and that was very important. I was very impressed with Lattie and Milt they were very encouraging and that was, that was the interview . . . they finished interviewing the candidates and making up their minds and called me, actually Milt Glick called me and gave me the offer . . . . So, I agreed to take the job contingent on my being able to start in January. And Alan Matheson who was the interim dean, who was of course anxious*

not to be the interim dean, had done it for that entire year after Dick Morgan had left, in his normal, saintly, institutionally generous beyond measure way agreed to stay interim Dean until January 1, 1999.[17]

Since she was not from Arizona, and knew no one on the faculty, arrangements were made with Paul Eckstein,[18] then-President of the Arizona State University Law Society, to introduce Trish to the legal community. At the time, he was the managing partner at Brown & Bain, one of Phoenix's most prestigious law firms.

I came down [to Phoenix] every month for several days from the time I accepted the job through December, until I actually moved here. During that period, that was something that was quite wonderful because I would come down here every month and I could do, I [had] no duties, I didn't have to run anything, but I could learn the lay of the land.... [Paul] Eckstein, who was just unbelievably generous with his time arranged each month a group of people for me to get to know and he would take two days off of his own billable time each month and take me around to meet people in the legal community, or the political community, or the judicial community that he thought I should know.... I met all of the leaders of the judiciary, I met all the leaders of the legislature, I met, he took me to receptions at firm after firm, after firm to introduce me. He had me meet key alumni who he thought I should know. It was just an extraordinary thing that he did. And I would use the time a little bit to spend, to get to know people here, the faculty, I went to a couple of faculty meetings, but that wasn't really what it was about, it was much more about getting to know the legal community and it was [Paul's] taking me around and introducing me. There could be no better person than [Paul] Eckstein to introduce you to the legal community.[19]

IT WAS ABOUT TIME—IT WAS A TERRIBLE TIME

She became the dean just when the James Hamm saga[20] roiled the legal, political, and alumni communities in Arizona. Ms. Alcorn covered that issue at some length because Dean White had a unique awareness of how bad it might be. She saw it as a debacle poorly handled by ASU.

> *[A]t this point the whole place was in kind of the doldrums and in despair because of the James Hamm debacle and alumni giving had pretty much dried up there was effectively no giving to the law school. Several people who had promised to give gifts had reneged on their gifts because they were so irritated and angry about James Hamm. It became clear that everybody in the community . . . knew somebody that hadn't gotten in to the law school, every one of those people would have been accepted had it not been for James Hamm . . . he took every denied, disappointed applicant seat. And in my view, the whole Hamm thing had been handled very poorly. It had been handled poorly because the school . . . had been very defensive about it, and so it hadn't done any kind of outreach, or understanding of why people might have reacted the way they did about James Hamm. So we had a situation where there was just terrible bad will in the community. I think that bad will had really hardened on the part of a lot of people. So what [Paul] did can't be over-estimated in terms of its importance in introducing me [to] people who didn't want to see me. They didn't want to meet anybody who was associated with this law school, but because I was a new person and because [Paul] Eckstein was taking me around they were at least willing to meet me . . . . And not only [Paul] Eckstein, but also Mike Gallagher was instrumental in trying to arrange luncheons and as personal favors saying would you have lunch with the new dean? I think you'll see that she isn't defensive about this.[21]*

A LOT OF WORK—A DOUBLE WHAMMY

In retrospect, to say that Trish White arrived at ASU knowing a lot of work had to be done was an understatement. She had been commuting between Salt Lake and Phoenix, learning about the job she'd already accepted, when James Hamm upped the ante. In December, as she was packing up for the official move to Phoenix and starting her new job in a matter of days, the game changed. It must have looked like someone stole the deck. The Oral History recorded by Ms. Alcorn captured the double-whammy.

> *The other thing that happened in December of '98, just before I arrived here I went to my mailbox at the University of Utah Law School two weeks or so before I was going to arrive only to see a delighted fax that had been*

> sent out by Joel Seligman,[22] then the dean at the University of Arizona law school to all the deans in America, and all the law professors in America announcing gleefully that they had just received a hundred million dollar gift from one James E. Rogers[23] for their school. So that happened two weeks before I was to actually take office and that was a little disconcerting... I didn't know quite what it meant at that point but I suddenly learned that the University of Arizona had a hundred million dollars, or at least seemed to have a hundred million dollars that I didn't have....[24]

NEW FRIENDS—NEW ALLEGIANCES— NEW WAYS TO CONNECT

As the first six months in the dean's office wound down, Dean White counted the many new ways the law school was reconnecting with the legal profession. She detailed much of it in her Oral History session with Ms. Alcorn:

> [W]ith this baggage that was here... I just can't tell you how much time I spent talking to law firms, meeting people, ... getting to know every regent, getting on a personal and friendly basis, getting to know large numbers of people in the legislature, getting to know ... the Secretary of Education [Lisa Keegan] ... getting to know the Governor [Jane Hull]. Fortunately Janet Napolitano and I became fast friends because she'd become Attorney General... [S]pent a lot of time with Ruth McGregor, and who also became a really good friend and was unbelievably generous with her time in introducing me around to the various members of the legal community.... It was an immersion, huge immersion, getting very active in the State Bar Board of Governors, at that point Don Bivens was the President of the State Bar he was incredibly welcoming, he's now a partner at Snell, was a partner at Meyer, Hendricks and Bivens, incredibly welcoming.... I really just jumped in to trying to become a very visible and active member of the legal community figuring that was the best way personally to try and bridge that gap.... I had bona fides with lawyers because I *was* a lawyer, and I was coming right out of an of-counsel relationship with Parsons, Bailey and Lattimer, which is, was at that point the largest firm in Salt Lake... So a lot of time was spent

with at that point the Provost [Milt Glick, and] the President Lattie Coor, who was much more an outside president than an inside president . . . .[25]

NEW RELATIONSHIPS WITH FACULTY AND STAFF

She became dean when Dean Morgan left to create the new law school at the University of Nevada, Las Vegas. He had succeeded Dean Paul Bender, who remained as a tenured faculty member. Ms. Alcorn went into some detail about Trish's building relationships with faculty and staff in the spring of 1999:

> *Paul [Bender] had done a very good job and Paul still today does a lot of very effective outside work and he is well regarded in the community . . . he had clearly been a force, an important force and still is in the community, but it had really been since Paul's deanship until I came in that there was any aggressive systematic involvement in the community by the dean because Dick [Morgan] just clearly, that's not what he did . . . [for me] it was a brand new school, I didn't know the faculty, except the people who had hired me . . . . I had to learn to know the institution, and get to spend time with everybody in the school, it wasn't just the faculty it was of course all the staff . . . people were all very nice . . . . I scheduled a half hour meeting with every single person, not just the faculty, but every staff member, and no matter what position . . . [including] people who hadn't been here long and didn't have high paid positions at all. And that really was a good thing to do; it would be very hard for someone to do now because the staff has probably tripled since I got here.*[26]

A NEW KIND OF FACULTY

It should be remembered, when assessing Dean White's makeover of Dean Pedrick's new law school, that he graduated from law school in 1939, sixty years before she became the eighth dean of the ASU College of Law. In his day, "faculty" meant men and women working full-time to join "The Academy." Trish White was about to blend part-time with full-time and downtown Phoenix lawyering with Tempe's Ivory Tower faculty. She was also ready to move a single-focused (law) faculty into a new interdisciplinary (scientific) world.

> *Noel Fidel was persuaded to join us after he stepped down from the Court of Appeals. . . . He'd been the Chief Judge of the Court of Appeals of Arizona. He has an enormously good reputation in the legal community for his intelligence and his fairness . . . as Associate Dean for student affairs . . . you might call him Dean of Discipline. . . . There are always cases I hate to say that rise to the level where the students get attorneys . . . plagiarism cases . . . cases where students are worried about dismissal . . . attorneys are now coming in and renegotiating with Noel and they all know Noel. . . . They know they are dealing with a very sophisticated judge . . . it's a person who speaks their language and who they know . . . this has been a wonderful thing to have Noel in that position . . . Gary Birnbaum has come in, fits the same model of getting people who are tops in their field, who are not doing this for the money. . . .*[27]

INTERDISCIPLINARY LANDS AT ASU LAW

"We're so interdisciplinary," Dean White told Ms. Alcorn in 2006.

> *We have so many complications. At least fifty-four. It's doubled. . . . who do you count as a faculty member . . . what do you do with the Guy Cardineaus of the world, he's a biochemist who teaches for us, who has an office here, who is a very important person, but he's not officially quite a faculty member, he's in the bio-design unit. How do you count him? How do you count, we have all kinds of administrative positions of people who teach and they are very important and very good teachers but they are not officially faculty members. Noel Fidel, Gary Birnbaum, Andy Askland, they're not faculty members but they are members of our teaching faculty and members of our intellectual community and our administrative community . . . There are a lot of people [from] the old days . . . who think the word faculty has special meaning. So they might want to argue about who's faculty, or who's not faculty. From a student's perspective the faculty are those people who are teaching them who are here, and who are playing a big role in the educational enterprise. I don't even know how many tenure-track faculty we have. What you do with clinical faculty if you count them in that way?*[28]

Dean Patricia White, 1997 to 2007

Dean White came in 1999 and left in 2010. The changes on her watch were monumental. But in retrospect paled in comparison with the changes that would come with moving the law school from its historic location on ASU's main campus in Tempe to its opulent new high-rise building in the center of ASU's Downtown Phoenix campus in 2016.

---

1 "Homepage," Steptoe & Johnson, LLC, last visited March 20, 2020, https://www.steptoe.com/en/.
2 "Caplin & Drysdale Attorneys," Caplin & Drysdale, last visited March 20, 2020, http://www.capdale.com/.
3 "Georgetown Law," Georgetown Law, last visited March 20, 2020, https://www.law.georgetown.edu/.
4 "About Bodman," Bodman, last visited March 20, 2020, http://bodmanlaw.com/about-Bodman/.
5 "History," Parsons, Behle, & Latimer, last visited March 20, 2020, https://www.parsonsbehle.com/parsons-approach/history.
6 "American College of Tax Counsel," American College of Tax Counsel, last visited March 20, 2020, https://www.actconline.org/.
7 From 1965, when it hired its first dean, to 2020, when Dean Sylvester serves as the school's eighth dean.
8 "'All but dissertation' (ABD) is a term identifying a stage in the process of obtaining a research doctorate or a research-oriented master's degree in the United States and other countries. In typical usage of the term, the ABD graduate student has completed the required preparatory coursework, passed any required preliminary and comprehensive examinations, and met all other requirements except for the research requirements, typically including the writing and defense of a dissertation." Wikipedia, s.v., "All but dissertation," last updated October 12, 2019 23:26, https://en.wikipedia.org/wiki/All_but_dissertation.
9 Dean Patricia White (Dean, Arizona State University College of Law), interview by Marianne Alcorn, September 8, 2006, Sandra Day O'Connor College of Law, transcript Sandra Day O'Connor College of Law, 1.
10 Ibid.
11 Ibid.
12 Ibid.
13 Ibid., 2.
14 "Professor Calleros is the Alan A. Matheson Fellow in Law at Sandra Day O'Connor College of Law. He is also a member of the American Law Institute. In addition to earning several teaching awards over the years, he has earned many awards for his work in mentoring programs and outreach to youth in the community, including the ABA's Spirit of Excellence Award in 2011, and the Los Abgados Lifetime Achievement Award in 2015. Prior to joining the ASU faculty in 1981, he clerked for Circuit Judge Procter Hug Jr., of the U.S. Court of Appeals. Professor Calleros is past-President of Region XIV of the Hispanic National Bar Association. Professor Calleros is a co-founder and drummer in a rhythm-and-blues band, The Repeat Offenders." "Charles Calleros," iSearch, last visited March 20, 2020, https://isearch.asu.edu/profile/22725.
15 Dean Patricia White (Dean, Arizona State University College of Law), interview by Marianne Alcorn, September 8, 2006, Sandra Day O'Connor College of Law, transcript Sandra Day O'Connor College of Law, 3–4.
16 Ibid., 4.
17 Ibid., 6 (emphasis added).
18 "Paul F. Eckstein," Perkins Coie, last visited March 20, 2020, https://www.perkinscoie.com/en/professionals/paul-f-eckstein.html.
19 Ibid., 7.
20 *See* Chapter 25 titled, "The James Hamm Saga."
21 Dean Patricia White (Dean, Arizona State University College of Law), interview by Marianne Alcorn, September 8, 2006, Sandra Day O'Connor College of Law, transcript Sandra Day O'Connor College of Law, 7–8.
22 Seligman was the Dean and Samuel M. Fegtly Professor of Law at the University of Arizona College

of Law (1995–1999).

23 The gift of $115 million to the University of Arizona College of Law was the largest gift to the University of Arizona and the largest gift to any American law school at that time. In November 1998, the Arizona Board of Regents renamed the University of Arizona college of Law James E. Rogers College of Law. University Relations – Communication, "UA Alumnus and Longtime Benefactor James E. Rogers Dies," UA News, June 16, 2014, https://uanews.arizona.edu/story/ua-alumnus-and-longtime-benefactor-james-e-rogers-dies.

24 Dean Patricia White (Dean, Arizona State University College of Law), interview by Marianne Alcorn, September 8, 2006, Sandra Day O'Connor College of Law, transcript Sandra Day O'Connor College of Law, 8–9.

25 Ibid., 9–10.

26 Ibid., 11–12.

27 Ibid., 16.

28 Ibid., 18–19.

CHAPTER 29

THE ARIZONA INNOCENCE PROJECT & LARRY HAMMOND, 1998

Larry Hammond often said there would be no Arizona Innocence Project without the ASU College of Law.[1] Tragically, Larry Hammond is no longer at the helm of the Arizona Innocence Project. He died on March 2, 2020, long before his time. Arizona has thousands of excellent lawyers. But he was not just one of a thousand; he was on every list that purported to chronicle the best of the best. He won more cases,

had more friends, had a renowned position in state and national legal circles and had more fun than anyone I ever knew. He loved the law and all of its glorious uncertainties, and will be missed by the thousands of people he helped and inspired.

Innocent eye. Is there such a thing? Can an innocent person be guilty in the eyes of the law? Isn't justice blind? What good is actual innocence if the prosecutor ignores presumed innocence? When does the innocence of one man outweigh the guilt of many? These are weighty questions. Sir John Fortescue, an English Chief Justice, answered the last one in 1470.[2] "I should indeed, prefer twenty guilty men to escape death through mercy, than one innocent to be condemned unjustly."[3]

Nationally, the Innocence Project is a nonprofit legal organization committed to exonerating wrongly convicted people through DNA testing and to reforming the criminal justice system to prevent future injustice. The group cites various studies estimating that in the United States, between 2.3 and 5 percent of all prisoners are innocent. The Innocence Project was founded in 1992 by Barry Scheck and Peter Neufeld.[4]

"The Arizona Justice Project was established in 1998 and became the fifth organization in the United States created to help inmates overturn wrongful convictions. Today, there are close to 70 similar organizations worldwide."[5]

What Barry Scheck and Peter Neufeld started nationwide, Larry Hammond did in Arizona. Both entities and the scores of lawyers they rely on every day stand for a simple, terrifying reality: America's vaunted criminal justice system makes mistakes. Not in every case, but in too many. For decades, the notion of actual innocence in America's vast prison population was not widely held. In fact, for many law-and-order mindsets, the notion was merely irritating. But in the waning decades of the twentieth century, a growing chorus of stories from the innocent surfaced and took on a life-form. Today we the public, and some legislators, and even a handful of prosecutors, know criminal justice is fallible. Committed advocates and DNA can prove it.

Barry Scheck, Peter Neufeld, and Larry Hammond share a common lawyer DNA. They advocate for men and women snared by a criminal justice system in traps set for the guilty. Sometimes they ignore 5 percent of those charged who are actually innocent, and who suffer the consequences of a fallible justice system. The calculus is unimpeachable. "Almost everyone would agree that it is wrong to put a person to death or in prison for something they actually didn't do, something for which they are 'actually innocent.'"[6]

We have scores of authoritative and irrefutable studies in the last century of *actual innocence*. Five come to mind. *Convicting the Innocent*[7] (1932), edited by Yale Law School Professor Edwin M. Borchard;[8] *The Court of Last Resort*[9] (1952) by Erle Stanley Gardner;[10] *The Death Penalty in America*[11] (1964) by Hugo Adam Bedau; *In Spite of Innocence: Erroneous Convictions in Capital Cases*[12] (1992) by Michael L. Radelet, Hugo Adam Bedau,[13] Constance E. Putnam; and *Innocent Until Interrogated* by this volume's author.[14]

LARRY A. HAMMOND, ESQ.

Without Larry Hammond,[15] there never would have been an Arizona *version* of the Innocence Project. And it is unquestioned that without ASU Law, the project would not have existed.[16] ASU Law was first in line to provide space and focus for the project at its infancy. It grew, first on the Tempe campus, and now on the Downtown Phoenix campus in the ASU Administration building at 411 North Central. While Arizona has many excellent lawyers, and ASU Law has many excellent teachers and supporters, it's fair to say that Hammond has met all the hallmark markers.

THE ARIZONA JUSTICE PROJECT

What began as a national project became an international network. The Arizona Justice Project is part of that network. It includes "law and journalism schools, and public defense offices that collaborate to help convicted felons prove their innocence. [Forty-six] states and several other countries are a part of the network . . . Australia, Canada, Ireland, New Zealand, and the United Kingdom."[17]

The statewide project is widely respected.[18]

- The Arizona Justice Project enjoys a collaborative relationship with Arizona's two law schools. The Arizona Justice Project receives the benefit of a close relationship with the law schools' nationally recognized experts in forensic science and DNA. The Arizona Justice Project works hand-in-hand with the Post-Conviction Clinic at ASU and the Wrongful Conviction Clinic at UofA.
- From 2008 to October 2013, the Arizona Justice Project partnered with the Attorney General's Office and the Arizona Criminal Justice Commission to undergo post-conviction DNA testing in cases of forcible rape, murder, and non-negligent homicide cases where the testing might demonstrate actual innocence.
- In January 2015, the Arizona Justice Project implemented a second grant from the National Institute of Justice to review DNA cases. This program was a joint effort between the Arizona Justice Project, ASU College of Law, and UofA College of Law.
- In March 2018, Arizona Justice Project and the ASU Post-Conviction Clinic worked as part of an innovative statewide hair-review Task Force funded by the NIJ. This effort, which grew out of the Arizona Forensic Science Advisory Committee, also includes Arizona DPS Crime Lab, the Phoenix Crime Lab, Arizona Attorney General's Office, and the Arizona Criminal Justice Commission. The hair-review Task Force

will examine hundreds of convictions where hair microscopy was used against the defendant. Where identity may be at issue, DNA testing can now resolve a claim of innocence.
- Most of the Arizona Justice Project's cases do not involve DNA, or the DNA would not provide convincing evidence of guilt or innocence.

The mission statement is crisp: "To seek justice for the innocent and the wrongfully imprisoned—the marginalized and forgotten of Arizona's criminal justice system."[19]

The management team, led by Lindsay Herf, executive director, includes Katherine Puzauskas, attorney; Kelly Dodd, paralegal; Kindra Fleming, staff attorney; Megan Ealick, development and communications director; and Shawnee Ziegler, operations manager.[20]

The Board of Directors, chaired by Larry Hammond, includes Christina Howden, Colleen Maring, Gregg Curry (Treasurer), Jane Caplan, MD, Jared Keenan, Jeffrey Willis, John Canby, Jordan Green, Jose Rivera, Katia Jones, Khalil Rushdan, Lee Stein (Vice President), Maria Baier, Michael Morrissey, Michael Piccarreta, Mikel Steinfeld, Molly Karlin, Noel Fidel (Secretary), Peter Akmajian, Randy Papetti, and Victor Flores.[21]

OUTCOMES & CONSEQUENCES

There have been over 2,400 exonerations in the United States since 1989.[22] The Arizona Justice Project receives, on average, 400 requests for assistance each year. Its lawyers have represented over fifty people in post-conviction relief proceedings or before the Arizona Board of Executive Clemency.[23] Most important, the Arizona Justice Project has helped free twenty-six people since its founding in 1998.[24]

STILL MORE COULD BE DONE

The cover page on the March 2019 *Red Book* magazine headlines the Arizona Justice Project with an evocative title: "Rebalancing the Scales of Justice—Arizona Justice Project—20 Years—24 People."[25]

Executive Director Lindsay Herf said, "'We see a variety of factors time and again that lead to wrongful convictions. . . . We've had cases where DNA evidence

The Arizona Innocence Project & Larry Hammond, 1998

has proven that the eyewitness identification was incorrect, and others where the defense counsel didn't investigate, or take steps prior to trial that might have saved their client.'" Herf named other "common issues that can put a thumb on the scales of justice, from prosecutorial misconduct, and flawed forensics, to false confessions, and jail informant testimony."[26]

Board Chairman and Founder Larry Hammond wants to see "numerous reforms in the criminal justice system, including public defender funding, indigent defendants' rights to experts, and curtailing of sentencing abuses. Moreover, Arizona doesn't have an expungement statute and remains one of 17 states without legislation to compensate the wrongly convicted." Hammond said, "'I'm gratified by how much support we've had from individual law school professors at ASU and U of A, because now it's part of the fabric. . . . It makes me hopeful that younger people in prosecuting agencies have grown up in law schools with Innocence Projects. They understand that mistakes can happen. And on a personal level, of all the cases that will live with me until I pass away, the most gratifying have been the things that we did because they had to be done." "Key collaborations include the Post-Conviction Clinic at Arizona State University (run by Katherine Puzauskas, former director of the Arizona Justice Project) and the Wrongful Conviction Clinic at the University of Arizona, which provide the assistance of law students, professors, and forensics and DNA experts. A recent partnership with the ASU School of Social Work helps freed clients; [they have] nothing but a Department of Corrections ID and a set of prison blues—with employment, housing, health care and counseling."

Sometimes the simplest truths come from the highest places. Justice Sonia Sotomayor,[27] when asked about her former role as a Manhattan prosecutor, quoted Perry Mason: "My job as a prosecutor is to do justice, and justice is served when a guilty man is convicted and when an innocent man is not."[28]

---

1 Larry Hammond, interview with Gary Stuart, November 2019.
2 "Sir John Fortescue of Ebrington in Gloucestershire was Chief Justice of the King's Bench and was the author of *De Laudibus Legum Angliae*, first published posthumously circa 1543, an influential treatise on English law. In the course of Henry VI's reign, Fortescue was appointed one of the governors of Lincoln's Inn three times and served as a Member of Parliament from 1421 to 1437." Wikipedia, s.v., "John Fortescue (judge)," last updated March 3, 2020, 21:16, https://en.wikipedia.org/wiki/John_Fortescue_ (judge).
3 David S. Shrager and Elizabeth Frost, *The Quotable Lawyer* (New England Publishing Associates, Inc., 1986), 136.
4 "About," Innocence Project—Help us put an end to wrongful convictions! last visited March 19, 2020, https://www.innocenceproject.org/.

5 "AZ Justice Project," Arizona Justice Project, last visited March 19, 2020, https://www.azjusticeproject.org/project.

6 "Work Innocence Project," *ForensicsMag*, February 2005, https://www.forensicmag.com/article/2005/01/work-innocence-project.

7 Edward M. Borchard, *Convicting the Innocent: Sixty-Five Actual Errors of Criminal Justice* (1932).

8 "Edwin Montefiore Borchard was an international legal scholar, jurist, and Sterling Professor at the Yale Law School. He was a leading advocate of innocence reform and compensation for victims of wrongful conviction as well as the use of declaratory judgments. His work in international law emphasized non-intervention and neutrality." Wikipedia, s.v., "Edwin Borchard," last updated April 15, 2019 00:22, https://en.wikipedia.org/wiki/Edwin_Borchard.

9 "*The Court of Last Resort* is an American television dramatized court show, which aired October 4, 1957 – April 11, 1958, on NBC. It was co-produced by Erle Stanley Gardner's Paisano Productions, which also brought forth the long-running hit CBS-TV law series, *Perry Mason*. Its approach to dealing with potential miscarriages of justice in an entirely extra-judicial format was adopted by the BBC series *Rough Justice* in the 1980s." Wikipedia, s.v., "*The Court of Last Resort*," last updated February 28, 2020 9:43, https://en.wikipedia.org/wiki/The_Court_of_Last_Resort.

10 "Erle Stanley Gardner was an American lawyer and author. He is best known for the Perry Mason series of detective stories, but he wrote numerous other novels and shorter pieces and also a series of nonfiction books, mostly narrations of his travels through Baja California and other regions in Mexico." Wikipedia, s.v., "Erle Stanley Gardner," last updated December 18, 2019 9:25, https://en.wikipedia.org/wiki/Erle_Stanley_Gardner.

11 Hugo Adam Bedau, *The Death Penalty in America* (Oxford University Press, 1982). "In *The Death Penalty in America: Current Controversies*, Hugo Adam Bedau, one of our preeminent scholars on the subject, provides a comprehensive sourcebook on the death penalty, making the process of informed consideration not only possible but fascinating as well. No mere revision of the third edition of *The Death Penalty in America*—which the *New York Times* praised as 'the most complete, well-edited and comprehensive collection of readings on the pros and cons of the death penalty'—this volume brings together an entirely new selection of 40 essays and includes updated statistical and research data, recent Supreme Court decisions, and the best current contributions to the debate over capital punishment." "The Death Penalty in America (9780195029871): Bedau, Hugo Adam: Books," Amazon.com, last visited March 19, 2020, https://www.amazon.com/Death-Penalty-America-Hugo-Bedau/dp/0195029879.

12 Michael L. Radelet, Hugo Adam Bedau, and Constance E. Putnam, *In Spite of Innocence: Erroneous Convictions in Capital Cases* (Northeastern University Press, 1992). "Few errors made by society can compare with the horror of executing a person wrongly convicted of a crime. This sobering book, which includes an expanded preface, tells the personal stories of over 400 innocent Americans convicted of capital crimes. Some were actually executed; most suffered years of incarceration, many on death row." "*In Spite of Innocence: Erroneous Convictions in Capital Cases*, Radelet, Michael L., Bedau, Hugo Adam, Putnam, Constance E.: 9781555531973: Books," Amazon.com, last visited March 19, 2020, https://www.amazon.com/Spite-Innocence-Erroneous-Convictions-Capital/dp/1555531970.

13 "Hugo Adam Bedau was the Austin B. Fletcher Professor of Philosophy, Emeritus, at Tufts University, and is best known for his work on capital punishment. He has been called a 'leading anti-death-penalty scholar' by Stuart Taylor Jr., who has quoted Bedau as saying 'I'll let the criminal justice system execute all the McVeighs they can capture, provided they'd sentence to prison all the people who are not like McVeigh.'" Wikipedia, s.v., "Hugo Bedau," last updated December 25, 2019 15:15, https://en.wikipedia.org/wiki/Hugo_Adam_Bedau.

14 Gary L. Stuart, *Innocent Until Interrogated: The True Story of the Buddhist Temple Massacre and the Tucson Four* (Tucson: University of Arizona Press, 2010). "On a sweltering August morning, a woman walked into a Buddhist temple near Phoenix and discovered the most horrific crime in Arizona history. Nine Buddhist temple members—six of them monks committed to lives of non-violence—lay dead in a pool of blood, shot execution style. The massive manhunt that followed turned up no leads until a tip from a psychiatric patient led to the arrest of five suspects. Each initially denied their involvement in the crime, yet one by one, under intense interrogation, they confessed. Soon after, all five men recanted, saying their confessions had been coerced. One was freed after providing an alibi, but the remaining suspects—dubbed "The Tucson Four" by the media—remained in custody even though no physical evidence linked them to the crime. Seven weeks later, investigators discovered—almost by chance—physical evidence that implicated two entirely new suspects. The Tucson Four were finally freed on November 22 after two teenage boys confessed to the crime." *Innocent Until Interrogated: The True Story of the Buddhist Temple Massacre and the Tucson Four:*

The Arizona Innocence Project & Larry Hammond, 1998

Stuart, Gary L.: 9780816529247: Books," Amazon.com, last visited March 19, 2020, https://www.amazon.com/Innocent-Until-Interrogated-Buddhist-Massacre/dp/0816529248.

15 Larry received his B.A at the University of Texas in 1967 and his J.D. at the University of Texas in 1970, after serving as the Editor-in-Chief of *Texas Law Review* and graduating Order of the Coif. "Larry A. Hammond < Lawyer," Osborn Maledon, last visited March 19, 2020, https://www.omlaw.com/attorneys/bio/larry-a-hammond/. "Larry Hammond is the most senior member of the Firm Osborn Maledon, and the Firm's investigations and criminal defense group. Larry's practice, for many years, has focused primarily on criminal defense – both white collar and general criminal representation. He has also been extensively involved in complex civil litigation . . . . He is a founder of the Arizona Justice Project, serving as its President for the last 20 years. He also helped found the Arizona Capital Representation Project to assist inmates charged or convicted of capital crimes, and has served as the Chair of the State Bar's Indigent Defense Task Force since its creation 20 years ago. He also served as President of the American Judicature Society – an organization devoted to improving the administration of justice in America." "Larry Hammond," AZ Justice Project, last visited March 19, 2020, https://www.azjusticeproject.org/larry-hammond. "Larry came to the predecessor of [Osborn Maledon] in 1974, after clerkships on the United States Court of Appeals for the District of Columbia, two Supreme Court Clerkships (for Justice Hugo L. Black and Lewis F. Powell, Jr.), and after serving as Assistant Watergate Special Prosecutor. Shortly after his arrival in Arizona, however, he left and spent the next four years as the First Deputy Assistant Attorney General in the Office of Legal Counsel at the Department of Justice. At the end of the Carter Administration, he returned to Osborn Maledon." Ibid.

16 Larry Hammond, multiple interviews with Gary L. Stuart, 2019.

17 Wikipedia, s.v., "Innocence Project," last updated February 26, 2020 18:35, https://en.wikipedia.org/wiki/Innocence_Project.

18 "AZ Justice Project," The Arizona Justice Project, last visited March 19, 2020, https://www.azjusticeproject.org/project.

19 "Mission and Vision – AZ Justice Project," The Arizona Justice Project, last visited March 19, 2020, https://www.azjusticeproject.org/mission-and-vision.

20 "Management Team – AZ Justice Project," The Arizona Justice Project, last visited March 19, 2020, https://www.azjusticeproject.org/management-team.

21 "Board of Directors – AZ Justice Project," The Arizona Justice Project, last visited March 19, 2020, https://www.azjusticeproject.org/board.

22 "The National Registry of Exonerations – Exoneration Registry," University of Michigan Law School, last visited March 19, 2020, http://www.law.umich.edu/special/exoneration/Pages/about.aspx.

23 "Facts and Figures – AZ Justice Project," The Arizona Justice Project, last visited March 19, 2020, https://www.azjusticeproject.org/facts-and-figures.

24 Ibid.

25 Jake Pointer, "Rebalancing the Scales of Justice—Arizona Justice Project—20 Years—24 People," *Redbook Magazine*, March 2019, https://issuu.com/theredbook/docs/trbm0319.issuu?fbclid=IwAR3MkrxzdpMMFKgnQnW8OcPGtaEpf_yKRHSiQnEO25NbVM4-N5WaTOM6Tug.

26 Ibid., 48–49.

27 "Sonia Maria Sotomayor is an American lawyer and jurist who serves as an Associate Justice of the Supreme Court of the United States. She was appointed by President Barack Obama in May 2009 and confirmed that August. She was the first Hispanic and Latina Justice." Wikipedia, s.v., "Sonia Sotomayor," last updated March 19, 2020 18:27, https://en.wikipedia.org/wiki/Sonia_Sotomayor.

28 "The Nation: Sotomayor's Reality Check," NPR.org, July 16, 2009, https://www.npr.org/templates/story/story.php?storyId=106679619.

CHAPTER 30

ASSOCIATE JUSTICE SANDRA DAY O'CONNOR NAMES THE LAW SCHOOL. 2006

She needs no introduction. There were about 1,116,967 lawyers in America in 2018.[1] It's a safe bet that each of the 1,116,967 active lawyers in the country knows her name. Thousands of them know her personally. Tens of thousands have had professional interactions with her. For that tiny handful of readers who do not recognize the name, Sandra Day O'Connor is a retired Associate Justice of the Supreme Court of the United States. President Ronald Reagan appointed her in 1981. She retired in 2006. She was the first woman to serve on the Court.[2] What many might not know is there are 237 law schools in America. Only one of them carries a woman's name. It is the *Sandra Day O'Connor College of Law*.[3]

RENAMING ASU LAW

On April 5, 2006, ASU Law was officially renamed the *Sandra Day O'Connor College of Law* at Arizona State University. She did not "give" her name to the school; she "lent" it. The press release clarified it: *"Founding Mother Lends Name to College."*

Jane Magruder said, "She's Arizona's favorite daughter, and a true pioneer, having been the first woman to lead a state senate, the first woman to serve on the United States Supreme Court, and, now, the first woman to have her name attached to a law school."[4]

ASU President Michael Crow called her "a founding mother in American History . . . She represents a unique thing among American intellectuals and that is a plain-spoken American intellect, it's understandable by many of us."[5]

Dean Patricia White, said, "We intend to use Justice O'Connor as a model, to break the mold and to move forward with great success."[6]

The November 17, 2006 naming ceremony was held at Armstrong Hall.[7] They built a special platform along the pathway between Armstrong Hall and the Ross-Blakley Law Library, just for this occasion. Congratulatory remarks by Dean Patricia White, Provost Betty Capaldi, President Michael Crow, and several students made the day sparkle, and the occasion humbling.

Alastair Gamble, a third-year law told the crowd a few little-known facts about Justice O'Connor's "golf prowess—she aced a hole-in-one six years ago . . . her admiration for the poet Aldous Huxley makes her a shining example to our generation . . . there has never been a time when we did not know the great Justice O'Connor . . . she has challenged us to make the most of our lives no matter how many setbacks there are."[8]

Justice O'Connor addressed the crowd.

> *I'm speechless. I'm also overwhelmed and greatly honored by having this law school named for me. There are about 190 law schools in the United States, almost four per state, two in the state of Arizona, and none of these many law schools until now named for a woman. That's a big step for the law school to take, and I am truly honored to have it bear my name. I grew up on a ranch over in Greenway County, Arizona, and Hidalgo County, New Mexico. Occasionally, as a youngster, my family would get in the car, and we would drive through Phoenix, and in doing that the highway used to come through Mesa and Tempe, and we would make that big turn down here just south of the university, and then go north, and we would pass by what was then Tempe Normal School, with its three red brick buildings. One of them is now the University Club, one of them is the old president's house, and then there's Old Main. Tempe Normal School taught people to be teachers. Over*

the years, as we still occasionally drove by, the university began to grow, and then it grew more, and it grew more.

After I got out of law school in 1957 when my husband, John, and I came back so that he could join a law firm in Phoenix and we would live in this community, I still couldn't get a job in a law firm. But that was all right. I opened a law office out in Maryvale with a partner, and we took whatever we could get—not the kind of thing usually heard at the United States Supreme Court—but we got along and John and I had a wonderful life in this marvelous place of Arizona. I loved this state, and I was so privileged to serve in all three branches of our state's government, and to watch it grow.

I was a member of the state legislature when a request was made to authorize funds to establish a law school at Arizona State University. I was on the appropriations committee. There was a lot of debate, many people did not want it to happen, they thought we had quite enough lawyers as it was, thank you very much, and we had a perfectly good law school down at the University of Arizona. But I guess wiser heads prevailed, and some money was appropriated to get this law school started. I was from Maricopa County, and ultimately I voted for that proposition, never dreaming of course that my name would ever be associated with it.

Luckily for the law school, Willard Pedrick became its first dean. He was enormously gifted, and talented, and had a very charming personality. He went a long way toward reconciling those people who had been opposed to the creation of a law school here. Now Phoenix is about the fifth-largest city in the nation, and it's altogether fitting that there be a great law school here in the Phoenix area, in Maricopa County, serving this enormous population center.

A law school, a good law school, becomes a voice in the public arena. I remember frequently in the legislature turning to professors here at the law school to help research and advise on particular legislative approaches to get their wisdom. A law school with its gifted faculty can make so many contributions to the business of the state and to how the state and the community progresses. Indeed, they can contribute nationally to the debates that we have. I learned very soon in serving in the state government that the problems faced in the states have their mirror images in the problems that the nation faces. The problems the states have are not limited to state boundaries.

And I am so touched to have my name now on this law school, but it is going to restrict my activities you know because I certainly don't want to bring any discredit now to this law school. So in my retirement I guess I am going to have to behave myself, but it will be a pleasure, and I hope that one of these days, in the not too distant future, I'll have a little more free time to spend a little more time here in Arizona, and come by the law school for various events, and various opportunities to visit with the very talented group of students, and a marvelously talented faculty. We are blessed today for me to see some friends in the audience who are here to observe this occasion, and I thank you for being here and to have the members of our state Supreme Court here for this occasion. You know of course, that Arizona has the best, most talented Supreme Court among the 50 states. If you don't know it, I'm here to tell you, we do.

This law school is already a wonderful law school, but what I want for it and what I see for it ahead is becoming a beacon among state university law schools throughout this country, and I think it will. It's gone a long way already.

So the main thing is just to tell all of you thank you. Those were beautiful words spoken by each of you on the podium today, very touching, and I respect what this law school stands for, what it has done, what it will do, and what this marvelous student body will do in the future, and all those that follow it. So bear with us, help us, and help make this just the best in the nation. Thank you.[9]

Justice O'Connor spent a good part of the day, after the ceremony, meeting with student groups, and visiting with old friends in the school's Rotunda. Speaking to a group of first-year students, she handed down a road map to law school success. "Read fast, write well, and look for opportunities to make something out of almost anything."[10]

She also talked about her interview with President Reagan in 1981, which apparently included a conversation about cattle, horses, and building fences. "I think he probably put me on the court because he liked my ranching background."[11]

THE SANDRA DAY O'CONNOR SYMPOSIUM—CONVERSATIONS ABOUT SANDRA DAY O'CONNOR

On March 23, 2007, the law school learned a good deal more about its namesake. It hosted the O'Connor Symposium. Melissa Bengtson, Editor-in-Chief, *Arizona State Law Journal,* and Dean Patricia White led the daylong event. The list of speakers and topics was as distinguished as it was topical.[12] The Symposium Notes include milestones on Justice O'Connor's road to the Supreme Court.

1946—Freshman year at Stanford.

1950—Graduation with BS from Stanford—starts law school—meets John O'Connor, III, fellow law student.

1952—Marries John.

1957—She and John are sworn in to the Arizona Bar.

1969—Appointed to fill an unexpired seat in Arizona State Senate.

1971—Elected to Arizona Senate Majority Leader; Writes to President Nixon, who is facing two Supreme Court vacancies, urging him to consider a woman—"It is my belief that citizens of this nation would warmly accept a woman on the Supreme Court"—Nixon names Louis Powell and William Rehnquist.

1975—Leaves the state legislature for a Maricopa County Superior Court judgeship.

1979—Gov. Bruce Babbitt appoints her to Arizona Court of Appeals.

1981—As she celebrates her fifty-first birthday in Phoenix, Supreme Court Justice Potter Stewart has a confidential meeting with Attorney General William French Smith and reveals his intent to step down at the end of his term. President Reagan creates a nomination process, and meets with her on July 1, 1981, at the Oval Office. After speaking with her, he interviews no one else. When he announces her nomination, he describes her as a "person for all seasons."

2005—Exactly twenty-four years later, she tells President George W. Bush she intends to retire to spend more time with John, her ailing husband. After a quarter-century on the Court, her legacy includes abortion rights, affirmative action, right to counsel, the death penalty, and separation of church and state. She shaped the law with her Western pragmatism and her feel for the American center.

EDUCATION

She went to Stanford University, earning a BA in Economics in 1950.[13] Two years later, she got her law degree from Stanford, and was on the Law Review with its presiding editor-in-chief, future Supreme Court Chief Justice William Rehnquist, who was the class valedictorian.[14] She was third in the class.[15] In 2003, she wrote a book titled *The Majesty of the Law—Reflections of a Supreme Court Justice*.[16] In 2005, she wrote a children's book, *Chico*, named for her favorite horse.[17]

Once on the Supreme Court, her higher education positions became clearer.[18] Law Professor Herman Schwartz called O'Connor "the Court's leader in its assault on racially oriented affirmative action."[19] She joined the Court majority in upholding the constitutionality of race-based admissions to universities.[20] In 2003, she authored a majority Supreme Court opinion, *Grutter v. Bollinger*.[21] It was a landmark case, upholding affirmative action admissions policies of the University of Michigan Law School. The court held, 5–4, that the University of Michigan Law School had a compelling interest in promoting class diversity. The majority opinion said a race-conscious admissions process may favor "underrepresented minority groups," but "[must also take] into account many other factors evaluated individually for every applicant, [cannot] amount to a quota system that would have been unconstitutional under *Regents of the University of California v. Bakke*."[22]

Justice O'Connor maintained her connections to Arizona, its law schools and courts after her retirement from the Supreme Court. In the spring semester, 2006, she taught a two-week course called "*The Supreme Court*" at the University of Arizona's James E. Rogers College of Law. In the fall of 2007, joined by one

Associate Justice Sandra Day O'Connor Names the Law School. 2006

of her former law clerks, Justice W. Scott Bales, she taught a course at the Sandra Day O'Connor College of Law. Additionally, she heard cases on a part-time basis in federal district courts and courts of appeals as a visiting judge. By 2008, O'Connor had sat for cases with the Second, Eighth, and Ninth Circuits.[23] She heard an Arizona voting rights case, which the Supreme Court later reviewed. In *Arizona v. Inter-Tribal Council of Arizona*,[24] a 7–2 majority affirmed O'Connor and the rest of Ninth Circuit panel, and struck down a provision of Arizona's voting registration law.[25]

In 2009, she founded the 501(c) 3 nonprofit organization now known as the *Sandra Day O'Connor Institute*. It promotes civil discourse, civic engagement, and civics education in the downtown Phoenix campus of the Sandra Day O'Connor College of Law.[26]

There are hundreds of books, essays, critiques, articles, and opinions about her, her life, her jurisprudence, and her incalculable impact on American law and culture. Perhaps the most recent is the most insightful. *First: Sandra Day O'Connor*, by Evan Thomas, is a 2019 biography that thrills and quells in almost equal proportions.[27] It was reviewed by many, bought by thousands, and will resonate with millions. Jeffery Toobin[28] reviewed it for the *New York Times*. The books' subtitle, *An Intimate Portrait of Sandra Day O'Connor, First Woman on the Supreme Court*, caught Toobin's well-trained eye for both the law and the great names associated with it. He said, "The book is billed as an 'intimate portrait' of O'Connor, and it certainly is. The O'Connor family gave Thomas open access to the justice's papers, including letters and diaries, and encouraged all who knew her, law clerks as well as colleagues, to speak with him. Thomas makes the most of this bounty, producing a richly detailed picture of her personal and professional life."[29]

Toobin's talent for connecting his subject's early life to a later career shows well in his review of Evan Thomas' brilliant work.

> *O'Connor's childhood on the Lazy B Ranch, which was situated on 160,000 rain-starved acres on the Arizona-New Mexico border. It was tough country. Sandra didn't have a pet cat; she had a pet bobcat. But her rugged father and refined mother wanted more than just a rural life for their precocious daughter, and that led to another toughening experience. When Sandra was just 6 years old, they sent her to live with her maternal grandparents in El Paso, where she attended a finishing school, ate on white tablecloths, and*

studied Latin and Greek. As Thomas notes, Sandra's childhood bred in her a passion for self-sufficiency and an aversion to whining. Much later, her orders to her law clerks were clear: "No excuses. Get the job done."[30]

His descriptive voice is clear about who she was in early life.

Her professional ascent is rapid. She wins a seat in the Arizona State Senate, tames that boys' club enough to become majority leader, and then moves to a judgeship on the state appeals court. Her life with John is a study—in that maddening phrase—in having it all. They hiked, skied and golfed; networked with big shots like Chief Justice Warren Burger; and raised three rambunctious boys (one of whom went on to climb Mount Everest). In her spare time, she cooked every recipe in Julia Child's "Mastering the Art of French Cooking." "Oh, for God's sake, Sandra," a friend lamented about that particular feat, "do you always have to overachieve?"[31]

Toobin, a constitutional scholar of sorts, crisply defines her jurisprudential voice. "There is no O'Connor doctrine—no overarching philosophy—just a series of practical accommodations to the issues before her. She respected traditions and institutions; as Thomas notes, one reason she embraced affirmative action was that the leaders of corporate America and the military, in amicus briefs, told her it was the right thing to do. (Marriage was another institution that O'Connor revered, and she was proud to be known as 'the Yenta of Paradise Valley')."[32]

It is also the case that Justice O'Connor always knew how hard it could be for women to succeed. That's on point in Toobin's review: "O'Connor knew what she wanted her legacy to be. While still a justice and in robust health, she gave instructions to her sons about the public portion of her funeral, writing, 'I hope I have helped pave the pathway for other women who have chosen to follow a career.' Notwithstanding her own extraordinary example, O'Connor recognized how difficult that still was."[33]

In October 2018, Justice O'Connor announced her effective retirement from public life after disclosing that she had been diagnosed with the early stages of Alzheimer's-like dementia.[34]

The ASU community, Arizona, and the nation no longer have a close connection to Justice O'Connor. We would do well to heed her own words.

Associate Justice Sandra Day O'Connor Names the Law School. 2006

It is the individual who can and does make a difference even in this increasingly populous, complex world of ours. The individual can make things happen. It is the individual who can bring a tear to my eye and then cause me to take pen in hand. It is the individual who has acted or tried to act who will not only force a decision but also have a hand in shaping it. Whether acting in the legal, governmental, or private realm, one concerned and dedicated person can meaningful affect what some consider an uncaring world. So give freely of yourself always to your family, your friends, your community, and your country. The world will pay you back many times over.[35]

---

1 According to the American Bar Association there are currently 1,116,967 lawyers practicing in the United States. That is approximately one for every 300 people, or approximately 0.36% of the total population. These statistics relate only to those currently practicing and maintaining their licenses. There are far more with inactive or retired status. "What Percent of the US Population do Lawyers Comprise?" *WiseGeek*, accessed April 6, 2020, https://www.wisegeek.com/what-percent-of-the-us-population-do-lawyers-comprise.htm.

2 Wikipedia, s.v. "Sandra Day O'Connor," last modified March 19, 2020, ttps://en.wikipedia.org/wiki/Sandra_Day_O%27Connor.

3 "On April 5, 2006, ASU Law was officially renamed the Sandra Day O'Connor College of Law at Arizona State University. This was, and still is, the only law school to be named after a woman. Seven months later on November 17, Justice O'Connor was the honored guest at a renaming celebration at Armstrong Hall in Tempe, Arizona. Under the banner of the Sandra Day O'Connor College of Law, ASU has jumped to No. 25 among all law schools and—like its namesake—has continued to increase its efforts to serve the community." "Celebrating 10 Years as the Sandra Day O'Connor College of Law," Newsletter, Sandra Day O'Connor College of Law, accessed March 27, 2020, https://law.asu.edu/asulaw-newsletter/oconnor-renaming.

4 See "*Constructive Notice, Commemorative Edition*," Sandra Day O'Connor College of Law, by Janie Magruder. Law library archives.

5 Ibid.

6 Ibid.

7 The author remembers her speech very well and was delighted to be among the invited guests. With only two exceptions, the entire Arizona Board of Regents was present for the naming and the reception in Armstrong Hall that followed. In addition to the occasional formal events I was privileged to attend, I tried two cases in her trial court, argued one appeal before her while she was on the Arizona Court of Appeals, and was thankful she let me sit in one of her two front row seats during Fifth Amendment oral arguments in three cases before the U.S. Supreme Court for oral arguments on Fifth Amendment cases in 2003. I also had the pleasure of teaching with her at the *National Institute of Trial Advocacy* in the early 1980s.

8 See "*Constructive Notice, Commemorative Edition,*" Sandra Day O'Connor College of Law, by Janie Magruder. Law library archives.

9 "Celebrating 10 Years as the Sandra Day O'Connor College of Law."

10 See "Constructive Notice, Commemorative Edition," Sandra Day O'Connor College of Law, by Janie Magruder. Law library archives.

11 Ibid.

12 See "Conversations About Sandra Day O'Connor—A Symposium. March 23, 2007," 39 Ariz. St. L.J. 777 (2007),Ross-Blakley Law Library, Arizona State University. Topics and speakers included: Session One—Biography of Justice O'Connor (Joan Biskupic, Journalist and Biographer; Barry MacBan, lawyer); Session Two—Former Law Clerks—Moderator Prof. Paul Bender—Speakers Justice Scott Bales, Justice Ruth McGregor, RonNell Anderson, Univ. of Arizona College of Law, Charles Blanchard, Perkins Coie Brown & Bain.; Session Three—Abortion Rights and Gender and Race Discrimination—Moderator Prof., George Schatzki, Prof. Jay Stewart, Prof. Paul Bender; Session Four—Politics and Judicial Independence, Prof. Arthur Hellman, Prof. Scot Powe.

13 Kevin Cool, "Front and Center," *Stanford Alumni Magazine,* January/February 2006, https://stanford mag.org/contents/front-and-center.

14 "Transcript: O'Connor on Fox." *Fox News,* July 1, 2005, https://web.archive.org/web/20070523084030/ http://www.foxnews.com/story/0, 2933, 161325, 00.html; Wikipedia, s.v. "William Rehnquist," last modified April 2, 2020, 08:11, https://en.wikipedia.org/wiki/William_Rehnquist.

15 "Transcript: O'Connor on Fox." *Fox News,* July 1, 2005, https://web.archive.org/web/20070523084030/ http://www.foxnews.com/story/0, 2933, 161325, 00.html.

16 Sandra Day O'Connor, *The Majesty of the Law: Reflections of a Supreme Court Justice* (New York: Random House, 2003).

17 Sandra Day O'Connor, *Chico* (New York: Dutton Children's Books, 2005).

18 *See* Wikipedia, s.v. "Sandra Day O'Connor," last modified March 19, 2020, 18:24, https://en.wikipedia.org/wiki/Sandra_Day_O%27Connor.

19 Herman Schwartz, "O'Connor as a 'Centrist'? Not When Minorities are Involved," *Los Angeles Times,* April 12, 1998, http://articles.latimes.com/1998/apr/12/opinion/op-38686.

20 James Taranto and Leonard Leo, *Presidential Leadership* (New York: Free Press, 2004), 235.

21 *Grutter v. Bollinger,* 539 U.S. 306 (2003).

22 *Regents of the University of California v. Bakke,* 438 U.S. 265 (1978). The court upheld affirmative action, allowing race to be one of several factors in college admission policy. However, the court ruled that specific racial quotas, such as the 16 out of 100 seats set aside for minority students by the University of California, Davis School of Medicine, were impermissible.

23 Wikipedia, s.v., "Sandra Day O'Connor," last updated January 28, 2021, 3:24, https://en.wikipedia.org/wiki/Sandra_Day_O%27Connor.

24 *Arizona v. Inter-Tribal Council of Arizona, Inc.,* 570 U.S. 1 (2013), revolving around Arizona's unique voter registration requirements, including the necessity of providing documentary proof of citizenship. In a 7–2 decision, the Supreme Court held that Arizona's registration requirements were unlawful because they were preempted by federal voting laws.

25 Wikipedia, s.v., "Sandra Day O'Connor," last updated January 28, 2021, 3:24, https://en.wikipedia.org/wiki/Sandra_Day_O%27Connor.

26 "Sandra Day O'Connor Institute," *Arizona Non-Profits,* last updated July 26, 2017, https://web.archive.org/web/20180510184142/http://arizonanonprofits.org/members/?id%3D42354572.

See also "Our Mission of Civic Duty," *Sandra Day O'Connor Institute,* accessed April 6, 2020, http://oconnor institute.org/about/missionopportunity/.

27 Evan Thomas, *First: Sandra Day O'Connor* (New York: Random House, 2019).

28 Toobin is a Harvard-trained lawyer, blogger, author, pundit, and legal analyst for CNN and *The New Yorker*. During the Iran–Contra affair, he served as an associate counsel in the Department of Justice, and moved from law into writing during the 1990s. He has written several books, including one on the O. J. Simpson murder case. It was adapted as a series, "The People v. O. J. Simpson: American Crime Story," and aired in 2016 as the first season of FX *American Crime Story.* It won numerous Emmy Awards. Wikipedia, s.v. "Jeffrey Toobin," last modified February 1, 2020, 09:00, https://en.wikipedia.org/wiki/Jeffrey_Toobin.

29 Jeffrey Toobin, "An Intimate Portrait of Sandra Day O'Connor, First Woman on the Supreme Court," *New York Times,* March 18, 2019, https://www.nytimes.com/2019/03/18/books/review/evan-thomas-first-sandra-day-oconnor.html.

30 Ibid.

31 Ibid.

32 Ibid.

33 Ibid.

34 Matthew Haag, "Sandra Day O'Connor, First Woman on Supreme Court, Reveals Dementia Diagnosis," *New York Times,* October 23, 2018, https://www.nytimes.com/2018/10/23/us/politics/sandra-day-oconnor-dementia-alzheimers.html.

35 O'Connor, *The Majesty of the Law,* 194.

CHAPTER 31

DEAN PAUL SCHIFF BERMAN. 2007 TO 2010

The press release dated May 8, 2008, was exciting news for the Sandra Day O'Connor College of Law. He was a "scholar with a vision."[1] He was "an administrator who could move with speed and agility."

Dean Berman replaced Dean Patricia White, ASU Law's seventh dean in forty-three years. It was a momentous change at a unique time in ASU Law's history. ASU President Michael Crow was obviously proud of his pick. "In Paul Berman, ASU has found a scholar and leader who reflects the core characteristics of the New American University . . . Paul is a bold thinker and will push the boundaries of what a law school can be. He will move swiftly and adroitly to elevate an already great law school into the top echelon of American legal education not by chasing the handful of law schools that represent the old 'gold standard' but rather by defining what 21st century legal education ought to be."

Dean Berman accomplished those goals in just over three years. Then he was lured back to the east coast to become the new dean of a much older (founded in 1865) and slightly higher-ranked law school, The George Washington University Law School[2] in Washington, DC.[3]

CREDENTIALS

Berman's legal pedigree[4] is outstanding. He graduated from Princeton in 1988 and earned his law degree from New York University School of Law in 1995.[5] He achieved the highest GPA and was valedictorian of his graduating class. He served as a law clerk first to Chief Judge Harry T. Edwards[6] of the U.S. Court of Appeals for the DC Circuit and then to Justice Ruth Bader Ginsburg[7] of the United States Supreme Court. When he joined ASU, his wife, Laura Dickinson, also joined the ASU Law Faculty. They met literally *at* the U.S. Supreme Court; she clerked for Justice Blackmun while he was clerking for Justice Ginsburg. Justice Ginsburg performed their wedding ceremony in 2004.

ASU Provost and Executive Vice President Elizabeth D. Capaldi was equally thrilled with his appointment. She said, "Paul Berman is incredibly creative and visionary. From [our] first meeting he impressed us all with his energy and ideas for building excellence in the law school, including greater interdisciplinary connections and new academic programs that will increase access, excellence and impact. He has terrific support from the faculty of the law school, and from the other deans. I am very excited we have attracted him here."[8]

In his first public announcement, he outlined what he hoped to accomplish at the ASU Law School: "Ultimately, I envision a truly multidisciplinary legal center, where future lawyers develop essential skills for both transnational and local legal practice, where leading scholars from around the world come to engage in high-level discourse on law's role in society, where policy-makers can address the pressing social issues of our time, where corporate leaders can find the latest information on the legal regulation of cutting-edge scientific and technological innovation, and where even those who do not intend to be lawyers can spend at least a year exploring law's crucial role in a multicultural democracy embedded within an increasingly interconnected world."[9]

A DIFFERENT APPROACH TO LEGAL EDUCATION

Berman brought a very different approach to legal education, based in part on his scholarly writing emphasis. He focused on how globalization affects the intersection between cyberspace law,[10] international law,[11] and the cultural analysis of law.

One of the books he co-authored, *Cultural Analysis, Cultural Studies, and the Law: Moving Beyond Legal Realism*,[12] is a field-defining collection of work. "Over the past few decades the marked turn toward claims and policy arguments based on cultural identity—such as ethnicity, race, or religion—has pointed up the urgent need for legal studies to engage cultural critiques. Exploration of legal issues through cultural analyses provides a rich supplement to other approaches—including legal realism, law and economics, and law and society. As Austin Sarat and Jonathan Simon demonstrate, scholars of the law have begun to mine the humanities for new theoretical tools and kinds of knowledge. Crucial to this effort is cultural studies, with its central focus on the relationship between knowledge and power."[13]

In retrospect, ASU Law might not have been ready for his high-level sense of global realism. It was Arizona, not Washington, DC. He explained this reality in 2012.

> *I start from the premise that we live in a world of legal pluralism, where a single act or actor is potentially regulated by multiple legal or quasi-legal regimes imposed by state, substate, transnational, supranational, and non-state communities. Yet law often operates based on a convenient fiction that nation-states exist in autonomous, territorially distinct, spheres and that activities therefore fall under the legal jurisdiction of only one regime at a time. Traditional legal rules have tied jurisdiction to territory: a state could exercise complete authority within its territorial borders and no authority beyond it. In the twentieth century, such rules were loosened, but territorial location remains the principal touchstone for assigning legal authority. If one could spatially ground a dispute, one could most likely determine the legal rule that would apply. But consider such a system in today's world. Should the U.S. government be able to sidestep the U.S. Constitution when it houses prisoners in "offshore" detention facilities in Guantánamo Bay or elsewhere around the world? Should spatially distant corporations that create serious local harms be able to escape local legal regulation simply because they are not physically located in the jurisdiction? When the U.S. government seeks to shut down the computer of a hacker located in Russia, does the virus transmitted constitute an act of war or a violation of Russia's sovereignty? How can we best understand the complex relationships among international, regional,*

national, and subnational legal systems? Does it make sense to think that satellite transmissions, online interactions, and complex financial transactions have any territorial locus at all? And in a world where nonstate actors such as industry standard-setting bodies, nongovernmental organizations, religious institutions, ethnic groups, terrorist networks, and others exert significant normative pull, can we build a sufficiently capacious understanding of the very idea of jurisdiction to address the incredible array of overlapping authorities that are our daily reality?[14]

LEGAL EDUCATION IN THE FUTURE TENSE

Tempe, Arizona, was not exactly the right place to discuss, research, or even convene twenty-first-century global, legal, or policy studies. But while dean at ASU, Berman was a force for the future of legal education. His signature theme, "Legal Education in the Future Tense," was part of his 2009–2010 report. In distributing that report, complete with pictures and tributes to the school's founders, Berman said, "Welcome to what I hope will be the first of a regular series of reports we will create informing you about the ongoing life of the Sandra Day O'Connor College of Law and featuring news on graduates who are making a real difference in their communities and throughout the nation. This is an exciting moment for the College of Law. As we celebrate the 40th anniversary of our first graduating class, we recognize those who built the school to its current level of excellence and national prominence. At the same time, in these pages we also highlight the astonishing array of new programs, initiatives, and student opportunities that are currently transforming the College of Law into an innovative national leader in legal education."

While not all his ideas were welcome in the faculty lounge, he accomplished much in his three years at the helm. He brought in many distinguished scholars, including Daniel M. Bodansky, Laura Dickinson, James G. Hodge, Jr., David Gartner, and Carl J. Artman. On his watch, he administered a program envied by many state law schools. In 2008, ASU Law enrolled 181 first-year students, 75 percent of whom arrived with LSAT scores above 162 and GPAs exceeding 3.7. Twenty-six percent were students of color, forty-nine were female, the average age was twenty-seven, and they ranged from twenty-one to sixty-five years of age. Concurrent degrees were offered: JD/MBA, JD/MD with the Mayo Medical School, JD/PhD in the Justice and Social Inquiry School, and JD/PhD in Psychology.

Dean Paul Schiff Berman. 2007 to 2010

He did not create ASU's nationally recognized centers. However, he supported them financially, intellectually, and administratively. They included the nation's first, largest, and most comprehensive Center for the Study of Law, Science, and Technology; the Center for Transnational Public-Private Governance; the Indian Law Program; and the Committee on Law and Philosophy. There were eight operating clinics for students, faculty, and local lawyers. Career Services reported the academic year of 2008–2009 results: a 95 percent placement rate and a 93 percent bar passage rate in Arizona. That year, the Arizona Supreme Court consisted of five justices—three were ASU Law graduates (Chief Justice Ruth McGregor, Vice-Chief Justice Rebecca White Berch, and Justice Michael D. Ryan). ASU Law was represented by three graduates on the Ninth Circuit Court of Appeals (Judges Barry G. Silverman, Judge Michael Hawkins, and Judge William C. Canby, Jr.—one of ASU Law's founding faculty members). Berman's message to the Arizona legal and professional communities was as broad as it was novel. "The Sandra Day O'Connor College of Law is pioneering a new model for 21st Century legal education, one that reinvents the modern law school as not just an institution that trains lawyers, but as a multifaceted legal studies center that engages in developing solutions to the world's global challenges and seeks to educate a broad cross section of contemporary society."

Dean Berman has fond memories of his deanship at ASU. He said, "Legal Education in the Future Tense was a way of encapsulating and branding a new vision for the college. It was a collaboration I helped establish between ASU and the New America Foundation, a DC think tank." Over the three years he was dean, the College of Law's *US News & World Report* ranking rose from 55 to 26, the largest and fastest move of any top school in the history of the rankings. Dean Berman, with a good deal of help from his associate deans, especially his successor in the dean's office, Douglas Sylvester, began the planning process to move the school from the Tempe campus to ASU's new Downtown Phoenix campus. In that process he developed the concept of making the law school more than just an academic institution, but a true "Center for Law & Society," housing resources for students, not-for-profit organizations, and members of the practicing bar. He initiated the nation's first post-graduate public interest fellowship to help graduating students secure jobs in the public sector. Though he longed to stay at ASU, family obligations ultimately took him back to the east coast where he became dean of the George Washington University Law School.

THE SANDRA DAY O'CONNOR COLLEGE OF LAW

BACK TO THE EAST COAST

In 2012, he left Arizona for Washington, DC, as the new dean at George Washington University's School of Law.

> *Paul Schiff Berman, currently the dean of the Arizona State University Sandra Day O'Connor College of Law, has been named dean by GW President Steven Knapp. . . . "Paul Berman stood out among the impressively diverse and accomplished group of finalists who emerged from an extensive national search," said Dr. Knapp. "He brings to this position exactly the right combination of vision, legal scholarship and proven administrative achievement." Mr. Berman will also serve as GW's Robert Kramer Research Professor of Law. His scholarship focuses on the ways in which globalization affects the interaction of legal systems, and his new book,* Global Legal Pluralism: A Jurisprudence of Law Beyond Borders, *will be published later this year by Cambridge University Press. "GW Law School is obviously already one of the top law schools in the country, but it is far more than that," Mr. Berman said. "It is a place where students and faculty work every day to help change the world: tackling the crucial challenges facing our society and integrating their academic pursuits with law in action in our nation's capital. This is the unique vision that the GW Law School is poised to pursue as we become the preeminent location for 21st-century global legal, and policy studies."*[15]

TROUBLE AT GW LAW

Berman's deanship at George Washington School of Law was tumultuous; he stepped down after just eighteen months.[16] But the University supported him. "I like him, respect him, and thought he did a very good job as dean," a source added. "But he's not someone who comes into a place and doesn't do anything, which is the norm in academia. He's hard-charging, he wants to change things, and that upset some people."[17] He retained his tenured professorship at GW Law. In addition, GW named him Vice Provost for Online Education and Academic Innovation. In this capacity, he oversaw all online operations for the University's 105 online degree and certificate programs and generated nearly $70 million in gross revenue annually. He also chaired the University's Strategic Planning Committee for Online Education and managed the creation of the University's eDesign Shop, a production facility and team of instructional designers, videographers, computer animation specialists, and supporting positions. Over a three-year period, he built GW University's eDesign Shop capacity to create state-of-the-art online programs.

THE TIDE TURNS AT GW LAW

By 2016, the tide at GW had turned in his favor. On June 29, 2016, University leaders, distinguished alumni, faculty, staff, and students gathered to celebrate the Law School Deanship of Paul Schiff Berman and to honor his extraordinary career, accomplishments, and impact, during the official unveiling of his commemorative portrait. The program was detailed online.

> *Paul Schiff Berman joined GW Law in July 2011, and served over five years—first as Dean and then as University Vice Provost for Online Education and Academic Innovation, where he oversaw more than 100 online degree and certificate programs. In January, he returned to full-time teaching as the Walter S. Cox Professor of Law. "It's a tremendous privilege to join so many distinguished guests, colleagues, friends, and members of the GW Law community today for this very special occasion," said GW Law Dean Blake D. Morant. "I have known Paul for 15 years and he is well deserving of this honor."... Mr. Burchfield recognized many new initiatives launched during Professor Berman's tenure, including new alumni mentoring programs, the innovative Inns of Court program for first-year students, an expansion of the school's Pathways to Practice Program to help support students entering the job market, and the creation of a unique interdisciplinary major on the Law and Business of Government Contracting. According to Burchfield, Berman also "reached out energetically to alumni, speaking with over 2500 alumni. This helped the law school raise an historic $11.5 million over a 14-month period, and allowed the law school to balance two consecutive budgets in a very challenging economic environment." Speakers emphasized Professor Berman's incredible dedication to students. Ben Gottesman, a former student, described him as "a student's dean...believing that the law school existed to serve students not the other way round. He really empowered the students to have a voice, and he really understood the value that they brought to the*

institution," said Monica Monroe, former Dean of Students. Mary Wells, former assistant to the Dean, added: "I found Paul always to be humble, passionate, and tireless, and I hope this portrait inspires current and future members of the law school to follow Paul's example and approach their work with humility and authentic self, a collaborative spirit, and a penchant for innovation." After listening to the speakers, Professor Berman expressed profound thanks to those in the room and all of the collaborators with whom he worked as Dean. "What I loved about being Dean," he said, "was creating a space where other people could feel safe to contribute ideas and then building a context where those ideas could take flight. It's not about implementing my ideas; it's about empowering others to create a better future together." Gavin Glakas, an award-winning Bethesda, Maryland artist whose work hangs in the U.S. Capitol, painted the portrait, which is now on permanent display on the second floor of Stockton Hall.[18]

FOND MEMORIES OF ASU LAW

When interviewed for this book in 2019, Dean Berman recalled an especially proud and happy moment. He held a celebratory party at his home each year for the student fellows at his signature creation—*The Center for Law and Global Affairs*. The students held forth on their summer work projects. Two planned to work in the Philippines as prosecutors on human trafficking. Three were working on a legal brief to be filed with the Inter-American Commission on Human Rights. Two others were working on a think-tank project regarding private military contractors. He said, "Those opportunities did not exist for students three years ago, and now they do. It was perhaps my proudest moment as Dean."[19]

---

1 Lisa Robbins, "Berman appointed as College of Law dean," ASU Now: Access, Excellence, Impact, Arizona State University, published May 20, 2008, https://asunow.asu.edu/content/berman-appointed-college-law-dean.
2 "GW Law," The George Washington University, accessed March 19, 2020, https://www.law.gwu.edu.
3 "New Dean of Law School Named," GW Today, The George Washington University, published April 28, 2011, https://gwtoday.gwu.edu/new-dean-law-school-named.
4 Juris Doctor *(summa cum laude),* New York University School of Law, 1995, Journal: Managing Editor, New York University Law Review, Awards: University Graduation Prize (for the graduating student with the highest cumulative GPA), Frank H. Sommer Memorial Award (for outstanding scholarship, character & professional activities), Frank T. Dierson Award (for writing that demonstrates technical accuracy & clarity of purpose), Orison Marden Moot Court Competition Prize for Best Oralist. Order of the Coif, American Jurisprudence Award for Contracts, Public Interest Summer Internship Grant; A.B. *(summa*

cum laude), Princeton University, 1988, Award: Louis B. Sudler Prize for the Arts; PROFESSIONAL HONORS = Queen Mary University of London, UK, Distinguished Visiting Professor at the School of Law, 2016–2022; Southern Cross University, Australia, Distinguished Visiting Professor at the School of Law, 2018; University of Bremen, Germany, Distinguished Visiting Scholar of the Centre for Transnational Studies, 2014; LegalTimes/National Law Journal, Champion and Visionary of the Law, 2012; Sandra Day O'Connor Institute Prize for Public Service, 2010; Princeton Program in Law and Public Affairs, Fellowship, 2006–2007; Yale Journal of International Law, Selection in Symposium Issue Competition (A Pluralist Approach to International Law); Yale/Stanford Junior Faculty Forum, Selected to Present in International Law category (The Globalization of Jurisdiction); University of Connecticut Provost's Research Fellowship, Spring 2004. He is the author of eight books:

The Oxford Research Handbook on Global Legal Pluralism (Oxford Univ. Press, forthcoming 2019); *Global Issues in Civil Procedure* (with Margaret Woo, West Publishing, forthcoming 2019); *Global Legal Pluralism: A Jurisprudence of Law Beyond Borders* (Cambridge Univ. Press, 2012); *Law & Society Approaches to Cyberspace,* Editor (Ashgate Publishing, 2007); *The Globalization of International Law,* Editor (Ashgate Publishing, 2005); *Cyberlaw: Problems of Policy and Jurisprudence in the Information Age,* 5th Edition (with Patricia L. Bellia, Brett Frischman & David G. Post, West Publishing, 2018); *Cyberlaw: Problems of Policy and Jurisprudence in the Information Age,* 4th Edition (with Patricia L. Bellia, Brett Frischman & David G. Post, West Publishing, 2010); *Cyberlaw: Problems of Policy and Jurisprudence in the Information Age,* 3d Edition (with Patricia L. Bellia & David G. Post, West Publishing, 2006); *Cyberlaw: Problems of Policy and Jurisprudence in the Information Age,* 2d Edition (with Patricia L. Bellia & David G. Post, West Publishing, 2004); *Cyberlaw: Problems of Policy and Jurisprudence in the Information Age.* He is also the author of several score law review articles, journal articles, newspaper op-ed pieces and a wide variety of other writings. As of June 2019, his author page at SSRN included 29 scholarly works. See "Paul Schiff Berman," SSRN, accessed March 18, 2020, https://papers.ssrn.com/sol3/cf_dev/AbsByAuth.cfm?per_id=159950.

5 ASU President Michael Crow was the Executive Provost at NYU when Dean Berman was a student at NYU Law.

6 Wikipedia, s.v. "Harry T. Edwards," last modified March 9, 2020, 21:38, https://en.wikipedia.org/wiki/Harry_T._Edwards. Harry Thomas Edwards, an American jurist and legal scholar, is currently a Senior United States Circuit Judge and chief judge emeritus of the United States Court of Appeals for the District of Columbia Circuit in Washington, D.C., and a professor of law at the New York University School of Law.

7 Wikipedia, s.v. "Ruth Bader Ginsberg," last modified March 19, 2020, 16:27, https://en.wikipedia.org/wiki/Ruth_Bader_Ginsburg. Ruth Bader Ginsburg is an American lawyer and jurist who is an Associate Justice of the U.S. Supreme Court. Ginsburg was appointed by President Bill Clinton and took the oath of office on August 10, 1993. She is the second female justice of four to be confirmed to the court. Following O'Connor's retirement, and until Sotomayor joined the court, Ginsburg was the only female justice on the Supreme Court. During that time, Ginsburg became more forceful with her dissents, which were noted by legal observers and in popular culture. She is generally viewed as belonging to the liberal wing of the court. Ginsburg has authored notable majority opinions, including *United States v. Virginia, Olmstead v. L.C.,* and *Friends of the Earth, Inc. v. Laidlaw Environmental Services, Inc.*

8 Lisa Robbins, "Berman appointed as College of Law dean," ASU Now: Access, Excellence, Impact, Arizona State University, published May 20, 2008, https://asunow.asu.edu/content/berman-appointed-college-law-dean.

9 Ibid., 3.

10 "Cyber Law: Everything You Need to Know," Up-Counsel, accessed March 19, 2020, https://www.upcounsel.com/cyber-law. Cyber law is any law that applies to the internet and internet-related technologies. Cyber law is one of the newest areas of the legal system. This is because internet technology develops at such a rapid pace. Cyber law provides legal protections to people using the internet.

11 Wikipedia, s.v. "International Law," last modified March 19, 2020, 02:27, https://en.wikipedia.org/wiki/International_law. International law is the set of rules generally regarded and accepted as binding in relations between states and between nations. It serves as a framework for the practice of stable and organized international relations. International law differs from state-based legal systems in that it is primarily applicable to countries rather than to private citizens.

12 Austin Sarat and Jonathan Simon, *Cultural Analysis, Cultural Studies, and the Law,* Duke University Press, July 2003, https://www.dukeupress.edu/Cultural-Analysis-Cultural-Studies-and-the-Law/.

13 Editor(s): Austin D. Sarat, Jonathan Simon; Contributor(s): Austin D. Sarat, Naomi Mezey, Tobey Miller, Paul Schiff Berman, Paul W. Kahn, Carol J. Greenhouse, Wai Chee Dimock, Peter Brooks, Shoshana Felman, Anthony Farley, Jonathan Simon, Alison Young. See book content described at https://www.dukeupress.edu/Cultural-Analysis-Cultural-Studies-and-the-Law/.

14 "Berman Book Discussion: Paul Berman on Global Legal Pluralist," Opinion Juris, published on June 16, 2012, www.opiniojuris.org/2012/06/18/opening-post-paul-berman-on-global-legal-pluralism/.

15 "Dean Berman," GW Law, The George Washington University, accessed March 19, 2020, http://www.law.gwu.edu/Dean/Pages/DeanBerman.aspx (site discontinued).

16 Cory Weinberg, "Law faculty plotted to oust dean," *The GW Hatchet,* published February 24, 2013, https://www.gwhatchet.com/2013/02/25/law-faculty-plotted-to-oust-dean/.

17 Ibid.

18 "GW Law Honors Former Dean Paul Schiff Berman with Portrait Unveiling," News & Events, GW Law, published September 13, 2016, https://www.law.gwu.edu/Paul-Berman-Portrait-Unveiling-Ceremony.

19 Email to author, June 18, 2019.

CHAPTER 32

DEAN DOUGLAS SYLVESTER, 2007 TO PRESENT

Presenting Doug Sylvester in this book is an opportunity to connect him to his seven legendary predecessors,[1] while simultaneously sketching his larger-than-life role in Sandra Day O'Connor College of Law's robust future. This book outlines fifty-three years of legal education at ASU, starting with the mere idea, and focusing on the Pedrick era and the 1970 inaugural graduating class.

Dean Sylvester was born in 1965, the same year ASU Law's founding dean, the inestimable Willard Pedrick, sketched the birth of the college on a yellow legal pad. Coincidently, Dean Sylvester also taught at Chicago's Northwestern School of Law, the same school that Dean Pedrick left in 1965 (Sylvester's birth year), to build ASU Law. Dean Pedrick was in charge for its first eight years. Dean Sylvester has been at the helm for the last eight years. Both periods proved to be deep searches for the rich intellectual environment that is today's Sandra Day O'Connor College of Law.

Dean Pedrick started in a few rooms in an already aging building in Tempe[2] on ASU's Tempe campus. Dean Sylvester now holds forth in six-story, 280,000-square-foot, masterpiece of a building, on ASU's Downtown Phoenix[3] campus. The journey from "little" Tempe to "gigantic" Phoenix is a breathtaking climb to a peak not even the most optimistic student or professor could have imagined fifty years ago.

Annie Dillard, a wordsmith of the finest order, could have been thinking of Dean Sylvester when she wrote, "Hone and spread your spirit, till you yourself are a sail, whetted, translucent, broadside to the merest puff."[4]

Dean Sylvester's story at the Sandra Day O'Connor College of Law starts in 2002 when he joined the law faculty as an associate professor and stretches through his deanship in 2011 to the much-anticipated 50th Anniversary Celebration in 2020. He is the eighth dean, and the fourth chosen from the existing faculty.[5]

RELEVANT ASU HISTORY TO THE ARRIVAL OF DEAN SYLVESTER

ASU got its start as a teachers college. No law, business, liberal arts, or football team. President Grady Gammage became president of Arizona State Teachers College at Tempe in 1933, after serving for six years as President of the Northern Arizona Teachers College in Flagstaff Arizona from 1927 to 1933. He was ASU's first and longest serving president—twenty-eight years at the helm.[6] He oversaw the construction of several buildings on the Tempe campus, guided the development of the university's graduate programs, and managed the school's name changes (Arizona State College in 1945, then Arizona State University in 1958). In the 1960s, under G. Homer Durham,[7] the university's eleventh president, ASU expanded its curriculum by establishing new colleges.

In 1965, the Arizona Board of Regents authorized the creation of ASU Law, and President Durham hired Dean Willard Pedrick. By 1969, when the law school was two years old, ASU had 23,000 students. It is now America's largest public university. "Arizona State University reached a new milestone in the 2017–18 school year, enrolling more than 100,000 students for the first time. Enrollment figures show ASU has 103,567 students, a 5-percent increase over last school year and 40 percent more than five years ago. Tempe remains the largest [of ASU's five campuses] with an enrollment of about 51,000."[8]

Dean Sylvester came to ASU Law in 2002, the same year Dr. Michael Crow[9] became ASU's President. They share remarkably similar talents, goals, and ambitions. Douglas Sylvester is the eighth dean of the Sandra Day O'Connor College of Law at Arizona State University. Under his leadership, ASU Law reached historic heights, ranked 24th in the nation (up from 40th in 2012, and 58th in 2008) and 9th among public law schools. From 2012–2017, the law school placed in the top

20 for employment (rising as high as #11 in 2014), hired more than 30 faculty members, and raised more than $70 million—twice the amount raised in the prior 45 years combined.

President Crow's leadership accomplishments are nothing short of stunning.[10] Those who know Michael Crow and Doug Sylvester will likely agree that Aristotle might have captured the driving force behind both men when he said, "The roots of education are bitter, but the fruit is sweet."[11] Comparing President Crow's success in leading the university to Dean Sylvester's success in leading the law college is essentially a matter of scale and focus. Both are master planners and accomplished leaders. They are widely successful because they understand the need to build at scale and produce at the highest possible level of quality. They build excellent staff; insist on on-time delivery, zero defects, satisfied students, economic competitiveness, and financial incentives for teachers, staff, students, employers, communities, and society at large.

Large universities create large colleges by sharing common ingredients—an examination of what makes anyone successful. The road to preeminent success in building a great university is identical to building a great college within a great university. They focus 24/7 on the outcome. They examine minutely every measure and every consequence of the endeavor. That is why they mirror one another.

Dean Sylvester was a driving force for the conceptualization and creation of the Beus Center for Law and Society in downtown Phoenix. It is now home to ASU Law and fifteen public spaces—legal-related organizations including the innovative ASU Alumni Law Group and the Arizona Legal Center.[12] Known colloquially as the BCLS, it uses form and function to connect students, visitors, and the general public to the role of justice in society. By careful design, and a great deal of communication between law school leaders, architects, builders, and designers, it is inviting, engaging, and accessible to everyone who is interested in learning about the law, and its effect on almost everyone.

APPOINTMENTS & EMPLOYMENT

Sylvester's appointment as dean is the culmination of a twenty-four-year run of successive appointments, universities, and clerkships. In reverse order:
- Dean of the Sandra Day O'Connor College of Law, 2011 to present.
- Professor of Law, 2006 to present.

- Associate Professor of Law, 2002 to 2006.
- Sandra Day O'Connor College of Law at Arizona State University Faculty Fellow, 2002 to present.
- ASU Center for the Study of Law, Science & Technology, 2002 to present.
- Attorney, 2000–2002, Baker & McKenzie, Global e-Commerce Practice Group.
- Lecturer-in-Law, 2000–2001, Northwestern University School of Law.
- Lecturer-in-Law, 2000–2001, University of Chicago Law School.
- Bigelow Fellow & Lecturer-in-Law, 1997–1999, University of Chicago Law School.
- Law Clerk, 1995–1997; United States District Court for the Southern District of Florida, Hon. C. Clyde Atkins.

EDUCATION & BAR MEMBERSHIPS

- New York University School of Law, LLM, 1995.
- Member of Legal History and International Law Faculty Colloquia.
- University of Buffalo School of Law, JD, *cum laude*, 1994.[13]
- Buffalo Law Review (Executive Editor); Jessup Moot Court (Best Oralist, Competitions Dir., Coach).
- University of Toronto,[14] BA (History), 1991.
- State of Illinois Bar Association, 2001.[15]

Law school faculty and deans who are not licensed to practice in Arizona, can practice on a limited basis under the rules of the Arizona Supreme Court.[16]

SCHOLARSHIP & PUBLICATIONS

Dean Sylvester understands the long history and oft-argued issues deeply embedded in defining both the law and the teaching of it. "Since the nineteenth century, the role of lawyers and the nature of law in U.S. society have been the subject of ongoing debate and scrutiny. Legal scholars and practitioners have discussed whether the law is a self-contained body of rules, displaying logic and reason. Some have embraced this view and have aspired to make law a science. Since the early twentieth century, however, other important legal figures have expressed skepticism about the inner logic of the law, preferring to see legal rulings as responses to immediate social, political, and economic pressures. These skeptics eventually became known as legal realists, a school of thought that can be traced to the scholar and jurist Oliver Wendell Holmes Jr."[17]

The debate surrounding legal scholarship notwithstanding, it is the case that substantially all law schools, and all full-time law professors engage in a life composed of teaching, scholarship, and writing. Why they write and publish is complicated. The dogmatic answer is, "Publish or perish. The whole game of academia is to publish articles so that one can get tenure, get promoted, and be on top of the world. This means publication in student-run law reviews, preferably at the highest U.S. News and World Report ranks."[18]

While true to a point, there are other reasons legal scholars like Dean Sylvester produce legal scholarship. They know the law is not static, often needs change, and good change demands careful analysis, and legal judgment. Who better to do that job than law professors?

Dean Sylvester has written at least thirty-four scholarly articles and reviews. His work has been read and reviewed 2,020 times and been cited 394 times.[19] The following are of particular notice in the legal world:

1. *Rule Violations and the Rule of Law: A Factorial Survey of Public Attitudes.*[20]
2. *Transnational Models For Regulation of Nanotechnology.*[21]
3. *United States Approaches to Trademark Law in Cyberspace.*[22]
4. *Counting on Confidentiality: Legal and Statistical Approaches to Federal Privacy Law After the USA PATRIOT Act.*[23]
5. *The Security of Our Secrets: A History of Privacy and Confidentiality in Law and Statistical Practice.*[24]
6. *Who Invented the Computer?*[25]
7. *Cyberspace Carcassonne: Nihilism and Normativity in Cyberspace Regulation.*[26]
8. *Myth in Restorative Justice History.*[27]
9. *Beyond Breard.*[28]
10. *International Law as Sword or Shield? Early American Foreign Policy and the Law of Nations.*[29]
11. Comment: *Customary International Law, Forcible Abductions and America's "Return to the Savage State."*[30]

Besides law review articles and essays, he also wrote chapters in three important legal books: (1) "*The Lessons of Nuremberg and the Trial of Saddam Hussein* in EVIL,

LAW & THE STATE: PERSPECTIVES ON STATE POWER AND VIOLENCE, 127–41 (John M. Parry, ed., 2006).[31] (2) *"Entrepreneur's Guide to Innovation Law."*[32] (3) *The Law of Online Privacy*, in INTERNET AND E-COMMERCE Law.[33]

MEDIA PUBLICATIONS & OTHER WRITINGS[34]

- Entries in Encyclopedia of American Civil Liberties (Paul Finkelman ed., Routledge Press).[35] Fair Credit Reporting Act of 1970
- Video Privacy Protection Act of 1988
- Privacy Protection Act of 1980
- Congressional Protection of Privacy
- Privacy Costs, ASU Forum (Dec. 2003)
- Baker & McKenzie, E-Commerce Practice Manual (2002) [contributor]
- Column for online Chicago Tribune.[36]
- "All Things Trademark: Co-Branding" (Feb. 16, 2001)
- "To Know Spam is to No Spam" (Feb. 19, 2001)
- "Pay Attention to Privacy" (Feb. 26, 2001)
- "Why International Privacy Matters" (Feb. 28, 2001)
- Columns have been reprinted in various online journals, including, the Orlando Sentinel, South Florida Sunsentinel,
- Baltimore Sun, Blackvoices.com, Hartford Courant, and Newsday.com
- Court Throws Mud on Adobe Argument in Software Dispute, Chic. Lawyer (Dec. 1, 2001)

GRANT APPLICATIONS[37]

- International Regulation of Nanotechnology (NSF Grant) (submitted Feb. 2006) [Dr. Gary Marchant, PI]
- International Intellectual Property and Barriers to Genomic Research (NSF Grant) (submitted Oct. 2004)
- [Dr. Dennis Karjala, PI]
- Negotiating Border Order (ASU Grant, funded Apr. 2004) [Dr. Michael Musheno, PI]
- 3/7

- Cyberspace Ethics (NSF Grant) (submitted 2002) [Dr. Forouzan Golshani, PI]

COURSES TAUGHT[38]

As is true across the law-college-dean spectrum in America, Dean Sylvester also teaches law students.

- International Intellectual Property, ASU College of Law (Spring 2007)
- Introduction to Intellectual Property, ASU College of Law (Fall 2005, 2006)
- Technology Ventures Co-requisite, ASU College of Law (Fall 2005)
- Technology Ventures Clinic, Faculty Director, ASU College of Law (Spring 2003–Summer 2006) Intellectual Property Decision-making & Portfolio Management, ASU College of Law & W.P. Carey School of Business (Spring 2004, 2005, 2007)
- e-Commerce Law, ASU College of Law (Fall 2003)
- Intellectual Property Commercialization & Technology Transfer, ASU College of Law (Fall 2003, 2004, 2005)
- Seminar in e-Commerce Law, ASU College of Law (Spring 2003)
- International Law & Politics, ASU College of Law (Fall 2002)
- Intellectual Property Strategies, Northwestern University College of Law, Kellogg Business School (Spring 2002)
- e-Commerce Contracting, Northwestern University College of Law, Summer Institute (Summer 2001) The World Trade Organization, University of Chicago, The Law School (Winter 2001)
- Sovereignty, Globalization and the Future of International Intellectual Property, University of Chicago, The Law School (Spring 2000)
- Research & Writing, University of Chicago, The Law School (Fall 1997–Spring 1999)
- Advanced Research & Writing, St. Thomas Univ. Law School (Miami) (Spring 1997)
- Research & Writing, University of Buffalo, (Teaching Assistant) (Spring 1994)

LECTURES, PRESENTATIONS, AND RELATED EVENTS[39]

- Plenary Speaker, "Real World Student Collaborations in Law, Science, and Technology – The Technology Ventures Clinic at Arizona State University College of Law," Association of American Law Schools, Clinical Education Conference, New York (May 2006).
- Presenter, "The Rule of Law: Public Perceptions of Rules and Rulemaking," The Clifford Symposium, DePaul Law School, Chicago (Apr. 2006).
- Lecture, "Patents and Technology Transfer," Science, Technology & Public Affairs (Mar. 2006) [course co-taught by Pres. Michael Crow and Prof. Daniel Sarewitz].
- Presenter and Panelist, "Privacy Enhancing Technologies" Surveillance and the Law Workshop, ASU (Feb. 2006).
- Presenter, "Patents and Patentability," Institute of Electrical and Electronics Engineers Society, DeVry University, Phoenix (Dec. 2006).
- Presenter, "Legal Regulation of Nanotechnology," International Association of Nanotechnology, San Francisco (Nov. 2005).
- Lecture, "Information Assurance and Cybersecurity," CSE: Information Assurance (prerequisite course for certification of ASU as a Center of Academic Excellence in Information Assurance Education to be certified by the National Security Agency and Department of Homeland Security) (Oct. 2005).
- Featured Presenter & Panelist, "Online Issues in Trademark and Patent Law in the United States," Conference on Intellectual Property Enforcement, Mykelos Romeris University, Vilnius, Lithuania (Jan. 2005).
- Presenter, "Loose Lips Sink Ships (and Studies): Maintaining Confidentiality of Data in Educational Research," Center for Research on Education in Science, Mathematics, Engineering, and Technology, ASU (Nov. 2004).
- Featured Presenter & Panelist, "Legal Pageantry and the Derogation of Due Process Norms in the Trial of Saddam Hussein—Law, Evil and the State," Mansfield College, Oxford (July, 2004).
- Commentator, "Gramscian Hegemony and International Law—Law War and Morality Conference, ASU, College of Law (April 2004). Response to Jose Alvarez.

- Featured Presenter & Panelist, "Head of State Immunity in International and United States Law," Sociedad Cubana de Ciencias Penales, Havana, Cuba (November 2003).
- Moderator, "Both Sides of the United States/Iraq Conflict," ASU College of Law (March 2003, November 2004).
- Presentation, "Legal Pageantry," ASU College of Law (May 2004).
- Presentation, "Introduction to Transactional Law Practice," ASU College of Law 1L Speakers Series, (February 2004).
- Lecture, "Introduction to Intellectual Property," CLEO, ASU College of Law (June 16, 2004).
- Lecture, "Cybersecurity," Introduction to Law, Science & Technology (course taught by Dr. Gary Marchant & Dr. Andrew Askland), ASU College of Law (March 4, 2003).
- Lecture, "Science and the Law," Capstone Course in Biotechnology, ASU School of Life Sciences (April 3, 2003).
- Presenter, "Cybersecurity for IT Companies," Association of Arizona Corporate Counsel (May 2003).
- Presenter, "Head-of-State Immunity in United States and International Law," ASU College of Law (May 2003).
- Presenter, "Cybersecurity and the USA PATRIOT Act," Bryan Cave Law Firm, Phoenix Arizona (February 2003).
- Presenter, "International Law and the Invasion of Iraq." ASU College of Law (February 2003).
- Presenter & Panelist, "Data Management and International Risks" E-CURE Electronic Records Conference (October 2002).
- Presenter & Panelist, "Intellectual History of Restorative Justice" Univ. of Utah Law School (March 2002).
- Featured Speaker, "Electronic Signatures in the Real World" E-Commerce World Forum (October 2001).
- Panelist, "International Law and E-Commerce Careers" at National Assoc. of Pre-Law Advisors. (September 2001).
- Featured Lecturer, "e-Contracting and e-Payments" at Northwestern Univ. Law School Summer Institute in Corp. Law (August 2001).

LEGAL CONSULTING

Testifying expert in case involving licensing and intellectual property (*Farnam Cos. v. Stabar Enters;*[40] Technology Mentor [volunteer mentoring of students in various technology competitions] (2004–present); Arizona Technopolis, Phoenix, AZ (2003–Present) [organization committed to the education and incubation of inventors and inventions in Arizona]. Midwestern University Medical School, Glendale, AZ & Peoria, Illinois (2003 & 2004).

ACADEMIC ACTIVITIES[41]

- Chair, Appointments Committee, ASU College of Law (2006–2007)
- Member, Appointments Committee, ASU College of Law (2005–2006)
- Ira A. Fulton School of Engineering, Office of Entrepreneurial Programs, Advisory Board (2005–Present)
- Member, LL.M. in Biotechnology and Genomics Committees on Admissions and Curriculum (2004–Present)
- Arizona Technology Enterprises, Technology Ventures Clinic Advisory Board (2003–Present)
- ASU Entrepreneurship 2004, Board of Directors, Competition Advisor, and Judge (2003–2004)
- Member, Law, Science, and Technology Center Advisory Committee, ASU College of Law (2002–2005)
- Faculty Advisor, Legal Alchemy and Entrepreneurship, ASU College of Law (2004–2005)
- Faculty Advisor, Student Association for International Law, ASU College of Law (2002–Present)
- Faculty Advisor, Jessup Moot Court, ASU College of Law (2002–Present)
- Member, Steering Committee for Proposed School of Global Studies, ASU (2003–2004)
- Member, Planning Committee for Innovation Institute, ASU (2004)
- Member, Executive Planning Committee and Proposal Committee for "Borders & Security," ASU (2004)

Dean Douglas Sylvester, 2007 to present

- Member, Senior Thesis Committee (for Mel Hedin), ASU Barrett Honors College (2003–2004)
- Referee, Jurimetrics (2002–Present)
- Chair, New Faculty Integration Committee, ASU College of Law (2004–Present)
- Chair, IT Advisory Committee, ASU College of Law (2002–2004)
- Member, Communications Group Advisory Committee, ASU College of Law (2004–Present)
- Member, Moot Court Advisory Board, ASU College of Law (2003–Present)
- Member, Curriculum Committee, ASU College of Law (2003–2004)
- Member, IT Advisory Committee, ASU College of Law (2004–Present)
- Member, Graduate Programs Committee, ASU College of Law (2002–2004)
- Member, Night School Curriculum Committee, ASU College of Law (2002–2003)
- Member, International Studies Committee, ASU College of Law (2004–Present)
- Chair, International Studies Committee, ASU College of Law (2002–2004)
- Orientation Leader, leading small group's discussion on Holmes' The Path of the Law, Arizona State University College of Law (Fall 2003)
- Faculty Advisor, Chicago Journal of International Law (1999–2000); Univ. of Chicago Jessup Moot Court (Coach, 2000–2001)
- Research Assistant, Dean Douglas Baird, University of Chicago Law School (1998–99)
- Research Assistant, Professor Amy Adler, Freedom Forum Media Center at Columbia Univ. (1996)
- Research Assistant, Professor Paulette Caldwell, New York University (1996)
- Research Assistant, Professor Guyora Binder, University of Buffalo Law School (1993–1994)
- Research Assistant, Professor Catherine Tinker, University of Buffalo Law School (1993–1994)

NOTABLE RECENT HISTORY AT SANDRA DAY O'CONNOR COLLEGE OF LAW

Under his leadership, from 2011 to date, the law school has established itself as one of the nation's best, offering a wide range of courses taught by excellent faculty. "Moved from its longtime home in Tempe into the brand-new Beus Center for Law and Society in downtown Phoenix, providing students with greater opportunities and access to the legal, political, and economic heart of Arizona. Remained focused on quality outcomes, maintaining high bar-passage rates and a consistent top-20 ranking for gainful employment. It offers an array of career-enhancing opportunities to alumni through the Law for Life program. It dramatically increased fundraising and the number of scholarships offered."[42]

The raw numbers confirm its high standing among America's 206 accredited law schools:

"It ranked seventh in public law schools; fifth in ranked programs; seventh in legal writing, tenth in dispute resolution, twenty-second in health law, twentieth is environmental law, twenty-fifth in international law, and twenty-fourth in bar passage. The entering class of 2019 was stunning in every category: 3710 Applications; 164 Median LSAT; 3.81 Median GPA; 100% of incoming JD students received a scholarship; 130+ Institutions represented; 69 Majors represented; 38 States represented; 30% Diversity."[43]

Dean Sylvester has consistently argued that effecting such change is a collaborative effort, not only among ASU Law staff, but also among the entire leadership team at ASU. Working as a loosely coupled sector within one of the largest schools in the country has required a great deal of cooperation, planning, and prioritization.[44] His leadership team includes:

- Adam Chodorow, Associate Dean, Academic Affairs[45]
- Zachary Kramer, Associate Dean, Faculty[46]
- Eric Menkhus, Associate Dean, New Education Initiatives & Clinical Professor[47]
- Diana Bowman, Associate Professor of Law[48]
- Victoria Ames, Assistant Dean, Legal Projects and External Engagement[49]
- Alfred Ray English, Assistant Dean, Office of Career and Employment Services[50]

- Andrew Jaynes, Assistant Dean, Admissions and Financial Aid[51]
- Thomas Williams, Assistant Dean and Chief of Staff[52]
- Karen Sung, Executive Director, Marketing and Communications[53]
- Terri Burkel, Senior Director of Development[54]

DEAN SYLVESTER'S BEST IDEAS

In assessing Sylvester's eight years as dean, it is helpful to examine what he did differently from his predecessors. They are remembered for modulated improvement and incremental change. Over the timespan of this book too many of America's law school deans were satisfied just by graduating law students and turning them over to bar examiners. None of the ASU Law deans settled for that. All pushed hard for students to be practice-ready, not just knowledgeable about the law. Dean Sylvester stands out because he helped to create two internal structures that define and stand for practice-ready graduates: The ASU Alumni Law Group[55] and the Arizona Legal Center.[56] He is a strong supporter of the college's outstanding trial advocacy program.[57]

Chief Justice Warren Burger, not known for coddling either law professors or trial lawyers, often talked about the reality of legal education in many law schools operating on limited budgets. "[I]n spite of all the bar examinations and better law schools, we are more casual about qualifying the people we allow to act as advocates in the courtroom than we are about licensing electricians. . . . The painful fact is the courtrooms of America all too often have 'Piper Cub' advocates trying to handle the controls of 'Boeing 747' litigation."[58]

Paul A. Freund[59] gave something close to a retort a few months later when he said, "We can't give up on specialized training in the highly complex structure of law today, but we do have to return to a feeling what the whole legal system stands for—how it relates to our own conception of the person as a human being."[60]

Doug Sylvester knew teaching a core law school curriculum was not enough. He created and managed more clinical legal education than any of his predecessors did. He expanded both faculty and the student body. He made the school more relevant in the profession. But those significant accomplishments are not what makes him stand out at the Sandra Day O'Connor College of Law; it's his ideas.

Sylvester is well known for both the originality of his ideas and his get-it-done attitude. He's an IP professor and pushes innovation as if he was shoveling a four-foot snow wall piled up at the entrance to his alma mater, the University of Buffalo School of Law.[61] Three of his best ideas are the ASU Alumni Law Group,[62] the Arizona Legal Center,[63] and the Beus Center for Law & Society.[64]

Dean Sylvester created *The ASU Law Group* as a not-for-profit law firm made up of experienced lawyers with a passion for mentoring the next generation of lawyers. Modeled after the concept of a teaching hospital, the ASU Law Group hires recent law graduates from the Sandra Day O'Connor College of Law at Arizona State University. The associates spend between two to three years learning how to practice quality law under the close supervision of senior attorneys who also oversee each associate.

He created the *Arizona Legal Center* to answer one question: "Do I have a case?" It is America's first legal triage system operating inside a law school, by working lawyers working on a pro bono basis, while giving law students a strong sense of how to triage legal problems. This central question is largely unanswered in the legal community unless and until those asking the question reach the inner office of a law firm. When it is available, it is neither quick nor free. Consequently, a large segment of the population does not seek legal assistance because they see legal fees as an impenetrable barrier. They may be able to identify that they have a legal problem but lack the resources or expertise to resolve that problem on their own. Doug's second great idea, the Arizona Legal Center, helps make the law accessible for all.

Dean Sylvester created, with the assistance of Leo Beus and scores of other committed supporters, the *Beus Center for Law and Society*. Once created and funded, the Beus Center took on a life of its own. It's the new home for the law school. It houses dozens of other entities committed to two things: First, to connect students, visitors, and the general public to the role of justice in society. Second, to further legacy and work of the college's namesake—Justice Sandra Day O'Connor—and her devotion to ensuring citizens learn about and understand the importance of rule of law and civic engagement.

It is the embodiment of collaboration among its occupants, the *Lincoln Center for Applied Ethics*, the *McCain Institute for International Leadership*, the *Sandra Day O'Connor Institute*, the *Arizona Voice for Crime Victims*, and the *Arizona Justice Project*.

Besides great ideas, and quick implementation, Dean Sylvester is a consummate "middle manager." University Presidents and Provosts run universities by appointing deans as middle managers of higher education. Deans are responsible up the university org chart for information, resources, and challenges in their individual colleges. Academic deans must be as smart as they are adroit. Senior administration, department chairs/conveners, faculty, and students all have and expect both immediate and ongoing access to the dean.[65]

Those closest to him know he is as influential as he is responsible. With the dedicated support of his associate deans, his leadership team advances new programs, seeks and supports faculty, and interacts, daily, with students, supporters, staff, and working lawyers, who are fast discovering the difference between the old law school in Tempe, and the new one in Phoenix. A few still remember the heady days when Dean Pedrick built this college. None will soon forget the soaring days when Dean Sylvester took it up into the stratosphere of legal education.

---

1 ASU Law Deans Willard Pedrick, Ernest Gellhorn, Alan Matheson, Paul Bender, Richard Morgan, Patricia White, and Paul Berman.

2 Wikipedia, s.v. "Matthews Hall (Tempe, AZ)," last modified August 12, 2019, 22:14, https://en.wikipedia.org/wiki/Matthews_Hall_ (Tempe, _Arizona). Matthews Hall is the oldest intact dormitory on the ASU Tempe campus. It was designed by L.G. Knipe and dedicated in 1920 as a men's dormitory. By 1930, it was a women's dormitory. The first library was placed in the building; it was renamed the Matthews Library in honor of Dr. Matthews's 30 years as president. It became the Matthews Center upon its conversion in the 1960s. Dean Pedrick and Associate Dean Alan Matheson had their first offices there in 1966–67 and taught their first classes in the two classrooms in 1967. It is now a photography gallery and offices for the Herberger Institute for Design and the Arts and home to the ASU Forensics (Speech & Debate) team.

3 "Projects," Buro Happold, accessed March 20, 2020, https://www.burohappold.com/projects/beus-center-for-law-and-society/. The Beus Center for Law and Society—dedicated in 2016. Located in downtown Phoenix, the new six-story, 280,000 square-foot building is an exemplary legal education facility designed to meet the demands of a changing law school program.

4 Wikipedia, s.v. "Pilgrim at Tinker Creek," last modified December 29, 2019, 04:52, https://en.wikipedia.org/wiki/Pilgrim_at_Tinker_Creek. This descriptive excerpt is found under "Self-Actualization" in a fine piece of work called *Metaphors Dictionary*, by Elyse Sommer with Dorrie Weiss (Visible Ink Press 1996, 376). In her book, *Pilgrim at Tinker Creek*, Ms. Dillard introduced herself and her subject, with "The secret of seeing is to sail on solar wind."

5 Ernie Gellhorn, then a professor at University of Virginia, succeeded inaugural dean Willard Pedrick, in 1976. Alan Matheson, the first dean to come from the existing faculty in 1978, succeeded Gellhorn. Matheson served four terms as interim dean, and one as dean. He was succeeded by Paul Bender, then a professor at the University of Pennsylvania in 1984. Richard Morgan succeeded Bender. Morgan came to ASU Law in 1980, from private practice in Los Angles California. He served as associate professor, associate dean, and full professor before he was appointed as dean in 1990. Patricia White, then a professor at the University of Utah, succeeded Morgan in 1999. She was succeeded by Paul Berman, then a professor at the University of Connecticut, in 2008. Sylvester was the fourth dean to be appointed from the existing faculty in 2011.

6 Wikipedia, s.v. "Grady Gammage," last modified January 1, 2020, 14:31, https://en.wikipedia.org/wiki/Grady_Gammage. Gammage served as president of NATC from 1927 until 1933, when he left to head Arizona State College. He served as president from 1933 to 1959. *See also* "The New ASU Story: Leadership," ASU Libraries, Arizona State University, https://www.asu.edu/lib/archives/asustory/pages/13lead.htm.

7 Wikipedia, s.v. "G. Homer Durham," last modified December 23, 2019, 01; 59, https://en.wikipedia.org/wiki/G._Homer_Durham. George Homer Durham (February 4, 1911 – January 10, 1985) was an American academic administrator and was a general authority of The Church of Jesus Christ of Latter-day Saints (LDS Church) from 1977 until his death. Durham earned a Ph.D. in political science from the University of California, Los Angeles. He became a professor at the University of Utah. Durham would serve as the

first head of the university's Political Science Department. He later served as the academic vice-president of the University of Utah. From 1960 to 1969, he was the president of Arizona State University. Under his presidency, the university increased both in size and in academic standing. From 1969 to 1976, he was the first commissioner and executive officer of the Utah System of Higher Education.

8 Anne Ryman, "Why is Arizona State so large and why does it keep growing?" *Arizona Republic*, published February 16, 2018, https://www.azcentral.com/story/news/local/arizona-education/2018/02/16/arizona-state-university-enrollment-size-asu-growth-online/1058167001/.

9 "Biography" Faculty and Staff, Arizona State University, https://isearch.asu.edu/profile/66195. Michael M. Crow became the sixteenth president of Arizona State University on July 1, 2002. An academic leader and educator, designer of knowledge enterprises, and science and technology policy scholar, he is guiding the transformation of ASU into one of the nation's leading public metropolitan research universities, an institution that combines the highest levels of academic excellence, inclusiveness to a broad demographic, and maximum societal impact—a model he terms the "New American University." Wikipedia, s.v. "Michael M. Crow," last modified August 13, 2019, 01:55, https://en.wikipedia.org/wiki/Michael_M._Crow. Dr. Crow was previously Executive Vice Provost of Columbia University, where he was also Professor of Science and Technology Policy in the School of International and Public Affairs. He is also chairman of the board for In-Q-Tel, the Central Intelligence Agency's venture capital firm.

10 "Biography" Faculty and Staff, Arizona State University, https://isearch.asu.edu/profile/66195. Under his leadership ASU has established more than a dozen new transdisciplinary schools and large-scale research initiatives such as the Biodesign Institute; Global Institute of Sustainability (GIOS), incorporating the School of Sustainability (SOS); Complex Adaptive Systems Initiative (CASI); Flexible Display Center; LightWorks; and initiatives in the humanities and social sciences, including the Center for the Study of Religion and Conflict. During his tenure the university has nearly tripled research expenditures, completed an unprecedented infrastructure expansion, and announced the eight largest gifts in the history of the institution, including three $50 million gifts, endowing the W. P. Carey School of Business; Ira A. Fulton Schools of Engineering; and Mary Lou Fulton Teachers College.

11 Diogenes Laertius, *Lives of Philosophers*, 5:18.

12 "Beus Center for Law and Society," Arizona State University, accessed March 20, 2020, http://beuscenterforlawandsociety.com/. "The Beus Center for Law and Society (BCLS) is the new home to the Sandra Day O'Connor College of Law at Arizona State University, as well as several other organizations. The building space uses form and function to connect students, visitors, and the general public to the role of justice in society. The BCLS was designed to be inviting, engaging, and accessible to everyone who is interested in learning about the law, its effect on our daily lives, and the many services and resources available through ASU and other BCLS partners. The BCLS fosters collaboration among its occupants, including the Lincoln Center for Applied Ethics, The McCain Institute for International Leadership, the Sandra Day O'Connor Institute, and Arizona Voice for Crime Victims, Arizona Justice Project, and the ASU Alumni Law Group—the nation's first teaching law firm that also helps the community gain access to affordable legal services. The building also includes Think Tank spaces for grant-funded, interdisciplinary research projects. The BCLS will further play a major role in helping members of the community understand their legal rights. To that end, a community outreach-focused organization—the Arizona Legal Center—will act as a conduit for the public to access legal support. ASU Law is proud to be a part of the BCLS, an endeavor that will further the legacy and work of the college's namesake—Justice Sandra Day O'Connor—who is devoted to ensuring citizens learn about and understand the importance of rule of law and civic engagement." *See also* Chapter 30 *infra*.

13 "University at Buffalo School of Law," University at Buffalo, accessed March 20, 2020, https://www.law.buffalo.edu/. "Founded in 1887, the University at Buffalo School of Law is a graduate professional school at the University at Buffalo. It is the State University of New York system's only law school. . . At the time of the school's founding in 1887, law was very much a craft that aspiring attorneys learned by apprenticing themselves to a practicing member of the bar. The system worked well enough for its time. But a handful of visionaries, seeing the limitations of law office training and acknowledging the presence of rigorous law schools in other cities, set out to change the landscape for legal education in Western New York."

14 Wikipedia, s.v. "University of Toronto," last modified March 20, 2020, 10:32, https://en.wikipedia.org/wiki/University_of_Toronto. "The University of Toronto is a public research university in Toronto, Ontario, Canada, located on the grounds that surround Queen's Park. It was founded by royal charter in 1827 as King's College, the first institution of higher learning in the colony of Upper Canada." *See also* "Home," University of Toronto, accessed March 20, 2020, https://www.utoronto.ca/.

15 Douglas Sylvester (Dean), Curriculum Vitae, Arizona State University, accessed March 21, 2020, https://isearch.asu.edu/profile/504321. Dean Sylvester holds an inactive license to practice in Illinois.

16 Arizona Supreme Court Rule 38 (c) was enacted, in part, to accommodate full-time law deans and professors the opportunity to practice law in Arizona without examination by the court's Committee on examinations. This rule was put in place, in part, to accommodate Dean Willard Pedrick's interest in engaging the Arizona Bar and our courts on an occasional basis. Arizona Supreme Court 38 (d) was adopted to encourage law schools to provide clinical instruction of varying kinds and to facilitate volunteer opportunities for students in pro bono contexts. These are limited practice rules designed to facilitate law faculty support in Arizona courts for both pro bono and educational purposes. Dean Sylvester is eligible to practice under Rule 38.

17 *West's Encyclopedia of American Law*, 2nd ed., s.v. "Legal Scholarship," accessed August 29, 2019, https://legal-dictionary.thefreedictionary.com/Legal+Scholarship.

18 LawProfBlawg (anonymous law professor and blogger), "Why Do Law Professors Write Law Review Articles?" *Above the Law*, May 9, 2017, https://abovethelaw.com/2017/05/why-do-law-professors-write-law-review-articles/.

19 ResearchGate, s.v. "Douglas J. Sylvester," https://www.researchgate.net/profile/Douglas_Sylvester. *See also* Dean Sylvester's SSRN Author page https://papers.ssrn.com/sol3/cf_dev/AbsByAuth.cfm?per_id=336250. This compilation notes 26 scholarly works with 6,381 downloads and 61 citations.

20 Douglas J. Sylvester, *Rule Violations and the Rule of Law: A Factorial Survey of Public Attitudes*, DePaul L. Rev. (2007). Invited symposium with Dr. Michael Saks and Nicholas Schweitzer.

21 Douglas J. Sylvester & Gary Marchant, *Transnational Models For Regulation of Nanotechnology*, J. Law Medicine & Ethics.

22 Douglas J. Sylvester, *United States Approaches to Trademark Law in Cyberspace*, 5 Jurisprudencija 20–28 (2006), Invited symposium, Law Journal of Mykolo Romero Universitetas, Vilnius, Lithuania.

23 Douglas J. Sylvester, *Counting on Confidentiality: Legal and Statistical Approaches to Federal Privacy Law After the USA PATRIOT Act*, 2005 Wisc. L. Rev. 1036 (2005), with Dr. Sharon Lohr.

24 Douglas J. Sylvester, *The Security of Our Secrets: A History of Privacy and Confidentiality in Law and Statistical Practice*, Denv. U. L. Rev. 147 (2005), with Dr. Sharon Lohr.

25 Douglas J. Sylvester, *Who Invented the Computer?* 44 Jurimetrics 367 (2004), review essay of Alice Rowe Burks, "Who Invented the Computer? The Legal Battle That Changed Computing."

26 Douglas J. Sylvester, *Cyberspace Carcassonne: Nihilism and Normativity in Cyberspace Regulation*, 43 Jurimetrics 369, (2003), review essay of Stuart Biegel, "Beyond Our Control? Confronting the Limits of Our Legal System in the Age of Cyberspace."

27 Douglas J. Sylvester, *Myth in Restorative Justice History*, 2003 Utah L. Rev. 1445 (2003), restorative justice symposium.

28 Douglas J, Sylvester, *Beyond Breard*, 17 Berkeley J. Int'l L. 147 (1999), with Prof. Erik G. Luna. Cited in *U.S. v. Jimenez-Nava*, 243 F.3d 192, 198–99, 5th Cir. 2001.

29 Douglas J. Sylvester, *International Law as Sword or Shield? Early American Foreign Policy and the Law of Nations*, 32 Nyu J. Int'l L. & Pol. 1 (1999).

30 Douglas J. Sylvester, *Comment: Customary International Law, Forcible Abductions and America's* "Return to the Savage State," 42 Buff. L. Rev. 555 (1994).

31 Douglas J. Sylvester, "The Lessons of Nuremberg and the Trial of Saddam Hussein in EVIL, LAW & THE STATE: PERSPECTIVES ON STATE POWER AND VIOLENCE," 127–41 (John M. Parry, ed., 2006), http://papers.ssrn.com/sol3/papers.cfm?abstract_id=789984).

32 Prepared for Arizona State University Technopolis Program, with Kari A. Granville and Eric Menkhus.

33 (Andre C. Frieden, ed. 2002) (with Neil B. Hayes), winner of "Best Publication"—Association for Continuing Legal Education 2002, www.law.asu.edu/files/Programs/Sci-Tech/Innovation%20Handbook%20Mailed%20To%20Terree2.pdf.

34 Douglas Sylvester (Dean), Curriculum Vitae, Arizona State University, accessed March 21, 2020, https://apps.law.asu.edu/files/faculty/cvs/douglasjsylvester.pdf.

35 Paul Finkelman, *Encyclopedia of American Civil Liberties*, Edition 1, Routledge Publishing, https://www.amazon.com/Encyclopedia-American-Civil-Liberties-Finkelman/dp/0415762375.

36 "Tech," *Chicago Tribune*, http://www.chicagotribune.com/tech.

37 Douglas Sylvester (Dean), Curriculum Vitae, Arizona State University, accessed March 21, 2020, https://apps.law.asu.edu/files/faculty/cvs/douglasjsylvester.pdf.

38 Ibid.

39 Ibid.

40 *Farnam Cos. v. Stabar Enters.*, 2005 U.S. Dist. LEXIS 32509.

41 Douglas Sylvester (Dean), Curriculum Vitae, Arizona State University, accessed March 21, 2020, https://apps.law.asu.edu/files/faculty/cvs/douglasjsylvester.pdf.

42 "Douglas J. Sylvester Dean and Professor," Sandra Day O'Connor College of Law, Arizona State University, http://napco4courtleaders.org/wp-content/uploads/2017/09/Mon_ASU-Law-Socratic-Panel.pdf.

43 "Why ASU Law," Sandra Day O'Connor College of Law, accessed March 20, 2020, https://law.asu.edu/why-asu-law.

44 "Douglas J. Sylvester Dean and Professor," Sandra Day O'Connor College of Law, Arizona State University, http://napco4courtleaders.org/wp-content/uploads/2017/09/Mon_ASU-Law-Socratic-Panel.pdf.

45 "Adam Chodorow," iSearch, accessed March 20, 2020, https://isearch.asu.edu/profile/709824.

46 "Zachary Kramer," iSearch, accessed March 20, 2020, https://isearch.asu.edu/profile/1599484.

47 "Eric Menkhus," iSearch, accessed March 20, 2020, https://isearch.asu.edu/profile/16983.

48 "Diana Bowman," iSearch, accessed March 20, 2020, https://isearch.asu.edu/profile/2712805.

49 "Victoria Ames," iSearch, accessed March 20, 2020, https://isearch.asu.edu/profile/940779.

50 "Ray English," iSearch, accessed March 20, 2020, https://isearch.asu.edu/profile/2953263.

51 "Andrew Jaynes," iSearch, accessed March 20, 2020, https://isearch.asu.edu/profile/2217379.

52 "Thomas Williams," iSearch, accessed March 20, 2020, https://isearch.asu.edu/profile/721880.

53 "Karen Sung," iSearch, accessed March 20, 2020, https://isearch.asu.edu/profile/3073630.

54 "Terri Burkel," iSearch, accessed March 20, 2020, https://isearch.asu.edu/profile/3429804.

55 *See* Chapter 33 *infra*.

56 *See* Chapter 34 *infra*.

57 "Trial Advocacy," Sandra Day O'Connor College of Law, Arizona State University, https://law.asu.edu/focus-areas/trial-advocacy. "The Trial Advocacy Certificate at the Sandra Day O'Connor College of Law at Arizona State University offers students the opportunity to focus their coursework on mastering the advocacy skills needed to effectively represent clients in court and other dispute-resolution processes. The program fuses traditional law and practice-oriented courses that draw upon the experience of distinguished trial lawyers and judges who serve as adjunct faculty. This select group of legal professionals serve as mentors for students seeking to hone their advocacy skills in a wide variety of practice areas."

58 Warren E. Burger, *The Special Skills of Advocacy: Are Specialized Training and Certification of Advocates Essential to Our System of Justice?* (originally a lecture given at Fordham Law School on November 26, 1973). 83 Fordham L. Rev. 1147 (2014).

59 Wikipedia, s.v. "Paul A. Freund," last modified August 28, 2019 05:52, https://en.wikipedia.org/wiki/Paul_A._Freund. Paul A. Freund was an American jurist and law professor. He taught most of his life at Harvard Law School and is known for his writings on the United States Constitution and the Supreme Court of the United States.

60 "The Quotable Lawyer," by David S. Shrager and Elizabeth Frost, New England Publishing Associates, Ind., 1986, Item 80.17, p. 205, quoting *U.S. News & World Report*, March 25, 1974.

61 Wikipedia, s.v "University at Buffalo Law School," last modified November 19, 2019, 14:12, https://en.wikipedia.org/wiki/University_at_Buffalo_Law_School. Founded in 1887, the University at Buffalo School of Law is a graduate professional school at the University at Buffalo. It is the State University of New York system's only law school.

62 ASU Law Group, Arizona State University, accessed March 20, 2020, http://asulawgroup.org/. *See also* Chapter 33, *supra*.

63 Arizona Legal Center, accessed March 20, 2020, https://arizonalegalcenter.org/ *See also* Chapter 34, *supra*.

64 Beus Center for Law and Society, Arizona State University, accessed March 20, 2020, http://beuscenterforlawandsociety.com/. *See also* Chapter 38, *supra*.

65 Emily Allen Williams, "The Delicate Balance of the Academic Dean," November 20, 2017, https://www.higheredjobs.com/Articles/articleDisplay.cfm?ID=1456.

CHAPTER 33

THE ASU ALUMNI LAW GROUP, 2014

Conceived by ASU Law Dean Douglas Sylvester in 2012 and enthusiastically approved by ASU President Michael Crow,[1] the ASU Alumni Group was an idea long in the planning, and long before any other law school would even try.

ABOUT

"The ASU Law Group is made up of experienced lawyers who have a passion for mentoring the next generation of lawyers. Modeled after the concept of a teaching hospital, the ASU Law Group hires recent law graduates from the Sandra Day O'Connor College of Law at Arizona State University. The associates spend between two to three years learning how to practice quality law under the close supervision of senior attorneys who also oversee each associate's casework to ensure that it meets the ASU Law Group's high standards. [It] provides a wide range of legal services for individuals and businesses. These services are provided at below market rates from what is standard in the greater Phoenix area. While prices vary based on . . . situation, the ASU Law Group is committed to providing the quality service you would expect from a top notch firm."[2]

LEADERSHIP

Marty Harper,[3] ASU Law class of 1973, is CEO and President of the ASU Law Group. "He brings over 40 years of litigation and law firm management experience to this unique non-profit firm. Marty is tasked with building and managing the Law Group, and is dedicated to its mission to train recent graduates from the Sandra Day O'Connor College of Law how to practice law well while providing quality legal services to clients who need legal services at affordable rates."[4]

Patricia K. Norris, class of 1977, is in charge of lawyer development at the ASU Law Group. "[She] served as a judge on the Arizona Court of Appeals from late 2003 until her retirement in June 2017. As a judge on the court, she authored over 1,000 decisions in civil, criminal, and administrative appeals."[5]

MISSION STATEMENT

"Inspiring the lawyers of tomorrow by serving the community today. The ASU Law Group is a not-for-profit law firm. Our purpose is to train recent graduates of the Sandra Day O'Connor College of Law, helping them to become practice-ready by providing on the job training. To accomplish this, we have adopted a residency model similar to those used for years by research hospitals and other professional organizations. In addition to practical experience, our firm includes a structured curriculum for associates. Our curriculum includes instruction in both the 'nuts and bolts' of practicing law and how to build a law practice, and provides further opportunities for associates to refine their writing, presentation, and analytic skills. We hope that our model will be not only sustainable, but also repeatable. Join us and become part of what we believe will be the first of many educational law firms. Together we can enhance the quality of young lawyers, and provide affordable legal solutions to our community."[6]

---

1 "Michael M. Crow," Office of the President, Arizona State University, accessed March 26, 2020, https://president.asu.edu/the-president. Dr. Michael M. Crow is an educator, knowledge enterprise architect, science and technology policy scholar and higher education leader. He became the sixteenth president of Arizona State University in July 2002 and has spearheaded ASU's rapid and groundbreaking transformative evolution into one of the world's best public metropolitan research universities. As a model "New American University," ASU simultaneously demonstrates comprehensive excellence, inclusivity representative of the ethnic and socioeconomic diversity of the United States, and consequential societal impact. He is ASU's 16th President.

2 "About the ASU Law Group," ASU Law Group, accessed March 26, 2020, http://asulawgroup.org/.

3 "Marty Harper," Attorneys and Professionals, ASU Law Group, accessed March 26, 2020, https://asulawgroup.org/1-marty-harper/. In the fall of 1970, Marty entered the ASU College of Law after serving more than five years in the U.S. Army. During his service, Marty was stationed in Europe, Vietnam and several bases stateside. He was a Captain when he resigned his commission. Beginning in 1973, Marty joined Lewis and Roca and practiced there for 24 years. Thereafter, he helped several firms, including Polsinelli, start and build full-service practices in Arizona. Throughout his legal career, Marty has been involved in building and managing law firms. At various times, he was a practice group leader, office managing partner and a member of various firm executive committees and boards of directors. In his

40 years of practice, Marty has represented a wide range of entities in a diverse array of large complex civil litigation matters. He is an AV® peer reviewed litigator who has been included in Best Lawyers in America for his experience in Commercial Litigation, Construction and Labor and Employment Law, and is recognized as a "bet the company" litigator.

4 Ibid.

5 "Pat Norris," Attorneys and Professionals, ASU Law Group, accessed March 27, 2020, http://asulawgroup.org/pat-norris/. Before joining the court, Pat was a partner at Lewis and Roca, Phoenix. During Pat's 25 years with the firm, her practice centered on civil, business, and commercial litigation and appeals.

Pat received her undergraduate degree from Arizona State University (1974) and JD degree, *magna cum laude* (1977), from Arizona State University College of Law. Pat clerked for Judge Mary M. Schroeder of the Arizona Court of Appeals from 1977–1978. Among her professional activities, Pat has served on the Arizona Committee on the Rules of Professional Conduct, participated in the Volunteer Lawyers Program, and served as an adjunct professor at the Sandra Day O'Connor College of Law, Arizona State University. She is also a member of the Lorna Lockwood Inn of Court. Pat served as president of the Arizona State University Alumni Association (1985–86). She has published articles on civil litigation and is co-editor and contributing author of the *Arizona Attorneys' Fees Manual* (6th ed. 2017) published by the State Bar of Arizona. She is also a frequent lecturer at State Bar and judicial continuing legal education programs. Pat is active in the State Bar of Arizona, and served as co-chair of the State Bar Convention in 2016. An active participant in community services, Pat is a member of the Board of Directors of Arizona Town Hall, and is currently Board Chair. Pat has been honored by the Arizona Women Lawyers Association and the Maricopa County Bar Association for her contributions to the legal profession and the judiciary. In 2016, the Arizona Association for Justice presented Pat with the Judicial Integrity Award, and in June 2017, the State Bar of Arizona awarded Pat the James A. Walsh Outstanding Jurist Award.

6 "Home," ASU Law Group, accessed April 13, 2020, http://asulawgroup.org/.

CHAPTER 34

THE ARIZONA LEGAL CENTER

The Arizona Legal Center, Inc.[1] (ALC) is the brainchild of ASU Law Dean Douglas Sylvester.[2] He invented it and is a member of the ALC Board of Directors with Assistant Dean Victoria Ames[3] as the President and CEO. It's on the third floor of the Beus Center for Law & Society. It is registered at the Arizona Corporation Center as a nonprofit corporation under the laws of Arizona and is a recognized 501(c) (3) tax-exempt organization under the Internal Revenue Code.[4] Its funding comes largely from donations that are tax deductible for qualifying taxpayers, and it is a qualified charitable organization enabling Arizona donors to take a tax credit of up to $800 on their state tax returns.

MISSION

Many Arizonans frequently face a core legal question. The question "Do I have a case?" is at the core of everything the ALC does.[5] It offers two symbiotic services to Arizona citizens at little or no cost. The ALC knows the question "is largely unanswered in the legal community unless and until you reach the inner office in a law firm. When it is available, it is neither quick nor free. Often, people do not seek legal assistance because they see legal fees as an impenetrable barrier. They may be able to identify that they have a legal problem, but lack the resources or expertise to resolve that problem on their own."[6] The ALC makes the law accessible. Its leadership team knows those in need of legal assistance have struggled to access justice. Many lawyers in private practice try to keep abreast of the ever-changing landscape while managing the multiple priorities a law practice demands. The ALC was created to remedy the justice challenge by offering legal assistance to the community and legal support to practicing attorneys. It works through two groundbreaking approaches.

The Gary L. Stuart Legal Triage and Referral Program assesses possible cases for legal "claims, defenses, and remedies. From there, a lawyer can identify possible resolutions/strategic options and ultimately provide appropriate referrals and resources for legal or other assistance on matters that are found to be valid and viable."[7] The ALC also coordinates special legal events for the public.

In addition, the Attorney Support Services cohort "serves as a resource for lawyers and law students, those who are new to the practice of law, those looking to change practice areas, and those who are veterans yet desire the opportunity to participate in creative solutions to everyday legal challenges."[8]

Dean Ames, in a 2018 interview, made the case for the ALC: "'We all think we know the general concepts of the law, but when we are thrown into a legal issue, it becomes abundantly clear that unless you really know how to navigate the legal system you can get yourself into trouble quickly . . . People come here, and we give them direction.'"[9]

Under her leadership, the ALC and its large team of ASU Law students and Arizona volunteer lawyers assisted over 2,000 people in 2018.[10]

1 "Arizona Legal Center | Making the Law Accessible to All," Arizona Legal Center, last visited April 13, 2020, https://arizonalegalcenter.org/.

2 *See* Chapter 3.

3 Ms. Ames is an accomplished lawyer uniquely qualified to lead the ALC. "Prior to establishing the ARTEMiS Law Firm, Victoria was in private practice with Jaburg & Wilk, P.C. where she practiced in the areas of commercial litigation and employment law. She also represented clients in healthcare matters both before the state and federal courts as well as in administrative proceedings before the medical board, nursing board, and physical therapy board. Before practicing law, Victoria Ames served as Chief Executive Officer of Make-A-Wish Foundation International . . . Her dedication to improving the lives of families faced with special needs is deeply rooted in her own experience as a parent of children with special needs. . . She serves on the Board of Directors of David's Hope, Arizona's Mental Health and Criminal Justice Coalition, an organization organized to promote and secure treatment for those with mental health disorders and addictions through increasing collaboration between our mental health and criminal justice system. She also serves on the American Bar Association Advisory Panel, is a member of the Special Olympics Advocacy Resource (SOAR) Program Committee, and volunteers with the Maricopa County Volunteer Lawyers Program. In addition to private practice, Victoria Ames directs the Arizona State University | Sandra Day O'Connor College of Legal Services Program, which provides free legal services to those unable to otherwise obtain legal assistance in various practice areas, teaching law students how to put their legal education to work in real-life situations. As part of her work with the College of Law, Victoria also supervises students in pro bono projects providing free legal consultations through the Medical-Legal Partnership and the Elder Law, Special Needs, and Mental Health Legal Assistance Program." "Victoria Ames," ARTEMiS Law Firm, last visited April 13, 2020, https://artemislawfirm.com/attorney/victoria-ames/. *See also* "Victoria Ames," iSearch, last visited April 13, 2020, https://isearch.asu.edu/profile/940779.

4 "Arizona Legal Center, Inc.," Arizona Corporation Commission, last visited April 13, 2020, https://ecorp.azcc.gov/BusinessSearch/BusinessInfo?entityNumber=20341944.

5 "Arizona Legal Center | Making the Law Accessible to All," Arizona Legal Center, last visited April 13, 2020, https://arizonalegalcenter.org/.

6 The State Press, "Student-based volunteer program helps more than 2000 people a year find legal guidance." October 9, 2018.

7 "New Arizona Legal Center to Serve Community," Sandra Day O'Connor College of Law Newsletter, last visited April 13, 2020, https://law.asu.edu/asulaw-newsletter/legal-center.

8 "Arizona Legal Center | Making the Law Accessible to All," Arizona Legal Center, last visited April 13, 2020, https://arizonalegalcenter.org/.

9 Marshall Terrill, "Arizona Legal Center Helps Residents Navigate the Law," ASU Now, October 9, 2018, https://asunow.asu.edu/20181009-arizona-impact-arizona-legal-center-helps-residents-navigate-law.

10 Ibid.

CHAPTER 35

THE SANDRA DAY O'CONNOR COLLEGE OF LAW AT WASHINGTON, DC. 2015

The Barrett & O'Connor Washington Center "expands ASU's presence in the nation's capital, spurring innovative national engagements and partnerships; providing one-of-a-kind learning, teaching and research opportunities for students and faculty members; facilitating ASU's participation in high-level idea exchanges; and expanding the impact of groundbreaking research efforts."[1] *The Washington Post*[2] covered the story behind ASU Law's programming in the nation's capital. Beth Luberecki[3] captured the excitement on November 12, 2018.

> *For more than a dozen years, Michael M. Crow, president of Arizona State University, has been on a mission to transform his school into a new kind of university, one that offers access to the broadest demographic possible and takes a new approach to higher education. A slew of changes and additions on the main Tempe campus have helped carry out that goal. So Crow started looking beyond Arizona's borders... Where is the greatest concentration of people from around the planet?.. that's Washington, D.C. Everybody's in Washington, D.C.*[4]

The Sandra Day O'Connor College of Law is part of ASU's presence in DC. The *Ambassador Barbara Barrett & Justice Sandra Day O'Connor Washington Center* is fully engaged in the eight-story building at 1800 I St. NW, just two blocks from the White House.[5] President Crow described the importance of being there: "We said to ourselves that we needed to build a transactional idea center in Washington,

D.C., and begin the process of engaging in new ideas, new solutions, and new ways to solve problems, new ways to teach and new ways to learn." For years, ASU has hosted students and faculty in the capital city, but the new building means lots of space for existing offerings and growth-space for new ideas. In addition to the law school, the building includes the DC operations for seven other ASU schools, centers and institutes: the Cronkite News Washington Bureau,[6] the McCain Institute for International Leadership,[7] the Center for Gender Equity in Science & Technology,[8] the Thunderbird School of Global Management,[9] the Consortium for Science Policy and Outcomes,[10] the School for the Future for the Innovation in Society,[11] and Issues in Science and Technology.[12]

One good argument for a large presence in Washington, DC, is the experience of Jordan Brunner, a third-year law student at the downtown Phoenix campus of the Sandra Day O'Connor College of Law. The center's renovation was funded in part by a Campaign ASU 2020 gift from Barbara Barrett and her husband, Craig Barrett. That gift supports student opportunities in ASU's new center in Washington, DC. It was special for Jordan Brunner, a third-year law student on the main campus in downtown Phoenix. He hopes to launch a career in Washington after spending a semester in DC in the International Rule of Law and Security program, formerly known as the Rule of Law and Governance program. He interned at the Brookings Institution, a research think tank, and took classes at night, including a course in which the students learned to function as embassy staff. "We simulated what it would really be like to give reports, to be ready to understand and respond with the correct information," said Brunner.[13] He had interned at the Brookings Institution where he wrote articles about national security issues and climate change at the National Security Agency. He said, "I worked with people who had been in D.C. a long time and were able to put in perspective what was happening. One of my bosses would say, 'This is how this operates in real life' . . . A lot of people think everything in D.C. has to be related to being a Democrat or a Republican, but the skills I learned were not political."[14]

LAW PROGRAMS AT THE DC CAMPUS

The externship program has been supporting students in Washington for a decade and continues to grow. "Our students may work in Washington for a single semester, or stay up to a full year, providing more opportunity to explore different areas

The Sandra Day O'Connor College of Law at Washington, DC. 2015

of law and grow their professional networks on the east coast. With an increasing number of externship placements and courses offered each semester, students interested in any area of law gain valuable experience in D.C. that can advance their career goals. In particular, D.C. positions students to explore federal regulation, legislative advocacy, tribal policy, intellectual property, international law and foreign policy, national security, and to work in agencies at the center of finance, business, health law, environmental law, and more."[15]

The International Rule of Law and Security program was permanently established in Washington, DC, in 2016 to educate students in protecting the rule of law globally. "Developed in partnership with the McCain Institute for International Leadership, IRLS includes coursework, events, international projects, and an externship component that immerse students in issues of global rule of law, governance, and national security and connect them with organizations such as the Department of State, Department of Justice, Congressional offices, and international NGOs and think tanks. JD, MLS, and LLM students can pursue a focus in international rule of law and security, with the option for IRLS MLS and LLM students to complete their degrees entirely in Washington."[16]

The long-standing Indian Legal Program now also offers a unique ILP DC Experience. "Federal policy has a huge impact on tribal governments and individual members. ASU Law and the Indian Legal Program (ILP) give students an opportunity to take classes and work in Washington, D.C. through the ILP Washington, D.C. Experience. Whether coming for one week with ILP's traveling classroom, or staying for a full year, students develop an informed insider perspective on Indian policy developments on Capitol Hill, learn how to navigate federal agencies, and build relationships that will help them when they begin to practice. The ILP faculty, staff and alumni use professional relationships to help students secure meaningful externship placements."[17]

---

1 "ASU in Washington D.C.", Arizona State University, accessed March 27, 2020, https://washingtondc.asu.edu/asu-in-washington-dc-building-launch.
2 *The Washington Post,* accessed March 27, 2020, https://www.washingtonpost.com/. "The Washington Post is a major American daily newspaper published in Washington, D.C., with a particular emphasis on national politics and the federal government. It has the largest circulation in the Washington metropolitan area. Its slogan *Democracy Dies in Darkness* began appearing on its masthead in 2017."
3 "Beth Luberecki," accessed March 28, 2020, http://www.bethluberecki.com/arts.html.
4 "With newly renovated campus ASU joins schools planting their flags in D.C.," *The Washington Post,* accessed March 28, 2020, https://www.washingtonpost.com/express/2018/11/13/with-newly-renovated-campus-asu-joins-schools-planting-their-flags-dc/?noredirect=on.

5 Kimberly Rapanut, "New center helps ASU make its mark in Washington, D.C.", The State Press, published March 13, 2018, https://www.statepress.com/article/2018/03/spcampus-new-asu-washington-dc-center-opening-week. "The Ambassador Barbara Barrett & Justice Sandra Day O'Connor Washington Center, a 32,000-square-foot, eight-story center, is located in a historic building just two blocks from the White House."

6 "Cronkite News Service to Launch Washington Bureau," Walter Cronkite School of Journalism and Mass Communication, Arizona State University, December 20, 2010, https://cronkite.asu.edu/news-and-events/news/cronkite-news-service-launch-washington-bureau.

7 "What We Do," McCain Institute, Arizona State University, https://www.mccaininstitute.org/. "The McCain Institute for International Leadership is a Washington, D.C.-based think tank in cooperation with Arizona State University whose mission is to 'advance leadership based on security, economic opportunity, freedom, and human dignity, in the United States and around the world.'"

8 "Center for Gender Equity in Science and Technology," Science@ASU, Arizona State University, accessed March 28, 2020, https://science.asu.edu/center-gender-equity-science-and-technology. "Arizona State University's Center for Gender Equity in Science and Technology is a research unit in the School of Social Transformation in the College of Liberal Arts and Sciences. The center strives to create an interdisciplinary, racially-ethnically diverse community of scholars, students, policymakers and practitioners who explore, identify and ultimately develop innovative scholarship about and best practices for under-represented girls in science, technology, engineering and mathematics (STEM)."

9 Thunderbird School of Global Management, Arizona State University, accessed March 26, 2020, https://thunderbird.asu.edu/. "Thunderbird School of Global Management at Arizona State University is a global management school in Phoenix, Arizona. Founded 1946 as an independent, private institution, it was acquired by Arizona State University in 2014."

10 "Consortium for Science, Policy and Outcomes," Science@ASU, Arizona State University, accessed March 26, 2020, https://science.asu.edu/consortium-science-policy-and-outcome. "The Consortium for Science, Policy & Outcomes is an intellectual network aimed at enhancing the contribution of science and technology to society's pursuit of equality, justice, freedom, and overall quality of life."

11 "Welcome," School for the Future of Innovation in Society, Arizona State University, accessed March 26, 2020, https://sfis.asu.edu/. "The School for the Future of Innovation in Society (SFIS) is a transdisciplinary unit at the vanguard of ASU's commitment to linking innovation to public value. We are pursuing a vision of responsible innovation that anticipates challenges and opportunities, integrates diverse knowledge and perspectives, and engages broad audiences. By examining the ways we translate imagination into innovation—and how we blend technical and social concerns along the way—we learn to build a future for everyone."

12 "About Us," Issues in Science and Technology, accessed March 26, 2020, https://issues.org/. "Issues in Science and Technology is a policy journal published by the United States National Academies of Sciences, Engineering, and Medicine; Arizona State University; and the University of Texas at Dallas. Issues is a forum for discussion of public policy related to science, technology, engineering, and medicine. This includes policy for science and science for policy, with emphasis on the latter."

13 Diverse Minds to Celebrate Opening of Barrett & O'Connor Washington Center, Plus Media Solutions, US Official News, March 8, 2018.

14 Ibid.

15 "D.C. Externship Program" Sandra Day O'Connor College of Law, Arizona State University, accessed March 28, 2020, https://law.asu.edu/about/locations/washington-dc.

16 Ibid.

17 Ibid.

CHAPTER 36

SANDRA DAY O'CONNOR COLLEGE OF LAW LEGAL CENTERS, CLINICS & PROGRAMS

The college is organized by Centers, Degrees, Programs and Clinics. It offers six degrees.[1] *Centers* are units within the college that provide law-specific study, research, and assistance to clients on a limited, pro bono basis. ASU Law has seven centers.[2] *Programs* are units within the college that focus on a particular area of law.

These organizing principles are important because students come to ASU Law for different reasons and with varied expectations. Most want to become lawyers. But some are interested in other fields and want to expand their legal knowledge, rather than practice law. ASU Law tailors its educational offerings to career goals.[3] The JD, JDAS, and LLM degrees are for people who want to practice law. The MLS and MSLB are for people who want to understand legal principles and apply them to their industry but do not intend to practice law. JD and MLS students may also pursue another degree while going through law school. The faculty delivers over 250 unique courses each year, giving students unparalleled opportunities to customize their degree to their areas of interest and career goals. Beyond taking classes, the school's myriad programs offer many opportunities to practice law or master legal principles in many fields, given that the legal landscape is undergoing systemic change.

Clinics are faculty/student offerings set up to provide practical and focused experience in a specific area of law. ASU Law has ten legal clinics premised on a basic understanding. "A legal education begins in the classroom but does not end there."[4] Clinics provide hands-on experience connecting students to clients in

461

courtrooms, boardrooms, meeting rooms, and design rooms. Arizona Supreme Court Rule 38 (d) governs much of the work of ASU's legal clinics and covers clinical law professors and law students.[5]

Jennifer Barnes[6] is the faculty director of clinical programs at ASU Law. She oversees all ten clinics. Renee Garcia, manager of clinical programs, coordinates activities from one clinic to another. Since 1969, the clinical program has helped students develop the legal expertise and professional judgment they need to bridge the gap between a law degree and practicing law. Under the direct supervision of faculty and practicing attorneys, clinics provide opportunities to take direct responsibility for clients in a law practice setting. Clinical courses are an integral part of a balanced legal education. In today's competitive legal environment, students with clinical experience have a decided edge in finding rewarding positions in their chosen fields.

THE CIVIL LITIGATION CLINIC

"Student attorneys in the Civil Litigation Clinic are certified by the Arizona Supreme Court to represent people without adequate resources to hire an attorney in cases such as consumer fraud, employment discrimination, unemployment insurance benefits, wage claims, and tenant's rights. Student attorneys are involved in all aspects of civil and administrative practice including interviewing and counseling clients, fact investigation, drafting pleadings, motions, and appellate briefs, conducting discovery such as taking depositions and propounding interrogatories and representing clients in trials, arbitrations, and mediation. Student attorneys may also present oral argument in appellate courts."[7]

The civil litigation clinic trains law students to "become effective, compassionate practitioners through direct representation of clients under close faculty supervision, classroom instruction, and individual mentoring. In fulfilling its mission, the clinic strives to promote access to justice by offering free legal services to people who do not have adequate resources to hire a private attorney."[8] The clinic is a one-semester course for six graded credits. Students are expected to spend at least 270 hours in the clinic during the semester. Included in those hours is a mandatory seminar class of at least five hours per week.[9]

FIRST AMENDMENT CLINIC

Gregg Leslie[10] is the director of ASU's First Amendment Clinic. Students are immersed in many aspects of a "First Amendment and media law practice, primarily concentrating on press freedom and access issues. The clinic's primary goal is to teach aspiring lawyers how to help journalists defend their rights and promote government accountability. Clinic students will be involved in all aspects of a media law practice, particularly emphasizing interviewing and counseling media clients, drafting of legal documents, such as briefs, pleadings, and motions, and representing clients in various legal settings."[11]

The First Amendment Clinic is a one-semester, three-credit experience, graded for two credits and pass/fail option on the third credit. Prerequisites are Professional Responsibility, Evidence, Criminal Law and Civil Procedure.

IMMIGRATION CLINIC

Evelyn H. Cruz[12] is the Faculty Director of the Immigration Clinic. It "collaborates with local nonprofits, governmental agencies, and community advocates to identify foster children needing immigration services. The clinic also provides legal advice and referral at events organized by community agencies, non-profits and elected officials. These services include:

1. Immigration Petitions for Special Juvenile Status (SIJ)
2. Naturalization through adoption by a US Citizen or for children who previously obtained lawful permanent status through SIJ
3. Retrieval of immigration documents or records to establish immigration status
4. General information sessions on immigration.

Certified limited practice students, who are mentored by Professor Cruz, represent foster children in the program. Students in the clinic "represent abused, neglected, abandoned children in immigration proceedings and state dependency cases. [They] draft motions, briefs, legal correspondence, closing statements, and direct examination questions. [They also] provide brief consultations at legal fairs to individuals with immigration law questions. [And they] research law and country conditions, interview and prepare experts/witnesses, investigate and document case facts."[13]

THE INDIAN LEGAL CLINIC

Patty Ferguson-Bohnee[14] is the faculty director for the Indian Legal Clinic *and* the Indian Law Program at ASU Law. The Indian Legal Program, established in 1988, is a larger, more comprehensive offering.[15] Arizona has twenty-two tribes, and ASU Law is a national leader in the developing field of Indian law. The nationally recognized faculty members in the Program are leading scholars in their fields and produce scholarly research and publications, and provide outreach and public service.

The Indian Legal Clinic "provides law students with an opportunity to participate in real cases dealing with native peoples and Indian issues. ILC serves both Indian country and the nation's urban Indian population by providing high-quality legal services, with attention to the special legal and cultural needs of native peoples. The ILC works with tribal courts handling criminal prosecutions and defense actions, undertakes tribal legal development projects, such as drafting tribal code provisions and court rules for Indian tribes, represents individuals in civil actions, and works on federal policy issues affecting native peoples, such as federal recognition."[16]

INNOVATION ADVANCEMENT PROGRAM

Raees Mohamed,[17] an attorney with Kelly Warner Law, is the director of the IAP. The Innovation Advancement Program at ASU Law is an off-campus clinic that "pairs inventors, technology entrepreneurs, tech transfer professionals, and emerging technology companies with some of ASU's brightest law students. The students, in teams of two or three law students undertake a wide array of legal services that help early stage ventures solidify their legal foundations, avoiding many of the mistakes and pitfalls often made when moving technology into the marketplace."[18]

It is a one-semester course for six credits (two graded and four pass/fail). The prerequisites are Evidence, Civil Procedure, and Criminal Law & Professional Responsibility. Students are expected to spend at least 270 hours in the clinic during the one semester.[19] The program's in-residence professionals provide additional supervision and guidance, especially Jon Coury, from the Hool Law Group[20] of Phoenix.

LISA FOUNDATION PATENT LAW

This clinic is "the brainchild of prominent Chicago patent attorney Steven G. Lisa,[21] a 1984 ASU Law alumnus. To date, through Lisa's foundation, the clinic has received $200,000 in donated funding. Students receive hands-on experience in real-world patent and trademark prosecution, and learn skills needed to recognize and obtain valuable and enforceable patents and trademarks for clients that may later be successfully licensed or litigated. Regardless of whether students plan to practice transactional patent and trademark law or intellectual property litigation, the clinic gives students insight into both areas of practice so that they may understand the impact that actions taken during the patent and trademark procurement processes have during a subsequent litigation."[22]

The clinic is a member of the U.S. Patent & Trademark Office (USPTO)'s Law School Clinic Certification Program[23] in which "students receive limited recognition practice numbers. Those who have a science or engineering background represent both patent and trademark clients whereas those without a technical background practice only on the trademark side of the clinic. The limited recognition practice numbers permit students to represent clients directly before the USPTO including signing and filing patent and trademark applications, office actions, maintenance and renewal documents, conducting examiner interviews and other official correspondence on behalf of clients."[24]

Students in the Lisa Foundation Patent Law Clinic "receive hands-on experience in real-world patent and trademark prosecution, including client interviewing and counseling, patentability and registrability searching and opinions, and drafting and filing patent and trademark applications and office action responses. Through their clinical experience, students work with independent inventors and start-up companies to assess clients' IP protection needs and draft and prosecute patent and trademark applications in the USPTO under the supervision of a licensed patent and trademark attorney."[25] It is a one-semester course but may be taken for a second semester with instructor approval. The course is for three graded credits for the first semester and up to three pass/fail credits for students returning for a second semester. Prerequisites are Patent Law, Comprehensive Patent Practice, Patent Drafting, Patent Preparation, Trademark Law and Prosecuting Trademark Applications. Students are expected to spend at least 135 total hours in the Clinic during the one semester.

LODESTAR MEDIATION CLINIC

The Lodestar Mediation Clinic is an integral component of the nationally recognized Lodestar Dispute Resolution Center.[26] It teaches students about the alternatives to litigation while providing practical experience about the mediation process. "Student attorneys experience an intensive training program focusing on the theory, strategy, and skills involved in the mediation of legal disputes, then act as mediators in civil (non-family) cases."[27]

Students "act as neutral third parties who help Justice Court litigants attempt to resolve their lawsuits before trial. [They] shadow and co-mediate with professional mediators from the EEOC and private practice [and] shadow judges in judicial settlement conferences."[28] It is a one-semester course, for four graded credits. Students are expected to spend at least 180 hours of clinical work during the one semester.

POST-CONVICTION CLINIC

Katherine Puzauskas[29] is the faculty director of ASU's Post-Conviction Clinic. It "investigates claims of wrongful conviction and manifest injustice from prisoners convicted of crimes in Arizona. Post-conviction work is a specialized practice area that delves into both fundamental and nuanced aspects of criminal law and criminal procedure—one that is becoming increasingly vital as over 400 prisoners nationwide have been exonerated either in full, or in part by DNA testing, and over 1,500 people have been exonerated by other means. Arizona is home to more than 40,000 prisoners and more than 5,000 on community supervision. Arizona incarcerates more people per capita than any other state in the west and ranks sixth in the country."[30]

Students "participate in the post-conviction investigation and litigation of criminal cases. [They] produce written work focused on reviewing and analyzing the history of the conviction and the potential reasons for any wrongful conviction, including the role DNA, or other newly discovered evidence could play in exonerating the inmate. Students interview witnesses and clients, locate biological evidence, and evaluate whether a given case should be submitted for DNA testing. [Finally, they] draft requests for post-conviction DNA testing, petitions for post-conviction relief, and petitions for clemency and parole. [They] may represent clients in court, or before the Arizona Board of Executive Clemency"[31] as permitted by Arizona Supreme Court Rule.

The Post-Conviction Clinic is a one-semester course for six credits (four-client component pass/fail and two-graded seminar). Prerequisites are Evidence, Civil Procedure, and Criminal Law & Professional Responsibility. Students are expected to spend at least 270 hours in the Clinic during the one semester.

PUBLIC DEFENDER CLINIC

Jeff Roth[32] is the faculty director of the Public Defender Clinic. "Under close attorney supervision, students who participate in the Public Defender Clinic represent indigent defendants in criminal cases in the Maricopa County Superior Court and Justice Courts. In the past, clinic students have represented clients charged with drug possession, aggravated assault, resisting arrest, promoting prison contraband, car theft and DUI, to name a few. Students interview clients and witnesses, draft motions, and handle preliminary hearings, plea proceedings, settlement conferences, sentencing, evidentiary hearings and jury trials. They receive regular feedback on their verbal and written work from adjunct professors, other experienced criminal defense attorneys, and sitting Superior Court judges."[33]

Evidence is a prerequisite. Students receive six units of graded credit. Students must complete 270 hours during the semester, including class time (approximately 20 hours per week during the school year or 27 hours per week in the summer). Students must attend a mandatory three-day training before the start of classes in fall and spring.

PROSECUTION CLINIC

Kenneth Vick[34] is the clinic director. "Under the supervision of experienced attorneys, Certified Limited Practice Students who participate in the Prosecution Clinic prosecute both misdemeanor and felony cases in Maricopa County and city courts. Students are responsible for a full range of trial-related tasks. They are initially assigned minor trials, then more difficult cases as the semester progresses. By the end of the semester, students may have an opportunity to participate in at least one jury trial.

"Criminal cases are assigned to students who are then responsible for preparing cases for trial and trying cases, if necessary. Classroom work helps equip students with the necessary skills needed for the courtroom, such as preparing opening statements, direct examination, cross-examination, and closing arguments." [35]

The clinic's goal is to give students the maximum amount of in-court trial experience. They should have the opportunity to participate in at least one jury trial. Students are assigned criminal cases, which they prepare for trial and try if necessary. Students are placed in various Maricopa County Attorney offices and are supervised by experienced prosecutors.

The Prosecution Clinic is a one-semester, six-credit course (three graded and three pass/fail). Prerequisites are Evidence, Civil Procedure, Criminal Law and Professional Responsibility. Students must work at least 260 hours per semester with their assigned agency per semester plus four hours per week of seminar.

ASU SPORTS LAW PROGRAM & BUD SELIG

Question—should the title be ASU Sports Law & Bud Selig, or should it be *déjà vu all over again?* [36] Answer—ASU Law offers a master's degree—MSLB—in "Sports Law and Business" in partnership with the W.P. Carey School of Business and in full cooperation with ASU's athletics department. And Bud Selig[37] plays on both teams.

As noted on its website, ASU's MSLB program "provides students with the training to understand the regulatory and revenue forces that drive the increasingly global sports industry: legal, policy, business, branding and marketing. The program uses a small class environment to deliver a problem- and project-based legal and business curriculum taught by recognized academic and professional leaders. That curriculum, together with an applied project, prepares students with the skills necessary to address the difficult issues present in the sports industry. This unique graduate program can be completed on a full-time basis in a 12-month period or in two or fewer years for part-time students working in the field. This is a program like no other: it blends sports, law and business. Phoenix is home to all four major professional sports, making it the perfect location to study this unique topic. Graduates land jobs at premier sports organizations around the country, and the program has 100 percent placement in sports law externships."[38]

RENAMING THE SPORTS LAW PROGRAM AFTER BUD SELIG

On Sept. 12, 2019, the law school announced the newly named Allan "Bud" Selig Master of Sports Law and Business program and the establishment of the Marie Selig Professorship in Selig's mother's name. The announcement was shared at the launch of the former Major League Baseball commissioner and Distinguished Professor of Sports in America.[39] The announcement was a pitch for Selig's new book, *For the Good of the Game*.[40]

Professor Zachary Gubler is the inaugural Marie Selig Professorship recipient. In announcing the Selig professorship, Dean Douglas Sylvester said, "The commissioner has been an instrumental part of the success of our Sports Law and Business program and we are honored that it will now be associated with such a legendary and transformative figure of professional sports. . . . With his long-term support and time spent here at the law school, we are deeply grateful to both Commissioner Selig and his wife, Sue."[41]

Selig has been a great supporter of the Sports Law and Business program. He was ASU Law's convocation speaker in 2017 and was the founding member of the Sports Law and Business Advisory Board. His teaching allows students a unique opportunity to learn from someone who has been on the front lines of sports administration. Distinguished Professor of Law and the Executive Director of the Selig Sports Law and Business Program Glenn Wong said, "We are grateful for the continued support of Commissioner Selig and his dedication to this program. . . . Through his naming of our Sports Law and Business program and his support of our Selig Scholars, ASU Law is able to provide access to an unparalleled law and graduate school experience."[42]

Investors Business Daily knows the Commissioner well. They said, "Allan Huber 'Bud' Selig went to his first baseball game when he was just 3 years old. His mom took him to Borchert Field, home of the Triple-A Milwaukee Brewers. Right then and there, the sport became his lifelong passion, which he focused on and excelled at. Selig's passion led him as a team owner and later Major League Baseball's commissioner to change the way the national pastime is run. He perhaps saved baseball from itself. But he also found ways to get the best from others, too."[43]

ACADEMY FOR JUSTICE—TAKING CRIMINAL JUSTICE ONE STEP FURTHER

A new website. A new idea. A new center at the Sandra Day O'Connor College of Law. In the summer of 2018, Erik Luna's focus on bridging the gap between academia and reform became real. With financial backing from the Charles Koch Foundation, ASU created a center for him to run. The Center's site tells the story. "Erik Luna's passion for criminal justice reform was ignited as a teenager during the height of America's 'war on drugs.' Growing up in the 1980s in a sleepy surfing community in San Diego, California, Luna noted that people in his white middle-class neighborhood seemed to peddle and consume drugs with little fear of punishment. Yet in southern California's poorer, mostly minority communities, drug busts and incarceration were far more common."

He knew "at an early age there was something terribly wrong about all of this." To help inform the ongoing debate about the system and its reform, Luna founded the ASU law school's new *Academy for Justice*.[44] Luna knew that academic research was "rarely reaching those working in the field. Our work tends to be buried in the bowels of university libraries or hidden behind internet pay walls, rather than going directly into the hands of people who could actually use it in the real world."[45] To change the reality, "Luna brought together more than 100 criminal justice scholars. In October 2017, the group published Reforming Criminal Justice, a four-volume report available free online that covers criminalization, policing, pretrial and trial processes, punishment, incarceration, and release. The report explains the reasons reform is needed in each area and offers possible solutions. In the few months since its release, the report has been distributed to reformers and policymakers, featured at conferences, discussed in the mass media, and cited in briefs before the U.S. Supreme Court. 'The four volume collection has already had a real impact,' says Brandon Garrett, the L. Neil Williams Professor of Law at Duke University, who has assigned multiple pieces from the report to his law students. 'And it will continue to influence criminal justice policy debates for years to come.'"[46]

PROFESSOR ERIK LUNA

Professor Luna holds an endowed chair at the law school; The Amelia D. Lewis Professor of Constitutional and Criminal Law. He is a man with ideas, ideals, and great conceptions of justice.[47] His academic and practice history is entirely consistent with one of Arizona's most famous lawyers, Amelia D. Lewis,[48] and the law and consequences of her most famous criminal law case—*In Re Gault*.[49] It seems poetic justice he now holds the endowed chair named after her.

His official ASU biography[50] defines him academically. "Professor Luna teaches and writes primarily in the areas of criminal law and criminal procedure. Luna has received two Fulbright awards.[51] In 2000, he served as the senior Fulbright Scholar to New Zealand at Victoria University Law School[52] (Wellington, NZ). In 2016–17, he was the Fulbright Distinguished Chair at the University of Birmingham (Birmingham, UK).[53] Luna has also been a visiting scholar with the Max Planck Institute for Foreign and International Criminal Law[54] (Freiburg, DE), a visiting professor with the Cuban Society of Penal Sciences (Havana, CU), a visiting professional in the Office of the Prosecutor of the International Criminal Court[55] (The Hague, NL), and a research fellow with the Alexander von Humboldt Foundation[56] (Bonn, DE).

"Prior to coming to ASU, Luna was the Sydney & Frances Lewis Professor of Law at Washington and Lee University, and before that, he was the Hugh B. Brown Chair in Law at the University of Utah. Luna is a member of the American Law Institute[57] and an adjunct scholar with the Cato Institute.[58] He graduated summa cum laude from the University of Southern California and received his J.D. with honors from Stanford Law School. Upon graduation, Luna was a prosecutor in the San Diego District Attorney's Office and a fellow and lecturer at the University of Chicago Law School." At ASU, his primary areas of scholarship and teaching are in criminal law, criminal procedure, and advanced topics in criminal justice, including sentencing, law of terrorism, and comparative criminal justice.

He has written, co-authored, and published eight book collections in the last ten years.[59] Between 1999 and 2017, he wrote or co-authored thirty-six law reviews, articles, or essays.[60] The breadth and reach of his short-form writing is evident in just six of his thirty-six published articles. (1) "The New Face of Racial Profiling"; (2) "Punishment Theory, Holism, and the Procedural Conception of Restorative Justice"; (3) Race, Crime, and Institutional Design"; (4) "The .22 Caliber Rorschach Test"; (5) "Sovereignty and Suspicion"; and (6) "What Is Legal Is Not Necessarily Ethical—The Limits of Law and Drug Testing Programs."

1 "Degree Programs," Sandra Day O'Connor College of Law, Arizona State University, accessed April 2, 2020, https://law.asu.edu/degree-programs. A law degree is the state of recognized completion of studies at a college or university. A degree is issued in recognition of having satisfactorily completed the prescribed course of study. ASU Law's degrees are Juris Doctor (JD); JD Advanced Standing (JDAS); JD Transfer Applicant; JD Visiting Applicant; Master of Laws (LLM); Master of Legal Studies (MLS); Master of Sports Law and Business (MSLB).

2 "Faculty & Research," Sandra Day O'Connor College of Law, Arizona State University, accessed April 2, 2020, https://law.asu.edu/faculty/centers. (1) Academy for Justice; (2) Center for Law, Science and Innovation; (3) Center for Public Health Law and Policy; (4) Indian Legal Program; (5) International Rule of Law and Security; (6) Lodestar Dispute Resolution Center; (7) Sports Law and Business.

3 "Degree Programs," Sandra Day O'Connor College of Law, Arizona State University, accessed April 2, 2020, https://law.asu.edu/degree-programs.

4 "Clinics," Sandra Day O'Connor College of Law, Arizona State University, accessed April 2, 2020, https://law.asu.edu/experiences/clinics.

5 The stated purpose for this rule is predicated on the inability of law students to actually practice law before graduating from an ABA-accredited law school, passing the bar exam, and securing the required approval from the court's Committee on Character & Fitness. "The rule is adopted as one means of providing assistance to practicing attorneys in providing such services to and to encourage law schools to provide clinical instruction in trial work of varying kinds and to facilitate volunteer opportunities for students in pro bono contexts." See ARSC 38, Special Exceptions to Standard Examination and Admission Process.

6 *See* Chapter 81 for her profile.

7 "Civil Litigation Clinic," Sandra Day O'Connor College of Law, Arizona State University, accessed April 2, 2020, https://law.asu.edu/experiences/clinics/civil-litigation.

8 Ibid.

9 Ibid.

10 "Gregg P. Leslie, Executive Director, ASU Law First Amendment Clinic," Walter Cronkite School of Journalism and Mass Communication, Arizona State University, accessed April 2, 2020, https://cronkite.asu.edu/about/faculty-and-leadership/faculty/gregg-leslie. Gregg Leslie is the executive director of the First Amendment Clinic at ASU's Sandra Day O'Connor College of Law, and is also a professor of practice at the school. Students in the clinic plan to work with Cronkite students on First Amendment and access issues.

Leslie previously served as legal defense director and staff attorney with the Reporters Committee for Freedom of the Press for 17 years. The Reporters Committee is a nonprofit organization dedicated to helping journalists with legal issues by maintaining a free hotline for reporters, producing publications to educate them about their rights and filing briefs on their behalf in cases around the country.

11 "First Amendment Clinic," Sandra Day O'Connor College of Law, Arizona State University, accessed April 2, 2020, https://law.asu.edu/experiences/clinics/first-amendment.

12 "Evelyn Cruz," Faculty and Staff, Arizona State University, accessed April 2, 2020, https://isearch.asu.edu/profile/833419. "Evelyn Cruz is a clinical professor of law, teaches immigration law and comprehensive law practice, and directs Sandra Day O'Connor's College of Law's Immigration Law and Policy Clinic, which represents unaccompanied minors in immigration removal proceedings and received the 2007 President's Medal for Social Embeddedness at ASU. Professor Cruz writes articles about immigration law, clinical education and therapeutic jurisprudence, and has co-authored several immigration law manuals used by immigration practitioners and pro-se detainees at Immigration Detention Centers throughout the country. She also comments at Immigration Prof Blog, A Member of the Law Professor Blog Network. Professor Cruz's paper, 'Competent Voices: Noncitizen Defendants and the Right to Know the Immigration Consequences of Plea Agreements,' discusses the Sixth Amendment's right to effective assistance of counsel in relation to the criminal prosecution of undocumented workers arrested at the 2009 Postville, Iowa immigration raids and the pending Supreme Court case Padilla v. Kentucky. The article appeared in the Harvard Latino Law Review (2010). Before joining ASU in 2005, Professor Cruz was the Robert M. Cover Clinical Teaching Fellow at Yale Law School, and an adjunct professor at both Golden Gate University School of Law and New College School of Law in San Francisco. She is a former staff attorney for the Immigration Legal Resource Center in San Francisco, and former acting director of Centro Legal de la Raza in Oakland, and she was an associate for the Law Offices of Francisco J. Barba in San Francisco."

13 "Immigration Clinic," Sandra Day O'Connor College of Law, Arizona State University, accessed April 2, 2020, https://law.asu.edu/experiences/clinics/immigration-law.

14 "Patricia Ferguson," Faculty and Staff, Arizona State University, accessed April 2, 2020, https://isearch.asu.edu/profile/1101447. Patty Ferguson-Bohnee has substantial experience in Indian law, election law and policy matters, voting rights, and status clarification of tribes. She is a clinical professor of law, the faculty director of the Indian Legal Program *and* the director of the Indian Legal Clinic at ASU.

15 *See* Chapter 13, *supra*, for a larger view of the program.

16 "Indian Legal Clinic," Sandra Day O'Connor College of Law, Arizona State University, accessed April 2, 2020, https://law.asu.edu/experiences/clinics/indian-legal.

17 "Raees Mohamed," Kelly Warner Law, accessed April 2, 2020, http://kellywarnerlaw.com/raees-mohamed-startup-lawyer/. Raeesabbas Mohamed is a partner at Kelly Warner Law who advises and guides entrepreneurs, executives and professionals through complicated and unpredictable legal issues. Raees is a master at crafting creative legal solutions, developing profitable business transactions and ligating technology issues.

18 "Innovation Advancement Legal Clinic," Sandra Day O'Connor College of Law, Arizona State University, accessed April 2, 2020, https://law.asu.edu/experiences/clinics/iap.

19 Ibid.

20 "Home," Hool Coury Law, accessed April 2, 2020, http://hoolcourylaw.com/. Hool Law Group "is committed to entrepreneurial success, representing investors and helping ventures scale from start-up to exit. We leverage our legal and business knowledge with our entrepreneurial spirit & connections."

21 "About the Law Offices of Lisa & Lesko." The Law Offices of Lisa & Lesko, LLC, accessed April 2, 2020, https://patentit.com/. "The Law Offices of Lisa & Lesko is a patent law firm with the skill, experience, and resources proven to succeed in the highly-specialized patent licensing and enforcement business. The Law Offices of Lisa & Lesko is unique in that our partners have a long history of successful contingent fee patent enforcement programs, including multiple highly lucrative, industry-wide enforcement programs throughout the last 35 years."

22 "Lisa Foundation Patent Law," Sandra Day O'Connor College of Law, Arizona State University, accessed April 2, 2020, https://law.asu.edu/experiences/clinics/lisa-foundation.

23 "Law School Clinic Certification Program," Unites States Patent and Trademark Office, last modified April 1, 2020, 06:35, https://www.uspto.gov/learning-and-resources/ip-policy/public-information-about-practitioners/law-school-clinic-1. The Law School Clinic Certification program allows law students enrolled in a participating law school's clinic program to practice Intellectual Property Law before the USPTO under the strict guidance of a Law School Faculty Clinic Supervisor. The program currently consists of students practicing in both patent and trademark law before the USPTO. The Office of Enrollment and Discipline administers the program. The Director of the Office of Enrollment and Discipline grants the law students limited recognition to practice before the Office.

Students gain experience drafting and filing either patent applications or trademark applications for clients of the law school clinic. Further, as they are authorized to practice before the USPTO, they gain experience answering Office Actions and communicating with either patent examiners or trademark examining attorneys for the applications they have filed.

24 Ibid.

25 Ibid.

26 "The Lodestar Dispute Resolution Center expands ASU Law's efforts to understand the nature of conflict and its impact on the effectiveness of dispute resolution. Through research, teaching, and service, students, lawyers, and non-legal professionals learn the problem-solving methods and skills that lawyers and other conflict resolution professionals employ regularly to prevent and resolve disputes." "Lodestar Mediation Clinic," Sandra Day O'Connor College of Law, Arizona State University, accessed April 2, 2020, https://law.asu.edu/faculty/centers/lodestar-dispute-resolution.

27 Ibid.

28 Ibid.

29 "Katherine Puzauskas," Management Team, AZ Justice Project, accessed April 2, 2020, https://www.azjusticeproject.org/katherine-puzauskas. Katie Puzauskas is the Director of the Post-Conviction Clinic at the Sandra Day O'Connor College of Law at Arizona State University. "She began her career as a lawyer with the nonprofit Arizona Justice Project, working with indigent Arizona prisoners who have claims of wrongful conviction, have suffered a manifest injustice such as an excessive sentence, or, who are seeking medical clemency. Katie continues her work with the Arizona Justice Project and supervises numerous volunteers and students in the review of post-conviction criminal cases. She provides direct representation in post-conviction proceedings, and, before the Arizona Board of Executive Clemency. Katie has managed multiple grants from the National Institute of Justice and the Bureau of Justice Assistance."

30 "Post-Conviction Clinic," Sandra Day O'Connor College of Law, Arizona State University, accessed April 2, 2020, https://law.asu.edu/experiences/clinics/post-conviction.

31 Ibid.

32 "Jeffrey Roth," Lawyer Directory, JUSTIA Lawyers, accessed April 2, 2020, https://lawyers.justia.com/lawyer/jeffrey-roth-677518.

33 "Public Defender Clinic," Sandra Day O'Connor College of Law, Arizona State University, accessed April 2, 2020, https://law.asu.edu/experiences/clinics/public-defender.

34 "Kenneth N. Vick," Lawyer.com, updated on July 3, 2019, https://www.lawyer.com/kenneth-n-vick.html.

35 "Prosecution Clinic," Sandra Day O'Connor College of Law, Arizona State University, accessed April 2, 2020, https://law.asu.edu/experiences/clinics/criminal-practice.

36 Wikipedia, s.v. "Yogi Berra," last modified April 1, 2020, 13:02, https://en.wikipedia.org/wiki/Yogi_Berra#"Yogi-isms. A veiled reference to one of Yogi Berra's most often quoted malapropisms. It is mildly apt since Yogi Berra and Bud Selig are baseball immortals.

37 Wikipedia, s.v. "Bud Selig," last modified March 26, 2020, 04:49, https://en.wikipedia.org/wiki/Bud_Selig. Allan Huber "Bud" Selig is an American baseball executive who currently serves as the Commissioner Emeritus of Baseball. Previously, he served as the ninth Commissioner of Baseball.

38 "Sports Law and Business, MSLB," Academic Programs, Arizona State University, accessed April 4, 2020, https://webapp4.asu.edu/programs/t5/majorinfo/ASU00/LWSLBMSLB/graduate/false?init=false&nopassive=true.

39 https://asunow.asu.edu/20190913-asu-law-allan-bud-selig-master-sports-law-and-business-program.

40 Eben Novy-Williams, "Bud Selig Was Baseball's Great Hero, Says Bud Selig, Critic," Bloomberg. published July 9, 2019, https://www.bloomberg.com/news/articles/2019-07-09/bud-selig-book-review-he-s-mlb-baseball-s-hero-in-new-memoir. "For 22 years, from 1992 to 2015, Bud Selig oversaw Major League Baseball, an era of massive change and growth for America's Pastime. He restructured the league's divisions and playoffs, initiated interleague play, introduced the World Baseball Classic, and helped grow a technology arm now worth billions of dollars."

41 Nicole Almond Anderson, "ASU Law names Sports Law and Business program for Alan 'Bud' Selig," ASU Now: Access, Excellence, Impact, Arizona State University, published September 13, 2019, https://asunow.asu.edu/20190913-asu-law-allan-bud-selig-master-sports-law-and-business-program.

42 Ibid.

43 Curt Schleier, "Baseball's Bud Selig Coaxed Greatness Out of Others," Leaders & Success, Investor's Business Daily, published August 22, 2019, https://www.investors.com/news/management/leaders-and-success/bud-selig-coaxed-greatness-out-others-mlb-baseball/.

44 The *Academy for Justice* brings together criminal justice scholars to form a world-class platform for academic research. Supported by a $6.5 million grant from the Charles Koch Foundation, the academy's goal is to ensure that those who create and enforce criminal justice policy draw on the best research in the field. In addition to publishing user-friendly scholarship, the academy will host conferences and workshops that connect scholars with think-tank experts, reformers, and policymakers, and create educational programs on the criminal justice system. *See also* http://academyforjustice.org/.

45 "Taking Criminal Justice Scholarship One Step Further," Charles Koch Foundation, published July, 28, 2018, https://www.charleskochfoundation.org/story/erik-luna-arizona-state-university/.

46 Ibid.

47 Chief Justice Warren E. Burger addressed the ABA at its annual convention in September of 1972. His full quote is, "Ideas, ideals and great conceptions are vital to a system of justice, but it must have more than that—there must be delivery and execution. Concepts of justice must have hands and feet or they remain sterile abstractions. The hands and feet we need are efficient means and methods to carry out justice in every case in the shortest possible time and at the lowest possible cost. This is the challenge to every lawyer and judge in America." *The Quotable Lawyer*, David S. Shrager and Elizabeth Frost. New England Publishing Company, 1986, p. 159. Full speech reported in ABA, Vital Speeches, Oct. 1, 1972.

48 Amelia Dietrich Lewis was born in New York City, June 25, 1903. She attended Hunter College and then graduated from St. Lawrence University School of Law (now Brooklyn Law School) with an LL.B., in 1925. She later received an LL.M. from New York Law School. She was legislative assistant to the minority leader of the New York City Council and was an attorney for the Legal Aid Society. During World War II, Lewis served with the Office of Price Administration. In 1957, after the death of her husband, Maxwell Lewis, she moved to Arizona. Upon being admitted to the Arizona Bar in 1958, Lewis accepted the post of Deputy County Attorney for Navajo County. In 1970, she moved and set up practice in Youngtown, later

moving her offices to Peoria. In 1964, Lewis undertook the representation of Gerald Gault, a minor, in an appeal of his case. She appealed, first to the Arizona Supreme Court, then to the United States Supreme Court, where Gault's conviction was overturned. "Amelia D. Lewis," Arizona Foundation for Legal Services & Education, accessed February 27, 2021,https://www.legallegacy.org/13-attorneys/26-amelia-lewis.

49 Gerald ("Jerry") Gault was a 15-year-old accused of making an obscene telephone call to a neighbor, Mrs. Cook, on June 8, 1964. After Mrs. Cook filed a complaint, Gault and a friend, Ronald Lewis, were arrested and taken to the Children's Detention Home. Gault was on probation when he was arrested, after being in the company of another boy who had stolen a wallet from a woman's purse. Mrs. Cook was again not present for the June 15th hearing, despite Mrs. Gault's request that she be there "so she could see which boy that done the talking, the dirty talking over the phone." Again, no record was made and there were conflicting accounts regarding any admissions by Gault. At this hearing, the probation officers filed a report listing the charge as lewd phone calls. An adult charged with the same crime would have received a maximum sentence of a $50 fine and two months in jail. The report was not disclosed to Gault or his parents. At the conclusion of the hearing, the judge committed Gault to juvenile detention for six years, until he turned 21. At that time, no appeal was permitted in juvenile cases by Arizona law; therefore, a habeas petition was filed in the Supreme Court of Arizona and referred to the Superior Court for a hearing. The Superior Court dismissed the petition, and the Arizona Supreme Court affirmed. The Supreme Court agreed to hear the case on *certiorari* to determine the procedural rights of a juvenile defendant in delinquency proceedings where there is a possibility of incarceration. On January 15, 1963, the Court reversed and remanded, unanimously overruling *Betts v. Brady*. "Facts and Case Summary – *In re Gault*," United States Courts, accessed February 28, 2021, https://www.uscourts.gov/educational-resources/educational-activities/facts-and-case-summary-re-gault.

50 "Erik Luna," iSearch, accessed February 27, 2021, https://isearch.asu.edu/profile/2698172.

51 The Council for International Exchange of Scholars (CIES), the scholar division of the Institute of International Education (IIE), is well known for its expertise and extensive experience in conducting international exchange programs for scholars and university administrators. For nearly seventy years, CIES (www.cies.org) has administered the Fulbright Scholar Program, the United States flagship academic exchange effort, on behalf of the United States Department of State, Bureau of Educational and Cultural Affairs (ECA). CIES was founded as a nonprofit organization in 1947 by four prestigious academic associations – the American Council of Learned Societies (ACLS), National Academy of Sciences (NAS), Social Science Research Council (SSRC), and American Council on Education (ACE). "About CIES," Council for International Exchange of Scholars, accessed February 27, 2021, https://www.cies.org/about-us/about-cies.

52 Our world-class, capital city Faculty of Law offers a stimulating and supportive learning environment. Ranked among the top 40 law schools in the world, home to scholars of international standing and based in the nation's vibrant legal and political heart, there is no better place to advance your knowledge of the law. "Faculty of Law," Victoria University of Wellington, accessed February 27, 2021, https://www.victoria.ac.nz/law.

53 Birmingham has been challenging and developing great minds for more than a century. Characterized by a tradition of innovation, research at the University has broken new ground, pushed forward the boundaries of knowledge and made an impact on people's lives. We continue this tradition today and have ambitions for a future that will embed our work and recognition of the Birmingham name on the international stage. "About Us," University of Birmingham, accessed February 27, 2021, https://www.birmingham.ac.uk/university/index.aspx.

54 Welcome to the website of the Max Planck Institute for Foreign and International Criminal Law. Comparative, international, and interdisciplinary research is conducted in the Departments of Criminal Law and Criminology. A third department, the Department of Public Security Law, is currently being set up. The overarching goal of all research conducted at the Institute is to provide national and supranational criminal policy solutions for the fundamental challenges of our time. Max Planck Institute for the Study of Crime, Security, and Law, accessed February 27, 2021, https://www.mpicc.de/en/.

55 The Prosecutor of the International Criminal Court is the officer of the International Criminal Court whose duties include the investigation and prosecution of the crimes under the jurisdiction of the International Criminal Court, namely genocide, crimes against humanity and war crimes as well as the crime of aggression once that crime comes under the Court's jurisdiction which will not be the case before 2017. Wikipedia, s.v., "Prosecutor of the International Criminal Court," last modified September 3, 2020, 7:12, https://en.wikipedia.org/wiki/Prosecutor_of_the_International_Criminal_Court.

56 We promote academic cooperation between excellent scientists and scholars from abroad and from Germany.

Our research fellowships and research awards allow you to come to Germany to work on a research project you have chosen yourself together with a host and collaborative partner. If you are a scientist or scholar from Germany, you can profit from our support and carry out a research project abroad as a guest of one of more than 29,000 Humboldt Foundation alumni worldwide—the Humboldtians. As an intermediary organization for German foreign cultural and educational policy, we promote international cultural dialogue and academic exchange. "About the Humboldt Foundation," Alexander von Humboldt Stifung Foundation, accessed February 28, 2021, https://www.humboldt-foundation.de/web/about-us.html.

57 The American Law Institute is the leading independent organization in the United States producing scholarly work to clarify, modernize, and otherwise improve the law. "About ALI," American Law Institute, accessed February 27, 2021, https://www.ali.org/about-ali/.

58 The Cato Institute is an American libertarian think tank headquartered in Washington, D.C. It was founded as the Charles Koch Foundation in 1974 by Ed Crane, Murray Rothbard, and Charles Koch, chairman of the board and chief executive officer of the conglomerate Koch Industries. In July 1976, the name was changed to the Cato Institute. Cato was established to have a focus on public advocacy, media exposure and societal influence. According to the 2017 Global Go To Think Tank Index Report, Cato is number 15 in the "Top Think Tanks Worldwide" and number 10 in the "Top Think Tanks in the United States." "Home," Cato Institute, accessed February 28, 2021, https://www.cato.org/.

59 (1) REFORMING CRIMINAL JUSTICE: INTRODUCTION AND CRIMINALIZATION (edited report, Academy for Justice 2017); (2) REFORMING CRIMINAL JUSTICE: POLICING (edited report, Academy for Justice 2017); (3) REFORMING CRIMINAL JUSTICE: PRETRIAL AND TRIAL PROCESSES (edited report, Academy for Justice 2017); (4) REFORMING CRIMINAL JUSTICE: PUNISHMENT, INCARCERATION, AND RELEASE (edited report, Academy for Justice 2017); (5) THE LAW OF TERRORISM (casebook with Wayne McCormack, Carolina Academic Press 2017); (6) UNDERSTANDING THE LAW OF TERRORISM (nutshell in "Understanding" series with Wayne McCormack, LexisNexis, 2014); (7) THE PROSECUTOR IN TRANSNATIONAL PERSPECTIVE (edited volume with Marianne Wade, Oxford University Press, 2012); (8) DRUGS AND JUSTICE: SEEKING A CONSISTENT, COHERENT, COMPREHENSIVE VIEW (monograph with Margaret Battin et al., Oxford University Press, 2007).

60 SELECTED LAW REVIEWS & JOURNALS (*refereed/peer reviewed).

"Drug War and Peace," 50 U.C. DAVIS LAW REVIEW 813 (2016) [article for symposium on marijuana legalization] "Charnel Knowledge," 34 CRIMINAL JUSTICE ETHICS 210 (2015) [solicited book review]* Prosecutor King, 1 STANFORD JOURNAL OF CRIMINAL LAW AND POLICY 48 (2014) [symposium article].

"Digital Innocence," 99 CORNELL LAW REVIEW 981 (2014) [article with Joshua Fairfield].

"The Open Society and Its Digital Enemies," 99 CORNELL LAW REVIEW ONLINE 217 (2014) [essay with Joshua Fairfield, replying to separate pieces by Jane Burnbaum and Brandon Garrett reviewing Digital Innocence].

"Rage Against the Machine, 97 MINNESOTA LAW REVIEW 2245 (2013) [response essay].

"Prosecutorial Decriminalization," 102 JOURNAL OF CRIMINAL LAW & CRIMINOLOGY 785 (2012) [article for symposium on over-criminalization].

"The Bin Laden Exception," 106 NORTHWESTERN UNIVERSITY LAW REVIEW 1489 (2012) [essay].

"Spoiled Rotten Social Background," 2 ALABAMA CIVIL RIGHTS AND CIVIL LIBERTIES LAW REVIEW 23 (2011) [article for symposium on "rotten social background" in criminal law].

"Sense and Sensibility in Mandatory Minimum Sentencing," 23 FEDERAL SENTENCING REPORTER 219 (2011) [essay with Paul Cassell, solicited for special issue].

"Prosecutors as Judges," 67 WASHINGTON AND LEE LAW REVIEW 1413 (2010)

[article with Marianne Wade, symposium on the future of prosecution] Symposium Introduction, 67 WASHINGTON AND LEE LAW REVIEW 1285 (2010) [introduction with Marianne Wade].

"Mandatory Minimalism," 32 CARDOZO LAW REVIEW 1 (2010) [lead article with Paul Cassell].

"The Curious Case of Corporate Criminality," 46 AMERICAN CRIMINAL LAW REVIEW 1507 (2009) [reply for symposium on corporate criminal liability].

"Criminal Justice and the Public Imagination," 7 OHIO STATE JOURNAL OF CRIMINAL LAW 71 (2009) [article for symposium on intersection of criminology and criminal law & procedure].

"Drug Détente," 20 FEDERAL SENTENCING REPORTER 304 (2008) [essay for special election issue].

"The Katz Jury," 41 U.C. DAVIS LAW REVIEW 839 (2008) [article for symposium on 40th anniversary of Katz].

"Cycles of Juvenile Justice: An Introduction to the Utah Criminal Justice Center Distinguished Lecture," 10 JOURNAL OF LAW & FAMILY STUDIES 1 (2008) [introduction to juvenile justice symposium].

"Traces of a Libertarian Theory of Punishment," 91 MARQUETTE LAW REVIEW 263 (2007) [article for plea bargaining symposium].

"Restorative Justice in Federal Sentencing: An Unexpected Benefit of Booker?" 37 MCGEORGE LAW REVIEW 787 (2006) [article for sentencing symposium, with Barton Poulson].

"Gridland: An Allegorical Critique of Federal Sentencing," 96 JOURNAL OF CRIMINAL LAW & CRIMINOLOGY 25 (2005) [article].

"System Failure," 42 AMERICAN CRIMINAL LAW REVIEW 1201 (2005) [essay for wrongful conviction symposium] "The Over-criminalization Phenomenon," 54 AMERICAN UNIVERSITY LAW REVIEW 703 (2005) [article for symposium on over-criminalization].

"Cuban Criminal Justice and the Ideal of Good Governance," 14 TRANSNATIONAL LAW & CONTEMPORARY PROBLEMS 529 (2004) [article for symposium on Cuba's future].

"Foreword: The New Face of Racial Profiling," 2004 UTAH LAW REVIEW 905 (2004) [introduction to racial profiling symposium].

"What Is Legal Is Not Necessarily Ethical—The Limits of Law and Drug Testing Programs," 4 AMERICAN JOURNAL OF BIOETHICS 41 (2004) [solicited commentary].

"A Place for Comparative Criminal Procedure," 42 BRANDEIS LAW JOURNAL 277 (2003–04) [article for criminal procedure symposium].

"Punishment Theory, Holism, and the Procedural Conception of Restorative Justice," 2003 UTAH LAW REVIEW 205 [article for restorative justice symposium].

"Introduction: The Utah Restorative Justice Conference," 2003 UTAH LAW REVIEW 1 [introduction to restorative justice symposium].

"Race, Crime, and Institutional Design," 66 LAW & CONTEMPORARY PROBLEMS 183 (2003) [article for race and crime symposium].

"Drug Exceptionalism," 47 VILLANOVA LAW REVIEW 753 (2002) [article for drug war symposium].

"The .22 Caliber Rorschach Test," 39 HOUSTON LAW REVIEW 53 (2002) [solicited comment for Frankel Lecture].

"Constitutional Road Maps," 90 JOURNAL OF CRIMINAL LAW & CRIMINOLOGY 1125 (2000) [article].

"Principled Enforcement of Penal Codes," 4 BUFFALO CRIMINAL LAW REVIEW 517 (2000) [article for M.P.C. symposium].

"Transparent Policing," 85 IOWA LAW REVIEW 1107 (2000) [article].

"Sovereignty and Suspicion," 48 DUKE LAW JOURNAL 787 (1999) [article] "The Models of Criminal Procedure," 2 BUFFALO CRIMINAL LAW REVIEW 389 (1999) [article for criminal procedure symposium]

"Beyond Breard, 17 BERKELEY JOURNAL OF INTERNATIONAL LAW 147 (1999) [article with Douglas Sylvester].

CHAPTER 37

SANDRA DAY O'CONNOR COLLEGE OF LAW DONATIONS & ENDOWMENT

The Sandra Day O'Connor College of Law is a public law school. Students who pay tuition fund the institution. It receives internal funding from its parent university. And it thrives because alumni, benefactors, and legal education supporters donate money. It could not exist without tuition funding. It could not meet its mission without university support. It could not deliver high-quality legal education, legal scholars, or effective lawyering and counseling without philanthropic support.

WHY GO TO LAW SCHOOL—WHY SUPPORT LEGAL EDUCATION

Most law students have made reasoned, well-thought-out, cautious decisions about the pivotal question—why go to law school? Law school benefactors have likewise made conscientious decisions about supporting legal education. It is no accident that students and benefactors share common goals and often follow similar career paths.

Success in either endeavor—learning the law or practicing philanthropy—is not inevitable. It does not happen only because it got off to a good start. It may not happen just because a finish line was crossed. The start (three years of study) and the finish (a law degree) are artificial constructs. Three factors determine whether they fit and fulfill. First, did the law professors do their job? Second, did the law students engage and absorb enough to make them competent, thoughtful, and ethical lawyers? Third, were both students and faculty financially supported such that they could start and finish their intertwining careers and donations?

The practice of law demands a rigorous, self-critical set of legal skills. Educating law students demands a deep understanding of those skills and protocols and processes that will ensure every student becomes sufficiently skilled to practice the art of lawyering. This giving and getting is the core of a legal education. Only when what the teachers taught is skillfully imbedded into the lawyer's brain will benefactors step up and give financial support.

Supporting legal education happens only when the law school's product—competent lawyers—are visible and engaged as lawyers, judges, and public officials. Benefactors will support a broad array of perspectives that enhance lawyering, economic, social, and political consequences based on sound legal philosophy, as well as a deep understanding of empirical and social science data.

THE CONSEQUENCES OF GOING TO LAW SCHOOL AND CHARITABLE GIVING TO LAW SCHOOLS

Learning the law and supporting it has always been of paramount importance in America. "The most useful and influential people in America are those who take the deepest interest in institutions that exist for the purpose of making the world better." –Booker T. Washington.[1]

It is not done lightly or without careful personal and public investigation. "The raising of extraordinarily large sums of money, given voluntarily and freely by millions of our fellow Americans, is a unique American tradition . . . Philanthropy, charity, giving voluntarily and freely . . . call it what you like, but it is truly a jewel of an American tradition." – John F. Kennedy.[2]

Great minds and great leaders put it in plain and simple terms. "We make a living by what we get; we make a life by what we give." –Winston Churchill.[3]

GIVING TO SUPPORT THE SANDRA DAY O'CONNOR COLLEGE OF LAW

Donor support[4] for the school began modestly in the 1960s. Today, it is a deeply embedded tradition. In the decade from 1968 to 1979, donor support was $112,135.00. Donor support jumped up 177 percent in the 1980s to $1,884,684.00. The 1990s produced $5,224,247.00, an increase of 204 percent. From 2000 to

2010, donations totaled $76,692,733.00. And from 2010 to 2019, donor support rose to $96,761,624.00, an increase of 26 percent.

Some of the earliest donors were the Estate of Blanche Farmer Strong, The William Polk Carey Foundation,[5] which created the John S. Armstrong Quasi-Endowment, and the Merriam Professorship Law Endowment, created by Charles J. Merriam.[6]

Over the last fifty years, students, alumni, and current and former faculty have created 125 annual scholarships. Today, this auspicious group of donors sees the college as "world-class education in a highly desirable location, [offering] unparalleled employment opportunities in Arizona and across the country, and a cost that is far below that of nearly every other top public law school." The relative low cost of attendance is directly due to the generosity of donors. "The combination of an active donor community, rich employment opportunities, and great value tuition allows us to attract students from all parts of the world. Students come from a wide variety of backgrounds, some who face social and economic challenges. Investing in ASU Law means supporting student success and the ability to positively contribute to our community. Contributions provide funding for scholarships, programs, faculty research, and much more."[7]

In addition to scholarship and professorship donations, a special library campaign to support the Ross-Blakley Law Library raised $1,247,370.39 between 1989 and 1991. Fifty thousand-dollar donations were made to support the library by five Phoenix law firms: Jennings, Strouss & Salmon, PLC[8]; Quarles & Brady, LLP[9]; Perkins Coie, LLP[10]; Lewis Roca Rothgerber Christie, LLP[11]; and Snell & Wilmer, LLP.[12] Many other firms supported the library with $20,000 gifts.

In 1999, JoAnn Pedrick made a $100,000 gift to establish the annual Willard H. Pedrick Lecture.[13] The lecture was given for many years; the fund is directed at student scholarship support. Many other top alumni and faculty donations have been made and consistently support the college:

- Bud & Suzanne Selig[14]
- Craig & Barbara Barrett Foundation[15]
- Estate of Dennis Karjala[16]
- Joe Sims[17]
- Michael & Rebecca Berch[18]
- Roslyn Silver[19]

The top non-alumni donors are:

- Leo and Annette Beus[20]
- W.P. Carey Foundation[21]
- Lodestar Foundation[22]
- Steele Foundation[23]
- Intel Foundation[24]

These current and former donors[25] are invaluable to the college because without them, it would be much smaller, less impactful, and unable to sustain a top-25 ranking in America's 203 ABA Accredited Law Schools. "Thanks to the generosity of our donors, ASU Law is able to award more than 125 scholarships annually. This alphabetically arrayed list includes all current scholarship donors.

- American Board of Trial Advocates Award
- Alan Matheson Moot Court Counseling Competition Scholarship
- Alan Matheson Service Award
- American Law Institute - American Bar Association Award
- Anthony Lucia Scholarship
- Arizona Chapter of the American Academy of Matrimonial Lawyers Scholarship
- Arizona Women Lawyers Honoring Justice O'Connor Scholarship
- ASU Alumni Association Outstanding Graduate Award
- ASU Sandra Day O'Connor College of Law Alumni Association Scholarship
- Augustine Jimenez Scholarship
- AZ Law Alliance Scholarship
- Ballard Spahr Diversity Scholarship
- Barnett E. Marks Scholarship
- Barrett Law Scholarship
- Benjamin Herbert Scholarship
- Birnbaum Family Fellowship
- Blanche Farmer Strong Scholarship
- Brett Aspey Memorial Scholarship
- C. Randall Bain Scholarship

Sandra Day O'Connor College of Law Donations & Endowment

- Carstens Family Fund Scholarship
- Charles E. Jones Scholarship
- Charles A. Pulaski Jr., Memorial Scholarship
- Chester H. Smith Scholarship
- Cohen Professionalism Scholars
- Curtis A. Jennings Scholarship
- Daniel Cracchiolo Scholarship
- Daniel Strouse Prize
- Daniel Strouse Scholars
- Donald and Marie Isaacson Endowed Scholarship
- Donald J. Winder Endowed Scholarship
- Doug and Anna Sylvester Scholarship
- Edward and Diane McDowell Scholarship
- Emily Burns Scholarship
- Fay T. Runyan Scholarship
- Fennemore Craig/Cal Udall Scholarship
- Frazier Ryan Goldberg Arnold Scholarship
- Frederick C. Berry Scholarship
- Gary L. Stuart Scholarship
- Getsinger Family Scholarship
- Gideon Fellowship
- Gold 'n Gavel Scholar
- Gordon Silver Scholarship
- Gust Rosenfeld Scholarship
- Harold and Lucille Dunn Memorial Law Scholarship
- Harriett Freye Scholarship
- Harris Powers & Cunningham Endowed Scholarship
- Harry J. Cavanagh Scholarship
- Hispanic Legacy Scholarship
- Hon. William C. Canby Jr., Scholarship
- Hon. John M. Gaylord Scholarship
- Hugo Zettler Scholarship
- Humberto Moreno Memorial Scholarship
- Indian Legal Program Scholarship
- International Academy of Trial Lawyers Award

- J. Reuben Clark Law Society Scholarship
- Jaburg/Wilk Scholarship
- James and Barbara Hennessy Scholarship
- James M. Koontz Memorial Scholarship
- Janet S. Mueller Oral Advocacy Award
- Jerry Hirsch Scholarship
- Jeremy Govekar Scholarship
- John A. Propstra Endowed Scholarship
- John H. Dick Memorial Scholarship
- John H. Killingsworth Scholarship
- John J. Dawson Memorial Scholarship
- John J. Ross Memorial Award
- John P. Morris Memorial Scholarship
- John R. Becker Scholarship
- John S. Armstrong Award
- Jonathan Rose Endowment
- Jon and Janelle Kappes Scholarship
- Joseph Feller Memorial Scholarship
- Judge Mary Anne Richey Scholarship
- Judge Roslyn Olson Silver Scholarship
- Kevin Kane Memorial Book Scholarship
- Leo & Annette Beus Top Scholars
- Liberty Project
- Los Abogados/Honorable Valdemar Cordova Endowed Scholarship for ASU
- M. David Shapiro Memorial Book Scholarship
- Marianne Alcorn Memorial Scholarship
- Mark Wilmer Scholarship
- Mary M. Schroeder Prize Endowment
- Mary Schroeder Public Federal Practice Award
- Michael Brophy Scholarship
- Michael D. Ryan Scholarship
- National Association of Women Lawyers Outstanding Graduate
- Navajo Law Fellowship
- Nussbaum Gillis & Dinner Scholarship

Sandra Day O'Connor College of Law Donations & Endowment

- Order of the Barristers
- Osborn Maledon Endowed Scholarship
- Palumbo Wolfe Scholarship
- Patricia D. White Scholarship
- Paul & Flo Eckstein Scholarship
- Paul Holloway Trial Advocacy Award
- Peter Baird Writing Prize
- Polk Aspiring Prosecutor Scholarship
- Pro Bono Scholarship
- Professor Rebecca Tsosie Spirit of Excellence Scholarship
- R. Kelly Hocker (Employment and Labor Law) Scholarship
- Richard Castillo Scholarship
- Rebecca & Michael Berch Scholarship
- Redfield and Susan Baum Scholarship
- Renaud Cook Drury Mesaros Scholarship
- Richard W. Effland Memorial Scholarship
- Robert Bartels Scholarship
- Ronald Jay Cohen Excellence in Advocacy Award
- Rosette LLP Scholarship
- S. Rex Lewis Scholarship
- Sandra Day O'Connor Award
- Simonson/Meyerson Family Scholarship
- Snell & Wilmer Law Journal Awards
- Snell & Wilmer Scholarship
- Soroosh Davani Memorial Scholarship
- State Bar Bankruptcy Section Scholarship
- State Bar Criminal Justice Section Scholarship
- State Bar Public Lawyers' Section Scholarship
- State Bar Real Property Section Scholarship
- Stevens Center Scholarship
- Sun Angel Scholarship
- Ted Karalis Scholarship
- Theodore Julian Memorial Scholarship
- Todd Nelson Scholarship
- Truman R. Young Jr. Prosecuting Fellowship

- Volunteer Lawyers Program Outstanding Volunteer Award
- W. P. Carey/Armstrong Prize for Achievement in Public Interest
- Walter E. Craig Scholarship
- Ward Family Future Legal Innovator Endowed Scholarship
- William H. Thomas Scholarship
- Women Law Students' Association Outstanding Graduate Award"[26]

Giving to the Sandra Day O'Connor College of Law is a pleasure, obligation, or onerous. It helps students and faculty help the world around them. That's what legislatures the world over are supposed to do. But would you give to support the Arizona Legislature or the U.S. Congress? Paul Ylvisaker got it right.[27] "Donors represent a private version of the legislative process—a deliberative process that selects goals, sets values, and allocates resources . . . an alternative vehicle for getting things done."[28]

---

1 "Philanthropic Quotes," Philanthropy Roundtable, last visited April 5, 2020, https://www.philanthropyroundtable.org/almanac/people/philanthropic-quotes. "Booker Taliaferro Washington was an American educator, author, orator, and advisor to multiple presidents of the United States. Between 1890 and 1915, Washington was the dominant leader in the African-American community and of the contemporary black elite." Wikipedia, s.v., "Booker T. Washington," last modified March 30, 2020 21:37, https://en.wikipedia.org/wiki/Booker_T._Washington.
2 "Philanthropic Quotes," Philanthropy Roundtable, last visited April 5, 2020, https://www.philanthropyroundtable.org/almanac/people/philanthropic-quotes.
3 Ibid.
4 All donor support data supplied by Terri Burkel, Senior Director of Development, Sandra Day O'Connor College of Law.
5 See "W.P. Carey Foundation," W.P Carey Foundation, last visited April 5, 2020, http://www.wpcareyfoundation.org/.
6 "Charles J. Merriam," Prabook, last visited April 5, 2020, https://prabook.com/web/charles_j.merriam/1066987.
7 "Give," Sandra Day O'Connor College of Law, last visited April 5, 2020, https://law.asu.edu/alumni-friends/give.
8 See "Jennings, Strouss & Salmon, PLC," Jennings, Strouss & Salmon, last visited April 5, 2020, https://jsslaw.com/.
9 See "Quarles & Brady LLP—Attorneys at Law," Quarles & Brady, last visited April 5, 2020, https://www.quarles.com/.
10 See "Perkins Coie LLP—An International Law Firm," Perkins Coie, last visited April 5, 2020, https://www.perkinscoie.com/en/.
11 See "Lewis Roca Rothberger Christie LLP," Lewis Roca Rothgerber Christie, last visited April 5, 2020, https://www.lrrc.com/.
12 See "Law Offices of Snell & Wilmer," Snell & Wilmer LLP, last visited April 5, 2020, https://www.swlaw.com/.
13 "JoAnn Pedrick, Widow of ASU Founding Dean Willard Pedrick, Passes Away," Sandra Day O'Connor College of Law, last visited April 5, 2020, https://law.asu.edu/content/joann-pedrick-widow-of-founding-dean-passes-away.

14 "ASU Law Names Sports Law and Business Program for Allan 'Bud' Selig," ASU Now, September 13, 2019, https://asunow.asu.edu/20190913-asu-law-allan-bud-selig-master-sports-law-and-business-program; Wikipedia, s.v., "Bud Selig," last updated March 26, 2020 4:49, https://en.wikipedia.org/wiki/Bud Selig.

15 "Craig and Barbara Barrett Foundation," GuideStar Profile, last visited April 5, 2020, https://www.guidestar.org/profile/7002608.

16 "Dennis S. Karjala was an intellectual property law professor at Arizona State University. His major interests in teaching and research were primarily in the area of intellectual property, specifically in copyright and its applications in digital technologies." Wikipedia, s.v., "Dennis Karjala," last updated November 26, 2019 1:55, https://en.wikipedia.org/wiki/Dennis_Karjala.

17 Joe Sims graduated from the Arizona State University College of Law in 1970 *magna cum laude*, after serving as a Comment Editor on the *Law Journal*. He received his B.S. from Arizona State University in 1967. "Joe Sims Biography," United States Department of Justice Antitrust Division, last visited April 5, 2020, https://www.justice.gov/atr/joe-sims-biography. *See* Chapter 10, *supra*.

18 For Michael Berch, *see* Chapter 8, *supra*. For Rebecca Berch, *see* Chapter 10, *infra*.

19 "Roslyn O. Silver is a Senior United States District Judge of the United States District Court for the District of Arizona. She served as Chief Judge for the district from 2011 to 2013." Wikipedia, s.v., "Roslyn O. Silver," last updated April 10, 2019 18:06, https://en.wikipedia.org/wiki/Roslyn_O._Silver. *See* Chapter 10, *supra*.

20 Leo and Annette are among the top donors to ASU in both law and science. *See* "Beus Gift to Law Center Reflects Affinity for ASU, Concern for Fellow Citizens," ASU Now, September 22, 2014, https://asunow.asu.edu/content/beus-gift-law-center-reflects-affinity-asu-concern-fellow-citizens;"Beuses' $10 Million Gift to Build World's First-of-its-Kind X-Ray Laser Lab at ASU," ASU Now, April 18, 2019, https://asunow.asu.edu/20190418-solutions-beus-10-million-gift-build-worlds-first-its-kind-x-ray-laser-lab-asu.

21 *See* "W.P. Carey Foundation," W.P Carey Foundation, last visited April 5, 2020, http://www.wpcareyfoundation.org/.

22 *See* "The Lodestar Foundation," Lodestar Foundation, last visited April 5, 2020, http://www.lodestarfoundation.org/.

23 *See* "The Steele Foundation," Steele Foundation AZ, last visited April 5, 2020, http://steeleaz.org/.

24 *See* "Intel Foundation," Intel, last visited April 5, 2020, https://www.intel.com/content/www/us/en/corporate-responsibility/intel-foundation.html.

25 Ibid.

26 "Give," Sandra Day O'Connor College of Law, last visited April 5, 2020, https://law.asu.edu/alumni-friends/give.

27 Paul Ylvisaker was an urban planner, government official, foundation executive, and educator. "Ylvisaker, Paul Norman," Encyclopedia.com, last updated March 10, 2020, https://www.encyclopedia.com/humanities/encyclopedias-almanacs-transcripts-and-maps/ylvisaker-paul-norman.

28 "Philanthropic Quotes," Philanthropy Roundtable, last visited April 5, 2020, https://www.philanthropyroundtable.org/almanac/people/philanthropic-quotes.

CHAPTER 38

THE BEUS CENTER FOR LAW & SOCIETY AS OF 2019

*I*s it a building? A law school? A grand collaboration? Yes it is. A one-word label would be *multifaceted*.[1]

Its website proudly proclaims the Beus Center as the "the new home to the Sandra Day O'Connor College of Law at Arizona State University . . . . The building space uses form and function to connect students, visitors, and the general public to the role of justice in society. The BCLS was designed to be inviting, engaging, and accessible to everyone who is interested in learning about the law, its effect on our daily lives, and the many services and resources available through ASU and other BCLS partners. The BCLS fosters collaboration among its occupants, including the Lincoln Center for Applied Ethics,[2] The McCain Institute for International Leadership,[3] the Sandra Day O'Connor Institute,[4] Arizona Voice for Crime Victims,[5] Arizona Justice Project,[6] the ASU Alumni Law Group—the nation's first teaching law firm that also helps the community gain access to affordable legal services.[7]

A community outreach program—the Arizona Legal Center[8]—is a conduit for public access to free legal support."[9]

Besides the seven direct legal source nonprofits listed above, "[t]he building also includes Think Tank spaces for grant-funded, interdisciplinary research projects. The BCLS will further play a major role in helping members of the community understand their legal rights. . . . ASU Law is proud to be a part of the BCLS, an endeavor that will further the legacy and work of the college's namesake—Justice Sandra Day O'Connor—who is devoted to ensuring citizens learn about and understand the importance of rule of law and civic engagement."[10]

THE BUILDING

The designer said the building took *50 Years of Innovation*. "This project stands out in Kovach's 50 year-portfolio as one of the most gratifying and unique projects we have ever completed. Ever since our inception half a century ago we have been known as an innovative team and ASU gave us the opportunity to expand our imagination at every turn. The design intent for the skin was to clad the exterior with a stone façade that was code compliant, fully warranted and would be durable enough to last a century. An aggressive schedule, working in downtown Phoenix required creative logistical solutions. Glass curtain wall, aluminum fins, and metal panels are part of the exterior scope. . . . To meet the unique demands of this project our team designed a unitized façade system that captured it all – stone, glass, and metal fins. To secure the stone into the units our engineering team designed a frame that attached to the mullions and a concealed anchor system secured the stone to the frame. The system allowed glazing to be installed in the same plane, while the stone could be articulated in a saw-tooth pattern. The male-female joinery of the unitized panels allowed the designer the freedom to alternate between slot glass and stone panels, as well as incorporate architectural fins on the east and west elevations of the building."[11]

It's a cement building, 50 percent from recycled materials. Buro Happold Engineering took on a unique challenge. "Located in downtown Phoenix, the new 280,000 square foot Beus Center for Law and Society provides an exemplary new education facility to meet the demands of a changing law school program. To accommodate growth in enrollment numbers, the building offers modern, flexible learning environments over eight stories. Classrooms, research clinics, and an extensive library are all equipped with the latest technology to support students and staff. . . . A key consideration for our client was increasing engagement between the law school, and the wider community by including shared amenities such as the café, library, public plaza and Alumni Law Group, which is the first organization of its kind to be associated with a law school. Our team had to consider how the building layout would accommodate these requirements. An additional challenge was the tight timescale in which the building needed to be completed, which required close collaboration between teams to devise an efficient delivery program."[12]

Rumor has it that a certain dean told the engineers to build a giant building out of slate, glass, and steel big enough to house a top-ranked law school, a law firm, a dozen legal entities, a library, a huge meeting hall with glass hangar doors, and a café, with its own liquor license, as soon as you can. And don't forget, it has to combine low energy use with high occupant comfort. It must have an extremely high-performance HVAC system, with chilled beams, and air displacement systems. When finished, we want it be a landmark piece of architecture, designed to serve ASU's educational needs and the social needs of Phoenix for generations to come. We want enough office space, conference rooms, classrooms, and mingle-space for a thousand students, several hundred faculty and staff, and lots of visitors, every day, right away.

In hardly any time at all, from a lawyer's perspective, the end result was a beautiful six-story building with two floors of underground parking, forty-two organizations inside a 280,000-square-foot easily navigated space, open to the air in all the right ways, with forty-three digital displays, and seventeen public-use spaces. ABOR bonds secured the base cost ($129M) and the students showed up in August of 2016. They found, much to their surprise, that they were steps away from the legal, political, and economic heart of Arizona in the nation's sixth-largest city. In a single stroke, law faculty and law students networked with alumni and prospective employers. The trial courts were three blocks away, and the appellate courts easily reached in minutes.

DESIGN

The Beus Center was designed by Tomas Rossant[13] / Ennead Architects,[14] in collaboration with Jones Studio.[15] From the outset, the design centered on "openness to the public in mind, as a unique urban environment where society and the study and practice of law converge. The building's breezeway between the West and East wings creates an inviting, engaging, and accessible pathway for people to connect with the law, as well as the law school. It also brings more daylight into the building. The law library is unconventionally configured to be without borders or thresholds: stacks and study spaces extend to the upper levels along all circulation paths, promoting informal intellectual and social interchange between students, faculty, and visitors. Open-air walkways bridge the east and west portions of the building, stitching together the breezeway and providing access to a suspended double-height reading room on the north, and two stories of legal think tank spaces on the south. The transparency of the expansive bi-folding glass door at the front of the W. P. Carey Foundation Armstrong Great Hall unifies the indoor and outdoor space and allows the hall to act as the public's 'legal living room.' An innovative retractable-tiered seating system allows the Great Hall to be converted from a socially dynamic arrangement to a more formal auditorium configuration, providing flexibility while offering a unique civic space to the downtown Phoenix community. Its welcoming gesture of openness clearly communicates and embodies the overarching message of ASU Law's new home—that our laws and the quality of our society are inextricably linked."[16]

SUSTAINABILITY

"Sustainability was a key driver throughout the design process. Beyond the naturally self-shading massing of the overall building, the saw-toothed configuration of the outer building facade, comprised of Arizona sandstone with aluminum and glass windows, has been designed to achieve a higher than standard level of thermal performance, responding to solar orientation, window size, and programmatic requirements. Mechanically, the building incorporates energy-efficient technologies, including chilled beams and under-floor displacement cooling. BuroHappold Engineering[17] provided integrated MEP engineering, structural engineering, lighting design, energy analysis, and sustainability consulting services, recognizing that the new Beus Center . . . demanded a highly integrated design approach in which building systems and key design elements work in concert in order to achieve design and performance goals. DPR Construction,[18] with its expertise in sustainable and Lean construction methods, also played a central role in this highly collaborative building process. DPR, an early adopter of integrated project delivery, Lean management, and other collaborative methods, strives to continuously push the industry forward with the help of IPD and Lean specialists. Given the complexity of the building process, the BCLS project team used Lean methodology and building information modeling (BIM) to eliminate unknown variables while successfully meeting cost, schedule, and design quality goals. DPR's award-winning Phoenix regional headquarters was the first of its size in the world to achieve Net-Zero Energy Building (NZEB) Certification from the International Living Future Institute.[19] [BCLS] serves as another example of how an adaptive response to an extreme desert environment may be integrated into an efficient, effective, and environmentally responsible building via innovative building solutions. BCLS is expected to reduce energy consumption by 37 percent compared to a baseline building and is calculated to have the fourth lowest EUI (Energy Use Intensity) of any of the 57 buildings analyzed at ASU."[20]

LANDSCAPING

"Designed by Colwell Shelor Landscape Architecture,[21] the landscape concept respects and celebrates the regional character of the Sonoran Desert, evoking a canyon where landscape and hardscape are carved out of a solid mass of stone. The outer edges of the site respond to the city grid and Taylor Mall, the three-block landscaped pedestrian walkway at the heart of the ASU Downtown Phoenix campus. The Snell & Wilmer[22] Plaza is comprised of faceted berms with flowering trees, evocative of sandbars in a canyon floor. The café and lobby spill out onto the north end of the plaza among lush planters and seating areas with platforms for events. The south end of the plaza highlights a lush, sunken garden naturally irrigated by surface run-off to support vegetation and contribute to recharging the local aquifer. The fifth floor 'green' courtyard features a balance of event space flanked with trees in raised planters, a community table, and both fixed and moveable seating. A primary design goal was the reduction of the demand on all landscaping systems. Desert-adaptive planting and water features activate the landscape, helping to minimize on-site irrigation demands. Landscape maintenance has further been reduced by virtue of chosen plant species requiring little to no pruning. Trees with high evapotranspiration rates provide natural cooling. Shaded benches allow visitors to comfortably appreciate the environmentally conscious solutions brought together in a beautiful, meaningful way, in which a variety of microclimates are created to provide multiple user experiences."[23]

"The BCLS is targeting LEED Gold certification and features a high-efficiency HVAC system that includes chilled beams and Airfloor heating/cooling. The building lighting system is 100 percent LED, with daylighting and occupancy controls also contributing to a low-energy lighting design . . . . Desert-adaptive plants are utilized in the building landscaping."[24]

TECHNOLOGY

"Every classroom (lecture halls and specialized rooms, not seminar rooms) is set up for lecture capture, as well as video streaming. They are further equipped with laser projectors to increase picture quality and reduce the cost of maintenance and repair. All features are integrated into a single control panel that professors will use to lower lights, blinds, etc. There is also technology throughout the BCLS to help people navigate the building and nearby areas, learn more about the law school and other occupants, keep a pulse on trending legal topics and events, and engage in trivia and games to connect the law and why it matters in our everyday lives. Central to that task is a Nano Display facing Taylor and First streets, a Media Mesh in the breezeway between the west and east wings of the building touch screens including a large display in the first-floor lobby, and other digital screens that share information passively. Ennead Architects teamed with Unified Field Inc.,[25] a pioneer in the field of interactive media, to create the new BCLS app, an educational and community-building tool developed specifically for the Beus Center. Created to take the building's 'pulse'—the activity within—and encourage greater connectivity between students, faculty, alumni, and their mobile devices, the app is part of a digital communication, dynamic wayfinding and messaging platform that creates a digital campus within the physical campus. Cutting-edge technology enables faculty, staff, students, alumni, prospective students, as well as members of the local legal and general public, to interact with each other and with the building itself, curating their own BCLS experience in real time. Establishing a new type of community, people can now connect and communicate in a way previously unknown in a university setting."[26]

THE DAN CRACCHIOLO EXECUTIVE CONFERENCE CENTER

The Executive Conference Center, named after one of Phoenix's leading lawyers, Dan Cracchiolo,[27] is "one of the most impressive pieces in current audiovisual technology. It features a large elliptical table with custom curved projection screens wrapped on the inside edge. Teaming up with the designers at JBL Architects, Level 3 AV was able to pull off this amazing blended technology using 20 projectors. Having this '360 degree' video wall allows meeting members to see face-to-face while still viewing presentation images on the inside screens. The conference center is also outfitted with three recessed ceiling mounted cameras with voice location automation technology that puts each person speaking into a clear view during video conferencing sessions. This two-part system of a 360-degree video wall and voice location automation technology gives all 30-people seated at the table the ability to be front and center for speaking and engagement for video conferencing."[28]

THE WILLIAM P. CAREY ARMSTRONG GREAT HALL

"The 150 seat lecture hall inside the building has the ability to 'open up' to a 'Great Hall' which is used for appellate court sessions and live TV broadcasts. It's a large, modular area with stadium bench seating. A 36-foot-wide motorized projection screen can drop down from a recessed area in the ceiling with a push of a button on the custom lectern. Two image-blended projectors create large format, multi window image capabilities so all 150 people seated in the hall have a clear line of sight. The space is beautiful, contemporary and constantly has students working in and around it."[29]

J. GRANT WOODS COURTROOM

No law school is complete without a mock-up courtroom. In the Beus Center, the courtroom "features 3 motorized projection screens that drop down via lifts from the ceiling. They are completely hidden when the room is not set to 'In-Use.' The lectern at the front of the room is out fitted with AMX and controls all of the rooms AV. Wired microphones are dropped in from the ceilings and speakers are installed throughout. PTZ cameras are used so students and faculty can view the courtroom proceedings as well as recording for future review."[30]

LECTURE HALLS & CLASSROOMS

"The lecture halls and classrooms at ASU are completely state-of-the-art. Each room has AMX scheduling panels on the outside confirming what classes are taking place. . . . [Students] are instantly engulfed in technology. Drop down projector screens come down from recessed ceiling panels to project two screens on each side of the room for maximum visibility. Each classroom and lecture hall has a lectern at the head of the class offering the instructor full control of the classroom. The lecterns can setup the entire room with the touch of one button. Each room is also equipped with several PTZ cameras offering students the ability to 'tune-in' to the classrooms when they are away from the building."[31]

COMMENTS, ACCOLADES, AND EXALTATIONS

"'[ASU President Michael Crow] felt like the law schools, historically, had done a very poor job of being involved with the communities and society,' said Tom Williams,[32] assistant dean for academic affairs and the institution. . . . When designing the Beus Center the need for a connection with the community was one of the main factors ASU asked the project's designers to take into consideration. Not only does the building connect law students with resources such as the ASU Alumni Law Group, a practice that hires law graduates, the school also plans to allow community engagement through lectures that will be open to the public. 'Education is supposed to go both ways,' Williams said, explaining that the Beus Center provides numerous resources to law students as well as helping to educate the community. . . . Williams said the city of Phoenix was a strong proponent of the plan, and also provided financial backing for the program."[33]

"Brian Masuda, Project Designer at Ennead Architects[34] said ASU wanted to move the law school from the Tempe campus to the Downtown Phoenix campus so that law students could engage with other Downtown Phoenix programs, such as nursing, journalism and social work, while also placing students in a geographically advantageous proximity to the legal community in Phoenix. 'The idea that the building would be open and be in a downtown setting really meant that they would get more exposure and have the opportunity to show people how law affects their lives on a daily basis.'"[35]

Tomas Rossant, Design Partner at Ennead Architects, said "the designers wanted to create a heart for the Downtown Phoenix campus, comparable to the traditional European piazza. 'The notion of the piazza and the heart are so important to the functioning of the city as a social context. . . . Finally there is a social heart of downtown. The placement of the law school, while not only providing students easy access to the Phoenix court systems, also serves as a resource for ASU students studying in closely related programs at the Downtown campus,' Rossant said. 'Nursing culture needs to understand medical liability. The press needs to understand legal constraints. There's a beautiful symmetry to the fact that at the very center of the campus . . . is also the institution that in effect, is the glue that connects every endeavor of American professional culture.' . . . The Beus Center's design is progressive compared to that of other law schools . . . they hope to dematerialize the barriers between the institution and the public. 'Universities are in crisis, and President Crow is leading a revolution,' Rossant said."[36]

LEO AND ANNETTE BEUS

It takes more than money to create something as important as a center inside a building, irrespective of how beautiful it is, or who resides in it, or even what it stands for. In the case of the Beus Center, it took Leo and Annette.[37] Without their generosity and commitment to the project, it would not be as grand as it is.

The ASU Foundation[38] knows them well and tells their story eloquently. "When Leo and Annette Beus arrived in Arizona in 1970, he was fresh out of law school and the young couple was, he says, 'starting out broke.' When it came time to donate to their most cherished causes, Arizona State University didn't make the list. As a graduate of Brigham Young University and the University of Michigan Law School, Leo says he was fiercely devoted to his alma maters and Annette to hers, the University of Utah. They still are, Leo Beus says, but their relationship with ASU is another story.

"During 43 years successfully practicing law in the Valley, Beus says he and Annette have forged strong ties to ASU that have given them an insiders' view of the university. They have seen ASU dramatically improve its academics and research, and become an invaluable asset to the community—one they are proud to support. The Beuses believe so strongly in ASU's potential they recently gave $10 million to the Sandra Day O'Connor School of Law's Center for Law and Society, scheduled to open in 2016 at the Downtown Phoenix campus. 'Leo and Annette Beus have long supported ASU because they recognize the meaningful ways this university can positively impact our communities and society in general,' said ASU President Michael Crow in announcing the gift. 'Their most recent investment is a reflection of their deep commitment to helping us build a center that will become a major part of our city and state's future; theirs is a contribution to the well-being of our fellow citizens.'"

"The gift is the most recent evidence of the Beuses' generosity to ASU, and brings their total commitment to $20 million. Past gifts have enriched a range of programs, including student scholarships and service groups; a teaching award and an endowed chair; the college of law; and Sun Devil Athletics. They felt drawn to contribute to the law school because Beus says it reflects ASU's commitment to access—allowing students of every economic background to earn a degree without accruing great amounts of debt. Leo Beus says he empathizes with students who struggle to pay for higher education. 'I grew up in humble circumstances,' he says. 'I grew up without the ability to attend a quality school without a scholarship.' ASU's commitment to include people who otherwise could never attain higher education meets a great need in society. 'I'm seeing ASU just close that gap,' he says. 'It's a blessing to the community, it's a blessing to the downtown and it's a blessing to the students.'

"He and Annette are also deeply impressed by Crow's vision to embed ASU within the community and produce scholarship that improves people's lives. The Center for Law and Society is a great example of that commitment, he says. The center is designed to be a model for public legal education. Situated in the heart of downtown near state and federal courts and many law offices, it will allow students unprecedented access to and cooperation with legal professionals. It will offer forums for continuing education, lectures and conferences. One of its greatest innovations will be the world's first nonprofit, teaching law firm that will serve

Arizonans. The Beuses' gift, the largest philanthropic investment to date on behalf of the law school, will be used for building and capital support."[39]

Dean Douglas Sylvester also knows the school's largest benefactor. "The concept from the start has been that the Center for Law and Society will be a community centerpiece that will strengthen our connections to those we serve. . . . With such generous support from Leo and Annette, this center will help transform the Sandra Day O'Connor College of Law, its students and faculty, our community and this great state for many generations to come. The Beuses have set a standard of support for what we are today and what we will become in the future."[40]

ASU's R.F. Shangraw, Jr.,[41] also knows them. "The Beuses' generosity also demonstrates the positive impact of private investment in ASU. . . . This most recent commitment to the Center for Law and Society is further evidence of Leo and Annette Beuses' belief in the vision of a New American University[42] that exists to better our communities . . . . Their continued support is making a meaningful difference in the lives of this university's students and faculty, and in the advancement of its programs."

Building relationships through service and faith is the story of how the couple created strong ties to ASU. "Many [of those relationships] were forged when he served as bishop with Annette of a Young Single Adult Ward at the LDS Institute at ASU. Each week they heard from students how ASU was changing their lives. Sometimes it was a scholarship that provided access to higher education; other times it was a program that nurtured a student's talents and ambitions. 'What ASU was doing for their lives was enormously important,' [Beus] recalls . . . . Leo Beus also notes his friendship with former law school dean Patricia White, with whom he worked to create an endowed chair named for Charles Jones, Jr., a former chief justice of the Arizona Supreme Court. Leo Beus credits White with laying the groundwork for the spirit of openness and cooperation between the law school and the wider community that will be realized in the new downtown center. . . . 'This donation was a big step for us . . . but we have been very fortunate in big-case litigation, and Annette and I are happy to do it.' He says private support from the community is a vital component to ASU's rise to excellence. 'If we could get ASU to the next level, the blessing it would be on the lives of the people of Arizona would be monumental.'"[43]

Leo Beus practiced law with Jennings, Strouss & Salmon, PLC[44] from 1970 to 1982. He and Paul Gilbert co-founded Beus Gilbert in 1982. Both are distinguished

Phoenix lawyers and ASU Law donors. Beus Gilbert McGroder PLLC[45] "is a boutique law firm concentrating on high stakes litigation, real estate and zoning law, and catastrophic personal injury. Demonstrating a relentless commitment to represent our clients' interests, our attorneys are listed among the best in the nation and described as tenacious, well respected, and highly successful. When it comes to representing our clients, we do what it takes to get the results you want and need."[46]

Leo Beus "leads the firm's high stakes litigation practice, with emphasis on representing plaintiffs in complex litigation involving securities, real estate, investment fraud, lender liability, professional malpractice, antitrust, trademark, intellectual property, and directorship liability."[47]

AN ACADEMIC PLACE—THE MANY WAYS LAW SHAPES SOCIETY

It is the case that every "old" law school (in existence for fifty years or more) that gets a "new" building in the twenty-first century is proud of its new digs. But ASU's new downtown Phoenix building is an *Academic Palace*.[48] It ". . . reinvents the traditional law school experience . . . . The relocation of the law school [to downtown Phoenix] . . . provides beneficial programmatic adjacencies to the Phoenix legal and criminal justice community and unique opportunities to advance the College's pedagogical mission.

"The Beus Center for Law and Society acts as an institutional change agent, dedicated to educating students and citizens on the importance of the law in shaping civil society. . . . [The facility] repositions the law school as a conduit for connecting the school's progressive legal scholarship with its commitment to the community by providing services like a public interest law clinic [the Arizona Legal Center] and the nation's first not-for-profit teaching law firm [the ASU Alumni Law Group] . . . . [Its] openness to the public . . . creates a unique urban environment that encourages vibrant connections between ASU, the College of Law and the local downtown Phoenix community. A north-south 'slice' through the courtyard massing creates an inviting and active public space with a pedestrian pathway that brings individuals directly into the central core of the law school, exposing them to the main lobby, and three double-height spaces located at the heart of the building. These three spaces are stacked vertically and serve as the core of the College, with the Great Hall on level one, the main library floor on level three and an outdoor courtyard on level five. Library stacks and study spaces extend up to the upper levels and serve as the primary circulation paths, which promote intellectual and social interchange between students, faculty and visitors. The 'slice' through the building is stitched together by open-air walkways that bridge east and west and provide access to a suspended double-height reading room at the north and two stories of think tank space at the south.

"The expansive bi-folding glass door at the front of the Great Hall blurs the line between indoor and outdoor space . . . the walkways that connects the east and west buildings [to] the suspended double-floor high reading room . . . . The self-shading, saw-toothed configuration of the main building façade, comprised of Arizona sandstone with aluminum and glass windows, changes in response to solar orientation, window size, and programmatic requirements . . . Desert-adaptive planting and water features activate the landscape, helping to minimize on-site irrigation demands . . . . [A]n innovative retractable seating system in the Great Hall allows the space to be converted from an everyday-tiered arrangement to a more formal auditorium configuration. Unlike traditional retractable seating where the chairs and tiered platform are attached and both retract together, the design team developed a motorized tray-like system that allows for each row of auditorium chairs to be deployed independently and concealed within the individual tiers. When the chairs are in their retracted position, the tiered array of wood steps serves as a unique social space and interior landscape that encourages interaction. The expansive bi-folding glass door at the front of the Great Hall blurs the line between indoor and outdoor space, providing flexibility while offering a unique civic space to the downtown Phoenix community.

"It's welcoming gesture of openness clearly communicates and embodies the overarching mission of the College of Law's new home as a place where the study and practice of law and society converge. In an area of downtown newly invigorated with the addition of retail spaces, a bookstore, and an independently owned and operated café, a large interior media display projects out towards Taylor Street and 1st Street and activates the street, featuring upcoming events, current legal topics, and other programmable content that informs and reminds the public of the many ways law shapes society."[49]

The Ross-Blakley Law Library "Fulfills the educational information needs of the faculty and students of the Sandra Day O'Connor College of Law. We have a superlative collection of legal and interdisciplinary research resources necessary to support faculty and students. The Law Library also provides materials and research assistance to the Phoenix legal community and to the public. We have a dedicated and knowledgeable staff to support the research needs of all our patrons."[50]

The collections of the Ross-Blakley Law Library meet the legal information needs of the faculty, the students, the university community and the public. "We maintain a collection of primary authority and secondary source materials. Some collection emphases include Indian Law, English Legal History and a student Study Skills Collection."[51]

WILLIAM C. BLAKLEY AND JOHN J. ROSS

"The Law Library is named in memory of William C. Blakley, a 1971 graduate of the Arizona State University Law School and member of the law firm of Mohr, Hackett, Pederson, Blakley, Randolf & Haga, PC,[52] at the time of his death, and John J. Ross, a graduate of Harvard Law School and senior partner of Brown & Bain PA[53] at the time of his death. The former Law Library building was made possible by an almost unprecedented capital campaign spearheaded by Sue Ross and Lynn Blakley Grant, and generously supported by a large number of individuals, law firms and organizations. Visitors will see a portrait of William C. Blakley and John J. Ross at the Law Library circulation desk."[54]

"Ross-Blakley Hall faculty, students and staff from 1968 to 2016 lived, learned, and sometimes slept in Armstrong Hall, the first law school building on ASU's Tempe campus. When the law school moved to the Downtown Phoenix campus, the Tempe Campus buildings were reconfigured and renamed—Ross-Blakley Hall.[55] It became the home of the ASU Department of English[56] and the Institute for Humanities Research[57] in 2017. Formerly the law library [adjacent to the "old" law school], the building housed law collections and served the ASU College of Law until their relocation to the ASU Downtown campus in 2016 . . . Built in 1993, Ross-Blakley Hall is named in memory of two prominent Phoenix attorneys, John J. Ross and William C. Blakley, who graduated from the ASU College of Law in 1971."[58]

ACCEPTANCE

"As the sixth-largest city in the country, Phoenix is home to some of the most prestigious law firms, making up a hot bed of legal opportunities for ASU students to explore. ASU students pursuing law-related careers should take advantage of the excellent legal opportunities in the state and explore the advantages that the Phoenix legal community has to offer. With ASU's Sandra Day O'Connor College of Law in close proximity to Maricopa County's judicial institutions, students have every opportunity to get hands-on experience within the legal system."[59]

"Charles Herf, faculty associate at ASU's Sandra Day O'Connor College of Law, has been involved in the Arizona legal community since the early 1970s. 'Phoenix has a very diverse community consisting of national firms, a large number of medium-sized local firms; many highly specialized and focused solo practitioners and a lot of public lawyers both in the civil and criminal area as well as the social services and public services lawyers.'"[60]

"Catherine Barnard, faculty associate at ASU's College of Law, has been practicing law in Phoenix for over three years, said that 'Phoenix has a tight-knit legal community, and is diverse in regards to attorneys, practice areas and specialties. It's an urban community with a lot to offer.'"[61]

The Steele Foundation[62] donated $2 million to the Sandra Day O'Connor College of Law at Arizona State University to endow the Daniel Cracchiolo Chair in Civil and Criminal Litigation.

The grant will establish a scholarship fund from the foundation, specifically for first-generation law students. "'With this type of support, we anticipate that our ability to draw an even more prominent pool of talent to ASU Law will be further strengthened,'" said ASU Law Dean Douglas Sylvester. In recognition of the gift, ASU Law will name its new downtown Phoenix executive conference room after Cracchiolo, who is the chairman and CEO of The Steele Foundation and co-founder of one of Phoenix's most prominent law firms, Burch & Cracchiolo.

"'It is wonderful to have my name associated with the ASU Law and I am equally ecstatic our grant will provide scholarships for first-generation law school students,' said Cracchiolo. 'For over 60 years I have practiced law in Arizona and I am excited to see ASU Law coming into downtown Phoenix.'"[63]

"Here are five facts about the school . . . (1) Marilyn Monroe slept there. The law school is being built on the site of the former Sahara Motor Inn. The motel opened in 1956, and actress Marilyn Monroe stayed in the three-room penthouse suite overlooking the pool while in town to shoot the movie *Bus Stop*.[64] The motel became a Ramada Inn in the 1960s. (2) Park it somewhere. Parking spaces can be highly sought after in downtown Phoenix. The law school will include two levels of underground parking. In fact, the parking-garage excavation was big enough to hold more than 9 million gallons of water. That's the equivalent of almost 14 Olympic-size swimming pools. (3) Digging up dirt. Dirt removal will take 3,614 truckloads. ASU estimates that if each truck were lined up end to end, the vehicles would stretch from the downtown Phoenix campus to ASU's Polytechnic campus in Mesa. Concrete used in the building would be enough to build a sidewalk from the downtown ASU campus to Payson. (4) Set in concrete. Once finished, the building structure will have more than 2,000 tons of steel, the equivalent of almost 730 Ford F-150 trucks. (5) Shed a little light on the situation. Workers plan to install 2,488 lights in the 280,000-square-foot building. That would be enough to light about 200 homes."[65]

"'In fall 2016, the benefits to ASU law students will further increase with our move to a new, multi-million dollar building in metropolitan Phoenix, just steps away from the legal, political and economic heart of Arizona,' Sylvester said. Last year, ASU's law college provided more than 300 externships—at least one for every eligible enrolled student—and clinical spots for every student, such as a unique opportunity to draft and prosecute patent applications at the United States Patent and Trademark Office. The college offers more than 150 courses per year for students who want to become lawyers, and customized, flexible Master of Legal Studies degrees for non-lawyer professionals who want grounding in legal basics but do not intend to practice law."[66]

"Leaders from courtrooms and capitols joined Arizona State University President Michael M. Crow on Monday evening to christen the Beus Center for Law and Society . . . Crow said [it] would stand as a monument to inclusion and accessibility. The grand opening highlighted how the building that Crow called a 'world-class facility in a world-class location,' would serve as more than home to ASU's Sandra Day O'Connor College of Law, whose namesake, a retired U.S. Supreme Court Justice, joined the ceremony. Crow and other speakers emphasized the center's aim of connecting the community, as much as students, to the law and justice . . . . ASU leaders said the building's expansive atrium, courtyard and public spaces are intended to encourage that openness. . . . The center was named for attorney Leo Beus and his wife, Annette, who contributed $10 million to help build it—the largest donation in the law school's history. The 2014 gift brought the Beus' ASU Law donation total to $15 million . . . . [Leo Beus said,] 'This University is transforming education across the country. . . . We were such a blessed community to have this here.'"[67]

---

1 Having many facets, as in a multifaceted approach to law *and* society. "Multifaceted," Merriam-Webster Dictionary, last visited April 5, 2020, https://www.merriam-webster.com/dictionary/multifaceted.

2 "The Lincoln Center for Applied Ethics advances teaching, research and community engagement efforts that explore how best to live together as a human community, so that we all may achieve purposeful, productive and prosperous lives." Lincoln Center for Applied Ethics, ASU, last visited April 5, 2020, https://lincolncenter.asu.edu/.

3 "[T]he McCain Institute for International Leadership at Arizona State University advances character-driven leadership based on security, economic opportunity, freedom and human dignity, [in the United States and] around the world. Inspired by the leadership of Senator John McCain and his family's legacy of public service, the McCain Institute implements concrete programs aimed at making a difference in people's lives across a range of critical areas: leadership development, human rights, rule of law, international security and combatting human trafficking." "What We Do," McCain Institute, last visited April 5, 2020, https://www.mccaininstitute.org/about/.

4 "Founded in 2009 by retired Supreme Court Justice Sandra Day O'Connor, the mission of the Sandra Day O'Connor Institute is to continue her distinguished legacy and lifetime work to advance civil discourse, civic engagement and civics education. The O'Connor Institute's vision is to create a nation where important policy decisions affecting our future are made through a process of civil discussion, critical analysis of facts and informed participation of all citizens." "A Mission of Civic Duty and Knowledge," The O'Connor Institute, last visited April 5, 2020, http://oconnorinstitute.org/about/missionopportunity/.

5 "The vision of Arizona Voice for Crime Victims is to establish a compassionate justice system in which crime victims are informed of their rights, fully understand those rights, know how to assert their rights, have a meaningful way to enforce those rights, and know how to seek immediate crisis intervention when they become victims of crime." "Mission and Vision Statement," Voice for Crime Victims, last visited April 5, 2020, http://voiceforvictims.org/.

6 *See* Chapter 29, *infra*.

7 *See* Chapter 33, *infra*.

8 At the Arizona Legal Center, we help make the law accessible for all. As long as justice has existed, those in need of legal assistance have struggled to access it and attorneys in practice have juggled to keep abreast of the ever-changing landscape while managing the multiple priorities a law practice demands. The Arizona Legal Center seeks to remedy both challenges by offering legal assistance to the community and legal support to practicing attorneys. We utilize volunteer lawyers and current law students to triage and assist pro bono clients. *See* "The Arizona Legal Center," Arizona Legal Center, last visited April 5, 2020, https://arizonalegalcenter.org/.

9 "Beus Center for Law and Society – Where Law Meets Society," Beus Center for Law and Society, last visited April 5, 2020, http://beuscenterforlawandsociety.com/.

10 Ibid.

11 "50 Years of Innovation: ASU Beus Center for Law and Society," Kovach, April 12, 2019, https://www.kovach.net/50-years-of-innovation-asu-beus-center-for-law-and-society/.

12 "Arizona State University, Beus Center for Law and Society," Buro Happold, last visited April 5, 2020, https://www.burohappold.com/projects/beus-center-for-law-and-society/.

13 "Tomas Rossant AIA," Ennead, last visited April 5, 2020, www.ennead.com/people/tomas-rossant.

14 *See* "Ennead Architects," Ennead, last visited April 5, 2020, http://www.ennead.com/.

15 "Jones Studio Inc.," Jones Studio, last visited April 5, 2020, http://jonesstudioinc.com/.
16 "Beus Center for Law and Society – Where Law Meets Society," Beus Center for Law and Society, last visited April 5, 2020, http://beuscenterforlawandsociety.com/.
17 *See* "Integrated engineers, consultants, and advisors – About Us," Buro Happold Engineering, last visited April 5, 2020, https://www.burohappold.com/what-we-do/.
18 *See* "DPR Construction," DPR Construction, last visited April 5, 2020, https://www.dpr.com/.
19 *See* "International Living Future Institute," International Living Future Institute, last visited April 5, 2020, https://living-future.org/.
20 "Beus Center for Law and Society – Where Law Meets Society," Beus Center for Law and Society, last visited April 5, 2020, http://beuscenterforlawandsociety.com/.
21 "Colwell Shelor Landscape Architecture—Vibrant and Unique Environments in Landscape Architecture," Colwell Shelor Landscape Architecture, last visited April 5, 2020, http://colwellshelor.com/.
22 "Law Offices of Snell & Wilmer," Snell & Wilmer LLP, last visited April 5, 2020, https://www.swlaw.com/.
23 "Beus Center for Law and Society – Where Law Meets Society," Beus Center for Law and Society, last visited April 5, 2020, http://beuscenterforlawandsociety.com/.
24 Ibid.
25 "Unified Field –Interactive Design Studio NYC," Unified Field, last visited April 5, 2020, http://www.unifiedfield.com/.
26 "Beus Center for Law and Society – Where Law Meets Society," Beus Center for Law and Society, last visited April 5, 2020, http://beuscenterforlawandsociety.com/.
27 "Daniel Cracchiolo," Burch & Cracchiolo, P.A., last visited April 5, 2020, https://www.bcattorneys.com/professionals/detail/daniel-cracchiolo.
28 "Arizona State University: The Beus Center for Law & Society: A Case Study by level 3 Audiovisual," Level 3AV, last visited April 5, 2020, https://level3av.com/wp-content/uploads/2018/09/ASU-LAW-CASE-STUDY-2017-min.pdf.
29 "Arizona State University, Beus Center for Law & Society: A Higher Education Campus AV Integration Case Study," Level 3AV, July 11, 2017, https://level3av.com/blog/arizona-state-university-beus-center-for-law-society/.
30 Ibid.
31 Ibid. A feature enjoyed by overachievers auditing one class while taking another.
32 "Thomas Williams," iSearch, last visited April 5, 2020, https://isearch.asu.edu/profile/721880.
33 Emi Kamezaki, "New Beus Center for Law and Society Reflects Administrators' Hopes of Engaging the Public in Law," *ASU State Press*, August 22, 2016, https://www.statepress.com/article/2016/08/asu-law-school-design.
34 "Ennead Architects," Ennead, last visited April 5, 2020, http://www.ennead.com/.
35 Emi Kamezaki, "New Beus Center for Law and Society Reflects Administrators' Hopes of Engaging the Public in Law," *ASU State Press*, August 22, 2016, https://www.statepress.com/article/2016/08/asu-law-school-design.
36 Ibid.
37 The author hopes readers will forgive the touch of familiarly in calling the principal donors at the Beus Center by their first names. He helped recruit them to Phoenix when Leo graduated from law school in Michigan and came to Arizona to practice law with his law firm, Jennings, Strouss & Salmon in 1970.
38 "ASU Foundation," Arizona State University, last visited April 5, 2020, https://www.asufoundation.org/.
39 Melissa Bordow, "Beus Gift to Law Center Reflects Affinity for ASU, Concern for Fellow Citizens," ASU Now, September 22, 2014, https://asunow.asu.edu/content/beus-gift-law-center-reflects-affinity-asu-concern-fellow-citizens.
40 Melissa Bordow, "Beus Gift to Law Center Reflects Affinity for ASU, Concern for Fellow Citizens," ASU Now, September 22, 2014, https://asunow.asu.edu/content/beus-gift-law-center-reflects-affinity-asu-concern-fellow-citizens.
41 "R.F. 'Rick' Shangraw Jr. (born August 17, 1959) was named chief executive officer of ASU Enterprise Partners on July 1, 2016 after the organization's launch. He previously served as chief executive officer of the ASU Foundation for A New American University from 2011 to July 1, 2017, after being appointed to the position by the Arizona State University Foundation board of directors on Oct. 31, 2011 succeeding Johnnie Ray. Previously, Shangraw worked in both the private and public sectors after beginning his career as an assistant professor at Syracuse University." Wikipedia, s.v., "Rick Shangraw," last edited August 8,

2019, https://en.wikipedia.org/wiki/Rick_Shangraw.

42 "Arizona State University exemplifies a new prototype for the American public research university. More than a decade ago, ASU set forth a new and ambitious trajectory to become a comprehensive knowledge enterprise dedicated to the simultaneous pursuit of excellence, broad access to quality education, and meaningful societal impact. From that point forward, and founded on a vision for a new 'gold standard,' all of its energy, creativity and manpower have been brought to bear on the design of a uniquely adaptive and transdisciplinary university committed to producing master learners." "New American University," Arizona State University, last visited April 5, 2020, https://newamericanuniversity.asu.edu/.

43 Melissa Bordow, "Beus Gift to Law Center Reflects Affinity for ASU, Concern for Fellow Citizens," ASU Now, September 22, 2014, https://asunow.asu.edu/content/beus-gift-law-center-reflects-affinity-asu-concern-fellow-citizens.

44 "Jennings, Strouss and Salmon, PLC," Jennings, Strouss and Salmon, last visited April 5, 2020, https://jsslaw.com/.

45 "Beus Gilbert McGroder," Beus Gilbert McGroder, last visited April 5, 2020, http://beusgilbert.com/.

46 Ibid.

47 "Leo R. Beus," Beus Gilbert McGroder, last visited April 5, 2020, https://beusgilbert.com/team/leo-beus/. "Mr. Beus has been the lead litigator in plaintiffs' cases resulting in verdicts and settlements totaling in excess of $4 Billion for his clients. In addition, Mr. Beus has successfully represented defendants against antitrust and shareholder derivative claims where the stakes have been up to $1 Billion. Mr. Beus has received numerous awards and recognitions in his profession and his community. Mr. Beus and his wife, Annette, serve as co-chairs of the President's Club of Arizona State University. He is recognized by his peers as an AV® Preeminent Lawyer with the highest rating in *Martindale-Hubbell* and is ranked among the highest rated lawyers in America in *Best Lawyers in America*, *Chambers & Partners USA Guide* and *Southwest Super Lawyers*. Mr. Beus was named Litigator of the Week by *Litigation Daily* and named as a Benchmark Litigation Star in the upcoming 2016 edition. He has been recognized in national business and industry media, including the *Wall Street Journal*, *New York Post*, *Crain's New York Business*, *Litigation Daily*, *Benchmark* and *Law360*, as well as the *Arizona Republic*, *Arizona Attorney*, *Phoenix Business Journal*, *Tucson Citizen* and *Deseret News*." Ibid.

48 *See* "Beus Center for Law and Society: Ennead Architects," Architect Magazine, August 18, 2016, https://www.architectmagazine.com/project-gallery/beus-center-for-law-and-society_o.

49 Ibid.

50 "About," Ross-Blakley Law Library, last visited April 5, 2020, https://lawlib.asu.edu/about.

51 "Collections," Ross-Blakley Law Library, last visited April 5, 2020, https://lawlib.asu.edu/about/collections.

52 "Mohr, Hackett, Pederson, Blakley & Randolph, P.C." Bizpedia, last updated April 27, 2016, https://www.bizapedia.com/az/mohr-hackett-pederson-blakley-randolph-pc.html.

53 Brown & Bain was merged into Perkins Coie in 2019. "Perkins Coie, LLP –International Law Firm," Perkins Coie, last visited April 5, 2020, https://www.perkinscoie.com/en/.

54 "About," Ross-Blakley Law Library, last visited April 5, 2020, https://lawlib.asu.edu/about.

55 "Ross-Blakley Hall," ASU Virtual Tour, last visited April 5, 2020, https://tours.asu.edu/tempe/ross-blakley-hall.

56 ASU English students engage in a diverse degree program, learning how to express themselves through traditional channels—literature analysis, rhetoric, linguistics, education, composition and creative writing—while studying contemporary themes, including environmental concerns, medical writing, human rights philosophies, digital narratives and computation. An English degree is applicable to just about any career and is a great springboard into graduate school, law school, medical humanities and more. "Department of English," Arizona State University, last visited April 5, 2020, https://english.asu.edu/.

57 The Institute for Humanities Research supports scholarship exploring human thought, expression and experience, and addressing many of the central challenges facing all of us. ASU humanities scholars of culture, language, literature, the arts, film, media, history, philosophy and religion work within their disciplines and in collaboration with scientists, social scientists, artists and others to advance research that makes a difference in the world. "The Institute for Humanities Research," Arizona State University, last visited April 5, 2020, https://ihr.asu.edu/.

58 "Ross-Blakley Hall," ASU Virtual Tour, last visited April 5, 2020, https://tours.asu.edu/tempe/ross-blakley-hall. Mr. Blakley and Mr. Ross were killed when Northwest Airlines Flight 255 crashed shortly after takeoff from Detroit Metropolitan Airport on August 16, 1987, killing all six crewmembers and 148 of its 149 passengers, along with two people on the ground. It was the second-deadliest aviation accident

at the time in the United States. Wikipedia, s.v., "Northwest Airlines Flight 255," last updated March 29, 2020, https://en.wikipedia.org/wiki/Northwest_Airlines_Flight_255.

59 Nina Plunkett, "ASU Students Should Take Advantage of Phoenix's Successful Legal Community," *The State Press*, November 9, 2017, https://www.statepress.com/article/2017/11/spopinion-asu-students-should-take-advantage-of-phoenixs-successful-legal-community.

60 Ibid.

61 Ibid.

62 "If we can't support the children in our community, how can we possibly ensure a bright future? That's the philosophy that guides the efforts of the Steele Foundation, which provides grants exclusively to programs that educate, protect, comfort and enrich the lives of Arizona's children. We're committed to helping kids throughout the state become confident and productive adults." "The Steele Foundation – Growing Stronger Families Through Education, Health and Community Enrichment," The Steele Foundation, last visited April 5, 2020, http://steeleaz.org/.

63 Janet Perez, "ASU Law School Receives $2M Gift From Steele Foundation," ASU Now, August 24, 2015, https://asunow.asu.edu/content/asu-law-school-receives-2m-gift-steele-foundation.

64 "*Bus Stop* is a 1956 American romantic comedy film directed by Joshua Logan for 20th Century Fox, starring Marilyn Monroe, Don Murray, Arthur O'Connell, Betty Field, Eileen Heckart, Robert Bray and Hope Lange. Unlike most of Monroe's films, Bus Stop is neither a full-fledged comedy nor a musical, but rather a dramatic piece; it was the first film she appeared in after studying at the Actors Studio in New York. Monroe does however sing one song: 'That Old Black Magic' by Harold Arlen and Johnny Mercer." Wikipedia, s.v., "*Bus Stop* (1956 film)," last updated March 25, 2020, 6:23, https://en.wikipedia.org/wiki/Bus_Stop_(1956_film).

65 Anne Ryman, "Last Beam Hoisted Atop ASU Law-School Project," *The Arizona Republic*, June 13, 2015.

66 Janet Perez, "ASU Law School Ranked One of Nation's Best," Sandra Day O'Connor College of Law, March 10, 2015, https://law.asu.edu/content/asu-law-school-ranked-one-nations-best-0.

67 Marshall Terrill, "University President Michael Crow Dedicates $130 Million Beus Center for Law and Society in Downtown Phoenix," ASU Now, August 15, 2016, https://asunow.asu.edu/20160816-arizona-impact-center-law-and-society-stands-inclusion.

EPILOGUE

*A*n epilogue should bring closure to the work. It flows from the story, allowing the author to speak directly to the reader, in first person voice. I know this story because I became an Arizona lawyer in the fall of 1967 just when Dean Willard Pedrick was inventing what is now a top American law school. By pure serendipity I got the chance to chronicle what he, his inaugural faculty, and those first fledging law students accomplished. My goal was to document the consequences—over a fifty-year period—of Ped's grand experiment. This book is about much more than the early years. It attempts to measure output, outcome, and value over fifty years. Who were they? What became of them? Did they do their jobs—as lawyers—judges—law professors, and respected leaders and protectors of the rule of law? Is Arizona and America the better for it?

Part One—The Pedrick Years, is the story of a remarkable experiment. One that far surpassed the expectations of its designers and gave Arizona and many other states lawyers, law professors, judges, diplomats, and elected officials at the highest possible levels. *Part Two—The Growth Years*, is about the legal and personal consequences of what the takeover deans, faculty, and students did from 1976 to 2000. *Part Three—The Success Years*—2000 to 2020, catalogues how far, how fast, and how high the Sandra Day O'Connor College of Law climbed to take its place in the top-25 law schools in America.

I've tried to identify the many people who taught, studied, researched, impacted, influenced, and innovated in ways that make our state and nation proud of its legal heritage and a proud advocate for the Rule of Law and our Independent Judiciary. My goal was a book that would memorialize the inaugural graduating class of 1970 and launch its 50th Anniversary in fall 2020. Covid-19 put that plan on hold.

The print version identifies just a small fraction of ASU Law's scholars and students. The new ASU website will add dimension and names to the print version by digitally displaying many student and faculty additional profiles. The audacious size of the school's most notable faculty and students would have made this book a "Tyee," at least in fishing terms.

What I thought would be a book became a tome. What I thought would be a chronicle of people and events turned out to be a story, not just a chronicle. This book began with one man, Willard Homer Pedrick. But as I said in the Prologue, it is not just his story—it belongs to the staff, students, faculty, donors, deans, and supporters in every part of Arizona and many parts of the U.S. It turned out to be what I hoped it would—a story about launching a legacy. Fifty years in the making, one lawyer at a time.

I knew Dean Pedrick, but not in the way the graduating class of 1970 did. They knew him from the inside. They were in front of him every day. They watched and engaged as he and his merry band of teachers experimented, designed a curriculum on the fly, and produced would-be lawyers from scratch, without a history, but with a bright future.

Who could have even imagined, forty years later, that a young woman then serving as an Assistant Attorney General in Arizona from 1965 to 1969 would in 2006 lend ASU Law her name and the law school would become the *Sandra Day O'Connor College of Law*?

Was it even remotely predictable that a 1974 graduate, Ruth McGregor, would eventually become Justice O'Connor's first law clerk, before her own intellectual brilliance led to becoming Chief Justice of the Arizona Supreme Court in 2004? Who knew then that a young Mike Hawkins, class of 1970, would later sit on the US Court of Appeals for the Ninth Circuit? And how about Mike Gallagher, '70, who came to ASU to play baseball, but instead founded a law firm that is today the sixth largest in the state?

And it wasn't just people; it was what they did. John Bates, '72, and Van O'Steen, '72, didn't know they would climb the law's highest mountain. They didn't even suspect it. But they shocked the legal world by making legal advertising acceptable, in no small part because their constitutional law professor at ASU, William Canby, carried them from a short disciplinary suspension to a giant victory in the U.S. Supreme Court. And was it "thinkable" that someday Professor Canby would become Judge Canby on the U.S. Court of Appeals for the Ninth Circuit?

The inaugural faculty and their first students from 1967 to 1972 included people who would literally create their own successors in law. Prof. Berch would

Epilogue

marry one of his students. She would become a professor herself, on her way to becoming Arizona Chief Justice Rebecca White Berch. They would produce a fine young graduate who herself would teach at her parents' law school (Prof. Jessica Berch). Judy Stinson would earn her law degree from the school, later become a professor at the school and retire from the school, all in less than the fifty years this book chronicles.

Who could have guessed that Joe Sims, '70, would become America's most highly touted anti-trust lawyer, or that Ed Pastor, '74, would become a shining light in the U.S. House of Representatives? And who could have predicted that Kyrsten Sinema, '04, would become the first woman elected to the U.S. Senate from Arizona?

Six ASU graduates would sit on the Arizona Supreme Court: Ruth McGregor, '74, Mike Ryan, Rebecca Berch, '79, John Lopez, '98, Ann Timmer, '85, and Bill Montgomery, '01.

At least thirteen graduates became state or federal court judges: Roslyn Silver, '71, Cecil Patterson, '71, Barry Silverman, '74, Chuck Case, '75, James Alan Soto, '75, Douglas Rayes, '76, Pat Norris, '77, Tena Campbell, '77, Bridget Bade, '90, Gloria Navarro, '92, Diane Humetewa, '93, John Tuchi, '94, and Jerod Tufte, '02.

Terry Woods, '72, would become an Air Force General. Grant Woods, '79, would become Arizona Attorney General. Hattie Babbitt, '72, would join the Foreign Service as a Diplomat. Barbara Barrett, 78, would become an Ambassador to Finland and Secretary of the United States Air Force. Joe Shoen, '81, would head one of America's largest companies. Many other graduates would go on to teach at other law schools.

Four ASU Law professors would be named as Regents Professors by the Arizona Board of Regents: Michael Saks, Jeffrie Murphy, Daniel Bodansky, and Gary Marchant. Three faculty members were promoted to Dean of the College: Alan Matheson, Richard Morgan, and Douglas Sylvester. Two members of the Adjunct Faculty also served as either state or federal judges—Scott Bales and Andrew Hurwitz. Every tenured professor would establish a record for high scholarship and be frequently quoted and asked to lecture across the planet.

There are 205 ABA-accredited law schools in America. ASU's Sandra Day O'Connor College of Law rose from brand-new to twenty-fourth by 2020, and ninth in public law schools. It highest rankings are in Clinical Training, Dispute Resolution, Environmental Law, Health Care Law, Intellectual Property Law, International Law, Legal Writing, Tax Law, and Trial Advocacy.

In 1970, the college only offered the JD degree. Today, it offers LLM, MLS, MSLB and MHREL degrees. Its first-year class in 1967 was 107. In 2020, it accepted 316 law students.[1] There were less than a dozen scholarships in 1967. One hundred percent of the 2020 JD entering class got a scholarship. In 1967, less than 4 percent of the class were female. In 2019, 53 percent of the class are female. The first classes in 1967 were taught in two large classrooms, in temporary building space. Today classes are taught in more than forty rooms in a six-story building. "ASU Law ranks No. 14 among all accredited law schools in the nation and No. 5 among public law schools in placing graduates in substantive jobs in the legal field. Within 10 months of graduation, 87 percent of ASU Law's graduating class of 2014 found employment in long-term, full-time positions where bar passage is required or a JD is preferred. This is well above the national employment average of 71 percent, according to data collected by the American Bar Association (ABA) on the nation's 204 ABA-accredited law schools. ASU Law's bar passage rate is No. 1 in Arizona at 89.1 percent, compared to 74 percent statewide."[2]

This book covers only a smidgen of those who taught, learned, led, and became lawyers all over America, and in many foreign countries. As of January 1, 2020, 7,935 lawyers hold law degrees from ASU Law. There are several hundred permanent and adjunct faculty members whose stories could not be included in this book for space reasons. I would have liked to profile many more. Nearly all of them are successful and all their children are above average.[3] As I said in Chapter 4, I do not pretend the list of "notable" teachers and graduates in this book is complete. There are many others that served the school and now the profession at the highest levels. I wrote about those whom the school itself has declared to be notable, and worthy of inclusion. The Sandra Day O'Connor College of Law's wiki page and its home page (https://law.asu.edu/) have much longer lists of notable clinical programs, centers, lecturers, professors, journals, and alumni. Some are squeezed in here.

The eight deans who served from 1965 to 2020 deserve special mention because they don't just manage the day-to-day operation of the school. They are the glue that binds the school's legacy. Law schools are foundational to free and democratic societies. They teach the Rule of Law and advocate constantly for an Independent Judiciary. All eight deans made sure the faculty and the student body understood their own roles in advancing and protecting our free and democratic society. Arizona is much the better for it.

Epilogue

Deans Pedrick, Gellhorn, Matheson, Bender, Morgan, White, Berman and Sylvester led in very different ways and advanced the school's reputation by the force of their intellect. They innovated, improved, and made good on their promises to the University Presidents and Provosts that hired them. Everyone connected to the school over the last fifty years owes them a debt of gratitude.

Their cumulative goal over the last fifty years was to produce lawyers, legal scholars, and leaders who would advance the rule of law in their own ways, at their own pace, ethically, and with gusto. They succeeded. The important lesson of this book is not that every ASU Law teacher or student excelled because they were taught, but rather that they learned the rule of law. There can be no higher reward for lawyers.

---

1 "Dean Douglas Sylvester welcomed 316 new students at ASU Law's Orientation on August 17, 2020. 217 first-year JD, 8 advanced standing JD, 11 LLM, 26 Master of Sports Law & Business, and 54 MLS students with a focus on patent practice, international law, and sustainability law." "ASU Law Welcomes Largest Class in School History," Arizona State University, accessed March 2, 2021, https://law.asu.edu/content/asu-law-welcomes-215-first-yr-jd-students.

2 Ibid.

3 Credit for this wonderfully impossible homily goes to Garrison Keeler, the creator of Lake Wobegone. Mr. Keeler created the fictional town "as the setting of the '*News from Lake Wobegon*' . . . a small rural town in central Minnesota . . . The closing words of the monologue were 'Well, that's the news from Lake Wobegon, where all the women are strong, all the men are good-looking, and all the children are above average.'" Wikipedia, s.v., "Lake Wobegon," last updated January 10, 2021, 7:25, https://en.wikipedia.org/wiki/Lake_Wobegon.

ACKNOWLEDGMENTS

I have been an adjunct faculty member of this law school for twenty-five years. I want to acknowledge the many other adjunct faculty who helped me teach law and advanced skills training. The fifty-year history of this law school is a big story and not entirely told in this book. The rest of the story will virtually emerge in fall 2021. There are twenty-one faculty and thirty-three student profiles in this book. During the writing phase, I wrote an additional seventy-eight student and faculty profiles I hoped would be in the book. However, given the space and cost limitations, these additional profiles will be published digitally on a new ASU Law College website, as part of the planned *Gold 'n Gavel Ceremony* in November 2021. Accordingly, I must acknowledge in advance faculty, staff and students who will make that website an extension of this print version of a great law school story.

This book would not have been possible without the authorization, direction, financial support and focus of Dean Douglas J. Sylvester. His early acceptance of my idea and his consistent engagement made the research, writing, design and production phases of the book seamless. His colleagues, Executive Associate Dean Zachary Kramer and Executive Director of Marketing and Communications Karen Sung, were always available and provided wise counsel. Many other staff members helped in myriad ways, including Lauren Dickerson, Terri Burkel, Melanie Knerr and Katie O'Brian, Carrie Rose and Emily McLallen.

Special thanks and recognition must go to Heather Robles, Class of 2020. She led the student research team, read every word of text, copyedited every chapter, and helped with sourcing and consistency. She generously gave me half of her time in the 2019 spring and fall semesters, and slightly less in 2020. She selected student researchers, Jacqueline Sager, Caitlin White, Alex Ronchetti, Yaseli Arellano, Tatianna Rawlings Dunne, and Bryan Shapiro. When Heather graduated, Caitlin White took over and spent a great deal of time re-organizing sources and checking evasive citations through fall 2020 and spring 2021. Heather and her student team checked my text, confirmed my sources, and constantly fixed my awkward footnotes. They blended the Blue Book and the Chicago Manual of Style into a consistent protocol. Associate Dean Tom Williams approved the retention of all student researchers and was always available.

The research and "finding" phases of the project were daunting but made manageable by law librarians, Victoria Trotta, Beth DiFelice, Carrie Henteleff, Tara Mospan and Andrea Gass.

Tammy Vavra, the law college Registrar, provided sound advice and direction for sources I might never have found without her.

As always, the Arizona Board of Regents provided documentation and research sources for many stories and profiles in the book. Special thanks to General Counsel Nancy Tribbensee, and Kim Edwards. My conversations with students over the last five years convinced me this was a book waiting for its day in the sun. I hope it comes this fall. I could never name them all, so I'll trust them to recognize this acknowledgment.

1106 Design led the production effort on the final manuscript. Many thanks to Michele DeFilippo and Ronda Rawlins. Their insight and oversight gave the book the shine and sense of accomplishment that the college's alumni and faculty deserve.

Last but hardly least, I got ideas, memories, and stories from scores of alumni about their experiences in and out of ASU Law. Most of them are in the book, if not by name, by reflection. I thank them all *in abstentia*.

INDEX

1Ls ('67–'69)
    curriculum, 211–213
    electives, 213
2Ls ('68–'69)
    costs, 215
    curriculum, 214–215
    internships, 215
    legal clinics, 215
    Moot Court, 214
    seminars, 215
3Ls ('69–'70), 216
3Ls grading system under Matheson, 286–287
25th Anniversary of ASU Law
    ASU Distinguished Achievement Award, 382–383
    Continuing Legal Education seminar, 380
    Coor, Lattie F., 381
    Eckstein, Paul, 379, 380
    Grant, Michael, 380
    Mahoney, Richard, 380
    Ortiz, David, 380
    Sims, Joe, 380
    speakers, 380

A

AALS Special Committee on Racial Discrimination, 14
Abbott, Joshua, 324–325
Abel v. United States, 338–339
ABOR (Arizona Board of Regents), 3, 7–8
    faculty speaking as private citizen, 199
    Kush, Frank, 296–300
    library approval, 110
    Starsky, Morris, 199–205
Academic Professionals, 75
Academy for Justice, 50, 470

accreditation
    inaugural dean's report, 111–112
    Indian Law program, 223
Administrative Law 550, 214
admissions
    admissions committee, 374
    baby boom and, 13–14
    interviews, 374–375
    LSAC (Law School Admissions Council), 375
    women, 14–15
advertising
    Arizona State Bar response, 273–274
    Bates, John, and, 272–276
    Bates v. State Bar of Arizona, 278–279
    Canons of Professional Ethics, 272
    Code of Professional Ethics, 276
    content, 279
    future of, 279–280
    Gordon, Frank, 276
    Hays, Jack, 276
    Holohan, William, 276–277
    O'Steen, Van, and, 272–276
    regional law firms, 280
    Supreme Court ruling, 277–278
advocacy training, 309–311
affirmative action, Paul Bender and, 347
Aguilar, Gloria, 229–230
Ahearn, Michael J., 52
Aiken, Jane H., 322
ALC (Arizona Legal Center)
    Gary L. Stuart Legal Triage and Referral Program, 454
    mission, 454
    Sylvester, Douglas, and, 453
Allen, Layman E., 315
Altman, Michael L., 262

alumni
  donor support, 481
  judicial officers, 156
  notable, 51–53
Ambassador Barbara Barrett & Justice Sandra Day O'Connor Washington Center, 457–459
Ames, Victoria, 442, 453
Antitrust Law 551, 214
Apollo 11, 24
applications
  1974–1975 school year, 246–247
  increases, 229–230
Ares, Charles, 39, 60, 65
Arizona Civil Remedies Book (Baum), 136
Arizona Innocence Project, 403–407
Arizona Justice Project, 403–407, 489
Arizona Legal Center, 444
Arizona Motor Vehicle Accident Deskbook (Diesel), 137
Arizona State College, 3
Arizona State Law Journal, 51, 315
Arizona State Sports and Entertainment Law Journal, 316
Arizona State Teachers College, 432
Arizona State University Archives, "The Willard Pedrick Papers," 46
Arizona v. Inter-Tribal Council of Arizona, 417
Arizona Voice for Crime Victims, 489
Armstrong, John S., 64–65
Armstrong, John S., III, 65
  Distinguished Achievement Award, 68
Armstrong, John S. IV, 64
Armstrong Great Hall, 495
Armstrong Hall, 8, 63–64
  dedication, 65–66
  inaugural dean's report, 110–111
  rededication, 67–69
  Starsky letter distribution, 198
Armstrong Prize, Armstrong Hall rededication, 68
Aspey, Fritz ('72), 134–135
Aspey, Watkins & Diesel PLLC, 134
ASU Alumni Law Group, 489
ASU California Center, 50
ASU College of Fine Arts, establishment, 7
ASU College of Law
  accreditation, 37–38
  establishment, 7
  move from Tempe, 425
  new building, 38
ASU Insight, Armstrong Hall rededication, 68
The ASU Law Group, 44, 449–450
Atkin, William F. ('75), 159–160

B

Babbitt, Bruce, 6
Babbitt, Hattie C. ('72), 51, 138–140
baby boom, admissions increase and, 13–14
Bade, Bridget Shelton, 52
Bailey, Michael G. ('75), 160
Bakke v. Regents of University of California, 265–267
Balder, Leland, 74
Bales, W. Scott, 417
Bank Officer's Handbook (Schroeder), 100
bar exam
  3Ls ('69–'70), 216
  core curriculum, 94
  legal education, 308, 310
Barnard, Catherine, 503
Barnes, Jennifer, 462
Barrett, Barbara ('78), 165–171
Barrett and O'Connor Center, 50
Barry, Jack, 44
Bates, John R., 271–280
Bates v. State Bar of Arizona, 278–279
Baum, Redfield T. ('72), 135–137
Beck, Shirley, 78
Bender, Paul, 74
  Abel v. United States, 338–339
  affirmative action and, 347
  Arizona Constitution victims' rights amendment, 340
  curriculum, 345
  The Federalist Society listing, 333–334
  future of school, 348
  Indian Law Program, 220, 343
  Mapp v. Ohio and, 337–338
  minority recruitment, 344
  Principal Deputy to Solicitor General, 345–346
  Supreme Court cases argued, 346–347
Berch, Michael A., 74, 97–98, 221, 262
Berch, Rebecca White, 52
Berman, Paul Schiff, 74
  bar passage rate, 425

Index

Center for the Study of Law, Science, and Technology, 425
Center for Transnational Public-Private Governance and, 425
College of Law ranking, 425
Committee on Law and Philosophy, 425
Cultural Analysis, Cultural Studies, and the Law: Moving Beyond Legal Realism, 423
George Washington University Law School, 421, 426–428
global realism, 422–424
goals, 422
Indian Law Program, 425
"Legal Education in the Future Tense," 424
legal education views, 422–424
memories of ASU, 425
placement rate, 425
Bernstein, Charles C., 60, 64
Beus, Annette, 497–500
Beus, Leo, 444, 497–500
Beus Center for Law and Society, 444, 489
    ALC (Arizona Legal Center), 453
    Arizona Justice Project, 489
    Arizona Legal Center, 490
    Arizona Voice for Crime Victims, 489
    Armstrong Great Hall, 495
    ASU Alumni Law Group, 489
    building facility, 490–491, 504
    as change agent, 500–501
    classrooms, 496
    Dan Cracchiolo Executive Conference Center, 495
    design
        BIM (building information modeling), 493
        Colwell Shelor Landscape Architecture, 493–494
        DPR Construction, 492–493
        Ennead Architects, 491
        EUI (Energy Use Intensity), 493
        Jones Studio, 491
        landscaping, 493–494
        NZEB (Net-Zero Energy Building), 493
        Rossant, Tomas, 491
    Ennead Architects
        Masuda, Brian, 496
        Rossant, Tomas, 497
    Great Hall, 500–501
    J. Grant Woods courtroom, 495
    lecture halls, 496
    Lincoln Center for Applied Ethics, 489
    McCain Institute for International Leadership, 489
    Sandra Day O'Connor Institute, 489
    Sylvester, Douglas, and, 433
    technology features, 494–496
    William P. Carey Armstrong Great Hall, 495
Birmingham movement, 29
Blakey, Robert, Jr. ('71), 124–126
Blakley, William C., 502
Boston Strangler, 24
Bowman, Diana, 442
Brown, Richard L., 322
Brown v. Board of Education of Topeka, 21
Bruff, Harold H., 74, 262
Brunner, Jordan, 458
Burger, Warren E., 248–249
Burkel, Terri, 443

C

Cameron, William, 5
Campbell, Tena, 51
campus residence, 215
Canby, William C., Jr., 10, 21, 74, 79–81, 262
    Conflict of Laws 553, 214
    Constitutional Law 510, 213
    Indian Law program, 220
Canons of Professional Ethics, 272
Caplan, Gerald, 74, 230–231
Carmel & Rossman architects, 64
Carr, Steven E., 52
Cartmell & Rossman architects, 8, 38
Case, Charles G., III, 51
Case, Charles G., Jr. ('75), 161
Case, Williby E., Jr., 65
Cases on Contracts (Havighurst), 85
CC&F (Committee on Character and Fitness), James Hamm, 356–357, 361–362
Center for Gender Equity in Science & Technology, 458
Center for Law, Science, and Innovation, 50, 322

"Governance of Emerging Technologies"
    conference, 325
    integrated training, 325–327
    Marchant, Gary, 324
    name change, 326–327
    programs at other universities, 327
Center for Law, Science, and Technology, 425
Center for Law & Global Affairs, 50
    Abbott, Joshua, 324–325
Center for Public Health Law and Policy, 50
Center for the Study of Law, Science & Technology, 319
    1989 Conference on Copyright Protection of Computer Software, 321
    1991 Workshop on the Human Genome Initiative, 321
    1993 Second International Conference on Forensic Statistics, 321
    1995 Workshop on Medical Futility, 321
    "Baby Doe" Symposium, 321
    faculty affiliates, 321–324
    interdisciplinary research and, 320
    Jurimetrics Journal of Law, Science, and Technology, 320
    student activities, 321
Center for Transnational Public-Private Governance, 425
centers, 50, 461. *See also* specific centers
charitable giving, 479–486
Chauncey, Tom II ('73), 141–142
Chodorow, Adam, 442
Civil Litigation Clinic, 462
Civil Rights Act of 1964, 22, 29
civil rights movement, 21–22, 25–29
classroom as training ground, 43
Cleary, Edward W., 9, 74, 81–83, 262
    Distinguished Teaching Award, 82
    Handbook on Illinois Evidence, 82
    McCormick on Evidence and, 82
clinical education, 230–231
    Bender, Paul, 341, 343–344
clinics. *See* legal clinics
Clutter family murders, 24
Code of Professional Ethics, 276
Cohen, Warren, 74
COINTELPRO, Morris Starsky and, 204
Colwell Shelor Landscape Architecture, 493–494
commencement address, inaugural, 238–240

Commercial Law 552, 214
Committee on Law and Philosophy, 425
Conflict of Laws 553, 214
Consortium for Science Policy and Outcomes, 458
Constitutional Law class, 21, 213
Coor, Lattie F., 69
Cordova, Valdamar, 5
core curriculum, 15–16
Corporate and Business Law Journal, 51, 316
Corporations 554, 214
Cracchiolo, Daniel, 503
Craig, Walter E., 60
Criminal Law and Procedure 509, 213
Cronkite News Washington Bureau, 458
Crow, Michael
    on Justice O'Connor, 412
    Sylvester, Douglas, and, 432–433
CSKI Executive council, 324
Culbertson, William, K., 142–144
Cultural Analysis, Cultural Studies, and the Law: Moving Beyond Legal Realism (Berman), 423
curriculum
    1Ls ('67), 211–213
    2Ls ('68–'69), 214–215
    Administrative Law 550, 214
    Antitrust Law 551, 214
    Bender, Paul, 345
    Commercial Law 552, 214
    Conflict of Laws 553, 214
    Constitutional Law 510, 213
    Contracts 501, 211
    core curriculum, 15–16
    Corporations 554, 214
    Criminal Law and Procedure 509, 213
    electives, 213
    Evidence 555, 214
    Federal Income Taxation 556, 214
    Gellhorn, Ernest, 259–260, 266
    inaugural dean's report, 111
    interdisciplinary programs, 345
    legal education definition, 10–12
    Legal Writing and Research, 212
    Matheson, Alan, 286
    Procedure 505, 211
    Procedure 557, 214
    Property 507, 211
    student challenges, 56–57

Index

Torts 505, 212
Trusts and Estates 559, 214

D

Dahl, Richard C., 76, 262
    law library, 77–79
    master's degree in history, 77
    obituary, 77
Dahl, Richard D., 10, 74
Dan Cracchiolo Executive Conference Center, 495
Daniel Cracchiolo Chair in Civil and Criminal Litigation, 503
Davis, Keith, 83
Davis, Michael, 375–376
deans. *See also* specific deans
    Ares, Charles, 43
    Bender, Paul, 74, 333–348
    Berman, Paul Schiff, 74, 421–428
    Gellhorn, Ernest, 74, 257–268
    Matheson, Alan, 74, 283–289
    Morgan, Richard, 74, 367–377
    Pedrick, Willard H., 6–9, 33–46
    Schroeder, Milton (associate), 99–100
    Sylvester, Douglas, 53–54, 74, 431–445
    White, Patricia, 74, 391–401
Dean's Report. *See* Report of the Law School Dean entries
degrees
    JD, 461
    JDAS, 461
    LLM, 461
    MLS, 461
    MLSB, 461
    MSLB, 468
Delgado, Richard, 75
Dennis, Karjala, 322
DePaul University law review, Willard Pedrick, 44–45
DeSalvo, Albert, 24
Devil's Advocate, 230
Diesel, Lou ('73), 134, 137
Distinguished Achievement Award, 127
Distinguished Alumnus Award, 151
Distinguished Teaching Award, 82
diversity
    affirmative action, 347
    Indian Law Program, 343
    minority recruitment, 344

Dix, George, 74
donor support, 480–481
    alumni, 481
    Beus, Annette, 497–500
    Beus, Leo, 497–500
    Estate of Blanche Farmer Strong, 481
    non-alumni, 482
    Ross-Blakley Law Library, 481
        Jennings, Strouss & Salmon PLC, 481
        Lewis Roca Rothgerber Christie LLP, 481
        Perkins Coie, LLP, 481
        Quarles & Brady, LLP, 481
        Snell & Wilmer LLP, 481
    scholarships, 481, 482–486
    The Steele Foundation, 503
    Willard H. Pedrick Lecture, 481
    William Polk Carey Foundation, 481
downtown campus, 504
DPR Construction, 492–493
Dred Scott v. Sandford, 21
Durham, G. Homer, 3, 7, 36–37, 60, 64
DuVal, Fred, 52

E

Effland, Richard W., 10, 74, 83, 211, 214, 262
Ekmark, Courtney, 52
elective classes, 213
Ellman, Ira, 322
English, Alfred Ray, 442
Ennead Architects, 491, 496
    Masuda, Brian, 496
    Rossant, Tomas, 497
Estate of Blanche Farmer Strong, 481
Evidence 555, 214
externships at DC campus, 458–459
extracurricular activities, inaugural dean's report, 108–109

F

fabric of the law, 240
faculty
    Academic Professionals, 75
    The Center for the Study of Law, Science & Technology, 321–324
    first women, 75
    inaugural, 9–10, 73, 74
        Beck, Shirley, 78

Berch, Michael A., 97–98
Canby, William C., Jr., 10, 79–81
Cleary, Edward W., 9, 81–82
Dahl, Richard C., 10, 76–79
Effland, Richard W., 10, 83
Furnish, Dale B., 84
Havighurst, Harold C., 9, 84–86
Knilans, Lorraine, 78
law professor, description, 73–74
Matheson, Alan A., 86–88, 283–289
Morris, John P., 88–95
Murray, William R., 78
Pedrick, Willard, 75
Ream, Carolyn S., 78
remaining "in the building," 74
Rose, Jonathan, 95–97
Schroeder, Milton R., 99–100
Taso, James J.C., 78
 notable, 51–53
 Pedrick's picks, 37–38
 salary scale, 232
Faculty Research Award, 83
Farr, H. Bartow III ('74), 147–148
Federal Grant Application, 8
Federal Income Taxation 556, 214
The Federalist Society, Paul Bender, 333–334
Feller, Joseph M., 322
Ferren, John M., 110
financial aid, inaugural dean's report, 109
First Amendment Clinic, 463
First: Sandra Day O'Connor (Thomas), 417–418
Fortescue, John, 403
Frank, John P., 278–279
Freedom Riders, 26
Furnish, Dale B., 74, 84, 262–263

G

Gallagher, Michael ('70), 60, 118–119, 238
Garcia, Renee, 462
Gary L. Stuart Legal Triage and Referral Program, 454
Gellhorn, Ernest, 74, 257–259, 262–268
Ginsberg, Ruth Bader, 14
Goddard, Terry ('76), 51, 163–164
Goldwater, Barry, 4
Gordon, Frank, 276
Gordon, Phil, 52

GPAs, median, 229
grading, third-year grading system, 245
graduates
 definition of graduate, 237–238
 first graduating class, 38–39
 inaugural, 117
  Aspey, Fritz ('72), 134–135
  Aspey, Watkins & Diesel PLLC and, 134
  Atkin, William F. ('75), 159–160
  Babbitt, Hattie C. ('72), 51, 138–140
  Bailey, Michael G. ('75), 160
  Barrett, Barbara ('78), 165–171
  Baum, Redfield T. ('72), 135–137
  Blakey, Robert, Jr. ('71), 124–126
  Case, Charles G., Jr. ('75), 161
  Chauncey, Tom II ('73), 141–142
  Culbertson, William, K., 142–144
  Diesel, Lou, 134
  Diesel, Lou ('73), 137
  Farr, H. Bartow III ('74), 147–148
  forty-year reunion, 238
  Gallagher, Michael ('70), 118–119
  Goddard, Terry ('76), 163–164
  Grant, Michael ('76), 164–165
  Harper, Marty ('73), 145
  Hawkins, Michael ('70), 119–122
  Macban, Barry ('72), 140
  McGregor, Ruth ('74), 148–151
  Pastor, Ed ('74), 152–153
  Patterson, Cecil B., Jr. ('71), 126–129
  Rayes, Douglas L. ('78), 171–172
  Sandweg, Bill ('74), 154
  Schiefelbein, Les ('71), 131–134
  Silver, Roslyn, 129–131
  Silverman, Barry G. ('76), 154–158
  Sims, Joe ('70), 122–123
  Smith, Jimmie Dee ('70), 123–124
  Soto, James Alan ('75), 161–163
  Watkins, Harold, 134
  Watkins, Harold ('73), 138
  Woods, Terrance P. ('73), 146–147
 initial salaries, 267
Grady Gammage Auditorium, Armstrong Hall dedication, 66
Grant, Michael ('76), 164–165
Great Hall, 69, 111, 495

Index

Armstrong Hall rededication, 67
moot court, 214
Green, Leon, 41, 67, 110
Griswold, Erwin N., 238–240
Guadalupe Project, 232
Gublar, Zachary, 469

H
Hall, Mark A., 322
Hamm, James, 52, 356–363
    Morgan, Richard and, 373–374
    White, Patricia and, 396–397
Hammond, Larry, 403–407
Handbook on Illinois Evidence (Cleary), 82
Harper, Marty ('73), 145
    ASU Law Group, 449–450
Hathaway, James D., 65
Havighurst, Harold C., 9, 74, 84–86, 214
    Cases on Contracts, 85
Hawkins, Michael ('70), 119–122
Hawkins, Michael Daly, 51
Hayden Library, 8
Hays, Jack, 5, 276
Hemrom-Maji, Shyam, 10
Herf, Charles, 503
Hickock, Richard, 24
Higher Education Facilities Act of 1962, 8
Holohan, William, 276–277
Humetewa, Diane, 52

I
ILP (Indian Law Program), 219
    25th Anniversary, 220
    accreditation, 223
    ASU School of Justice Studies, 221
    Bender, Paul, on, 220, 343
    Berman, Paul, on, 425
    Canby, William C., 220
    DC campus, 459
    Indian country, 224
    Inter-Tribal Council of Arizona, 221
    Monteau-Nabors, Autumn, on, 222
    National Indian Justice Center, 221
    outcomes, 224–225
    planning committee, 221–222
    recruiting Indian students, 221
    Southwest Indian Court Judges
        Association, 221
    timeline, 222–224

Immigration Clinic, 463–464
In Cold Blood (Capote), 24
inaugural class
    current events during, 55–58
    recruitment, 16–17
inaugural faculty. *See* faculty
inaugural graduation ceremony, 235–237
    commencement address, 238–240
    Griswold, Erwin, N., 238
Indian Law Program. *See* ILP (Indian Law
    Program)
Indian Legal Clinic, 464
Indian Legal Program, 50
Innocence Project
    Arizona Justice Project, 403–407
    Neufeld, Peter, 404
    Scheck, Barry, 404
Innovation Advancement Program, 464
interdisciplinary education, Patricia White,
    400
interdisciplinary research
    The Center for the Study of Law, Science
        & Technology, 320
    conferences, 321
International Rule of Law and Security, 459
internships, 2Ls, 215–216
Issues in Science and Technology, 458

J
J. Grant Woods courtroom, 495
Jarvi, Ted, 229
Jaynes, Andrew, 443
JD degree, 461
JDAS degree, 461
John S. Armstrong Quasi-Endowment, 481
John S. Lancy Award, 121
Johnson, Kay, 10
Johnson, Lyndon Baines, 29
Jones, Owen, 322
Jones Studio, 491
judicial offers graduated, 156
*Jurimetrics: The Journal of Law, Science, and
    Technology*, 51, 315, 320

K
Kaufman, Irving R., 249
Kaye, David H., 83, 322
Kennedy, John F., 22, 27–29
King, Martin Luther, Jr., 29

Knilans, Lorraine, 78
Kramer, Zachary, 316, 442
Kush, Frank, 291
 ABOR, 296–297
 All-Americans coached, 292
 alumni on firing, 301
 early career, 292
 firing, 293, 302–303
 media coverage of trial, 299–300
 rehire, 302
 Rutledge, Kevin, 292–293
 Rutledge vs. Kush, 293–299
 settlement, 302–303
 Sport Illustrated, 294
 Sun Angel Foundation, 301
 suspension, 293
 Wikipedia page, 300

L

La France, Arthur, 230–231
LaSota, John, Jr., 74
Law Alumni Association growth, 267
Law and the Social Order, 315
The Law and Regulation of Financial Instruments (Schroeder), 100
Law Journal for Social Justice, 51, 316
Law Journal luncheon 1980, 255
law journals
 Arizona State Law Journal, 51, 315
 Arizona State Sports and Entertainment Law Journal, 316
 Corporate and Business Law Journal, 51, 316
 Jurimetrics: The Journal of Law, Science, and Technology, 51, 315
 Law and the Social Order, 315
 Law Journal for Social Justice, 51, 316
 M.U.L.L. (Modern Users of Logic in Law), 315
 Sports and Entertainment Law Journal, 51
law library
 Beck, Shirley, 78
 Dahl, Richard, 77–78
 inaugural dean's report, 110
 Knilans, Lorraine, 78
 law librarian, inaugural faculty, 9–10
 Murray, William R., 78
 Ream, Carolyn S., 78
 Taso, James J.C., 78

law professor, description, 73–74
law reviews, 51
Law Revue, 244–245
law skills training. *See* skills training
The Law Society of Arizona State University, 39, 59–61
 Rehnquist, William, 232
 Sixth Annual Dinner, 232
Laws, Lawyers, and Texts: Studies in Medieval Legal History in Honor of Paul Brand (ed. Rose), 96
lawyer advertising. *See* advertising
lawyering skills, 260
lawyers, service to country, 66
Lee, Stephen E., 74, 263
LeFrance, Arthur, 74
legal clinics, 50, 461–468
 2Ls, 215–216
legal education, 10–12
 charitable giving, 479–486
 dean's report 1967–1968, 111–114
 future of, 424–425
 inaugural Dean's report, 111–114
 Litchfield Law School, 12
 music and, 40–41
 Sylvester, Douglas, 443–444
legal realism, 55–56
legal writing, inaugural dean's report, 111
Legal Writing and Research class, 212
Leshey, John D., 322
Leslie, Douglas, 74
Levin, A. Leo, 110
Levy, Leon, 66
Lincoln Center for Applied Ethics, 489
Lisa Foundation Patent Law, 465
Litchfield Law School, 12
LLM degree, 461
Lockwood, Lorna E., 5, 64
Lodestar Dispute Resolution Center, 50
Lodestar Mediation Clinic, 465
Lopez, John IV, 52
Loving v. Virginia, 21
LSAC (Law School Admissions Council), 375
LSAT, application trends and, 13
LSI. *See* Center for Law, Science, and Innovation
Luna, Erik, 470–471
Lyons, John D., 39

Index

M

Macban, Barry ('72), 140
Macerate Report, 371–372
Mahoney, Richard D., 52
Maintenance in Medieval England (Rose), 96
The Majesty of the Law—Reflections of a Supreme Court Justice (O'Connor), 416
Mangum, H. Karl, 66, 67
Mapp v. Ohio, 337–338
March on Washington, 21, 29
Marchant, Gary, 324
Maricopa County Bar Association Hall of Fame, 45
Marie Selig Professorship, 469
Matheson, Alan A., 74, 86–88, 263, 268
    3Ls, grading system and, 286–287
    Administrative Law 550, 214
    changes, 285
    clinic program, 285
    curriculum, 286
    forty years at ASU, 284
    interview with Ped, 34–46
    legal advisor position, 283–284
    Oral History, 283, 287–288
    on Willard Pedrick, 285
Matthews Center Building, 109–110
McCain Institute for International Leadership, 458, 489
McCaskey, George, 52
McCormick on Evidence (Cleary, ed.), 82
McFarland, Ernest W., 5, 64, 66, 110
McGregor, Ruth V. ('74), 51, 69, 148–151
Melvin, Bob, 220
Mendlovitz, Saul H., 110
Menkhus, Eric, 442
Merriam, Charles J., 481
Merriam Professorship Law Endowment, 481
minority recruitment, 344
Misner, Robert L., 263
Mitchell, Rachel, 52
MLS degree, 461
MLSB degree, 461
Mondale, Walter (Fritz), 80
Monroe, Marilyn, 504
Moore, Carleton, 83
Moot Court, 2Ls and, 214
Moot Court Hall, 110–111
moral character. *See* CC&F (Committee on Character and Fitness)
Morgan, Richard J., 69, 74, 370–377
Morris, Earl F., 66, 67
Morris, John P., 74, 88–95, 264
    remembrances, 89–91
    The Way We Were, 92
Morris, Norval, 110
Moulton, Beatrice A., 75, 264
MSLB degree, 468
Muecke, Carl, 202–203
M.U.L.L. (Modern Users of Logic in Law), 315
Murphy, Jeffrey, Indian Law program, 221
Murray, William R., 78
music, legal education and, 40–41

N

NAACP (National Association for the Advancement of Colored People), 26
Navarro, Gloria, 52
Neufeld, Peter, 404
Norris, Patricia K., 450
notable, definition, 49

O

O'Connor, Sandra Day
    address at naming ceremony, 412–414
    Alzheimer's diagnosis, 418
    Arizona Court of Appeals, 6
    Arizona v. Inter-Tribal Council of Arizona, 417
    career milestones, 415–416
    courses taught, 416–417
    education, 416
    letter to Nixon, Supreme Court vacancies, 5
    The Majesty of the Law—Reflections of a Supreme Court Justice, 416
    Maricopa County Superior Court, 6
    Supreme Court career, 416–417
        Associate Justice appointment, 6
Office of Indian Law, 220
Oliver Wendell Holmes Devise Lecture Series, 229
Ong, Wing, 5
Oral History
    Barrett, Barbara, 169, 170
    Bender, Paul, 337–338
    Fred M. Vinson Oral History Project, 35
    Matheson, Alan, 283, 287–288
    Morgan, Richard, 370–371

Patterson, Cecil B., Jr., 126, 127
Rose, Jon, 96
Schroeder, Milton R., 100
White, Patricia, 392, 397–399
O'Steen, Van, 271–280
Outstanding Alumni Award
    Aspey, Fritz, 135
    McGregor, Ruth, 151
Outstanding Alumnus Award
    Chauncy, Tom, 142

P

Parker, Kellis E., 309
parking at law school, 504
part-time employment, 215
Pastor, Ed ('74), 51, 152–153
Patterson, Cecil B., Jr. ('71), 126–129
Pedrick, Willard H., 4, 75, 264
    accreditation and, 38
    DePaul University law review, 44–45
    Distinguished Achievement Award, 382
    educational background, 34–36
    faculty appointments, 36–37
    faculty choices, 37–38
    family background, 34–36
    first visit to Tempe, 36–37
    as founding dean, 7–8
    Fred M. Vinson Oral History Project, 35
    inaugural faculty, 74
    job interview, 38–39
    legal ideology, 44–45
    love of dean position, 42–43
    Maricopa County Bar Association Hall of Fame, 45
    organizational plan, 8–9
    Philosophy of the College of Law, 246–247
    publications, 45
    Report of the Law School Dean
        Academic Year 1967–1968, 107–114
        Academic Year 1971–1972, 229–232
        Last Hurrah (Academic Year 1974–1975), 243–251
    teaching methods, 42–43
    "The Willard Pedrick Papers," 46
    Torts 505, 212
    Vinson, Frederick M., and, 35–36
Pedrick follies, 40–41
Philosophy of Legal Education, 248
"Philosophy of the ASU College of Law," 246–247, 251
Phoenix, 4–5
physical facilities, inaugural dean's report, 109–110
Plessy v. Ferguson, 21
policing, protests and, 22–23
Post-Conviction Clinic, 465–467
Powell, Lewis, 5
Powell v. Alabama, 21
Procedure 505, 211
Procedure 557, 214
Program Development, inaugural dean's report, 111
programs, 50, 461
    Academy for Justice, 50
    Indian Legal Program, 50
    Sports Law and Business, 468–469
Property 507, 211
Prosecution Clinic, 467–468
Prosser, William, 40–42
Prosser and Keeton on Torts, 41
Prosser on Torts (Prosser), 41
protests, 22–23
    Newark riots, 25–26
    race riots, 25–26
Public Defender Clinic, 467

R

race, school integration, 26–27
race riots, 25–26
racism
    1960s, 26–27
    anti-racism rallies, 199–200
Raushenbush, Walter B., 83
Rayes, Douglas L. ('78), 52, 171–172
realism, 55–56
Ream, Carolyn S., 78
recruitment
    first class, 16–17
    minorities, 344
Reeve, Tapping, 12
Rehnquist, William, 5, 232
Renaut, Samuel, 316
Report of the Law School Dean Academic Year 1967–1968, 59–60, 107–112
Report of the Law School Dean Academic Year 1971–1972, 229–231

Index

Report of the Law School Dean Academic Year 1974–1975, 243–250
Report of the Law School Dean Academic Year 1975–1976, 258–265
Report of the Law School Dean Academic Year 1976–1977, 265–268
Richard Grand Foundation of Tucson, 61
Rogers, Joe, 52
Romley, Rick, 52
Rose, Jonathan, 12, 74, 95, 264, 322
    Contracts 501, 211
    Laws, Lawyers, and Texts: Studies in Medieval Legal History in Honor of Paul Brand (ed.), 96
    Maintenance in Medieval England, 95
    Oral History, 96
Rosenthal Lecture, Harold Havighurst, 85
Ross, John J., 502
Rossant, Tomas, 491
Ross-Blakley Hall, 502
Ross-Blakley Law Library, 481, 500–502
Rothschild, Ed, 44
Rutledge vs. Kush, 293–299
Ryan, Michael D., 51

S

Saks, Michael, 83
Salmon, Riney B., 60, 66
Sandra Day O'Connor College of Law
    ASU presence in Washington, D.C., 457–458
    naming ceremony, 411–415
Sandra Day O'Connor Inn of Court, 12–13
Sandra Day O'Connor Institute, 417, 489
Sandra Day O'Connor Symposium, 415–416
Sandweg, Bill ('74), 154
Scheck, Barry, 404
Schiefelbein, Les ('71), 131–134
scholarships
    donations, 481
    donors, 482–486
    incoming JD students class of 2019, 442
    Patterson, Cecil B., 126
    Richard Grand Foundation of Tucson, 61
    Rose, Jonathan, 96–97
    Sylvester, Douglas, 434–435
School for the Future for the Innovation in Society, 458

school integration, 26–27
Schroeder, Milton R., 74, 99–100, 264–265
SCLC (Southern Christian Leadership Conference), 26, 31n35
Selig, Bud, 468–469
service to country, lawyers', 66
sexual revolution, 22
Shelley v. Kraemer, 21
Silver, Roslyn O., 51, 129–131
Silverman, Barry G. ('76), 51, 154–158
Sims, Joe ('70), 122–123
Sinema, Kyrsten, 52
skills training, 248–249
    1970s, 307–311
    advocacy training, 309–311
    Morgan, Richard, on, 372
    "What are Law Schools Training Students For?" *(Forbes Magazine),* 311
Smith, Jimmie Dee ('70), 123–124
Smith, Perry, 24
Sneed, Joseph, 66
Soto, James Alan ('75), 161–163
specialization, deciding on, 215–216
Spivak, Susan, 75
Sports and Entertainment Law Journal, 51
Sports Law and Business program, 468–469
    Marie Selig Professorship, 469
standing in class, 42–43
Stanford Plan, 247
Starsky, Morris J., 197–205
State Bar of Arizona, ASU Law class of 1970, 5
The Steele Foundation, 503
Stevens, Henry S., 65
Stevens, John Paul, 44
Strong, Robert, Jr., 74, 265
Strouse, Daniel S., 322
Struckmeyer, Fred C., 64
Students for Democratic Society, 199
Sugarman, Steven, 42
sui generis, 87
Sung, Karen, 443
Supreme Court
    Bender, Paul and, 346–347
    O'Connor career, 6, 416–417
    ruling on lawyer advertising, 277–278
Sylvester, Douglas, 6, 74, 431–444
    ALC (Arizona Legal Center), 453
    Arizona Legal Center, 444

The ASU Law Group, 444
Beus Center for Law and Society, 433, 444
publications, 435–436
welcome message, web page, 53

T
Tang, Thomas, 5
Task Force on Law Schools and the Profession: Narrowing the Gap, 371–372
Taso, James J.C., 78
Teson, Fernando R., 322
third-year grading system, 245
Thomas, Evan, *First: Sandra Day O'Connor*, 417–418
Thunderbird School of Global Management, 458
Timmer, Ann Scott, 52, 280
Toobin, Jeffery, 417–418
tort law, 41–42
Torts 505, 212
trial advocacy, 248–249
Trusts and Estates 559, 214
Tufte, Jerod E., 52

U
Udall, Jesse, 5, 64
Udall, Nick, 4
University of Arizona, 3
U.S. Supreme Court. *See* Supreme Court

V
Venable, Gilbert T., 74, 265
Vietnam War, 21
  Starsky, Morris, 198–199
  uniting behind war effort, 57
Vinson, Frederick Moore, 7, 35–36
Volker, John F., 3
von Ammon, Phil, 39
Voting Rights Act of 1965, 22

W
Wallace, George, 27
Ware, Kent, 220
Warren, Earl, 66, 110
Watkins, Harold ('73), 134, 138
Watson, Andrew S., 110
The Way We Were (Morris), 92
Webb, Del E., 64
Wessel, Milton R., 322
White, Patricia, 74, 391–400
Whitman, Charles, 24
Whittaker, Charles Evans, 80
Willard H. Pedrick Lecture, 481
William P. Carey Armstrong Great Hall, 495
"The Willard Pedrick Papers," Arizona State University Archives, 46
William Polk Carey Foundation, 481
William S. Boyd School of Law, 377
Williams, Thomas, 443
Winer, Laurence H., 322
Wirtz, W. Willard, 110
women, admittance to law school, 14–15
Woods, Grant, 52
Woods, Terrance P. ('73), 146–147
Woodstock, 23

Y
Yale, legal realism, 56
Yerushalmi, David, 52

Z
Zillman, Donald N., 265
Zimmerman, Donald, 75

www.ingramcontent.com/pod-product-compliance
Lightning Source LLC
Chambersburg PA
CBHW081505080526
44589CB00017B/2655